SOURCEBOOK ON MEDICAL LAW

Marc Stauch MA (Oxon),
Solicitor, Senior Lecturer in Law

and
Kay Wheat BA,
Solicitor, Senior Lecturer in Law

with
John Tingle BA, M Ed,
Barrister, Reader in Health Care Law

all at
The Nottingham Trent University

Cavendish
Publishing
Limited

London • Sydney

First published in 1998 by Cavendish Publishing Limited, The Glass House, Wharton Street, London WC1X 9PX, United Kingdom

Telephone: +44 (0) 171 278 8000   Facsimile: +44 (0) 171 278 8080

E-mail: info@cavendishpublishing.com

Visit our Home Page on http://www.cavendishpublishing.com

ISBN 1 85941 103 7

Printed and bound in Great Britain by
Biddles Ltd, Guildford and King's Lynn

SOURCEBOOK ON MEDICAL LAW

Cavendish
Publishing
Limited

London • Sydney

PREFACE

Medical law is an exciting and challenging subject, whose dilemmas are the focus of intense and ongoing public debate. The fact that it is a relatively young discipline, which must attempt to keep pace with the constant advance of medical science, makes it of considerable jurisprudential interest. Moreover, the questions which it addresses are ones of fundamental human concern, bearing ineluctably upon the lives of each one of us and the shape of the society we inhabit. In fact, few other legal subjects display so clearly the interaction between law and morality.

This *Sourcebook on Medical Law* aims to draw together a wide range of material (much of it very recent), including extracts from statutes, judgments, and academic commentaries. It is primarily designed for use as a core text by law students taking medical (or health care) law at undergraduate level. However, it is hoped that it may also be of some interest to postgraduate students, including those in the burgeoning field of bioethics, as well as to health care professionals.

While the authors take collective responsibility for the book, primary responsibility for the individual chapters was as follows: Marc Stauch, Chapters 7, 8, 11 and 12; Kay Wheat, Chapters 1, 3, 4, 5 and 9; John Tingle and Marc Stauch, Chapter 2; Marc Stauch and Kay Wheat, Chapter 10. Finally, Chapter 6 was contributed to by all three authors, though overall responsibility was taken by Marc Stauch.

We should like to express our thanks to Terry Hanstock of The Nottingham Trent University Library and Information Services, and to Chris Garratt, formerly of The Nottingham Trent LIS, now of Hammond Suddards, for their assistance in tracking down material and references for inclusion in the work.

Crown copyright is reproduced with the permission of the Controller of Her Majesty's Stationery Office. Every effort has been made to trace copyright holders, but if any have been inadvertently overlooked the publishers will be pleased to make the necessary arrangements.

We have aimed to state the law as at 1 March 1998, though it has been possible to include more recent material in places.

MS, KW and JT
Nottingham,
June 1998

CONTENTS

Contents

Contents

TABLE OF CASES

TABLE OF LEGISLATION

EUROPEAN LEGISLATION

STATUTORY INSTRUMENTS

STATUTES

TABLE OF ABBREVIATIONS

Atlantic Reporter	A
Appeal Cases	AC
Australian Law Journal Reports	ALJR
All England Law Reports	All ER
American Journal of Law and Medicine	Am J Law & Med
British Columbia Law Reports	BCLR
British Medical Journal	BMJ
Butterworths Medico-Legal Reports	BMLR
Californian Appellate Cases	Cal App
Californian Reporter	Cal Rptr
Chancery Division	Ch
Chancery Division	Ch D
Cambridge Law Journal	CLJ
Current Legal Problems	CLP
Cox's Criminal Cases	Cox
Criminal Appeal Reports	Cr App R
Criminal Law Review	Crim LR
Dominion Law Reports	DLR
European Human Rights Reports	EHRR
Federal Reporter	F
Family Division	Fam
Family Law	Fam Law
Family Law Reports	FLR
Industrial Relations Law Reports	IRLR
Journal of Social Welfare Law	J Soc Wel L
Journal of Law and Society	JLS
Journal of Medical Ethics	JME
King's Bench Law Reports	KB
Knight's Industrial Reports	KIR
Lloyd's Law Reports: Medical	Lloyd's Rep Med
Law Quarterly Review	LQR

Massachussetts Supreme Judicial Court Reports	Mass
Medical Law Review	Med L Rev
Medical Law Reports	Med LR
Modern Law Review	MLR
North Eastern Reporter	NE
New Jersey Supreme Court Reports	NJ
New Law Journal	NLJ
New Law Journal Reports	NLJR
Nottingham Law Journal	Nott LJ
New South Wales Law Reports	NSWLR
North Western Reporter	NW
New York Court of Appeal Reports	NY
New York Supplement	NYS
New Zealand Law Reports	NZLR
Oxford Journal of Legal Studies	OJLS
Ontario Reports	OR
Pacific Reporter	P
Pennsylvania District and County Reports	Pa D & C
Queen's Bench Law Reports	QB
Road Traffic Reports	RTR
Supreme Court Reporter	S Ct
South Australian State Reports	SASR
Session Cases	SC
Canada Law Reports: Supreme Court	SCR
Solicitor's Journal	SJ
Scots Law Times	SLT
Southern Reporter	SO
South Western Reporter	SW
United States Supreme Court Reports	US
United States Law Week	USLW
Victorian Reports	VR
Weekly Law Reports	WLR
Western Weekly Reports	WWR

PART ONE

CHAPTER ONE

ETHICS AND MEDICINE

INTRODUCTION TO ETHICS

This chapter will examine the ways in which ethical issues are part of the practice of medicine. In this first section we will look, briefly, at a number of ethical theories and concepts and the ways in which they might relate to medicine. Next, we consider the doctor-patient relationship and the way in which medicine has given rise to particular ways of describing this relationship and its ethical implications. Although it is by no means a clear cut dichotomy, generally it can be said that many of the problems in medical ethics, and certainly many of the conflicting opinions, are based upon the debate between paternalism and the patient's right to autonomy. First, the view that paternalism is central to the doctor-patient relationship means that because of the doctor's superior knowledge and his ethical obligation to do good, the medical view of what is best for the patient should prevail. The opposing view is that the patient has a right to autonomous decision making and that this should not be overridden by 'doctor knows best'. Later in the chapter we will study these two different ways of looking at the doctor-patient relationship, question whether it is helpful to use either of these models as frameworks for medical decision making, and look at alternatives. Finally, we will look at justice and fairness in the allocation of treatment between competing patients when resources dictate that not all can be treated, and at the distribution of health care resources on a national level.

However, although the current chapter looks at general principles, when appropriate, ethical problems in particular areas of medical practice will be examined in other chapters.

Why study ethics?

Why should ethics be so important in medicine? In other fields of activity, such as commerce, ethics plays a small role. As long as business is operated on the right side of the law, little consideration is given to whether it is practised ethically. Although many may protest, for example, that 'it isn't fair' for large supermarkets to put small shops out of business, the 'ethics' of this plays a minor role in the general discourse about such matters, which is much more likely to be concerned with convenience and consumer choice. That is not to say that it is not relevant. It is simply that the language of ethics has not permeated the world of business in the way in which it has the practice of medicine. The reason may be that much of medicine is about issues of life and death: for example, abortion, infertility treatment, the threat to life through negligent treatment, or insufficiency of health resources, the treatment of the terminally ill and so on. Perhaps the heart of the doctor-patient relationship is this: the doctor does things to the body of the patient, thereby invading his physical integrity. This is neither good nor bad in itself, but is instrumentally good if the likely effect is the cure or amelioration of the patient's condition, and if it is done with the real consent and co-operation of the patient. However, in so far as it can be ascertained, it must be done in the patient's best medical interests. If there is no real consent, or if the treatment is unsuitable or negligently carried out, then it could be regarded as a violation of the patient's physical integrity.

Although, as we shall see, there is some argument that the doctor-patient relationship has been wrongly accorded this special status, there is no doubt that since the time of ancient Greece, it has given rise to ethical codes prescribing the extent of the doctor's duties.

Mason, JK and McCall Smith, RA, *Law and Medical Ethics*, 1994, London: Butterworths, p 4:

Medicine in the Middle East

The first effective example of organised medicine is to be found in Egypt where the father figure of medicine practised – Imhotep, who was the archetypal combination of physician, priest and court official. The Papyri discovered in the 19th century indicate that Egyptian medicine was comparatively advanced as early as the second millennium BC. Several features of that organisation are outstanding in their relation to modern practice. In the first place, the concept of a national health service seems to have been well developed – patients were not charged for visits to the healers who, themselves, were supported by the community. Secondly, rather rigid rules were laid down as to experimental treatment – there was no culpability in failure to cure so long as the standard textbooks were followed. Severe penalties were, however, threatened for those who ignored the instructions, the reason being that very few men would be expected to know better than the best specialists who had gone before – an interesting attitude towards negligence which was still being adopted by the courts at the turn of this century ... More importantly, the notion of specialisation was deeply instilled. Medical treatment, however, remained very much the practice of the priest caste – indeed, the aura of mystique surrounding the physician in comparison with the overt technical expertise of his surgical colleagues has persisted until recent times.

The extension of surgical practice into lay hands was steady and was demonstrated in the parallel practice of Babylonian medicine.

It is from here that the first known legal code originated – the Code of Hammurabi (c 1900 BC). This contained an element of medical ethics and laid down, *inter alia*, a system of payment based on results and, to some extent, on the ability to pay and on the status of the patient; it also tabled penalties for negligent failure, some of which were draconian to an extent which must have deterred many from entering the profession.

Greek medicine

For the origin of our modern ethics, however, one must look to Greece where early medical practice must have been derived from both Egypt and Babylon. By 500 BC, the originally strong influence of the priest had waned and had been taken over by the philosophers who, through the processes of logical thought, observation and deduction, transformed the practice of medicine. Inevitably, this led to the formation of schools involving close association, paternalism and the elements of the 'closed shop'; a code of intraprofessional conduct evolved – the dawn of what has become known as medical etiquette. In addition, the new concepts of practice dictated that the physician went to the patient rather than the patient to the temple. A standard of practice relevant to the new ideals was required and has survived as the Hippocratic Oath ...

Hippocrates remains as the most famous figure in Greek philosophical medicine but he was not alone and, indeed, it is probable that the Oath predates his own school. It therefore indicates a prevailing ethos rather than a professorial edict and it is still regarded as the fundamental governance of the medical profession. We are not, here, concerned with medical etiquette. As to medical ethics, the Oath lays down certain guidelines. First, it implies the need for co-ordinated instruction and registration of doctors – the public is to be protected, so far as is possible, from the dabbler or the charlatan. Secondly, it is clearly stated that a doctor is there for the benefit of his patients – to the best of his ability he must do them good and he must do nothing which he knows will cause harm. Thirdly, euthanasia and abortion are proscribed; the reference to lithotomy probably prohibits mutilating operations (castration) but has been taken by many to indicate a proper limitation of practice to that in which one has expertise. Fourthly, the nature of the doctor-patient relationship is outlined and an undertaking is given not to take advantage of that relationship. Finally, the Oath expresses the doctrine of medical confidentiality.

In fact, the Hippocratic Oath did not become an integral part of ethical teaching until well into the Christian era; it lapsed with the decline of Greek civilisation and was restored with the evolution of university medical schools. It is doubtful if any British medical school now requires a reiteration of the Oath at graduation – although Edinburgh, for one, requires assent by students to a modified version – but, avowed or not, all doctors would admit to its persuasive influence. The language of the Oath is, however, archaic and a modernised version was introduced by the World Medical Association as the Declaration of Geneva. This was amended at Sydney in 1968 and provides the basis of an International Code of Medical Ethics.

What is the study of ethics about? The purpose of ethics is to try and find principles for living good lives. It will be seen that there is much overlap between ethical theories, and within each, there are contradictions and tensions. Words like 'equality', 'rights' and 'liberty' all sound good, and we all like to think that we approve of these things. However, in deciding what we mean by them we may find that we are making all sorts of value judgments and interpretations which suit the end we would like to achieve.

A fundamental starting point in discussions about ethics is universalisation. This means that one must move away from what is right or beneficial for the individual and seek principles that can apply to everyone. Peter Singer describes the way this has permeated ethical thinking.

Singer, P, *Practical Ethics,* **1979, Cambridge: CUP, p 10:**

From ancient times, philosophers and moralists have expressed the idea that ethical conduct is acceptable from a point of view that is somehow *universal*. The 'Golden Rule' attributed to Moses tells us to go beyond our own personal interests and 'do unto others as we would have them do unto us'. The same idea of putting oneself in the position of another is involved in the Christian commandment that we love our neighbour as ourselves. The Stoics held that ethics derives from a universal natural law. Kant developed this idea into his famous formula: 'Act only on that maxim through which you can at the same time will that it should become a universal law.' Kant's theory has itself been modified and developed by RM Hare, who sees 'universalisability' as a logical feature of moral judgments. The 18th century British philosophers Hutcheson, Hume and Adam Smith appealed to an imaginary 'impartial spectator' as the test of a moral judgment, and this theory has its modern version in the Ideal Observer Theory. Utilitarians from Jeremy Bentham to JJC Smart take it as axiomatic that in deciding moral issues 'each counts for one and none for more than one'; while John Rawls, a leading contemporary critic of utilitarianism, incorporates essentially the same axiom into his own theory by deriving basic ethical principles from an imaginary choice in which those choosing do not know whether they will be the ones who gain or lose by the principles they select. Even Continental philosophers like the existentialist Jean-Paul Sartre and the Marxist Jürgen Habermas, who differ in many ways from their English-speaking colleagues – and from each other – agree that ethics is in some sense universal.

One could argue endlessly about the merits of each of these characterisations of the ethical; but what they have in common is more important than their differences. They agree that the justification of an ethical principle cannot be in terms of any partial or sectional group. Ethics takes a universal point of view. This does not mean that a particular ethical judgment must be universally applicable. Circumstances alter causes, as we have seen. What it does mean is that in making ethical judgments we go beyond our own likes and dislikes. From an ethical point of view the fact that it is I who benefit from, say, a more equal distribution of income and you, say, who lose by it, is irrelevant. Ethics requires us to go beyond 'I' and 'you' to the universal law, the universalisable judgment, the standpoint of the impartial spectator or ideal observer, or whatever we choose to call it.

Can we use this universal aspect of ethics to derive an ethical theory which will give us guidance about right and wrong? Philosophers from the Stoics to

Hare and Rawls have attempted this. No attempt has met with general acceptance. The problem is that if we describe the universal aspect of ethics in bare, formal terms, a wide range of ethical theories, including quite irreconcilable ones, are compatible with this notion of universality; if, on the other hand, we build up our description of the universal aspect of ethics so that it leads us ineluctably to one particular ethical theory, we shall be accused of smuggling our own ethical beliefs into our definition of the ethical – and this definition was supposed to be broad enough, and neutral enough, to encompass all serious candidates for the status of 'ethical theory'.

As Singer says, the principle of universalisation has appealed to many and it cannot be said to belong to any particular theory.

Consequences v deontological absolutes

One way of deciding whether an action is ethically right or wrong is to look at the consequences of *this* act; or we might consider it important to look at the consequences of translating this act into an ethical proposition about what should be done generally, ie, by framing an ethical principle which will produce the best consequences. So, for example, we might make a rule about keeping promises which is generally a good thing to do, even though in some circumstances the consequences of breaking a promise may be better than keeping it. Another way is to ask whether the act or principle would be right or wrong *regardless of its consequences*. This leads to a somewhat crude distinction between theories which judge the moral correctness of an action by its consequences alone, and those which state there are certain principles, rights or whatever, which are inviolable, whatever the consequences. However, it is by no means a neat division. Most consequentialists try to incorporate certain things such as respect for individual rights into their theories with varying degrees of success. Those who believe in the paramountcy of absolute values cannot disregard consequences entirely. Advocates of certain principles such as the sanctity of life (one of those so called inviolable principles) may oppose, say, the withdrawal of nutrition from a permanently unconscious patient (see below, Chapter 12). However, they may argue that one of the reasons for their view is the 'slippery slope' argument, which says that once a certain course of action is carried out (as here), then the next step will be to withdraw food from a patient who is gravely disabled, but not unconscious. This argument is an appeal to consequentialism.

Consequentialism

The theory that the rightness of a course of action is to be judged by its consequences is an attractive one and it is tempting to embrace this view as being self-evidently right. Human actions have outcomes. We believe that we need to know what these are in order to decide what is the right thing to do. However, a moment's reflection will make us realise that whilst it may be correct, as it stands, it is full of holes. First, consequences for whom? If we are looking at types of medical treatment or the allocation of health resources we must ask whether we are looking at these sorts of patients or society as a whole? What sorts of consequences are going to be relevant? If the consequences of treating these patients may be that they will live, but live in pain or be dependent upon others for their most basic needs, is this right?

The most well known consequentialist view is that of utilitarianism. This theory, of whom Jeremy Bentham was one of the earliest exponents, states that ethical principles should produce the greatest happiness for the greatest number of people, and 'happiness' is defined by means of pleasure. The rightness of a decision is judged by deciding whether it produces, on balance, more pleasure than pain. When we consider the treatment of say, very seriously disabled new-born children, we might discount treating them because they will live (we believe) painful lives. But we also tend to think that there is more to life than the pursuit of pleasure and the avoidance of pain. JC Smart has put forward the example of the 'pleasure machine' (see his contribution to *Utilitarianism: For and Against*, 1993, Cambridge: CUP). This is a machine that can be connected to the brain to give pleasure, without the 'inconvenience' of the means of obtaining pleasure, for example, from books, sex, sport and so on. Once we acknowledge the absurdity of this and realise that we do not pursue pleasure as such, but an infinite number of pursuits, the pain-pleasure dichotomy is not so attractive. We tend to think that to be human is to be more than the repository of the sensations of pleasure and pain. Although the most well known utilitarian philosopher, John Stuart Mill, referred to the maximising of pleasure, and described utilitarianism as the 'happiness' theory, he was aware that this might be interpreted as pandering to selfish and, perhaps, base, tastes. Mill tried to deal with this by distinguishing between different kinds of pleasure.

Mill, JS, *Utilitarianism*, 1863, London: Routledge, p 15:

It must be admitted ... that utilitarian writers in general have placed the superiority of mental over bodily pleasures chiefly in the greater permanency, safety, uncostliness, etc, of the former – that is, in their circumstantial advantages rather than in their intrinsic nature. And, on all these points, utilitarians have fully proved their case, but they might have taken the other, and, as it may be called, higher ground, with entire consistency. It s quite compatible with the principle of utility to recognise the fact that some *kinds* of pleasure are more desirable and more valuable than others. It would be absurd that while, in estimating all other things, quality is considered as well as quantity, the estimation of pleasures should be supposed to depend on quantity alone.

Singer describes his own version of utilitarianism:

Singer, P, *Practical Ethics*, 1979, Cambridge: CUP, p 12:

Suppose I then begin to think ethically, to the extent of recognising that my own interests cannot count for more, simply because they are my own, than the interests of others. In place of my own interests, I now have to take account of the interests of all those affected by my decision. This requires me to weigh up all these interests and adopt the course of action most likely to maximise the interests of those affected. Thus I must choose the course of action which has the best consequences, on balance, for all affected. This is a form of utilitarianism. It differs from classical utilitarianism in that 'best consequences' is understood as meaning what, on balance, furthers the interests of those affected, rather than merely what increases pleasure and reduces pain. (It has, however, been suggested that classical utilitarians like Bentham and John Stuart Mill used 'pleasure' and 'pain' in a broad sense which allowed them to include achieving what one desired as a 'pleasure' and the reverse as a 'pain'. If this interpretation is correct, the difference between classical utilitarianism and utilitarianism based on interests disappears.)

What does this show? It does not show that utilitarianism can be deduced from the universal aspect of ethics. There are other ethical ideals – like individual rights, the sanctity of life, justice, purity and so on – which are universal in the required sense, and are, at least in some versions, incompatible with utilitarianism. It does show that we very swiftly arrive at an initially utilitarian position once we apply the universal aspect of ethics to simple, pre-ethical decision making. This, I believe, places the onus of proof on those who seek to go beyond utilitarianism. The utilitarian position is a minimal one, a first base which we reach by universalising self-interested decision making. We cannot, if we are to think ethically, refuse to take this step. If we are to be persuaded that we should go beyond utilitarianism and accept non-utilitarian moral rules or ideals, we need to be provided with good reasons for taking this further step. Until such reasons are produced, we have some grounds for remaining utilitarians.

It has been suggested that utilitarianism fails to deal with the problem of people's unacceptable preferences.

Beauchamp, TL and Childress, JF, *Principles of Biomedical Ethics*, 1994, Oxford: OUP, p 53:

Problems arise for utilitarians who appeal to preferences when individuals have what our considered judgments tell us are morally unacceptable preferences. For example, if a research investigator derived supreme satisfaction from inflicting pain on animals or on human subjects in experiments, we would condemn this preference and would seek to prevent it from being actualised. Utilitarianism based on subjective preferences is a defensible theory only if a range of acceptable preferences can be formulated, where 'acceptability' is determined independently of the preferences of agents. This task seems inconsistent with a pure preference approach, but will utilitarians be destroyed by a second level that delineates what counts as an acceptable preference?

Critics of utilitarianism have pointed out that the theory can be upheld and still permit an awful lot of wrongdoing. In other words, the great majority of society can be wealthy and healthy, but a small minority may live in appaling circumstances, with no access whatsoever to basic facilities, such as health care. This is a powerful argument. Although Mill does incorporate concepts such as justice into his theory, is this not coming perilously close to maintaining that there are ideals or principles which are worthy and must be supported regardless of the consequences? Consequentialist theories do not have to be utilitarian, ie, the maximisation of happiness or welfare can be replaced by some other concept of what is good. For example, one may try to incorporate some role for distributive justice. This may be possible, but it is not necessarily part of a consequentialist theory, which may lead us to conclude that judging actions by consequences alone is an insufficient guide to ethical behaviour.

Utilitarianism, however, is an attractive theory when one considers certain specific issues such as the doctor's obligation of confidentiality, where the obligation can be justified on the basis that patients would be less than candid when consulting a doctor if they had doubts that the information would be kept confidential (see below, Chapter 5). The fact that the obligation can be broken if it is in the public interest to do so is also an appeal to consequentialism.

Absolutism/deontology

Having recognised the inadequacies of consequentialism, John Mackie considers alternatives:

> **Mackie, JL, *Ethics Inventing Right and Wrong*, 1977, Harmondsworth: Penguin, p 149:**
>
> ... we could reject the consequentialist structure, and develop a moral system built not round the notion of some goal that is to be attained, but rather round the notions of rules or principles of action or duties or rights or virtues, or some combination of these – in a very broad sense, some kind of deontological system. Of course a consequentialist theory will usually give some place to items of all these sorts, but a subordinate place: a utilitarian takes virtues, for example, to be good just because and in so far as they tend to issue in behaviour that increases the general happiness. But in a deontological theory actions of the kinds held to be virtuous are seen as being intrinsically obligatory or admirable, and goodness of character too may be seen as having intrinsic value; actions and characters may have a merit of their own not wholly derived from what they bring about.

The term 'deontology' comes from *deon* – the Greek word for 'duty'. Probably the most well known exponent of this is Immanuel Kant.

Paton, HJ, *The Moral Law*, 1948, London: Hutchinson University Library, p 19:

> *A human action is morally good, not because it is done from immediate inclination – still less because it is done from self-interest – but because it is done for the sake of duty.*

This is Kant's first proposition about duty, though he does not state it in this general form.

An action – even if it accords with duty and is in that sense right – is not commonly regarded as morally good if it is done solely out of self-interest. We may, however, be inclined to attribute moral goodness to right actions done solely from some immediate inclination – for example, from a direct impulse of sympathy or generosity. In order to test this we must *isolate* our motives: we must consider first an action done solely out of inclination and *not* out of duty, and then an action done solely out of duty and *not* out of inclination. If we do this, then, we shall find – to take the case most favourable to immediate inclination – that an action done solely out of natural sympathy may be right and praiseworthy, but that nevertheless it has no distinctively moral worth. The same kind of action done solely out of duty does have distinctively moral worth. The goodness shown in helping others is all the more conspicuous if a man does this for the sake of duty at a time when he is fully occupied with his own troubles and when he is not impelled to do so by his natural inclinations.

Kant's doctrine would be absurd if it meant that the presence of a natural inclination to good actions (or even of a feeling of satisfaction in doing them) detracted from their moral worth. The ambiguity of his language lends some colour to this interpretation, which is almost universally accepted. Thus he says that a man shows moral worth if he does good, not from inclination, but from duty. But we must remember that he is here contrasting two motives taken in *isolation* in order to find out which of them is the source of moral worth. He would have avoided the ambiguity if he had said that a man shows moral worth, not in doing good from inclination, but in doing it for the sake of duty. It is the motive of duty, not the motive of inclination, that gives moral worth to an action.

Just as happiness was central to Mill's view, it plays a significant role in Kant's philosophy: 'the natural end which all men seek is their own happiness'. However, this happiness will only be produced, says Kant, if human beings, as rational beings, make rules to govern their own lives and the lives of others, and have reverence for the moral law. Crucial to Kant's philosophy is the maxim that no one should be treated merely as a means to an end, but always, as well, as an end in themselves. As we shall see, this Kantian rule is particularly pertinent to issues such as medical research and organ donation (see below, Chapters 10 and 11).

Beauchamp and Walters comment on deontological theories as follows:

Beauchamp, TL and Walters, L, *Contemporary Issues in Bioethics,* **1982, Belmont, Calif: Wadsworth Publishing, p 19:**

Deontological theories

We have seen that utilitarianism conceives the moral life in terms of intrinsic value and the means to produce this value. Deontologists, by contrast, argue that moral standards exist independently of utilitarian ends and that the moral life should not be conceived in terms of means and ends ... An act or rule is right, in the view of a deontologist, in so far as it satisfies the demands of some overriding principle(s) of obligation.

Deontologists urge us to consider that actions are morally wrong not because of their consequences but because the action type – the class of which the actions are instances– involves a moral violation. Because of the wide diversity in these theories it is hard to find the unity, but the following two conditions are close to the heart of deontological theories. First, the justification of principles and actions is not entirely by appeal to the consequences of adopting the principles or performing the actions. Second, some principles must be followed or actions performed irrespective of the consequences. Thus, there are not only justificatory grounds of obligation that are independent of the production of good consequences, but these grounds are at least sometimes sufficient to defeat the consequences no matter what the consequences are.

A radical deontologist will argue that consequences are irrelevant to moral evaluations: an act is right if and only if it conforms to an overriding moral obligation and wrong if and only if it violates the overriding moral duty or principle. Many deontological theories are not so radical, however, holding that moral rightness is only in part independent of utilitarian conceptions of goodness. The fairness of distribution, keeping a personal promise, repaying a debt, and abiding by a contract would be right, according to these theories, whether or not utility was maximised.

Deontologists believe that our duties to others are manifold and diverse, some springing from special relationships that utilitarians unjustifiably ignore. These relationships include, for example, those of parent and child, physician and patient, and employer and employee. Physicians have obligations to their patients that they do not have to other individuals, no matter the utilitarian outcome of treating their patients and not treating others. Children incur special obligations to their parents, and vice versa; parents have a moral obligation to oversee and support the health and welfare needs of their children that they do not have in regard to other children in their neighbourhood. This is not to suggest that utilitarians denigrate or downgrade these relationships. They do not. The point is that deontologists do not believe that these relationships can be justified on consequentialist grounds.

Deontologists also believe that utilitarians give too little consideration to the performance of acts in the past that create obligations in the present. If a person has promised something or has entered into a contract, he or she is bound to the terms of the agreement, no matter what the consequences of keeping it are. If one person harms another, the person who inflicted the injury is bound to compensate the injured one, whether the compensation serves utilitarian goals or not.

As an example of differences in utilitarian and deontological thinking, consider a survey conducted by researchers K Ann Coleman Stolurow and Dale W Moeller. Stolurow and Moeller were interested in the frequency with which x-rays are routinely used as part of dental checkups. They conducted a telephone survey of dental offices in the Boston area and found that in 95% of the offices surveyed x-ray procedures are customarily ordered in connection with the initial investigation of new patients, and that in nearly half of those offices the procedures employed involve full-mouth x-rays to obtain accurate information. These researchers misrepresented themselves over the telephone as new residents in the Boston area inquiring about available dental services and they asked a series of specific questions that followed a prepared written survey instrument wholly undisclosed to the dentists or their offices. This misrepresentation apparently contributed significantly to the accuracy of the results, because the data obtained showed a frequency of dental x-ray use far greater than that reported by an earlier study in which the researchers did not conceal their purposes.

This use of deception raises ethical issues of whether the researchers violated the moral rights of the participants or unjustifiably invaded privacy. Many act utilitarians would likely consider this study justifiable: there are public benefits of obtaining accurate information about dental x-rays. The information, for instance, might form the basis on which the American Dental Association would refocus its ongoing efforts to reduce unnecessary x-ray exposure, from lessening dosage levels to cutting down on the frequency of exposure. One also might draw an analogy with consumer surveys, noting that the survey seeks to evaluate a contractual service between providers and customers. The utilitarian could then argue that the terms of the contract give potential customers grounds to know accurate information about the service, and that this customer interest overrides conflicting rights of dental office owners and employees. A deontologist, by contrast, may find indefensible the deception and invasion of privacy essential to the conduct of the study. In any event, the deontologist will not frame the moral problem exclusively in terms of a weighing of consequences.

Since deontologists believe that moral standards are independent of utilitarian ends, what is the source of these standards and how is moral obligation based on these standards? Throughout the history of philosophy deontologists have identified starkly different ultimate principles of obligation as the final moral standards. Although these many different views cannot be surveyed here, it is possible to briefly distinguish several different grounds to which they have appealed. Perhaps the best known deontological account is the divine command theory. The will of God is the ultimate standard in this account and an action or action type is right or wrong if and only if commanded or forbidden by God. Other deontologists hold that some actions or action types are naturally right or wrong, good or evil, requiring no reason having to do with religion, politics, or social organisation.

Finally, some deontologists appeal to a social contract reached under conditions of absolute fairness as the source of moral obligation. The ultimate principle of obligation is action in accordance with moral rules fairly derived from a situation of mutual agreement. Many writers in this volume appeal to the recent work of John Rawls on the topic of justice, and Rawls is one representative of the social contract point of view.

We also talk about absolutism, ie, the belief in absolute values which can be regarded as inviolable, regardless of what they may bring about in any given set of circumstances. For example, it could be said that torture is *always* wrong. This is illustrated by the prohibition on torture in the Declaration of Tokyo, issued by the World Medical Association:

Declaration of Tokyo 1975:

1   The doctor shall not countenance, condone or participate in the practice of torture or other forms of cruel, inhuman or degrading procedures, whatever the offence of which the victim of such procedures is suspected, accused or guilty, and whatever the victim's beliefs or motives, and in all situations, including armed conflict and civil strife ...

This implies that under no circumstances could torture ever be justified, but it is by no means clear that we can be sure about this. Simmonds gives the following example:

Simmonds, NE, *Central Issues in Jurisprudence*, 1986, London: Sweet & Maxwell, p 34:

... if a madman had hidden a nuclear device which was set to destroy the whole of South East England at a pre-set time, we might feel justified in torturing him if this really was the only way of discovering the location of the bomb so as to defuse it.

The sanctity of life principle might also be said to be an absolute, but, again, this is questionable. Most people accept the fact that innocent people's lives will be lost in the cause of a just war. In medicine, the right of people to refuse life-saving treatment is respected, even though it conflicts with the sanctity of life principle, and, as we shall see below, in Chapter 12, many doctors believe that it is right not to treat a person if the treatment will not 'benefit' him, even if his death will result because of this.

Gillon describes the view of the intuitionist philosopher WD Ross, and his account of what happens when principles conflict:

Gillon, R, *Philosophical Medical Ethics*, 1985, Chichester: John Wiley, p 18:

Ross described various moral principles that he believed any reflective person would intuitively accept: duties of fidelity (the obligations to keep promises and not to deceive); duties of beneficence (obligations to try and help others); the duty of non-maleficence (the obligations, more stringent than the obligation to help others, not to harm others); duties of justice (obligations to promote the distribution of happiness or pleasure in accord with merits – probably meaning deserts – of the persons concerned); duties of reparation (obligation to compensate others for harms we have caused them); duties of gratitude (obligations to repay in some way those who have helped us); and a duty of self-improvement.

According to Ross, it is self-evident to any mature person on reflection that all these principles of conduct are *prima facie* moral obligations or moral rules of conduct that should undoubtedly prevail unless to obey them would result in a clash with some other rule of conduct. Although he did not claim that the list was exhaustive, he had no doubts that it was 'correct as far as it goes', and that the 'moral order expressed in these propositions is just as much part of the fundamental nature of the universe ... as is the spatial or numerical structure expressed in the axioms of geometry or arithmetic'.

What should be done when these *prima facie* principles conflict in any given circumstances? Ross did not believe that they could be immutably ranked or weighted so that we could know in advance which principles should take precedence over which. He also did not believe in any decisive overarching principle such as the Kantian supreme moral principle or the utilitarian greatest happiness principle by reference to which moral conflicts could be settled. Our moral life was far more complicated that the systematisers and simplifiers of ethics accepted, and when it came to specific cases of moral conflict we could only have opinions, not knowledge about which principle took precedence.

This idea that principles can be weighed up against each other depending upon the circumstances is attractive and is reflected in the writings of Ronald Dworkin, who describes the role principles have in legal decision making (see *Taking Rights Seriously*, 1977, London: Duckworth). As we shall see, this 'weighing up' of different principles is frequently a feature of medical law cases.

Rights, duties and liberties

When considering absolutist theories we questioned whether there was, for example, a right not to be tortured which could never be overridden. It leads us to try to get to grips with what we mean by rights. Rights are often described in terms of the corresponding duties which go with them. The jurist WN Hohfeld was a well known exponent of this, incorporating into his scheme the role of liberties and powers.

Simmonds, NE, *Central Issues in Jurisprudence*, 1986, London: Sweet & Maxwell, p 133:

Correlativity of rights and duties

In Hohfeld's analytical scheme, claim-rights are correlative to duties in a very strict way. When we say that X has a claim-right of a certain kind, a part of what we mean (according to Hohfeld) is that Y owes a duty of some kind to X. Liberties are not correlative to duties: they are correlative to the absence of a claim-right, or what Hohfeld calls a 'no-right' (thus if X has a liberty to wear a hat, Y has 'no-right' that X should not wear a hat). Powers are correlative to liabilities (being liable to have one's legal position changed by the act of another) and immunities are correlative to disabilities (ie, the inability to change another person's legal position).

The idea of strict correlativity between rights (ie, claim-rights) and duties is a controversial one, and the controversy is important for two quite different sets of reasons, which we may summarise as follows:

1   If rights are strictly correlative to duties, then a person has established legal rights only in so far as there are established duties corresponding to those rights. The law on this account has a static appearance: it could be represented as a long list of duties. If, on the other hand, it makes sense to talk of established rights without established correlative – we may think of the law as imposing duties, and perhaps creating new duties, in order to protect established rights. On this account, there may at any one time be established legal rights which are inadequately protected by legal duties: such rights provide a legal reason for creating new legal duties. Seen from this perspective, the law is not static but has an inner dynamic of its own. It is not a long list of duties that is added to whenever moral and policy considerations make this desirable: new duties may be recognised as a response to specifically legal considerations, in the attempt to give better legal protection to established legal rights.

2   Politicians and others make frequent use of the concept of rights. People are said to have rights of this and that kind, and rights are generally regarded as a 'good thing'. But if rights (in this case moral, rather than legal, rights) are correlative to duties, such claims are always open to the question 'on whom do the correlative duties rest?' People are much more willing to assert the existence of rights to various amenities than they are to ascribe specific duties. Moreover, if rights are correlative to duties, we may feel that they are not necessarily an unqualified good: for if rights entail duties, they entail greater restrictions on freedom. If therefore we believe that freedom is a 'good thing' we will not wish to see an unlimited expansion in people's rights (meaning, I repeat, 'claim-rights').

Kant distinguished between perfect and imperfect duties. Paton gives examples of these:

Paton, HJ, *The Moral Law*, 1948, London: Hutchinson University Library, p 31:

A perfect duty is one which admits of no exception in the interests of inclination. Under this heading the examples given are the ban on suicide and on making a false promise in order to receive a loan. We are not entitled to commit suicide because we have a strong inclination to do so, nor are we entitled to pay our debt to one man and not to another because we happen to like him better. In the case of imperfect duties the position is different: we are bound only to adopt the maxim of developing our talents and of helping others, and we are to some extent entitled to decide arbitrarily which persons we will help. There is here a certain 'latitude' or 'playroom' for mere inclination.

In terms of medicine, this could be translated as follows. Doctors are under a perfect duty to be just in the way in which they decide who to treat. They have only an imperfect duty to provide medical treatment to everyone who requests it. Under the Hohfeldian scheme there is no right to medical treatment, only the right to be considered in accordance with just criteria. In the next chapter we refer to the European Social Charter of 1961, which enshrines the 'right to protection of health, and the right to social and medical assistance'. However, as we shall see, in the context of the provision of medical treatment, the clinical discretion of the doctor as to the provision of treatment is paramount.

We might look for perfect duties in medical law, or we might consider the question the other way round and ask whether there are any absolute rights. Ronald Dworkin argues that there is a right to be treated with equal respect (see *Taking Rights Seriously*, 1977, London: Duckworth). Are mentally impaired people to be treated with the same respect as the non-impaired? There are a number of controversial cases where mentally impaired young women have been sterilised for contraceptive purposes even though there was little likelihood of them becoming pregnant (see below, Chapter 4). Were they being treated with the same respect as non-impaired women?

The principle of self-determination is frequently asserted in medical law and ethics. It could be said that there is an absolute right to self-determination as long as the person has the capacity to make decisions. We often talk of people being competent to make decisions. Problems may arise in deciding whether the person is competent, but once it is established then the right to physical integrity seems to be inviolable. But could the right still be overridden – for example, in an emergency? As we shall see, this 'right' is overridden when the doctor has no time to consult with, for example, an unconscious patient: he will successfully raise the defence of necessity to an action in battery. However, is it arguable that the right to self-determination has not been overridden at all because the patient was incapable of exercising it? In English law the foetus has no legal 'rights'. We will examine this below, in Chapter 8, in relation, in particular, to abortion and women who refuse Caesarean section operations even though the refusal may gravely risk their own lives and the survival of the foetuses. Does the foetus have no rights because it cannot enforce them? If this were the case, then children and the seriously mentally disordered would not have rights, but we often speak about the rights of children and the mentally ill. In one of the sterilisation cases referred to above it was said that a woman's 'right' to reproduce meant nothing to her (*Re B (A Minor) (Wardship: Sterilisation)* [1988] AC 199). Because of the dangers of dismissing rights in this way, it might be preferable to consider the rights of the incompetent in terms of the duties others have towards them. With regard to children, Carl Wellman states:

Wellman, C, *An Approach to Rights*, 1997, Dordrecht: Kluwer Academic, p 132:

The moral right to freedom of movement contains several other associated elements, but let me mention only one – the State's moral duty to enforce the parental duty of non-interference with the child's freedom of movement.

Although this duty is very limited in scope, it can be of crucial importance in extreme cases. Imagine that a parent keeps a young child restrained in a crib so much of the time that the child has no opportunity to learn to walk ... Under such circumstances, the State would have a moral obligation to intervene in the family and force the parent to cease and desist from such grossly unjustified interference with the freedom of movement of the child. Although this moral duty of the State begins as merely a duty regarding the child, in due course it grows into a moral duty to the child when the child becomes capable of claiming State intervention vis à vis the parent.

Wellman goes on to examine the right of the child to protection. In medical law the tension between granting the child the freedom it needs to develop and the protection it may need will be apparent when we look at the ability of the child to consent to treatment (see below, Chapter 3).

Liberty and equality are two other general ethical concepts that are open to a number of different interpretations. In Mill's philosophy they are interdependent. Mill stresses the liberty of the individual is paramount, and his liberty to pursue his own choices has to be no more than the equal liberty of everyone else. He can only be restrained from any activity which interferes with the liberty of others:

Mill JS, *On Liberty*, 1982, Harmondsworth: Penguin, p 68:

The object of this essay is to assert one very simple principle, as entitled to govern absolutely the dealings of society with the individual in the way of compulsion and control, whether the means used be physical force in the form of legal penalties or the moral coercion of public opinion. That principle is that the sole end for which mankind are warranted, individually or collectively, in interfering with the liberty of action of any of their number is self-protection. That the only purpose for which power can be rightfully exercised over any member of a civilised community, against his will, is to prevent harm to others. His own good, either physical or moral, is not a sufficient warrant.

Mill's principle is reflected in the right to self-determination.

Respect for persons

We have referred to Dworkin's equal respect for persons, but do we know what we mean by a person? This may sound like a silly question, but if we pose the question in a different way and ask what we mean by respect for human life it is not an easy one to answer. (There are those who argue that respect for life generally is what matters, so that animals should be treated with respect, and this has relevance to medical research and the development of xenotransplantation (animal to human), see below, Chapter 11).

Harris asks when human life begins to matter morally and examines the potentiality argument which says that human life begins when the human egg is fertilised, ie, when there is the potential for human life.

Harris, J, *The Value of Life,* **1985, London: Routledge and Kegan Paul, p 11:**

There are two sorts of difficulty with the potentiality argument which are jointly and severally fatal to it. The first is that the bare fact that something will become X (even if it will inevitably become X, which is far from being the case with the fertilised egg and the adult human being) is not a good reason for treating it now as if it were in fact X. We will all inevitably die, but that is, I suppose, an inadequate reason for treating us now as if we were dead.

The second difficulty is that it is not only the fertilised egg that is potentially a human being. The unfertilised egg and the sperm are equally potentially a human being. The unfertilised egg and the sperm are equally potentially new human beings. To say that a fertilised egg is potentially a human being is just to say that if certain things happen to it (like implantation), and certain other things do not (like spontaneous abortion), it will eventually become a human being. But the same is also true of the unfertilised egg and the sperm. If certain things happen to the egg (like meeting a sperm) and certain things happen to the sperm (like meeting an egg) and thereafter certain other things do not (like meeting a contraceptive), then they will eventually become a new human being.

It is sometimes objected that it is only the fertilised egg that has all the necessary potential present in one place, so to speak, and it is this that is crucial. It is only when the egg has been fertilised, so the argument goes, that a new unique entity exists that itself has all the potential necessary to become a new human being. This seems plausible enough until we remember that something had the potential to become that fertilised egg; and whatever had that potential, had also the potential to become whatever it is that the fertilised egg has the potential to become!

If then we ignore the first difficulty with the potentiality argument, and concede that we are somehow morally required to actualise all human potential, we are all in for a highly exhausting time. And it is clear that if we put the maximal effort into procreation that this imperative demands, our endeavours will ultimately be self-defeating.

Harris goes on to say that what we really value is a *person*:

Harris, J, *The Value of Life,* **1985, London: Routledge and Kegan Paul, p 18:**

... a person will be any being capable of valuing its own existence. Apart from the advantage of its simplicity, this account has two other major advantages. The first is that it is value- and species-neutral. It does not imply that any particular kind of being or any particular mode of existence is more valuable than any other so long as the individual in question can value its mode of existence. Once this threshold is crossed, no individual is more of a person or more valuable than any other. This concept of the person sets out to identity which individuals and which forms of life have the sort of value and importance that makes appropriate and justifies our according to them the same concern, respect and protections as we grant to one another. And it tries to do so without begging any questions as to the sort of creatures that will be found to qualify.

The second advantage is that it is capable of performing the two tasks we require of a concept of a person. These are that it should give us some grasp of why persons are valuable and make intelligible the moral difference between persons and other beings. The second task is that it should enable us, in principle, to tell persons from non-persons.

On this concept of the person, the moral difference between persons and non-persons lies in the value that people give to their own lives. The reasons it is wrong to kill is that to do so robs that individual of something they value, and of the very thing that makes possible valuing anything at all. To kill a person not only frustrates their wishes for their own futures, but frustrates every wish a person has. Creatures that cannot value their own existence cannot be wronged in this way, for their death deprives them of nothing that they can value.

Of course non-persons can be harmed in other ways, by being subjected to pain for example, and there are good reasons for avoiding subjecting any sentient creatures to pain if this can be avoided.

It is important to note that Harris is talking about the *capacity* to value one's own existence, so a new-born child would have that capacity. However, would a foetus also have the capacity?

Justice

By now it will be apparent that the language of morals can slip easily between rights, duties and liberties. The concept of 'justice' is no less an elusive concept. Although its importance usually lies in the realm of politics, it can be relevant both to the wider issues of allocating health resources on a national basis, and when deciding which patients to treat when local resources are limited. This will be examined further at the end of this chapter and in Chapter 2.

Relativism and feminist ethics

It is arguable that we approach ethical problems from the standpoint of a white Western man (see Hart's criticism of Mill, below, p 32). Increasingly, therefore, there are thinkers who want to move away from this and explore the issues from the perspective of women or of people from different cultures.

We commenced this section with the suggestion that ethical principles are universal. Some would argue that this does not address the way in which cultural differences might give rise to different ethical norms.

Beauchamp, TL and Walters, L, *Contemporary Issues in Bioethics*, 1982, Belmont, Calif: Wadsworth Publishing, p 8:

[Cultural] relativists defend their position by appeal to anthropological data indicating that moral rightness and wrongness vary from place to place and that there are no absolute or universal moral standards that could apply to all persons at all times. They add that rightness is contingent on cultural beliefs and that the concepts of rightness and wrongness are therefore meaningless apart from the specific contexts in which they arise. The claim is that patterns of culture can only be understood as unique wholes and that moral beliefs about normal behaviour are thus closely connected in a culture to other cultural characteristics, such as language and fundamental political institutions. Studies show, they maintain, that what is deemed worthy of moral approval or disapproval in one society varies, both in detail and as a whole pattern, from moral standards in other societies.

Similarly, some feminists have taken the view that the language of moral philosophy is male-centred, and dominated by an undue reverence for 'reason'. This is particularly pertinent to medical ethics, as the medical profession has traditionally been dominated by men, particularly in its upper reaches. It has been said that the traditional approach to medical ethics reinforces the practice of patriarchal medicine and the patriarchal institutions within society (for example, by Susan Sherwin – see 'Feminist and medical ethics: two different approaches to contextual ethics' in Bequaert Holmes, H and Purdy, LM, *Feminist Perspectives in Medical Ethics*, 1992, Bloomington: Indiana University Press). Some feminist writers have spoken of the need for an 'ethics of care', whereby the emotions have an important role to play in ethical theories (see Gilligan, C, *In a Different Voice*, 1982, Cambridge, Mass: Harvard University Press). Beauchamp and Childress describe the care ethic as follows:

Beauchamp, TL and Childress, JF, *Principles of Biomedical Ethics*, **1994, Oxford: OUP, p 89:**

Having a certain emotions attitude and expressing the appropriate emotion in acting are morally relevant factors, just as having the appropriate motive for an action is morally relevant. The person who acts from rule-governed obligations without appropriately aligned feelings such as worry when a friend suffers seems to have a moral deficiency ... Insight into the needs of others and considerate alertness to their circumstances often come from the emotions more than reason. In the history of human experimentation, for example, those who first recognised that some subjects of research were being brutalised, subjected to misery, or placed at unjustifiable risk were persons who were able to feel compassion, disgust, and outrage through insight into the situation of these research subjects.

The care ethic, however has its weaknesses, in that it is arguable that it is not sufficient as a moral theory. Beauchamp and Childress comment as follows:

Beauchamp, TL and Childress, JF, *Principles of Biomedical Ethics*, **1994, Oxford: OUP, p 90:**

On at least some occasions we need an impartial judgment to arbitrate between conflicting moral judgments or feelings. It is doubtful that many who endorse the ethics of care want their theory to be interpreted so narrowly as to exclude all impartial judgments and considerations of justice and the public good. But the problem remains about whether the theory can successfully incorporate these moral notions without losing much of its critical thrust and uniqueness. The ethic of care, as Gilligan and others have defended it, recognises that two perspectives exist, but can they be made *coherent*? ...

Although initiated by feminist writers, the ethics of care has been sharply criticised by some feminists who worry that it attends to women's experiences as givers of care in traditional roles of self-sacrifice, but often neglects feminist insights into problems of oppression and dominance ...

Without a broader framework, the ethics of care is too confined to the private sphere of intimate relationships and may serve to reinforce an uncritical adherence to traditional social patterns of assigning caretaker roles to women.

THE DOCTOR-PATIENT RELATIONSHIP

Beneficence

Doctors are generally regarded as having a positive duty to do good. Raanan Gillon comments as follows:

Gillon, R, *Philosophical Medical Ethics*, 1985, Chichester: John Wiley, p 73:

Whatever the case in general ethics, it is undoubtedly true that members of the medical profession undertake to place the interests of their patients before their own in many circumstances. This undertaking differentiates them from, for instance, merchants, who, while they may also on occasion put their clients' interests first, will do so (*qua* merchants) only to further their own longer term interests – for example, when it is good for business to put themselves out for their clients. Although an element of such self-interest undoubtedly exists in the practice of medicine and although the grandiose claim that interests of patients always come first is false as a description and undesirable as a prescription, the medical profession nonetheless conceives itself, and is conceived by society, as having a duty of beneficence to the sick in general and to its patients in particular. One does not hear the Tannoy ringing out during a ball with the request, 'Would any architect present please report to the manager's office', and if one did, no architect there would feel the slightest moral obligation to respond.

Is this a sentimental view of the role of doctors and can it be justified? Gillon uses the example of an architect, but what about a plumber – might not he be called upon to act in an emergency? Referring to the duty of the doctor as going beyond what can reasonably be expected of everyone else, Downie comments:

Downie, RS, 'Traditional medical ethics and economics in health care: a critique', in Mooney, G and McGuire, A (eds), *Medical Ethics and Economics in Health Care*, 1988, Oxford: OUP, p 45:

[A main ingredient in a code of medical or other professional ethics] consists of some generalised exhortations to care for patients, which can be summed up by saying that the medical and perhaps all the professions are governed to a much greater extent than other jobs by the principle of benevolence. Indeed,

Gillon (1986) goes so far as to describe the doctor's duty as one of supererogatory benevolence, in that it goes beyond what can reasonably be expected of the rest of us.

A short way to dispose of this claim might be to argue that it confuses conceptual points about the definition of the aims of a profession with moral duties; definitional 'oughts' have been confused with moral 'oughts'. Thus, it sounds like a high ideal to say that the doctor ought to care for the health or the welfare of his patient, but in fact this is simply a definition of the job of a doctor. The shepherd *qua* shepherd ought to care for his sheep, the gardener *qua* gardener ought to care for his flower beds and grass, and the pilot *qua* pilot ought to aim at transporting his passengers with safety. These are just definitions of occupations in terms of their aims. Of course, one might say that the person who happens to be a doctor ought to do the best he can as a doctor. Yes, and the person who happens to be a gardener ought to do the best he can for his flower beds. We all ought to work hard in our respective spheres. In other words, if medical ethics is made to seem grander than ordinary morality it is because a conceptual claim has become confused with a perfectly ordinary moral claim.

An argument of this kind is usually thought by doctors to be too superficial. They reply that patients are vulnerable and that health care must be delivered through the uniquely special doctor-patient relationship. But that uniquely special relationship requires a special morality to protect it, and so we need medical ethics as traditionally understood.

Yet what is uniquely special about the doctor-patient relationship? What emerges after any attempt to answer this question is that it is difficult to find a set of necessary and sufficient conditions, which justify the description 'uniquely special' of the doctor-patient relationship. Note to begin with that there is no one relationship which is *the* doctor-patient relationship. For example, an anaesthetist might see a patient once before an operation, but adding this to the anaesthetist's function during an operation hardly creates a 'relationship', and in any case it is certainly different from the 'relationship' which a community health doctor might have with the population who live in a given geographical area. But even waiving this objection and concentrating on certain typical sorts of doctor-patient relationships we cannot easily say what is uniquely special about them. Certainly, patients are lacking in information and power when, say, a coronary artery bypass operation is prescribed, but so are most of us when the garage mechanic prescribes an engine transplant! In each case most of us must trust in the knowledge, skills, and good faith of our helpers. Perhaps car engines are not so important as our bodies, but then we also commit the latter to the care of airline pilots and taxi drivers. Again, doctors may have access to our bodies; but teachers, clergymen, and advertisers have access to our minds and can influence to varying degrees our very perceptions of our own identities. The conclusion seems to be that if there are *uniquely* defining conditions of the doctor-patient relationship they are likely to be trivial and not special in the sense of important, and if there are special or important features they are likely to be shared with a variety of occupations such as the lifeboat service, the police, the clergy, teachers, and many others, some of which are 'professions' and some not. It seems more profitable, then, to drop the whole idea of uniquely special features of the doctor-patient relationship and to draw attention to 'family resemblances' between that relationship and a whole variety of others.

To argue, as I have done, that there is nothing uniquely special about the doctor-patient relationship certainly weakens the claim that there is a need for a special sort of morality. But it does not dispose of it entirely. I wish now to argue that medical ethics as traditionally understood is actually harmful to health care, and that the need is really to drop the traditional approach and to re-assert the claims of ordinary morality (Downie and Calman, 1987).

The first respect in which traditional medical ethics has been harmful to health care concerns the distortions it has created in the doctor-patient relationship. For example, traditional codes are expressed in terms of the duties of the doctor, and while this has certainly inspired an idealistic practice it has also created a professional ethos of elitism and paternalism. Thus, generations of medical students have been given the impression that there is an esoteric set of rules – 'medical ethics' – which govern their professional activities. It is easy to extrapolate from this to the conclusion that such a code is different from and superior to ordinary morality. Doctors are not as other men; other men are guided by right and wrong, but doctors have medical ethics. For example, in ordinary life the assumption, if not the reality, is that people speak the truth to each other, but this is not an assumption of those governed by medical ethics; for medical ethics says that the first responsibility of the doctor is to the well-being of his patient, and it is generally thought to follow that it is up to the doctor to decide how far, in his opinion, a patient's well-being will be furthered by telling the truth. Medical ethics in this respect distorts the doctor-patient relationship, for any true human relationship must have sincerity as its necessary condition, and that condition is discouraged by the attitude built into traditional medical ethics: benevolence (if that is what it is) has swamped sincerity. This criticism might be summed up by saying that the duties of doctors should not be regarded, as they are in the tradition, as duties of benevolence, but rather as duties correlative to the *rights of patients*. To give this emphasis to the doctor-patient relationship is to cut out the distortion caused by the tradition. Indeed, an emphasis on rights – consumer rights, social and political rights, human rights of all kinds – is one moral characteristic of our time.

A second criticism which can be made of the tradition is that its fraternal, inward-looking nature discourages frank and open co-operation with other caring professions. For example, nurses and social workers are not part of the fraternity, so it has been a matter for debate how far they should be admitted into the inner counsels. One consequence of this is inefficiency in the delivery of health care due to uncertainty or lack of co-operation among all the members of a health care team. Where objectives are not shared and discussed among the caring professions there is a diminution of job satisfaction, friction, and a consequent damage to patient care. For example, one member of a team, a nurse, say, may not know how much a patient has been told or what the overall prognosis is. It is then difficult for the nurse to be fully supportive of the patient. This is not good morality.

A third respect in which the traditional approach to medical ethics is deficient is that it suggests that morality is about selected issues, rather than that it is all-pervasive. The discussion of medical ethics has tended to highlight the dramatic issues which happen to be topical at any one time. Although euthanasia, abortion, resuscitation, surrogate motherhood, and human experimentation are undoubtedly important matters, their prominence has obscured the fact that, not just once but many times in the course of a working day, moral stances, value judgments and decisions will result in actions considered to be right or wrong by the doctor. This is partly, but only partly, due to the uncertain nature of medical diagnosis and prognosis. The doctor, lacking certainty, must estimate what in his opinion is for the total good of the patient. This concept of 'total good' is not just a matter of technical expertise but involves values. For example, let us imagine a 70 year old man who wants to be allowed home soon after an operation. The doctor's judgment here will involve technical expertise, but will also involve economic and value judgments of a total good, including knowledge of the home circumstances and many other factors. Again, whether we do a job only moderately well when we are capable of doing it better is a question of morality, of deciding which direction we want to take. Allowing ourselves to become professionally socialised into routinised working patterns which keep things going but diminish patients' dignity and freedom requires as much a moral justification as a sociological explanation. These moral demands are all-pervasive and inescapable in health care.

Fourth, the traditional distinction between 'medical ethics' and 'private morality' suggests that one can deal with moral questions in a professional context without examining personal values and convictions. But I am arguing that it follows from the inescapable and all-pervasive nature of morality that we encounter moral problems in our personal lives which are not fundamentally different from those we may have to explore in our working environment. Whatever values we may feel to be important to us as individuals are almost certainly influencing and directing the decisions that we make as professional health care workers. If we have or lack the skills which allow us to approach moral dilemmas in a rational and methodical way in ordinary life, this will affect how we attempt to solve moral problems in a professional context. In other words, morality is 'indivisible'.

On the other hand, this fundamental assumption about the 'indivisibility' of morality does not lead to a rejection of the very special place that the maintenance of acceptable professional standards of behaviour must have in the work of people whose primary responsibility is to care for vulnerable fellow men and women. The potential harm that can come to people who are in some ways and by definition dependent on the knowledge and skills of others will undoubtedly heighten the moral concern in situations which, outside the professional context, might not be perceived as quite so threatening or acute. For example, a critical or sarcastic remark, which might be acceptable in ordinary circumstances, could be devastating to a sick person.

Another aspect of the 'indivisibility' of morality is that hospitals and other health care organisations ought not to be immune to general attitudinal changes in society. Moral dilemmas arise frequently from the attempts which the professions make or do not make to accommodate social change. Likewise, what professional people do, or often more pertinently what they would refuse to do, reflects the moral standards of their society in the same way in which actions of the individual doctor or nurse, psychologist or speech therapist, social worker or dietician reflect his or her standards of personal morality. The dilemmas created by social change can be obscured by an emphasis on medical ethics traditionally understood as a product.

A fifth criticism of traditional medical ethics is that it tends to underestimate the fact that medical decisions ought to be made in the real world of technological and economic facts. This point is much stressed in the papers of Mooney and McGuire, and Jennett ... Traditionally medical ethics tends to be seen in terms of pure moral absolutes – the doctor must do all that is medically possible for his (or her) patient regardless of the cost. I am asserting that in the real world compromises must be made. As an example of compromise we can point to renal dialysis. It is not helpful to say that there is an absolute value on human life if there are two patients who would benefit from dialysis but facilities for treating only one. The moral requirement here is to reflect on the scientific and economic facts of the cases as well as the quality of life of the potential recipients. This point can be expressed in the form of a distinction between compromising our consciences, which is wrong, and conscientious compromises, which consist in making the moral best of a bad job in the light of scientific and economic constraints. This distinction is compatible with the view that in some circumstances no compromises should be made.

These five criticisms of traditional medical ethics ... suggest that an enlightened medical ethics will be in terms of a 'process' – the process of applying the principles of everyday morality to the scientific and economic complexities of patient care. Moral decisions in medicine are what can be called 'consequential' or 'resultant' in that they arise out of the professional, economic, and legal facts of given cases. Ethics is no substitute for a good diagnosis of the problem, skillfully carried out treatment or clearly communicated information, but equally in doing these things the doctor is at the same time engaging in moral and economic activity.

However, it may be arguable that there is a difference between a doctor and others who provide vital services. It might be said that if a doctor were to refuse to treat in an emergency, he would be the subject of moral condemnation in a way that, say, an off-duty fireman who refused to help in a rescue, would not. It is important to remember that here we are talking about moral, not legal obligations. In the UK, a doctor has no legal obligation to stop at the scene of an accident and treat the injured. If he does, then he is obliged to treat with reasonable skill and care and he may be liable in negligence (see below, Chapter 6). The position of a non-medically qualified volunteer who assists at the scene of an accident is exactly the same – it is simply that the standard of care is different. The legal duty not to harm is the same for doctor and lay person alike. Is the doctor's moral obligation different? Harris suggests it is not:

Harris, J, *The Value of Life*, 1985, London: Routledge and Kegan Paul, p 54:

We believe ... that we should rescue trapped miners and other victims of accidents, or those shipwrecked, or the victims of hijackers of other hostage-takers; and, not least, those who can be rescued only by medical care. Some of these rescues can be performed by anyone who is on hand; others require all sorts of expertise from that of potholers, sailors, miners, engineers, firemen and so on, to specialised military personnel and those with medical skills. Very often, those of us who lack these skills can best help, and thus discharge our obligation to those at risk, by keeping well out of the way. All of this is perhaps obvious enough, but it helps us to see two important features of the obligation of health care professionals. The first is that *there is nothing special about their obligation in particular*. Just as there is no special category of person whose unique and first obligation it is to refrain from inflicting death, injury or suffering on the rest of us, so there is no one who is specially required, morally speaking, to undertake rescues.

It is also illuminating to consider the duty of beneficence in terms of Kant's perfect/imperfect duties. Kant considers generosity or beneficence as imperfect duties, which an individual has no right to demand, as he has a right, for example, to demand justice.

Of course, the doing of 'good' may, in the short term, necessitate the infliction of pain. Beauchamp and McCullough describe the 'balancing exercise' that may arise as follows:

Beauchamp, TL and McCullough, LB, *Medical Ethics*, 1984, Englewood Cliffs: Prentice Hall, p 30:

The basic roles and concepts that give substance to the principle of beneficence in medicine are as follows: the positive benefit the physician is under obligation to seek is the cure of disease and injury if there is a reasonable hope of cure; the harms to be avoided, prevented, or removed are the pain and suffering of injury and disease. In addition, the physician is enjoined from doing harm. This consideration, too must be included in the beneficence model because physician interventions themselves can inflict unnecessary pain and suffering on patients. The Hippocratic texts hold that inflicting pain and suffering is permissible in those cases in which the physician is attempting to reverse a threat to health, eg, administering an emetic after the accidental ingestion of a poison. Inflicting such pain and suffering on a patient in order to eliminate a deadly substance from the body is justified because the patient is on balance benefited. When the patient cannot be benefited by further intervention, the inflicted pain and suffering is unnecessary and to be avoided. Thus, in its first formulation in Western medical ethics, the beneficence model of moral responsibility adapts the principle of beneficence to patient care by providing a medically oriented account of how to balance goods over harms.

The rosy spectacled view of the special role of beneficence is questioned by Pellegrino and Thomasma:

Pellegrino, ED and Thomasma, DC, *For the Patient's Good: The Restoration of Beneficence in Health Care*, 1988, Oxford: OUP, p 4:

According to the Hippocratic Oath, the physician promises to 'follow that system of regimen which according to my ability and judgment I consider for the benefit of my patients'. Nowhere in the Hippocratic corpus is there any provision for the patient's view of things. In fact, in one place the relationship is described as being between 'one who orders and one who obeys'.

We shall see that this traditional principle, however, may be tempered to take into account the wishes of the patient (see below, p 42).

The work of a doctor in the late 20th century is often highly technical in nature, depending upon pharmacy, engineering, computer technology and so on. It might be argued that this diminishes the particular duty of beneficence in some way. Beauchamp and McCullough suggest that it does not:

Beauchamp, TL and McCullough, LB, *Medical Ethics*, 1984, Englewood Cliffs: Prentice Hall, p 35:

In the history of medicine, the physician has primarily functioned in care-giving and comforting roles, with beneficence serving as the moral foundation of these roles. As medical science exploded in the 20th century, medicine was transformed into a more scientific and technical enterprise. It might be argued that this change has transformed the physician's role, stripping it of its moral core and making it a sheerly technical enterprise. However, this hypothesis is misleading. Beneficent intervention remains, as ever, the moral foundation of the physician's role, a role powerfully augmented by medical science and technology. These remarkable new capacities created some moral problems in medicine, especially problems concerning the physician's authority, but they did not destroy medicine's tradition of beneficence.

But is this confidence that the traditional role of the physician has not been undermined misplaced? Much of the research which leads to treatment at the disposal of the physician has not been developed by physicians at all. Developments in genetics are a case in point. Once opportunities for genetic manipulation, for example, have been unleashed, how much power does the physician have to resist them?

The principle of beneficence is at work when we consider the doctrine of 'double effect'. Imagine a gravely ill patient in the last stages of terminal cancer. The patient is in pain and only a substantial dose of morphine will relieve the pain. However, such a large dose will also hasten the patient's death. As far as the law is concerned this is not homicide (see below, Chapter 12), and as far as medical ethics is concerned, the principle of beneficence means that the doctor's only intention is to do good, ie, relieve pain. The fact that death would also be hastened does not undermine the beneficent motive of the doctor. However, as we shall see, there are aspects of medical law where the principle of beneficence is undermined. First, in medical research patients may be subjected to randomised control trials (RCTs) (see below, Chapter 10). This means that some patients will not be receiving any treatment at all, but unknown to them, will be given placebos, so that the researchers can compare their progress with that of the patients who are given drug treatment. It is arguable that this can never be consistent with the principle of beneficence unless the principle is interpreted as meaning beneficence towards patients in the sense of a *general* benefit to the sick. Similarly, it is accepted that doctors may breach their duty of confidentiality in respect of an individual patient in the wider public interest. In these circumstances, it can be argued, the principle of beneficence is only upheld if it is equated with some form of consequentialism.

Non-maleficence

The traditional duty to do good has been accompanied by the obligation to do no harm – *primum non nocere* (first, do no harm). Gillon describes this in terms of Kant's perfect/imperfect duties distinction, and sees this as a wider obligation than that of beneficence:

Gillon, R, *Philosophical Medical Ethics*, 1985, Chichester: John Wiley, p 81:

The claim that avoiding harm has priority over doing good is vigorously contested in moral philosophy. An interesting sample of the detailed arguments appears in a paper by Phillippa Foot in which she argues for the claim that 'other things being equal, the obligation not to harm people is more stringent that the obligation to benefit people' [Foot, P, 'The problem of abortion and the doctrine of double effect', reprinted in Steinbock, *Killing and Letting Die*, 1980, Englewood Cliffs: Prentice Hall] and in a detailed criticism of her paper Nancy Davis, who argues, primarily by counterexamples, that no such general priority can be defended [Davis, N, 'The priority of avoiding harm', reprinted in Steinbock] ... At first sight Foot's thesis is undoubtedly plausible. We seem to have what Kant called a perfect (though, many would add, only *prima facie*) duty to all other people not to harm them. On the other hand, we do not have a duty to benefit all other people; apart from everything else it is incoherent to talk of a duty which is impossible to fulfil. Thus at most we can have a duty only to benefit some other people (an imperfect duty), while we have a perfect duty to everybody not to harm them.

While it seems entirely plausible to claim that we owe non-maleficence, but not beneficence, to everybody, it does not follow from this that avoidance of doing harm (non-maleficence) takes priority over beneficence. All that follows is that the scope of non-maleficence is general, encompassing all other people, whereas the scope of beneficence is more specific, applying only to some people not to harm them. Thus we can accept that each of us has a (*prima facie*) moral duty not to harm anybody else without being committed to believing that this *prima facie* duty must always take priority if it conflicts with any duty, including any duty of beneficence, we may have to particular people or groups of people.

This principle might, for example, be used to justify the 'acts and omissions' distinction in the law relating to euthanasia. As we shall see (below, Chapter 12), in the case of a very seriously ill patient, a doctor may not be obliged to continue to treat that patient. In other words, he can withdraw or omit to treat, and remain within the confines of the law. This is because the doctor may decide that the treatment is not benefiting the patient. That is consistent with the principle of beneficence because the doctor will say that the treatment is not, or would not, benefit the patient. The omission to treat is acceptable. However, the doctor is not legally permitted to give the patient a lethal injection to bring about death, even when 'natural' death is very close, as, it is argued, it would infringe the principle of non-maleficence. But it is arguable that the lethal injection would not be harmful as it might be the kindest way of treating a patient who is terminally ill and in great pain.

The nature of illness

Why is it necessary to consider this? It could be said that the presence of 'illness' or 'disease' is a straightforward factual matter. However, it is interesting to try and formulate a definition. Culver and Gert review the medical literature and select a number of definitions:

Culver, CM and Gert, B, *Philosophy in Medicine*, 1982, New York: OUP, p 66:

Some past definitions of 'disease'

There have been many attempts to set out a formal definition of 'disease,' but among physicians only rarely has a distinction among 'disease', 'illness', 'injury' and related terms been recognised. Consequently, 'illness' is often used interchangeably with 'disease', and injuries are regarded merely as a subclass of diseases. What most of the following authors have intended to define is what we call a malady, so that in addition to diseases they have included injuries, illnesses, headaches and the like in their definitions. By not realising what they have done, however, they have often been misled by some particular feature of the term 'disease'.

Some definitions are general, vague, and too inclusive. Thus, a pathology textbook (Peery and Miller, 1971) states:

> Disease is any disturbance of the structure or function of the body or any of its parts; an imbalance between the individual and his environment; a lack of perfect health.

This seems to offer three separate but equivalent definitions. According to the first definition, clipping nails and puberty are diseases, as well as asymptomatic *situs inversus* (right-left reversal of position of bodily organs) and being tied to a chair. The second definition is too vague to be of any use, and the third is circular. A textbook on internal medicine (Talso and Remenchik, 1968) says:

> ... disease may be defined as deprivation or lack of ease, a discomfort or an annoyance, or a morbid condition of the body or of some organ or part thereof.

There are similar problems here. Two separate definitions are offered. The first is too sweeping and would include inflation, quarrelsome in-laws, poor television reception, and ill-fitting shoes, while the second is circular and depends on the phrase 'morbid condition', which is merely a synonym for 'disease'.

Most texts on medicine and pathology make no attempt to define disease, which is appropriate enough since the exercise is irrelevant to their purposes. Thus, it might be said in defence of the above attempts that they were probably not meant to be taken very seriously.

One cluster of definitions which is meant to be taken seriously utilises a dynamic metaphor in which a person is pictured as constantly interacting and adapting to changes in his environment; disease then corresponds to a failure in that adaptation. An early expression of this definition is found in White's 1926 book, *The Meaning of Disease*:

> Disease can only be that state of the organism that for the time being, at least, is fighting a losing game whether the battle be with temperature, water, micro-organisms, disappointment or what not. In any instance, it may be visualised as the reaction of the organism to some sort of energy impact, addition or deprivation.

Thus, one wrestler held down by another is suffering a disease. A more modern version is found in Engel's 1962 book, *Psychological Development in Health and Disease*:

> When adaptation or adjustment fail and the pre-existing dynamic steady state is disrupted, then a state of disease may be said to exist until a new balance is restored which may again permit the effective interaction with the environment.

Aside from the ambiguities and the question begging inherent in 'adaptation' and 'balance', the emphasis in this definition (and the preceding one) on the deterioration of a previously more normal state seems to rule out all congenital and hereditary diseases ...

JG Scadding (1959, 1963, 1967) has written a series of papers on the definition of disease. In the most recent of these, he offers the following 'formal definition':

> A disease is the sum of the abnormal phenomena displayed by a group of living organisms in association with a specified common characteristic or set of characteristics by which they differ from the norm for their species in such a way as to place them at a biological disadvantage.

Scadding's definition is an improvement over those previously cited. He explicitly introduces the notion of deviation from a norm for a species which, though it does not deserve the prominence he gives it, is necessary for understanding the essential elements of the concept of malady. His 'biological disadvantage' criterion also points in the right direction but is too vague. Kendell, in a recent paper (1975), interprets 'biological disadvantage' as meaning decreased fertility or longevity. But this does not work. Even Kendell recognises that his revision of Scadding's definition leaves one with the 'rather disconcerting' result that a condition such as psoriasis would not qualify as a disease.

Several recent authors have also correctly identified aspects of disease. Spitzer and Endicott (1978) include in their definition of 'a medical disorder' that it is intrinsically associated with distress, disability, or certain types of disadvantage. We think this definition is on the right track. Goodwin and Guze (1979) consider as a disease 'any condition associated with discomfort, pain, disability, death, or an increased liability to these states, regarded by physicians and the public as properly the responsibility of the medical profession ...

Note the concluding phrase 'regarded by physicians and the public as properly the responsibility of the medical profession'. Is 'illness' that which a doctor thinks should be treated? A doctor faced with a hypochondriac may well form the conclusion that the symptoms complained of are imagined and that the person is not ill, and therefore no treatment is given regardless of the fact that the patient may have some organic disorder, which would be treated by another doctor who did not know about the hypochondria. This may sound simplistic, but consider treatment for infertile people. Are they ill? Or diseased? The answer is no, but they receive 'treatment' because doctors think that they should. It may be argued that it is society which decides what conditions merit treatment and what do not, but does that underestimate the power of information and medical technology, concentrated as it is, if not in the hands of doctors exclusively, in the hands of medical science? Society did not demand heart transplants until the first operation had been performed. The developments in genetic research have implications here. There is evidence that genes which 'cause' things such as baldness may be isolated and eradicated. This would be a 'medical' procedure. Would it mean that baldness would become an illness?

THE CASE FOR PATERNALISM

Introduction

In this and the following sections, we will look at the arguments which may be advanced, respectively, in favour of a paternalistic approach to medicine, and in favour of the primacy of patient autonomy. These two theories are described by Pellegrino and Thomasma:

Pellegrino, ED and Thomasma, DC, *For the Patient's Good: The Restoration of Beneficence in Health Care*, 1988, Oxford: OUP, p 3:

Two major ethical theories are today vying for dominance in medical ethics. The first, inherited from the Enlightenment, stresses the liberty and autonomy of the individual. It gathered strength in the 19th century in response to the depreciation of personal worth that accompanied the Industrial Revolution. This theory grounds ethics in rights, duties and obligations. The second theory stresses social utility rather than individual autonomy. Ironically, it too gained ascendancy during the Industrial Revolution to counter the social atomism of a purely individualistic ethic. This theory stresses social good, rules of conduct, and social accountability. Mill laid the foundation for such theories when he proposed the principle of autonomy, on the one hand, and the principle of utility, on the other.

Applied to physician-patient relationship, the first theory imposes on the physician the obligation of respect for the patient's self-determination. The second theory requires that the physician act to maximise benefits and goods even if this might demand acting without the patient's consent. It sanctions overriding the patient's autonomous decision if that decision is not judged by the physician to be in the patient's or society's good.

When considering the respective positions of the paternalist and the anti-paternalist, it is important to consider two things. First, as we shall see, the consent of the patient is necessary before any medical treatment can take place. This might be said to reflect the anti-paternalist view. The patient can refuse simple life-saving treatment and there is no mechanism for imposing it upon him. However, at least in English law, the arbiter of what the patient needs to know before he consents or refuses is the doctor. It might be said that this reflects a paternalist viewpoint. Secondly, the patient must be competent, ie, have sufficient mental capacity to make a treatment decision. The doctor will decide whether the patient is competent. If he lacks competence, he may be treated in his 'best interests'. When reading the following, keep these points in mind.

What is paternalism?

When we considered the principle of beneficence, we noted that it is a one-sided principle: the doctor is *doing good to/for the patient*. Beneficence does not mean the same as paternalism (the recognition of the patient's right to self-determination may be part of beneficence), but a narrower view of beneficence is compatible with paternalism. The paternalistic doctor 'knows best' and regards himself as being the best judge as to what is for the patient's own good. It is interesting to consider the duty of beneficence in relation to the parent-child relationship (the term paternalistic meaning to act like a father): although the parent may be said to have a duty of non-maleficence towards his child, does he have a positive duty to do good?

John Harris distinguishes paternalism from moralism:

Harris, J, *The Value of Life*, 1985, London: Routledge and Kegan Paul, p 194:

When health care professionals accept that their first duty is to act always in the best interests of their patients they are in effect saying that they are concerned for the welfare of their patients and that this is in no way inconsistent with manifesting 'respect for persons'. Welfare is not here used as a technical term – it means what it usually means, 'the state or condition of doing or being well', which will include things like happiness, health and living standards.

An initial problem is that concern for the welfare of others is compatible both with paternalism and with moralism. Briefly, paternalism is the belief that it can be right to order the lives of others for their own good, irrespective of their own wishes or judgments. The characteristic cry of the paternalist is: 'Don't do that, it isn't good for you.' *Moralism*, on the other hand, is the belief that it can be right to order the lives of others so that 'morality' may be preserved. The characteristic cry of the moralist is: 'Don't do that, it's wicked.'

Both the paternalist and the moralist are genuinely concerned for the welfare of others. They argue that it cannot be in your interest, nor can it be conducive to your being in a state of doing or being well, if you either do what isn't good for you or act immorally. Despite the genuineness of this moral concern, both paternalism and moralism involve treating the agent as an incompetent. They deny the individual control over her own life and moral destiny and treat her as incompetent to run her own life as she chooses. While both involve genuine concern for the welfare of others, neither can lay claim to demonstrating respect for their wishes.

But although Harris is right in saying that we are not respecting the wishes of the person whom we exhort to do good, or refrain from doing bad, we would nevertheless argue that we are entitled to do it. If you intervene to prevent another from picking someone's pocket, you are certainly not respecting the pickpocket's wishes, but you are not wrong to do this. Cannot we say the same thing about paternalism? The paternalist's argument would be that, although you are not respecting the patient's wishes when he says he does not want a life-saving operation and you go ahead and perform it anyway, nevertheless you are not wrong to save his life.

Hart describes paternalism as the protection of people against themselves, and maintains that, although respect for individual autonomy is very much a part of 20th century life, there has been a general decline in the belief that we are the best judges of our own best interests. Referring to the libertarian views of JS Mill, Hart says:

Hart, HLA, *Law, Liberty and Morality*, 1963, Oxford: OUP, p 33:

[There is] an increased awareness of a great range of factors which diminish the significance to be attached to an apparently free choice or to consent. Choices may be made or consent given without adequate reflection or appreciation of the consequences; or in pursuit of merely transitory desires; or in various predicaments when the judgment is likely to be clouded; or under inner psychological compulsion; or under pressure by others of a kind too subtle to be susceptible of proof in a law court. Underlying Mill's extreme fear of paternalism there perhaps is a conception of what a normal human being is like which now seems not to correspond to the facts. Mill, in fact, endows him with much of the psychology of a middle-aged man whose desires are relatively fixed, not liable to be artificially stimulated by external influences; who knows what he wants and what gives him satisfaction or happiness; and who pursues these things when he can.

As far as medicine is concerned, this argument states that paternalism is justified when, in the judgment of the doctor, the patient does not exhibit sufficient of the features of Hart's middle-aged man. The patient may be too young; the patient may have limited intelligence or limited education or may have a volatile personality given to acts of impetuosity. The doctor, on the other hand, is educated, impartial, knowledgeable and has only the best interests of the patient at heart. This grading of patients – and in consequence the way in which a doctor is entitled to regard them – is reflected in some of the case law (see, for example, the case of *Sidaway v Board of Governors of the Bethlem Royal Hospital and the Maudsley Hospital* [1985] AC 871, where Lord Diplock (p 895) states that an educated judge would 'naturally' want to ask questions about the risks of medical treatment before he consented to it – see further below, Chapter 3).

Strong and weak paternalism

It is arguable that the above view, ie, that some patients do not have sufficient education, etc, to make valid decisions, does not support paternalism in any form, but only where the patient's views are disregarded because of the circumstances, or something in the patient's own character. Writers sometimes refer to the difference as that between 'strong' and 'weak' (or 'limited') paternalism.

Childress describes the justification for limited paternalism as follows:

Childress, JF, *Who Should Decide? Paternalism in Health Care*, 1982, Oxford: OUP, p 102:

Conditions for justified paternalism

The principle of limited paternalism

Parents sometimes override their children's wishes in order to protect them. Such parental actions are often justified because of children's incompetence and risk of harm or loss of some good. This example from familial relations yields two conditions that are frequently invoked to justify medical paternalism: (1) the defects, encumbrances, and limitations of a person's decision making and acting, and (2) the probability of harm to that person unless there is intervention.

If the second condition – probable harm – is held to be sufficient to justify paternalism, apart from the person's incapacity for decision making, we have extended or strong paternalism. According to this position, paternalistic interventions can be justified when a patient's risk-benefit analysis is unreasonable even though he is competent and his wishes, choices, or actions are informed and voluntary. If, however, the first set of conditions is held to be necessary, we have limited or weak paternalism, which allows paternalistic interventions only when a person's wishes, choices, or actions are defective because of incompetence, ignorance, or some internal or external constraint.

Both conditions, yet to be explained and amplified, are jointly necessary to justify active paternalism ... To intervene merely because a person suffers some defect, encumbrance, or limitation in decision making or in acting is unwarranted. It would be intervention for the sake of intervention. As 'paternalism' implies, intervention requires justification in terms of the patient's interests as well as in terms of the patient's defects in deciding or acting. If the patient is not at risk, intervention is not warranted, however much his or her capacity to make decisions is reduced. Even a person with diminished capacity for decision making should be free except when he or she is at risk. This is an implication of holding that both conditions are jointly necessary.

If these two conditions are jointly necessary for justified active paternalism, and if only limited paternalism is justified, we are able to express both the principle of beneficence and the principle of respect for persons. In limited paternalism, agents meet the needs of other persons without insulting them. For example, if another person is incompetent to make decisions and is also at risk, interventions even against that person's express wishes do not signify disrespect or constitute an indignity. Not to intervene might even violate the principle of respect for persons; certainly, it would violate the principle of beneficence in some circumstances.

Since both of these conditions are necessary to justify paternalistic acts, it is possible to start with either one. An apparent reason to start with prevention or removal of harm, or provision of benefit, is that this consideration frequently triggers paternalistic actions. In the order of experience, perception of risk to the patient, apart from intervention, usually precedes and provokes an assessment of the patient's competence to decide. Indeed ... Carlton's studies indicate that a patient's competence to consent to treatment is rarely examined unless there is a conflict between the physician's recommendation and the patient's wishes. Thus, an apparent conflict of values provides the occasion for an examination of the patient's competence. In view of customary medical practice, there are two good reasons for beginning with the patient's incompetence as a necessary condition for justified paternalism. First, to begin with the prevention or removal of harm may appear to give this condition priority and may play into the hands of strong paternalists. Second, even though in practice there may be little interest in the patient's competence unless there are risks, from a moral point of view the assessment of the patient's competence should be somewhat independent of the risks. Otherwise, strong paternalism could masquerade as weak paternalism, since – the argument might go – no competent person would knowingly and voluntarily accept some risks.

Culver and Gert put forward two examples of paternalism, one of which they maintain is justified, the other, not:

Culver, CM and Gert, B, *Philosophy in Medicine*, 1982, New York: OUP, p 146:

Case 8-1

Mr K was brought to the emergency room by his wife and a police officer. Mrs K had confessed to her husband earlier that evening that she was having an affair with one of his colleagues. He had become acutely agitated and depressed and, after several hours of mounting tension, told her he was going to kill himself so 'you'll have the freedom to have all the lovers you want'. She became frightened and called the police because there were loaded guns in the house and she knew her husband was an impulsive man.

In the emergency room Mr K would do little more than glower at Dr T, his wife, and the officer. He seemed extremely tense and agitated. Dr T decided that for Mr K's own protection he should be hospitalised but Mr K refused. Dr T therefore committed Mr K to the hospital for a 72 hour emergency detention.

How could Dr T attempt to justify his paternalistic commitment of Mr K? He could claim that by depriving Mr K of his freedom, there was a great likelihood that he was preventing the occurrence of a much greater evil: Mr K's death, or serious injury. Dr T could further claim that in his professional experience the overwhelming majority of persons in Mr K's condition who were hospitalised did subsequently recover from their state of agitated depression and acknowledge the irrational character of their former suicidal desires.

Note that Dr T need not claim that self-inflicted death is an evil of such magnitude that paternalistic intervention to prevent it is always justified. Rather, he could claim that it is justified in Mr K's case on several counts. First, Mr K's desire to kill himself seems irrational; while one may explain his desire, using psychodynamic concepts, he appears to have no adequate reason for killing himself. An adequate reason would be a belief on his part that his death would result in the avoiding of great evil(s) or the attaining of great goods for himself or others. (His statement to his wife ['You'll have ... all the lovers you want'] sarcastically expresses an altruistic reason which, even if taken literally, would not be an adequate reason for his suicide.) Second, there is evidence that he suffers from a condition that is well known to be transient. Third, the violation of a moral rule (deprivation of freedom) which Dr T has carried out results in Mr K's suffering a much lesser evil than the evil (death) which Mr K may perpetrate on himself.

But it is not sufficient justification for Dr T merely to show that the evils prevented for Mr K by his paternalistic action outweigh the evils caused to Mr K; he must also be willing to publicly advocate the deprivation of Mr K's freedom in these circumstances. That is, he must be willing to advocate to all rational persons that in these circumstances everyone may be deprived of his freedom for a limited period of time. We believe that, accepting the case as described, not only could Dr T advocate to all rational persons that Mr K may be deprived of his freedom but also that, if they accepted the facts of the case and the conditions of public advocacy, all rational persons would agree with Dr T's judgment completely. Thus, Dr T's paternalistic behaviour is strongly justified.

By contrast, Culver and Gert consider the following:

Case 8-2

Mrs R, a 29 year old mother, is hospitalised with symptoms of abdominal pain, weight loss, weakness, and swelling of the ankles. An extensive medical workup is inconclusive, and exploratory abdominal surgery is carried out which reveals a primary ovarian cancer with extensive spread to other abdominal organs. Her condition is judged to be too far advanced for surgical relief, and her life expectancy is estimated to be at most a few months. Despite her oft-repeated requests to be told 'where I stand and what I face', Dr E tells both the patient and her husband that the diagnosis is still unclear but that he will see her weekly as an out-patient. At the time of discharge she is feeling somewhat better than at admission, and Dr E hopes that the family will have a few happy weeks together before her condition worsens and they must be told the truth.

Dr E's behaviour is clearly paternalistic: he has deceived Mrs R for what he believes is her benefit; he knows that he is violating the moral rule against deception without her consent; and he views her as someone who is competent to give or refuse valid consent to being told the truth.

Dr E could attempt to justify his paternalistic act by claiming that the evil – psychological suffering – he hoped to prevent by his deception is significantly greater than the evil, if any, he caused by lying. While this might be true in this particular case, it is by no means certain. By his deception, Dr E is depriving Mrs R and her family of the opportunity to make those plans that would enable her family to deal more adequately with her death. In the circumstances of this case as described, Mrs R's desire to know the truth is a rational one; in fact, there is no evidence of any irrational behaviour or desires on her part. This contrasts sharply to Mr K's desire to kill himself, which is clearly irrational. Furthermore, although we regard Mr K's desire not to be deprived of freedom, considered in isolation, as a rational one, we would not consider it rational for one to choose a high probability of death over the loss of a few days of freedom.

Arguably, we can see a weak form of paternalism operating when we consider our attitude to organ donation and non-therapeutic medical research. It is unlawful in the UK to sell a non-regenerative organ for transplant (see below, Chapter 11). Similarly, we prevent anything other than modest payments for those who undergo non-therapeutic research (ie, healthy volunteers). Many people who would not regard themselves as paternalists in the context of medical treatment might support these prohibitions on the basis that it is offensive for there to be a 'trade' in human organs or for people to sell their bodies for the purposes of research. However, is this not a form of paternalism, albeit one based upon the principle of non-maleficence, (as opposed to paternalism in relation to medical treatment which is based upon the principle of beneficence)?

Paternalism and the sanctity of life principle

Both Mill and Kant would accept the sanctity of life principle as this stems from the inherent value of the individual. The duty of beneficence has this principle at its heart. A paternalist might argue that the doctor's duty to do good and to uphold the sanctity of life principle will, on occasion, justifiably, override patient autonomy. For example, in Chapter 8 we look at several cases where the courts have had to consider the refusal by women of consent to Caesarean section operations to deliver their children. It has been held that the women's refusals must be respected, even if there is a strong likelihood that both mother and foetus will not survive. However, there is an argument that the principle of the sanctity of life might, in certain circumstances, override the woman's refusal.

Paternalism and the doctor's duty of beneficence

It might be said that it is bad for those involved in health care to be forced to stand helpless in the face of a refusal of life-saving treatment and witness an unnecessary death. This view might be illustrated by the role of doctors and other health care workers in the treatment of suicide attempts. Someone who attempts to take their own life can be treated without their consent. From what arises the right to override the patient's wish to die? Is it because the true wishes of the patient may not be known (it could be a 'cry for help' or an accident), or is it because of the dominance of the sanctity of life principle? It should be noted that health authorities have been held liable when a patient has committed suicide whilst under their care, if there has been inadequate supervision (see below, Chapter 3). Again, arguably this is about sanctity of life and beneficence: it is inappropriate that hospitals should be places of avoidable and self-inflicted deaths; they are places for healing and the saving of lives.

Paternalism and a duty to oneself?

In Culver and Gert's example of the patient at risk of suicide, it was assumed that paternalism would eventually give way to autonomy. Is there a sustainable ethical argument that one has a duty to oneself to live and to live a healthy life, and, therefore, treatment against one's wishes may be justifiable? It will be recalled that the intuitionist philosopher, WD Ross, said that one of the intuitively good principles was the duty of self-improvement.

Similarly, Kant, whose moral philosophy stated that human life is intrinsically valuable, puts duty before 'natural inclinations'. For example, he thought suicide permissible only if it was to avoid moral degradation. This was based upon the principle that only human beings can uphold the moral law and, therefore, for as long as they are not morally degraded, they have a duty to do that. Would this justify medical paternalism on the basis that the patient has a duty to live a healthy life and if, in the opinion of his doctors, he is not doing so, he must be treated against his will?

THE CASE FOR PATIENT AUTONOMY

Paternalism has an old-fashioned ring to it. Two American academics, Pellegrino and Thomasma, comment as follows:

Pellegrino, ED and Thomasma, DC, *For the Patient's Good: The Restoration of Beneficence in Health Care,* 1988, Oxford: OUP, p 5:

The sources of ... resistance to medical paternalism are many: the political and ethical philosophy of individual rights; the higher educational level of today's public; the latter's awareness of the powers and dangers of medical technology; a distrust of experts; the rise of consumerism; and the moral challenges of the Vietnam War, the civil rights movement, and the campus revolts of the sixties and early seventies. The convergence of these forces has been powerful enough to erode the 2,500 year old tradition of medical status contained in beneficent authoritarianism.

Autonomy

It is in the assertion that the right to autonomous medical decision making is paramount that Mill's libertarian philosophy is most evident: the only justification for imposing medical treatment on a patient against his will is to prevent harm to others. (In the section on utilitarianism and autonomy we will consider whether non-consensual medical treatment may ever by justified on the basis that it will prevent harm to others, but let us assume for the present that it will not.) Beauchamp and McCullough describe the development of the autonomy principle:

Beauchamp, TL and McCullough, LB, *Medical Ethics*, 1984, Englewood Cliffs: Prentice Hall, p 42:

A key feature of the principle of respect for autonomy has been developed in legal contexts, where 'self-determination' has a venerable history and is taken to be synonymous with what we are calling autonomy – that is, the ability to understand one's situation and pursue personal goals free of governing constraints. The principle of self-determination means that one has sovereignty over one's life – a sovereignty that protects privacy as well as rights to control what happens to one's person and property. In its original development in the law, the intrinsic worth of the individual, including the right to personal sovereignty, was advanced primarily as a check or limit on the authority of the State or another person. For example, the Bill of Rights and the 'due process' amendments to the United States Constitution were so fashioned. The central theme is that a person's sovereignty limits the sphere into which others may legitimately intrude.

Individual sovereignty needs protection for two reasons. First, there is a danger of imbalance in power between the individual and the State (or other parties) in favour of the latter. Individual rights provide a corrective to this imbalance by ensuring that individuals as individuals will be given due consideration and respect. Second, conflicts arise between an individual's perception of his or her best interests and another's perception of those interests. Rights of individual sovereignty protect an individual's freedom to choose his or her best interests. The legal principle of respect for self-determination is applied to questions concerning the physician's responsibility because patients and physicians are unequal in their possession of information and their power to control the circumstances under which they meet. Typically, one party is fit and medically knowledgeable, the other sick and medically ignorant. Legal rights are a way of limiting the physician's power and of protecting the patient from unwarranted intrusions – such as surgery without consent, involuntary commitment to a mental institution, and public disclosure of information contained in hospital records.

Conflicts also arise between medicine's understanding of a patient's best interests and the patient's understanding of those interests. This conflict occurs in the case [of a young woman who wishes to be sterilised as a contraceptive measure as she had decided that her life would be better without children] A physician ... may view this patient's best interests in quite another way by following the beneficence model. Thus, the law dictates that the physician who performs an invasive procedure without the patient's permission may be found guilty of a *battery*, though usually only *negligence* is charged. The underlying rationale behind the battery theory of liability for failure to obtain the patient's agreement has been closely linked in law to autonomy. This rationale burst on the scene in a crucial 1914 case and has since been widely offered as the basic right underlying the legal doctrine of informed consent: 'Every human being of adult years and sound mind has a right to determine what shall be done with his own body; and a surgeon who performs an operation without his patient's consent commits an assault.'

This right is an autonomy right. The language in which the law has expressed it is quite striking. Among the most important formulations is the following from a 1960 landmark case, *Natanson v Kline*: 'A doctor might well believe that an operation or form of treatment is desirable or necessary, but the law does not permit him to substitute his own judgment for that of the patient by any form of artifice or deception.' In a later case, Warren Burger, who later became Chief Justice of the United States Supreme Court, amplified the legal concept of self-determination, with a reflection on the character of the reasons or values of a patient that are meant to be protected. He argued that nothing in the right to be left alone means that an individual possesses these rights only regarding sensible beliefs, reasonable emotions, and the like. Hence many eccentric and even absurd ideas may validly form the basis of a patient's autonomous choices.

Much of the debate surrounding the principle of autonomy concerns the right of a patient to refuse life-saving treatment. Earlier we considered how far there may be an obligation to prevent suicide. It is interesting to note that it has been said that the liberty to commit suicide may be seen as 'an index of high civilisation', because the act goes against the most basic of our instincts, that of self-preservation (see Alvarez, A, *The Savage God: A Study of Suicide*, 1971, London: Weidenfeld and Nicolson).

The right to self-determination

Is the principle of autonomy equivalent to the right to self-determination? Is this 'right' really a liberty in the sense that there is no claim against anyone in the Hohfeldian sense? Certainly the right to self-determination could not be relied upon to impose duties on others to provide medical treatment.

Although not part of English law, other jurisdictions, such as the United States, recognise the right to privacy. (The right to privacy is also protected by Art 8 of the European Convention on Human Rights, which is soon to be incorporated into English law.) There is some debate as to whether autonomy is part of the right to privacy. Wellman considers the issue:

> **Wellman, C, *An Approach to Rights*, 1997, Dordrecht: Kluwer Academic, p 185:**
>
> ... how is this right [to privacy] related to personal autonomy? A tempting hypothesis is that autonomy is located within one portion of this right because one of the constitutionally protected areas of privacy is that of private decisions. Thus, even though the right to privacy is not the liberty-right to make and act on private decisions, it includes the claim-right that others not interfere with these private decisions, for any such interference would be an invasion of a protected area of privacy. I very much doubt, however, that this direct and essential connection between privacy and autonomy has ever been recognised by the courts. For one thing, the expression 'a private decision' is conspicuous by its absence from the opinions in the privacy cases, even in *Roe* [*v Wade*] and *Quinlan* that centre on the abortion decision and the decision to refuse medical treatment, respectively. Moreover, this interpretation misrepresents the reasoning of the courts. The argument in *Roe* is not that the abortion decision is constitutionally protected because it is a private decision, but that it is encompassed by the right to privacy because it involves the exercise of one of the fundamental liberties recognised in the US Constitution. Hence, the emphasis is upon how fundamental, not how personal and private, the decision is.

The political approach and the rejection of 'social control'

Those who support the overriding importance of the autonomy principle are lent support by the way in which psychiatry was used in the former Soviet Union, where some political dissidents were diagnosed as being 'psychiatrically ill' and compulsorily detained in hospital. The writer Thomas Szasz, whose work is considered further below, in Chapter 9, cites this abuse of medicine in a number of his publications (see, for example, Szasz, TS, *Law, Liberty and Psychiatry: An Inquiry into the Social Uses of Mental Health Practices*, 1974, London: Routledge and Kegan Paul). The argument is that illness is a value-laden concept and any form of paternalism runs the risk of doctors branding patients with 'illness' and subsequent treatment. It is easy to see how this abuse can take place with something as nebulous as mental illness, but could this sort of abuse take place in respect of other forms of illness? Perhaps alcoholism, for example, could be so regarded – and see above, p 30, where it is suggested that 'imperfections' such as baldness might be categorised as illnesses.

Utilitarianism and autonomy

It is interesting to consider the interaction of these two concepts, because both were embraced in the philosophy of JS Mill. His libertarian views imply that one must be free to pursue a conception of life that is conducive to human flourishing. However, is there one conception of the good life, and if not, how do we maximise welfare? Similarly, if one is looking at the consequences of actions, if the exercise of one's autonomy adversely affects other people, then are not the two principles incompatible? In the context of refusal of life-saving treatment, it may be said that the right to self-determination is in conflict with utility because the consequences of the refusal may be bad for the family left behind: the loss of a breadwinner (the family is now dependent upon society for support) and the infliction of grief. It is arguable that this reflects one of the deficiencies in the utilitarian approach: it allows only a limited role for basic rights. Alternatively, it could be said that subjecting people to violation of their physical integrity has worse consequences for society than does respecting their bodily integrity. If this argument were accepted then respect for autonomy would be an essential element of any utilitarian account of medical ethics.

Rationality

Giving effect to autonomy in relation to medical treatment presupposes that the patient is competent to make decisions about such treatment. Do these decisions have to be rational? GEM Anscombe (see *Intention*, 1963, Oxford: Blackwells) gives an interesting example of having a reason for doing something. She cites the example of a man who wants a saucer of mud. He is asked whether he wants it to study its chemistry, whether he finds mud aesthetically pleasing, whether he has a practical use for it and so on; he answers all questions in the negative: he just wants a saucer of mud for no reason. Surely we would want to conclude that he doesn't want a saucer of mud at all. By analogy, there would have to be reasons for making decisions about medical treatment. However, these can be and, as we shall see, often are, bizarre. Do we conclude that, because of this, the patient lacks decision making capacity? As we shall see from examining the case law in Chapter 3, the answer is 'no'. Decision making capacity may be present despite the fact that a patient holds a number of strange and, apparently, unsupportable, beliefs. Perhaps the correct view is that if these beliefs are genuinely held, and form part of the patient's 'world view', then they should be respected. In other words, unlike the man who wants the saucer of mud for no reason whatsoever, the patient has reasons that *make sense to him* and, as such, should be respected.

Autonomy and beneficence

Even the most ardent proponent of the principle of autonomy would accept that it would be wrong to deny someone medical treatment because they were incapable of consenting. If it were otherwise, no mentally incompetent patient would ever receive treatment. However, the argument would be that in the cases of children and adults lacking capacity, such treatment is not contrary to the principle of autonomy because they are not autonomous human beings. Similarly, people suffering from certain forms of mental disorder may be compulsorily detained and treated for that disorder without consent, and it is argued that this is carried out to *restore* their autonomy, and therefore entirely consistent with the principle (see below, Chapter 9).

PATERNALISM V AUTONOMY – A FALSE DICHOTOMY?

Using the principle of beneficence, the paternalist will justify treating patients against their will, or withholding information from them which is 'bad for them'. We have seen that, even within the philosophy of autonomy, there may be justified intervention, although the advocate of autonomy would argue that the patient in those cases is not truly autonomous. However, when we look at decision making capacity below, in Chapter 3, we will find that it is by no means easy to decide whether someone has sufficient capacity to make truly autonomous decisions. It might be thought that this adds fuel to the argument of the paternalists. However, it is arguable that precisely because it can be difficult to assess capacity, it is all the more important to guard against the paternalist declaring someone incapable in order to do what he thinks is best for them. These difficulties might make us wonder whether the traditional opposition of paternalism and autonomy might not give way to something which recognises the best in each of them. Some writers have endeavoured to find a more conciliatory approach, which accommodates both models.

Collaborative decision making

Pellegrino and Thomasma say that there can never be a single model to describe the doctor-patient relationship adequately. They set down a beneficence model as follows:

Pellegrino, ED and Thomasma, DC, *For the Patient's Good: The Restoration of Beneficence in Health Care*, 1988, Oxford: OUP, p 32:

... one of the seductions of the autonomy and paternalism models is their comparative ease of decision making: Either the physician makes all the decisions or the patient does so. Both models abandon the trials and rewards of a mutual dialogue and exchange between doctor and patient. Both also can assault the moral agency of the patient or the physician ...

... The values of patient autonomy – which translate into the corresponding moral duties of beneficence and respect for persons – may come into conflict with each other. In our view, however, these duties cannot remain in conflict if medicine is to achieve its goal of healing.

But healing, as we define it, is a form of assistance in making the patient whole again by working through his or her body. If the values of patient welfare and patient autonomy remain in conflict, then authentic healing cannot take place. A physician, therefore, must become both a moderate autonomist and a moderate welfarist ...

Another way of arriving at this position is to consider the principle of respect for persons. This principle leads to at least two moral duties. The first is to respect the self-determination or autonomy of others. The second, often neglected duty is to help restore that autonomy or help establish it when it is absent. Looked at in this way, beneficence is seen to be a direct consequence of a fundamental moral principle and the guiding duty of medicine. If this is true, then the autonomy model is necessarily incomplete. So, too, is the paternalistic model.

In this regard, other writers have suggested that it would be preferable for medical decision making to be conceived of as a kind of collaborative effort:

Teff, H, 'Consent to medical procedures: paternalism, self-determination or therapeutic alliance' [1985] 101 LQR 450:

It has been argued that the pursuit of a therapeutic alliance, in the sense of a genuine collaborative effort, is desirable in so far as it can facilitate a beneficial outcome. Quite apart from the fact that for many medical conditions there is either no specific remedy or the effectiveness of treatment is unknown, the doctor cannot intuitively know precisely what constitutes health or well being for a particular patient. The optimum 'outcome' is not necessarily to be equated with the technically successful result of a given operation, but may embrace a prognosis of the patient's subsequent medical and psychological condition and ability to function, as well as other social and financial considerations where relevant.

When medical procedures, especially invasive ones, are contemplated, doctor-patient relationships are often fraught with uncertainty and ambiguity. There is no *a priori* reason to assume that a doctor or surgeon possesses the kind of psychological or moral insight that would enable him to decide unaided what is most appropriate. The relative importance which patients attach, for example, to quality as against length of life, and to physical integrity or appearance as against diminution of pain, may reflect personal values, circumstances and priorities of which the surgeon, in particular, is initially unaware and may never become sufficiently apprised. It is apparently common practice in English hospitals for the information deemed relevant to patient consent to be provided by 'the most junior and inexperienced doctor, who will not perform the operation and who knows nothing of the likely complications' ...

A fiduciary relationship

That the doctor-patient relationship might be a fiduciary relationship has yet to be accepted by the English courts (see, for example, the judgment of Lord Scarman in *Sidaway v Board of Governors of the Bethlem Royal Hospital and the Maudsley Hospital* [1985] AC 871). However, some commentators have suggested that this may be a plausible analysis of the relationship. What is a fiduciary relationship? Peter Bartlett describes it as follows:

> **Bartlett, P, 'Doctors as fiduciaries: equitable regulation of the doctor-patient relationship' [1997] Med L Rev 193:**
>
> A fiduciary relationship attracts the attention of equity. The term apparently arose in the 19th century, when a variety of relationships held by equity to be 'on trust' were no longer necessarily flowing from 'trusts' themselves in any meaningful sense. With this motley origin, it is not surprising that fiduciary relationships themselves differ widely in the duties equity imposes on them. Consider the examples of lawyers and trustees. Certainly, one would expect a duty of undivided loyalty to the beneficiary or client in each case, and one would not expect the fiduciary to make a profit from the relationship outside that expressly authorised. There are equally firm differences, however. Unless inconsistent with his or her duty to the court, the lawyer acts on the instructions of the client, even when the instructions do not reflect the lawyer's view of the client's best interest. Trustees, by comparison, act in the beneficiary's best financial interest in any event. Where the beneficiary is in a relatively weak position in the control of the trust, the client is in control of the legal matter.
>
> This has led a number of scholars to argue that it is inappropriate to think of the application of fiduciary relationships as a class at all, but rather specific relationships attracting specific collections of fiduciary duties ...
>
> Further flexibility is introduced through the distinction between fact-based and status-based fiduciary obligations, the latter being based in relationships traditionally recognised by equity and attracting a broader array of fiduciary obligations, and the former based in specific fact situations and attracting only some fiduciary obligations. The advantage of this approach is that the courts may perceive an increased flexibility to extend obligations beyond the traditional fiduciary situations to offer specific equitable remedies in specific situations, without setting broad precedent.

Is it arguable that the fiduciary model could remove the paternalism-autonomy divide? For example, could the relationship of trust justify paternalistic treatment as long as the doctor was totally candid with the patient? But there may be an inherent problem here: if the doctor is candid and the patient refuses the treatment, then the 'fiduciary' nature of the relationship does not assist in resolving the problem. However, it is clear that aspects of the doctor-patient relationship can be fiduciary in nature, such as the duty of confidentiality, and whilst the English courts have been reluctant to accept the model in the context of access to medical records, a fiduciary duty may be applicable (see below, Chapter 5).

JUSTICE IN THE ALLOCATION OF HEALTH RESOURCES

The foregoing sections have considered the treatment of patients when they have not wanted treatment, or where the patients' medical conditions have not been fully revealed to them, or where treatment information has been withheld or restricted. A scenario we have not yet considered consists of a patient requiring treatment, and being refused, or a doctor ready and willing to treat a patient, but unable to do so because of lack of resources.

Most of us would agree that resources should be distributed fairly, or in accordance with justice. However, this bland statement gets us nowhere unless we decide the basis of a fair distribution. Concepts of justice often present three different models for distribution. First, resources may be distributed in accordance with merit. This would mean that the most deserving persons, for example, in terms of moral worth or contribution to society, would receive health care as a matter of priority. Secondly, resources may be distributed 'equally'. However, this presupposes that we have a test for deciding whether the persons concerned are equal. Certainly they are entitled to equal respect and consideration, but that in itself may not be enough. This tempts us to adopt the third model, which is that resources be distributed in accordance with need.

What effect does a shortage of resources have on the doctor-patient relationship? Christopher Newdick argues as follows:

Newdick, C, *Who Should We Treat?*, 1995, Oxford: Clarendon Press, p 277:

A   Rationing and the Hippocratic Oath

One of the most pressing problems in medical law concerns the current status of the Hippocratic Oath and the many international codes which have followed it. Under the Oath doctors promise: 'I will follow that system of regimen which, according to my ability and judgment, I consider for the benefit of my patients ... Into whatever house I enter, I will go into them [sic] for the benefit of the sick.

The modern statement of the principle is contained in the Declaration of Geneva, published by the World Health Organisation. It says, *inter alia*, that the 'health of my patient will be my first consideration'. Similarly, the International Code of Medical Ethics provides that 'a physician shall act only in the patient's best interests when providing medical care which might have the effect of weakening the physical and mental condition of the patient'.

Exactly what counts as a patient's 'best interests' is not, and probably never could be, specified in detail. Patients present doctors with an infinite variety and combination of illnesses and reasonable doctors will naturally differ as to the best way of responding to them. Also, although the Hippocratic Oath presumes that doctors will always promote the best interests of the individual, finite resources have long meant that difficult decisions between patients may sometimes be unavoidable. In all this, however, there is nothing new. Resources have never been infinite and unenviable decisions between patients have always been made, though in a manner less visible in the past. Doctors care for groups of patients and know very well that the use of a bed or operating theatre for one patient may mean that the treatment of another will be delayed or denied altogether. For this reason elderly people have found it more difficult to be referred for surgery, infertility treatment has not always been made available, those suffering mental illness have not always obtained care in hospital, and kidney dialysis has been available to relatively few. In reality, therefore, the idea of absolute clinical freedom may long have been an unaffordable myth. It is debatable whether true clinical freedom in fact ever existed and, if it did, whether it should have been allowed.

Our ethical dilemmas have previously been about the nature of the doctor-patient relationship in a one to one sense. Now we are looking at the relationship between the doctor and many of his patients. Does this undermine the cosy beneficence model, where the doctor's only concern is to do his best for the patient?

Newdick comments further on the issue of clinical freedom:

Newdick, C, *Who Should We Treat?*, 1995, Oxford: Clarendon Press, p 278:

... pressure is now being exerted on doctors to comply with clinical practice guidelines, to undertake medical audit of their procedures, and to be prepared to justify substantial differences between them. To what extent will the differing instincts of doctors continue to be supportable? Some have individual patients uppermost in their minds and have always prescribed the best available treatment. Others with an eye on reducing expenditure may try a 'second best' treatment first, and use the best only if that fails. Modern medical ethics demands that doctors understand the economic impact of their decisions, of what economists call 'opportunity costs', ie, the range of treatments, the opportunities, that will be forgone if the money to pay for them is diverted elsewhere. Thus, the British Medical Association has said: 'Wastage of resources is unethical because it diminishes society's capacity to relieve suffering through the other uses that could be made of the wasted resources. Doctors working within the NHS need to be aware of cost-effectiveness as well as clinical effectiveness in the care provided for the patient.

But 'waste' is not a neutral word. Governments, health service managers, doctors and patients all have differing ideas about how resources should be spent. Used as a way of insisting that individual patients receive only the most effective treatment, it may not threaten the idea of clinical freedom. Doctors will be eager to uphold this usage of the word. Many believe the relationship of trust between doctor and patient is precious and that doctors should never compromise their clinical commitment to the individual. The General Medical Council endorses this view and encourages doctors to adhere to their traditional Hippocratic priorities. Recognising the importance of limited resources, it says: 'The Council endorses the principle that a doctor should always seek to give priority to the investigation and treatment of patients solely on the basis of clinical need.'

By contrast, health economists will stress the need to distribute national resources efficiently and give 'waste' a different meaning. They will stress the 'macro' goals and priorities of health spending. This approach tends to emphasise the clinical benefits to whole communities, rather than to individuals, and could have considerable potential in modifying the relationship between doctors and patients. One set of guidelines, for example, has recommended that the distribution of resources by hospitals and doctors should always be consistent with the policies established by governments at national level so that: 'Health care professionals at the clinical level ought not to make any treatment decision that undermines legitimate attempts at a higher level to establish just and efficient use of resources.'

This view is likely to gain ground although it is currently still in its infancy because firm evidence of the cost and effectiveness of medical treatment is unavailable. Its implications, however, are important. Were such an approach to be adopted, doctors would become more openly involved in shaping and implementing social and economic policies and their clinical freedom with respect to individuals would have to be modified as a result. This poses the most clear and coherent threat to the traditional notion of the Hippocratic Oath. On the other hand, in this most delicate and fundamental area of practice, doctors have little training in the principles (whatever they may be) which might assist them. 'Unfortunately, physicians have little experience with the task of bringing moral and social norms to bear on particular disputes and situations. [And] ethicists and jurists are not familiar with the medical and emotional nuances associated with the care of acutely ill and dying patients.'

There is an urgent need for both doctors and the community to address the questions raised by these pressures.

The administration and efficient running of the National Health Service is looked at further below, in Chapter 2.

It is highly likely in practice that many doctors will frequently have to choose who to treat, or who to treat as a matter of priority, and that this will mean that he is not doing his best for those who are not treated, or not treated in a timely fashion. Some doctors have been frank about these issues and have suggested to their patients that a ballot takes place to decide on priority.

'Editorial' (1980) 6 JME 171:

Who shall die?

A British gynaecologist recently chose by ballot the patients who were to be admitted to the inadequate number of beds at his disposal. He had already selected those patients with gynaecologically urgent problems, and finding not much to chose medically between the rest, he obtained their consent to select by lot. He was subsequently criticised on radio by a medically qualified administrator for not using a better method of selection.

Well, what *is* a better method? The question – an extremely complex one – is raised in a more obviously serious context by two articles in this issue of the *Journal*. In the first Drs Parsons and Lock discuss the results of a survey they carried out among British nephrologists on their criteria for triage among patients with chronic renal failure. In the second Gavin H Mooney, the health economist, argues for the central importance of cost-benefit analysis in the allocation of limited medical resources.

Parsons and Lock, disturbed by increasingly inadequate funds for dialysis and transplantation, asked 25 British nephrologists to reject 10 out of 40 realistically described patients, ticking their reasons for rejection from a checklist under the categories of age, marital status, home facilities, underlying disease, and additional disease. All the nephrologists completed the questionnaire except for one who felt unable to accept any of the reasons suggested as valid grounds for rejection. Their responses make important reading. Interestingly, of the 10 patients most generally rejected, 'we found that at least six of them had been successfully treated by our own unit'; and not one of the patients was rejected by all the respondents.

Accepting for the time being that such choices must in practice be made, whereby some individuals are to be allocated life-saving resources while others with the same problem are to be refused them (microallocation or triage) it may be worthwhile distinguishing different criteria upon which such choices might conceivably be made. Perhaps the one most commonly used in practice is that favoured by many of the respondents, notably the medical or technical criterion, whereby triage is based on the probability of successful medical outcome. In clear cases this criterion seems unproblematic; for example, other things being equal, a doctor faced with two patients needing blood transfusion and only enough blood for one would surely be not merely absurd but downright wicked to transfuse the patient with an incompatible blood group when the other's blood group matched that of the available blood. The criterion for proper choice here is quite clearly likelihood of medical success.

The first of the criteria, the probability of successful medical outcome, seems, as the editorial states, unproblematic. However, the example given of the blood transfusion is perhaps too simplistic. It is beyond doubt that in this example there is one, and only one, ethical choice. Indeed there is no ethical dilemma here at all. Many predictions of 'successful medical outcome', however, might be covert value judgments. From time to time the newspapers report cases of smokers being refused heart surgery. Hospitals are at pains to point out that the refusal is not because they are smokers, but because the cardiac specialists state that the surgery will not be a lasting success if the patient, who has no plans to give up smoking, continues to smoke. However, might, at least in part, these decisions be based on other factors?

'Editorial' (1980) 6 JME 171:

A second criterion for selection might be the candidates' value or disvalue to society; thus those respondents who rejected patients positive for Australia antigen on grounds of the risk to other patients and staff of potentially lethal hepatitis were explicitly or implicitly using this social criterion, as were any respondents who wished to stop treatment on the grounds that resources are being drained by the heavily handicapped and homeless from other less demanding patients.

There may be concern about the restriction on treatment in the cases of elderly people. Doctors may well find it easier to justify this on the basis of successful medical outcome. Is age a good reason for refusing treatment? The following are some of the arguments explored by Harris for and against:

Harris, J, *The Value of Life*, **1985, London: Routledge and Kegan Paul, p 89:**

The anti-ageist argument

All of us who wish to go on living have something that each of us values equally, although for each it is different in character, for some a much richer prize than for others, and we none of us know its true extent. This thing is of course 'the rest of our lives'. So long as we do not know the date of our deaths, then for each of us the 'rest of our lives' is of indefinite duration. Whether we are 17 or 70, in perfect health or suffering from a terminal disease, we each have the rest of our lives to lead. So long as we each fervently wish to live out the rest of our lives, however long that turns out to be, then if we do not deserve to die, we each suffer the same injustice if our wishes are deliberately frustrated and we are cut off prematurely. Indeed there may well be a double injustice in deciding that those whose life expectation is short should not benefit from rescue or resuscitation. Suppose I am told today that I have terminal cancer with only approximately six months or so to live, but I want to live until I die, or at least until I decide that life is no longer worth living. Suppose I then am involved in an accident and because my condition is known to my potential rescuers and there are not enough resources to treat all who could immediately be saved I am marked among those who will not be helped. I am then the victim of a double tragedy and a double injustice. I am stricken first by cancer and the knowledge that I have only a short time to live and I'm then stricken again when I'm told that because of my first tragedy a second and more immediate one is to be visited upon me. Because I have once been unlucky I'm now no longer worth saving.

The point is a simple but powerful one. However short or long my life will be, so long as I want to go on living it then I suffer a terrible injustice when that life is prematurely cut short. Imagine a group of people all of an age, say a class of students all in their mid twenties. If fire trapped all in the lecture theatre and only 20 could be rescued in time should the rescuers shout 'youngest first!'? Suppose they had time to debate the question or had been debating it 'academically' before the fire? It would surely seem invidious to deny some what all value so dearly merely because of an accident of birth. It might be argued that age here provides no criterion precisely because although the lifespans of such a group might be expected to vary widely, there would be no way of knowing who was most likely to live longest. But suppose a reliable astrologer could make very realistic estimates or, what amounts to the same thing, suppose the age range of the students to be much greater, say 17 to 55. Does not the invidiousness of selecting by birth-date remain? Should a 17 year old be saved before a 29 year old or she before the 45 year old and should the 55 year old clearly be the last to be saved or the first to be sacrificed?

Our normal intuitions would share this sense of the invidiousness of choosing between our imaginary students by reason of their respective ages, but would start to want to make age relevant at some extremes, say if there were a 2 day old baby and a 90 year old grandmother. We will be returning to discuss a possible basis for this intuition in a moment. However, it is important to be clear that the anti-ageist argument denies the relevance of age or life expectancy as a criterion absolutely. It argues that even if I know for certain that I have only a little space to live, that space, however short, may be very precious to me. Precious, precisely because it is all the time I have left, and just as precious to me on that account as all the time you have left is precious to you, however much those two timespans differ in length. So that where we both want, equally strongly, to go on living, then we each suffer the same injustice when our lives are cut short or are cut further short.

It might seem that someone who would insist on living out the last few months of his life when by 'going quietly' someone else might have the chance to live for a much longer time would be a very selfish person. But this would be true only if the anti-ageist argument is false. It will be true only if it is not plausible to claim that living out the rest of one's life could be equally valuable to the individual whose life it is irrespective of the amount of unelapsed time that is left. And this is of course precisely the usual situation when individuals do not normally have anything but the haziest of ideas as to how long it is that they might have left.

I think the anti-ageist argument has much plausibility. It locates the wrongness of ending an individual's life in the evil of thwarting that person's desire to go on living and argues that it is profoundly unjust to frustrate that desire merely because some of those who have exactly the same desire, held no more strongly, also have a longer life expectancy than the others. However, there are a number of arguments that pull in the opposite direction and these we must now consider.

The fair innings argument

One problem with the anti-ageist argument is our feeling that there is something unfair about a person who has lived a long and happy life hanging on grimly at the end, while someone who has not been so fortunate suffers a related double misfortune, of losing out in a lottery in which his life happened to be in the balance with that of the grim octogenarian. It might be argued that we could accept the part of the anti-ageist argument which focuses on the equal value of unelapsed time, if this could be tempered in some way. How can it be just that someone who has already had more than her fair share of life and its delights should be preferred or even given an equal chance of continued survival with the young person who has not been so favoured? One strategy that seems to take account of our feeling that there is something wrong with taking steps to prolong the lives of the very old at the expense of those much younger is the fair innings argument.

The fair innings argument takes the view that there is some span of years that we consider a reasonable life, a fair innings. Let's say that a fair share of life is the traditional three score and ten, 70 years. Anyone who does not reach 70 suffers, on this view, the injustice of being cut off in their prime. They have missed out on a reasonable share of life; they have been short-changed. Those, however, who do make 70 suffer no such injustice, they have not lost out but rather must consider any additional years a sort of bonus beyond that which could reasonably be hoped for. The fair innings argument requires that everyone be given an equal chance to have a fair innings, to reach the appropriate threshold but, having reached it, they have received their entitlement. The rest of their life is the sort of bonus which may be cancelled when this is necessary to help others reach the threshold.

The attraction of the fair innings argument is that it preserves and incorporates many of the features that made the anti-ageist argument plausible, but allows us to preserve our feeling that the old who have had a good run for their money should not be endlessly propped up at the expense of those who have not had the same chance. We can preserve the conclusion of the anti-ageist argument, that so long as life is equally valued by the person whose life it is, it should be given an equal chance of preservation, and we can go on taking this view until the people in question have reached a fair innings.

There is, however, an important difficulty with the fair innings argument. It is that the very arguments which support the seeing of the threshold at an age which might plausibly be considered to be a reasonable lifespan, equally support the setting of the threshold at any age at all, so long as an argument from fairness can be used to support so doing. Suppose that there is only one place available on the dialysis programme and two patients are in competition for it. One is 30, and the other 40 years of age. The fair innings argument requires that neither be preferred on the grounds of age since both are below the threshold and are entitled to an equal chance of reaching it. If there is no other reason to choose between them we should do something like toss a coin. However, the 30 year old can argue that the considerations which support the fair innings argument require that she be given the place. After all, what's fair about the fair innings argument is precisely that each individual should have an equal chance of enjoying the benefits of a reasonable lifespan. The younger patient can argue that from where she's standing, the age of 40 looks much more reasonable a span than that of 30, and that she should be given the chance to benefit from those 10 extra years.

This argument generalised becomes a reason for always preferring to save younger rather than older people, whatever the age difference, and makes the original anti-ageist argument begin to look again the more attractive line to take. For the younger person can always argue that the older has had a fairer innings, and should now give way. It is difficult to stop whatever span is taken to be a fair innings collapsing towards zero under pressure from those younger candidates who see their innings as less fair than that of those with a larger share.

But perhaps this objection to the fair innings argument is mistaken? If 70 years is a fair innings it does not follow that the nearer a span of life approaches 70 years, the fairer an innings it is. This may be revealed by considering a different sort of threshold. Suppose that most people can run a mile in seven minutes, and that two people are given the opportunity to show that they can run a mile in that time. They both expect to be given seven minutes. However, if one is in fact given only three minutes and the other only four, it's not true that the latter is given a fairer running time: for people with average abilities four minutes is no more realistic a time in which to run a mile than is three. Four minutes is neither a fair threshold in itself, nor a fairer one than three minutes would be.

Nor does the argument that establishes seven minutes as an appropriate threshold lend itself to variation downwards. For that argument just is that seven is the number of minutes that an average adult takes to run a mile. Why then is it different for lifespans? If three score and ten is the number of years available to most people for getting what life has to offer, and is also the number of years people can reasonably expect to have, then it is a misfortune to be allowed anything less, however much less one is allowed, if nothing less than the full span normally suffices for getting what can be got out of life. It's true that the 40 year old gets more time than the 30 year old, but the frame of reference is not time only, but time normally required for a full life.

This objection has some force, but its failure to be a good analogy reveals that two sorts of considerations go to make an innings fair. For while living a full or complete life, just in the sense of experiencing all the ages of man, is one mark of a fair innings, there is also value in living through as many ages as possible. Just as completing the mile is one value, it is not the only one. Runners in the race of life also value ground covered, and generally judge success in terms of distance run.

What the fair innings argument needs to do is to capture and express in a workable form the truth that while it is always a *misfortune* to die when one wants to go on living, it is not a tragedy to die in old age; but it is on the other hand, both a tragedy and a misfortune to be cut off prematurely. Of course, ideas like 'old age' and 'premature death' are inescapably vague, and may vary from society to society, and over time as techniques for postponing death improve. We must also remember that while it may be invidious to choose between a 30 and a 40 year old on the grounds that one has had a fairer innings than the other, it may not be invidious to choose between the 30 and the 65 year old on those grounds.

If we remember, too, that it will remain wrong to end the life of someone who wants to live or to fail to save them, and that the fair innings argument will only operate as a principle of selection where we are forced to choose between lives, then something workable might well be salvaged.

While 'old age' is irredeemably vague, we can tell the old from the young, and even the old from the middle-aged. So that without attempting precise formulation, a reasonable form of the fair innings argument might hold; and might hold that people who had achieved old age or who were closely approaching it would not have their lives further prolonged when this could only be achieved at the cost of the lives of those who were not nearing old age. These categories could be left vague, the idea being that it would be morally defensible to prefer to save the lives of those who 'still had their lives before them' rather than those who had 'already lived full lives'. The criterion to be employed in each case would simply be what reasonable people would say about whether someone had had a fair innings. Where reasonable people would be in no doubt that a particular individual was nearing old age *and* that that person's life could only be further prolonged at the expense of the life of someone that no reasonable person would classify as nearing old age, then the fair innings argument would apply, and it would be justifiable to save the younger candidate.

In cases where reasonable people differed or it seemed likely that they would differ as to whether people fell into one category or the other, then the anti-ageist argument would apply and the inescapable choice would have to be made arbitrarily.

But again it must be emphasised that the fair innings argument would only operate as a counsel of despair, when it was clearly impossible to postpone the deaths of all those who wanted to go on living. In all other circumstances the anti-ageist argument would apply.

One influential proposal for allocating health care resources fairly has been by means of calculating QALYs (see, for example, *The Measurement of Health*, published by the Office of Health Economics in 1985, and Williams, A, 'The value of QALYs' (1985) Health and Social Services Journal). John Harris describes this approach as follows:

Harris, J, 'QALYfying the value of life' (1987) 13 JME 117:

1 What are QALYs?

It is important to be as clear as possible as to just what a QALY is and what it might be used for. I cannot do better than let Alan Williams, the architect of QALYs, tell you in his own words:

> The essence of a QALY is that it takes a year of healthy life expectancy to be worth one, but regards a year of unhealthy life expectancy as worth less than one. Its precise value is lower the worse the quality of life of the unhealthy person (which is what the 'quality adjusted' bit is all about). If being dead is worth zero, it is, in principle, possible for a QALY to be negative, ie, for the quality of someone's life to be judged worse than being dead.

> The general idea is that a beneficial health care activity is one that generates a positive amount of QALYs, and that an efficient health care activity is one where the cost-per-QALY is as low as it can be. A high priority health care activity is one where the cost-per-QALY is low, and a low priority activity is one where cost-per-QALY is high.

The plausibility of the QALY derives from the idea that given the choice, a person would prefer a shorter healthier life to a longer period of survival in a state of severe discomfort and disability. The idea that any rational person would endorse this preference provides the moral and political force behind the QALY. Its acceptability as a measurement of health then depends upon its doing all the theoretical tasks assigned to it, and on its being what people want, or would want, for themselves.

Harris subsequently became involved in a debate with John McKie *et al* about the application of QALYs (a series of articles was published in (1996) 22 JME 204–21). Part of the debate centred on John Rawls' famous 'veil of ignorance' argument in *A Theory of Justice*, 1972, Oxford: OUP. Rawls was attempting to find a system of distributive justice whilst accepting the proposition that people tend to be self-interested rather than altruistic. The scenario he envisages is as follows. Imagine that you are one of a number of people who are aware of the way in which the so called laws of economics work, but do not know their place in society. So, for example, you may be rich and powerful, or you may be unemployed with no resources whatsoever. Behind this 'veil of ignorance' you are asked to agree a set of principles which will govern the way in which the benefits and burdens in society are distributed. Assume, too, that you are motivated by self-interest. Rawls argues that because you do not know your position in society you will take care to ensure that conditions for those at the bottom of the pile are as good as possible. Rawls' theory is open to the objection that it assumes that the self-interested person will choose to play safe in this way. It can be argued that those behind the veil might choose to take a gamble. McKie *et al* state that QALYs would be chosen by those behind the veil of ignorance because QALYs maximise utility. In other words, they take a wider view of self-interest. Harris states that they would not, because the persons behind the veil, ie, typical human beings, are cautious risk-averse persons, who would weigh the downside more than the upside. This is a difficult dispute to resolve. Does it depend upon the view one takes of human psychology, and won't there always be at least two views?

Harris also maintains that the problem with the QALY approach is that a person's life is valued more even if the difference in life expectation is very small. For example, the patient who would survive for just two days more than another would be preferred. McKie *et al* acknowledge this, but point out that Harris' insistence upon treating all needy patients equally means that the patient who would survive for 30 years if treated, and the patient who would survive for two days if treated, would be regarded as equally deserving of that treatment. Is the Harris-McKie debate another example of utility versus absolutism? On the basis of the former, at least the traditional way of looking at utilitarianism, some pretty ruthless decisions could be made about health care rationing. So, for example, the denial of treatment to anyone over 75 years old would provide more resources for younger people who would be in the majority. The utilitarian response would be that such a rule would morally impoverish society, leaving a lot of people to suffer a painful and distressing old age, a spectacle which, far from being good for the majority of younger people, would make them positively unhappy.

Both Harris and McKie agree that any form of resource allocation which creates social divisiveness is wrong. But if the wider issues relating to health are examined, there is a great deal of evidence that poverty and health are inextricably linked. See, for example, Black *et al*, *Inequalities in Health: The Black Report*, 1982, Harmondsworth: Penguin. The latter produced evidence on the link between health and wealth, and reported that life expectancy at birth was seven years higher in social class one (professional) than in social class five (manual). There is therefore a cogent argument in favour of a redistribution of health resources to redress the imbalance. Furthermore, it points up the fact that 'health care' decisions are strongly linked to economic policy and social justice.

CHAPTER TWO

HEALTH CARE IN ENGLAND AND WALES

BACKGROUND

The international framework

The UK Government has committed itself under international law to the promotion of its citizens' health and the prevention of disease. The key aspirations to this end are contained in the European Social Charter of 1961 (as revised in 1996), which is an offshoot from the scheme of political and civil rights found in the 1950 European Convention for the Protection of Human Rights and Fundamental Freedoms and is overseen by the same body, the Council of Europe. Articles 11 and 13 of the Social Charter provide as follows:

Article 11 – The right to protection of health

With a view to ensuring the effective exercise of the right to protection of health, the Parties undertake, either directly or in co-operation with public or private organisations, to take appropriate measures designed *inter alia*:

1 to remove as far as possible the causes of ill health;

2 to provide advisory and educational facilities for the promotion of health and the encouragement of individual responsibility in matters of health;

3 to prevent as far as possible epidemic, endemic and other diseases, as well as accidents.

Article 13 – The right to social and medical assistance

With a view to ensuring the effective exercise of the right to social and medical assistance, the Parties undertake:

1 to ensure that any person who is without adequate resources and who is unable to secure such resources either by his own efforts or from other sources, in particular by benefits under a social security scheme, be granted adequate assistance, and, in case of sickness, the care necessitated by his condition;

2 to ensure that persons receiving such assistance shall not, for that reason, suffer from a diminution of their political or social rights ...

National provisions

Unlike the position in respect of the Convention, the failure by a State to protect these social 'rights' will not allow one of its citizens to complain to the European Commission of Human Rights. However, the broad commitment on this country's part to the goal of access to health care for all is clear, and in fact predates the salient international law: it is found in the existence and operation of the National Health Service (NHS), which was established in 1948.

The National Health Service Act 1977

The NHS Act 1977, which consolidated a number of previous statutes in the area, remains the key piece of legislation governing the obligations of the Government – as devolved to the relevant minister, the Secretary of State for Health, and the Department of Health under him – to make provision for health care. The key provisions of this Act are as follows:

1   **Secretary of State's duty as to health service**

(1) It is the Secretary of State's duty to continue the promotion in England and Wales of a comprehensive health service designed to secure improvement–

(a) in the physical and mental health of the people of those countries; and

(b) in the prevention, diagnosis and treatment of illness;

and for that purpose to provide or secure the effective provision of services in accordance with this Act.

(2) The services so provided shall be free of charge except in so far as the making and recovery of charges is expressly provided for by or under any enactment, whenever passed.

2   **Secretary of State's general power as to services**

Without prejudice to the Secretary of State's powers apart from this section, he has power–

(a) to provide such services as he considers appropriate for the purpose of discharging any duty imposed on him by this Act; and

(b) to do any other thing whatsoever which is calculated to facilitate, or is conducive or incidental to, the discharge of such a duty.

This section is subject to s 3 (3) below.

3   **Services generally**

(1) It is the Secretary of State's duty to provide throughout England and Wales, to such extent as he considers necessary to meet all reasonable requirements–

(a) hospital accommodation;

(b) other accommodation for the purpose of any service provided under this Act;

(c) medical, dental, nursing and ambulance services;

(d) such other facilities for the care of expectant and nursing mothers and young children as he considers are appropriate as part of the health service;

    (e) such facilities for the prevention of illness, the care of persons suffering from illness and the after-care of persons who have suffered from illness as he considers are appropriate as part of the health service;

    (f) such other services as are required for the diagnosis and treatment of illness.

(2) Where any hospital provided by the Secretary of State in accordance with this Act was a voluntary hospital transferred by virtue of the National Health Service Act 1946, and–

    (a) the character and associations of that hospital before its transfer were such as to link it with a particular religious denomination, then

    (b) regard shall be had in the general administration of the hospital to the preservation of that character and those associations.

(3) Nothing in s 2 above or in this section affects the provisions of Part II of this Act (which relates to arrangements with practitioners for the provision of medical, dental, ophthalmic and pharmaceutical services).

4 Special hospitals

The duty imposed on the Secretary of State by s 1 above to provide services for the purposes of the health service includes a duty to provide and maintain establishments (in this Act referred to as 'special hospitals') for persons subject to detention under the Mental Health Act 1959 who in his opinion require treatment under conditions of special security on account of their dangerous, violent or criminal propensities.

5 Other services

(1) It is the Secretary of State's duty–

    (a) to provide for the medical inspection at appropriate intervals of pupils in attendance at schools maintained by local education authorities or at grant-maintained schools and for the medical treatment of such pupils;

    (b) to arrange, to such extent as he considers, necessary to meet all reasonable requirements in England and Wales, for the giving of advice on contraception, the medical examination of persons seeking advice on contraception, the treatment of such persons and the supply of contraceptive substances and appliances.

(1A) It is also the Secretary of State's duty to provide, to such extent as he considers necessary to meet all reasonable requirements–

    (a) for the dental inspection of pupils in attendance at schools maintained by local education authorities or at grant-maintained schools;

    (b) for the dental treatment of such pupils; and

    (c) for the education of such pupils in dental health.

(2) The Secretary of State may–

(a) provide invalid carriages for persons appearing to him to be suffering from severe physical defect or disability and, at the request of such a person, may provide for him a vehicle other than an invalid carriage (and the additional provisions set out in Sched 2 to this Act have effect in relation to this paragraph);

(b) arrange to provide accommodation and treatment outside Great Britain for persons suffering from respiratory tuberculosis;

(c) provide a microbiological service, which may include the provision of laboratories, for the control of the spread of infectious diseases and carry on such other activities as in his opinion can conveniently be carried on in conjunction with that service;

(d) conduct, or assist by grants or otherwise (without prejudice to the general powers and duties conferred on him under the Ministry of Health Act 1919) any person to conduct, research into any matters relating to the causation, prevention, diagnosis or treatment of illness, and into any such other matters connected with any service provided under this Act as he considers appropriate.

(2A) Charges may be made for services or materials supplied by virtue of para (c) of sub-s (2) above; and the powers conferred by that paragraph may be exercised both for the purposes of the health service and for other purposes ...

Outside the hospital setting, general practitioners (GPs) are required to provide general medical services (known as 'primary care') to patients registered with them pursuant to a statutory contract with the relevant health authority, whose terms are fixed under the NHS (General Medical Services) Regulations 1992 SI 1992/635 (as amended). (Further statutory provisions for community and primary care – provided, *inter alia*, by community nurses – are found in a number of miscellaneous statutes and statutory instruments, including s 2(1) of the Chronically Sick and Disabled Persons Act 1970; s 47 of the National Health Service and Community Care Act 1990; the National Health Service (Primary Care) Act 1997; and the National Health Service (Fund-Holding Practices) Regulations 1996 as amended.)

The NHS is a vast public health care system as the following statistics illustrate: in 1995 the total public expenditure on health services amounted to £33.3 billion, compared with £13.9 billion in 1985 (Department of Health Press Release 96/336, 31 October 1996); the total number of staff employed in the NHS hospital and community health services in England, as at 30 September 1995, was 764,210 (DoH Statistical Bulletin 1996/19, August 1996); between 1994–95 and 1995–96 the total number of finished consultant episodes (ordinary admissions plus day cases) rose by 6.5% to 11.2 million. Within this total, ordinary episodes rose by 3.9% to 8.4 million and day cases rose by 15% to 2.8 million (DoH Statistical Bulletin 1996/23, 17 October 1996). Within this large activity and expenditure range the population is treated generally at no cost to itself.

Beyond the broad aim of providing comprehensive care to all, which is free at the point of delivery (based on clinical need rather than ability to pay), the objectives of the NHS are not articulated in legislation. However, some evidence of its success can arguably be found in the increasing life expectancy of citizens in the UK. In 1994, the average expectation of life at birth was estimated to be 74.5 years in males and 79.7 years in females; projections for 1995 indicated marginally lower figures than in 1994, but substantially higher than a decade earlier. The infant mortality rate reached its lowest ever level of 6.1 per 1,000 live births in 1994, and this was maintained in 1995 (*On the State of The Public Health for the Year 1995: Introduction to the Annual Report of the Chief Medical Officer of the DoH to the Secretary of State*, September 1996, DoH).

Nevertheless, during its 50 year history, the NHS has remained the focus of continued and deeply felt public concern and debate, and the service has, from time to time, been the subject of important reforms. The major controversies have centred on achieving accountability within the NHS in relation to two issues: *cost of provision* and *quality of care*. We shall next be looking in more detail at the mechanisms which have been tried in order to ensure that the NHS delivers both efficient and high quality care, before returning later in the chapter to the question of how far, in law, the individual citizen enjoys a right to obtain the particular treatment he desires.

STRUCTURE OF HEALTH CARE IN THE UK

In economic terms, health care as a commodity has the clear potential for generating an anticompetitive market situation, given that the demand for services is in the hands of the same profession (doctors making patient referrals) as is responsible for its supply. The manner in which this may encourage inefficiency in the delivery of care has been commented upon by Christopher Newdick:

Newdick, C, *Who Should We Treat?*, 1995, Oxford: Clarendon Press, pp 41–43:

Two features of expenditure in the NHS prompted the Government to reconsider its system of funding. The first was a method of distributing financial resources to hospitals largely according to the perceived 'needs' of a resident population, to its mortality and morbidity [propensity for illness], without considering the 'efficiency' of the hospitals responsible for providing treatment. This became known as the 'efficiency trap'. Those hospitals which reduced their unit costs and became more efficient were unable to admit more patients because they were limited by their financial allocation. Arguably, hospitals which are funded simply according to the requirements of their population's needs may feel no incentive to manage their funds as effectively as those whose funding is performance-related. Indeed, when there is no relationship between the amount of money allocated to a district and the number of patients it is able to treat, the more efficient hospital appears to suffer a penalty. By treating more patients it spends its allocation more quickly and exhausts its funds before the end of the financial year. [A Enthoven,] who influenced the eventual shape of the health service reforms, wrote of the NHS in 1984:

> The NHS runs on the ability and dedication of the many people who work in it ... But other than the satisfaction of a job well done – which I do not wish to minimise – the system contains no serious incentives to guide the NHS in the direction of better quality care and service at reduced cost ... In the non-competitive NHS, the manager who attempts to implement efficiency-improving changes is more likely to be seen as a cause of problems.

> In fact, the structure of the NHS contains perverse incentives. For example, a District that develops an excellent service in some specialty that attracts more referrals is likely to get more work without getting more resources to do it. A District that does a poor job will 'export' patients and have less work, but not correspondingly less resources, for its reward ... management and consultants in a District risk weakening the case for a new hospital wing they have been campaigning for by solving their waiting list problem by referring patients to other districts with excess capacity ... [and] GPs have weak or no incentives to reduce referrals. They have neither the incentives nor the resources to make extra efforts to keep people out of hospital.

One solution to this trap is to enable efficient hospitals with spare capacity to offer their services to larger numbers of patients. Obviously, an incentive is required for such a hospital to fund the additional work and logic suggests that the money ought to come from those hospitals which work below full capacity. Those hospitals which achieve most, at least cost and at highest quality, ought to receive more funding than those that do less.

The second feature of the system which gave cause for concern was that those responsible for spending had no direct interest in controlling costs. The argument was: so long as GPs and consultants are not asked to account for the medicines they prescribe or the procedures they recommend, there may be a tendency to overtreat patients. Why refuse to prescribe antibiotics to a patient who mistakenly expects that they will cure his cold, or antidepressants to the patient who, for entirely non-medical reasons, has good reason to be depressed? Not only might it cause the patient upset and distress, but also doctors are increasingly concerned about the time, expense, and anxiety caused by patients' complaints. On one view, it makes more sense to satisfy patients' misplaced expectations than to spend time trying to explain the medical risks associated with pointless treatment.

The internal market

In a drive to make the NHS more competitive and better serve the interests of patients, reforms came into effect with the National Health Service and Community Care Act 1990. The key provisions of this Act are extracted below:

4   NHS contracts

(1) In this Act the expression 'NHS contract' means an arrangement under which one health service body ('the acquirer') arranges for the provision to it by another health service body ('the provider') of goods or services which it reasonably requires for the purposes of its functions.

(2) In this section 'health service body' means any of the following, namely–

(a) a health authority;

(b) a health board;

(c) the Common Services Agency for the Scottish Health Service;

(d) a Family Health Services Authority;

(e) an NHS trust;

(f) a recognised fund-holding practice;

(g) the Dental Practice Board or the Scottish Dental Practice Board;

(h) the Public Health Laboratory Service Board; and

(i) the Secretary of State.

(3) Whether or not an arrangement which constitutes an NHS contract would, apart from this sub-section, be a contract in law, it shall not be regarded for any purpose as giving rise to contractual rights or liabilities, but if any dispute arises with respect to such an arrangement, either party may refer the matter to the Secretary of State for determination under the following provisions of this section.

(4) If, in the course of negotiations intending to lead to an arrangement which will be an NHS contract, it appears to a health service body–

(a) that the terms proposed by another health service body are unfair by reason that the other is seeking to take advantage of its position as the only, or the only practicable, provider of the goods or services concerned or by reason of any other unequal bargaining position as between the prospective parties to the proposed arrangement; or

(b) that for any other reason arising out of the relative bargaining position of the prospective parties any of the terms of the proposed arrangement cannot be agreed;

that health service body may refer the terms of the proposed arrangement to the Secretary of State for determination under the following provisions of this section.

(5) Where a reference is made to the Secretary of State under sub-s (3) or sub-s (4) above, the Secretary of State may determine the matter himself or, if he considers it appropriate, appoint a person to consider and determine it in accordance with regulations.

(6) By his determination of a reference under sub-s (4) above, the Secretary of State or, as the case may be, the person appointed under sub-s (5) above may specify terms to be included in the proposed

arrangement and may direct that it be proceeded with; and it shall be the duty of the prospective parties to the proposed arrangement to comply with any such directions ...

NHS trusts are hospitals, community or ambulance services and are full corporate bodies with legal personality. Each trust has a statutory establishment order which along with the provisions of the NHS and Community Care Act 1990 determines its functions.

Section 5 of the 1990 Act provides in regard to such trusts as follows:

5   NHS trusts

(1)   Subject to sub-s (2) or, as the case may be, sub-s (3) below the Secretary of State may by order establish bodies, to be known as National Health Service trusts (in this Act, referred to as NHS trusts)–

(a)   to assume responsibility, in accordance with this Act, for the ownership and management of hospitals or other establishments or facilities which were previously managed or provided by Regional, District or Special Health Authorities; or

(b)   to provide and manage hospitals or other establishments or facilities.

(2)   In any case where the Secretary of State is considering whether to make an order under sub-s (1) above establishing an NHS trust and the hospital, establishment or facility concerned is or is to be situated in England, he shall direct the relevant Regional Health Authority to consult, with respect to the proposal to establish the trust–

(a)   the relevant Community Health Council and such other persons or bodies as may be specified in the direction; and

(b)   such other persons or bodies as the Authority considers appropriate;

and, within such period (if any) as the Secretary of State may determine, the relevant Regional Health Authority shall report the results of those consultations to the Secretary of State.

(3)   In any case where the Secretary of State is considering whether to make an order under sub-s (1) above establishing an NHS trust and the hospital, establishment or facility concerned is or is to be situated in Wales, he shall consult the relevant Community Health Council and such other persons and bodies as he considers appropriate.

...

(5)   Every NHS trust–

(a)   shall be a body corporate having a board of directors consisting of a chairman appointed by the Secretary of State and, subject to para 5(2) of Sched 2 to this Act, executive and non-directors who, subject to executive directors (that is to say, directors who, subject to sub-s (7) below, respectively are and are not employees of the trust); and

(b) shall have the functions conferred on it by an order under sub-s (1) above and by Sched 2 to this Act.

(6) The functions specified in an order under sub-s (1) above shall include such functions as the Secretary of State considers appropriate in relation to the provision of services by the trust for one or more health authorities.

Schedule 2 to the Act articulates the powers and duties given to NHS trusts:

Part II

Duties, powers and status

Specific duties

6 (1) An NHS trust shall carry out effectively, efficiently and economically the functions for the time being conferred on it by an order under s 5(1) of this Act and by the provisions of this Schedule and, with respect to the exercise of the powers conferred by s 5(10) of this Act and paras 10–15 below, shall comply with any directions given to it by the Secretary of State, whether of a general or a particular nature.

(2) An NHS trust shall comply with any directions given to it by the Secretary of State with respect to all or any of the following matters–

(a) the qualifications of persons who may be employed as officers of the trust;

(b) the employment, for the purpose of performing functions specified in the direction, of officers having qualifications or experience of a description so specified;

(c) the manner in which officers of the trust are to be appointed;

(d) prohibiting or restricting the disposal of, or of any interest in, any asset which, at the time the direction is given, the Secretary of State reasonably considers to have a value in excess of such sum as may be specified in an order under s 5(1) of this Act and in respect of which the Secretary of State considers that the interests of the National Health Service require that the asset should not be disposed of;

(e) compliance with guidance or directions given (by circular or otherwise) to health authorities, or particular descriptions of health authorities; and

(f) the implementation of awards relating to the distinction or merit of medical practitioners or dental practitioners or any class or classes of such practitioners.

7 (1) For each accounting year an NHS trust shall prepare and send to the Secretary of State an annual report in such form as may be determined by the Secretary of State.

(2) At such time or times as may be prescribed, an NHS trust shall hold a public meeting at which its audited accounts and annual report and any report on the accounts made pursuant to sub-s (3) of s 15 of the Local Government Finance Act 1982 shall be presented.

(3) In such circumstances and at such time or times as may be prescribed, an NHS trust shall hold a public meeting at which such document as may be prescribed shall be presented.

8   An NHS trust shall furnish to the Secretary of State such reports, returns and other information, including information as to its forward planning, as, and in such form as, he may require.

...

Specific powers

10 In addition to carrying out its other functions, an NHS trust may, as the provider, enter into NHS contracts.

11 An NHS trust may undertake and commission research and make available staff and provide facilities for research by other persons.

12 An NHS trust may–

(a) provide training for persons employed or likely to be employed by the trust or otherwise in the provision of services under the principal Act; and

(b) make facilities and staff available in connection with training by a university or any other body providing training in connection with the health service.

...

General powers

16 (1) Subject to Sched 3 to this Act, an NHS trust shall have power to do anything which appears to it to be necessary or expedient for the purpose of or in connection with the discharge of its functions, including in particular power–

(a) to acquire and dispose of land and other property;

(b) to enter into such contracts as seem to the trust to be appropriate;

(c) to accept gifts of money, land or other property, including money, land or other property to be held on trust, either for the general or any specific purposes of the NHS trust or for all or any purposes relating to the health service; and

(d) to employ staff on such terms as the trust thinks fit.

(2) The reference in sub-para (1)(c) above to specific purposes of the NHS trust includes a reference to the purposes of a specific hospital or other establishment or facility which is owned and managed by the trust.

...

Status

18 An NHS trust shall not be regarded as the servant or agent of the Crown or, except as provided by this Act, as enjoying any status, immunity or privilege of the Crown; and an NHS trust's property shall not be regarded as property of, or property held on behalf of, the Crown.

A useful summary of the manner in which the NHS is presently organised is provided in the following extract:

Department of Health, *A Guide to the National Health Service*, May 1996, Leeds: NHS Executive, pp 19–22:

How is the NHS organised?

With almost a million employees, the sheer size of the NHS requires careful organisation. Recent reforms have concentrated on improving patient care, making the service more responsive to individual patients and achieving better value for money. This has been achieved by linking funding to the quality and quantity of the health care provided and by giving local staff greater freedom to innovate and manage their resources more effectively.

Overall responsibility for the NHS in England lies with the *Secretary of State for Health*. Supported by the *Department of Health* in London, the Secretary of State sets the strategic direction for the NHS and answers to parliament.

Responsibility for NHS policy and operation lies with the *NHS Executive*, a part of the Department of Health, with headquarters in Leeds and eight regional offices. The Executive implements the health policies laid down by the Secretary of State and manages the funding and the way the Service operates. Since the NHS is now structured to promote local initiative and diversity, one of the NHS Executive's prime responsibilities is to establish common objectives. National priorities are therefore reflected in corporate contracts agreed between the Executive and the professionals organising health care locally.

Funding

NHS management and funding are organised on the principle of separating the 'purchasers' and 'providers' of care.

Purchasers are local *health authorities* and GP *fund-holders*, responsible for assessing the health needs of their local populations or patients and for purchasing the best possible care for them. Providers, such as hospitals, ambulance and community services, have the freedom to manage their own resources to provide the most effective care.

Because purchasers, and to an extent patients, have freedom to choose the best care, the system places competitive pressure on providers to offer greater quality, efficiency and value for money.

Purchasers

On 1 April 1996, 100 new unitary health authorities (HAs) replaced the previous structure of 105 separate District Health Authorities and 90 Family Health Services Authorities.

The new HAs are responsible for health and health services in their areas. They are also responsible for assessing the health care needs of the local population and developing integrated strategies for meeting those needs in partnership with GPs and in consultation with the public, hospitals and others.

The new HAs have a key role in taking forward the strategy for developing a 'primary care-led NHS'. This will see HAs involved in promoting the involvement of GPs in purchasing by developing increasingly primary care-led purchasing, especially GP fund-holding, and improving the provision of all the primary care services.

GP fund-holders carry out a similar role and have the budgetary freedom to buy what they consider to be the most effective services to meet their patients' needs. Like the health authorities, GP fund-holders agree annual contracts with their providers. Although GP fund-holding is a voluntary scheme, the number of fund-holders is growing, now caring for more than 50% of the population.

They purchase a range of services including most elective (non-emergency) surgery, out-patient and specialist nursing care. Some practices will pilot buying all the community, secondary and emergency care their patients need. Some smaller practices purchase a limited range of services, including most community health services but excluding all hospital treatment.

Providers

Almost all hospitals, community services and ambulance services run themselves as self-governing *NHS trusts* with the freedom to decide staff numbers and rates of pay. Within boundaries, trusts also have some powers to invest and borrow money. In 1994–95, 433 trusts managed more than 98% of all NHS hospitals and community health services. To discharge this responsibility effectively, each trust has a chairperson and board of directors, whose members are drawn not just from the health service but also from local organisations, bringing in considerable expertise and experience of running successful enterprises, both commercial and voluntary.

Though independent of local health authority control, trusts remain part of the NHS, reporting directly to the Secretary of State. Codes of Conduct and Accountability define the roles and responsibilities of the trust and health authority boards and chairpersons; their performance is monitored through the eight NHS Executive regional offices.

In effect, the current scheme is designed to comprise an internal market with purchasers and providers working to (legally unenforceable) contracts, with disputes between them being resolved extra-judicially at a local management level. If the dispute remains unresolved then there may be a reference to an adjudicator under a special statutory dispute resolution scheme (NHS Contracts (Dispute Resolution) Regulations 1996 SI 1996/623). McHale, Hughes and Griffiths discuss this quasi-contractual framework as follows:

McHale, JV, Hughes, D and Griffiths, L, 'Disputes in the NHS internal market: regulation and relationships' (1996) 2(3) Medical Law International 215–27:

The procedure

While the Secretary of State may determine references personally it is likely that, in all but the most exceptional cases, s/he would appoint a nominee. The

Secretary of State has the power to impose directions needed to resolve the dispute including directions to give effect to variation or termination. These are to be treated as though they were the result of agreement between the parties themselves, retaining the illusion of the contract as a meeting of minds ...

NHS contract disputes, whether through statutory or other procedures for non-statutory agreed arbitration and conciliation set out in guidance, are to be resolved by appointees who will almost invariably be drawn from within the NHS management structure. The exception to this is Wales where guidance states that conciliation may be undertaken by a suitable academic. Internal arbiters will be able to draw upon the special expertise that an external person would lack. Comparisons can be drawn with the arbitration of commercial disputes which are habitually referred to arbitrators with appropriate specialisms. Perceived independence may be maintained by such decision makers being drawn from NHS managers outside the areas involved in the dispute. Nevertheless the focus upon internal arbiters may perhaps also be indicative of a desire to maintain control of dispute resolution within the organisational structure.

The statutory instrument provides that, in making a decision, the adjudicator must seek written submissions from the parties, the Regional Health Authority and the Secretary of State. There is no right to demand to make oral representations. The dispute resolution process sets out a detailed timescale within which issues are to be resolved. For example, Welsh Office guidance provides that between notice of dispute through conciliation and up to formal dispute resolution the period will be some 10 weeks. Time limits may facilitate the efficient resolution of the dispute but they also provide a further indication of the fact that the dispute resolution procedure is closely regulated by central government. It remains to be seen how this process will operate and to what extent parties will be held to their contract. It is uncertain whether, in considering contracts, a legalistic interpretation will be given or whether a more flexible approach will be used. One pointer may be found in guidance from the National Health Service Executive which states that disputes should be resolved to give effect to what the parties decided, not to what they should have decided. What is clear is that the decisions reached by the adjudicators should not amount to precedents to be referred to in subsequent disputes ...

In practice the statutory procedure has been used only once. This may be related to the fact that other mechanisms exist for defusing disputes ... but there are perhaps other reasons for its limited use. First, guidance stated that the adjudicator's ultimate decision should take what is known as a 'pendulum form':

> The Secretary of State is minded to stipulate that the arbiter should be free to find for one party or another and not be able to compromise. This is known as pendulum arbitration and would impose the maximum pressure on both the parties to make sensible final offers to each other.

Some evidence exists that the all or nothing nature of this procedure has deterred contracting parties from making use of the statutory procedure, particularly in view of the fact that these decisions may be taken in a context in which contracting parties are endeavouring to resolve what are complex matters of resource allocation. Second, most of the disputes which have arisen have not involved decided contracts but have related to pre-contractual disputes. This may be because, where disagreement arises regarding the terms of a concluded contract, the contracting parties may very well decide not to resolve their differences at that time but instead defer the matter to the next annual contracting round. A pre-contractual dispute may be less likely to be referred to the statutory procedure than a contractual dispute. A party who wishes to refer a pre-contractual dispute to statutory arbitration would have to show that the dispute arose out of the fact that the provider was the 'only practical provider' of services or that the dispute arose because the parties were in an unequal bargaining position.

On the NHS internal market see, further, Health Service Guideline HSG (94) 55, *The Operation of the NHS Internal Market*, 12 December 1994, London: NHS Executive.

Beyond the internal market

The New Labour Government is going to introduce major changes into the NHS and these have been highlighted in the Government White Paper, *The New NHS: Modern, Dependable*, Cm 3807, 1997, London: The Stationery Office and *Executive Summary*, 1997, London: DoH. The Government is committed to abolishing the internal market and is going to replace it with a system of integrated care based on partnerships between NHS bodies and other local agencies.

Department of Health, *Executive Summary*, December 1997, London: DoH, pp 8–9:

New roles and responsibilities

The new NHS will mean new roles and responsibilities for Health Authorities and NHS trusts and the Department of Health. Primary Care Groups will be developed across the country ...

Health Authorities will be leaner bodies with stronger powers to improve the health of their residents and oversee the effectiveness of the NHS locally. Over time, they will relinquish direct commissioning responsibility. Working with local authorities, NHS trusts and Primary Care Groups, they will take the lead in drawing up three year Health Improvement Programmes which will provide the framework within which all local NHS bodies will operate. These will be backed by a new duty of partnership. Health Authorities will allocate funds to Primary Care Groups on an equitable basis, and hold them to account. Links with social services will be strengthened. Fewer Health Authorities covering larger areas will emerge as a product of these changes.

Primary Care Groups comprising all GPs in an area together with community nurses will take responsibility for commissioning services for the local community. They will work closely with social services. There will be four options for the form that Primary Care Groups can take ... including the opportunity to become free standing Primary Care trusts, with responsibility for running community hospitals and community health services. None of these options affects the independent contractor status of GPs. The new arrangements will replace the thousands of existing commissioning and fund-holding groups. Typical Groups may serve about 100,000 patients, but this will vary according to local circumstances. Primary Care Groups will mean fewer commissioners with more clout. They will have freedom to make decisions about how to use their resources, consistent with the Health Improvement Programme. They will control a single unified budget which will give maximum choice to GPs and community nurses about how best to meet individual patient needs, since no individual elements within it will be artificially capped.

NHS trusts will have devolved operational responsibility, but will also be party to the local Health Improvement Programme. They will agree long term service agreements with Primary Care Groups. These service agreements will generally be organised around a particular care group (such as children) or disease area (such as heart disease) linked to the new National Service Frameworks. In this way, hospital clinicians will be able to make a more significant contribution to service planning. NHS trusts will have new statutory duties of quality and partnerships. NHS trusts will also be more accountable to the public and will publish details of their performance. They will need to demonstrate the development and involvement of their staff.

The private sector

The private sector is subject to statutory regulation pursuant to Part II of the Registered Homes Act 1984. This provides for health authorities to operate a system of registration and (at least twice yearly) inspection in respect of private hospitals in their areas, and is designed to ensure that patients are offered a suitable standard of care. Moreover, as Jonathan Montgomery notes, as well as being vulnerable, like their NHS counterparts, to malpractice actions brought in negligence (see below, Chapter 6), private hospitals can also be sued for breach of contract:

Montgomery, J, *Health Care Law*, 1997, Oxford: OUP, p 166:

Outside the NHS actions may also be brought in contract law. This is not possible under the NHS, because NHS patients do not have a contract with those who treat them. In private medicine, where patients pay their professionals (even if the fees are later reimbursed under some form of insurance), there will be a contract. The patient would be able to sue in both negligence and contract. In theory it is possible for a health professional to contract to provide a standard of care that is higher than that required in negligence. However, the courts have shown themselves very reluctant to accept that they have done so.

REGULATING THE QUALITY OF HEALTH CARE

As previously noted, one perennial concern in relation to the NHS is ensuring that minimum standards are maintained throughout the service in terms of all aspects of provision and care. Clearly this is also an important way of reducing the expenditure of resources on the fighting and settling of malpractice suits brought by dissatisfied patients (a subject dealt with at length below, in Chapter 6). In this section, we shall first consider the role of a number of agencies, which oversee and influence the implementation of decision making within the service at the 'macro level', before moving on to address the mechanisms to regulate and provide redress in the context of individual treatment decisions (the 'micro level'). In respect of the latter, there is the possibility for complaints to be brought by aggrieved patients either through the NHS' own complaints system, or, where unprofessional conduct on the part of a particular member of the NHS' medical staff is alleged, through the latter's professional licensing body – in the case of a doctor, the General Medical Council (GMC).

'Macro' decision making: the role of the NHS Executive

The NHS Executive (NHSE) is a branch of the Department of Health and is responsible for overall strategic planning, as well as drafting and disseminating numerous guidelines and circulars on a multitude of topics bearing on the provision of health care in the UK. Such guidance may be addressed either to purchasers (health authorities and GP fund-holders) or providers (NHS trusts) and will often take the form of setting priorities in terms of what services should be contracted for between them: in this regard, it can sometimes be quite specific, for example, detailing particular treatments that health authorities should secure the provision of. In this way, the NHSE is able to ensure a measure of uniformity in the types of health care available on the NHS to citizens up and down the country, albeit at some cost to the exercise of local autonomy within the service. Though the directives in question may be described as 'soft law' in that they are non-legislative in character and do not provide for any direct sanction in case of non-observance, failure on the part of a health authority to have regard to them may well form the basis of an action in judicial review. A good illustration of this is found in the recent case of *R v North Derbyshire HA ex p Fisher*.

R v North Derbyshire HA ex p Fisher [1997] 8 Med LR 327, QBD (Dyson J)

Kenneth Fisher, who suffered from the relapsing/remitting form of multiple sclerosis, challenged the refusal of his health authority, North Derbyshire, to finance his treatment with a new form of drug therapy, beta-interferon, which he had been assessed as suitable to receive by doctors at the NHS trust in

Sheffield where he was being treated. North Derbyshire's refusal reflected the view of its own experts that beta-interferon (which was expensive) was of unproven therapeutic benefit, but contrasted with the terms of an NHS Circular, EL (95) 97, in which the NHSE asked health authorities to assist in implementing the use of the drug.

> **Dyson J**: [The] lawfulness [of the authority's policy] must be judged in accordance with *Wednesbury* principles against the background of national policy which was set out fully and firmly in the guidance to be found in the Circular. The respondents had to have regard to that national policy. They were not obliged to follow the policy, but if they decided to depart from it, they had to give clear reasons for so doing, and those reasons would have been susceptible to a *Wednesbury* challenge ... Moreover, if the respondents failed properly to understand the Circular, then their policy would be as defective as if no regard had been paid to the policy at all. It is accepted on behalf of the respondents that they were under a duty to give serious consideration to each aspect of the Circular. Mr Seys Llewllyn submits that the respondents' policy was an honest and conscientious way of managing the introduction into the NHS of the new drug, and was at least consistent with the Circular.

> In my judgment the policy was plainly not in accordance with the Circular. The Circular asked for purchasing authorities and providers:

> > To develop and implement local arrangements to manage the entry of such drugs into the NHS ... and in particular to initiate a continued prescribing of beta-interferon through hospitals.

> One of the key aims was to 'target the drug appropriately at patients who were most likely to benefit from treatment'. In other words, the Circular was giving guidance as to how most effectively beta-interferon could be introduced into the NHS as a drug to be prescribed to treat patients ... I do not consider that the respondents' policy could at any time have fairly been described as a reasonable way of giving effect to the Circular. The respondents, like others, no doubt honestly and conscientiously believed that the efficacy of beta-interferon had not been sufficiently tested. The assumption that underpinned the Circular was that it had been sufficiently tested ... This is not a case in which a health authority departed from the national policy because there were special factors which it considered exceptionally justified departure. The respondents failed to implement any aspect of national policy, principally because they disagreed with it altogether. They now seek to argue that at least they acted consistently with that policy, although for the reasons that I have given that is plainly not the case. Accordingly, they do not seek to justify their policy as a rational exception to the national policy. That is hardly surprising, since I expect that the situation in which the respondents found themselves when the Circular was issued was not materially different from that faced by most other health authorities. The respondents did not take the Circular into account and decide exceptionally not to follow it. They decided to disregard it altogether throughout 1996, because they were opposed to it. That is something which in my judgment they were not entitled to do.

Regional level – the role of Community Health Councils

A further form of control over the manner in which NHS bodies organise their affairs and take decisions affecting the availability and quality of services can be found at regional or local level, which lies between generalised policy, as administered by the NHSE, and decisions bearing directly on the care of individual patients (see below, p 88). Particularly important in this regard is the role of Community Health Councils (CHCs) which are designed to promote accountability to the public in relation to the NHS services they consume in their own locality. CHCs (which are government-funded bodies staffed by lay members of the local community) were initially set up in 1974 and cover each health authority district. Their broad function, pursuant to the CHC Regulations 1996 SI 1996/640, is to monitor the activities of their local NHS bodies and, where appropriate, to recommend improvements in the service they provide. As in the case of non-observance of NHSE guidance discussed previously, a failure on the part of a health authority to consult the local CHC over a decision substantially affecting the provision of health care in its area may be challenged in the courts through judicial review.

R v North and East Devon HA ex p Pow (1997) 39 BMLR 77, QBD (Moses J)

The respondent health authority decided in June 1997 to close, temporarily, a small hospital at Lynton in order to reduce its borrowing deficit. Though the CHC Regulations 1996 normally obliged the local CHC to be consulted over such a step, the authority claimed that it was released from this obligation in view of the urgency of the matter. However, the applicants produced evidence that the initial proposal to close Lynton had been formulated in April, when time for consultation was still available.

> **Moses J**: This case is not concerned with the merits of the decision to order temporary closure. The case is concerned with the procedure by which the decision to close was reached.
>
> The applicants are three elderly patients at present in the hospital. No point has been taken before me as to their locus to bring this application. Lynton Hospital commands widespread local support. It is understandable that the decision to close the hospital, although temporarily, has caused dismay and a determination to resist the action of the health authority. I am not concerned as to whether this response is well founded or not ...
>
> **The statutory framework**
>
> The Secretary of State is under a duty imposed by the National Health Service Act 1977 to promote in England and Wales a comprehensive health service. He has power to provide such services as he thinks appropriate to discharge that duty. His duties in relation to provision of services have been delegated to health authorities, such as the respondent, by virtue of the National Health Service (Functions of Health Authorities and Administration of Arrangements) Regulations 1996 SI 1996/708.

An internal market for the provision and purchase of health services was created by the National Health Service and Community Care Act 1990. Health authorities purchase services from NHS trusts, who are, in the main, the service providers.

Funds for such purchases are provided by central government annually, based on formulae designed to take into account local characteristics. Health authorities' financial years run from 1 April, the amount available being determined by the national budget (in this case the budget of 26 November 1996) and by the allocation formula announced in December 1996. Health authorities are required, by s 97A of the 1977 Act, to balance their books, that is to secure that expenditure does not exceed income. Deficits from previous years must be carried forward and they impose an additional demand upon annual income.

Under the statutory scheme created by the 1990 Act, health authorities are not in law responsible for the provision of services such as those provided at Lynton. They are the responsibility of the trust. If a health authority decides not to purchase services hitherto provided by a trust, then the service will have to cease. In this case ... in the course of negotiations as to the contract between the health authority and the trust for 1997–98 the respondent decided not to purchase the Lynton Hospital in-patient services and the trust cannot therefore, at least temporarily, provide them. But it has been agreed that that process should be regarded as an instruction to close temporarily those services. The trust has been served as a person directly affected. Mr Engelman appears for both the health authority and the trust and both have agreed that the health authority should take responsibility for the decision.

Community Health Councils

By 1996, the government had resolved to make the National Health Service more responsive to the needs of its consumers (see Circular EL (90) 185). To this end, Community Health Councils were established by the Community Health Councils Regulations 1996 SI 1996/640 pursuant to the Secretary of State's powers to issue directions under the National Health Service Act 1977. Part IV of those Regulations identifies the functions of a Community Health Council. I should read reg 17 and reg 18. Regulation 17 provides:

> It shall be the duty of each Council to keep under review the operation of the health service in its district, to make recommendations for the improvement of that service and to advise any relevant health authority upon such matters relating to the operation of the health service within its district as the Council thinks fit.

Regulation 18 is headed by the rubric 'Consultation of Councils by relevant health authorities':

> (1) Subject to para (2) and (3), it shall be the duty of each relevant health authority to consult a Council on any proposals which the health authority may have under consideration for any substantial development of the health service in the Council's district and on any proposals to make any substantial variation in the provision of such service.

> ...

(3) Paragraph (1) shall not apply to any proposal on which the health authority is satisfied that, in the interest of the health service, a decision has to be taken without allowing time for consultation; but, in any such case, the health authority shall notify the Council immediately of the decision taken and the reason why no consultation has taken place.

Thus, a health authority is obliged to consult a Community Health Council if in relation to this case, two conditions are satisfied: (a) there is a proposal to make any substantial variation in the health service; and (b) that proposal is under consideration by the health authority.

The essential issue

The real decision which is impugned is not the decision temporarily to close, but the decision, made on 4 June 1997, to do so without consultation with the Community Health Council. The essential issue is whether the health authority acted lawfully in issuing instructions to close Lynton Hospital without consulting the North Devon Community Health Council. The decision not to consult was made pursuant to reg 18(3), and it was notified on 28 May to the Community Health Council. The letter of notification gives the reasons for the decision not to consult. It states:

Consultation is not possible because of the urgent need to release resources to 1997–98 and 1998–99 to allow the Authority to meet its statutory requirements. Closure of the in-patient services by 15 August is necessary to allow the cost of the contract with North Devon Healthcare Trust to be reduced to affordable levels. Neither the trust nor the Authority can agree an unaffordable contract.

... Consultation involves the opportunity for representations to be made and for them to be conscientiously taken into account before the proposals are finalised. Thus, it must take place while the proposals are still at a formative stage (see Auld J in *R v London Borough of Barnet ex p B* [1994] ELR 357, pp 370–71).

Circular EL (90) 185 refers to consultations as an integral part of the management process. It says that consultation responds to the desire of the public to have influence in the delivery of health services. Thus the process envisaged by the regulation is a process whereby the Community Health Council and the health authority jointly seek to reach a solution to the problem with which the health authority is presented. The health authorities are under a duty, once they are considering a proposal, to consult the Community Health Council before that proposal has evolved into a definite solution.

In my judgment, a proposal to close Lynton and Winsford's health services temporarily was of sufficient cogency by 9 April 1997 as to trigger the duty to consult with the Community Health Council.

Complaints and discipline

Finally, in relation to decisions or other conduct bearing upon the treatment of individual patients, there are a number of mechanisms in place for monitoring the quality of care. We first look at the procedures in place to deal with complaints brought by patients in respect of their treatment (which are an important alternative to formal litigation in the courts), before considering the wider question of disciplinary sanctions available against health professionals who are shown to have behaved in an unbefitting manner.

The complaints system

After widespread and long standing criticism of its excessive complexity and bureaucracy, the NHS complaints system has recently been the subject of radical reform in the light of the recommendations of a government committee of inquiry chaired by Professor Alan Wilson (*Being Heard*, 1994, London: DoH). The key principles of the new system, which became operational from 1 April 1996, are outlined by Jonathan Montgomery:

Montgomery, J, *Health Care Law*, 1997, Oxford: OUP, pp 116–18:

The NHS complaints procedures are intended to achieve a number of key objectives. These are expressed as being ease of access, simplicity (with common features for complaints in all parts of the NHS), separation of complaints from disciplinary matters, fairness (for both complainants and staff), speed, openness, honesty, and thoroughness. It is also intended that the new procedure should make it easier for lessons to be learnt from complaints in order to improve the system. It is hoped that most complaints will be resolved by an immediate informal response by front line staff. Where this is not possible, there should be a procedure for resolving complaints internally. If that fails to satisfy the complainant, they may seek an independent review, although they are not absolutely entitled to have one held. The ultimate level of complaint is the Health Service Commissioner.

To put this system into place, health service bodies are required to adopt and publicise written complaints procedures which explain the arrangements for local resolution and independent review, how to initiate them, the role of the community health council, and the way to complain to the Health Service Commissioner. Trusts and health authorities must identify a designated complaints manager, readily accessible to the public, to oversee the procedure. They must also appoint at least one person to act as 'convenor' for the purposes of the independent review stage of the procedure ... General practices must nominate someone to administer the complaints procedure, and identify them to patients and clients.

The guidance also explains the application of the NHS procedures in cases of mixed sector complaints ...

Where complaints are made that involve more than one NHS body, then they are expected to co-operate in resolving the complaint ...

The Directions and Guidance on the complaints system identify 'complainants' (ie, those who may use the system) as existing or former patients using the services of the body complained about, and those who complain on behalf of the patient, with the patient's consent. Third parties may make oral complaints on behalf of a patient without that patient's consent. It is also recognised that third parties can complain on behalf of patients who are unable to complain themselves ...

Like the courts in malpractice actions, the NHS system operates a time limit within which complaints are expected to be brought. This should normally be within six months of the incident, or of awareness that there is a problem, providing that it is still within a year of the incident. There is a discretion to extend these time limits where the complaints manager thinks that it would have been unreasonable for the complainant to make a complaint within the normal period, and that it will still be possible to investigate the complaint properly. In those circumstances, the complaint shall be investigated. The only example given in the Guidance refers to cases where the complainant has suffered such distress or trauma as to prevent a complaint being made earlier.

Initial reactions to the new complaints procedure have been largely positive, it being recognised that the opportunity for patients to air grievances, and for providers to receive such feedback in a more positive way, is not only conducive to a better run service, but also the best means of avoiding litigation, which is likely to be costly and traumatic for both sides. Una Whetung, a manager of consumer services for a health authority in London, comments as follows:

Whetung, U, 'The NHS complaints procedure: a consumer service manager's opinion' (1997) 3(3) Health Care Risk Report 18:

The Wilson Committee was set the task of reviewing complaints handling in the NHS and recommended changes in a system long considered outdated and bureaucratic. The recommendations were for a simpler, more accessible procedure that would apply no matter which aspect of NHS care had caused the concern ...

New procedures

From 1 April 1996 the new procedures applied, with two stages for dealing with complaints. Emphasis is placed on the first stage, which is local resolution. Front line staff should be trained to handle and resolve complaints as they arise and the information should be logged and reviewed.

Health authorities, trusts, independent providers and health authority providers should all have in place their own complaints procedures and timescales are laid down for what are considered acceptable response times.

Someone who is dissatisfied with a response at the end of local resolution can ask for an independent review. Health authorities and trusts have appointed non-executive directors to deal with these requests. Health authorities' convenors also deal with requests about the family health services' practitioners in contract and about providers in the independent sector ...

The 'independence' of the independent review procedure is provided by the appointment of a chair by the regional office of the NHSE. Before a decision can be made about calling a panel the convenor must discuss the request with a person nominated through that office. The intention is that health authorities and trusts would not be able to build up relationships with particular chairs so that this ingredient of independence would be preserved. When an independent review is set up it is chaired by a regional nominee on terms of reference set by the convenor ...

The lead-up to changes

Prior to 1 April complaints concerning family health services practitioners had involved them in a rigid 'complainant-led' disciplinary procedure (service committees). The procedure was formal and based on an adversarial model. Most people agreed that the changes were overdue and welcome. After the Wilson Committee report some [health authorities] acted on its recommendations in advance of statutory change and in 1994 the author was appointed to lead a consumer services team of three including a conciliator.

The main difference in the approach of the team was to move away from a formalised response to complaints; contacting the complainant by telephone or in person and using conciliation as a means of resolving people's concerns. When a close relative or partner has died, the survivor often complains, feeling that the GP must be at fault. There may indeed be fault or medical negligence, but in the first instance it is necessary to recognise that as part of a bereavement process many people want someone to blame.

A bureaucratic system culminating in an appearance before a panel of five people some 10 months later is unlikely to be the best way of resolving the complainant's concerns. Their first need is usually for a prompt and sympathetic response with information and an explanation as to why this person died.

There is some point in recognising that no complaint is in a vacuum. In other words, behind every complaint there is a complainant whose concerns may be wider than those expressed in a formal letter. To address the complaint it is necessary to address the complainant.

An important role within the general framework of the complaints system is that of the Health Service Commissioner, who, as Parliamentary Commissioner for Administration, acts as Ombudsman to the NHS. He is given wide ranging powers under the Health Service Commissioners Act (HCSA) 1993 (as amended) to investigate complaints by the public, be they of maladministration or of individual treatment. Normally, however, he will only do so where complainants have exhausted other procedures for complaint (s 4(5) of the HSCA 1993). In his Annual Report for 1996–97, London: HMSO, the present Commissioner, Michael Buckley, notes some recent changes to his role as well as the number of complaints with which his office now deals:

1.1 This is my first report as Health Service Commissioner. I took up my office in January 1997 on the retirement of Sir William Reid KCB. Like him and all his five predecessors I was appointed to the three separate statutory offices of Health Service Commissioner for England, Scotland and Wales.

1.2 In accordance with tradition this Annual Report covers my responsibilities in all three offices. For most of the year the offices were under the stewardship of Sir William, to whose work and achievements as Commissioner I am happy to add my own appreciation to those expressed in parliament and elsewhere. I hope to fill this office with the same diligence and success.

1.3 The year has not only seen a change in Commissioner. From 1 April 1996, as a result of the Health Service Commissioners (Amendment) Act 1996, my jurisdiction received its first major change since it was established in 1973. The new Act means that I can now investigate complaints about family health service practitioners, as well as about hospital and community health services. It also enables me to investigate complaints arising from the exercise of clinical judgment by health service professionals, whether in hospitals, community or primary health care. In the past this office has had to reject many complaints because they related to those two areas, so the extensions are potentially very significant. They provide equal access to my office for anyone who has a complaint about any aspect of the services they have received from any part of the National Health Service. Over the last year my office has had to prepare for, and begin to deal with complaints in these important new areas as well as continuing work under my previous jurisdiction.

...

1.12 In terms of the number of complaints to my office 1996–97 has also been a record year – 2,219 complaints, 24% up on the previous year. My office also dealt with 2,207 items of supplementary correspondence, an increase of 30%. Three-quarters of all correspondence received a reply within 18 days, compared with under two-thirds in the previous year. The average was 14 days, compared with 40 and 22 days in 1994–95 and 1995–96 respectively.

Discipline

In the wake of the Wilson Committee's report, discipline is the subject of separate procedures to those which govern complaints. Nevertheless, it may become apparent as the result of a complaint (or indeed in the course of a malpractice action, see below, Chapter 6) that the conduct of a particular medical professional is deserving of censure. In this regard there are two parallel systems for disciplining the professional concerned. First, disciplinary procedures internal to the NHS may be invoked as set out in DoH Circular (90) 9: this provides for a number of distinct procedures depending on the nature of the alleged misdemeanour, and the ultimate sanction is dismissal from employment. (Slightly different procedures apply to GPs in so far as they are found to be in breach of their statutory contract with the relevant health authority: see the NHS (Committee and Tribunal) Regulations SI 1992/664 (as amended).)

Secondly, and perhaps of even greater consequence for the professional, their conduct may be investigated by the responsible governing and licensing body for their profession. In respect of doctors this is the General Medical Council (GMC), and the equivalent body for nurses is the United Kingdom Central Council for Nursing, Midwifery and Health Visiting (UKCC). Such self-regulatory organisations have a long tradition of enunciating and administering the standards of professional practice to which their members are required to adhere, and their power to discipline and, ultimately, to 'strike off' the register the names of those found guilty of serious misconduct has been codified in statute. In the case of the GMC, the relevant provisions are found in Part V of the Medical Act 1983:

Professional conduct and fitness to practise

35 General Council's power to advise on conduct or ethics

The powers of the General Council shall include the power to provide, in such manner as the Council think fit, advice for members of the medical profession on standards of professional conduct or on medical ethics.

36 Professional misconduct and criminal offences

(1) Where a fully registered person–

    (a) is found by the Professional Conduct Committee to have been convicted in the British Islands of a criminal offence, whether while so registered or not; or

    (b) is judged by the Professional Conduct Committee to have been guilty of serious professional misconduct, whether while so registered or not;

the Committee may, if they think fit, direct–

    (i) that his name shall be erased from the register;

    (ii) that his registration in the register shall be suspended (that is to say, shall not have effect) during such period not exceeding 12 months as may be specified in the direction; or

    (iii) that his registration shall be conditional on his compliance, during such period not exceeding three years as may be specified in the direction, with such requirements so specified as the Committee think fit to impose for the protection of members of the public or in his interests.

(2) Where a fully registered person whose registration is subject to conditions imposed under sub-s (1) above by the Professional Conduct Committee or under s 42(3)(e) below by the Preliminary Proceedings Committee is judged by the Professional Conduct Committee to have failed to comply with any of the requirements imposed on him as conditions of his registration the Committee may, if they think fit, direct–

    (a) that his name shall be erased from the register; or

(b) that his registration in the register shall be suspended (that is to say, shall not have effect) during such period not exceeding 12 months as may be specified in the direction ...

(Similar powers reside in the UKCC pursuant to the provisions of the Nurses, Midwives and Health Visitors Act 1997.)

Erasure from the register is clearly a very serious sanction for the professional, in that henceforth (unless they succeed at some future date in having their name restored to it) they will be deprived of their professional livelihood. In so far as a doctor is unhappy with the decision of the GMC in this matter, he or she may appeal (pursuant to s 40 of the 1983 Act) to the Privy Council. A recent case in point, in which the meaning of 'serious professional misconduct' under s 36 of the Act was considered, is that of *McCandless v GMC* [1996] 1 WLR 167:

> **Lord Hoffmann**: Dr David McCandless, a general practitioner in Deeside, appeals against a determination and direction of the Professional Conduct Committee of the General Medical Council. At a hearing on 16 March 1995 the Committee found that he was guilty of serious professional misconduct and directed that his name should be erased from the Register of Medical Practitioners.
>
> The charges alleged errors in his diagnoses of three patients and failure to refer them to hospital. Two subsequently died and the other was found on her eventual admission to hospital to be seriously ill. It is not necessary to go further into the details because Mr Mitting, who appeared for Dr McCandless, accepted that the Committee's findings of fact were not open to any material dispute. He also accepted that in each case Dr McCandless had been negligent. The chairman of the Committee gave the following brief reasons for its finding that he had been guilty of serious professional misconduct:
>
> > Dr McCandless, the Committee take a very serious view of the evidence which they have heard about the poor standard of medical care which you provided to all three patients in this case. The care which you provided fell deplorably short of the standard which patients are entitled to expect from their general practitioners.
>
> Mr Mitting submits that these reasons reveal an error of law by the Committee. He says that the Committee applied the wrong test for what amounts to serious professional misconduct. It thought that it was enough that the treatment given to the three patients fell 'deplorably short' of the standard which would reasonably be expected. Mr Mitting says that poor treatment is not enough. The doctor may nevertheless have been doing his best. He may have been overworked or just not particularly good at the job. But 'serious professional misconduct' means, he said, conduct which is morally blameworthy. This cannot be determined simply by deciding whether the treatment measured up to an objective standard. One has to look at why the doctor gave the treatment which he did. If it fell short of a reasonable standard because he was, for example, too lazy or drunk to examine the patient properly, then he would be guilty of misconduct. But not if he made an honest mistake.

Their Lordships think that some support can be found for Mr Mitting's submission in old cases on the meaning of 'infamous conduct in a professional respect' – the words which were used in 19th century Medical Acts and which continued to be used until replaced by the words 'serious professional misconduct' in the Medical Act 1969 ...

[However] ... the authorities on the old wording do not speak with one voice and ... they are of little assistance in the interpretation of the new. Secondly, although there remains the single disciplinary offence now styled 'serious professional misconduct', the possible penalties available to the Committee, which used to be confined to the ultimate sanction of erasure, have been extended to include suspension and the imposition of conditions upon practice. This suggests that the offence was intended to include serious cases of negligence. Thirdly, the public has higher expectations of doctors and members of other self-governing professions. Their governing bodies are under a corresponding duty to protect the public against the genially incompetent as well as the deliberate wrongdoers. Fourthly, the meaning of the new wording has been authoritatively stated by this Board in *Doughty v General Dental Council* [1988] AC 164, p 173 in objective terms:

> ... judged by proper professional standards in the light of the objective facts about the individual patients ... the dental treatments criticised as unnecessary [were] treatments that no dentist of reasonable skill exercising reasonable care would carry out.

This test appears to their Lordships to be, *mutatis mutandis*, equally applicable to treatment by doctors ...

Once it is accepted that seriously negligent treatment can amount to serious professional misconduct, then it seems to their Lordships that the appeal must fail. The eminent medical practitioners who sat on the Committee came to the conclusion that Dr McCandless' treatment of his three patients fell deplorably short of the standard to which patients are entitled to expect from general practitioners. In the circumstances, it is scarcely surprising that they concluded that Dr McCandless was guilty of serious professional misconduct. Their Lordships can see no basis for interfering with that conclusion. Nor can they see any ground for interfering with the Committee's decision that the offences merited the penalty of erasure from the register.

(Pursuant to terms of the Nurses, Midwives and Health Visitors Act 1997, an appeal from a decision of the UKCC in similar circumstances will lie to the High Court.)

Role of (criminal) law

Of course, the disciplinary mechanisms with which we have so far been concerned operate alongside, and independently of, the sanctions provided by the legal system in relation to doctors and other persons who, by their conduct, inflict harm upon others. In Chapters 3 and 6 below, we shall be focusing upon the civil remedies, in the torts of battery and negligence respectively, available to patients in relation to maltreatment they receive during medical care. However, it is important to note that the criminal law may also be of relevance in some cases. In this regard, where a patient is injured, or simply handled non-consensually, a doctor could in theory be prosecuted for an offence, either in battery at common law, or under the Offences Against the Person Act 1861. Where the patient actually dies, then a charge in murder or manslaughter may be brought depending on the *mens rea* of the doctor. The former charge, in particular, is a possibility in certain cases of euthanasia (see further below, Chapter 12).

Although it is generally very rare for criminal charges to be preferred against doctors (it usually not being thought in the public interest for prosecutions to be brought), the fact that ultimately doctors do not belong to any special category of citizen – and must answer for the serious consequences of deficient conduct – was recently illustrated by the conviction for manslaughter of an anaesthetist in *R v Adomako*.

R v Adomako [1994] 5 Med LR 27:

Lord Mackay of Clashfern LC: The conviction arose out of the conduct of an eye operation carried out at the Mayday Hospital, Croydon on 4 January 1987. The appellant was, during the latter part of that operation, the anaesthetist in charge of the patient.

The operation was carried out by two surgeons supported by a team of five nurses and a theatre sister. Anaesthesia commenced at about 9.45 am ...

At approximately 11.05 am a disconnection occurred at the endotracheal tube connection. The supply of oxygen to the patient ceased and this led to cardiac arrest at 11.14 am. During this period the appellant failed to notice or remedy the disconnection.

The appellant first became aware that something was amiss when an alarm sounded on the Dinamap machine, which monitors the patient's blood pressure. From the evidence it appears that some four and a half minutes would have elapsed between the disconnection and the sounding of this alarm. When this alarm sounded the appellant responded in various ways by checking the equipment and by administering atropine to raise the patient's pulse. But at no stage before the cardiac arrest did he check the integrity of the endotracheal tube connection. The disconnection itself was not discovered until after resuscitation measures had been commenced.

For the prosecution it was alleged that the appellant was guilty of gross negligence in failing to notice or respond appropriately to obvious signs that a disconnection had occurred and that the patient had ceased to breathe. In particular the prosecution alleged that the appellant had failed to notice at various stages during the period after disconnection and before the arrest either occurred or became inevitable that the patient's chest was not moving, the dials on the mechanical ventilating machine were not operating, the disconnection in the endotracheal tube, that the alarm on the ventilator was not switched on and that the patient was becoming progressively blue. Further the prosecution alleged that the appellant had noticed but failed to understand the correct significance of the fact that during this period the patient's pulse had dropped and the patient's blood pressure had dropped.

Two expert witnesses gave evidence for the prosecution. Professor Payne described that standard of care as 'abysmal' while Professor Adams stated in that in his view a competent anaesthetist should have recognised the signs of disconnection within 15 seconds and that the appellant's conduct amounted to 'a gross dereliction of care'.

On behalf of the appellant it was conceded at his trial that he had been negligent. The issue was therefore whether his conduct was criminal ...

... [I]n my opinion the ordinary principles of the law of negligence apply to ascertain whether or not the defendant has been in breach of a duty of care towards the victim who has died. If such breach of duty is established the next question is whether that breach of duty caused the death of the victim. If so, the jury must go on to consider whether that breach of duty should be characterised as gross negligence and therefore as a crime. This will depend on the seriousness of the breach of duty committed by the defendant in all the circumstances in which the defendant was placed when it occurred. The jury will have to consider whether the extent to which the defendant's conduct departed from the proper standard of care incumbent upon him, involving as it must have done a risk of death to the patient, was such that it should be judged criminal.

It is true that to a certain extent this involves an element of circularity, but in this branch of the law I do not believe that is fatal to its being correct as a test of how far conduct must depart from accepted standards to be characterised as criminal. This is necessarily a question of degree and an attempt to specify that degree more closely is I think likely to achieve only a spurious precision. The essence of the matter which is supremely a jury question is whether, having regard to the risk of death involved, the conduct of the defendant was so bad in all the circumstances as to amount in their judgment to a criminal act or omission ...

In my view the summing up of the learned judge in the present case was a model of clarity in analysis of the facts and in setting out the law in a manner which was readily comprehensible by the jury. The summing up was criticised in respect of the inclusion of the following passage ([1991] 2 Med LR 291):

> Of course you will understand it is not for every humble man of the profession to have all that great skill of the great men in Harley Street but, on the other hand, they are not allowed to practise medicine in this country unless they have acquired a certain amount of skill. They are bound to show a reasonable amount of skill according to the circumstances of the case, and you have to judge them on the basis that they are skilled men, but not necessarily so skilled as more skillful men in the profession, and you can only convict them criminally if, in your judgment, they fall below the standard of skill which is the least qualification which any doctor should have. You should only convict a doctor of causing a death by negligence if you think he did something which no reasonably skilled doctor should have done.

The criticism was particularly of the latter part of this quotation in that it was open to the meaning that if the defendant did what no reasonably skilled doctor should have done it was open to the jury to convict him of causing death by negligence. Strictly speaking this passage is concerned with the statement of a necessary condition for a conviction by preventing a conviction unless that condition is satisfied. It is incorrect to treat it as stating a sufficient condition for conviction. In any event I consider that this passage in the context was making the point forcefully that the defendant in this case was not to be judged by the standard of more skilled doctors but by the standard of a reasonably competent doctor. There were many other passages in the summing up which emphasised the need for a high degree of negligence if the jury were to convict and read in that context I consider that the summing up cannot be faulted.

For these reasons I am of the opinion that this appeal should be dismissed ...

(Lords Keith, Goff, Browne-Wilkinson, and Woolf agreed.)

ACCESS TO HEALTH CARE

Background – scarcity of NHS resources

Demand for NHS resources has always outstripped supply:

Timmins, N, *NHS 50th Anniversary: A History of the NHS*, 1996, London: DoH, p 3:

The new service uncovered a vast well of unmet need. GPs of the time recall women with prolapsed uteruses, who had been unable to afford the hospital treatment, suddenly pouring into the surgery, along with men with huge hernias held in by trusses. Bevan, who had declared the NHS would 'lift the shadow from millions of homes', had been right.

But there was also some abuse as GPs were inundated with people wanting wigs, or free cotton wool for padding, and free surgical spirit and aspirin. 'One would think the people saved up their illness for the first free day', one GP complained and Bevan himself, when the service had been running for 18 months, declared: 'I shudder to think of the ceaseless cascade of medicine which is pouring down British throats at the present time'.

Nonetheless, the NHS transformed health care – and not just for the poor, who were spared the indignity of means tests, but also for the middle classes, who no longer faced the fear of bills. It did so too for doctors. 'I used to charge 1/6d for a consultation', one Clydeside GP recalled. 'They laid the money on the desk as they came in. It was all rather embarrassing. I used to charge 2/6d to 7/6d for a visit, the highest rate for foremen and undermanagers. We'd send out the bills, but about a quarter would be bad debts and some you simply didn't bill because you knew they couldn't pay. The NHS thankfully got rid of all that.'

In doing so, however, the service instantly faced the first of the great financial crises which were periodically to mark its history. Spending in the first nine months proved two thirds higher than expected. The sea of unmet need, the sheer difficulty of predicting in advance the costs of the new service, the rising expectations it generated and the costs of medical advance had all combined to blow the early budgets.

If this sounds familiar it is because it is the history of health services the world over. Take medical advance. The first antibiotic – penicillin – had become available, for troops, during the war. But the year 1948 saw new types of penicillin developed. Streptomycin, the first drug to successfully tackle tubercular meningitis – TB in the forties was a major scourge – became available. In both Britain and America, other new antibiotics were developed. Tubocurarine, the muscle relaxant still used in surgery today, was introduced.

Clearly, pressures on NHS resources are not simply a consequence of inefficiencies in the way the service is run (the issue that reforms such as the internal market have sought to address). Rather, in the light of constant advances in medical technology, they are to be regarded as inherent and inescapable in nature. As Christopher Newdick writes:

Newdick, C, *Who Should We Treat?*, 1995, Oxford: Clarendon Press, pp 5–6:

Medicine no longer focuses on opportunist and acute illness. It routinely deals with chronic conditions such as the diseases of the cardiovascular system, of the respiratory system, the gastrointestinal system, the central nervous system, and joint diseases such as arthritis. Treatments for these conditions are usually long term, and often last many years. Combined together, they accounted for some 63.6% of the total drugs bill in England in 1992. These are the diseases associated with relative affluence and old age which, for the moment, are likely to put increasing pressure on resources. As a result of these pressures, some treatments are not routinely provided by the NHS. For example, tattoo removal is often not offered by hospitals, and many health authorities have restricted the availability of *in vitro* fertilisation, gender reassignment, reversal of sterilisation, cosmetic surgery, and complementary medicine.

Matters will soon become more complicated still. The pharmaceutical industry stands on the edge of a new generation of medicines which will revolutionise our ideas about sickness and health. But they may be so expensive that health service providers will be forced to reassess the question of priorities. Just the past year has seen a paradigm shift in modern biology because it is revealing so much information about the basic mechanisms of disease for which drugs can be developed. In the past, pharmaceutical firms relied on serendipity to find new drugs. In future that is not the way to go if the idea is to produce medicines of value.

Today, as a result of the Human Genome Project, we have sufficient knowledge of the basic structures of DNA in the human body to consider genetic treatments for chronic conditions of illness which were hitherto entirely beyond the reach of doctors and medicines. We may soon be in a position to attack the genetic causes of chronic illness. Cystic fibrosis, for example, is being treated in this way. Similar developments are occurring in the field of medical devices and technology, in both diagnosis and treatment of illness. Such techniques offer the potential for considerable savings on conventional, long term treatment of conditions such as heart and liver disease, diabetes and cancer and may be attractive on health and financial grounds. On the other hand, their cost may be so prohibitive as to threaten the availability of other, less expensive treatments. They also raise fundamental questions about the meaning of the words 'health' and 'illness'. Curative treatment may become available for a range of conditions which are explained in societal or personal terms, rather than as illnesses. Obesity, alcoholism, cigarette smoking and drug addiction provoke arguments of this nature. Should they qualify for care in the same way as other conditions? These issues raise questions about the very purpose of a 'health' service.

Disputes over obtaining treatment

Following the drafting of, and publication by, the Government of the Patient's Charter (*The Patient's Charter and You*, 1995, London: DoH), patients are invited to expect prompt and efficient treatment on the NHS. However, as Jonathan Montgomery notes, the Charter functions primarily to define targets for NHS bodies to aim at, rather than conferring a set of enforceable rights upon patients:

Montgomery, J, *Health Care Law*, 1997, Oxford: OUP, pp 60–61:

... the NHS has committed itself to attaining certain standards through its Patient's Charter. This Charter does not create legally enforceable rights. If the rights it contains are enforceable, it is because they are already recognised by the law, not because they are set out in the Charter ...

The Charter states that NHS patients possess 10 general rights. Six refer to access to health care; to receive it on the basis of clinical need rather than ability to pay, to be registered with a general practitioner (and therefore receive primary care), to receive emergency care, to be referred to a consultant or for a second opinion, to information on the quality of local services (according to measures chosen by the Government or NHS rather than the patient), to be admitted for in-patient treatment within two years of being placed on a waiting list by a consultant. Three refer to the position of patients once they are receiving care; to a clear explanation of the proposed treatment (including alternatives and risks), to have access to records (which are guaranteed to be confidential), and to be permitted to choose whether or not to be involved in research or training. The final Charter right is to have complaints investigated and receive a full and prompt written reply.

The general charter rights have been supplemented by specific targets (aspirations rather than rights) in relation to waiting times in hospital and community appointments. All patients must be admitted to hospital within 18 months of a consultant deciding that treatment is necessary. Ninety per cent of people referred should be seen as out-patients within 13 weeks, and all within 26 weeks. Urgent cases should be seen more quickly, and by January 1995, nearly half of all NHS patients waiting for treatment were admitted within five weeks. Out-patients should be given a specific appointment time and be seen within 30 minutes of that time. Visits to a patient's own home should take place within a two hour time band agreed with the patient. These targets have had a considerable influence on the behaviour of NHS trusts.

How far can a patient who is denied NHS treatment bring an action in the courts in order to secure its provision?

Judicial review

Given the public status of the health service, and the constituent bodies within it (ie, health authorities, NHS trusts, etc), a decision not to provide some given treatment may be susceptible to challenge in public law. This means that such a decision, if viewed as *Wednesbury* unreasonable (see *Associated Provincial Picture Houses v Wednesbury Corporation* [1947] 2 All ER 680), can be quashed by the courts. Lord Diplock in *Council of Civil Service Unions v Minister for the Civil Service* [1985] AC 374, p 410, described the power of judicial review in the following terms:

> **Lord Diplock**: It applies to a decision which is so outrageous in its defiance of logic or of accepted moral standards that no sensible person who had applied his mind to the question to be decided could have arrived at it. Whether a decision falls within this category is a question that judges by their training and experience should be well equipped to answer, or else there would be something badly wrong with our judicial system.

In the course of a number of actions brought in judicial review, however, the courts have shown themselves to be unwilling to interfere with decisions of NHS bodies in relation to the treatment of individual patients. In so doing, judges have recognised that the NHS has limited resources and that it is not for them to assume the role of organisers and arbiters of hospital waiting lists.

One of the first cases in which patients invoked judicial review in an attempt to assert a direct right to receive specified health care was that of *R v Secretary of State for Social Services et al ex p Hincks*.

R v Secretary of State for Social Services, West Midlands RHA and Birmingham AHA (Teaching) ex p Hincks and Others (1980) 1 BMLR 93, CA (Lord Denning MR, Bridge and Oliver LJJ)

This case was principally concerned with the meaning of s 3(1) of the National Health Service Act 1977 (see above, p 58), and in particular whether it imposed an absolute duty on the Secretary of State to provide services regardless of available funding. Four people who had been on the waiting list for orthopaedic surgery sought a declaration that the Secretary of State was in breach of his duty when plans for additional orthopaedic services at a hospital could not be carried out because of lack of funding. In refusing the declaration, the Court of Appeal noted that the Secretary of State has to have regard to the money made available to him:

> **Lord Denning MR**: Mr Blom-Cooper has urged before us all that can be said. He has referred us to the fact that there are no provisions in the statute which limit the expenditure of the Department. Section 3(1) of the National Health Service Act 1977 provides:

It is the Secretary of State's duty to provide throughout England and Wales, to such extent as he considers necessary to meet all reasonable requirements – (a) hospital accommodation ... (c) medical, dental, nursing and ambulance services ... (f) such other services as are required for the diagnosis and treatment of illness.

So that is his duty. It is a short point, and an important point that Mr Blom-Cooper raises. He says that that duty must be fulfilled. If the Secretary of State needs money to do it, then he must see that parliament gives it to him. Alternatively, if Parliament does not give it to him, then a provision should be put in the statute to excuse him from his duty. Mr Blom-Cooper says that that duty is plain and imperative, and it ought to be fulfilled by the Secretary of State.

That is an attractive argument, because there is no express limitation on the duty of the Secretary of State in the statute. But, in the course of the argument, many illustrations have been taken showing how necessary it is for a Secretary of State to have regard to forward planning (as it is called), to estimated changes in the population, for instance – or maybe the ageing population. He has to estimate for the future. For instance, when in 1971 the Good Hope Hospital scheme was approved, it was necessarily contemplated that it would be possible within the resources available. Indeed, as the discussion proceeded, it seemed to me inevitable that this provision had to be implied into s 3, 'to such extent as he considers necessary to meet all reasonable requirements such as can be provided within the resources available'. That seems to me to be a very necessary implication to put on that section, in accordance with the general legislative purpose. It cannot be supposed that the Secretary of State has to provide all the latest equipment. As Oliver LJ said in the course of argument, it cannot be supposed that the Secretary of State has to provide all the kidney machines which are asked for, or for all the new developments such as heart transplants in every case where people would benefit from them. It cannot be that the Secretary of State has a duty to provide everything that is asked for in the changed circumstances which have come about. That includes the numerous pills that people take nowadays: it cannot be said that he has to provide all these free for everybody.

I would like to read a few words from the judgment of Wien J, who gave a very comprehensive and good judgment in this matter.

He said:

> The question remains: has there been a breach duty? Counsel for the (Secretary of State) submits that s 3 does not impose an absolute duty. I agree. He further submits it does, by virtue of the discretion given, include an evaluation of financial resources or the lack of them is at the root of the whole problem in this case.
>
> If funds were unlimited, then of course regions and areas could go ahead and provide all sorts of services. But funds are not unlimited. The funds are voted by parliament, and the health service has to do the best it can with the total allocation of financial resources.

I agree with that approach of the judge in this case. But there is a further aspect which he dealt with.

He said, instead of looking at the health service as a whole, could you pinpoint a particular hospital or a particular area like the Good Hope Hospital in Birmingham, and say, that does require an extension, and it is a breach of duty for the Secretary of State not to provide for that hospital and that area? It seems to me – as, indeed, Mr Roland Moyle said in the course of his letter – that you cannot pinpoint any particular hospital or any particular area. The Secretary of State has to do his best having regard to his wide responsibilities. For instance, there are 12 hospitals in this particular area. The service has to be provided over the whole country. Upon that point, the judge said:

> I have come to the conclusion that it is impossible to pinpoint any breach of statutory duty on the part of the Secretary of State. If he is entitled to take into account financial resources, as in my judgment he is, then it follows that every thing that can be done within the limit of the financial resources available has been done in the region and in the area. I doubt very much whether under s 3(1) it is permissible to put the spotlight, as it were, upon one particular department of one particular hospital and say that conditions there are unsatisfactory.

It seems to me that those two paragraphs in the judge's judgment express the position very accurately. It is an interesting point, and it is important from the public point of view because of the grievances which many people feel nowadays about the long waiting list to get into hospital. So be it. The Secretary of State says that he is doing the best he can with the financial resources available to him: and I do not think that he can be faulted in the matter.

I think that the judge was quite right, and I would dismiss the appeal.

Margaret Brazier comments on the *Hincks* case, discussing the possibility of a future claim in the area:

Brazier, M, *Medicine, Patients and the Law*, 1992, Harmondsworth: Penguin, p 22:

The courts did not entirely abdicate control over the minister. A public-spirited patient resigned to getting no damages himself might try again for an order against any minister who he alleged had totally subverted the health service, for example a minister using his position and powers exclusively to benefit private medicine at the expense of the NHS. Chances of success are not high, and of course the government of the day could always change the law, but they can be made to do it openly and not permitted to pay lip service to a duty to a health service which may have been abandoned.

The decision shows the very difficult health resource policy issues involved and the extent to which to which there are often no immediate solutions. The lives of patients can be seen to be at stake in some of the cases.

R v Central Birmingham HA ex p Walker, R v Secretary of State for Social Services and Another ex p Walker (1987) 3 BMLR 32 (MacPherson J)

David Barber Walker was a premature baby who needed a heart operation. He had been cared for in hospital since his birth. and was not in any immediate danger. His operation had been postponed on a number of occasions because of a shortage of specially trained nurses in the intensive care unit where he would have to go after the operation. His mother applied for leave to apply for judicial review of the decision to postpone the operation, seeking *certiorari* to quash the decision to postpone on the ground that it had been arrived at unlawfully and unreasonably, and mandamus to require the authority to carry out the operation.

> **MacPherson J:** It seems to me that this case is not truly an attack upon the actual decision made (although that is the matter set out in the application itself) and I detect a general criticism of the decisions as to the staffing and financing of the National Health Service and of those who provide its funds and facilities. It has been said before, and I say it again, that this court can no more investigate that on the facts of this case than it could do so in any other case where the balance of available money and its distribution and use are concerned. Those, of course, are questions which are of enormous public interest and concern – but they are questions to be raised, answered and dealt with outside the court.
>
> I am wholly convinced that this decision of the health authority is not justiciable, that is to say that it is not a matter in which the court should intervene. If it were so, then any question of priority or clinical judgment of which case came first could be subject to review where it may depend on the location of available facilities.
>
> I pause to say that there is no possible basis for suggesting that there could be any 'policy' of the health authority to deprive the hospital of staff other than for financial and general reasons which are well known.
>
> In my judgment the court would do a great disservice to those who have to work in difficult and straitened circumstances if it were to contemplate making an order in this case. No surgeon should be ordered to perform an operation by the court in the circumstances which this case reveals. I deprecate any suggestion that patients should be encouraged to think that the court has a role in a case of this kind.
>
> Mr De Mello has to satisfy me that he has an arguable case, upon the facts set out in this application and in the light of the principles which govern judicial review. He has wholly failed so to persuade me. Of course everybody hopes that this matter will be resolved as soon as is humanly possible. But in my judgment I would simply raise false hopes by giving leave. I am convinced that there are no prospects of success in this court in this application – and it must be dismissed.

The applicant's appeal to the Court of Appeal (Sir John Donaldson MR, Nicholls LJ and Caulfield J) was dismissed:

Sir John Donaldson MR: It is not for this court, or indeed any court, to substitute its own judgment for the judgment of those who are responsible for the allocation of resources. This court could only intervene where it was satisfied that there was a *prima facie* case, not only of failing to allocate resources in the way in which others would think that resources should be allocated, but of a failure to allocate resources to an extent which was *Wednesbury* unreasonable, if one likes to use the lawyers' jargon, or, in simpler words, which involves a breach of a public law duty ... Even then, of course, the court has to exercise a judicial discretion. It has to take account of all the circumstances of the particular case with which it is concerned.

The Court of Appeal (Stephen Brown, Neill, and Ralph Gibson LJJ) subsequently considered the case of *R v Central Birmingham HA ex p Collier* (1988) LEXIS Transcript, 6 January, which had similar facts to *Walker*, except that here there was some evidence of an immediate danger to the patient's health.

Stephen Brown LJ: The situation in this case, in my judgment, is not different in any relevant respect from that which obtained in the *Walker* case.

Mr De Mello has sought to distinguish the factual situation in this case by submitting that here, on the evidence of Mr Collier's affidavit, there is an immediate danger to health. I am not sure that I can accept that the affidavit establishes that fact. We have no medical evidence before us, but, even assuming that it does establish that there is immediate danger to health, it seems to me that the legal principles to be applied do not differ from the case of *In re Walker*. This court is in no position to judge the allocation of resources by this particular health authority. Mr De Mello recognises that there is no hint of criticism, let alone of complaint, of any action on the part of the surgeon, or any other doctor at the hospital. There is no complaint of bad faith by the health authority. It is not suggested that they are in any way dragging their feet. Mr De Mello asserts that, on the basis of what he would say is 'general knowledge', there is a lack of sufficient resources to enable every bed to be in use at the hospital; but there is no suggestion here that the hospital authority has behaved in a way which is deserving of condemnation or criticism. What is suggested is that somehow more resources should be made available to enable the hospital authorities to ensure that the treatment is immediately given.

Of course this is a hearing before a court. This is not the forum in which a court can properly express opinions upon the way in which national resources are allocated or distributed. There may be very good reasons why the resources in this case do not allow all the beds in the hospital to be used at this particular time. We have no evidence of that, and indeed, as the Master of the Rolls has said, it is not for this court, or any court, to substitute its own judgment for the judgment of those who are responsible for the allocation of resources.

From the legal point of view, in the absence of any evidence which could begin to show that there was a failure to allocate resources in this instance in circumstances which would make it unreasonable in the *Wednesbury* sense to make those resources available, there can be no arguable case. I am bound to say that, whilst I have for my part every sympathy with the position of Mr Collier and his family and can understand their pressing anxiety in the case of their little boy, it does seem to me unfortunate that this procedure has been adopted. It is wholly misconceived in my view. The courts of this country cannot arrange the lists in the hospital, and, if it is not evidence that they are not being arranged properly due to some unreasonableness in the *Wednesbury* sense on the part of the authority, the courts cannot, and should not, be asked to intervene.

Having regard to the very recent decision of *In re Walker* it seems to me unfortunate that the step has been taken of bringing the matter before a court again.

It may be hoped that the publicity will assist in bringing pressure to bear upon the hospital; I do not know. This court cannot be concerned with matters of that kind. But simply upon the basis – which is a purely legal basis – that the matter comes before this court I can see no ground upon which the application can be granted.

Ralph Gibson LJ: I agree. I add very little. If I were the father of this child, I think that I would want to be given answers about the supply to, and use of, funds by this health authority. No doubt the health authority would welcome the opportunity to deal with such matters so that they could explain what they are doing and what their problems are. But this court and the High Court have no role of general investigator of social policy and of allocation of resources. The court's jurisdiction, as is very well known, is limited to dealing with breach of duties under law, including decisions made by public authorities which are shown to be unreasonable.

There is in my view no evidence whatever of any arguable breach of law on the part of this health authority. The court by this application is being asked to conduct an investigation which it has no power to conduct, and I agree that the application must be dismissed.

A more recent case which considered the meaning of s 3(1) of the NHS Act 1977, and the scope of a health authority's duty to provide medical services was *R v Sheffield HA ex p Seale*.

R v Sheffield HA ex p Seale (1994) 25 BMLR 1, QBD (Auld J)

Julie Anne Seale sought *in vitro* fertilisation treatment from the respondent health authority. She was refused it on the grounds that, at 37 years of age, she was outside the age range within which the authority provided such treatment.

Auld J: Mr Straker challenges the decision made in this case, based on the criteria set out in the letter of 22 April 1994, under three heads. The first is illegality. As I understand his submission, it is that as the Secretary of State has given no directions or imposed no limitations on the provision of *in vitro* fertilisation, and it is not for the district health authority, once it has committed itself to providing such a service, to restrict that provision if in the case of any patient there is a chance, a reasonable probability, a possibility – I do not quite know where the line is to be drawn – of the treatment being effective. As I understand Mr Straker's argument, it is that if any such qualification beyond efficacy is to be introduced, that is for the Secretary of State, and she has not done it here.

In my view, it is not possible to erect out of the absence of a direction by the Secretary of State, or of the imposition by her of a limitation on the provision of such a service, a denial to the regional or district health authority of itself determining the circumstances in which such a service can be provided. It is not arguable, in my view, that it is bound, simply because it has undertaken to provide such a service, to provide it on demand to any individual patient for whom it may work, regardless of financial and other constraints upon the authority. Accordingly, I reject as unarguable any submission based on illegality here.

In my view it is clear that if the Secretary of State has not limited or given directions as to the way in which such a service, once undertaken, should be provided; the authority providing it is entitled to form a view as to those circumstances and when they justify provision and when they do not.

The second argument of Mr Straker is that the decision here is irrational, that is, absurd. That is what he has to show as arguable to succeed on this application for leave. He says it is irrational because it is not founded on any sustainable, clinical approach. The basis of that argument appears to be that there is more than one view of the appropriate 'cut-off' age for such treatment. In short, he submits, and refers me to the views of other doctors, that 35 years old is too low an age. It is possible to achieve success certainly up to the age of 42. I cannot, nor could the court when deciding the matter as a substantive issue, if it came to that, form a view as to the rightness or wrongness of competing medical views on the effective cut-off date for the utility of such treatment. The decision letter does not say that the treatment cannot be effective after the age of 35, but merely that it is 'generally less effective in women aged over 35 years'.

If that is so, can Mr Straker challenge the decision as irrational on the basis that it is absurd to apply the age of 35 years as a blanket cut-off point, taking no account of individual circumstances? His submission is that every case should be considered individually. Clinically speaking there is no doubt good sense in such a submission. And a clinical decision on a case by case basis is clearly desirable and, in cases of critical illness, a necessary approach. However, it is reasonable, or it is at least not *Wednesbury* unreasonable (see *Associated Provincial Picture Houses Ltd v Wednesbury Corp* [1947] 2 All ER 680), of an authority to look at the matter in the context of the financial resources available to it to provide this and the many other services for which it is responsible under the National Health Service legislation. I cannot say that it is absurd for this authority, acting on advice that the efficacy of this treatment decreases with age and that it is generally less effective after the age of 35, to take that as an appropriate criterion when balancing the need for such a provision against its ability to provide it and all the other services imposed upon it under the legislation.

The third matter upon which Mr Straker relied as part of his argument based on irrationality was a reference to a particular condition from which this applicant suffers for which pregnancy is said to be a cure. However, that matter does not appear to have loomed large, or at all, in the circumstances giving rise to the decision of 22 April. Nor does it appear to have been particularly prominent as a reason for special treatment in this case in the correspondence that followed that decision.

Under the heading of 'Irrationality' Mr Straker relies upon the fact that privately paying patients can secure such treatment until the age of 42. It seems to me that that argument does not meet the central problem here of an authority coping with a finite budget and a myriad of services which it is bound to provide under it. I am, therefore, of the view that there is no arguable case that this decision was irrational, applying the high test that that word imports under the *Wednesbury* decision.

Lastly, Mr Straker submits that there was a procedural impropriety here. I confess I find it difficult to see any procedural hook on which Mr Straker could base his application. It seems to me, to whatever extent there was a procedural element upon which he relied, it falls to be considered under the heading of 'Irrationality'. I certainly can see no procedural basis upon which he can challenge this decision.

Accordingly, despite the very well organised and highly persuasive arguments of Mr Straker, I feel bound to refuse this application.

(On the provision of fertility treatment generally, see further below, Chapter 7.)

Seale is a useful decision as it shows a slightly less resolute approach being taken to resource allocation issues compared with cases such as *Collier*. Christopher Newdick has commented on the case as follows:

Newdick, C, 'Resource allocation in the NHS' (1997) 23(2–3) Am J Law & Med 291:

Although the application was refused on its merits the case distinguishes between 'critical', and other, illnesses. If critical illness necessitates an individual clinical decision of the case the *Wednesbury* test of managerial reasonableness is presumably limited to other areas of elective or optional health care. Note how uncomfortably this approach to clinical merits sits with *Collier*. This case is useful on its own facts for identifying that some care may fall into a category in which a clinical assessment is necessary. It says nothing however, about the components of such a decision, who is responsible for making it, or where the line should be drawn.

It does not of course follow, from the fact that the patient may sometimes be entitled to have their own circumstances and condition clinically assessed, that treatment need actually be provided. Indeed, as a corollary of the general ethical obligation on doctors to act in their patients' best interests, it may be that in a particular case no doctor will be found who is willing to carry it out, for example where it involves serious side effects for the patient and is believed to be of little or no therapeutic benefit. Certainly, the fact that the patient, where competent, wishes to receive the treatment will usually be a strong indicator that such treatment is in his best interests. Nevertheless, there will be exceptions, especially where terminal illness has been diagnosed, and claims for treatment brought on behalf of incompetent patients may also present difficulties.

A recent and well known case, which raised issues of this nature, as well as the question of how far financial considerations should play a part in the deliberations of the treatment provider, was that of *R v Cambridge HA ex p B*.

R v Cambridge HA ex p B (A Minor) (1995) 23 BMLR 1, CA (Sir Thomas Bingham MR, Sir Stephen Brown P, Simon Brown LJ)

In this case a 10 year old girl was refused the resources for further remedial treatment. She was suffering from acute myeloid leukaemia. The doctors responsible for her care believed that no further treatment could be usefully given to her beyond palliative care. Her father sought further medical treatment by chemotherapy with a view to a second bone marrow transplant. Taking into account clinical judgment, the nature of the treatment requested and its very low chances of success, the health authority declined the father's request. He sought judicial review of the health authority's decision, which was granted by Laws J at first instance. The authority appealed:

> **Sir Thomas Bingham MR**: In the course of his judgment, quashing the decision of the authority, the judge made four criticisms of the manner in which the authority had reached its decision. Before I turn to those, however, it is important that I should state very clearly, as the judge did, that this is a case involving the life of a young patient and that that is a fact which must dominate all consideration of all aspects of the case. Our society is one in which a very high value is put on human life. No decision affecting human life is one that can be regarded with other than the greatest seriousness.
>
> The second general comment which should be made is that the courts are not, contrary to what is sometimes believed, arbiters as to the merits of cases of this kind. Were we to express opinions as to the likelihood of the effectiveness of medical treatment, or as to the merits of medical judgment, then we should be straying far from the sphere which under our constitution is accorded to us. We have one function only, which is to rule upon the lawfulness of decisions. That is a function to which we should strictly confine ourselves.
>
> The four criticisms made by the judge of the authority's decision were these. First, he took the view that Dr Zimmern as the decision maker had wrongly failed to have regard to the wishes of the patient, as expressed on behalf of the patient by her family, and in particular by her father. Our attention was directed to the affidavits that I have mentioned. The point was made that nowhere does one see an express statement that among the factors that led Dr Zimmern to his decision was a consideration of the wishes of the family. In that situation, the judge held that the authority had failed to take a vitally important factor into consideration and that the decision was accordingly flawed.
>
> I feel bound for my part to differ from the judge. It seems to me that the judge's criticism entirely fails to recognise the realities of this situation. When

the case was first presented to the authority, it was presented on behalf of the patient, B, as a case calling for the co-operation and funding of the authority. At all times Dr Zimmern was as vividly aware as he could have been of the fact that the family, represented by B's father, were urgently wishing the authority to undertake this treatment; by 'undertake' I mean, of course, provide the funding for it. He was placed under considerable pressure by the family and, in the first instance, perhaps unfortunately, made reference to his policy of not corresponding directly with patients or their relatives about what he called 'extra-contractual referrals', meaning requests for the purchase of medical services outside the health authority.

The inescapable fact is, however, that he was put under perfectly legitimate, but very obvious, pressure by the family to procure this treatment and he was responding to that pressure. It was because he was conscious of that pressure that he obviously found the decision which he had to make such an agonising one and one calling for such careful consideration. To complain that he did not in terms say that he had regard to the wishes of the patient as expressed by the family, is to shut one's eyes to the reality of the situation with which he was confronted. It is also worthy of note, and there is no hint of criticism in this, that the accusation that he did not take the patient's wishes into account was not made in the grounds annexed to Form 86A. It was not, therefore, recognised as an accusation calling for a specific rebuttal.

The second criticism that is made is of the use of the expression 'experimental' to describe this treatment. The judge took the view, and Mr McIntyre on behalf of B urges, that that is not a fair or accurate description given the estimates of success which have been put by reputable practitioners, and given the willingness of Dr Gravett to accept that there was a worthwhile chance of success. The fact, however, is that even the first course of treatment had a chance of success of something between 10 and 20%. It was only if, contrary to the probabilities, that was totally successful, that it would be possible to embark on the second phase of the treatment which itself had a similar chance of success.

The plain fact is that, unlike many courses of medical treatment, this was not one that had a well tried track record of success. It was, on any showing, at the frontier of medical science. That being so, it does not, in my judgment, carry weight to describe this decision as flawed because of the use of this expression.

The third criticism that is made by the judge is of the reference to resources. The learned judge held that Dr Zimmern's evidence about money consisted only of grave and well rounded generalities. The judge acknowledged that the court should not make orders with consequences for the use of health service funds in ignorance of the knock-on effect on other patients. He went on to say that 'where the question is whether the life of a 10 year old child might be saved by however slim a chance, the responsible Authority ... must do more than toll the bell of tight resources'. The judge said that 'They must explain the priorities that have led them to decline to fund the treatment', and he found they had not adequately done so here.

I have no doubt that in a perfect world any treatment which a patient, or a patient's family, sought, would be provided if doctors were willing to give it, no matter how much it cost, particularly when a life was potentially at stake. It would, however, in my view, be shutting one's eyes to the real world if the court were to proceed on the basis that we do live in such a world. It is common knowledge that health authorities of all kinds are constantly pressed to make ends meet. They cannot pay their nurses as much as they would like; they cannot provide all the treatments they would like; they cannot purchase all the extremely expensive medical equipment they would like; they cannot carry out all the research they would like; they cannot build all the hospitals and specialist units they would like. Difficult and agonising judgments have to be made as to how a limited budget is best allocated to the maximum advantage of the maximum number of patients. That is not a judgment which the court can make. In my judgment, it is not something that a health authority such as this authority can be fairly criticised for not advancing before the court.

Mr McIntyre went so far as to say that if the authority has money in the bank which it has not spent, then they would be acting in plain breach of their statutory duty if they did not procure this treatment. I am bound to say that I regard that submission as manifestly incorrect. Unless the health authority had sufficient money to purchase everything which in the interests of patients it would wish to do, then that situation would never ever be reached. I venture to say that no real evidence is needed to satisfy the court that no health authority is in that position.

I furthermore think, differing, I regret, from the judge, that it would be totally unrealistic to require the authority to come to the court with its accounts and seek to demonstrate that if this treatment were provided for B then there would be a patient, C, who would have to go without treatment. No major authority could run its financial affairs in a way which would permit such a demonstration.

The fourth criticism which the judge made was that the authority had wrongly treated the problem which they faced as one of spending £75,000 when, in the first instance, the treatment only involved the expenditure of £15,000. It was therefore a two stage process, so it was held and submitted to us, and not a one stage process, as the authority wrongly thought. Again, I regret that I differ from the judge's view. It is, of course, true that if the first stage were unsuccessful, then £15,000, or even less than £15,000, would be the maximum that the authority would end up spending. It would not, however, be reasonable for the authority to embark on this expenditure on that basis since, quite plainly, they would have to continue if, having expended the £15,000, it proved successful and the call for the second stage of the treatment came. It was, therefore, an inescapable decision whether they should embark on this process at all. Having weighed the matter up and taken advice, particularly bearing in mind the suffering which even embarking on the treatment would inflict, the authority thought that they should not fund the treatment at all. I regret that I find it impossible to fault that process of thinking on their part.

The treatment was subsequently paid for by an anonymous benefactor, though B eventually died in March 1996. She did however survive well beyond the six to eight weeks estimate that the health authority had originally given her to live.

Richard Mullender has commented upon the case as follows:

Mullender, R, 'Judicial review and the rule of law' (1996) 112 LQR 182:

Laws J [at first instance] takes the novel step, in his judgment, of treating the fundamental right to life as providing a constraint upon the health authority's decision making discretion. To justify doing so, he first expresses 'the greatest doubt' as to *Wednesbury*'s adequacy as a standard of review (on account of its uncertainty) and, secondly, notes that, where such uncertainty exists, there are *dicta* which support the view that fundamental rights (viz, those occupying a place of central importance in the European Convention for the Protection of Human Rights and Fundamental Freedoms (Cmnd 8969, 1953)) can be invoked in order to resolve uncertainties in the common law ... With this justification for invoking the right to life in place, he determines that the health authority's decision constitutes an interference with it and addresses the question as to whether they have provided a substantial public interest justification for doing so. This question he answers in the negative, rejecting both their argument that further remedial treatment would not be in B's interests (because of the suffering to which it would expose her) and their argument that funding the treatment would not be an effective use of their limited resources. In the light of these findings, he concludes that B's right to life has been violated and quashes the respondent's decision. While the bulk of the judge's analysis concerns the right to life, he, nonetheless, states that the same result can be reached by applying *Wednesbury* and identifies four forms of unreasonableness manifested by the health authority: viz, failure to consider the wishes of B's family, wrongly characterising the treatment sought as 'experimental', failure to explain the priorities that led to the decision not to provide it, and an inaccurate estimate of its cost.

In contrast to the judgment of Laws J, the right to life plays no part in that of Bingham MR, notwithstanding his observing both that 'our society is one in which a very high value is put on human life' and that 'no decision affecting human life ... can be regarded with other than the greatest seriousness'. While, in the light of these comments, the Master of the Rolls' decision not to invoke the right to life might seem surprising, his not doing so can be explained by his commitment to the principle that, in judicial review proceedings, judges must merely scrutinise the lawfulness of a public body's decision and must not adjudicate upon its merits – a commitment to which he gives emphatic expression thus: 'we have one function only, which is to rule upon the lawfulness of decisions. That is a function to which we should strictly confine ourselves.' It is, hence, unsurprising to find him basing his decision not on the right to life, but, rather, on the ground of *Wednesbury* unreasonableness, which specifies a modest standard of review and, thus, leaves public bodies with broad scope for making discretionary decisions. The interpretation placed by Bingham MR on *Wednesbury* diverges radically from that of Laws J: he rescinds the judge's quashing order, identifying as unsustainable all four of the grounds on which the latter found the health authority's denial of treatment to be unreasonable.

An interesting question, given the Labour Government's determination to incorporate the European Convention on Human Rights into national law, is how far in the future courts will feel bound to adjudicate substantively on decisions by NHS bodies to deny potentially life-prolonging treatment, in the light of the (patient's) right to life enshrined in Art 2 of the Convention.

As previously discussed (see above, p 72), a health authority or trust's decision on the allocation of health care resources could also be challenged on the basis of procedural irregularity. This could include a failure to consult appropriately with the local Community Health Council or the maintenance of a policy directly opposed to Department of Health Circulars and advice: see *R v North and East Devon HA ex p Pow* (1997) 39 BMLR 77, and *R v North Derbyshire HA ex p Fisher* [1997] 8 Med LR 327.

Breach of statutory duty

Rather than bringing a claim in judicial review, could a plaintiff challenge a decision over health care resource allocation in private law? Jonathan Montgomery addresses the possibility here of an action being maintained for breach of statutory duty, but sees little scope for the successful use of this tort in relation to the National Health Service Act 1977:

Montgomery, J, *Health Care Law*, 1997, Oxford: OUP, pp 70–71:

Breach of statutory duty

In an action for the tort of breach of statutory duty, it is alleged that damage has been caused to the plaintiff due to the failure to perform a statutory duty which exists for the benefit of the aggrieved individual, and which parliament intended to be enforceable, through the courts, by that individual. Thus, patients denied services could argue that the NHS body responsible had failed to perform its statutory obligations and had harmed them. The prospects for success of this form of action depend in part upon the particular statutory duty in question. However, the courts have shown themselves to be reluctant to permit actions for the breach of duties to provide welfare services, and it is unlikely that such an action could be brought under the NHS Act 1977.

The House of Lords has noted that there has been no case in which statutory social welfare schemes, established for the benefit of the public at large, have been held to give rise to a private law action for damages. In *Re HIV Haemophilic Litigation*, the Court of Appeal accepted (in a preliminary action) that the general duties to provide services under the 1977 Act did not provide a foundation for such a suit. They also noted that Wien J had taken a similar view, *obiter*, in the High Court in *R v Secretary of State for Social Services ex p Hincks*. However, the point was not considered in the Court of Appeal in that case. Against this authority, there was a suggestion in *R v Ealing DHA ex p Fox* that a specific duty to provide services for discharged mental patients could be spelt out from the provisions of s 3(1) of the NHS Act 1977. It was not necessary for the judge in this case to consider this point, as such a duty was explicitly set out in s 117 of the Mental Health Act 1983, and he was not concerned with the issue of compensation. Consequently, it would be dangerous to rely on his comment.

It is possible that the courts will prove themselves less reticent where the statutory duties are more specific, because it is easier to show that the individual was entitled to expect a service to be provided. Thus, a failure to provide after-care services under the Mental Health Act 1983, s 117, might more readily form the basis of an action for breach of statutory duty. There, it will be clear that the individual patient, who has now been discharged, should be receiving help. It is not a general duty owed to the public, but a specific one owed to an identified individual. It may also be possible to use the action for breach of statutory duty where patients are promised specific services after an assessment of their needs, and are then not given them because the relevant authority failed to execute their decision. However, this sort of failure may be more amenable to a claim in negligence.

Negligence and health resources

Patients who are denied treatment might also attempt to argue that a health authority or trust has acted carelessly towards them and they have suffered injury as a result. General principles of the law of tort would be applied and the action framed as a malpractice suit (see further below, Chapter 6). To the extent that treatment is provided, then it is apparent that lack of resources cannot be used as an excuse for failure to reach the requisite standard of care: see *Wilsher v Essex AHA* [1987] QB 730, CA and *Bull v Devon AHA* [1993] 4 Med LR 117. However, it is unlikely that an action in negligence would lie where, due to lack of resources, a decision is taken not to treat in the first place. Certainly, where the NHS body simply refused to make a given facility available, it is difficult to see how any duty of care would arise between it and the patient.

Compulsory treatment and care

Finally, it should be noted that, exceptionally, treatment may be *imposed* upon citizens in the wider interests of public health, in particular when they are found to be suffering from serious contagious disease. This area, which is governed by the Public Health (Control of Disease) Act 1984 and associated secondary legislation, is looked at further below, in Chapter 3, in relation to consent.

CHAPTER THREE

CONSENT TO TREATMENT

ETHICAL CONSIDERATIONS

The requirement that a patient must give a valid consent to medical treatment, and its corollary, that it is the patient's prerogative to refuse treatment, even that which will save his life, are issues at the heart of medical law. It is necessary therefore, to examine the essential elements which have to be satisfied in order for a patient to give a valid consent.

However, it is also important to consider the ethical underpinnings of the high regard in which society holds the whole concept of consent. In Chapter 1 we looked at the conflict between the patient's right to autonomous decision making and medical paternalism and nowhere is this more apparent than in the issue of consent to treatment.

Autonomy

The basis of requiring consent to any form of medical treatment is that of bodily inviolability. To breach this, even in the most well meaning way, is an affront to our notion of our personal bodily integrity. It will be recalled that Mill's libertarian philosophy is particularly relevant to the issue of consent.

> **Mill, JS, *On Liberty*, 1982, Harmondsworth: Penguin, p 68:**
>
> ... the only purpose for which power can be rightfully exercised over any member of a civilised community, against his will, is to prevent harm to others. His own good, either physical or moral, is not a sufficient warrant. He cannot rightfully be compelled to do or forbear because it will be better for him to do so, because it will make him happier, because, in the opinions of others, to do so would be wise, or even right.

This approach also echoes the Kantian view (see above, Chapter 1) that persons are ends in themselves and not simply a means to the ends of other people. Every student of medical law is familiar with the statement made by Justice Cardozo in *Schloendorff v New York Hospital* (1914) 105 NE 92:

> **Cardozo J**: Every human being of adult years and sound mind has a right to determine what shall be done with his own body; and a surgeon who performs an operation without his patient's consent, commits an assault ...

The importance of bodily inviolability is entrenched in the law of Western societies. In *McFall v Shimp* (1978) 10 Pa D & C (3d) 90, a patient required a bone marrow donation to avoid almost certain death. The procedure for donation was virtually risk free, and if a donation from a suitable donor went ahead, the prognosis was excellent. The patient's cousin had volunteered for a compatibility test, but when the test showed him to be a suitable donor, he declined to undergo further tests or to donate the bone marrow. The patient sought an injunction to compel his cousin to go ahead.

> **Flaherty J**: The common law has consistently held to a rule which provides that one human being is under no legal compulsion to give aid or to take action to save that human being or to rescue. A great deal has been written regarding this rule which, on the surface, appears to be revolting in a moral sense. Introspection, however, will demonstrate that the rule is founded upon the very essence of our free society. It is noteworthy that counsel for the plaintiff has cited authority which has developed in other societies in support of the plaintiff's request in this instance. Our society, contrary to many others, has as its first principle, the respect for the individual, and that society and government exist to protect the individual from being invaded and hurt by another. Many societies adopt a contrary view which has the individual existing to service the society as a whole. In preserving such a society as we have it is bound to happen that great moral conflicts will arise, and will appear harsh in a given instance. In this case, the Chancellor is being asked to force one member of society to undergo a medical procedure which would provide that part of that individual's body would be removed from him and given to another so that the other could live. Morally, this decision rests with the defendant, and, in the view of the court, the refusal of the defendant is morally indefensible. For our law to *compel* the defendant to submit to an intrusion of his body would change every concept and principle upon which our society is founded. To do so would defeat the sanctity of the individual, and would impose a rule which would know no limits, and one could not imagine where the line would be drawn.

Paternalism

Doctors who believe that a medical procedure is appropriate and necessary for a patient's well being, can, perhaps, be forgiven for believing that the principle of autonomy should be sacrificed in the best interests of the patient. As we saw above, in Chapter 1, even a strong libertarian such as Mill accepted a limited form of paternalism when it was necessary to intervene temporarily to restore autonomy. However, this is not, perhaps, true paternalism: if autonomy has to be restored then arguably it could not have been exercised in the first place.

In the context of consent to treatment, a decision that autonomy is absent is generally expressed by saying that the patient lacks the necessary mental capacity (ie, understanding) to make valid decisions about treatment. It will be seen, however, that it may be tempting here for the paternalistically inclined to 'reason backwards' and infer that a patient, who refuses treatment which the doctor recommends, lacks such requisite understanding.

THE LEGAL FRAMEWORK

Introduction

Battery

A valid consent to medical treatment is required, because without it, the doctor will be committing a trespass to the person, ie, a battery. This is both a crime and a tort. A battery takes place when there is a non-consensual touching. It is sometimes said that an 'assault' has taken place (see the statement of Cardozo J in *Schloendorff v Society of New York Hospital* (1914) 105 NE 92, above, p 103). Technically, of course, an assault cannot take place unless the victim apprehends some immediate threat, and this would not be the case if the patient were unconscious. Although for the purposes of the criminal law, assault includes battery, in tort they are distinct (but see *AG's Reference (No 6 of 1980)* [1981] QB 715), and the correct term, in the case of non-consensual touching, is battery.

The favoured opinion is that there is no requirement that the touching be hostile. This is reflected in early case law, such as *Mohr v Williams* (1905) 104 NW 12, which concerned a patient who had consented to an operation on her right ear. During the course of the operation, the doctor discovered that the right ear did not, in fact, need surgery, but the left ear was in a more serious condition which required an operation. He performed the operation, which was successful. The patient sued in battery and was also successful.

In the case of *Wilson v Pringle* [1986] 2 All ER 440, the Court of Appeal suggested that the touching must be 'hostile' in order to constitute a battery. Although the court was prepared to adopt a very wide view of hostility so as not to confine it to acts of ill will, this view has been questioned since by the House of Lords (see *Re F (Mental Patient: Sterilisation)* [1990] 2 AC 1). Further, it must be the case that if a wide definition is adhered to then 'hostile' will mean little more than 'non-consensual', in which case its use is otiose. The reason for the hostility requirement imposed in *Wilson v Pringle* is the need to eliminate actions in battery as a result of things such as physical contact in crowded streets; Lord Goff in *Re F* dealt with the matter by stating that there could simply be no liability for physical contact which is generally acceptable in the ordinary conduct of everyday life.

Is it possible to envisage a non-consensual medical procedure which would not amount to a battery? Given that the essence of the tort/crime is *touching*, it is possible to imagine a scenario in which no touching has taken place. Suppose a doctor prescribes a drug, which the patient self-administers, and it turns out to be the wrong drug, but the mistake is quickly discovered, and the patient suffers no physical harm. Would the patient still have a cause of action in battery?

Countervailing interests that justify non-consensual treatment?

It is clear from the law of battery that, in relation to consent to treatment, paternalism will not override autonomy. However, might it be argued that there are countervailing State interests, as opposed to private acts of paternalism, which justify overriding a patient's refusal of certain forms of treatment? Four State interests with potential for limiting patient rights were identified in the New Jersey case *In the matter of Claire Conroy* 486 A 2d 1209 (1985). These were: preserving life, preventing suicide, safeguarding the integrity of the medical profession, and protecting innocent third parties.

> **Schrieber J**: The State's interest in preserving life ... may be seen as embracing two separate but related concerns: an interest in preserving the life of the particular patient, and an interest in preserving the sanctity of life ...
>
> While both of these State interests in life are certainly strong, in themselves they will usually not foreclose a competent person from declining life-sustaining medical treatment for himself. This is because the life that the State is seeking to protect in such a situation is the life of the same person who has competently decided to forgo the medical intervention; it is not some other actual or potential life that cannot adequately protect itself ...
>
> It may be contended that in conjunction with its general interest in preserving life, this State has a particular legislative policy of preventing suicide ... [However] this State interest in protecting people from direct and purposeful self-destruction is motivated by, if not encompassed within, the State's more basic interest in preserving life. Thus, it is questionable whether it is a distinct State interest worthy of independent consideration.
>
> In any event, declining life-sustaining medical treatment may not properly be viewed as an attempt to commit suicide. Refusing medical treatment merely allows the disease to take its natural course; if death were eventually to occur, it would be the result, primarily, of the underlying disease, and not the result of a self-inflicted injury ...
>
> The third State interest that is frequently asserted as a limitation on a competent patient's right to refuse medical treatment is the interest in safeguarding the integrity of the medical profession. This interest is not particularly threatened by permitting competent patients to refuse life-sustaining medical treatment. Medical ethics do not require medical intervention in disease at all costs ...
>
> Moreover, even if doctors were exhorted to attempt to cure or sustain their patients under all circumstances, that moral and professional imperative, at least in cases of patients who were clearly competent, presumably would not require doctors to go beyond advising the patient of the risks of forgoing treatment and urging the patient to accept the medical intervention ...
>
> The fourth asserted State interest in overriding a patient's decision about his medical treatment is the interest in protecting innocent third parties who may be harmed by the patient's treatment decision. When the patient's exercise of his free choice could adversely and directly affect the health, safety, or security of others, the patient's right of self-determination must frequently give way.

Thus, for example, the courts have required competent adults to undergo medical procedures against their will if necessary to protect the public health: *Jacobson v Massachusetts* 197 US 11 ... (1905) (recognising enforceability of compulsory smallpox vaccination law); to prevent a serious risk to prison security: *Myers* ... 379 Mass 263 [379 Mass 255; 399 NE 2d 452 (1979)] ... (compelling prisoner with kidney disease to submit to dialysis over his protest rather than acquiescing in his demand to be transferred to a lower-security prison) ... or to prevent the emotional and financial abandonment of the patient's minor children: *Application of President and Directors of Georgetown College Inc* 331 F 2d 1000, p 1008 (DC Cir), cert denied, 377 US 978 ... (1964) (ordering mother of seven month old infant to submit to blood transfusion over her religious objections because of the mother's 'responsibility to the community to care for her infant'); *Holmes v Silver Cross Hosp* 340 F Supp 125, p 130 (NDIII 1972) (indicating that patient's status as father of a minor child might justify authorising blood transfusions to save his life despite his religious objections).

It must be said that these latter cases 'to protect innocent parties' are of very dubious validity. Whilst public health arguments may, in the right circumstances, result in the overriding of a patient's refusal of treatment, in the UK this would have to be by express statutory provision, (see, for example, below, p 161, on the provisions of the Public Health (Control of Disease) Act 1984) as the common law would not permit it, unless under the doctrine of necessity (see below, Chapter 4). The cases referred to in *Conroy* relating to the emotional and financial abandonment of children are not in accordance with US or UK law. There is no principle which regards the parents as a means to the ends of their children. Whilst the welfare of the child is paramount in English law, the necessary protection is given, not by compelling parents to care for their children (except financially), but by removing the children from the parents. It is unthinkable that a parent would be ordered to undergo a blood transfusion on the grounds that her children would be motherless if she died.

The interest of the State in preserving life and preventing suicide was considered by the California Court of Appeal in the case of *Bouvia v Superior Court* 179 Cal App 3d 1127 (1986). Elizabeth Bouvia was a severely disabled quadriplegic, almost totally immobile, and entirely dependent upon others for all her needs. In addition, she was in continual and severe pain. Mentally, however, she was intelligent and aware. She was spoon fed, but found it difficult to take sufficient food orally because of nausea. It was, therefore, decided to feed her by nasogastric tube. She sought a court order that such 'treatment' could be refused (see below, Chapters 9 and 12 on feeding as treatment), and her right to self-determination was upheld. Associate Justice Beach reviewed the Californian authorities and the Presidential Commission for the Study of Ethical Problems in Medicine and Biomedical and Behavioural Research, and concluded:

> **Beach J**: It is ... immaterial that the removal of the nasogastric tube will hasten or cause Bouvia's eventual death. Being competent she has the right to live out

the remainder of her natural life in dignity and peace. It is precisely the aim and purpose of the many decisions upholding the withdrawal of life support systems to accord and provide as large a measure of dignity, respect and comfort as possible ...

Overlooking the fact that a desire to terminate one's life is probably the ultimate exercise of one's right to privacy, we find no substantial evidence to support the [trial] court's conclusion [that Bouvia's refusal of tube feeding amounted to a suicide attempt] ... As a consequence of her changed condition, it is clear she has now merely resigned herself to accept an earlier death, if necessary, rather than live by feedings forced upon her by means of nasogastric tube. Her decision to allow nature to take its course is not equivalent to an election to commit suicide with real parties aiding and abetting therein ...

Moreover, the trial court seriously erred by basing its decision on the 'motives' behind Elizabeth Bouvia's decision to exercise her rights. If a right exists, it matters not what 'motivates' its exercise. We find nothing in the law to suggest the right to refuse medical treatment may be exercised only if the patient's motives meet someone else's approval. It certainly is not illegal or immoral to prefer a natural, albeit sooner, death than a drugged life attached to a mechanical device.

These issues relating to positive acts of killing and omissions to treat, will be examined further below, in Chapter 12. Consider, however, what difference (if any) it would have made, if Elizabeth Bouvia had stated categorically that she was refusing food, not because it was difficult for her to swallow, but because she wished to die? On the analysis of Beach J, the motives are irrelevant. However, if that is the case, why was he at pains to point out that she did not intend to kill herself?

If, on the other hand, the patient requires life-saving treatment as the result of *self-inflicted* injuries, it is arguable that a doctor may treat them, despite their refusal to consent. As Skegg has written:

Skegg, PDG, *Law, Ethics and Medicine*, 1984, Oxford: Clarendon Press, pp 110–12:

Where someone has done something in an apparent attempt to kill himself, doctors will often be justified in taking action to avert the consequences of the action. Prior to the abolition of the offence of suicide, there was no difficulty in explaining the legal basis for a doctor acting to prevent a person from attempting to commit suicide, or to avoid death resulting from such an attempt. Suicide was a felony, so the doctor was simply exercising the general liberty to prevent a felony. [*R v Duffy* [1967] 1 QB 63, p 67] ... However, since the enactment of the Suicide Act 1961 it has continued to be accepted that doctors are sometimes free – sometimes, indeed, under a duty – to prevent patients from committing suicide.

In some cases, the person who has apparently attempted to commit suicide will be suffering from a mental disorder which prevents the giving or withholding of consent. But in many cases the person will have a sufficient understanding to give, or withhold, consent. This is so, even though the act will often result from a passing impulse or temporary depression, rather than from a rational and fixed decision. If restrained and given assistance, the majority are glad that their action did not result in death. Hence, even if it is accepted that a person should not be prevented from carrying out a calm or a reasoned decision to terminate his own life, there is an overwhelming case for intervention where there is reason to believe that, if given help, the person will be glad he did not kill, or seriously injure, himself. Doctors are constantly intervening in these circumstances and there can be little doubt that, were their conduct to be questioned, the courts would hold it justified.

As regards the third State interest, protecting the integrity of the medical profession, Schrieber J suggested in *Conroy* that this will not justify overriding a refusal of treatment. What, though, of someone who is no longer competent to refuse it? In another case, that of *Brophy v New England Sinai Hospital* 497 NE 2d 626 (1986), a Massachusetts court held that a hospital need not compromise its own principles by withdrawing feeding from a patient in PVS (who had made it clear he would not wish to survive in such a state), but should permit his transfer to another hospital sympathetic to this course. (The general problems that arise in relation to the treatment of patients in PVS are discussed below, in Chapter 12.)

The categorisation of the four State interests in *Conroy* has been endorsed in a number of subsequent US authorities, and was adopted by Thorpe J (as he then was) in the English High Court in *Secretary of State v Robb*.

Secretary of State v Robb [1995] 1 All ER 677 (Thorpe J)

The respondent, a prison inmate with a personality disorder, went on hunger strike. The application concerned the question of whether it was lawful for his doctors and nurses to abstain from force feeding him in such circumstances:

> Thorpe J: The only reference to the duty of the Home Office in modern authority is the briefest passage in the speech of Lord Keith of Kinkel in *Airedale NHS Trust v Bland* [1993] 1 All ER 821, p 861; [1993] AC 789, p 859, in which he said:
>
> > ... the principle of the sanctity of life ... is not an absolute one. It does not compel a medical practitioner on pain of criminal sanctions to treat a patient, who will die if he does not, contrary to the express wishes of the patient. It does not authorise forcible feeding of prisoners on hunger strike. It does not compel the temporary keeping alive of patients who are terminally ill where to do so would merely prolong their suffering.
>
> There have been much fuller developments in other common law jurisdictions, particularly in the United States, and all counsel have drawn attention to and relied upon a number of decisions, all of which consider the right of the individual to refuse nutrition in differing circumstances. I will refer only to recent decision in the United States that is directly concerned with adult prisoners on hunger strike. The most recent, and for me the most helpful, is the decision of the Supreme Court of California, *Thor v Superior Court* 5 Cal 4th

725 (1993). That authority upheld a decision at first instance that the prison authorities failed in their application for an order authorising force feeding of a quadriplegic prison inmate who had determined to refuse food and medical treatment necessary to maintain his life. The conclusion of the court was that the right of self-determination prevailed, but the court recognised that the right of self-determination was not absolute and that there were four specific State interests that might countervail. They were specifically: (i) preserving life; (ii) preventing suicide; (iii) maintaining the integrity of the medical profession; and (iv) protecting innocent third parties. The other United States case which is relevant to these arguments is the case of *Re Caulk* 125 NH 226 (1984). There, the Supreme Court of New Hampshire identified a very similar balancing exercise but found that the balance tipped against the right of self-determination. It seems that that decision was not specifically considered in the judgments given in the later case of *Thor*, and I have to say that I find more persuasive the dissenting judgment of Douglas J than the judgment of the majority given by Bachelder J.

These decisions are obviously relevant and helpful in reaching a decision as to how the law stands in this jurisdiction. I consider specifically the four countervailing State interests that were set against the individual's right of self-determination.

The first, namely the interest that the State holds in preserving life, seems to me to be but part and parcel of the balance that must be struck in determining and declaring the right of self-determination. The principle of the sanctity of human life in this jurisdiction is seen to yield to the principle of self-determination. It is within that balance that the consideration of the preservation of life is reflected.

The second countervailing State interest, preventing suicide, is recognisable, but seems to me to be of no application in cases such as this where the refusal of nutrition and medical treatment in the exercise of the right of self-determination does not constitute an act of suicide.

The third consideration of maintaining the integrity of the medical profession is one that I find hard to recognise as a distinct consideration. Medical ethical decisions can be acutely difficult and it is when they are at their most acute that applications for declaratory relief are made to the High Court. I cannot myself see that this is a distinct consideration that requires to be set against the right of self-determination of the individual.

The fourth consideration of protecting innocent third parties is one that is undoubtedly recognised in this jurisdiction, as is evidenced by the decision of Sir Stephen Brown P in *Re S (Adult: Refusal of Medical Treatment)* [1992] 4 All ER 671; [1993] Fam 123. Also recognised within this jurisdiction is a consideration that was given weight in the decision of *Re Caulk*, namely the need to preserve the internal order, discipline and security within the confines of the jail. But neither of these considerations arise in the present case.

The case of *Re S*, referred to in the last paragraph, concerned the refusal of a pregnant woman to submit to a Caesarean necessary to save the life of her foetus and (probably) her own life, and is considered further below, in

Chapter 8. In our respectful view, however (and notwithstanding the terms of the President's declaration in the case, which referred to the 'vital interests of the ... child'), the decision is not really to be understood as a matter of the court protecting an innocent third party. Rather, in so far as it is supportable, it belongs in our view within the first category adverted to by Thorpe J in *Robb*. In short, though normally, in a case of passive refusal of treatment, the State's interest in preserving life yields to the patient's right of self-determination, there might be an argument that this is not the case where the exercise of the right will cause excessive damage to the sanctity of life principle (as when both mother and foetus stand to die in a macabre fashion).

Maim and statutory criminal offences

As already stated, battery is a crime as well as a tort. However, if one considers the nature of non-consensual surgical procedures, it is clear that more serious offences may be committed. In cases of non-consensual surgery, it is clear, at least in theory, that the statutory offences of wounding and causing grievous bodily harm contrary to ss 18 and 20 of the Offences Against the Person Act 1861 may have been committed. It is also interesting to contemplate the relevance of the old common law offence of maim. Skegg comments as follows:

Skegg, PDG, *Law, Ethics and Medicine*, 1984, Oxford: Clarendon Press, p 40:

In practice, the common law offence of maim has long been supplanted by statutory offences. But it has not been expressly abolished, and a judge has made an extra-judicial statement which suggests that there is at least a theoretical possibility of the offence of maim applying to operations in which a kidney is removed from a healthy living donor, for transplantation into a person who is in need of it. It is therefore desirable to consider the extent to which the offence of maim would apply to medical procedures, and the related issue of whether consent would be effective to prevent liability.

The authorities have long distinguished between acts which permanently disable and weaken a man, rendering him less able in fighting; and acts which simply disfigure. The former are maims, which fall within one category rather than the other ...

The fact that a particular injury has in the past been classified as a maim need not be decisive in any future case. Changes in military practice, or increased medical knowledge, could lead to certain injuries ceasing to be regarded as maims, and other injuries coming to be regarded as maims ...

Most medical procedures do not permanently disable a person and render that person less able in fighting. They therefore fall outside even the potential scope of any offence of maim. This is as true of the removal of a healthy kidney for transplantation as it is of the removal of a diseased appendix. But even if a medical procedure did come within the potential scope of an offence of maim, it would not follow that a doctor would commit an offence of maim in going ahead with it. Just as the infliction of a maim was sometimes permitted in self-defence, so a maiming operation would not amount to the offence of maim if there was a good reason for it. Hence, even if castration could still be regarded as coming within the potential scope of maim, it would be justified if performed for a therapeutic purpose.

Express and implied consent

Express consent

In both the NHS and in private health care, the patient will be required to sign a consent form. There is a standard form that covers most forms of medical treatment, although modified types of form are used in certain treatments such as sterilisations. The standard NHS form is reproduced opposite.

By signing the form, it may be thought that the patient is confirming that he has received an explanation of the medical procedures and cannot later deny this. However, in *Chatterton v Gerson* [1981] 1 All ER 257, Bristow J (p 265) stated:

> **Bristow J**: I should add that getting the patient to sign a pro forma expressing consent to undergo the operation 'the effect and nature of which have been explained to me', as was done here in each case, should be a valuable reminder to everyone of the need for explanation and consent. But it would be no defence to an action based on trespass to the person if no explanation had in fact been given. The consent would have been expressed in form only, not in reality.

This approach has been endorsed by the appeal courts (for example by Lord Donaldson MR in *Re T (Adult: Refusal of Treatment)* [1992] 4 All ER 649) and is acknowledged by the NHS Executive in its 1990 publication, *A Guide to Consent for Examination or Treatment* (London: NHS Executive), which gives general guidance to doctors and other health care workers:

> It should be noted that the purpose of obtaining a signature on the consent form is not an end in itself. The most important element of a consent procedure is the duty to ensure that patients understand the nature and purpose of the proposed treatment. Where a patient has not been given appropriate information then consent may not always have been obtained despite the signature on the form.

The consent form requires the patient to acknowledge that the procedure need not be carried out by any particular doctor. There are examples of patients in America who have successfully sued following surgery carried out competently and in accordance with the patient's consent, but performed by a different doctor to that expected by the patient (see *Perna v Pirozzi* (1983) 457 A 2d 431). However, it is implied by the form that if the procedure is not carried out by *this* doctor, it will be carried out by *a* doctor. Much controversy surrounds the issue of treatment by medical students, and even nurses.

CONSENT FORM

APPENDIX A (1)

For medical or dental investigation, treatment or operation

Health Authority ....

Patient's Surname ....

Hospital ....

Other Names ....

Unit Number ....

Date of Birth ....

Sex (please tick)   Male ☐   Female ☐

DOCTORS OR DENTISTS (This part to be completed by doctor or dentist. See notes on the reverse)

TYPE OF OPERATION INVESTIGATION OR TREATMENT

I confirm that I have explained the operation investigation or treatment, and such appropriate options as are available and the type of anaesthetic, if any (general/regional/sedation) proposed, to the patient in terms which in my judgment are suited to the understanding of the patient and/or to one of the parents or guardians of the patient

Signature ....   Date   .../ .../ .....

Name of doctor or dentist ....

PATIENT/PARENT/GUARDIAN

1. Please read this form and the notes overleaf very carefully.

2. If there is anything that you don't understand about the explanation, or if you want more information, you should ask the doctor or dentist.

3. Please check that all the information on the form is correct. If it is, and you understand the explanation, then sign the form.

I am the patient/parent/guardian (delete as necessary)

I agree	■	to what is proposed which has been explained to me by the doctor/dentist named on this form.
	■	to the use of the type of anaesthetic that I have been told about.
I understand	■	that the procedure may not be done by the doctor/dentist who has been treating me so far.
	■	that any procedure in addition to the investigation or treatment described on this form will only be carried out if it is necessary and in my best interests and can be justified for medical reasons.
I have told	■	the doctor or dentist about any additional procedures I would not wish to be carried out straightaway without my having the opportunity to consider them first.

Signature   ....

Name   ....

Address   ....

(if not the patient)   ....

....

NHS *Management Executive*

Kennedy, I and Grubb, A, *Medical Law,* **2nd edn, 1994, London: Butterworths, p 168:**

There are at least two factual situations ... which do give rise to legal difficulties if the patient is unaware that the person is a student.

First, a student may, in fact, examine (ie, touch) a patient solely so as to acquire knowledge or experience for himself. The touching plays no part in the care of the patient. In such a circumstance, the consent given by the patient is probably invalid since the identity of the person touching affects the nature of what is being done to the patient, ie, training rather than caring.

Secondly, a student may touch a patient as part of the patient's care. Does the lack of awareness by the patient of the identity of the person touching (identity being status here) affect the validity of the patient's consent? ... It could be said that the difference between a lay person and a doctor is material whereas the difference between a medical student (presumably supervised) and a doctor is not. In our view, unless the patient suffered harm and could establish that the medical student was negligent, an English court would reject any claim by a patient.

The patient also acknowledges on the form that any other procedure will only be carried out if it is necessary and in his best interests and justified for medical reasons. Michael Jones comments as follows:

Jones, M, *Medical Negligence,* **1996, London: Sweet & Maxwell, p 295:**

At best, this probably amounts to little more than providing information to the patient, bearing in mind that any procedure which was *not* in the best interest of the patient or could not be justified for medical reasons would run the risk of being held to be negligent.

Consider whether the patient's acknowledgment that other treatments may also be carried out is a true consent to those other treatments, even if they are in the patient's best interests. It is a standard form, which most patients will feel they are unable to object to: is there not an element of coercion here? How many patients, about to undergo surgery, are likely to delete or alter a standard consent form? The disturbing consequences of such 'blanket' consent forms was illustrated in the case of *Breen v Baker* (1956) *The Times,* 27 January, where a woman consented to surgery which she believed would be dilatation and curettage, but was subsequently given a total hysterectomy. There was found to be no battery because the consent form stated: 'I agree to leave the nature and extent of the operation to be performed to the discretion of the surgeon.' Jones goes on to comment on the NHS form as follows:

Jones, M, *Medical Negligence,* **1996, London: Sweet & Maxwell, p 295:**

The model consent form also states that: 'I have told the doctor or dentist about any additional procedures I would not wish to be carried out straightaway without my having the opportunity to consider them first.' The purpose of this provision is obscure, to say the least. Even if it were remotely practical for patients to identify all the potential procedures to which they did not wish to be subjected (which, clearly, it is not), there is no obligation in law for a patient to specify what he does not want to have done to him. In the absence of some valid justification, such as the patient's consent to the specific procedure that is contemplated, or necessity, all other procedures which involve physical contact with the person are unlawful, as battery. To suggest otherwise, even by implication, as the new model consent form appears to do, misrepresents the true position in law.

Implied consent

In the case of *Mohr v Williams* (1905) 104 NW 12 (see above, p 105), the defendant tried to argue (*inter alia*) that the fact that the patient had consented to the operation on her right ear was relevant to the lawfulness of the operation on the other ear. In other words, the suggestion was that the patient had consented to 'an ear operation'. Could it be argued that she had given an implied consent to an operation on the other ear? The judge in that case took the view that there was no implied consent because the diseased condition of the patient's left ear was not discovered in the course of an authorised examination of that ear, but in the course of an examination which had not been authorised. In other cases, however, the patient's consent may be implied by their conduct, as in *O'Brien v Cunard Steamship Co* (1891) 28 NE 266, in which a ship's passenger who held out her arm to be vaccinated was subsequently unable to succeed in battery against the doctor.

THE ELEMENTS TO A VALID CONSENT

Introduction

The essential elements to a valid consent to treatment can be summed up as follows:

(a) the patient must have sufficient understanding, variously described as mental capacity or mental competence, to make the decision;

(b) the patient must consent to (or refuse) the treatment of his own free will, with no duress or undue influence; and

(c) the patient must have been given sufficient information about the proposed treatment.

We shall address each of these requirements in turn.

Capacity to consent

The Law Commission has identified three different approaches to capacity (*Mental Incapacity*, Report No 231, 1995). These are the 'status', 'outcome' and 'functional' approaches. The status approach is most easily explained in relation to children. This would simply state that a child under a certain age lacked capacity and there would be no examination of other issues such as the child's understanding. The Law Commission rejects this as being contrary to a policy of encouraging self-determination.

The 'outcome' approach is described by the Commission as follows:

Law Commission, *Mental Incapacity*, Report No 231, 1995, London: HMSO, para 3.4:

An assessor of capacity using the 'outcome' method focuses on the final content of an individual's decision. Any decision which is inconsistent with conventional values, or with which the assessor disagrees, may be classified as incompetent. This penalises individuality and demands conformity at the expense of personal autonomy. A number of our respondents argued that an 'outcome' approach is applied by many doctors; if the outcome of the patient's deliberations is to agree with the doctor's recommendations then he or she is taken to have capacity, while if the outcome is to reject a course which the doctor has advised then capacity is found to be absent.

Again, the Commission rejected this approach. It must, in fact, be arguable that such an approach would make a nonsense of the whole issue of consent to treatment. To take an outcome approach would mean that the patient's consent would only be required when a doctor did not recommend a type of treatment, and described a number of alternatives to a patient inviting him to decide which to choose. In any situation when there was one recommendation only, a patient who refused it would be deemed to lack capacity, and the treatment could go ahead on the ground that it was in the best interests of the patient to treat him without consent (see below, Chapter 4). Not only does it undermine the way in which we have traditionally approached capacity, it would destroy the very basis of the need to obtain a valid consent to treatment at all.

Accordingly, the Law Commission recommended the 'functional' approach. Here, the assessor asks whether an individual is able, at the time when a particular decision has to be made, to understand its nature and effects.

The Commission favoured this view not least because it is reflected in the approach the courts have taken. In *Re T (Adult: Refusal of Treatment)* [1992] 4 All ER 649, Lord Donaldson MR (p 661) stated as follows:

Lord Donaldson MR: Doctors faced with a refusal of consent have to give very careful and detailed consideration to the patient's capacity to decide at the time when the decision was made. It may not be the simple case of the patient having no capacity because, for example, at that time he had hallucinations. It may be the more difficult case of a temporarily reduced capacity at the time when his decision was made. What matters is that the doctors should consider whether at that time he had a capacity which was commensurate with the gravity of the decision which he purported to make. The more serious the decision, the greater the capacity.

In fact, it is arguable that this approach is wrong. If by 'serious' it is meant that the consequence of non-treatment is likely to be death, then why should this require more capacity than a case in which the patient is faced with a choice between two forms of complex treatment for a non-life-threatening condition? It may also be tempting to use this 'varying threshold' approach to deny that a patient has capacity when his decision is going to result in his death. However, Lord Donaldson went on to say:

> **Lord Donaldson MR**: ... [T]he patient's right of choice exists whether the reasons for making that choice are rational, irrational, unknown or even non-existent. That his choice is contrary to what is to be expected of the vast majority of adults is only relevant if there are other reasons for doubting his capacity to decide. The nature of his choice or the terms in which it is expressed may then tip the balance.

There is surprisingly little authority on capacity to consent to medical treatment, but further guidance was given in *Re C (Adult: Refusal of Treatment)*, a case startling in a number of ways.

Re C (Adult: Refusal of Treatment) [1994] 1 WLR 290, Fam Div (Thorpe J)

The patient was an elderly man, diagnosed as suffering from paranoid schizophrenia. He had been a patient in Broadmoor special hospital for 30 years. One of his delusional beliefs was that he had been a great doctor who had never failed to cure a patient. He also believed that he had the ability to cure damaged limbs. Following an injury to his foot in 1993, he was diagnosed as suffering from gangrene and the doctors at the local general hospital considered that, unless his foot was amputated, because of the highly toxic nature of gangrene, he was 85% likely to die. Mr C objected to amputation and made an application to the court for an injunction restraining the health authorities from amputating his foot then *or at any time in the future*. Consent to treatment, other than treatment for the mental disorder, is required even if the patient is mentally ill, as long as they have the necessary capacity (see s 63 of the Mental Health Act 1983 and below, Chapter 9), so in this case the decision would turn on C's capacity, regardless of his long history as a patient suffering from what is generally regarded as serious mental illness. Thorpe J held that there is a rebuttable presumption in favour of capacity. C's evidence was that, he did not believe the gangrene would kill him; that he had been born into the world with four complete limbs and he intended to go out with those limbs, and that he did not believe that God wanted him to have his foot amputated.

> **Thorpe J**: [Counsels'] submissions divide over the definition of the capacity which enables an individual to refuse treatment. Mr Gordon argues for what he calls the minimal competence test, which he defines as the capacity to understand in broad terms the nature and effect of the proposed treatment. It is common ground that C has the legal capacity to initiate these proceedings without a next friend, within the terms of RSC Ord 80. Mr Gordon contends that the capacity to refuse treatment is no higher and is equally no higher than the capacity to contract. I reject that submission. I think that the question to be decided is whether it has been established that C's capacity is so reduced by his chronic mental illness that he does not sufficiently understand the nature, purpose and effects of the proffered amputation.

I consider helpful Dr Eastman's analysis of the decision making process into three stages: first, comprehending and retaining treatment information, second, believing it and, third, weighing it in the balance to arrive at choice. The Law Commission has proposed a similar approach in para 2.20 of Law Commission Consultation Paper No 129, *Mentally Incapacitated Adults and Decision Making*. Applying that test to my findings on the evidence, I am completely satisfied that the presumption that C has the right of self-determination has not been displaced. Although his general capacity is impaired by schizophrenia, it has not been established that he does not sufficiently understand the nature, purpose and effects of the treatment he refuses. Indeed, I am satisfied that he has understood and retained the relevant treatment information, that in his own way he believes it, and that in the same fashion he has arrived at a clear choice.

The prevalence of paternalism in English medical law had been dealt a blow: the patient's beliefs can be more important than medical opinion. (And it is interesting to note that Mr C did, in fact, respond to more conservative treatment.)

The approach in *Re C* was approved by the Court of Appeal in the case of *Re MB (Medical Treatment)* [1997] 2 FLR 426, which concerned a woman who was admitted to hospital when she was 40 weeks pregnant. The foetus was in the breech position and because a vaginal delivery would pose a serious risk of death or injury to the foetus, the woman agreed to a Caesarean operation to deliver the child. However, because of a phobia that she had about needles, she panicked and, at the last moment, withdrew her consent. The High Court granted a declaration that it would be lawful to carry out the operation because, on the evidence, she was suffering from a temporary impairment to her mental functioning and was, therefore, not competent. The Court of Appeal (Butler-Sloss, Saville and Ward LJJ) upheld the first instance decision, finding that the needle phobia had robbed the patient of her decision making capacity:

> **Butler-Sloss LJ** (delivering the judgment of the court): A person lacks capacity if some impairment or disturbance of mental functioning renders the person unable to make a decision whether to consent to or to refuse treatment. That inability to make a decision will occur when:
>
> (a) the patient is unable to comprehend and retain the information which is material to the decision, especially as to the likely consequences of having or not having the treatment in question;
>
> (b) the patient is unable to use the information and weigh it in the balance as part of the process of arriving at the decision. If, as Thorpe J observed in *Re C* ... a compulsive disorder or phobia from which the patient suffers stifles belief in the information presented to her, then the decision may not be a true one. As Lord Cockburn CJ put it in *Banks v Goodfellow* (1870) LR 5 QB 549, p 569:
>
>> ... one object may be so forced upon the attention of the invalid as to shut out all others that might require consideration.

Interestingly in this passage, which echoes the test for capacity proposed by the Law Commission in its 1995 report, *Mental Incapacity*, there is no reference to the need for the patient to believe the information. Elsewhere in its judgment, however, the Court of Appeal cited Thorpe J's full, three stage formulation of the test in *Re C* without demur. Some of the problems that may arise when applying the test will now be examined in more detail.

Assessing capacity

Understanding

As we have seen, those caring for the patient must be satisfied that he comprehends or understands the treatment information. Arguably this notion of 'understanding' can be manipulated to facilitate a finding of incapacity against the latter: see Lee, S, 'Towards a jurisprudence of consent', in *Oxford Essays in Jurisprudence*, 1987, Oxford: Clarendon Press, in which Lee states that few adults could meet Lord Scarman's criteria in relation to a child's understanding, set out in *Gillick v West Norfolk and Wisbech AHA* [1986] 1 AC 112 (see below, p 133). It remains open as to whether this was intended simply to stress the importance of certainty in the case of children, whether it was imposing a different test of understanding for children, or whether those criteria were intended to apply to adults too.

The question has also been raised as to whether the requirement for 'understanding' means that the patient actually understand the nature of the information about the treatment and its consequences, or merely that he is *capable* of understanding.

> **Kennedy, I and Grubb, A, *Medical Law*, 2nd edn, 1994, London: Butterworths, p 120:**
>
> If the test of understanding is *actual understanding* ... then whether or not the girl understands *and therefore is competent* to consent may turn on what she is told. Indeed, this seems to have been Lord Donaldson's approach in *Re R* ... If the girl is not given certain information she may not understand enough, but this would not be the product of any lack of competence but merely that she decided in relative ignorance. It would be an unsatisfactory state of law if doctors could be controlling the information given to a patient and thereby grant or deny her competence ... It must, therefore, be the law that competence is determined by reference to the unvarying conceptual standard of capacity or ability to understand.

In the case of *Re R (A Minor) (Wardship: Consent to Medical Treatment)* [1991] 4 All ER 177, referred to here, a 15 year old girl with a fluctuating mental state, who was refusing antipsychotic drugs, was treated without her consent after the courts (Waite J and a unanimous Court of Appeal) held her to be incompetent.

Subsequently, in *Re W (A Minor) (Medical Treatment)* [1992] 4 All ER 627, Thorpe J concluded that the patient, a 17 year old girl, had the necessary capacity to make a decision. This was doubted in the Court of Appeal on the basis that she did not understand the nature of her condition. She was suffering from anorexia nervosa, and one of the symptoms of that condition is that the patient wants to decide herself when to eat.

> **Lord Donaldson MR:** ... [I]t is a feature of anorexia nervosa that it is capable of destroying the ability to make an informed choice. It creates a compulsion to refuse treatment or only to accept treatment which is likely to be ineffective. This attitude is part and parcel of the disease and the more advanced the illness, the more compelling it may become. Where the wishes of the minor are themselves something which the doctors reasonably consider need to be treated in the minor's own best interests, those wishes clearly have a much reduced significance.

What is being said is that she did not actually understand the nature of her condition, even though she may well have been capable, in intellectual terms, of understanding it. On the face of it, there seems to be an inconsistency with the view of Kennedy and Grubb. However, the inconsistency is more apparent than real. It simply means that the capability test will not apply in cases where there is evidence that the patient, perhaps because of the nature of the medical condition, does not actually understand.

Another important factor is the stability of the patient's mental profile, so that a fluctuating mental state as in *Re R* may affect understanding, as might temporary factors such as pain and exhaustion. However, it is imperative that the latter are stringently defined. There are a number of cases, such as *Re MB (Medical Treatment)* [1997] 2 FLR 426 (see above, p 118), which concern the refusals of Caesarean sections when, in the course of labour, difficulties have arisen which have put the life of both woman and foetus at risk. These are dealt with in more detail later (see below, Chapter 8), but it is important to note here that, in all those cases where a Caesarean is refused after labour has commenced, there could be a temptation to use the argument that the labour process has produced temporary factors which have inhibited understanding (see, in particular, the judgment of Johnson J in *Rochdale Healthcare (NHS) Trust v C* [1997] 1 FCR 274). The temporary loss of decision making capacity was the basis of the decision in *Re L (An Adult: Non-Consensual Treatment)* [1997] 1 FCR 609, in which, as in *Re MB (Medical Treatment)* [1997] 2 FLR 426, a patient panicked during attempts to anaesthetise her for a Caesarean because of her phobia about needles.

Belief

It may be that the distinction between actual understanding and the capacity to understand should apply by analogy to belief. The patient in *Re C* was capable of believing he was going to die, but as a matter of fact did not. He believed that the doctors believed that he was going to die, as Thorpe J said, he believed 'in his own way'. However, it can be questioned whether the patient would be required to believe that the doctor's belief was true.

Another approach may be to say that the patient believes the information he has been given about his condition and the proposed treatment, but that it is not necessary for him to believe in the prognosis, with or without treatment. There would be nothing illogical about this, although it might be argued that the prognosis is inescapably bound up with the belief about the medical condition itself. However, unless the prognosis is such that the doctor believes that the patient has a 100% risk of death (eg, in the case of a refused blood transfusion), it is arguable that the patient may be told that he has, say, only a 5% chance of survival without treatment, but that it is still not unreasonable for him to believe that he will fall into the 5% category. There will also be cases where understanding and belief are intertwined. In contrast to the case of *Re C*, consider the facts of the following American decision.

State of Tennessee v Northern **563 SW 2d 197 (1978), Tenn Ct App:**

Todd J: On 24 January 1978 the Tennessee Department of Human Services filed this suit alleging that Mary C Northern was 72 years old, with no available help from relatives; that Miss Northern resided alone under unsatisfactory conditions as a result of which she had been admitted to and was a patient in Nashville General Hospital; that the patient suffered from gangrene of both feet which required the removal of her feet to save her life; that the patient lacked the capacity to appreciate her condition or to consent to necessary surgery ...

Capacity means mental ability to make a rational decision, which includes the ability to perceive, appreciate all relevant facts and to reach a rational judgment upon such facts.

Capacity is not necessarily synonymous with sanity. A blind person may be perfectly capable of observing the shape of small articles by handling them, but not capable of observing the shape of a cloud in the sky.

A person may have 'capacity' as to some matters and may lack 'capacity' as to others ...

In the present case, this court has found the patient to be lucid and apparently of sound mind generally. However, on the subjects of death and amputation of her feet, her comprehension is blocked, blinded or dimmed to the extent that she is incapable of recognising facts which would be obvious to a person of normal perception. For example, in the presence of this court, the patient looked at her feet and refused to recognise the obvious facts that the flesh was dead, black, shrivelled, rotting and stinking.

The record also discloses that the patient refuses to consider the eventuality of death which is or ought to be obvious in the face of such dire bodily deterioration.

As described by the doctors and observed by this court, the patient wants to live and keep her dead feet, too, and refuses to consider the impossibility of such a desire. In order to avoid the unpleasant experience of facing death and/or loss of feet, her mind or emotions have resorted to the device of denying the unpleasant reality so that, to the patient, the unpleasant reality does not exist. This is the 'delusion' which renders the patient incapable of making a rational decision as to whether to undergo surgery to save her life or to forgo surgery and forfeit her life.

The physicians speak of probabilities of death without amputation as 90% to 95% and the probability of death with surgery as 50:50 (one in two). Such probabilities are not facts, but the existence and expression of such opinions are facts which the patient is unwilling or unable to recognise or discuss.

If, as repeatedly stated, this patient could and would give evidence of a comprehension of the facts of her condition and could and would express her unequivocal desire in the face of such comprehended facts, then her decision, however unreasonable to others, would be accepted and honoured by the courts and by her doctors. The difficulty is that she cannot or will not comprehend the facts.

Accordingly, the court found that the patient was incompetent. Did the patient in this case lack understanding or belief, or both?

Weighing treatment information in the balance

Undoubtedly, the patient's appreciation of the consequences of non-treatment is very much part of capacity, but even when the consequences of non-treatment are likely to be grave, the patient with sufficient understanding and belief can still refuse as long as he is capable of balancing the risks of refusal against his other needs. Carrying out this sort of balancing exercise would, on the face of it, require the patient to provide reasons for those needs, and, if necessary, reasons for preferring those needs to taking the recommended medical treatment. However, to recall Lord Donaldson MR's *dictum* in *Re T*, 'the patient's right of choice exists whether the reasons for making that choice are rational, irrational, unknown or even non-existent'. The latter reference to a non-existent reason raises some interesting questions, which we examined above, in Chapter 1 (see p 41).

It will be recalled that when we there looked at 'rational' decision making, we concluded that if the decision fitted in with the patient's world view, then it should be respected. If this subjective test is adopted, then genuinely held beliefs that fit in with an internally coherent body of thought will not disqualify the patient from decision making, even if the 'internal coherence' contains a number of bizarre beliefs which can be clearly shown to be unsustainable, eg, Mr C's belief that he had once been a successful doctor. Ian Kennedy favours this approach.

> **Kennedy, I, 'Consent to treatment: the capable person', in Dyer, C (ed), *Doctors, Patients and the Law*, 1992, Oxford: Blackwell Science, p 56:**
>
> ... if the beliefs and values of the patient, though incomprehensible to others, are of long standing and have formed the basis for all the patient's decisions about his life, there is a strong argument to suggest that the doctor should respect and give effect to a patient's decision based on them. That is to say that

the doctor should regard such a patient as capable of consenting (or refusing). To argue otherwise would effectively be to rob the patient of his right to his own personality which may be far more serious and destructive than anything that could follow from the patient's decision as regards a particular proposed treatment.

Could it be argued, in this regard, that the functional approach to capacity (see above, p 116), currently favoured by the courts and the Law Commission, is deficient in failing properly to address a patient's refusal of treatment in context? In particular, the view that a patient may refuse life-saving medical treatment either irrationally or indeed 'for no reason at all' could be felt to sit uneasily with certain conceptions of autonomy.

Stauch, M, 'Court-authorised Caesareans and the principle of patient autonomy' (1997) 6 Nott LJ 74:

Whilst autonomy, as it figures in the writings of jurists and philosophers, lacks a single fixed meaning, it broadly amounts to a right of self-determination; the ability to choose one's own life plan and the values that will inform it, and to shape one's destiny, so far as possible, in accordance with those values. Essentially, it appears to be a medium to long term concept and is thus to be contrasted with 'liberty', which is used here to denote the freedom to act upon impulses of a more transient nature ...

Of course ... there will be situations in which refusals of medical treatment are consonant with autonomy: this is true where treatment, if given, will at best secure the patient a quality of life insufficient for him to continue to pursue the goals and values central to his conception of himself. It may also be so where the nature of the treatment itself would radically infringe those values (an example here is of a Jehovah's Witness who refuses a blood transfusion because receiving blood is inconsistent with a core value governing the lives of members of that faith). On the other hand, the refusal of treatment on a whim cannot be regarded as falling within such a category.

... To say that an irrational choice may be upheld is ambiguous, so far as giving effect to patient autonomy is concerned, for such a choice may or may not be autonomous. What should instead be required is that the choice 'fits' in the general scheme of the patient's life (though there is no need for the scheme itself to be 'rational', whatever that might mean). Clearly, this is a question which cannot be resolved without some inquiry into the patient's reasons for making the choice.

... The above argument, if accepted, suggests *a fortiori* that we should reject the ... view that a [patient] may refuse [treatment] (with, very likely, serious consequences for [his] future) for 'no reason at all'.

As discussed earlier, the courts are clearly right not to insist that a competent refusal *must* be a rational one (in according with the patient's best interests, objectively considered). Indeed, concentration on the rational/irrational raises the image of a neat dichotomy which is misleading. Many of the factors which influence decisions about medical treatment cannot be categorised as one or the other. For example, fear of pain cannot be said to be irrational, but what of a patient who anticipates pain which he has been assured will not result from the treatment. Can this patient be properly accused of irrationality? Pain, after all, is subjective. In other cases there may be a subtle blend of reasons which result in a refusal of treatment, again belying the rational/irrational distinction.

The US case of *Re Maida Yetter* 96 D & C 2d 619 (1973) illustrates the difficulties which can arise when there is an interplay of reasons, some of which are delusional. The patient in that case, a chronic schizophrenic, refused breast surgery, potentially needed to alleviate a malignant condition. It was generally accepted that when surgery was first suggested to her, her reasons for refusing were largely based on fear of surgery, and that she appreciated the consequences of refusal, including death.

Williams J: Mrs Yetter was committed to Allentown State Hospital in June 1971, by the Courts of Northampton County, after hearings held pursuant to s 406 of the Mental Health and Mental Retardation Act of 20 October 1966 .... Her diagnosis at that time was schizophrenia, chronic undifferentiated. It appears that late in 1972, in connection with a routine physical examination, Mrs Yetter was discovered to have a breast discharge indicating the possible presence of carcinoma. The doctors recommended that a surgical biopsy be performed together with any additional corrective surgery that would be indicated by the pathology of the biopsy. When this recommendation was first discussed with Mrs Yetter in December of 1972 by her caseworker, Mrs Perhac, who had weekly counselling sessions with Mrs Yetter for more than a year, Mrs Yetter indicated that she would not give her consent to the surgery. Her stated reasons were that she was afraid because of the death of her aunt which followed such surgery and that it was her own body and she did not desire the operation. The caseworker indicated that at this time Mrs Yetter was lucid, rational and appeared to understand that the possible consequences of her refusal included death.

Mr Stauffer, who indicated that he visits his sister regularly, and Dr Bischoff, whose direct contacts with Mrs Yetter have been since March 1973, testified that in the last three or four months it has been impossible to discuss the proposed surgery with Mrs Yetter in that, in addition to expressing fear of the operation, she has become delusional in her reasons for not consenting to surgery. Her tendency to become delusional concerning this problem, although no others, was confirmed by Mrs Perhac. The present delusional nature of Mrs Yetter's reasoning concerning the problem was demonstrated at the hearing when Mrs Yetter, in response to questions by the court and counsel, indicated that the operation would interfere with her genital system, affecting her ability to have babies, and would prohibit a movie career. Mrs Yetter is 60 years of age and without children.

Dr Bischoff testified that Mrs Yetter is oriented as to time, place and her personal environment, and that her present delusions are consistent with the diagnosis and evaluation of her mental illness upon admission to the hospital in 1971. The doctor indicated that, in her opinion, at the present time Mrs Yetter is unable, by reasons of her mental illness, to arrive at a considered judgment as to whether to undergo surgery.

Mr Stauffer testified that the aunt referred to by Mrs Yetter, although she underwent a similar operation, died of unrelated causes some 15 years after surgery. He further indicated that he has been apprised by the physicians of the nature of the proposed procedures and their probable consequences as well as the probable consequences if the procedures are not performed. He indicated that if he is appointed guardian of the person for his sister he would consent to the surgical procedures recommended.

At the hearing Mrs Yetter was alert, interested and obviously meticulous about her personal appearance. She stated that she was afraid of surgery, that the best course of action for her would be to leave her body alone, that surgery might hasten the spread of the disease and do further harm, and she reiterated her fears due to the death of her aunt. On several occasions during the hearing she interjected the statements that she would die if surgery were performed. It is clear that mere commitment to a State hospital for treatment of mental illness does not destroy a person's competency or require the appointment of a guardian of the estate or person: *Ryman* (1940) 139 Pa Superior Ct 212. Mental capacity must be examined on a case by case basis.

In our opinion, the constitutional right of privacy included the right of a mature competent adult to refuse to accept medical recommendations that may prolong one's life and which, to a third person at least, appear to be in his best interests; in short, that the right of privacy includes a right to die with which the State should not interfere where there are no minor or unborn children and no clear and present danger to public health, welfare or morals. If the person was competent while being presented with the decision and in making the decision which she did, the court should not interfere even though the decision might be considered unwise, foolish or ridiculous ...

The testimony of the caseworker with respect to her conversations with Mrs Yetter in December 1972, convinces us that at that time her refusal was informed, conscious of the consequences and would not have been superseded by this court. The ordinary person's refusal to accept medical advice based upon fear is commonly known and while the refusal may be irrational and foolish to an outside observer, it cannot be said to be incompetent in order to permit the State to override the decision.

The obvious difficulty in this proceeding is that in recent months Mrs Yetter's steadfast refusal has been accompanied by delusions which create doubt that her decision is the product of competent, reasoned judgment. However, she has been consistent in expressing the fear that she would die if surgery were performed. The delusions do not appear to us to be her primary reason for rejecting surgery. Are we then to force her to submit to medical treatment because some of her present reasons for refusal are delusional and the result of mental illness? Should we now override her original understanding but irrational decision?

There is no indication that Mrs Yetter's condition is critical or that she is in the waning hours of life, although we recognise the advice of medical experts as to the need for early detection and treatment of cancer symptoms. Upon reflection, balancing the risk involved in our refusal to act in favour of compulsory treatment against giving the greatest possible protection to the individual in furtherance of his own desires, we are unwilling now to overrule Mrs Yetter's original irrational but competent decision.

The importance in this context of cultural awareness, on the part of those assessing capacity, was highlighted by Michael Gunn, when examining the Consultation Paper which preceded the Law Commission's Report (*Mental Incapacity*, Report No 231, 1995, London: HMSO).

Gunn, M, 'The meaning of incapacity' (1994) 2 Med L Rev 8:

It is clearly the case that capacity is a value-laden concept. Undoubtedly, the approach recommended by the Law Commission is one very much within the tradition of Western cultures. Care must therefore be taken in its application to people from other cultures. More specifically, any person assessing the competence of another individual must be aware of their own values so that assumptions and decisions are not made which are unjustifiable. It is the values of the person being assessed which must be respected. The assessor needs to be able to identify where her values vary from those of the person being assessed. Values cannot be removed from any assessment, but assessors of capacity can be educated to be aware of their own values and thus to take care in assessing capacity not to be prejudiced when meeting someone with a different value base.

Suicide and capacity

It is generally accepted that a choice to take one's own life is not necessarily indicative of mental illness and/or lack of capacity, and in circumstances where the person is capable of making such a choice, it can be argued, on the basis of individual autonomy, that their wishes should be respected (see Battin, MP, *Ethical Issues in Suicide*, 1982, Englewood Cliffs: Prentice Hall). On the other hand, as noted earlier, the courts have recognised a State interest in the prevention of suicide. Given this tension, what is the position of the patient who is admitted to hospital, having been discovered unconscious after taking a drug overdose, who is treated without his consent? Unconscious patients can be treated without consent under the doctrine of necessity (see below, Chapter 4), but this is based upon reasoning that there is no possibility of knowing that the patient would not wish to be treated. However, in a suicide case, is not the act of attempted suicide a clear expression of the patient's wish to die? There are two initial reasons why treatment is justified: first, there may be no way of knowing whether the patient had capacity (it would be a rare case where, under the exigency of trying to save the life, a doctor would have had time to be convinced that the patient was competent), and, secondly, it is well known that suicide attempts are often not intended to succeed, ie, so called 'gesture' suicides. In so far as the doctor is, or ought to be, aware that the attempt was genuine and well considered, it is a moot point as to whether the patient would subsequently be able to claim in battery. A court may take the view that allowing such an action would be contrary to public policy.

Indeed, there are cases where it has been held that there is a duty to prevent suicide. In *Selfe v Ilford and District Hospital Management Committee* (1970) 114 SJ 935, damages were recovered after the patient made a further suicide attempt after being admitted to hospital following a drug overdose, and in *Kirkham v Chief Constable of Greater Manchester Police* [1990] 2 WLR 987 the Court of Appeal upheld the claim of a widow of a prisoner who killed himself while on remand in custody. The police had failed to pass on to the prison authorities details of the prisoner's suicidal tendencies. The defence had argued that the claim should be rejected on the basis of *ex turpi causa non oritur actio* (ie, the defence of illegality), arguing that this would apply to acts which were wrong in a civil, as well as a criminal, sense. Lloyd LJ held that this defence did not apply to suicide if there was evidence that the suicide was not in full possession of his mind, but went on to say that the defence of *volenti non fit injuria* would apply where a man 'of sound mind' commits suicide or injures himself in an unsuccessful attempt. Although this is not a medical case, it raises awkward questions in relation to autonomy and paternalism. Lloyd LJ's dichotomy of 'sound mind' and 'not in full possession of his mind' sounds very much like 'competent' and 'incompetent'. Does this mean that a hospital will not be liable for a suicide if the patient is competent, even though he is also a known suicide risk? It is submitted that the hospital will not escape liability in such circumstances if reasonable steps are not taken to prevent the suicide. Although *Kirkham* concerned a prisoner described as being 'of unsound mind', the Court of Appeal held in *Reeves v Commissioner of Police of the Metropolis* [1998] 1 All ER 381, that the police owed a duty of care to take reasonable steps to prevent the suicide of a 'sane' prisoner. The state of mind of the prisoner was irrelevant to the establishment of such a duty. By analogy, it is submitted, a patient, known to be a suicide risk, would be owed the same duty by any hospital authority purporting to care for him. (See also *Knight v Home Office* [1990] 3 All ER 237 and below, Chapter 9, generally, on the difficult issue of consent and treatment for mental disorder.)

Consent must be voluntary

The case of *Freeman v Home Office* [1984] 1 All ER 1036 concerned a prisoner who had been injected with certain drugs, apparently for the treatment of a personality disorder. It gave rise to a number of issues: did the prisoner, as a matter of fact, consent to this treatment, and, more interestingly, could it be argued that a prisoner could not give a valid consent to treatment by a prison medical officer where the officer was not acting in his capacity as a doctor but as a disciplinarian. As to the judge's finding of fact in respect of whether consent had been given, the Court of Appeal would not disturb this. On the wider point of doctor *qua* disciplinarian, Sir John Donaldson MR stated (p 1044):

Sir John Donaldson MR:

Legal inability to consent

Counsel for the plaintiff submitted that such were the pressures of prison life and discipline that a prisoner could not, as a matter of law, give an effective consent to treatment in any circumstances. This is a somewhat surprising proposition since it would mean that, in the absence of statutory authority, no prison medical officer could ever treat a prisoner. The answer of counsel for the plaintiff was in part that outside medical officers could be brought in, but I am not persuaded that this would reduce the pressures, whatever they may be ...

The maxim *volenti non fit injuria* can be roughly translated as 'You cannot claim damages if you have asked for it', and 'it' is something which is and remains a tort. The maxim, where it applies, provides a bar to enforcing a cause of action. It does not negative the cause of action itself. This is a wholly different concept from consent which, in this context, deprives the act of its tortious character. Volenti would be a defence in the unlikely scenario of a patient being held not to have in fact consented to treatment, but having by his conduct caused the doctor to believe that he had consented.

The judge expressed his view on this aspect of the argument by saying ([1983] 3 All ER 589, p 597 ...):

> The right approach, in my judgment, is to say that where, in a prison setting, a doctor has the power to influence a prisoner's situation and prospects, a court must be alive to the risk that what may appear, on the face of it, to be a real consent is not in fact so.

I would accept that as a wholly accurate statement of the law. The judge said that he had borne this in mind throughout the case. The sole question is therefore whether, on the evidence, there was a real consent.

Although *Freeman* endorses the need for particular vigilance when a patient may be in a vulnerable situation, on the evidence in this case, the patient was being administered drugs 'because of his obvious hostility and cantankerous behaviour'. The question arises whether this was treatment at all? The patient had been told that the drugs would 'make him feel like a new man', but there is a very clear indication that the drugs would make him a much easier prisoner to deal with. Arguably a rather complacent view of the medical interests of prison inmates was also taken in the case of *Thor v Superior Court* 5 Cal 4th 725 (1993), in which the Supreme Court of California stated:

> There is no reason to believe that the prison environment, with its possible inadequacy of medical and related support services for ill or injured prisoners, inherently jeopardises the voluntariness of a prisoner's decision to forgo life-sustaining treatment. Any individual who suffers a debilitating or life-threatening disease or injury inevitably faces choices in medical decision making affected or even dictated by his life circumstances, and the prison environment (although in some respects unique) is simply one such circumstance in the individual's personal calculus.

Commenting upon the *Thor* case, Ian Kennedy wrote as follows:

Kennedy, I, 'Commentary on *Thor v Superior Court*' (1994) 2 Med L Rev 224:

Medical law as it relates to those in prison is a distinctly murky world. The California Supreme Court could perhaps be excused for not examining in any detail the tensions between the conflicting claims which arise. The impression which is left, however, is one of too great a willingness to defer to the needs of security over the claims of the prisoner, whether to refuse or, just as important, to obtain medical treatment. English law sadly is no less murky. There is, of course, the statement by Lord Keith in the course of his speech in *Bland* [[1993] 1 All ER 821] that concern for the principle of the sanctity of life 'does not authorise forcible feeding of prisoners on hunger strikes'. But the wider questions of the refusal of medical treatment by prisoners, their ability to gain access to treatment and the involuntary treatment of them with, for example, psychotropic drugs are greatly underexamined. One obvious reason is the inability to obtain reliable information. The instant case should serve as a reminder that such an examination is long overdue. [See now, *Health Care of Detainees in Police Stations*, 1994, London: BMA.]

Given these justifiable concerns, should there be additional criteria for a valid consent in such situations? The earlier US case of *Kaimowitz v Michigan Department of Mental Health* had suggested a more protective approach to someone in a potentially coercive situation.

Kaimowitz v Michigan Department of Mental Health 42 USLW 2063 (1973):

It is impossible for an involuntarily detained mental patient to be free of ulterior forms of restraint or coercion when his very release from the institution may depend upon his co-operating with the institutional authorities and giving consent to experimental surgery.

... Even Dr Yudashkin, in his testimony, pointed out that involuntarily confined patients tend to tell their doctors what the patient thinks these people want to hear.

... Involuntarily confined mental patients live in an inherently coercive institutional environment. Indirect and subtle psychological coercion has profound effect upon the patient population. Involuntarily confined patients cannot reason as equals with the doctors and administrators over whether they should undergo psychosurgery. They are not able to voluntarily give informed consent because of the inherent inequality in their position.

What of the possibility of coercive behaviour on the part of doctors in the normal setting of patient care (ie, general hospital or GP's surgery)?

Culver, CM and Gert, B, *Philosophy in Medicine*, 1982, New York: OUP, p 51:

Valid consent requires the absence of any coercion by the doctor or the medical staff. Coercion involves any threat of sufficient force that no rational person would reasonably be expected to resist it ... A threat of this kind means that the person being threatened has been deprived of his freedom and so has an excuse for doing what he has been coerced to do. We do not regard strong recommendations, forcefully given, as coercive. To extend the term 'coercion', so that any pressure by a doctor on a patient to accept the doctor's recommendations would count as coercive, and hence in need of justification, seems to us undesirable. We wish to allow doctors considerable leeway in supporting their views. Patients often have irrational fears that must be overcome, so we do not want to set unrealistic limits. But, given the tremendous authority of doctors and the vulnerable position of patients, no threats of lack of care should be allowed.

Culver and Gert may be right in stating that 'strong recommendations' are not coercive (in the sense of amounting to duress), but given the power imbalance between doctor and patient, and the likelihood of the latter enjoying reduced autonomy due to illness, does the doctor exercise undue influence?

The question of undue influence in respect of the conduct of a relative rather than a doctor was considered in the case of *Re T (Adult: Refusal of Medical Treatment)*.

Re T (Adult: Refusal of Medical Treatment) [1992] 4 All ER 649, CA (Lord Donaldson MR, Butler-Sloss and Staughton LJJ)

The patient (an adult), who was pregnant, was admitted to hospital after a road accident. The patient's mother was a devout Jehovah's Witness, although the patient herself was not of the faith. Shortly after being visited by her mother she informed doctors that she did not want a blood transfusion. She asked doctors if there were alternative treatments and was told that there were. Prior to a Caesarean section she signed a form refusing blood transfusions, but was not told that one might be necessary to save her life or prevent serious injury. After the stillbirth of her baby, the patient's condition deteriorated, and the judge at first instance granted a declaration that it would be lawful to administer a blood transfusion.

Lord Donaldson MR:

The vitiating effect of outside influence

A special problem may arise if at the time the decision is made the patient has been subjected to the influence of some third party. This is by no means to say that the patient is not entitled to receive and indeed invite advice and assistance from others in reaching a decision, particularly from members of the family. But the doctors have to consider whether the decision is really that of the patient. It is wholly acceptable that the patient should have been persuaded by others of the merits of such a decision and have decided accordingly. It matters not how strong the persuasion was, so long as it did not overbear the independence of the patient's decision. The real question in each such case is: does the patient really mean what he says or is he merely saying it for a quiet life, to someone else or because the advice and persuasion to which he has been subjected is such that he can no longer think and decide for himself? In other words, is it a decision expressed in form only, not in reality?

When considering the effect of outside influences, two aspects can be of crucial importance. First, the strength of the will of the patient. One who is very tired, in pain or depressed will be much less able to resist having his will overborne than one who is rested, free from pain and cheerful. Second, the relationship of the 'persuader' to the patient may be of crucial importance. The influence of parents on their children or of one spouse on the other can be, but is by no means necessarily, much stronger than would be the case in other relationships. Persuasion based upon religious belief can also be much more compelling and the fact that arguments based upon religious beliefs are being deployed by someone in a very close relationship with the patient will give them added force and should alert the doctors to the possibility – no more – that the patient's capacity or will to decide has been overborne. In other words the patient may not mean what he says.

Lord Donaldson acknowledged that awareness of the possibility of undue influence should not preclude genuine consultation by the patient with others, particularly family members. However, given that the doctors will rarely be privy to these consultations, it is hard to see how they could have sufficient evidence of undue influence, unless this was revealed to them by the patient. It is arguable that the decision in this case should have revolved more around the genuineness of the consent in relation to the information given by the doctors to the patient (ie, risk of death, possibility of no alternative treatment and so on) and/or on the possible temporary incapacity of the patient, rather than on the issue of undue influence.

Children

Consent to treatment

Although the English age of majority is 18 years, and up until that date minors are still subject to the jurisdiction of the courts, the Family Law Reform Act 1969 provides that minors who have attained the age of 16 may give a valid consent to medical treatment:

Family Law Reform Act 1969:

8 (1) The consent of a minor who has attained the age of 16 years to any surgical, medical or dental treatment which, in the absence of consent, would constitute a trespass to his person, shall be as effective as it would be if he were of full age; and where a minor has by virtue of this section given an effective consent to any treatment it shall not be necessary to obtain any consent for it from his parent or guardian.

Just as mental illness without more will not remove capacity, neither will tender years. The case of *Gillick v West Norfolk and Wisbech AHA* had to consider the capacity of children to consent to treatment. In *Gillick* it was acknowledged that there was no magic in the age of 16, and that younger children may be able to consent to medical treatment, depending on their level of understanding, ie, what is generally known as '*Gillick* competence'.

Gillick v West Norfolk and Wisbech AHA **[1986] 1 AC 112, HL (Fraser, Scarman, Bridge, Brandon, and Templeman LL)**

Following concern about the number of under age pregnancies, the Department of Health and Social Security issued guidance to area health authorities on family planning services containing particular provisions relating to young people. Although it stressed the importance of the parents of children under 16 being involved in the consultation, it went on to say that, in exceptional cases, it was for a doctor to decide whether to prescribe contraception without informing the parents of the child. Mrs Gillick, who had a number of daughters under the age of 16, sought a declaration that the guidance gave advice which was unlawful and which adversely affected parental rights and duties. Woolf J refused the declaration. Mrs Gillick succeeded before the Court of Appeal (Eveleigh, Fox and Parker LJJ). The House of Lords allowed the Department of Health and Social Security's appeal by a majority of 3:2.

> **Lord Fraser**: It would, therefore, appear that, if the inference which Mrs Gillick's advisers seek to draw from the provisions [of the FLRA 1969] is justified, a minor under the age of 16 has no capacity to authorise any kind of medical advice or treatment or examination of his own body. That seems to me so surprising that I cannot accept it in the absence of clear provisions to that effect. It seems to me verging on the absurd to suggest that a girl or a boy aged 15 could not effectively consent, for example, to have a medical examination of some trivial injury to his body or even to have a broken arm set. Of course the consent of the parents should normally be asked, but they may not be immediately available. Provided the patient, whether a boy or a girl, is capable of understanding what is proposed, and of expressing his or her own wishes, I see no good reason for holding that he or she lacks the capacity to express them validly and effectively and to authorise the medical man to make the examination or give the treatment which he advises. After all, a minor under the age of 16 can, within certain limits, enter into a contract. He or she can also sue and be sued, and can give evidence on oath. Moreover, a girl under 16 can give sufficiently effective consent to sexual intercourse to lead to the legal result that the man involved does not commit the crime of rape – see *R v Howard* [1966] 1 WLR 13, p 15, when Lord Parker CJ said:
>
> > ... in the case of a girl under 16, the prosecution, in order to prove rape, must prove either that she physically resisted, or if she did not, that her understanding and knowledge were such that she was not in a position to decide whether to consent or resist ... there are many girls under 16 who know full well what it is all about and can properly consent.
>
> Accordingly, I am not disposed to hold now, for the first time, that a girl aged less than 16 lacks the power to give valid consent to contraceptive advice or treatment, merely on account of her age.

Lord Fraser suggested a five point test for doctors contemplating whether to provide such a girl with contraceptive advice and treatment without reference to her parents.

Lord Fraser: ... [T]he doctor will, in my opinion, be justified in proceeding without the parents' consent or even knowledge provided he is satisfied on the following matters: (1) that the girl (although under 16 years of age) will understand his advice; (2) that he cannot persuade her to inform her parents or to allow him to inform the parents that she is seeking contraceptive advice; (3) that she is very likely to begin or to continue having sexual intercourse with or without contraceptive treatment; (4) that unless she receives contraceptive advice or treatment her physical or mental health or both are likely to suffer; (5) that her best interests require him to give her contraceptive advice, treatment or both without the parental consent.

Lord Scarman, in his judgment, emphasised the increasing autonomy of minors as they approach adulthood.

Lord Scarman: ... I would hold that as a matter of law the parental right to determine whether or not their minor child below the age of 16 will have medical treatment terminates if and when the child achieves sufficient understanding and intelligence to enable him or her to understand fully what is proposed. It will be a question of fact whether a child seeking advice has sufficient understanding of what is involved to give a consent valid in law. Until the child achieves the capacity to consent, the parental right to make the decision continues save only in exceptional circumstances. Emergency, parental neglect, abandonment of the child or inability to find the parent are examples of exceptional situations justifying the doctor proceeding to treat the child without parental knowledge and consent; but there will arise, no doubt, other exceptional situations in which it will be reasonable for the doctor to proceed without the parent's consent.

When applying these conclusions to contraceptive advice and treatment it has to be borne in mind that there is much that has to be understood by a girl under 16 if she is to have legal capacity to consent to such treatment. It is not enough that she should understand the nature of the advice which is being given: she must also have a sufficient maturity to understand what is involved. There are moral and family questions, especially her relationship with her parents; long term problems associated with the emotional impact of pregnancy and its termination; and there are the risks to health of sexual intercourse at her age, risks which contraception may diminish but cannot eliminate. It follows that a doctor will have to satisfy himself that she is able to appraise these factors before he can safely proceed on the basis that she has capacity at law to consent to contraceptive advice and treatment. And it further follows that ordinarily the proper course will be for him, as the guidance lays down, first to seek to persuade the girl to bring her parents into consultation, and, if she refuses, not to prescribe contraceptive advice and treatment unless he is satisfied that her circumstances are such that he ought to proceed without parental knowledge and consent.

Lord Bridge agreed with Lords Fraser and Scarman. Dissenting judgments were given by Lords Brandon and Templeman. Lord Templeman accepted the general principle that consent is a function of understanding, not status, but dissented on the specific matter of contraceptive advice and treatment.

Lord Templeman: The effect of the consent of the infant depends on the nature of the treatment and the age and understanding of the infant. For example, a doctor with the consent of an intelligent boy or girl of 15 could, in my opinion, safely remove tonsils or a troublesome appendix. But any decision on the part of a girl to practise sex and contraception requires not only knowledge of the facts of life and of the dangers of pregnancy and disease but also an understanding of the emotional and other consequences to her family, her male partner and to herself. I doubt whether a girl under the age of 16 is capable of a balanced judgment to embark on frequent, regular or casual sexual intercourse fortified by the illusion that medical science can protect her in mind and body and ignoring the danger of leaping from childhood to adulthood without the difficult formative transitional experiences of adolescence. There are many things which a girl under 16 needs to practise but sex is not one of them. Parliament could declare this view to be out of date. But in my opinion the statutory provisions discussed in the speech of my noble and learned friend, Lord Fraser of Tullybelton, and the provisions of s 6 of the Sexual Offences Act 1956, indicate that as the law now stands an unmarried girl under 16 is not competent to decide to practise sex and contraception ...

The position seems to me to be as follows. A doctor is not entitled to decide whether a girl under the age of 16 shall be provided with contraceptive facilities if a parent who is in charge of the girl is ready and willing to make that decision in exercise of parental rights. The doctor is entitled in exceptional circumstances and in emergencies to make provision, normally temporary provision, for contraception but in most cases would be bound to inform the parent of the treatment. The court would not hold the doctor liable for providing contraceptive facilities if the doctor had reasonable grounds for believing that the parent had abandoned or abused parental rights or that there was no parent immediately available for consultation or that there was no parent who was responsible for the girl. But exceptional circumstances and emergencies cannot be expanded into a general discretion for the doctor to provide contraceptive facilities without the knowledge of the parent because of the possibility that a girl to whom contraceptive facilities are not available may irresponsibly court the risk of pregnancy. Such a discretion would enable any girl to obtain contraception on request by threatening to sleep with a man.

Lord Brandon relied on public policy arguments based upon the criminalisation of acts of sex with girls under the age of 16:

Lord Brandon: The Sexual Offences Act 1956 represents the latest pronouncement of parliament on these matters. Sections 5 and 6 provide, so far as material:

5   It is a felony for a man to have unlawful sexual intercourse with a girl under the age of 13.

6   (1)   It is an offence ... for a man to have unlawful sexual intercourse with a girl not under the age of 13 but under the age of 16.

Further, by s 37 and Sched 2, the maximum punishment for an offence under s 5 is imprisonment for life, and that for an offence under s 6 imprisonment for two years. Since the passing of the Act of 1956 the distinction between felonies and misdemeanours has been abolished. For the purposes of this case, however, nothing turns on this change of terminology.

My Lords, the inescapable inference from the statutory provisions of the Acts of 1885 and 1956 to which I have referred is that parliament has for the past century regarded, and still regards today, sexual intercourse between a man and a girl under 16 as a serious criminal offence so far as the man who has such intercourse is concerned. So far as the girl is concerned, she does not commit any criminal offence, even if she aids, abets or incites the having of such intercourse. The reason for this, as explained earlier, is that the relevant statutory provisions have been enacted by parliament for the purpose of protecting the girl from herself. The having of such intercourse is, however, unlawful, and the circumstance that the man is guilty of a criminal offence, while the girl is not, cannot alter that situation.

On the footing that the having of sexual intercourse by a man with a girl under 16 is an unlawful act, it follows necessarily that for any person to promote, encourage or facilitate the commission of such an act may itself be a criminal offence, and must, in any event, be contrary to public policy. Nor can it make any difference that the person who promotes, encourages or facilitates the commission of such an act is a parent or a doctor or a social worker.

[T]o give such a girl advice about contraception, to examine her with a view to her using one or more forms of protection, and finally to prescribe contraceptive treatment for her, necessarily involves promoting, encouraging or facilitating the having of sexual intercourse, contrary to public policy, by that girl with a man.

However, as Lord Brandon himself observed, on this logic Mrs Gillick's desire to have the girl's parents involved would also be problematic, since they too would become accessories to an offence. Moreover, it is interesting to reflect upon the earlier judgment of Lord Brandon in the case of *R v D* [1984] AC 778, which was cited with approval by both Lords Fraser and Scarman. That judgment clearly implied that a mature child could make decisions about medical treatment. It seems that the nature of the treatment in *Gillick* influenced Lord Brandon to take a restrictive approach.

Refusals of treatment

Although *Gillick* makes it clear that, depending on the nature of the treatment, a child may have the capacity to consent, the case has been interpreted subsequently by the Court of Appeal as relating only to consent and not *refusal*, so that a child's refusal of treatment can still be overridden by his parents or others *in loco parentis*.

Re R (A Minor) (Wardship: Consent to Treatment) [1991] 4 All ER 177, CA (Lord Donaldson MR, Staughton and Farquharson LJJ)

The mental health of a 15 year old girl in the care of the local authority deteriorated and she was placed in an adolescent psychiatric unit. Her condition fluctuated between periods of lucidity and, what was described as 'florid psychotic behaviour'. However, she objected to receiving antipsychotic drugs, and the local authority applied under the wardship jurisdiction for leave to administer the drugs regardless of her lack of consent. The judge at first instance (Waite J) decided that if she had the necessary capacity, then her refusal could not be overridden, but, on the facts, decided that she lacked capacity. The Court of Appeal accepted that she was not mentally competent due to the fluctuating nature of her mental illness, but went on to assert, *obiter*, that the wardship jurisdiction could not in any event be ousted by the decision of a *Gillick* competent child. The basis of the *Gillick* decision was interpreted by Lord Donaldson (p 184):

> **Lord Donaldson MR:** ... [C]onsent by itself creates no obligation to treat. It is merely a key which unlocks a door. Furthermore, whilst in the case of an adult of full capacity there will usually only be one keyholder, namely the patient, in the ordinary family unit where a young child is the patient there will be two keyholders, namely the parents, with a several as well as a joint right to turn the key and unlock the door. If the parents disagree, one consenting and the other refusing, the doctor will be presented with a professional and ethical, but not with a legal, problem because, if he has the consent of one authorised person, treatment will not without more constitute a trespass or a criminal assault.
>
> If Mrs Gillick was to succeed in her claim to a declaration that the memorandum of guidance issued by the department was unlawful, she had to show that no child under the age of 16 could be a keyholder in respect of contraception advice and treatment or that the parents' key overrode the child's. As Lord Fraser put it ([1985] 3 All ER 402, p 412, [1986] AC 112, p 173): 'She has to justify the absolute right of veto in a parent.' If she was to succeed in her claim against the area health authority, she had also to show that it was under a duty to inform all medical staff employed by it that Mrs Gillick was exercising that right of veto, but in the light of the House's finding that there was no such right, this additional factor can be ignored.
>
> In the instant appeal Mr James Munby QC, appearing for the Official Solicitor, submits that: (a) if the child has the right to give consent to medical treatment, the parents' right to give or refuse consent is terminated; and (b) the court in the exercise of its wardship jurisdiction is only entitled to step into the shoes of the parents and thus itself has no right to give or refuse consent. Whilst it is true that he seeks to modify the effect of this rather startling submission by suggesting that, if the child's consent or refusal of consent is irrational or misguided, the court will readily infer that in the particular context that individual child is not competent to give or withhold consent, it is necessary to look very carefully at the *Gillick* decision to see whether it supports his argument and, if it does, whether it is binding upon this court.
>
> The key passages upon which Mr Munby relies are to be found in the speech of Lord Scarman ([1985] 3 All ER 402, pp 423–24):
>
> > ... as a matter of law the parental right to determine whether or not their minor child below the age of 16 will have medical treatment terminates if and when the child achieves a sufficient understanding and intelligence to

enable him or her to understand fully what is proposed. It will be a question of fact whether a child seeking advice has sufficient understanding of what is involved to give a consent valid in law ...

... What Mr Munby's argument overlooks is that Lord Scarman was discussing the parents' right *'to determine* whether or not their minor child below the age of 16 will have medical treatment' (my emphasis) and this is the 'parental right' to which he was referring in the latter passage. A right of determination is wider than a right to consent. The parents can only have a right of determination if either the child has no right to consent, ie, is not a keyholder, or the parents hold a master key which could nullify the child's consent. I do not understand Lord Scarman to be saying that, if a child was *'Gillick* competent', to adopt the convenient phrase used in argument, the parents ceased to have an independent right of consent as contrasted with ceasing to have a right of determination, ie, a veto. In a case in which the *'Gillick* competent' child refuses treatment, but the parents consent, that consent enables treatment to be undertaken lawfully, but in no way determines that the child shall be so treated. In a case in which the positions are reversed, it is the child's consent which is the enabling factor and again the parents' refusal of consent is not determinative. If Lord Scarman intended to go further than this and to say that in the case of a *'Gillick* competent' child, a parent has no right either to consent or to refuse consent, his remarks were *obiter*, because the only question in issue was Mrs Gillick's alleged right of veto. Furthermore I consider that they would have been wrong.

One glance at the consequences suffices to show that Lord Scarman cannot have been intending to say that the parental right to consent terminates with the achievement by the child of *'Gillick* competence'. It is fundamental to the speeches of the majority that the capacity to consent will vary from child to child and according to the treatment under consideration, depending upon the sufficiency of his or her intelligence and understanding of that treatment. If the position in law is that upon the achievement of *'Gillick* competence' there is a transfer of the right of consent from parents to child and there can never be a concurrent right in both, doctors would be faced with an intolerable dilemma, particularly when the child was nearing the age of 16, if the parents consented, but the child did not. On pain, if they got it wrong, of being sued for trespass to the person or possibly being charged with a criminal assault, they would have to determine as a matter of law in whom the right of consent resided at the particular time in relation to the particular treatment. I do not believe that that is the law.

The Court of Appeal subsequently considered the status of consent under s 8 of the Family Law Reform Act 1969 in relation to a 16 year old child's refusal of treatment. It will be seen from the section (see above) that it merely states that there is no need to obtain the consent of a parent or guardian if a child gives consent. However, on the face of it, there is no *obligation* on a doctor to obtain the consent of the child in preference to that of the parent or guardian.

Re W (A Minor) (Medical Treatment) **[1992] 4 All ER 627, CA (Lord Donaldson MR, Balcombe and Nolan LJJ)**

A 16 year old girl was suffering from anorexia nervosa and was in the care of the local authority in an adolescent residential unit. Her condition deteriorated and the local authority sought authorisation from the court for removal of the girl to a specialist unit for treatment without her consent. As she had attained the age of 16, she resisted the application on the ground that s 8 of the Family Law Reform Act 1969 conferred on her the same right as an adult to refuse treatment without her consent. Although there is some suggestion in the judgments that, because of her condition, Miss W may not have been competent, the essence of the Court of Appeal's decision was that s 8 did not in any event confer an absolute right upon a child, and could be overridden by the court exercising its inherent jurisdiction.

Lord Donaldson MR:

Is s 8 ambiguous?

The wording of sub-s (1) shows quite clearly that it is addressed to the legal purpose and legal effect of consent to treatment, namely, to prevent such treatment constituting in law a trespass to the person, and that it does so by making the consent of a 16 or 17 year old as effective as if he were 'of full age'. No question of '*Gillick* competence' in common law terms arises. The 16 or 17 year old is conclusively presumed to be '*Gillick* competent' or, alternatively, the test of '*Gillick* competence' is bypassed and has no relevance. The argument that W or any other 16 or 17 year old can, by refusing to consent to treatment, veto the treatment notwithstanding that the doctor has the consent of someone who has parental responsibilities, involves the proposition that s 8 has the further effect of depriving such a person of the power to consent. It certainly does not say so. Indeed if this were its intended effect, it is difficult to see why the sub-section goes on to say that it is not necessary to obtain the parents' consent, rather than providing that such consent, if obtained, should be ineffective. Furthermore, such a construction does not sit easily with sub-s (3), which preserves the common law as it existed immediately before the Act which undoubtedly gave parents an effective power of consent for all children up to the age of 21, the then existing age of consent ...

The most promising argument in favour of W having an exclusive right to consent to treatment and thus, by refusing consent, to attract the protection of the law on trespass to the person, lies in concentrating upon the words 'as effective as it would be if he were of full age'. If she were of full age her ability to consent would have two separate effects. First, her consent would be fully effective as such. Second, a failure or refusal to give consent would be fully effective as a veto, but only *because no one else would be in a position to consent*. If it is a possible view that s 8 is intended to put a 16 or 17 year old in exactly the same position as an adult and there is thus some ambiguity, although I do not think that there is, it is a permissible aid to construction to seek to ascertain the mischief at which the section is directed.

The Latey Committee Report

It is common ground that the Family Law Reform Act 1969 was parliament's response to the *Report of the Committee on the Age of Majority*, Cmnd 3342, 1967.

The relevant part is contained in paras 474–84. These show that the mischief aimed at was twofold. First, cases were occurring in which young people between 16 and 21 (the then age of majority) were living away from home and wished and needed urgent medical treatment which had not yet reached the emergency stage. Doctors were unable to treat them unless and until their parents had been traced and this could cause unnecessary suffering. Second, difficulties were arising concerning

> ... operations whose implications bring up the question of a girl's right to privacy about her sexual life. A particularly difficult situation arises in the case of a girl who is sent to hospital in need of a therapeutic abortion and refuses point blank to enter the hospital unless a guarantee is given that her parents shall not be told about it.

The committee had recommended that the age of majority be reduced to 18 generally. The report, in para 480, records that all the professional bodies which gave evidence recommended that patients aged between 16 and 18 should be able to give an effective consent to treatment and all but the Medical Protection Society recommended that they should also be able to give an effective refusal. The point with which we are concerned was therefore well in the mind of the committee. It did not so recommend. It recommended that:

> ... *without prejudice to any consent that may otherwise be lawful*, the consent of young persons aged 16 and over to medical or dental treatment shall be as valid as the consent of a person of full age. (My emphasis.)

Conclusion on s 8

I am quite unable to accept that parliament in adopting somewhat more prolix language was intending to achieve a result which differed from that recommended by the committee.

On reflection I regret my use in *Re R* ... of the keyholder analogy because keys can lock as well as unlock. I now prefer the analogy of the legal 'flak jacket' which protects the doctor from claims by the litigious whether he acquires it from his patient who may be a minor over the age of 16, or a *'Gillick* competent' child under that age or from another person having parental responsibilities which include a right to consent to treatment of the minor. Anyone who gives him a flak jacket (that is, consent) may take it back, but the doctor only needs one and so long as he continues to have one he has the legal right to proceed.

It is interesting to compare Lord Donaldson's interpretation of s 8(3) of the 1969 Act with that of Lord Scarman in *Gillick*. It will be recalled that Lord Scarman said (p 182) that 'sub-s 3 leaves open the question whether the consent of a minor *under* 16 could be an effective consent', whereas Lord Donaldson interprets it as safeguarding parental rights in cases of minors over 16. In the light of this conflict, it should be noted that in Scottish law a child under the age of 16 has legal capacity to consent to medical treatment if 'he is capable of understanding the nature and possible consequences of the procedure or treatment' (s 2(4) of the Age of Legal Capacity (Scotland) Act 1991), and in *Houston, Applicant* (see (1997) 5 Med LR 237), the Sheriff's Court confirmed that the child's power to consent could not be overridden by a guardian, even though s 5(1) of the Act provides that the guardian of a person under 16 has the same powers after the passing of the Act as before. It was said that it would be illogical to grant a power to consent to medical treatment if this decision could be overridden by a guardian.

Certainly *Re R* and *Re W* sit rather uneasily with the *Gillick* decision. It is hard to see how, for example, Lord Scarman's wide ranging approach to the issue of understanding and the gradual attainment of the age of discretion can simply have been constructed to provide the doctor with protection from legal action. On the other hand, the recommendation of the Latey Committee does appear to support Lord Donaldson's view. However, could it not be argued that the committee was leaving the question open, and that the *Gillick* decision has since decided the position? Not surprisingly, the cases have drawn a large amount of critical comment.

Bainham, A, 'The judge and the competent minor' (1992) 108 LQR 194:

[In *Re R*] Lord Donaldson sought to draw a distinction between 'determination' and 'consent', the former being a wider concept than the latter, since it implied a right of veto. In his view, Lord Scarman in *Gillick* was referring to the parent's right to determine whether or not a child should receive medical treatment. This right of determination, which amounted to a definitive right to decide, would be removed where the child also had a capacity to consent. But, according to Lord Donaldson, Lord Scarman was not saying that the parent's independent right to consent would be lost in these circumstances. There would, according to this interpretation, be concurrent independent rights in parent and child and it would be open to a doctor to act on either consent ...

There are fundamental objections to this position. It can only work on the assumption that a doctor is dealing solely with the parent or solely with the child and is unaware of any disagreement between them. Where he is aware of a disagreement then, in the absence of judicial intervention, he must choose between the conflicting views. This is so where the parent is proposing action and the child is objecting, or conversely, where the child is in favour of action and the parent is objecting. If the doctor decides to proceed, or not to proceed, on the basis of the parent's view, he is in reality giving effect to a parental veto over the child's view. He is allowing the parent to 'determine' the matter, and the suggested distinction between 'determination' and 'consent' falls apart. And it is difficult to see how medical personnel seeking to administer drugs with the consent of a parent (or, as here, someone else with parental responsibility) could possibly be unaware of the child's objection. The dilemma referred to by Lord Donaldson of choosing between two potentially valid consents (either of which might subsequently be held invalid) is inevitable in the absence of a mandatory judicial procedure.

However Lord Donaldson did not stop there. Surprisingly, he took the view that the same principles governed the situation of a young person over 16. Section 8(1) of the Family Law Reform Act 1969 provides that where this age has been attained, the child's consent 'to any surgical, medical or dental treatment ... shall be as effective as it would be if he were of full age' and that 'it shall not be necessary to obtain any consent for it from his parent or guardian'. He adopted a literal interpretation to the effect that, while it was unnecessary for a doctor to secure parental consent in relation to a 16 year old, there was nothing to preclude him from acting on a parent's consent alone. This flies in the face of the settled interpretation of this provision that it was intended to confer complete autonomy on a young person of this age and that by implication this must outweigh any parental claim to decide.

The majority in *Gillick* were clearly aware of the potential for conflict between two independently valid consents and gave precedence to the views of the competent child. Lord Scarman could hardly have been more definite about this. Even Lord Fraser, who was anxious to ensure that the parental contribution was properly explored, also supported a doctor's right in specified circumstances to act on the child's consent alone. There is nothing in either speech which gives the remotest hint that a parent's view could lawfully be allowed to prevail over that of the mature child. Lord Donaldson's remarks, if accepted, would have the effect of turning the clocks back on *Gillick* and would surely be unlikely to survive the scrutiny of the House of Lords.

However, there has also been support for the Court of Appeal's interpretation.

Lowe, N and Juss, S, 'Medical treatment – pragmatism and the search for principle' (1993) 56 MLR 865:

Whether one uses Lord Donaldson MR's 'keyholder analogy' or his 'flak jacket' approach, the effect is the same. It enables the court to prevent, in the words of the Latey Committee, 'permanent disability' or 'unnecessary pain and suffering'.

In our view, the decision in *Re W* should not be reversed by the House of Lords. Similarly, we would support the outcome in *Re R* and in *Re E* ... [T]hese decisions establish two grounds upon which a child's refusal can be overridden: namely (1) the inability to make an informed judgment, in which case the refusal carries no weight; and (2) where the child is capable of making an informed view, that preference is balanced against the harm to the child's welfare which will ensue if these wishes are observed.

We would support the decisions on either basis because it seems to us wrong for the court to allow a child to refuse treatment that would do him or her irreparable harm. After all, it is perhaps all too easily forgotten that, in the final analysis, a child is still only a child. Moreover, the entire thesis based on the premise of Lord Scarman's child of 'sufficient understanding and intelligence' who is able 'to understand fully what is proposed' is, it is submitted, in one sense open to question. Is a child of sufficient understanding and intelligence if he or she acts irrationally? Is autonomy meaningful if it is irrational? The point is well illustrated by *Re W* itself. At first instance, Thorpe J, with support from W's consultant psychiatrist who specialised in anorexia nervosa, had 'no doubt at all' that she was '*Gillick* competent'. Lord Donaldson MR, however, had serious doubts, contending 'it is a feature of anorexia nervosa that it is capable of destroying the ability to make an informed choice' being 'an illness which is not the fault of the sufferer' but which in its clinical manifestations contains 'a firm wish not to be cured'. Balcombe LJ recognised that if W's refusal not to take solid food was not shortly reversed 'she would be likely to suffer permanent damage to her brain and reproductive organs and not be able to bear children. Can it humanely be argued, in these circumstances, that the court ought not to have intervened? We agree with Ward J [in *Re E*] that a court should be slow to let a child martyr himself. To those who question how a child can be held able to give a valid consent yet be unable to exercise a power of veto, we would reply that there is a rational distinction to be made between giving consent and withholding it. We must start with the assumption that a doctor will act in the best interests of his patient. Hence, if the doctor believes that a particular treatment is necessary for his patient, it is perfectly rational for the law to facilitate this as easily as possible and hence allow a *'Gillick* competent' child to give a valid consent, and also to protect the child against parents opposed to what is professionally considered to be in its best medical interests. In contrast, it is surely right for the law to be reluctant to allow a child of whatever age to be able to veto treatment designed for his or her benefit, particularly if a refusal would lead to the child's death or permanent damage. In other words, the clear and consistent policy of the law is to protect the child against wrong-headed parents and against itself with the final safeguard, as *Re W* unequivocally establishes, of giving the court the last word in cases of dispute.

On this view, a child may be deemed to be *Gillick* competent, but still lacking the necessary capacity that an adult would enjoy, to the extent that the outcome of its decision is not deemed to be in its own best interests. However, the support Lowe and Juss seek to derive from the Latey Committee report – that it sought to prevent 'unnecessary pain and suffering' – is in our view not justified. The pain and suffering at issue was caused, not by 'unacceptable' treatment decisions by minors, but by the fact that – pre-*Gillick* – they had no legal power to make any decisions. The Court of Appeal seems to be substituting the functional view of capacity (at the heart of the later adult case of *Re C*) with a bare 'all or nothing' test: either under or over 18 years of age, either competent or incompetent. Whatever view is taken it can be seen that the effect of *Re W*, so far as refusals of treatment are concerned, is to re-establish the very 'status' approach which the House of Lords were at pains to reject in *Gillick* in relation to consent. The 'all or nothing' aspect is illustrated by the train of events during and after the case of *Re E (A Minor) (Wardship: Medical Treatment)* [1993] 1 FLR 386, referred to in the Lowe and Juss article. The patient was 15 and, like his parents, a devout Jehovah's Witness. He was suffering from leukaemia, the treatment of which included blood transfusions. Ward J ordered the carrying out of the treatment, which continued until the boy reached 18. At this point he refused further medical treatment and died.

Informing the patient

It is common to come across the expression 'informed consent' in relation to medical treatment. However, this expression has a number of interpretations and is often misused. In relation to the validity of consent to medical treatment, it means no more than an understanding of the broad nature of the treatment proposed. As long as the patient understands this, then much of the detail can be left out, and the patient will still have given a valid consent. It does not matter, for example, that a risk of which the patient was not informed later materialises. It is important to keep in mind that we are here considering the validity of the patient's consent so as to negate a subsequent action in battery, and not whether a doctor may have been *negligent* in not giving certain information. The nature of the consent was considered in *Chatterton v Gerson* [1981] QB 432.

> **Bristow J**: In my judgment, once the patient is informed in broad terms of the nature of the procedure which is intended, and gives her consent, that consent is real, and the cause of the action on which to base a claim for failure to go into risks and implications is negligence, not trespass. Of course, if information is withheld in bad faith, the consent would be vitiated by fraud. Of course, if by some accident, as in a case in the 1940s in the Salford Hundred Court, where a boy was admitted to hospital for tonsillectomy and due to administrative error was circumcised instead, trespass would be the appropriate cause of action against the doctor, though he was as much the victim of the error as the boy. But in my judgment it would be very much against the interests of justice if actions which are really based on a failure by the doctor to perform his duty adequately to inform were pleaded in trespass.

This approach is also found in the Canadian case of *Reibl v Hughes* (1980) 114 DLR (3d) 1:

> **Laskin CJ**: I can appreciate the temptation to say that the genuineness of consent to medical treatment depends on proper disclosure of the risks which it entails, but in my view ... a failure to disclose the attendant risks, however serious, should go to negligence rather than to battery. Although such a failure relates to an informed choice of submitting to or refusing recommended and appropriate treatment, it arises as the breach of an anterior duty of due care, comparable in legal obligation to the duty of due care in carrying out the particular treatment to which the patient has consented. It is not a test of the validity of consent.

In *Davis v Barking, Havering and Brentwood HA* [1993] 4 Med LR 85, the High Court considered the case of a woman who signed a consent form to undergo a general anaesthetic, but, who subsequently received a caudal block (ie, an injection of anaesthetising drug into part of the body to interrupt nerve function), and who suffered some damage as a result of this. McCullough J rejected the argument that the failure to obtain consent to this procedure amounted to a battery.

> **McCullough J**: If one is to treat the administration of an injection for analgesic purposes while the patient is generally anaesthetised (eg, the caudal block given to Mrs Davis) as something requiring separate consent, why should separate consent not also be sought for an injection of, for example, morphine to provide analgesia when the patient begins to come round from the general anaesthetic?
>
> ... And once this degree of sectionalisation is accepted, how long will it be before the court is invited to say that separate consent should be sought for separate steps in the surgical procedure itself? A sectionalised approach of this

kind would encourage – indeed necessitate – what has been called the 'deplorable' prospect of actions being brought in trespass rather than in negligence.

What of, say, carrying out tests on specimens of bodily fluids or tissue which have not been specifically authorised by the patient, although consent to the taking of specimens was given? This is particularly relevant to HIV testing. In April 1994 a number of Harrods' staff had tests carried out on their blood samples without explicit consent (some were also carried out in the face of an express refusal of consent). In the light of this sort of reasoning, would a battery be found to have taken place here? Unfortunately, there has been no judicial consideration of the issue, and expert opinions have differed. The British Medical Association took advice from Michael Sherrard QC and Ian Gatt, who formed the view the explicit consent is necessary, as did Kennedy and Grubb and Gordon Langley QC, whilst Leo Charles QC, advising the Central Committee for Hospital Medical Services, advised that explicit consent was not necessary.

Commenting upon the difference of opinion, with reference to the 'broad nature of the treatment' test in *Chatterton v Gerson*, John Keown states:

Keown, J, 'The ashes of AIDS and the phoenix of informed consent' (1989) 52 MLR 790:

The doctor who tells the patient that a sample of blood is to be taken for 'tests' has surely discharged this duty. The fact that he does not inform the patient that one of the tests is for HIV does not alter the general nature of the procedure as part of a process of therapeutic diagnosis.

The Sherrard opinion's invention of a distinction between 'routine' and 'non-routine' tests, a distinction which apparently turns on the seriousness of the consequences of a positive result suffers not only from vagueness (what is meant by 'seriousness' and does the requirement to inform extend to other tests and treatments?) but is unsupported by authority or argument, as are the opinion's assertions of an implied representation by the doctor that he will only do 'routine' tests without express consent, and that this representation vitiates the uninformed patient's consent. Curiously, the most copious use of authority in the opinion is its lengthy quotation from the *dissenting* opinion of Lord Scarman in *Sidaway*. Whereas it is understandable that a distinction could be made between 'therapeutic' and 'non-therapeutic' testing (an example of the latter being where the sample is taken purely as part of a research programme) such as to render the latter a procedure of a different nature to the former, a distinction between 'routine' and 'non-routine' seems to be insupportable.

No less insupportable, with respect, is Kennedy and Grubb's analogy between the removal of a sample of blood for HIV testing and off-the-ball kicks and punches on the sports field, an analogy which can hardly be described as obvious.

It is one thing to say that a person cannot, as a matter of public policy, consent to the deliberate infliction of bodily harm without good reason (and hence to regard off-the-ball kicks and punches as assaults). It is quite another to extend this reasoning to touchings which involve no infliction, deliberate or otherwise, of bodily harm.

Not only is no relevant authority cited to warrant such an extension, but the supporting argument that consent should be required because of the possible far-reaching implications of the test presumably entails the conclusion that on those, doubtless many, occasions when a doctor takes a sample from a patient to perform a test which may have far-reaching implications (such as for cancer) the doctor is guilty of battery if he does not obtain the patient's specific consent to it.

A second argument advanced by Kennedy and Grubb is that *Chatterton* in fact supports their case. They argue that although the doctor need only inform the patient in broad terms of the nature of the procedure, the 'procedure' is not merely the use of the syringe to obtain a blood sample, but to obtain a blood sample for an HIV test. Merely to have assented to a particular touching will not necessarily amount to consent if there is no comprehension of the quality of the touching. In support of this argument they cite the case of *Flattery* (as explained by Dunn LJ in *Sidaway*) and state that it is clear that a woman who consents to sexual intercourse, knowing it is sexual intercourse but believing it is being done as a surgical operation, has not given a valid consent to the intercourse because she is unaware of the underlying quality of the touching ...

In sum, *Chatterton* merely requires the patient to be informed in broad terms of the nature of the procedure. The doctor who tells his patient that blood is to be removed for testing, even though he does not say that it is to be tested for HIV, has surely satisfied this requirement.

One reason that the courts stress the distinction between battery and negligence is because otherwise a doctor would theoretically be guilty of a criminal offence, as well as a breach of civil law, if he were found to have battered the patient in failing to give sufficient information. Although such a failure may be thought culpable, it is likely that public policy generally militates against imposing criminal liability upon the doctor. What also of the situation where a doctor changes his mind about what to do with blood that he has *previously* removed – at this point can he be guilty retrospectively of committing a battery?

However, there are cases where doctors have clearly battered their patients. One example is provided by the Canadian case of *Allan v Mount Sinai Hospital* (1980) 109 DLR (3d) 634, in which Linden J found a battery when an anaesthetic injection was given in the patient's left arm, after she had specifically requested that it not be given there. In *Devi v West Midlands RHA* (1981) CA, Transcript 491, the patient had consented to a repair to a perforation in her uterus, and the surgeon, believing it to be in her best interests, sterilised her instead. This was, not surprisingly, found to be a battery. In *Cull v Royal Surrey County Hospital* (1932) 1 BMJ 1195, there was a battery when a patient had consented to an abortion but received a sterilisation in addition.

THE DUTY TO DISCLOSE IN NEGLIGENCE

What is 'informed consent'?

As indicated above, this expression is not always used with sufficient precision. It does not relate to patient information as described above (ie, the broad nature of the procedure which is all that needs to be explained in order for a doctor to avoid an action in battery). The doctrine is primarily American, and relates to the amount of information that a patient should be given in addition to the broad nature requirement to avoid an action in negligence. It has been confirmed in English case law that 'informed consent' has no application (see, for example, *Freeman v Home Office* [1987] 1 All ER 1036). Though some additional information should be given, the test is much weaker than in, for example, the USA. However, the language of English case law is frequently misleading, with judges using this expression when referring to the English test (see, for example, Lord Bridge's speech in *Sidaway* [1985] AC 871).

The nature of the information that a patient must have in order to give an 'informed consent' in the American sense is often described as subjecting it to the 'prudent patient' test.

The prudent patient test

This can be summed up by reference to the following passage in the court's judgment in the District of Columbia case of *Canterbury v Spence*.

Canterbury v Spence **464 F 2d 772 (1972):**

Robinson J: There are, in our view, formidable obstacles to acceptance of the notion that the physician's obligation to disclose is either germinated or limited by medical practice. To begin with, the reality of any discernible custom reflecting a professional consensus on communication of option and risk information to patient is open to serious doubt. We sense the danger that what in fact is no custom at all may be taken as an affirmative custom to maintain silence, and that physician witnesses to the so called custom may state merely their personal opinions as to what they or others would do under given conditions. We cannot gloss over the inconsistency between reliance on a general practice respecting divulgence and, on the other hand, realisation that the myriad of variables among patients makes each case so differing that its omission can rationally justified only by the effect of its individual circumstances. Nor can we ignore the fact that to bind the disclosure obligation to medical usage is to arrogate the decision on revelation to the physician alone. Respect for the patient's right of self-determination on particular therapy demands a standard set by law for physicians rather than one which physicians may or may not impose upon themselves ...

Once the circumstances give rise to a duty on the physician's part to inform his patient, the next inquiry is the scope of the disclosure the physician is legally obliged to make. The courts have frequently confronted this problem but no uniform standard defining the adequacy of the divulgence emerges from the decisions. Some have said 'full' disclosure, a norm we are unwilling to adopt literally. It seems obviously prohibitive and unrealistic to expect physicians to discuss with their patient every risk of proposed treatment – no matter how small or remote – and generally unnecessary from the patient's viewpoint as well. Indeed, the cases speaking in terms of 'full' disclosure appear to envision something less than total disclosure, leaving unanswered the question of just how much.

The larger number of courts, as might be expected, have applied tests framed with reference to prevailing fashion within the medical profession. Some have measured the disclosure by 'good medical practice', others by what a reasonable practitioner would have done under the circumstances, and still others by what medical custom in the community would demand. We have explored this rather considerable body of law but are unprepared to follow it. The duty to disclose, we have reasoned, arises from phenomena apart from medical custom and practice. The latter, we think, should no more establish the scope of the duty than its existence. Any definition of scope in terms purely of a professional standard is at odds with the patient's prerogative to decide on projected therapy himself. That prerogative, we have said, is at the very foundation of the duty to disclose, and both the patient's right to know and the physician's correlative obligation to tell him are diluted to the extent that its compass is dictated by the medical profession.

In our view, the patient's right of self-decision shapes the boundaries of the duty to reveal. That right can be effectively exercised only if the physician's communications to the patient, then, must be measured by the patient's need, and that need is the information material to the decision. Thus the test for determining whether a particular peril must be divulged is its materiality to the patient's decision: all risks potentially affecting the decision must be unmasked. And to safeguard the patient's interest in achieving his own determination on treatment, the law must itself set the standard for adequate disclosure.

However, as the court noted, a difficulty with the prudent patient test is in deciding whether it is objective or subjective:

Robinson J: Of necessity, the content of the disclosure rests in the first instance with the physician. Ordinarily it is only he who is in a position to identify particular dangers; always he must make a judgment, in terms of materiality, as to whether and to what extent revelation to the patient is called for. He cannot know with complete exactitude what the patient would consider important to his decision, but on the basis of his medical training and experience he can sense how the average, reasonable patient expectably would react. Indeed, with knowledge of, or ability to learn his patient's background and current condition, he is in a position superior to that of most others – attorneys, for example – who are called upon to make judgments on pain of liability in damages for unreasonable miscalculation.

From these considerations we derive the breadth of the disclosure of risks legally to be required. The scope of the standard is not subjective as to either the physician or the patient; it remains objective with due regard for the patient's informational needs and with suitable leeway for the physician's situation. In broad outline, we agree that '[a] risk is thus material when a reasonable person in what the physician knows or should know to be the patient's position would be likely to attach significance to the risks or cluster of risks in deciding whether or not to forgo the proposed therapy'.

Does this ultimately imply an objective or a subjective approach in the court's assessment of what the doctor should tell a patient?

The prudent doctor test

The 'prudent doctor test' is the stance currently adopted by the English courts, following the decision of the majority of the House of Lords in *Sidaway*:

Sidaway v Board of Governors of the Bethlem Royal Hospital and the Maudsley Hospital and Others [1985] 1 AC 871, HL (Diplock, Bridge, Scarman, Templeman and Keith LL)

The patient underwent an operation which carried an inherent risk (ie, even if performed with all reasonable care) of damage to the spinal cord of between 1% and 2%. The patient was not warned of this risk, and when it subsequently materialised and she became severely disabled, she brought an action in negligence. The judgments refer to the *Bolam* test (which will be examined further in relation to medical malpractice, see below, Chapter 6). This means that a doctor is not negligent if he acts in accordance with a responsible body of medical opinion. Here it is being applied to the amount of information he chooses to give a patient, not simply to the type of treatment he recommends, or surgical procedures he carries out.

> **Lord Diplock**: My Lords, no convincing reason has in my view been advanced before your Lordships that would justify treating the *Bolam* test as doing anything less than laying down a principle of English law that is comprehensive and applicable to every aspect of the duty of care owed by a doctor to his patient in the exercise of his healing functions as respects that patient. What your Lordships have been asked to do – and it is within your power to do so – is to substitute a new and different rule for that part only of the well established *Bolam* test as comprises a doctor's duty to advise and warn the patient of risks of something going wrong in the surgical or other treatment that he is recommending ...
>
> My Lords, I venture to think that in making this separation between that part of the duty of care that he owes to each individual patient, which can be described as a duty to advise upon treatment and warn of its risks, the courts have misconceived their functions as the finders of fact in cases depending upon the negligent exercise of professional skill and judgment. In matters of diagnosis and the carrying out of treatment the court is not tempted to put

itself in the surgeon's shoes; it has to rely upon and evaluate expert evidence, remembering that it is no part of its task of evaluation to give effect to any preference it may have for one responsible body of professional opinion over another, provided it is satisfied by the expert evidence that both qualify as responsible bodies of medical opinion. But when it comes to warning about risks, the kind of training and experience that a judge will have undergone at the Bar makes it natural for him to say (correctly), it is my right to decide whether any particular thing is done to my body, and I want to be fully informed of any risks that may be involved of which I am not already aware from my general knowledge as a highly educated man of experience, so that I may form my own judgment as to whether to refuse the advised treatment or not.

No doubt if the patient in fact manifested this attitude by means of questioning, the doctor would tell him whatever it was the patient wanted to know; but we are concerned here with volunteering unsought information about risks of the proposed treatment failing to achieve the result sought or making the patient's physical or mental condition worse rather than better. The only effect that mention of risks can have on the patient's mind, if it has any at all, can be in the direction of deterring the patient from undergoing the treatment which in the expert opinion of the doctor it is in the patient's interest to undergo. To decide what risks the existence of which a patient should be voluntarily warned and the terms in which such warning, if any, should be given, having regard to the effect that the warning may have, is as much an exercise of professional skill and judgment as any other part of the doctor's comprehensive duty of care to the individual patient, and expert medical evidence on this matter should be treated in just the same way. The *Bolam* test should be applied.

Consider here Lord Diplock's reference to the 'highly educated' lawyer requesting medical information. Is there not a suggestion here that 'ordinary' people will not make such inquiries, and is there not something offensive about this, reflecting dual standards which depend upon the sophistication of the patient?

Note that Lord Diplock also suggests that information may deter the patient from undergoing treatment.

McLean, S, *A Patient's Right to Know*, 1989, Aldershot: Dartmouth, p 114:

The decision whether or not to disclose information can be regarded as merely the professional exercise of the doctor's skills *qua* doctor, only if it is thought likely to have a significant impact on the patient's choice as to whether or not to accept the recommended therapy; and in fact, only if it is thought likely that the patient would not agree with the professional assessment made by the doctor that therapy, or particular therapy, should be undertaken. When seen in this light, the statement in effect is suggesting that, when the doctor thinks – in the exercise of his or her professional judgment – that the patient should undergo a particular therapy, then the patient should not be given the opportunity to decline. In other words, the perceived value of therapy takes precedence over the patient's rights to reject it (however medically irrational this may seem) and to exercise his or her self-determination knowledgeably and in a calculated fashion.

Lord Bridge (in *Sidaway* [1985] AC 871, p 897) also took a stance which tends to defer to clinical judgment.

Lord Bridge: The important question which this appeal raises is whether the law imposes any, and if so what, different criterion as to the measure of the medical man's duty of care to his patient when giving advice with respect to a proposed course of treatment. It is clearly right to recognise that a conscious adult patient of sound mind is entitled to decide for himself whether or not he will submit to a particular course of treatment proposed by the doctor, most significantly surgical treatment under general anaesthesia. This entitlement is the foundation of the doctrine of 'informed consent' which has led in certain American jurisdictions to decisions, and in the Supreme Court of Canada to dicta, on which the appellant relies, which would oust the *Bolam* test and substitute an 'objective' test of a doctor's duty to advise the patient of the advantages and disadvantages of undergoing the treatment proposed and more particularly to advise the patient of the risks involved.

There are, it appears to me, at least theoretically, two extreme positions which could be taken. It could be argued that, if the patient's consent is to be fully informed, the doctor must specifically warn him of *all* risks involved in the treatment offered, unless he has some sound clinical reason not to do so. Logically, this would seem to be the extreme to which a truly objective criterion of the doctor's duty would lead. Yet this position finds no support from any authority, to which we have been referred, in any jurisdiction. It seems to be generally accepted that there is no need to warn of the risks inherent in all surgery under general anaesthesia. This is variously explained on the ground that the patient may be expected to be aware of such risks or that they are relatively remote. If the law is to impose on the medical profession a duty to warn of risk to secure 'informed consent' independently of accepted medical opinion of what is appropriate, neither of these explanations for confining the duty to special as opposed to general surgical risks seems to me wholly convincing.

At the other extreme it could be argued that, once the doctor has decided what treatment is, on balance of advantages and disadvantages, in the patient's best interest, he should not alarm the patient by volunteering a warning of any risk involved, however grave and substantial, unless specifically asked by the patient. I cannot believe that contemporary medical opinion would support this view, which would effectively exclude the patient's right to decide in the very type of case where it is most important that he should be in a position to exercise that right and, perhaps even more significantly, to seek a second opinion as to whether she should submit himself to the significant risk which has been drawn to his attention.

The final paragraph contains a somewhat oblique endorsement of the *Bolam* test. On the omission to warn of risks – 'I cannot believe that contemporary medical opinion would support this view ...' – is Lord Bridge suggesting that if medical opinion *did endorse* such a view, then such a view would prevail?

Lord Keith agreed with Lord Bridge; and Lord Templeman, though his judgment makes no express reference to the *Bolam* test, appears to have taken a similar view.

> **Lord Templeman**: The patient is free to decide whether or not to submit to treatment recommended by the doctor and therefore the doctor impliedly contracts to provide information which is adequate to enable the patient to reach a balanced judgment, subject always to the doctor's own obligation to say and do nothing which the doctor is satisfied will be harmful to the patient. When the doctor himself is considering the possibility of a major operation the doctor is able, with his medical training, with his knowledge of the patient's medical history and with his objective position to make a balanced judgment as to whether the operation should be performed or not ... The duty of the doctor in these circumstances, subject to his overriding duty to have regard to the best interests of the patient, is to provide the patient with information which will enable the patient to make a balanced judgment if the patient chooses to make a balanced judgment.

Elsewhere, Lord Templeman referred rather mysteriously to a distinction between general and special risks.

> **Lord Templeman**: In the case of a general danger the court must decide whether the information afforded to the patient was sufficient to alert the patient to the possibility of serious harm of the kind in fact suffered. If the practice of the medical profession is to make express mention of particular kind of danger, the court will have no difficulty in coming to the conclusion that the doctor ought to have referred expressly to this danger unless the doctor can give reasons to justify the form or absence of warning adopted by him. Where the practice of the medical profession is divided or does not include express mention, it will be for the court to determine whether the harm suffered is an example of a general danger inherent in nature of the operation.

What is the real difference between general and special risks, and is the distinction a useful one? Lord Templeman seems to be saying that they would be treated differently *by the court,* as opposed to the medical profession, and to suggest that *Bolam* only applies to special risks, and even then, will not apply if the medical profession is divided. However, it will be seen in Chapter 6 that if the profession is divided, the usual application of *Bolam* means that the doctor will not have been negligent just because there is a body of medical opinion which differs from the body of opinion to which he belongs.

However, it is at any rate apparent from the majority judgments in *Sidaway* (Lords Bridge, Keith and Templeman) that certain risks must be warned about.

> **Lord Bridge:** I am of the opinion that the judge might in certain circumstances come to the conclusion that disclosure of a particular risk was so obviously necessary to an informed choice on the part of the patient that no reasonably prudent medical man would fail to make it. The kind of case I have in mind would be an operation involving a substantial risk of grave adverse

consequences, as, for example, the 10% risk of a stroke from the operation which was the subject of the Canadian case of *Reibl v Hughes*, 114 DLR (3d) 1. In such a case, in the absence of some cogent clinical reason why the patient should not be informed, a doctor, recognising and respecting his patient's right of decision, could hardly fail to appreciate the necessity for an appropriate warning.

(See also Lord Templeman's reference to the possibility of 'some danger which by its nature or magnitude or for some other reason requires to be separately taken into account by the patient in order to reach a balanced judgment'.)

What about the need for more general matters to be disclosed? For example, should a doctor tell a patient that he has never performed this operation before? It may be thought that the training of surgeons is such, that they will always have assisted and observed before carrying out a surgical procedure, and therefore, they will always have 'done' the operation in various ways before taking responsibility for it. However, this will not be the case when new procedures and techniques are developed, for example, keyhole surgery. What sort of disclosure should be made then? It is likely that many patients would be very interested to know that their surgeons had never done this before, particularly if there was alternative treatment (ie, conventional surgery), but what would a responsible body of medical opinion decide? This point is considered further below, in Chapter 6, in relation to innovative treatment. It is also a moot point as to whether there is any obligation to disclose matters such as success, or, crucially, failure rates for the type of treatment proposed. This is particularly pertinent in the light of the GMC disciplinary proceedings against three doctors at the United Bristol Healthcare Trust (see (1998) *The Guardian*, 30 May). The doctors were found to be in breach of professional standards in continuing to carry out heart operations on babies in the knowledge that the death rates of the children they were treating were well above the average for such operations. There can surely be no doubt that patients would regard such statistical disparity as a risk factor of which they should be made aware.

Consider whether the giving of information always differs from other aspects of the doctor's duty of care in that the decision about what to tell a patient is not really a *medical* one. Although he agreed that the plaintiff's appeal should be dismissed on its facts, Lord Scarman delivered a dissenting judgment on this aspect of the law. His view accords much more with the US 'prudent patient' approach:

Lord Scarman: My Lords, I think the *Canterbury* propositions reflect a legal truth which too much judicial reliance on medical judgment tends to obscure. In a medical negligence case where the issue is the advice and information given to the patient as to the treatment proposed, the available options, and the risk, the court is concerned primarily with a patient's right. The doctor's duty arises from his patient's rights. If one considers the scope of the doctor's duty by beginning with the right of the patient to make his own decision whether he will or will not undergo the treatment proposed, the right to be informed of significant risk and the doctor's corresponding duty are easy to understand: for the proper implementation of the right requires that the doctor be under a duty to inform his patient of the material risks inherent in the treatment ...

Ideally, the court should ask itself whether in the particular circumstances the risk was such that this particular patient would think it significant if he was told it existed. I would think that, as a matter of ethics, this is the test of the doctor's duty. The law, however, operates not in Utopia but in the world as it is: and such an inquiry would prove in practice to be frustrated by the subjectivity of its aim and purpose. The law can, however, do the next best thing, and require the court to answer the question, what would a reasonably prudent patient think significant if in the situation of this patient? ...

As we have seen, the *Canterbury v Spence* approach, favoured by Lord Scarman, very much equates the need for information and the right to decide upon its materiality, with the patient's right of self-determination.

On the other hand, there is arguably room for an even more patient-friendly standpoint to be adopted. In the case of *Rogers v Whitaker* (1993) 4 Med LR 79, the Australian High Court had to consider the case of a patient who was not warned of a very small risk of blindness. The patient was a woman who had been almost completely blind in her right eye after a childhood injury. Nearly 40 years later she was referred to an eye surgeon who said that removal of the scar tissue would considerably improve the appearance of the eye and might also restore some sight. He failed to warn her that, as a result of surgery, there was a risk (one in 14,000) of her developing sympathetic ophthalmia in her left, good eye. Unfortunately, this risk materialised, leaving the patient totally blind in the left eye and with none of the hoped-for improvement in the right eye. There was no negligence in the performance of the operation, so the question turned on the warning of the risk.

Mason CJ: One consequence of the application of the *Bolam* principle to cases involving the provision of advice or information is that, even if a patient asks a direct question about the possible risks or complications, the making of that inquiry would logically be of little or no significance; medical opinion determines whether the risk should or should not be disclosed and the express desire of a particular patient for information or advice does not alter that opinion or the legal significance of that opinion ...

There is a fundamental difference between, on the one hand, diagnosis and treatment and, on the other hand, the provision of advice or information to the patient. In diagnosis and treatment, the patient's contribution is limited to the narration of symptoms and relevant history; the medical practitioner provides diagnosis and treatment according to his or her level of skill. However, except in cases of emergency or necessity, all medical treatment is preceded by the patients choice to undergo it. In legal terms, the patient's consent to the treatment may be valid once he or she is informed in broad terms of the nature of the procedure which is intended. But the choice is, in reality, meaningless unless it is made on the basis of relevant information and advice. Because the choice to be made calls for a decision by the patient on information known to the medical practitioner but not to the patient, it would be illogical to hold that the amount of information to be provided by the medical practitioner can be determined from the perspective of the practitioner alone or, for that matter, of the medical profession.

Although the majority of the court in *Rogers* relied on the US 'prudent patient' test from *Canterbury v Spence* (including its reference to 'material risks') it appears to have taken a subjective approach to the test, ie, what did *this* patient need to know? The decision did not turn on how the risk would have presented itself to a reasonable patient, but on how important it was to her as an individual. There had been findings of fact that in the nature of the consultation the patient had expressed anxiety about losing her sight, in particular by asking for assurance that it would be clear which was her good eye and which was her damaged eye, to ensure that the operation was carried out on the correct one.

UK developments post-*Sidaway*

The Court of Appeal, in *Gold v Haringey HA* [1988] 1 QB 481, followed the *Bolam* approach to patient information, relying upon the unequivocal judgment of Lord Diplock in *Sidaway*. In this case the court had to consider whether there was any difference between information given in the context of non-therapeutic treatment. The 'non-therapeutic' treatment here was a sterilisation carried out for contraceptive purposes, and the allegation was a negligent failure to warn the plaintiff of the risk of failure of the operation, and of the respective failure rate of vasectomy operations. Lloyd LJ endorsed the application of the *Bolam* test.

> **Lloyd LJ**: ... In the first place the line between therapeutic and non-therapeutic medicine is elusive. A plastic surgeon carrying out a skin graft is presumably engaged in therapeutic surgery; but what if he is carrying out a face-lift, or some other cosmetic operation?
>
> In the second place, a distinction between advice given in a therapeutic context and advice given in a non-therapeutic context would be a departure from the principle on which the *Bolam* test is itself grounded. The principle does not depend on the context in which any act is performed, or any advice given. It depends on a man professing skill or competence in a field beyond that possessed by the man on the Clapham omnibus. If the giving of contraceptive advice required no special skill, then I could see an argument that the *Bolam* test should not apply. But that was not, and could not have been, suggested. The fact (if it be the fact) that giving contraceptive advice involves a different sort of skill and competence from carrying out a surgical operation does not mean that the *Bolam* test ceases to be applicable. It is clear from Lord Diplock's

speech in *Sidaway* that a doctor's duty of care in relation to diagnosis, treatment and advice, whether the doctor be a specialist or general practitioner, is not to be dissected into its component parts. To dissect a doctor's advice into that given in a therapeutic context and that given in a contraceptive context would be to go against the whole thrust of the decision of the majority of the House of Lords in that case. So I would reject Mr Lewis's argument under this head, and hold that judge was not free, as he thought, to form his own view of what warning and information ought to have been given, irrespective of any body of responsible medical opinion to the contrary.

Latterly, though, the lower courts have been more willing to apply the majority judgments in *Sidaway* and to impugn failures by doctors to disclose risk even where there is an accepted practice not to do so (see especially the judgment of Morland J in *Smith v Tunbridge Wells HA* [1994] 5 Med LR 334). In fact, there may be grounds for thinking that the courts in the future will move beyond the *Bolam* test altogether in this area, towards a true doctrine of informed consent as proposed by Lord Scarman. In this regard, the terms of the new Patient's Charter (which refers to the 'right' of patients to receive a clear explanation of risks: see above, Chapter 2) are apposite, as are the somewhat ambiguous comments of Lord Browne-Wilkinson in *Bolitho v City and Hackney HA* [1997] 4 All ER 771 (see below, Chapter 6).

Miscellaneous issues

Answering questions

Consider the following comments of Lord Bridge (p 898) in *Sidaway*:

Lord Bridge: I should perhaps add at this point, although the issue does not strictly arise in this appeal, that, when questioned specifically by a patient of apparently sound mind about risks involved in a particular treatment proposed, the doctor's duty must, in my opinion, be to answer both truthfully and as fully as the questioner requires.

Lord Diplock (p 895) also stated in the same case:

Lord Diplock: No doubt if the plaintiff in fact manifested this attitude by means of questioning, the doctor would tell him whatever it was the patient wanted to know.

Has this difference between the silent patient and the inquiring one been recognised since *Sidaway*? Consider the Court of Appeal case of *Blyth v Bloomsbury HA* [1993] 4 Med LR 151. The case concerned a patient (a qualified nurse) who was given an injection of the contraceptive Depo-Provera following her pregnancy. She alleged it had caused numerous side effects and maintained that she would not have had the drug if she had known of these. The trial judge had accepted that some of the side effects had been caused by the drug, and that the health authority were negligent in failing to answer inquiries made by her.

Kerr LJ: In the particulars of negligence the plaintiff included an allegation that the defendants were negligent by '... (iv) failing to answer the plaintiff's inquiries concerning Depo-Provera accurately and of failing to obtain answers to her questions before attempting to give her the said assurances about the said drug' ...

The question of what a plaintiff should be told in answer to a general inquiry cannot be divorced from the *Bolam* test, any more than when no such inquiry is made. In both cases the answer must depend upon the circumstances, the nature of the inquiry, the nature of the information which is available, its reliability, relevance, the condition of the patient, and so forth. Any medical evidence directed to what would be the proper answer in the light of responsible medical opinion and practice – that is to say, the *Bolam* test – must in my view equally be placed in the balance in cases where the patient makes some inquiry, in order to decide whether the response was negligent or not.

Neill LJ gave a short judgment supporting this view and Balcombe LJ agreed with both of them. This is a surprising decision given that even Lord Diplock in *Sidaway*, the hard-liner when it came to *Bolam*, had made the confident assertion that a doctor would tell an inquiring patient 'whatever it was the patient wanted to know'. Can it be that the case simply reflects the fact that doctors and courts fear that too much time may be taken up with questions from a particularly inquisitive patient? The decision must in any event now be in doubt following the more recent developments since *Sidaway* referred to above, p 155.

Therapeutic privilege

The issue of therapeutic privilege was considered in *Canterbury v Spence* (1972), where it was stated that where the patient is likely to become so distraught by medical information that he is incapable of making a rational decision, information may be withheld on the grounds of the doctor's privilege.

In *Sidaway*, Lord Scarman stressed that the burden of proof is on the doctor: '... there is the need that the doctor should have the opportunity of proving that he reasonably believed that disclosure of the risk would be damaging to his patient or contrary to his best interests.' Would it be preferable to remove all question of 'best interests' and use therapeutic privilege only to mean positive damage to the patient? Otherwise it would appear that doctors could use the defence generally to avoid telling patients of risks to treatment that they feel is in the patient's interests to have. Moreover, such positive damage should arguably only be of such a magnitude as would render the patient incapable of making a decision. In other words, therapeutic privilege would be inextricably linked to capacity.

Causation

Causation does not have to be proved in cases of battery, because trespass to the person is actionable *per se*, with no requirement of damage, so there does not have to be anything which has been caused, and therefore it is irrelevant whether the patient would have gone ahead and consented to the procedure if informed of its nature. Obviously, if the non-consensual procedure does result in damage, then this will affect the amount of compensation awarded. In negligence, however, the patient must establish that if he had been given sufficient information, he would not have gone ahead and had the (injurious) treatment. This issue is looked at below, in Chapter 6.

Battery, negligence and capacity

An interesting problem arises as to the amount of information to be disclosed to patients of impaired or partial capacity. Does the test of capacity differ in deciding whether the patient is capable of consenting (thereby avoiding an action in battery), from the test of capacity in deciding the amount of information that should be given to avoid an action in negligence? If so, might a doctor find that he must accept the consent of a patient of only limited understanding, only to find that he will almost certainly be negligent in not having warned of risks which he thinks the patient would not understand? Or would the prudent doctor test let him off the hook? And, further would the prudent patient test also let him off the hook because the patient would not wish for further information, or because therapeutic privilege would be used to justify the lack of information given?

Mistake

What of the situation where a doctor mistakenly believes the patient has consented? In *Re T (Adult: Refusal of Medical Treatment)* [1992] 4 All ER 649, p 663, Lord Donaldson stated that misinformation, whether given innocently or not, may well vitiate a consent or a refusal. If the patient has not been given enough information so as to be aware of the broad nature of the procedure then a battery will be committed, otherwise there may be the possibility of an action in negligence. On the question of mistake as to capacity, Kennedy and Grubb point out that unreasonable mistakes would give rise *prima facie* to a negligence action. On reasonable mistakes they comment as follows:

> **Kennedy, I and Grubb, A, *Medical Law*, 2nd edn, 1994, London: Butterworths, p 242:**
>
> Deciding which action may be brought is by no means simple: the difficulty lies in whether the mistaken view of the doctor is as to a matter of fact or of opinion ... If it is a mistake of fact, then on first principles an action in battery would lie since mistake is not ordinarily a defence to such an intentional tort

(see *John Lewis and Co Ltd v Tims* [1952] AC 676). There are however exceptions where mistake may be a defence. For example, a policeman making an arrest in the mistaken belief, based on reasonable grounds, that a crime has been committed, would at common law, quite apart from statute, be excused.

Since the House of Lords' decision in *Re F (Mental Patient: Sterilisation)* [1990] 2 AC 1, the doctor will have a defence based upon necessity if on the facts the treatment was in the incompetent patient's best interest. Of course, *Re F* would not apply in the converse position where the doctor decides in good faith that a patient is incompetent when this is not so. *Prima facie* the law in these circumstances would consider the doctor to have committed a battery if he treats the patient in the face of a refusal ...

If, by contrast, in law the mistaken view of the doctor as to the patient's understanding is regarded as relating to a matter of *opinion*, assuming the doctor acts in good faith, then the answer may be different ... On grounds of public policy it may be desirable that the law should recognise a legal excuse for the doctor in these circumstances.

In fact it is submitted that there is no obvious reason why mistakes (whether they be as to the patient's capacity, the information they have been given, or what they have consented to) should be treated differently in themselves. In each case it is arguable that non-negligent mistakes should not be actionable; negligent mistakes should sound in negligence and grossly negligent mistakes should result in an action in battery.

Consent to non-therapeutic procedures

It has been established that there are certain procedures which cannot be carried out lawfully, even with the consent of the patient (see *R v Brown et al* [1993] 2 All ER 75). They usually will not apply to medical procedures because these are almost always therapeutic. However, there are a number of interventions which are not therapeutic and have to be justified by other means. The issue of consent to non-therapeutic research and to organ donation will be considered later in those chapters relating to those topics, but three examples of other, possibly non-therapeutic, procedures are given here.

Gender re-assignment

This is now generally regarded as therapeutic, as such an operation is normally carried out when the patient has exhibited serious and continuing manifestations of the personality of someone of the opposite sex, and is psychologically disturbed by being 'in the wrong body'. Such operations are performed under the NHS as well as privately, and it is highly unlikely that a challenge to their legality would succeed. However, it is important to note that such an operation, carried out on the cosmetic whim of a patient who did not have a history of doubts about his sexual identity, may well constitute a serious criminal offence (see *R v Brown et al*).

Sterilisation/vasectomy

Despite the judgment of Denning LJ in *Bravery v Bravery* [1954] 1 WLR 1169 when he suggested that sterilisation operations carried out for contraceptive purposes were injurious to the public interest, there can be no doubt nowadays that such operations are lawful, and, it must be said, even in that 1954 case, Denning LJ was not supported by his fellow Court of Appeal judges.

Circumcision

Female circumcision is a much more drastic procedure than male circumcision, and results in pain, discomfort, sexual and childbirthing difficulties which do not follow in the case of men. As a result of a number of well publicised cases, female circumcision was criminalised by the Prohibition of Female Circumcision Act 1985.

However, there is no doubt that, even in the male, these operations, when undergone for religious or cultural reasons, are non-therapeutic, yet they are carried out almost without question. Further, they are usually carried out on children, at the behest of their parents, and often without anaesthetic. Although failure to be circumcised may inhibit family relationships, it is also said that it is a practice which results in diminished sexual enjoyment. Christopher Price points out that, historically, the practice has been seen as a means of counteracting excessive lust (12th century), and as a preventive for masturbation (19th century England). He also notes that the medical profession justify carrying out such operations on the basis that they will be performed anyway, and therefore are better done in a clinical setting. He notes that the Bradford Royal Infirmary provide such a service under the NHS. However, he suggests on a number of grounds that the practice should be outlawed.

Price, C, 'Male circumcision: an ethical and legal affront' (1997) Bulletin of Medical Ethics (May) 13:

Rejoicing in our multicultural society does not mean that we should be blind to practices, whatever their source and motive, which are themselves abusive and discriminatory of others, directly and inevitably diminishing the freedoms, human rights, integrity and dignity of others ...

The UN Convention on the Rights of the Child makes the position clearer in respect to circumcision. Article 24(3) provides: 'States Parties shall take all effective and appropriate measures with a view to abolishing traditional practices prejudicial to the health of children.' Some have sought to argue that this provision was only aimed at female circumcision; but this argument cannot hold when the Convention is read with the interpretative provisions of the Vienna Convention on the Law of Treaties 1969.

Referring to the conflict with religious freedom, Price states:

> Customary international law provides that an individual's exercise of his freedoms can legitimately be restrained when so to exercise them is to damage or deny those freedoms to another. Thus, Art 9(2) of the European Convention on Human Rights provides:
>
> > Freedom to manifest one's religion or beliefs shall be subject only to such limitations as are prescribed by law and are necessary in a democratic society in the interests of public safety, for the protection of public order, health or morals, or *for the protection of the rights and freedoms of others'* (emphasis added).
>
> The Convention thus distinguishes between the unfettered right to freedom of thought, and the more restricted right to manifest one's religion.
>
> ... Non-therapeutic circumcision is clearly discriminatory, unethical and illegal. Its prehistoric origins, and its kinship with subincision and other forms of penile mutilation, show its essential barbarity ...

These are strong words, but it is hard to disagree that the procedure is non-therapeutic, and constitutes an assault against the person. Is it tolerated simply to avoid the outcry from the religious communities if action were taken against those who carry it out?

STATUTORY EXCEPTIONS TO THE NEED FOR CONSENT

There are a number of miscellaneous statutory exceptions to the need normally to obtain a person's consent prior to giving medical treatment and care. One relates to the removal to a place of safety of those who, through age or infirmity, are no longer able to care for themselves.

National Assistance Act 1948:

Removal to suitable premises of persons in need of care and attention

47 (1) The following provisions of this section shall have effect for the purposes of securing the necessary care and attention for persons who–

(a) are suffering from grave chronic disease or, being aged, infirm or physically incapacitated, are living in insanitary conditions, and

(b) are unable to devote to themselves, and are not receiving from other persons, proper care and attention.

(2) If the medical officer of health certifies in writing to the appropriate authority that he is satisfied after thorough inquiry and consideration that in the interest of any such person as aforesaid residing in the area of the authority, or for preventing injury to the health of, or serious nuisances to, other persons, it is necessary to remove any such person as aforesaid from the premises in which he is residing, the

appropriate authority may apply to the court of summary jurisdiction having jurisdiction in the place where the premises are situated for an order under the next following sub-section.

It is, however, questionable how far this provision extends to the administration of medical treatment, as conventionally understood. Treatment may also be given without consent under the Mental Health Act 1983, if it is treatment for the mental disorder of a compulsorily detained patient (see further below, Chapter 9).

Finally, a patient who suffers from a contagious disease which may pose risks to the health of the community at large may be compulsorily detained and treated pursuant to the Public Health (Control of Disease) Act 1984. Section 37 of the Act provides:

37 (1) Where a justice of the peace (acting, if he deems it necessary, *ex parte*) is satisfied, on the application of the local authority, that a person is suffering from a notifiable disease and–

(a) that his circumstances are such that proper precautions to prevent the spread of infection cannot be taken, or that such precautions are not being taken; and

(b) that serious risk of infection to other persons is thereby caused to other persons; and

(c) that accommodation for him is available in a suitable hospital vested in the Secretary of State or, pursuant to arrangements made by a health authority (whether under an NHS contract or otherwise), in a suitable hospital vested in an NHS trust or other person,

the justice may, with the consent of the health authority in whose area lies the area, or the greater part of the area, of the local authority, order him to be removed to it.

(2) An order under this section may be addressed to such officer of the local authority as the justice may think expedient, and that officer and any officer of the hospital may do all acts necessary for giving effect to the order.

A list of 'notifiable diseases' is contained in the Public Health (Infectious Diseases) Regulations 1988 SI 1988/1546 and includes meningitis, dysentery, polio, typhoid, malaria, tuberculosis and AIDS.

CHAPTER FOUR

TREATING THE INCOMPETENT PATIENT

There can be no doubt that patients who lack capacity should nevertheless receive medical treatment. The difficulties arise when considering the legal framework in which treatment decisions are made, and the criteria used to decide on the suitability of treatment.

The treatment of the incompetent patient will be considered in later chapters in relation to particular forms of treatment (for example, organ donation – Chapter 11; medical research – Chapter 10; and particular medical situations – where the patient is terminally ill or gravely incapacitated – Chapter 12). In this chapter we will concentrate on the basic legal framework, and general principles, making particular reference to so called non-therapeutic areas relating to the control of fertility by sterilisation and abortion.

THE LEGAL FRAMEWORK

A doctor who treats without a valid consent may still not be liable in an action in battery if he can raise the defence of necessity and has treated the patient in the patient's best interests. Although the defence of necessity must be equated with acting in the best interests of the patient, the defence of necessity is frequently used to refer to emergency treatment carried out on unconscious patients, whilst the best interests defence tends to be referred to when dealing with patients who are permanently lacking in capacity, whether emergency cases or not. It must be stressed, however, that there is no strict dichotomy, and, arguably, the distinction is meaningless.

The temporarily incompetent – necessity

As indicated in the previous chapter, there have been attempts to argue that, for example, when faced with an unconscious patient, a doctor can assume that there is an implied consent to treatment. These attempts, however, have not been successful, and the favoured view is that, in such circumstances, the doctor treats without any consent, but can raise the defence of necessity.

> **Mason, JK and McCall Smith, A, *Law and Medical Ethics*, 1994, London: Butterworths, p 220:**
>
> It is widely recognised in both criminal and civil law that there are circumstances in which acting out of necessity legitimates an otherwise wrongful act ...

Necessity will be a viable defence to any proceedings for non-consensual treatment when an unconscious patient is involved and there is no known objection to treatment. The treatment undertaken, however, must not be more extensive than is required by the exigencies of the situation ... A doctor cannot, therefore, 'take advantage' of unconsciousness to perform procedures which are not essential for the patient's survival.

The defence of necessity, therefore, must necessarily entail the doctor acting in the best interests of the patient. The difference lies in the nature of the treatment. In an emergency, the treatment must be confined to that which is necessary to preserve life and limb, when it is impossible to obtain consent. However, as we shall see, the best interests test will apply to all forms of medical treatment carried out on permanently incompetent patients.

The nature of necessity was examined in the case of *Re F*:

Re F (Mental Patient: Sterilisation) [1990] 2 AC 1:

Lord Goff, p 73: Upon what principle can medical treatment be justified when given without consent? We are searching for a principle upon which, in limited circumstances, recognition may be given to a need, in the interests of the patient, that treatment should be given to him in circumstances where he is (temporarily or permanently) disabled from consenting to it. It is this criterion of a need which points to the principle of necessity as providing justification ...

We are concerned here with action taken to preserve the life, health or well being of another who is unable to consent to it. Such action is sometimes said to be justified as arising from an emergency; in Prosser and Keeton, *Handbook on Torts*, 5th edn, 1984, p 117, the action is said to be privileged by the emergency. Doubtless, in the case of a person of sound mind, there will ordinarily have to be an emergency before such action taken without consent can be lawful; for otherwise there would be an opportunity to communicate with the assisted person and to seek his consent. But this is not always so ...

We can derive some guidance as to the nature of the principle of necessity from the cases on agency of necessity in mercantile law. When reading those cases, however, we have to bear in mind that it was there considered that (since there was a pre-existing relationship between the parties) there was a duty on the part of the agent to act on his principal's behalf in an emergency. From these cases it appears that the principle of necessity connotes that circumstances have arisen in which there is a necessity for the agent to act on his principal's behalf at a time when it is in practice not possible for him to obtain his principal's instructions so to do. In such cases, it has been said that the agent must act bona fide in the interests of his principal: see *Prager v Blatspiel Stamp and Heacock Ltd* [1924] 1 KB 566, p 572, *per* McCardie J. A broader statement of the principle is to be found in the advice of the Privy Council delivered by Sir Montague Smith in *Australasian Steam Navigation Co v Morse* (1872) LR 4 PC 222, p 230, in which he said:

> ... when by the force of circumstances a man has the duty cast upon him of taking some action for another, and under that obligation, adopts the course which, to the judgment of a wise and prudent man, is apparently

the best for the interest of the persons for whom he acts in a given emergency, it may properly be said of the course so taken, that it was, in a mercantile sense, necessary to take it.

In a sense, these statements overlap. But from them can be derived the basic requirements, applicable in these cases of necessity, that, to fall within the principle, not only (1) must there be a necessity to act when it is not practicable to communicate with the assisted person, but also (2) the action taken must be such as a reasonable person would in all the circumstances take acting in the best interests of the assisted person.

On this statement of principle, I wish to observe that officious intervention cannot be justified by the principle of necessity. So intervention cannot be justified when another more appropriate person is available and willing to act; nor can it be justified when it is contrary to the known wishes of the assisted person, to the extent that he is capable of rationally forming such a wish. On the second limb of the principle, the introduction of the standard of a reasonable man should not in the present context be regarded as materially different from that of Sir Montague Smith's 'wise and prudent man', because a reasonable man would, in the time available to him, proceed with wisdom and prudence before taking action in relation to another man's person or property without his consent. I shall have more to say on this point later. Subject to that, I hesitate at present to indulge in any greater refinement of the principle, being well aware of many problems which may arise in its application – problems which it is not necessary, for present purposes, to examine. But as a general rule, if the above criteria are fulfilled, interference with the assisted person's person or property (as the case may be) will not be unlawful. Take the example of a railway accident, in which injured passengers are trapped in the wreckage. It is this principle which may render lawful the actions of other citizens – railway staff, passengers or outsiders – who rush to give aid and comfort to the victims: the surgeon who amputates the limb of an unconscious passenger to free him from the wreckage; the ambulance man who conveys him to hospital; the doctors and nurses who treat him and care for him while he is still unconscious. Take the example of an elderly person who suffers a stroke which renders him incapable of speech or movement. It is by virtue of this principle that the doctor who treats him, the nurse who cares for him, even the relative or friend or neighbour who comes in to look after him, will commit no wrong when he or she touches his body. The two examples I have given illustrate, in the one case, an emergency, and in the other, a permanent or semi-permanent state of affairs. Another example of the latter kind is that of a mentally disordered person who is disabled from giving consent. I can see no good reason why the principle of necessity should not be applicable in his case as it is in the case of the victim of a stroke. Furthermore, in the case of a mentally disordered person, as in the case of a stroke victim, the permanent state of affairs calls for a wider range of care than may be requisite in an emergency which arises from accidental injury. When the state of affairs is permanent, or semi-permanent, action properly taken to preserve the life, health or well being of the assisted person may well transcend such measures as surgical operation or substantial medical treatment and may extend to include such humdrum matters as routine medical or dental treatment, even simple care such as dressing and undressing and putting to bed.

The distinction I have drawn between cases of emergency, and cases where the state of affairs is (more or less) permanent, is relevant in another respect. We are here concerned with medical treatment, and I limit myself to cases of that kind. Where, for example, a surgeon performs an operation without his consent on a patient temporarily rendered unconscious in an accident, he should do no more than is reasonably required, in the best interests of the patient, before he recovers consciousness. I can see no practical difficulty arising from this requirement, which derives from the fact that the patient is expected before long to regain consciousness and can then be consulted about longer term measures. The point has, however, arisen in a more acute form where a surgeon, in the course of an operation, discovers some other condition which, in his opinion, requires operative treatment for which he has not received the patient's consent. In what circumstances he should operate forthwith, and in what circumstances he should postpone the further treatment until he has received the patient's consent, is a difficult matter which has troubled the Canadian courts (see *Marshall v Curry* (1933) 3 DLR 260; and *Murray v McMurchy* (1949) 2 DLR 442), but which it is not necessary for your Lordships to consider in the present case.

But where the state of affairs is permanent or semi-permanent, as may be so in the case of a mentally disordered person, there is no point in waiting to obtain the patient's consent. The need to care for him is obvious; and the doctor must then act in the best interests of his patient, just as if he had received his patient's consent so to do. Were this not so, much useful treatment and care could, in theory at least, be denied to the unfortunate. It follows that, on this point, I am unable to accept the view expressed by Neill LJ in the Court of Appeal ... that the treatment must be shown to have been necessary.

Lord Goff referred to the Canadian case of *Marshall v Curry* [1933] 3 DLR 260, where a patient brought an action in battery against a surgeon who had removed a diseased testicle during the course of a hernia operation. The surgeon tried to argue that it was necessary to remove the testicle because it seriously threatened the health of the patient. In other words, though couched in terms of necessity, the defence, in reality, was that it was in the best interests of the patient to perform this operation. The court held that the removal of the testicle was necessary and that it would have been unreasonable to put the procedure off to a later date. This is a somewhat troubling decision, and was not followed in a later Canadian case. In *Murray v McMurchy* [1949] 2 DLR 442, the patient was a woman who had been sterilised without her consent in the course of a Caesarean section. The defence was that the condition of her uterus was such as to make it dangerous for her to go through another pregnancy. The court held that it would have been reasonable to postpone this operation in order to seek her consent.

It should be recalled that difficulties are raised by the NHS standard consent form, which contains the acknowledgment by the patient that any other procedure will only be carried out if it is necessary and in the patient's best interests and justified for medical reasons (see above, Chapter 3).

The long term incompetent and proxy decision making

The expression 'long term' is used here because, as well as permanently incompetent patients, we are considering the situation of children, and mentally disordered adults who may regain competence at some time, but where the treatment concerned is not emergency treatment. Aside from those patients compulsorily detained under the Mental Health Act 1983 who can be treated for the mental disorder itself without consent (s 63), the presumption is that consent is necessary. As we shall see, this is not always the case, but in cases where there is a lawful proxy or surrogate decision maker, consent may, and sometimes must, be obtained from that source.

The case of *Gillick v West Norfolk and Wisbech AHA* [1986] AC 112 has been considered in Chapter 3, together with the restrictive interpretations of the case in the Court of Appeal in *Re R (A Minor) (Wardship: Medical Treatment)* [1991] 4 All ER 177 and in *Re W (A Minor) (Medical Treatment)* [1992] 4 All ER 627. Regardless of these differences in approach, it is clear that if the child is incompetent consent can be given by parents (or someone *in loco parentis*).

If an adult patient is permanently incompetent, then medical procedures may be carried out without consent. However, it will be seen that the law is significantly different in respect of adults than it is in regard to children. Having said that, however, it must be noted that although the court's jurisdiction in respect of children is much wider, in the case of both adults and children, dubious treatment decisions can only be challenged if there is an interested party willing to bring the matter before the courts. In cases where the patient's family and the patient's doctors agree a course of action there may be no such interested party. In the case of *Re D (A Minor) (Wardship: Sterilisation)* [1976] 1 All ER 326 (considered in detail below, p 199), the proposed sterilisation of a child only came before the court because of the chance intervention by an educational psychologist at the child's school.

Children and the rights of parents

In *Gillick*, on the subject of parental rights Lord Fraser said:

Gillick v West Norfolk and Wisbech AHA [1986] AC 112:

Lord Fraser, p 171: In practice most wise parents relax their control gradually as the child develops and encourage him or her to become increasingly independent. Moreover, the degree of parental control actually exercised over a particular child does in practice vary considerably according to his understanding and intelligence and it would, in my opinion, be unrealistic for the courts not to recognise these facts. Social customs change, and the law ought to, and does in fact, have regard to such changes when they are of major importance ...

In times gone by the father had almost absolute authority over his children until they attained majority. A rather remarkable example of such authority being upheld by the court was *In re Agar-Ellis* (1883) 24 Ch D 317 which was much relied on by the Court of Appeal. The father in that case restricted the communication which his daughter aged 17 was allowed to have with her mother, against whose moral character nothing was alleged, to an extent that would be universally condemned today as quite unreasonable. The case has been much criticised in recent years and, in my opinion, with good reason ...

... In *J v C* [1970] AC 668 Lord Guest and Lord MacDermott referred to the decision in *Agar-Ellis* (1883) 24 Ch D 317 as an example of the almost absolute power asserted by the father over his children before the Judicature Act 1873 and plainly thought such an assertion was out of place at the present time: see Lord MacDermott, pp 703–04. In *Reg v D* [1984] AC 778 Lord Brandon of Oakbrook cited *Agar-Ellis* as an example of the older view of a father's authority which his Lordship and the other members of the House rejected. In my opinion, the view of absolute paternal authority continuing until a child attains majority which was applied in *Agar-Ellis* is so out of line with present day views that it should no longer be treated as having any authority. I regard it as a historical curiosity ...

Once the rule of the parents' absolute authority over minor children is abandoned, the solution to the problem in this appeal can no longer be found by referring to rigid parental rights at any particular age. The solution depends upon a judgment of what is best for the welfare of the particular child. Nobody doubts, certainly I do not doubt, that in the overwhelming majority of cases the best judges of a child's welfare are his or her parents. Nor do I doubt that any important medical treatment of a child under 16 would normally only be carried out with the parents' approval. That is why it would and should be 'most unusual' for a doctor to advise a child without the knowledge and consent of the parents on contraceptive matters. But, as I have already pointed out, Mrs Gillick has to go further if she is to obtain the first declaration that she seeks. She has to justify the absolute right of veto in a parent. But there may be circumstances in which a doctor is a better judge of the medical advice and treatment which will conduce to a girl's welfare than her parents. It is notorious that children of both sexes are often reluctant to confide in their parents about sexual matters, and the DHSS guidance under consideration shows that to abandon the principle of confidentiality for contraceptive advice to girls under 16 might cause some of them not to seek professional advice at all, with the consequence of exposing them to 'the immediate risks of pregnancy and of sexually transmitted diseases'. No doubt the risk could be avoided if the patient were to abstain from sexual intercourse, and one of the doctor's responsibilities will be to decide whether a particular patient can reasonably be expected to act upon advice to abstain. We were told that in a significant number of cases such abstinence could not reasonably be expected ...

... the doctor will, in my opinion, be justified in proceeding without the parents' consent or even knowledge provided he is satisfied on the following matters: (1) that the girl (although under 16 years of age) will understand his advice; (2) that he cannot persuade her to inform her parents or to allow him to inform the parents that she is seeking contraceptive advice; (3) that she is very likely to begin or to continue having sexual intercourse with or without contraceptive treatment; (4) that unless she receives contraceptive advice or treatment her physical or mental health or both are likely to suffer; (5) that her best interests require him to give her contraceptive advice, treatment or both without the parental consent.

Lord Scarman took a similar view (p 182):

Lord Scarman: Mrs Gillick relies on both the statute law and the case law to establish her proposition that parental consent is in all other circumstances necessary. The only statutory provision directly in point is s 8 of the Family Law Reform Act 1969. Sub-section (1) of the section provides that the consent of a minor who has attained the age of 16 to any surgical, mental or dental treatment which in the absence of consent would constitute a trespass to his person shall be as effective as if he were of full age and that the consent of his parent or guardian need not be obtained. Sub-section (3) of the section provides:

> Nothing in this section shall be construed as making ineffective any consent which would have been effective if this section had not been enacted.

I cannot accept the submission made on Mrs Gillick's behalf that sub-s (1) necessarily implies that prior to its enactment the consent of a minor to medical treatment could not be effective in law. Sub-section (3) leaves open the question whether the consent of a minor under 16 could be an effective consent. Like my noble and learned friend Lord Fraser of Tullybelton, I read the section as clarifying the law without conveying any indication as to what the law was before it was enacted. So far as minors under 16 are concerned, the law today is as it was before the enactment of the section ...

The law has, therefore, to be found by a search in the judge-made law for the true principle. The legal difficulty is that in our search we find ourselves in a field of medical practice where parental right and a doctor's may point us in different directions. This is not surprising. Three features have emerged in today's society which were not known to our predecessors: (1) contraception as a subject for medical advice and treatment; (2) the increasing independence of young people; and (3) the changed status of women. In times past contraception was rarely a matter for the doctor: but with the development of the contraceptive pill for women it has become part and parcel of everyday medical practice, as it made clear by the department's *Handbook of Contraceptive Practice*, 1984 revision, particularly para 1.2. Family planning services are now available under statutory powers to all without any express limitation as to age or marital status. Young people, once they have attained the age of 16, are capable of consenting to contraceptive treatment, since it is medical treatment: and, however extensive be parental right in the care and upbringing of children, it cannot prevail so as to nullify the 16 year old's capacity to consent which is now conferred by statute. Furthermore, women have obtained by the availability of the pill a choice of lifestyle with a degree of independence and of opportunity undreamed of until this generation and greater, I would add, than any law of equal opportunity could by itself effect.

The law ignores these developments at its peril ...

... The principle of the law, as I shall endeavour to show, is that parental rights are derived from parental duty and exist only so long as they are needed for the protection of the person and property of the child. The principle has been subjected to certain age limits set by statute for certain purposes: and in some cases the courts have declared an age of discretion at which a child acquires before the age of majority the right to make his (or her) own decision. But these limitations in no way undermine the principle of the law, and should not be allowed to obscure it.

Let me make good, quite shortly, the proposition of principle ...

... It is abundantly plain that the law recognises that there is a right and a duty of parents to determine whether or not to seek medical advice in respect of their child, and, having received advice, to give or withhold consent to medical treatment. The question in the appeal is as to the extent, and duration, of the right and the circumstances in which, outside the two admitted exceptions to which I have earlier referred, it can be overridden by the exercise of medical judgment ...

Although statute has intervened in respect of a child's capacity to consent to medical treatment from the age of 16 onwards, neither statute nor the case law has ruled on the extent and duration of parental right in respect of children under the age of 16. More specifically, there is no rule yet applied to contraceptive treatment, which has special problems of its own and is a latecomer in medical practice. It is open, therefore, to the House to formulate a rule. The Court of Appeal favoured a fixed age limit of 16, basing themselves on a view of the statute law which I do not share and upon their view of the effect of the older case law which for the reasons already given I cannot accept. They sought to justify the limit by the public interest in the law being certain. Certainty is always an advantage in the law, and in some breaches of the law it is a necessity. But it brings with it an inflexibility and a rigidity which in some branches of the law can obstruct justice, impede the law's development, and stamp upon the law the mark of obsolescence where what is needed is the capacity for development. The law relating to parent and child is concerned with the problems of the growth and maturity of the human personality. If the law should impose upon the process of 'growing up' fixed limits, where nature knows only a continuous process, the price would be artificiality and a lack of realism in an area where the law must be sensitive to human development and social change. If certainty be thought desirable, it is better that the rigid demarcations necessary to achieve it should be laid down by legislation after a full consideration of all the relevant factors than by the courts, confined as they are by the forensic process to the evidence adduced by the parties and to whatever may properly fall within the judicial notice of judges. Unless and until Parliament should think fit to intervene, the courts should establish a principle flexible enough to enable justice to be achieved by its application to the particular circumstances proved by the evidence placed before them ...

The modern law governing parental right and a child's capacity to make his own decisions was considered in *Reg v D* [1984] AC 778. The House must, in my view, be understood as having in that case accepted that, save where statute otherwise provides, a minor's capacity to make his or her own decision depends upon the minor having sufficient understanding and intelligence to make the decision and is not to be determined by reference to any judicially fixed age limit ...

In the light of the foregoing I would hold that as a matter of law the parental right to determine whether or not their minor child below the age of 16 will have medical treatment terminates if and when the child achieves a sufficient understanding and intelligence to enable him or her to understand fully what is proposed. It will be a question of fact whether a child seeking advice has sufficient understanding of what is involved to give a consent valid in law. Until the child achieves the capacity to consent, the parental right to make the decision continues save only in exceptional circumstances. Emergency, parental neglect, abandonment of the child, or inability to find the parent are examples of exceptional situations justifying the doctor proceeding to treat the child without parental knowledge and consent: but there will arise, no doubt, other exceptional situations in which it will be reasonable for the doctor to proceed without the parent's consent.

When applying these conclusions to contraceptive advice and treatment it has to be borne in mind that there is much that has to be understood by a girl under the age of 16 if she is to have legal capacity to consent to such treatment. It is not enough that she should understand the nature of the advice which is being given: she must also have a sufficient maturity to understand what is involved. There are moral and family questions, especially her relationship with her parents; long term problems associated with the emotional impact of pregnancy and its termination; and there are the risks to health of sexual intercourse at her age, risks which contraception may diminish but cannot eliminate. It follows that a doctor will have to satisfy himself that she is able to appraise these factors before he can safely proceed upon the basis that she has at law capacity to consent to contraceptive treatment. And it further follows that ordinarily the proper course will be for him, as the guidance lays down, first to seek to persuade the girl to bring her parents into consultation, and if she refuses, not to prescribe contraceptive treatment unless he is satisfied that her circumstances are such that he ought to proceed without parental knowledge and consent.

Most medical decisions made by parents on behalf of their children will be uncontroversial. However, in certain areas, such as the control of fertility, there can be a real conflict between parental wishes and the interests of the child. Bernard M Dickens examines the concept of parental rights.

Dickens, BM, 'Function and limits of parental rights' [1981] 97 LQR 462:

The modern function of parental rights, it is proposed, is not to enforce duties children owe their parents, or simply to enforce against third parties powers of custody and control parents enjoy over their children. It is to permit parents to discharge their duties to their children. These duties are not positively to do good, but to avoid harm. It is obvious that to the extent that ill health and, for instance, illiteracy are considered harm, parents are bound by positive duties to provide health care and education. This proposition may be derived from an abundance of case law and legislation. The duty to avoid harm is more elastic, however, since it affords licence to control a child not for its benefit, but in non-beneficial and non-therapeutic ways falling short of causing or risking harm. The issue to be critically addressed is the point at which an exercise of parental choice over a child's management and future is so potentially harmful to the welfare or interests of the child as to require State intervention and possibly a countermanding of parental choice.

Not surprisingly, the courts recognise that there are limits to the rights of a parent. The case of *Re S (A Minor) (Medical Treatment)* [1993] 1 FLR 376 is a clear illustration of this. The patient was a young child suffering from T-cell leukaemia, treatable only by chemotherapy which necessitated blood transfusions. The parents of the child were devout Jehovah's Witnesses and therefore were fundamentally opposed to blood transfusions. The local authority invoked the inherent jurisdiction of the court under s 100 of the Children Act 1989, and sought an order permitting such treatment to be given.

> **Thorpe J:** ... [T]he test must remain the welfare of the child as the paramount consideration. Specifically, in this case, the choice is not between two medical procedures with similar, if differing, prospects of success. Here the stark choice is between one medical procedure with no prospect of success and one medical treatment with a prospect of success which is put at even.
>
> So, as I put to Mr Daniel in argument: are the religious convictions of the parents to deny their child a 50% chance of survival? Are those convictions to deny him that 50% chance and condemn him to inevitable and early death? Mr Daniel realistically saw that this was an extreme case and one in which it is difficult to pursue the argument that the religious convictions of the parents should deny the child the chance of treatment.
>
> Finally, Mr Daniel invites the court to look ahead to the later years of childhood. If this treatment is applied in the face of parental opposition what would be the difficulties and stresses for S in years to come – parented by parents who believe that his life was prolonged by an ungodly act? Well, that consideration seems to me one that has little foundation in reality. The reality seems to me to be that family reaction will recognise that the responsibility for consent was taken from them and, as a judicial act, absolved their conscience of responsibility.

Parental opposition to clinical decisions was considered in the case of *Re C (A Minor)* [1998] 1 Lloyd's Rep Med 1. The patient was a 16 month old baby, suffering from spinal muscular atrophy, and said to be seriously disabled and severely emaciated. For a few weeks before the case came before the court, the child had been ventilated to support her own breathing. The opinion of the consultant paediatric neurologist in charge of the child's care was that no further ventilation should take place, and if, following withdrawal of the ventilation, the child should undergo further respiratory arrest, she should not be resuscitated. The evidence was that further respiratory arrest would mean long term ventilator dependency. The parents of the child, who were religious orthodox Jews, were opposed to this. They agreed that ventilation should be withdrawn, but would not agree that no attempt at resuscitation be made. A second medical opinion was obtained which supported the opinion of the treating doctor. Sir Stephen Brown P held that support of the parents' view would be tantamount to requiring doctors to undertake a course of treatment which they were unwilling to do, and no order would be made to this effect. Clinical judgment, however, will not always prevail, as will be seen from the case of *Re T (A Minor) (Wardship: Medical Treatment)* [1997] 1 All ER 906.

In the case of *Re S* above, Thorpe J was considering a case where the treatment objected to (the blood transfusion) carried virtually no risk, and nothing more than inconvenience to the child. What about the case of a parent who refuses to agree to a difficult form of treatment which may be lengthy and painful? This was considered in the case of *Re T (A Minor) (Wardship: Medical Treatment)* [1997] 1 All ER 906. The child was born with a serious liver defect and underwent surgery at the age of three and a half weeks. The operation caused pain and distress and was unsuccessful. The medical prognosis was that without a liver transplant the child would not live more than a couple of years. The mother refused consent to a transplant. The child's father (to whom she was not married) agreed with her. Both patents were described as 'health care professionals' with experience of caring for sick children. The mother had moved out of the country at the time of the hearing of the local authority's application for permission for the operation to be carried out. The application had been brought at the behest of the consultants who had treated the child. The judge at first instance granted the application on the basis that it was in the child's best interests for it to be carried out and that the mother was being 'unreasonable'. The Court of Appeal allowed the mother's appeal.

> **Waite LJ**: ... The law's insistence that the welfare of a child shall be paramount is easily stated and universally applauded, but the present case illustrates, poignantly and dramatically, the difficulties that are encountered when trying to put it into practice. Throughout his clear and able judgment, the judge demonstrated his appreciation of the dilemma to which the case gives rise. Loving and devoted parents have taken, after anxious consideration, a decision to withhold consent to operative transplant treatment. Although it is relatively novel treatment, still unavailable in many countries, doctors of the highest expertise have unanimously recommended it for this child on clinical grounds, taking the view that it involves a relatively minor level of risk which they regard as well worth taking in the child's long term interests (which in this instance include an extension of life itself). The parents' opposition is partly instinctive and (being based on their own awareness of the procedures involved) partly practical. It has sufficient cogency to have led one of the principal medical experts in the field of this operation to say that his team would decline to operate without the mother's committed support.

What is the court to do in such a situation? It is not an occasion – even in an age preoccupied with 'rights' – to talk of the rights of a child, or the rights of a parent, or the rights of the court. The cases cited by Butler-Sloss LJ are uncompromising in their assertion that the sole yardstick must be the need to give effect to the demands of paramountcy for the welfare of the child. They establish that there are bound to be occasions when such paramountcy will compel the court, acting as a judicial parent, to substitute the judge's own views as to the claims of child welfare over those of natural parents – even in a case where the views of the latter are supported by qualities of devotion, commitment, love and reason. The judge, after anxious consideration, reached the conclusion that this case provides such an occasion. Was he right to do so?

Of course if his decision was founded on a correct application of legal principle, it is unassailable, however tempted individual members of an appellate court might be to substitute a judgment of our own. These decisions, not least because they are so difficult and finely balanced, are best left to the discretion of the experienced judges who have the task, often a lonely and worrying one, of weighing the numerous delicate elements (including the view taken of the parties and witnesses) which enable a cumulative picture to be formed of the demands of welfare in a particular case, and taking the momentous decision which the child patient cannot take for himself.

In this instance, however, in agreement with Butler-Sloss LJ, I consider that the judge was betrayed into an error of law by his concern with the need to form a judgment about the reasonableness of the mother's approach. An appraisal of parental reasonableness may be appropriate in other areas of family law (in adoption, for example, where it is enjoined by statute), but when it comes to an assessment of the demands of the child patient's welfare, the starting point – and the finishing point too – must always be the judge's own independent assessment of the balance of advantage or disadvantage of the particular medical step under consideration.

In striking that balance, the judge will of course take into account as a relevant, often highly relevant, factor the attitude taken by a natural parent, and that may require examination of his or her motives. But the result of such an inquiry must never be allowed to prove determinative. It is a mistake to view the issue as one in which the clinical advice of doctors is placed in one scale and the reasonableness of the parent's view in the other. Had the judge viewed the evidence more broadly from the standpoint of his own perception of the child's welfare when appraised in all its aspects, he would have been bound, in my view, to take significant account of other elements in the case. Those include the parents' ties in country AB, and – crucially – the evidence of Dr P.

No one disputes that in the aftermath of the operation the child would remain in the primary care of the mother. Dr P maintained a very clear view that – even assuming that the operation proved wholly successful in surgical terms – the child's subsequent development could be injuriously affected if his day to day care depended upon the commitment of a mother who had suffered the turmoil of having her child being compelled against her will to undergo, as a result of a coercive order from the court, a major operation against which her own medical and maternal judgment wholeheartedly rebelled.

All these cases depend on their own facts and render generalisations – tempting though they may be to the legal or social analyst – wholly out of place. It can only be said safely that there is a scale, at one end of which lies the clear case where parental opposition to medical intervention is prompted by scruple or is of a kind which is patently irreconcilable with principles of child health and welfare widely accepted by the generality of mankind; and that at the other end lie highly problematic cases where there is genuine scope for a difference of view between parent and judge. In both situations it is the duty of the judge to allow the court's own opinion to prevail in the perceived paramount interests of the child concerned, but in cases at the latter end of the scale, there must be a likelihood (though never of course a certainty) that the greater the scope for genuine debate between one view and another the stronger will be the inclination of the court to be influenced by a reflection that in the last analysis the best interests of every child include an expectation that difficult decisions affecting the length and quality of its life will be taken for it by the parent to whom its care has been entrusted by nature. I too would allow this appeal.

Is the distinction between the 'welfare of the child' approach and the 'reasonableness of the parent' approach one of semantics only? In other words, was the first instance decision that the mother was being unreasonable only another way of saying that she was not acting in the best interests of the child, and that the Court of Appeal was wrong to disturb the decision?

It is also of some concern that the Court of Appeal was relying too heavily upon the judgment of the mother to whom the child's care 'has been entrusted by nature'. Marie Fox and Jean McHale, referring to Butler-Sloss LJ's judgment, comment as follows:

Fox, M and McHale, J, 'In whose best interests?' [1997] 60 MLR 700:

... a significant feature is the emphasis in the Court of Appeal judgments on the parents' status as health care professionals, with experience of paediatric care. However it is questionable whether such significance should have been attributed to the parents' profession. It should be noted that, in the context of medical treatment, there is some evidence that health care professionals are actively discouraged from treating their families. However, amongst the professional bodies there appears to be uncertainty about the ethics of the practice. While the General Medical Council and United Kingdom Council for Nursing, Midwifery and Health Visiting do not censure health professionals who treat themselves or their family members, the British Medical Association regards such practice as unethical. In *Re T*, however, the Court of Appeal drew an implicit distinction between medical treatment on the one hand and 'caring' on the other. This calls into question whether the same objections apply when health professionals are involved in caring for their own children, and what weight their views should carry in this context. Pinpointing the divide between treatment and care is a process fraught with difficulties, especially since caring may be entrusted to either professionals or lay persons. Such difficulties become particularly acute where parents are also health practitioners. Significantly, this policy issue was not addressed in *Re T*. In part, the Court of Appeal was able to avoid the issue by downplaying the importance of medical opinion. A striking feature of the judgments is that there is virtually no reference to medical evidence. This is in stark contrast to earlier cases, such as *Re C* and *Re J*, where a wealth of expert evidence was cited. Indeed, in *Re T*, greater weight appeared to be placed on a fact sheet published by the Children's Liver Disease Foundation (which highlighted the general complications of liver transplantation, thus endorsing the parental reservations about treatment) than on the specific medical evidence pertaining to this child. Thus, rather than focusing on the evidence which would have justified treatment, the judges focused on the implications for the carers should treatment be authorised against their will. A further point is that the judgments do not clarify whether the significance of the parents' occupations lies simply in their status as health professionals or is derived from their greater competence as decision makers.

Since the legitimacy of according carers an enhanced decision making role by virtue solely of their status as health care professionals is questionable, we need to explore whether other special features of this case justify the weight accorded to the position of the carers. In this regard Butler-Sloss LJ noted that:

> Some of the objections of the mother, such as the difficulties of the operation itself, turned out ... to be less important than the mother believed. Underlying those less important objections by the mother was deep-seated concern of the mother as to the benefits to her son of the major invasive surgery and post-operative treatment, the dangers of failure long term as well as short term, the possibility of the need for further transplants, the likely length of life and the impact upon her son of all these concerns.

Thus, the mother's opposition to the procedure is represented as rooted in caring attitudes. Butler-Sloss LJ also refers to 'the enormous significance of the close attachment between the mother and baby'. Yet there are unresolved tensions in this portrayal of the mother. We are given little evidence to support the court's opinion that this mother was exceptionally devoted. Furthermore, even assuming that this representation is accurate, two troublesome issues arise. First, if we accept the court's depiction of her as especially caring, it was surely incumbent upon the judges to examine why she was so reluctant to undertake the care of her son following a procedure which could save his life, particularly in view of her professional expertise in this area. Secondly, there is no exploration of the relationship between caring and reasonableness. It must be doubted whether the decisions of an exceptionally caring parent, even one who is a health professional herself, may automatically be deemed reasonable ones ...

A further noteworthy point is the manner in which caring was construed as the mother's responsibility rather than that of both the parents. Nowhere in the judgments was the role of the father clearly articulated. In the circumstances this may have been largely because the parents were unmarried so that parental responsibility was vested in the mother alone. Certainly, the effect of the relative marginality of the father was to make it easier for the court to depict the mother as sole carer and then to conflate the interests of mother and child. This occurs most strikingly in the following passage of Butler-Sloss LJ's judgment:

> This mother and child are one for the purpose of this unusual case and the decision of the court to consent to the operation jointly affects the mother and son and it also affects the father. The welfare of this child depends upon his mother.

... It may be questioned what the broader implications of this line of reasoning are for the autonomy of the mother in cases where no clinical support exists for her views, with the result that they are not upheld by the court.

Nevertheless, in this case, construing the mother and child as one permitted the Court of Appeal to minimise the potential conflict between the interests of the woman and child. It effectively allowed the court to encompass within the best interests test the interests of the mother as carer as well as the interests of the child. The problem of disentangling the determination of best interests from the question of who decides is rendered still more intractable by the court's reasoning in this case. Thus, it is significant that when Butler-Sloss LJ considered the consequences of upholding the judge's original order that the child should be returned to England for treatment, her emphasis was upon the difficulties and inconvenience of such an outcome for the mother:

> She will have to comply with the court order; return to this country and present the child to one of the hospitals. She will have to arrange to stay in this country for the foreseeable future ... If [the father] does not come she will have to manage unaided. How will the mother cope? Can her professionalism overcome her view that her son should not be subjected this distressing procedure? Will she break down? How will the child be affected by the conflict with which the mother may have to cope?

... surely the Court of Appeal's approach in this case is exceptional, given that in the Jehovah's Witness cases cited above doctors were prepared to undertake treatment in the face of intransigent parental opposition?

Certainly, there is cause for concern in intertwining the interests of a child and its mother, or indeed a child and its parents. It is difficult to see the difference between *Re T* and cases where sincere religious views of caring parents are overridden in the best interests of the child.

In the case of *Re T*, the parents purported to care for their child, despite the potentially tragic consequences of their views holding sway. In a case where the parents simply do not want the child to live, judicial decision making is more clear cut. The case of *Re B (A Minor) (Wardship: Medical Treatment)* [1981] 1 WLR 1421 may have been such a case. The child was a newly born Down's syndrome baby who also had an intestinal complaint that required surgery in order for the child to survive. The parents refused consent. Their view was that the child would be better off dead. This may have been because they anticipated a poor life ahead for the child, or it may have been the fact that they did not want a Down's syndrome child. In that case, the Court of Appeal authorised the treatment. Templeman LJ described the choice as a stark one between authorising the operation so that the child may live for 20 or 30 years as a mongoloid, or terminating the life of a mongoloid child because she also has an intestinal complaint. (See below, Chapter 12 for further discussion of this and other cases of gravely incapacitated children.)

The question of parental rights was considered in the case of *Re P (A Minor)* (1982) 80 LGR 301, when Butler-Sloss J made an order for the termination of a 15 year old girl's pregnancy in the face of her parents' opposition. The girl already had a baby and resided in a special mother and baby unit. Her parents wanted to care for the second child she was carrying, and her father objected to abortion on religious grounds.

> **Butler-Sloss J:** I would not like it to be thought that because she says she does not want the child her wishes should be given such paramount importance as to mean that for that reason only she should have an abortion. But where her wishes coincide with the facts that she is in danger of injury to her mental health; that she is undoubtedly – when I consider her interests, as I do, as the first and paramount consideration – unable to fulfil her own growing up as a child at her schooling as a consequence of this second pregnancy; where she is endangering the future of her current child; and where I take into account all the aspects of her actual and reasonably foreseeable environment, I have no doubt that this case comes within s 1(a) of the Abortion Act 1967 ...
>
> I must take into account in considering the welfare of Shirley – and her welfare is what is paramount in my mind because she is a ward of court – and through her the effect on her son of having this unwanted child, the important aspect of her parents. I was helpfully reminded of what had been said in the House of Lords in *J v C* [1970] AC 668 about the rights and obligations of parents. These parents are in certain difficulties in that they do not have the day to day care of Shirley since she is in care, and they are not able to offer to take over the day to day care of Shirley. In the circumstances, although I must give weight to their feelings as a factor in the case to be taken into consideration, and I must take into account their deeply and sincerely held religious objection, in considering the best interest of the minor as to whether she should have her pregnancy terminated I draw to some extent an analogy with Jehovah's Witnesses and blood transfusions ... I am satisfied ... that there is a risk of injury to the mental health of this minor, the factors raised by the grandfather on behalf of himself and his wife – which I have taken into account – cannot weigh in the balance against the needs of this girl so as to prevent the termination which I have decided is necessary in her best interests.

This may be thought to be in stark contrast with the views expressed by Butler-Sloss LJ in the much later case of *Re T*, above, p 176. However, even if it had been in issue, the closeness of the parent/child relationship, which was regarded as so important in *Re T*, would not have been relevant here as, unlike the case of a young, sick child, there was no question of this child needing her parents to care for her.

Note that in *Re P* the judge had to take into account the provisions of the Abortion Act 1967, where, *inter alia*, there has to be a risk to the health of the pregnant woman (see below, Chapter 8), and therefore the decision could not be made on the basis of her wishes alone. However, in abortion cases, it is always arguable that a child who does not want to continue with her pregnancy is going to be mentally damaged if she is compelled to continue it. In the context of other areas of medicine and surgery, however, might the wishes of the child also override those of the parents if the child's welfare demands it?

See also the case of *Re Z (A Minor) (Freedom of Publication)* [1995] 4 All ER 961.

Children and the role of the court

Decisions concerning the treatment of children can come before the court via the Children Act 1989 (specific issue orders under s 8), or via the jurisdiction of the High Court. The wardship jurisdiction must be distinguished from the inherent jurisdiction of the High Court. In the former case parental authority is vested in the court; in the latter the court is dealing only with the particular treatment issue put before it. The inherent jurisdiction of the court may be invoked by local authorities, as the wardship jurisdiction is unavailable to them. Regardless of the nature of the judicial proceedings, the welfare of the child is paramount.

Adults and the rights of others

In a number of the sterilisation cases we are about to consider, it was argued that the views of the close relatives of the patients were relevant to the final outcome of the cases. However, though taken into account by the courts, as they were in the case of *Re P*, the case concerning a child, the argument that a close relative's views could in any way be determinative has been rejected. In the Canadian case of *Re Eve* (1986) 2 SCR 388, La Forest J stated:

> **La Forest J**: One may sympathise with Mrs E [the adult patient's mother]. To use Heilbron J's phrase, it is easy to understand the natural feelings of a parent's heart. But the *parens patriae* jurisdiction cannot be used for her benefit. Its exercise is confined to doing what is necessary for the benefit and protection of persons under disability like Eve. And a court ... must exercise great caution to avoid being misled by this all too human mixture of emotions and motives.

(See below, p 180, for explanation of the *parens patriae* jurisdiction.)

Commenting upon the use of surrogate decision makers, Pellegrino and Thomasma state:

> **Pellegrino, ED and Thomasma, DC,** *For the Patient's Good,* **1988, Oxford: OUP, p 164:**
>
> Some have argued that the family is almost always the best surrogate because of the family member's 'bonding' to the patient. This may not always be the case. The physician's first responsibility ... is to ascertain the moral validity –

that is to say, the moral acceptability – of the surrogate decision maker. This is the only way the physician can fulfil his or her own responsibility as steward of the patient's interests.

The criteria for a morally valid surrogate decision are as follows:

(1) First, the surrogate must provide some evidence that he or she really knows the patient and his or her values. This is not necessarily the case even with families. In our mobile society parents and children are often separated geographically; they may be estranged from each other, or may not have seen each other for a long time. Friends may have a closer, or more recent, knowledge of what the patient would want. Nurses may know more about a patient in a long term care setting than does the patient's family.

(2) Further, the surrogate or proxy must not have a conflict of interest with the patient's best interests. The desire for gain – settlement of an estate, inheritance of property, changing a will, and so on – can impel surrogates, consciously or not, to hasten a patient's death by undertreatment.

(3) Also to be guarded against is the deleterious effect of psychological antipathies – the unconscious desire to overtreat a patient whom one has neglected or maltreated for many years, or, conversely, the motivation to undertreat and thus act vindictively to settle old scores.

The relevance of blood ties was considered by the Court of Appeal in the case of *Re S (Hospital Order: Court's Jurisdiction)* [1995] 3 All ER 290. The plaintiff was the patient's cohabitee and the defendant, his son. Hale J, at first instance, (approved in the Court of Appeal, p 295):

Hale J: Yet although his relationship to the patient is a close one, and his wishes are of course worthy of respect, he has no more legal right to decide the patient's future than has the plaintiff. Indeed, were this to be a Mental Health Act case, the facts might be such that the plaintiff (rather than the wife) would be the patient's nearest relative for the purposes of s 26 of the Mental Health Act 1983.

It will be seen in Chapter 9 that, under the Mental Health Act, a blood relative is readily capable of displacement as the patient's 'nearest relative'.

Adults and the role of the court

It may seem odd, but in English law there is no mechanism whereby someone may be sanctioned to make decisions about medical treatment on behalf of an adult patient. Incompetent adults once had protection: there was an inherent power in the courts (known as the *parens patriae* jurisdiction) to act on behalf of the incapacitated adult in very much the same way as minors are still protected today. This is the jurisdiction extant in the Canadian legal process referred to by La Forest J in the judgment in *Re Eve* above, p 179. However, the royal warrant by which this power was delegated to the courts was revoked shortly after the 1959 Mental Health Act came into force because it was believed that the Act made all necessary provision for mental patients. However, whilst there is power to appoint a guardian in respect of the patient's financial affairs, who is then overseen by the Court of Protection, no such power exists in respect of the personal welfare or health of the patient. The result is that, although it is possible to bring cases before the courts when a doctor wants to treat a patient who is incapable of giving consent, the mechanism is such that the court can only make a declaration that the proposed treatment is lawful (pursuant to RSC Ord 15 r 16); it cannot make a decision *on behalf* of a patient, either directly, or through an appointed guardian. This may mean that forms of treatment which are alternatives to that proposed by the physicians in the case cannot be authorised by the court. Brenda Hoggett examines the situation of children and mentally impaired adults, and considers how far they may be comparable:

> Hoggett, B, 'The royal prerogative in relation to the mentally disordered: resurrection, resuscitation or rejection' in Freeman, MD (ed), *Medicine, Ethics and the Law*, 1988, London: Stevens, pp 88–89:
>
> ... the analogy between the protection of children and the protection of adult handicapped people can never be exact. First, the court's jurisdiction over children can arise automatically by reference to the objectively determinable fact of age; a similar automatic jurisdiction does not and cannot apply to the handicapped. Secondly, the court's powers in wardship are there to supplement, override or replace the powers and responsibilities of parents; although the court's powers may be somewhat more extensive, at least in their enforceability, they are operating against a background of existing powers over and responsibilities for the upbringing of children. No such powers and responsibilities can be assumed in respect of adult handicapped people. Thirdly, therefore, if the court does not intervene to take a particular decision about a child, it may generally be assumed that somebody else would be able to do so; depending upon the nature of the decision and the capacities of the child, this may be either the parents or the child himself. As we have already seen, if the adult handicapped person does not himself have the capacity to take the particular decision, there is usually no one who can take it on his behalf. These distinctions may support rather than undermine the case for some protective machinery, but they also suggest that it cannot be quite like the machinery applied to children.

Doctors wishing to carry out, say, a sterilisation operation on a teenage girl may, therefore, do so in the knowledge that the safeguards for the patient are much less effective once she has reached the age of 18, and no longer subject to the jurisdiction of the court as a minor.

Doctors make decisions about medical treatment and the incompetent purely on the basis of what they, the doctors, believe to be best for the patient. The great majority of these decisions will be uncontroversial, but some can have huge ethical significance, and, in those circumstances, although doctors would be wise to seek the appropriate declaration from the court, they are under no obligation to do so. The case of *In re F (Mental Patient: Sterilisation)*

[1990] 2 AC 1 concerned the sterilisation of a mentally impaired woman aged 36, but said to have an overall mental age of four or five. The case is considered in further detail below, p 192, but on the subject of the court's role, Lord Brandon said as follows (p 56):

> **Lord Brandon**: ... [The] question is whether, in the case of an operation for the sterilisation of an adult woman of child-bearing age, who is mentally disabled from giving or refusing her consent to it, although involvement of the court is not strictly necessary as a matter of law, it is nevertheless highly desirable as a matter of good practice. In considering that question, it is necessary to have regard to the special features of such an operation. These features are: first, the operation will in most cases be irreversible; secondly, by reason of the general irreversibility of the operation, the almost certain result of it will be to deprive the woman concerned of what is widely, and as I think rightly, regarded as one of the fundamental rights of a woman, namely, the right to bear children; thirdly, the deprivation of that right gives rise to moral and emotional considerations to which many people attach great importance; fourthly, if the question whether the operation is in the best interests of the woman is left to be decided without the involvement of the court, there may be a greater risk of it being decided wrongly, or at least of it being thought to have been decided wrongly; fifthly, if there is no involvement of the court, there is a risk of the operation being carried out for improper reasons or with improper motives; and, sixthly, involvement of the court in the decision to operate, if that is the decision reached, should serve to protect the doctor or doctors who perform the operation, and any others who may be concerned in it, from subsequent adverse criticisms or claims.
>
> Having regard to all these matters, I am clearly of the opinion that, although in the case of an operation of the kind under discussion involvement of the court is not strictly necessary as a matter of law, it is nevertheless highly desirable as a matter of good practice.
>
> There may be cases of other special operations to which similar considerations would apply. I think it best, however, to leave such other cases to be examined as and when they arise.

Only Lord Griffiths dissented from the view that an application to the court remains within the discretion of the doctors concerned (p 70):

> **Lord Griffiths**: ... I cannot agree that it is satisfactory to leave this grave decision with all its social implications in the hands of those having the care of the patient with only the expectation that they will have the wisdom to obtain a declaration of lawfulness before the operation is performed. In my view the law ought to be that they must obtain the approval of the court before they sterilise a woman incapable of giving consent and that it is unlawful to sterilise without that consent. I believe that it is open to your Lordships to develop a common law rule to this effect ...
>
> The *parens patriae* jurisdiction is in any event now only available in the case of minors through their being made wards of court. I would myself declare that on grounds of public interest an operation to sterilise a woman incapable of giving consent either on grounds of age or mental incapacity is unlawful if performed without the consent of the High Court.

Similarly, in the earlier case of *Re B (A Minor) (Wardship: Sterilisation)* [1988] AC 199, only Lord Templeman took the view that court approval should always be obtained. However, in the Australian High Court's decision in *Department of Health v JWB and SMB* (1992) 66 ALJR 300, although the judges did not express the view that it is mandatory to apply to the court in the case of a therapeutic sterilisation, in the case of a non-therapeutic sterilisation (ie, a sterilisation carried out where the physical health of the patient does not demand it), the court held that it required prior court approval. Although this case and the case of *Re B* concerned children, it is arguable that exactly the same view should be taken in the case of an incompetent adult.

When *Re F* was heard in the Court of Appeal, the view was taken that the declaratory process was unsatisfactory (p 20):

> **Lord Donaldson MR:** For my part, I do not think that this [the declaration procedure] is an appropriate procedure. A declaration changes nothing. All that the court is being asked to do is to declare that, had a course of action been taken without resort to the court, it would have been lawful anyway. In the context of the most sensitive and potentially controversial forms of treatment the public interest requires that the courts should give express approval before the treatment is carried out and thereby provide an independent and broad-based 'third option'. In the case of wards of court, the performance of any such operation without first obtaining the approval of the court would in any event constitute a very grave contempt of court. In the case of other minors, the law will impose a very heavy burden of justification on those who carry out the treatment without first ensuring that the minors are made wards of court and the court's consent obtained. In the case of adults who are themselves incompetent to consent, the law will impose an equally heavy burden of justification if those who carry out the treatment do not first seek a determination of the lawfulness of the proposed treatment by enabling the court to approve or disapprove.

Most of the cases using the declaratory jurisdiction have been brought by the health carers involved with the patient. However, it was used in the case of *Re S (Hospital Order: Court's Jurisdiction)* [1995] 3 All ER 290 to decide a dispute between the wife and the mistress of a elderly Norwegian who had become incompetent following a stroke. Both wife and mistress wanted to care for him. The court held that the declaratory jurisdiction could be used by anyone with a genuine and legitimate interest in obtaining a decision on a serious justiciable issue. The dispute in this case was found to be such an issue.

In the context of abortion, in *Re SG (A Patient)* [1993] 4 Med LR 75, the High Court has held that it is not necessary to seek the specific approval of the court:

> **Sir Stephen Brown P:** I have no doubt on the facts of this case that, if a declaration such as was considered in the case of *Re F* is required as a matter of good practice, I should make it, but in the light of the present state of the law I accept the submissions of the Official Solicitor that it is not necessary that the specific approval of the High Court should be a condition precedent to the

carrying out of a termination of pregnancy. I consider that the Abortion Act 1967 provides fully adequate safeguards for the doctors who are to undertake this treatment. Accordingly, I am prepared to indicate that in my judgment a formal declaration is not required for this particular treatment. However, it is important that I should also make it clear that the conditions of s 1 of the Abortion Act 1967 must be complied with.

This is an unsatisfactory decision. It will be seen (in Chapter 8) that the provisions of the Abortion Act are very easily complied with, and, in a case such as this, where the doctors were firmly decided that an abortion should take place, the Act does not safeguard an incompetent patient.

The Law Commission, *Report on Mental Incapacity*, Report No 231, 1995, London: HMSO put forward a number of recommendations which would include a form of guardianship in respect of medical decision making, a new Court of Protection, and court-appointed managers of the personal welfare affairs of the mentally incapacitated. In December 1997, the Lord Chancellor's Department published a Green Paper, 'Who Decides?', which is closely based upon the Law Commission's report.

DECISION MAKING CRITERIA

The therapeutic/non-therapeutic distinction

Most medical procedures performed on mentally incompetent patients will be carried out to cure or ameliorate the effects of disease and disorder. However, this will not always be the case. In the case of medical research on healthy volunteers (see below, Chapter 10), and the control of fertility (see below, p 195), there is no physical or mental disorder which is being treated. It is common to refer to these latter cases as instances of non-therapeutic 'treatment'. Of course, they are not really 'treatment' cases at all. However, when the patient is incompetent and the procedure is being carried out on the basis of his 'best interests', the English courts have questioned whether the distinction has any useful purpose.

The validity of making such a distinction was accepted by the Australian High Court in the case of *Secretary, Department of Health and Community Services v JWB and SMB* (1992) 66 ALJR 300. However, although accepting that there is a distinction, all seven judges acknowledged that it was not easy to draw the line. Brennan J suggests the following distinguishing factors:

> **Brennan J**: ... It is necessary to define what is meant by therapeutic medical treatment. I would define treatment (including surgery) as therapeutic when it is administered for the chief purpose of preventing, removing or ameliorating a cosmetic deformity, a pathological condition or a psychiatric disorder, provided the treatment is appropriate for and proportionate to the purpose for which it is administered. 'Non-therapeutic' medical treatment is descriptive of

treatment which is inappropriate or disproportionate having regard to the cosmetic deformity, pathological condition or psychiatric disorder for which the treatment is administered and of treatment which is administered chiefly for other purposes.

In the Canadian case of *Re Eve* (1986) 2 SCR 388, the distinction was crucial to the decision of the court. The case concerned a 24 year old woman suffering from extreme expressive aphasia, which is a condition inhibiting the patient from communicating thoughts and feelings. She was described as being mildly to moderately retarded. It was accepted that she may be able to carry out the physical aspects of child care, but due to her severe lack of communication skills she would not make a suitable mother in the wider sense. As a result of what was described as a close relationship with a male student at the school for retarded adults that she attended, her mother became concerned and wished her to be sterilised.

> **La Forest J:** ... [I]t is difficult to imagine a case in which non-therapeutic sterilisation could possibly be of benefit to the person on behalf of whom a court purports to act, let alone one for in which that procedure is necessary in his or her best interest. And how are we to weigh the best interests of a person in this troublesome area, keeping in mind that an error is irreversible? Unlike other cases involving the use of the *parens patriae* jurisdiction, an error cannot be corrected by the subsequent exercise of judicial discretion. That being so, one need only recall Lord Eldon's remark ... that 'it has always been the principle of this court, not to risk damage to children which it cannot repair' to conclude that non-therapeutic sterilisation may not be authorised in the exercise of the parens patriae jurisdiction.
>
> McQuaid J was, therefore, right in concluding that he had no authority or jurisdiction to grant the application.

In the case of *Re B (A Minor) (Wardship: Sterilisation)* [1988] AC 199, the distinction was rejected. The child in this case was 17 years old and described as having the mental age of a five or six year old. She was in the care of the local authority, and, when it was thought that she was exhibiting signs of some sexual appetite, it applied to the High Court for leave for her to be sterilised. The case eventually reached the House of Lords.

> **Lord Hailsham of St Marylebone LC:** We were also properly referred to the Canadian case of *Re Eve* ... I find, with great respect, [La Forest J's] conclusions ... that the procedure of sterilisation 'should never be authorised for non-therapeutic purposes' (my emphasis) totally unconvincing and in startling contradiction to the welfare principle which should be the first and paramount consideration in wardship cases. Moreover, for the purposes of the present appeal I find the distinction he purposes to draw between 'therapeutic' and 'non-therapeutic' purposes of this operation in relation to the facts of the present case above as totally meaningless, and, if meaningful, quite irrelevant to the correct application of the welfare principle.
>
> ... To say that the court can never authorise sterilisation of a ward as being in her best interests would be patently wrong. To say that it can only do so if the

operation is 'therapeutic' as opposed to 'non-therapeutic' is to divert attention from the true issue, which is whether the operation is in the ward's best interests, and remove it to an area of arid semantic debate as to where the line is to be drawn between 'therapeutic' and 'non-therapeutic' treatment.

Kennedy and Grubb comment as follows on the rejection of the distinction by the English courts:

Kennedy, I and Grubb, A, *Medical Law*, 2nd edn, 1994, London: Butterworths, pp 316–17:

In the light of the views expressed by the Canadian Supreme Court and Australian High Court, it could therefore be argued that the House of Lords' rejection of the distinction is out of step. It could be said that the distinction is rejected out of a misunderstanding of its true basis. It is not entirely a descriptive distinction to be applied or not mechanistically to any particular intervention. This is because the distinction is also, in part, normative, reflecting prior value judgments as to what types of medical interventions are legitimate and acceptable to society. A differing set of values are at the heart of the different results in *Re B* and *Re Eve*. The misunderstanding of the House of Lords in *Re B* is that they applied the simplistic 'best interests' approach, instead of proceeding in two stages. First, the court must determine in general terms the permissible limits of medical interventions. Secondly, the court must then determine whether the particular doctor did what he did with the intention of producing those permissible ends. The value of the distinction between therapeutic and non-therapeutic interventions is that ordinarily, *ex hypothesi*, the court will regard a therapeutic intervention as legitimate. By contrast the court will need to be persuaded that an intervention which has no therapeutic purpose is legitimate ...

It may be that the insistence of the Australian High Court on the distinction need not in fact produce any different result in any particular case from an application of the 'best interests' test. This is because the 'best interests' test also proceeds from judicial and societal values. The question then has to be put, if the result may be the same why should we be concerned? The answer is that the criterion of 'best interests' contains within it, as Brennan J is anxious to point out, virtually no explicit guidelines as to the values it embraces and thereby allows the court free rein and provides no guidance to proxy decision makers. By contrast, the distinction between therapeutic and non-therapeutic causes the court to identify the values underlying the notion of treatment and then places a not inconsiderable burden on those who would engage in a non-therapeutic intervention to justify it. Finally, we may speculate that the true reason for the House of Lords' preference for the 'best interests' test rested on pragmatic rather than theoretical grounds. It may well be that their Lordships thought that the therapeutic/non-therapeutic distinction limited them to a consideration of medical matters whereas the 'best interests' test allowed a consideration of wider matters. Wanting the freedom to take account of non-medical factors, their Lordships opted for the 'best interests' approach.

Does this interpretation suggest that the Law Lords were rejecting the distinction because it worked against the interests of the person concerned? Clearly, there is a good argument that the courts should not be fettered by having no discretion to consider 'wider' issues, but, by implication, adopting the therapeutic/non-therapeutic distinction means that these wider issues can be considered, even though, as, in *Re Eve*, non-therapeutic treatment of a certain nature is rejected.

The case of *R v Human Fertilisation and Embryology Authority ex p Blood* [1997] 2 WLR 806 concerned the legality of using the sperm of the woman's deceased husband after his death (see further below, Chapter 7). The argument before the court was about the application of the Human Fertilisation and Embryology Act 1990. However, it was accepted that at least some of the sperm was taken from the man before his death (see below, Chapter 11 for a discussion of the rights anyone may have when tissue is removed from a dead body). Surprisingly, the Court of Appeal passed little comment on the common law, despite the fact that the procedure was non-therapeutic, carried out without consent, and therefore, probably constituted a battery. However, consider the position if the patient would have wished for his sperm to be taken in this way and used after his death (as his widow tried to argue): would it mean that the 'battery' would be transformed into something done in his best interests? Consider also the 'substituted judgment' test, dealt with below, p 190.

The case of *S v S* [1972] AC 24 concerned two disputed cases of paternity. The parents of the children had agreed that blood samples be taken from the children in question for the appropriate tests to be carried out. The Official Solicitor had argued that the blood tests could not be carried out unless it was in the interests of the children. The House of Lords considered the matter.

> **Lord MacDermott**: In exercising what I have called the ancillary jurisdiction in relation to infants the court must also observe and, if need be, exercise its protective jurisdiction. For instance, if the court were satisfied that – as might possibly be the case on rare occasions – a blood test would prejudicially affect the health of the infant it would, no doubt, exercise its discretion against ordering the test. And, again, if the court had reason to believe that the application for a blood test was of a fishing nature, designed for some ulterior motive to call in question the legitimacy, otherwise unimpeached, of a child who had enjoyed a legitimate status, it would be justified in refusing the application. I need not, however, pursue such instances as they do not arise on these appeals. The point to be made is that the protective jurisdiction, if of the nature I have described, would not ordinarily afford ground for refusing a blood test merely because it might, in revealing the truth, prove the infant's illegitimacy in duly constituted paternity proceedings.

The implications of this are considered further below, but would it be possible to argue that the child has an interest in knowing the identity of his father, and therefore, this 'procedure' would be 'therapeutic' in the sense that it would have psychological benefits for the child? Arguably it would not. It is pure speculation as to the outcome of the paternity dispute and its effect upon the child, and therefore whether it would make him *feel* better is unascertainable. However, this raises a crucial factor in the concept of the 'therapeutic' – the making life better for the person concerned. It must be remembered that we are not talking here about patients. The healthy volunteer in a research programme is not a patient. The mentally handicapped person whom it is proposed to sterilise because she may become pregnant is not a patient (she may or may not live in a hospital, but her residence there would not be because of gynaecological disorder). That is not to say that these procedures may never be carried out, but the decision is not a medical decision. It is arguable that it is important to label the procedure as 'non-therapeutic' so as not to lose sight of this.

However, might the converse be the case? We consider below, p 217, a number of cases where sterilisations have been carried out on women for the purposes of 'managing menstruation'. These have been regarded as 'therapeutic' because the purpose was not to render the women sterile. By describing them thus, it could be said that the distinction might be used to mask a real 'non-therapeutic' intention.

The 'best interests' test

In *Re F (Mental Patient: Sterilisation)* [1990] 2 AC 1 the House of Lords held that medical treatment can be given to an incompetent patient if it is in the 'best interests' of the patient. What does this mean?

The Law Commission, *Report on Mental Incapacity*, Report No 231, 1995, London: HMSO recommends a new general rule that anything done for a person who is without capacity should be done in that person's 'best interests'. The expression is not defined, although there are four factors listed in the report which should be considered in deciding whether something is done in the patient's best interests, and these are: the ascertainable past and present wishes and feelings of the person concerned and the factors which he or she would consider if able to do so; the need to permit and encourage the person concerned to participate, or to improve his or her ability to participate, in anything done for and any decision affecting him or her; whether the purpose for which any action or decision is required can be as effectively achieved in a manner less restrictive of the person's freedom of action; and, if it is practicable and appropriate to consult them, the views of people such as those who care for the patient, anyone named by the patient as a person to be consulted, any donee of an enduring power of attorney (a special power of attorney, pursuant to the Enduring Powers of Attorney Act 1985, which remains in force even if the donor subsequently loses mental capacity), and any manager appointed by the court.

Consider, once again, the case of *S v S* (see above, p 187). Here, it was found that there were no reasons why the tests should not be carried out, as opposed to there being positive reasons in favour. However, Kennedy and

Grubb (*Medical Law*, 2nd edn, 1994, London: Butterworths, p 258), suggest that this decision, ie, that the carrying out of blood tests was not *against* the interests of the child, may be interpreted as being special on the facts, ie, it relates to the ancillary jurisdiction of the court to make orders to ensure a fair trial. Any other interpretation would mean that the emphasis would change. Instead of examining the reasons for the treatment and how these may be for the positive benefit of the patient, the court would be left to decide whether there was any likelihood of detriment to the patient. In practice, might such a change of emphasis be disadvantageous to the patient?

The House of Lords in *Re F* gave no definition of 'best interests', dealing with the case on its particular facts. The lack of judicial guidance has been criticised:

> **Kennedy, I, 'Patients, doctors and human rights', in Blackburn, R and Taylor, J (eds), 1991, *Human Rights for the 1990s*, London: Mansell, p 90:**
>
> ... [the best interests test] allows lawyers and courts to persuade themselves and others that theirs is a principled approach to law. Meanwhile, they engage in what to others is clearly a form of 'ad hocery'. The best interests approach of family law allows the courts to atomise the law, to claim that each case depends on its own facts. The court can then respond intuitively to each case while seeking to legitimate its conclusion by asserting that it is derived from the general principle contained in the best interests formula. In fact, of course, there is no general principle other than the empty rhetoric of best interests; or rather, there is some principle (or principles) but the court is not telling. Obviously the court must be following some principles, otherwise a toss of a coin could decide cases. But these principles, which serve as pointers to what amounts to the best interests, are not articulated by the court. Only the conclusion is set out. The opportunity for reasoned analysis and scrutiny is lost.

This view was supported by Brennan J in his dissenting judgment in the Australian case of *Department of Health v JWB and SMB* (1992) 66 ALJR 300:

> **Brennan J:**
>
> 14 ... the best interests approach offers no hierarchy of values which might guide the exercise of a discretionary power to authorise sterilisation, much less any general legal principle which might direct the difficult decisions to be made in this area by parents, guardians, the medical profession and courts. It is arguable that, in a field where the law has not developed, where ethical principles remain controversial and where each case turns on its own facts, the law should not pretend to too great a precision. Better, it might be said, that authority and power be conferred on a suitable repository – whether it be parents or guardians, doctors or the court – to decide these difficult questions according to the repository's view as to the best interests of the child in the particular circumstances of the case. In that way, it can be said, the blunt instrument of legal power will be sharpened according to the exigencies of the occasion. The absence of a community consensus on ethical principles may be thought to

support this approach. But it must be remembered that, in the absence of legal rules or a hierarchy of values, the best interests approach depends upon the value system of the decision maker. Absent any rule or guideline, that approach simply creates an unexaminable discretion in the repository of the power.

15   Of course the variable circumstances of each case require evaluation and judicial evaluations of circumstances vary, but the power to authorise sterilisation is so awesome, its exercise is so open to abuse, and the consequences of its exercise are generally so irreversible, that guidelines if not rules should be prescribed to govern it. The courts must attempt the task in the course of, and as a necessary incident in, the exercise of their jurisdiction. That is not to say that the courts should arrogate to themselves the power to authorise sterilisations of intellectually disabled children, but it is to say that it has become the duty of the courts – and, in the present case, specifically the duty of this court – to define the scope of the power to authorise sterilisations of intellectually disabled children and the conditions of exercise of the power, and to determine the repository of the power. The power cannot be left in a state so amorphous that it can be exercised according to the idiosyncratic views of the repository as to the 'best interests' of the child. That approach provides an insubstantial protection of the human dignity of children; it wraps no cloak of protective principle around the intellectually disabled child.

The potentially broad scope of the best interests test is illustrated in the organ transplant cases, where it has been argued that it may be in the best interests of the donor to be treated as an altruistic member of the wider community (see below, Chapter 11).

The best interests test is considered in more detail below, pp 195 *et seq*.

The 'substituted judgment' test

Is it possible to look at the situation from the point of view of the patient, and to make medical decisions on the basis of what he would have wanted, regardless of what may be thought by others to be good for him? The English courts have not adopted the 'substituted judgment' test used by some American courts (see *Re Eve* (1986) 2 SCR 388). In any event, the test cannot be used when the patient has never had sufficient understanding to form genuine personal opinions on such matters, but is relevant to the status of Advance Directives (see further below, Chapter 12).

The 'substituted judgment' test was considered, and rejected, in *Airedale NHS Trust v Bland* [1993] 1 All ER 821, p 872:

Lord Goff: I wish however to refer at this stage to the approach adopted in most American courts under which the court seeks, in a case in which the patient is incapacitated from expressing any view on the question whether life-prolonging treatment should be withheld in the relevant circumstances, to determine what decision the patient himself would have made had he been able to do so. This is called the substituted judgment test, and it generally involves a detailed inquiry into the patient's views and preferences: see, for example, *Re Quinlan* 70 NJ 10 (1976) and *Belchertown State School Superintendent v Saikewicz* 373 Mass 728 (1977). In later cases concerned with PVS patients it has been held that, in the absence of clear and convincing evidence of the patient's wishes, the surrogate decision maker has to implement as far as possible the decision which the incompetent patient would make if he was competent. However, accepting on this point the submission of Mr Lester, I do not consider that any such test forms part of English law in relation to incompetent adults, on whose behalf nobody has power to give consent to medical treatment. Certainly, in *F v West Berkshire HA* your Lordships' House adopted a straightforward test based on the best interests of the patient ... Of course, consistent with the best interests test, anything relevant to the application of the test may be taken into account; and, if the personality of the patient is relevant to the application of the test (as it may be in cases where the various relevant factors have to be weighed), it may be taken into account, as was done in *Re J (A Minor) (Wardship: Medical Treatment)* [1990] 3 All ER 930; [1991] Fam 33.

It is reasonable to conclude that the views of a patient will not be taken into account if he has never been capable of making an anticipatory decision: his views will be subsumed under the 'best interests' test, as indicated in the Law Commission's recommendations:

Law Commission, *Report on Mental Incapacity*, Report No 231, 1995, London: HMSO:

3.25 We explained in our overview paper that two criteria for making substitute decisions for another adult have been developed in the literature in this field: 'best interests' on the one hand and 'substituted judgment' on the other. In Consultation Paper No 128 we argued that the two were not in fact mutually exclusive and we provisionally favoured a 'best interests' criterion which would contain a strong element of 'substituted judgment'. It had been widely accepted by respondents to the overview paper that, where a person has never had capacity, there is no viable alternative to the 'best interests' criterion. We were pleased to find that our arguments in favour of a 'best interests' criterion found favour with almost all our respondents, with the Law Society emphasising that the criterion as defined in the consultation papers was in fact 'an excellent compromise' between the best interests and substituted judgment approaches.

The Law Commission does state that the wishes of the patient are relevant to best interests, as past wishes and feelings may conflict with feelings the person is still able to express. The Commission concludes that present wishes and feelings must be taken into account, and, where necessary, balanced with past wishes and feelings.

The *Bolam* test

The test set down in *Bolam v Friern Hospital Management Committee* [1957] 1 WLR 582 provides that a doctor will not be negligent if he follows a medical practice which is supported by a responsible body of medical opinion, and recent case law indicates that the 'body' of opinion to support the actions of the doctor can be small (see *Defreitas v O'Brien and Another* [1995] 4 Med LR 108). This test has been subjected to much criticism on the basis that it results in judicial abstentionism, leaving the standard of care to be set exclusively by a single faction within the medical profession (see Chapter 6). In the case of *Re F (Mental Patient: Sterilisation)* [1990] 2 AC 1, which concerned a non-therapeutic sterilisation, it was held that decisions by doctors in respect of incompetent patients should be judged by the *Bolam* test.

> **Lord Bridge**: The common law should be readily intelligible to and applicable by all those who undertake the care of persons lacking the capacity to consent to treatment. It would be intolerable for members of the medical, nursing and other professions devoted to the care of the sick that, in caring for those lacking the capacity to consent to treatment they should be put in the dilemma that, if they administer the treatment which they believe to be in the patient's best interests, acting with due skill and care, they run the risk of being held guilty of trespass to the person, but if they withhold that treatment, they may be in breach of a duty of care owed to the patient. If those who undertake responsibility for the care of incompetent or unconscious patients administer curative or prophylactic treatment which they believe to be appropriate to the patient's existing condition of disease, injury or bodily malfunction or susceptibility to such a condition in the future, the lawfulness of that treatment should be judged by one standard, not two. It follows that if the professionals in question have acted with due skill and care, judged by the well known test laid down in *Bolam v Friern Hospital Management Committee* [1957] 1 WLR 582, they should be immune from liability in trespass, just as they are immune from liability in negligence. The special considerations which apply in the case of the sterilisation of a woman who is physically perfectly healthy or of an operation upon an organ transplant donor arise only because such treatment cannot be considered either curative or prophylactic.

In the Court of Appeal, the *Bolam* test had been rejected by Neill LJ, with whom Butler-Sloss LJ agreed.

> **Neill LJ**: A doctor may defeat a claim in negligence if he establishes that he acted in accordance with a practice accepted at the time as proper by a responsible body of medical opinion skilled in the particular form of treatment in question. This is the test laid down in *Bolam* ... But to say that it is not negligent to carry out a particular form of treatment does not mean that that treatment is necessary. I would define necessary in this context as that which the general body of medical opinion in the particular speciality would consider to be in the best interests of the patient in order to maintain the health and to secure the well being of the patient. One cannot expect unanimity but it

should be possible to say of an operation which is necessary in the relevant sense that it would be unreasonable in the opinion of most experts in the field not to make the operation available to the patient. One must consider the alternatives to an operation and the dangers or disadvantages to which the patient may be exposed if no action is taken. The question becomes: what action does the patient's health and welfare require?

Commenting upon this in the House of Lords, Lord Brandon stated (p 68):

> **Lord Brandon**: With respect to the Court of Appeal, I do not agree that the *Bolam* test is inapplicable to cases of performing operations on, or giving other treatment to, adults incompetent to give consent. In order that the performance of such operations on, and the giving of such other treatment to, such adults should be lawful, they must be in their best interests. If doctors were to be required, in deciding whether an operation or other treatment was in the best interests of adults incompetent to give consent, to apply some test more stringent than the *Bolam* test, the result would be that such adults would, in some circumstances at least, be deprived of the benefit of medical treatment which adults competent to give consent would enjoy. In my opinion it would be wrong for the law, in its concern to protect such adults, to produce such a result.

Whilst in the context of, say, diagnosis, there is much force in the argument that there should be the same standard of care regardless of whether the patient is competent or incompetent, in the context of non-therapeutic treatment the *Bolam* test is not sufficiently rigorous. By its very nature, the decision can only be made on *non-medical* grounds and there is no reason why a doctor should be privileged to make such decisions. Clearly, as we shall see, in cases such as *Re F*, the best interests of the patient will be concerned with her best 'social' or 'personal' interests, and the *Bolam* test is far too weak to safeguard these. Josephine Shaw comments as follows:

> **Shaw, J, 'Sterilisation of mentally handicapped people rules OK' (1990) 53 MLR 91:**
>
> It is unfortunate, but not surprising, that the *Bolam* test, which attaches great weight to clinical freedom, should have penetrated still further into the realm of consent to treatment. The construction of decision making concerning mental disability within the courtroom as an aspect of the doctor-patient relationship in which the doctor's word is paramount fits in with a general pattern which devalues the power of patient autonomy in medical decision making generally. Yet the *Bolam* test has never been either academically or judicially uncontroversial and Lord Scarman, for one, has argued vehemently against its application in the realm of consent, preferring a more patient-centred approach to the disclosure of the risks of medical treatment which places weight on the factors which a reasonable patient, rather than a reasonable doctor would consider significant.
>
> It is not insignificant that English law should have been criticised for failure to give adequate weight to both patient autonomy in the field of informed consent and the rights of mentally handicapped people in the field of

reproduction. It cannot be correct entirely to equate the standard of care to which a doctor must adhere if he or she is not to run the risk of paying compensation for damage caused and the standard which governs the application of a strictly limited exception to the consent principle encapsulating a fundamental right to self-determination. In the latter case there is an overriding public interest in ensuring that the fundamental rights of a class of person not able to operate autonomously in society are respected and that other interests will only prevail where there is a clear and precise benefit thereby to be gained. The application of the *Bolam* test provides no guarantee that this goal will be realised.

The Law Commission has also considered the relationship of best interests and negligence:

Law Commission, *Report on Mental Incapacity*, Report No 231, 1995, London: HMSO:

3.27 It should be made clear beyond any shadow of a doubt that acting in a person's best interests amounts to something more than not treating that person in a negligent manner. Decisions taken on behalf of a person lacking capacity require a careful, focused consideration of that person as an individual. Judgments as to whether a professional has acted negligently, on the other hand, require a careful, focused consideration of how that particular professional acted as compared with the way in which other reasonably competent professionals would have acted. Lord Mustill, who was both a member of the appellate committee of the House of Lords which decided the case of *Airedale NHS Trust v Bland* and a member of the House of Lords Select Committee on Medical Ethics, said during oral evidence to the latter committee that:

> ... one of the things that is not very good is that the phrase 'best interests' has been put into play without any description of what it means. This, I think, actually increases the difficulties for the doctors rather than helps to solve them. What is at the back of my mind is whether perhaps Parliament could give some more specific definition of ... what are the relevant factors ...

However, it must be noted that the *Bolam* test was not considered in the case of *Re T*, where the Court of Appeal said that the welfare of the child was better served by overriding majority medical opinion (see above, p 173). Was this because the *parental* views in the case of a very young child were of greater importance? In the case of an incapacitated adult, would be the decision be the same? It is also important to note that, in *Re F*, best interests were rolled up with necessity. It is arguable that this implies a more stringent test than *Bolam*.

THE CONTROL OF FERTILITY AND THE INCOMPETENT

Introduction

The sterilisation of incompetent patients raises profound ethical issues. Furthermore, these procedures are inevitably associated with the practice of eugenics carried out by the Nazis during the 1930s and 1940s. However, as Davies points out, the practice was by no means unknown before this:

Davies, M, *Medical Law*, 1996, London: Blackstone Press, p 262:

13.3.1 Historical development of sterilisation

The debate on sterilising the mentally handicapped has been a long, and as the case law will show, a vociferous one. The debate has as its emotive backdrop the history of late 19th and early 20th centuries. The case law will show that the judiciary of a number of common law jurisdictions are aware of the dark side of this history. Sterilisation for eugenic purposes was not a product of Nazi Germany, although that regime was the most horrific expression of the perversion of the concept of eugenics. The theory that the species could be improved or perfected by a cleansing of the gene pool through selective breeding was introduced by Sir Francis Galton at University College London in 1869. It was not long before a number of US State reformatories were using the concept to justify the sterilisation of what were deemed to be those carrying undesirable traits within society ... One of the best known, and to some most frightening, judicial justifications for the performance of these irreversible operations was found in *Buck v Bell* 274 US 200 (1927). Carrie Buck was described as the 'feeble-minded' daughter of a mother who was herself described (among other things) as 'feeble-minded'. Her proposed sterilisation was challenged on 'due process' as a 'cruel and unusual punishment' grounds under the US Constitution. The Supreme Court's view was that it was not going to be done as a punishment, but as a means to facilitate her freedom within the community. One of the most chilling quotes comes from Mr Justice Oliver Wendell Holmes (p 207):

> We have seen more than once that the public welfare may call upon the best citizens for their lives. It would be strange if it could not call upon those who already sap the strength of the State for these lesser sacrifices, often not felt to be such by those concerned, in order to prevent our being swamped with incompetents. It is better for all the world, if instead of waiting to execute degenerate offspring for crime, or to let them starve for their imbecility, society can prevent those who are manifestly unfit from continuing their kind. The principle that sustains compulsory vaccination is broad enough to cover cutting the fallopian tubes. Three generations of imbeciles are enough.

Freeman charts the American experience after *Buck v Bell*:

Freeman, MD, 'Sterilising the mentally handicapped', in *Medicine, Ethics and the Law*, 1988, London: Stevens, p 57:

There have been a number of significant cases in the USA since *Buck v Bell*. There have been attempts to reverse the decision. That this has not happened is in part attributable to the fact that the line of argument has changed. Eugenics (or rather negative eugenics) is out of fashion: instead, the appeal is grounded on the burden placed on society by the need to care for the handicapped. The most interesting of the recent cases is *North Carolina Association for Retarded Children v State of North Carolina* in 1976. The statute challenged authorised both voluntary and involuntary sterilisations. There was a duty to institute sterilisation proceedings when the relevant official felt it was either in (i) the best interests of the retarded person, or (ii) the public at large, or (iii) where the retarded person would be likely, unless sterilised, to procreate children with a tendency to serious physical, mental or nervous disease or deficiency or would be unable to care for the child, or (iv) when the next of kin or legal guardian of the retarded person 'requests' that he file the petition. The court found (iv) irrational and irreconcilable with (i), (ii) and (iii). But it thought the first three provisions made out 'a complete and sensible scheme'. The fourth, however, granted to the retarded person's next of kin or legal guardian 'the power of a tyrant'. The scheme was thus found constitutional with the exception of the fourth provision. The language and ideology of Holmes' 'incantation' was rejected. 'Medical and genetical experts', the court noted, 'are no longer sold on sterilisation to benefit either retarded patients or the future of the Republic'. The case is also significant for containing a number of general propositions about the origins of mental retardation, about expression of sexuality, about the ability of the handicapped to use contraceptive methods. Finally, the opinion holds that in rare unusual cases it can be medically determined that involuntary sterilisation is in the best interests of either the mentally retarded persons, or the State, or both.

A lot of people have been sterilised in the USA pursuant upon the compulsory programmes depicted here. By 1964, by which time the programmes had long passed their peak, 63,678 such sterilisations had taken place. Those sterilised were mainly young women and for the large part they were poor and came from socio-economically and culturally deprived environments. Whether it was, as Gonzales indicates, a popular way of controlling reproduction, it certainly was a convenient method for controlling the reproductive urges of the populace. Given the population concerned and the imperfections of classification, the dangers of labelling with sterilisation merely an incident of stigmatisation were difficult to overcome. The evidence suggests they were not surmounted.

It is not surprising, therefore, that the case of *Re B (A Minor)* [1988] 1 AC 199, which concerned the sterilisation of a mentally handicapped girl, caused a considerable amount of controversy. Freeman, in a BBC interview, had described the approval of the sterilisation by the Court of Appeal as 'Nazi-like'. In the House of Lords, Lord Hailsham, no doubt bearing in mind this reaction, had sought from the outset to distinguish this case from the practice of eugenics (p 202):

> **Lord Hailsham**: There is no doubt that, in the exercise of its wardship jurisdiction, the first and paramount consideration is the well being, welfare, or interests (each expression occasionally used, but each, for this purpose, synonymous) of the human being concerned, that is the ward herself or himself. In this case I believe it to be the only consideration involved. In particular there is no issue of public policy other than the application of the above principle which can conceivably be taken into account, least of all (since the opposite appears to have been considered in some quarters) any question of eugenics.

When the case of *Re F (Mental Patient: Sterilisation)* [1990] 2 AC 1 was in the Court of Appeal, Lord Donaldson had taken the view that sterilisation operations were special cases (p 19):

> **Lord Donaldson:**
>
> **Is sterilisation in a special category?**
>
> ... Mr Munby seeks to persuade us that it is in a special category and in this I think he is right, although I would include in the same category abortion and surgical intervention to enable an incompetent adult to donate an organ during lifetime. However, there is a real distinction between medical treatment undertaken with a view to securing abortion or sterilisation and that undertaken for a different purpose, for example the excision of a malignant tumour, which has this incidental result. It is only the former type of treatment which the law regards as being in a special category, probably because of its irreversible and emotive character in the light of the history of our times.

As stated by Lord Donaldson, sterilisation operations can be carried out for exclusively therapeutic purposes, for example, when the ovaries or uterus are damaged or diseased. Those operations do not concern us here. The cases we will examine fall into two categories. First, 'social' sterilisations, where it is proposed to render sterile those who, it is said, are simply incapable of understanding parenthood and caring for a child. Secondly, there have been a number of cases where young women have been sterilised to avoid difficulties with menstruation. The question arises as to whether these can properly be called 'therapeutic'.

Non-therapeutic sterilisations

We have considered above, p 184, whether there is any meaningful distinction between a therapeutic and a non-therapeutic procedure, and saw that La Forest J in the case of *Re Eve* (1986) 2 SCR 388 favoured such a distinction. (See above, p 185, for the facts of the case.) In the following extract, the court considers issues raised by the proposed 'non-therapeutic' sterilisation, ie, for social reasons:

La Forest J: Another factor merits attention. Unlike most surgical procedures, sterilisation is not one that is ordinarily performed for the purpose of medical treatment. The Law Reform Commission of Canada tells us this in *Sterilisation*, Working Paper [No] 24, 1979, a publication to which I shall frequently refer as providing a convenient summary of much of the work in the field. It says at p 3:

> Sterilisation as a medical procedure is distinct, because except in rare cases, if the operation is not performed, the physical health of the person involved is not in danger, necessity or emergency not normally being factors in the decision to undertake the procedure. In addition to its being elective, it is for all intents and purposes irreversible.

As well, there is considerable evidence that non-consensual sterilisation has a significant negative psychological impact on the mentally handicapped; see *Sterilisation* ... pp 49–52. The Commission has this to say at p 50:

> It has been found that, like anyone else, the mentally handicapped have individually varying reactions to sterilisation. Sex and parenthood hold the same significance for them as for other people and their misconceptions and misunderstandings are also similar. Rosen maintains that the removal of an individual's procreative powers is a matter of major importance and that no amount of reforming zeal can remove the significance of sterilisation and its effect on the individual psyche.

> In a study by Sabagh and Edgerton, it was found that sterilised mentally retarded persons tend to perceive sterilisation as a symbol of reduced or degraded status. Their attempts to pass for normal were hindered by negative self-perceptions and resulted in withdrawal and isolation rather than striving to conform ...

The psychological impact of sterilisation is likely to be particularly damaging in cases where it is a result of coercion and when the mentally handicapped have had no children.

In the present case, there is no evidence to indicate that failure to perform the operation would have any detrimental effect on Eve's physical or mental health. The purposes of the operation, as far as Eve's welfare is concerned, are to protect her from possible trauma in giving birth and from the assumed difficulties she would have in fulfilling her duties as a parent. As well, one must assume from the fact that hysterectomy was ordered, that the operation was intended to relieve her of the hygienic tasks associated with menstruation ...

The justifications advanced are the ones commonly proposed in support of non-therapeutic sterilisation (see *Sterilisation*). Many are demonstrably weak. The Commission dismisses the argument about the trauma of birth by observing at p 60:

> For this argument to be held valid would require that it could be demonstrated that the stress of delivery was greater in the case of mentally handicapped persons than it is for others. The generally known wide range of *post-partum* response would likely render this a difficult cause to prove.

The argument relating to fitness as a parent involves many value-loaded questions. Studies conclude that mentally incompetent parents show as much fondness and concern for their children as other people; see *Sterilisation* ... pp 33 *et seq*, pp 63–64. Many, it is true, may have difficulty in coping, particularly with the financial burdens involved. But this issue does not relate to the benefit of the incompetent; it is a social problem, and one, moreover, that is not limited to incompetents. Above all it is not an issue that comes within the limited powers of the courts, under the *parens patriae* jurisdiction, to do what is necessary for the benefit of persons who are unable to care for themselves. Indeed, there are human rights considerations that should make a court extremely hesitant about attempting to resolve a social problem by this means. It is worth noting that in dealing with such issues, provincial sterilisation boards have revealed serious differences in their attitudes as between men and women, the poor and the rich, and people of different ethnic backgrounds; see *Sterilisation* ... at p 44.

As far as the hygienic problems are concerned, the following view of the Law Reform Commission (p 34) is obviously sound:

> ... if a person requires a great deal of assistance in managing their own menstruation, they are also likely to require assistance with urinary and faecal control, problems which are much more troublesome in terms of personal hygiene.

The grave intrusion on a person's rights and the certain physical damage that ensues from non-therapeutic sterilisation without consent, when compared to the highly questionable advantages that can result from it, have persuaded me that it can never safely be determined that such a procedure is for the benefit of that person ...

One of the first English cases to examine the issue was *Re D (A Minor) (Wardship: Sterilisation)*. The case concerned an 11 year old child, who suffered from Sotos syndrome, a condition characterised by epilepsy, clumsiness, unusual facial appearance, behavioural problems such as emotional instability and aggression and impairment of mental function. She was described as having an IQ of 80 (described as 'dull normal'), some reading and writing skills, good conversational skills and the understanding of a nine or nine and a half year old. An application was made to the court under the wardship jurisdiction for authorisation of a sterilisation. The reasons are outlined in the judgment of Heilbron J (p 330):

Re D (A Minor) (Wardship: Sterilisation) [1976] 1 All ER 326:

Heilbron J:

The background to the decision to operate

When Mrs B first realised that she had given birth to a handicapped child, she recalled with deep concern that, many years before, she had lived near a family who had the misfortune to have three mentally retarded children, and their plight and their troubled lives had deeply affected her. She and her husband not unnaturally were extremely worried about D's future, as at that time they thought D could never improve, and so even when D was a very young child they decided that when she reached the age of about 18 they would take the necessary steps to prevent her from having any children, and would apply to have her sterilised. From the decision made in those early days Mrs B has never resiled, and she has in consequence, over the years, had several discussions about this operation with Dr Gordon. When D reached puberty by the age of 10 Mrs B's concern increased, and so she discussed the operation once again with Dr Gordon on 7 January 1975. Mrs B said, and I accept, that when she reiterated to Dr Gordon that she would like D sterilised when she was older, the doctor said: 'We can do it now.' This is indeed confirmed by the doctor in his affidavit when he says that rather than wait any longer the decision could be taken then. Mrs B agreed that the operation should be performed. She was very worried lest D might be seduced and possibly give birth to a baby, which might also be abnormal. She had always believed that D would not, or should not, marry and in any event would be incapable of bringing up a child. Her anxieties are genuine and understandable.

Dr Gordon took the view that there was a real risk that D might give birth to an abnormal foetus. I have already referred to some of his other anxieties. As to the possibility of producing an abnormal child, the evidence of Dr Snodgrass and Dr Newton, the well known consultant psychiatrist called on behalf of the Official Solicitor, confirmed that there was, as Dr Gordon stated, an increased risk of such an eventuality. On the other hand, they pointed out that no one with this particular syndrome had ever been known to have a baby, and it is not therefore possible to make any precise predictions whether or not they are able to do so.

At that consultation in January Dr Gordon, with Mrs B's agreement, came to a decision provided that Miss Duncan, the consultant gynaecologist, who is a senior lecturer and gynaecologist to the Sheffield and Northern General Hospital, to whom he referred, concurred in his recommendation that the operation should be performed. Miss Duncan saw and interviewed both D and Mrs B on 7 February 1975, but she did not examine the child, and I think there is little doubt that Miss Duncan did not give very much independent consideration to the wider implications of this operation, but was content in large measure to rely on Dr Gordon's recommendation and assessment of the situation. She did, however, agree to perform the sterilisation, namely a hysterectomy, and I am satisfied that D was booked to enter hospital on 4 May for that operation to be carried out on 6 May. No one else was consulted prior to that decision. It is surprising that Dr T, the child psychiatrist, was not, for, prior to the date of the recommendation, he had on a number of occasions interviewed and examined the child, and his views, as Dr Gordon later agreed in evidence, must have been of considerable importance in evaluating the numerous problems, medical, social, educational and psychiatric, which such a vital decision involved.

Dr Gordon maintains, however, that his recommendation was one which was based on clinical judgment as a doctor, and that he and the gynaecologist should be the sole judges whether or not it should be performed, provided of course that they had the parent's consent.

Despite Dr Gordon's assertion that his decision should be upheld because it was based on his clinical judgment, he nevertheless, in putting forward his grounds for recommending this operation, stated that such reasons or such grounds were of a twofold character, ie, that they were both medical and social. The medical reasons included the possibility that she might give birth to an abnormal child, that her epilepsy might cause her to harm a child, and that the only satisfactory method of birth control was this operation. The social reasons included his opinion that D would be unable in the future to maintain herself save in a sheltered environment, her inability due to epilepsy and other handicaps to cope with a family if she were to marry, without substantial support, the deterioration in her behaviour for which he said there was no known method of improvement and the possibility that she might have to enter an institution as he alleged for social or criminal reasons in the future. Certain persons concerned with D's welfare, however, took a different view. They were the former and present headmaster of her school, Mrs Hamidi and the social worker involved with the family. They believed that an operation for sterilisation in the case of a minor, particularly a girl of 11, being irreversible and permanent, was a matter of grave concern, and so on 26 March Mrs Hamidi wrote on their behalf and on her own to the senior school medical officer, pointing out in detail the conflict between Mrs B and the school and the welfare services in regard to D's attainments and their concern in regard to the proposed operation, which they pointed out could affect the whole of her future.

On 21 April there was a meeting between Dr Gordon and those professionals working with the child and her family, at which Dr Gordon's social and behavioural reasons for performing this operation were seriously challenged. Dr Gordon, however, refused to acknowledge that these views could possibly be wrong or exaggerated or premature. I think Dr Gordon, whose sincerity cannot be challenged, was persuaded by his emotional involvement with Mrs B's considerable problems and anxieties, and his strong personal views in favour of sterilisation – as he stated in his affidavit, 'Sterilisation is now an emotive word, and we must try to change its image' – to form a less than detached opinion in regard to a number of matters which were not in my view in reality matters of clinical judgment, but which were concerned, to a large extent, with grounds which were other than medical. I feel it is a pity that he was not prepared to accept that others, whose duties, training and skills were directed to the assessment and amelioration of many of these problems, had much to contribute in the formulation of a decision of this gravity.

In my judgment Dr Gordon's views as to D's present and future social and behavioural problems were somewhat exaggerated and mistaken. I think in this area his views were clouded by his resentment at what he considered unjustified interference.

In the event Dr Gordon did not accept the alternative views, and he and Miss Duncan refused to defer the operation despite the grave implications for the child. Mrs Hamidi and the others, therefore, wrote to the area administrator of the health authority requesting an urgent and independent review of this decision. The area administrator consulted the local authority's specialist in community medicine (child health) and he later replied saying that she had made a very careful appraisal of the case, but could not interfere. Mrs Hamidi and her colleagues, however, were not daunted and they thereupon consulted solicitors, and in due course these proceedings got under way. It is only right that I should pay tribute to their courage, persistence and humane concern for this young girl.

... I am dealing here with the case of this particular young girl, but the evidence, including that which disclosed that Dr Gordon has recommended and Miss Duncan has performed two prior operations of this nature on handicapped children in Sheffield, indicates the possibility that further consideration may need to be given to this topic, consideration which would involve extensive consultation and debate elsewhere.

Dr Gordon's reason for wishing this operation to be performed was, of course, to prevent D ever having a child. He recognised, as did Mrs B, that there are other methods of achieving that objective, but his view was that D could not satisfactorily manage any form of contraception. Mrs B was concerned lest D might be seduced and become pregnant ...

Mrs B's genuine concern ... cannot be disregarded. A body of evidence was produced, therefore, to indicate the advantages and disadvantages of various forms of contraception. I shall not, however, burden this judgment with any detailed examination of it, save to say that I do not accept on the evidence Dr Gordon's contention that this young girl, if and when the time arrived, would not be a suitable subject for one of the various methods described by the doctors ...

It was common ground that D had sufficient intellectual capacity to marry, in the future of course, and that many people of a like kind are capable of, and do so. Dr Gordon agreed that this being so, she and her future husband would then be the persons most concerned in a question of sterilisation, and such an operation might have a serious and material bearing on a future marriage and its consequences.

The purpose of performing this operation is permanently to prevent the possibility of reproduction. The evidence of Professor Huntingford, consultant and professor of obstetrics and gynaecology at the University of London and at St Bartholomew's Hospital and the London Hospital Medical Colleges, was that in his view such an operation was normally only appropriate for a woman who consented to it, possibly at the conclusion of child-bearing, and then only after careful and anxious consideration by her and her husband of many factors and, what is most important, with full knowledge of all its implications.

Professor Huntingford, Dr Snodgrass and Dr Newton were all agreed that such an operation was not medically indicated in this case, and should not be performed. Dr Snodgrass said he was firmly of the view that it was wrong to perform this operation on an 11 year old, on the pretext that it would benefit her in the future. Dr Newton said:

> In my opinion sterilisation of a child before the age of consent can only be justified if it is the treatment for some present or inevitable disease. In this case, sterilisation is not a treatment for any of the signs or symptoms of Sotos syndrome, from which she suffers. I am totally against this operation being performed on D.

... Dr Gordon, however, maintained that, provided the parent or parents consented, the decision was one made pursuant to the exercise of his clinical judgment, and that no interference could be tolerated in his clinical freedom.

The other consultants did not agree. Their opinion was that a decision to sterilise a child was not entirely within a doctor's clinical judgment, save only when sterilisation was the treatment of choice for some disease, as, for instance, when in order to treat a child and to ensure her direct physical well being, it might be necessary to perform a hysterectomy to remove a malignant uterus. Whilst the side effect of such an operation would be to sterilise, the operation would be performed solely for therapeutic purposes. I entirely accept their opinions. I cannot believe, and the evidence does not warrant the view, that a decision to carry out an operation of this nature performed for non-therapeutic purposes on a minor, can be held to be within the doctor's sole clinical judgment ...

A review of the whole of the evidence leads me to the conclusion that in a case of a child of 11 years of age, where the evidence shows that her mental and physical condition and attainments have already improved, and where her future prospects are as yet unpredictable, where the evidence also shows that she is unable as yet to understand and appreciate the implications of this operation and could not give a valid or informed consent, but the likelihood is that in later years she will be able to make her own choice, where, I believe, the frustration and resentment of realising (as she would one day) what had happened, could be devastating, an operation of this nature is, in my view, contra-indicated.

Three things in particular are noteworthy: first, the apparent lack of concern by the gynaecologist; secondly, the intransigence of Dr Gordon; and thirdly, the chance way in which the case came before the court. As far as the first two are concerned, would the combined opinions of Miss Duncan and Dr Gordon have constituted a responsible body of medical opinion for the purposes of the *Bolam* test? Even if two opinions were deemed insufficient, it is likely that, if necessary, other doctors could have been found to endorse their views. On an application of the *Bolam* test, would Heilbron J have been able, nevertheless, to reject these opinions on the ground that they were not 'responsible' or that they were 'illogical'? Or would the 'welfare of the child' principle relegate the *Bolam* test to a secondary position (see *Re T* above). Consider this and the other sterilisation cases when looking at the application of the *Bolam* test in Chapter 6.

Commenting on the way in which this case reached the court, Freeman writes as follows:

Freeman, MD, 'Sterilising the mentally handicapped', in *Medicine, Ethics and the Law*, 1988, London: Stevens, p 57:

... the Sheffield girl in *Re D* was not the first English victim, or even the first in Sheffield. The chance intervention by an educational psychologist and the financial support of the NCCL for once converted a private matter into a public concern. Just how many young persons have been sterilised in Britain is something that will never be known. Dr David Owen in 1975 said the Ministry of Health kept no comprehensive statistics. He quoted figures from two out of 14 regional health authorities. According to *The Sun* in September 1975, the DHSS believed that in 1973 and 1974 11 girls and four boys under 16 had been sterilised and 29 girls and 34 boys of between 16 and 18. Figures in the Journal of Medical Ethics do not tally with these. It is indicated there (by Sir George Porter) that at least 14 sterilisations were performed in this period on under 16 year olds and another 22 on those in the age range 16 to 18. According to the *Birmingham Evening Mail* (in January 1976), one West Midlands leading child psychiatrist had himself recommended 12 adolescents under 16 for sterilisation. In *Re D* there is reference to two sterilisations having been carried out in Sheffield. Figures released by the Department of Health in March 1987 indicate that about 90 sterilisations are performed a year in England on females under 19. The department is unable to break the figures down into those aged under 18, and those who have reached the age of majority, nor to give the reasons for the sterilisations.

The case of *Re B (A Minor) (Wardship: Sterilisation)* [1988] 1 AC 199 (the case of 'Jeanette') concerned a 17 year old girl. She was a voluntary patient in a local authority residential unit. The facts are outlined in the judgment of Lord Oliver (p 207):

Lord Oliver: ... [Jeanette] suffers from what is described as a 'moderate' degree of mental handicap but has a very limited intellectual development. Her ability to understand speech is that of a six year old, but her ability to express herself has been described as comparable to that of a two year old child. No cause for her mental handicap has been established but the report of Dr Berney, a consultant psychiatrist who gave evidence before the judge, indicates that her epilepsy and the degree of her mental incapacity suggest an underlying abnormality of the brain. It is not envisaged that she will ever be capable of caring for herself in the community or reach a stage where she could return permanently to her mother's care. She is capable of finding her way round a limited locality, of dressing and bathing herself and performing simple household tasks under supervision and she has been taught to cope with menstruation; but the evidence is that she is unlikely to show an improvement in mental capacity beyond that of a six year old child. She has, in the past, shown evidence of extremes of mood and can become violent and aggressive, a phenomenon associated with premenstrual tension. Since the middle of 1986 there has been prescribed for her a drug known as Danazol to help in controlling her irregular periods and relieving premenstrual tension, whilst her epilepsy is controlled by anti-convulsant drugs. She suffers from obesity and an earlier attempt to treat her outbursts of violence with Microgynon 30 (a combined oral contraceptive) had to be abandoned because it produced a significant increase in weight. Another behavioural feature of significance is her high tolerance of pain. There is evidence that she bites her arm and that if injured she interferes with the process of healing by opening and probing the wounds.

What prompted the application to the court was the consciousness on the part of her mother and officers of the council responsible for her care that she was beginning to show recognisable signs of sexual awareness and sexual drive exemplified by provocative approaches to male members of the staff and other residents and by touching herself in the genital area. There was thus brought to their attention the obvious risk of pregnancy and the desirability of taking urgent and effective contraceptive measures. Although at present she is subject to effective supervision, her degree of incapacity is not such that it would be thought right that she should, effectively, be institutionalised all her life. The current approach to persons of her degree of incapacity is to allow them as much freedom as is consistent with their own safety and that of other people and although the likelihood is that she will, for the foreseeable future, continue to live at the residential institution, she visits her mother and her siblings at weekends and will, inevitably, be much less susceptible to supervision when she goes to an adult training centre. At the same time the risks involved in her becoming pregnant are formidable. The evidence of Dr Berney is that there is no prospect of her being capable of forming a long term adult relationship, such as marriage, which is within the capacity of some less mentally handicapped persons. She has displayed no maternal feelings and indeed has an antipathy to small children. Such skills as she has been able to develop are limited to those necessary for caring for herself at the simplest level and there is no prospect of her being capable of raising or caring for a child of her own. If she did give birth to a child it would be essential that it be taken from her for fostering or adoption although her attitude towards children is such that this would not cause her distress. So far as her awareness of her own sexuality is concerned, she has, as has already been mentioned, been taught to manage for herself the necessary hygienic mechanics of menstruation, but it has not been possible to teach her about sexuality in any abstract form. She understands the link between pregnancy and a baby but is unaware of sexual intercourse and its relationship to pregnancy. It is not feasible to discuss contraception with her and even if there should come a time when she becomes capable of understanding the need for contraception, there is no likelihood of her being able to develop the capacity to weigh up the merits of different types of contraception or to make an informed choice in the matter. Should she become pregnant, it would be desirable that the pregnancy should be terminated, but because of her obesity and the irregularity of her periods there is an obvious danger that her condition might not be noticed until it was too late for an abortion to take place safely. On the other hand, the risks if she were permitted to go to full term are serious, for although it is Dr Berney's opinion that she would tolerate the condition of pregnancy without undue distress, the process of delivery would be likely to be traumatic and would cause her to panic. Normal delivery would be likely to require heavy sedation, which could be injurious to the child, so that it might be more appropriate to deliver her by Caesarean section. If this course were adopted, however, past experience of her reaction to injuries suggests that it would be very difficult to prevent her from repeatedly opening up the wound and thus preventing the healing of the post-operative scar. It was against this background and in the light of the increasing freedom which must be allowed her as she grows older and the consequent difficulty of maintaining effective supervision that those having the care of the minor concluded that it was essential in her interests that effective contraceptive measures be taken. Almost all drugs appear to have a bad effect upon her and the view was formed, in which her mother concurred, that the only appropriate course offering complete protection was for her to undergo sterilisation by occluding the fallopian tubes, a relatively minor operation carrying a very small degree of risk to the patient, a very high degree of protection and minimal side effects. There is, however, no possibility that the minor, even if of full age, would herself have the mental capacity to consent to such an operation. Hence the application to the court.

... Your Lordships' attention has, quite properly, been directed to the decision of Heilbron J in *In re D (A Minor) (Wardship: Sterilisation)* [1976] Fam 185, a case very different from the instant case, where the evidence indicated that the ward was of an intellectual capacity to marry and would in the future be able to make her own choice. In those circumstances, Heilbron J declined to sanction an operation which involved depriving her of her right to reproduce. That, if I may say so respectfully, was plainly a right decision. But the right to reproduce is of value only if accompanied by the ability to make a choice and in the instant case there is no question of the minor ever being able to make such a choice or indeed to appreciate the need to make one. All the evidence indicates that she will never desire a child and that reproduction would in fact be positively harmful to her.

Was this operation in Jeanette's best interests? Much of the reasoning behind the court's decision was that the operation was necessary to protect her. Lord Oliver said, p 210:

> **Lord Oliver:** My Lords, I have thought it right to set out in some detail the background of fact in which this appeal has come before your Lordships' House because it is, in my judgment, essential to appreciate, in considering the welfare of this young woman which it is the duty of the court to protect, the degree of her vulnerability, the urgency of the need to take protective measures and the impossibility of her ever being able at this age or any later age either to consent to any form of operative treatment or to exercise for herself the right of making any informed decision in matters which, in the case of a person less heavily handicapped, would rightly be thought to be matters purely of personal and subjective choice.

Note that, in the judgment of Lord Oliver, he moves from reference to 'provocative gestures' to the 'risk of pregnancy' without pausing to consider that there is no inevitable progression from one to the other. The somewhat hollow ring of the efficacy of this procedure as a protective measure may be, at least in part, related to the fact that it is at odds with much of the evidence. If Jeanette was so limited in her understanding, and this was stressed by carers and judges alike, then the operation was arguably unnecessary *for precisely this very reason*. She would simply never have the opportunity to have sexual intercourse. The concern that she would not be supervised sufficiently at the adult training centre which she was shortly due to attend is not entirely consistent with the negative assertions about her uncontrolled behaviour.

De Cruz, SP, 'Sterilisation, wardship and human rights' (1988) 18 Fam Law 6:

> ... since Jeanette could not even be allowed on the streets unsupervised, as she could not understand traffic, she would certainly need close and constant

attention for a great deal of the time. Admittedly, provided she was indoors, the supervision need not be quite so intensive or intrusive, once this alarming prospect of pregnancy no longer existed. Yet given the prospect of sexual exploitation, of course, sterilisation would give no protection against rape or sexual abuse. Furthermore, the operation would certainly not free her, as Lord Hailsham seemed to imply, from 'incarceration', nor give her the liberty to satisfy the sexual desires she was experiencing, when she would certainly experience difficulties in relationships with the opposite sex. If anything, the ruling accentuates her vulnerability and, tragically, results in her being treated very differently from 'normal' people, which would undermine all the advances made in the last decade or so in the achievements of mental health groups in their efforts to integrate people with mental disabilities into the community at large.

The lack of consistency in the evidence and the conclusions drawn from the statements made about Jeanette's abilities and difficulties were highlighted by Lee and Morgan:

Lee, R and Morgan, D, 'Sterilisation and mental handicap: sapping the strength of the State?' (1988) 15 JLS 229:

... a curious pattern emerges. It is of a girl who can manage 'the necessary hygienic mechanics of menstruation', but could not cope with contraception; who can understand the link between pregnancy and babies, but 'is unaware of sexual intercourse and its relationship to pregnancy'. No information is offered about Jeanette's sex education and why it has failed to overcome her ignorance of one of the outcomes of sexual intercourse. Nothing explains why her carers are able successfully to manage the regime of medication necessary to control her epilepsy, but would be unable to supervise the use of an oral contraceptive because 'it would not be possible in the light of her swings of mood and considerable physical strength to ensure the administration of the necessary daily doses'.

Lord Oliver had said that the concern of the court had been about 'what is in the best interests of this unfortunate young woman and how best she can be given the protection which is essential to her future well being so that she may lead as full a life as her intellectual capacity allows' (p 212). It is tempting, however, to conclude that the 'full life' was a life which relieved her carers of many of their duties to protect her.

Might someone in Jeanette's position be in need of protection from exploitation from those responsible for her safety? Freeman comments upon this as follows:

Freeman, MD, 'Sterilising the mentally handicapped', in *Medicine, Ethics and the Law*, 1988, London: Stevens, p 68:

If it was really unlikely that Jeanette would become pregnant, was sterilisation the right answer? If she understood as little as the law report seems to indicate, she certainly needed (and needs) protection, in particular from exploitation. It is noticeable how many parents of mentally handicapped daughters complain about their daughters being 'raped' by employees of institutions, for example, drivers employed to take them back and forth. One right that the mentally handicapped undoubtedly have is the right not to be sexually abused. Sterilisation does nothing to protect them from sexual exploitation. Saner employment policies (for example the employment of female drivers) and better sex education might achieve rather more.

In this regard, see the case of *Re LC (Medical Treatment: Sterilisation)* [1997] 2 FLR 258, where an application for authority to perform a sterilisation operation on a 25 year old mentally impaired woman, came before the court because of her mother's anxiety following an indecent assault upon her by a member of staff at her former residential home. In the event, the operation was not authorised, as the woman was now resident in a home where the care was described as 'of exceptionally high quality', and, on balance, the operation was not justified. Whilst not disputing the correctness of this decision, is it right for the outcome to depend upon the quality of care? If this woman had been in a home where the quality of care was poor, would the operation have been authorised? If so, the woman would have been exposed to a double jeopardy: the imposition of major, invasive and irreversible surgery, together with risk of sexual abuse and exploitation.

It is also questionable that there was any significant likelihood that Jeanette would have become pregnant. Freeman (Freeman, MD, 'Sterilising the mentally handicapped', in *Medicine, Ethics and the Law*, 1988, London: Stevens, p 68) cites evidence that the majority of those with serious impairment do not have effective fertility. Furthermore, as De Cruz says ('Sterilisation, wardship and human rights' (1988) 18 Fam Law 6) 'mere provocative gestures are not necessarily to be equated with an invitation to have sex'.

> **Lee, R and Morgan, D, 'Sterilisation and mental handicap: sapping the strength of the State?' (1988) 15 JLS 229:**
>
> The fears of undetected pregnancy, abortion, and traumatic childbirth must all be subject to some real likelihood of Jeanette's becoming pregnant. Moreover, had Jeanette been sexually active, pregnancy is not the only risk she would face; the hazards of AIDS and other sexually transmitted diseases are ignored.

It is, of course, possible that an incompetent patient may not be suited to pregnancy and motherhood. Likewise, in the case of a competent woman there may be circumstances which would mean that pregnancy and motherhood would be similarly undesirable. In such a case would sterilisation be thought to be the only solution, particularly when she was not sexually active, was aged only 17 and her future development was uncertain? Surely, it is highly unlikely that sterilisation would even be considered at that stage in her life. However, it is essential to compare Jeanette with a competent woman, otherwise Jeanette is being treated differently *because of her mental impairment*. The comparison with 'normal' people was made in the dissenting judgment of Brennan J in *Department of Health v JWB and SMB* (1992) 66 ALJR 300, where the majority of the High Court of Australia sanctioned a 'non-therapeutic' sterilisation on a 14 year old girl.

Brennan J:

22 ... a variety of different purposes may appear which many would regard as of significant value in assessing the 'best interests' of an intellectually disabled child. The purposes which fall into this category can be gathered under the broad description of 'preventative': to prevent the risk of a pregnancy which the child could not properly understand and the concomitant risk of parenthood with responsibilities beyond the capacity of the child to discharge. These risks are an understandable source of anxiety to parents, guardians and others who have a genuine concern for the welfare of an intellectually disabled child. These are risks which create an understandable anxiety in many parents, guardians and others who have a genuine concern for the welfare of a normal child. In the case of a normal female child, it would be wholly unacceptable to permit sterilisation in order to prevent pregnancy or parenthood, though those events might be thought to be tragedies in particular circumstances by reasonable persons concerned with the welfare of the child. Depending on the circumstances, the use – or, *a fortiori*, the exploitation – of the sexual attributes of a female child may entail tragic consequences, yet the risk or even the likelihood of tragic consequences affords no justification for her sterilisation. What difference does it make that the risk is occasioned by an intellectual disability? The answer to this question depends on the view taken of the proposition earlier set out in the Declaration on the Rights of Mentally Retarded Persons: they are entitled to the same rights as other humans to the maximum degree of feasibility. To accord in full measure the human dignity that is the due of every intellectually disabled girl, her right to retain her capacity to bear a child cannot be made contingent on her imposing no further burdens, causing no more anxiety or creating no further demands. If the law were to adopt a policy of permitting sterilisation in order to avoid the imposition of burdens, the causing of anxiety and the creating of demands, the human rights which foster and protect human dignity in the powerless would lie in the gift of those who are empowered and the law would fail in its function of protecting the weak.

23 ... In any event, though pregnancy be a possibility, sterilisation, once performed, is a certainty. If a non-therapeutic sterilisation could be justified at all, it could be justified only by the need to avoid a tragedy that is imminent and certain. Such a situation bespeaks a failure of care, and sterilisation is not the remedy for the failure. Nor should it be forgotten that pregnancy and motherhood may have a significance for some intellectually disabled girls quite different from the significance attributed by other people. Though others may see her pregnancy and motherhood as a tragedy, she, in her world, may find in those events an enrichment of her life.

Were the alternatives properly explored by the court, and, indeed, by Jeanette's carers? Most forms of contraceptive pill were thought to be unsuitable because of her obesity, although it was argued by the Official Solicitor that insufficient consideration had been given to the use of a progestogen contraceptive pill less likely to have that effect. The prospect of a *daily* dose, however, was daunting to Jeanette's carers, although other drugs were administered to her for her epilepsy, apparently without undue difficulty. In addition, it was thought undesirable for the contraceptive drug to be administered to her for 30 years or more. Why should this have been regarded as a foregone conclusion? Again, it is instructive to consider the comparison with a competent woman.

The possibility of Jeanette making progress, socially, was considered by Lee and Morgan:

Lee, R and Morgan, D, 'Sterilisation and mental handicap: sapping the strength of the State?' (1988) 15 JLS 229:

The certainty of the sterilisation operation, compared with Jeanette's developmental prognosis, is striking. All the judges seem prepared to accept that from her present position she will never be able to develop, either on her own or in the company of a sympathetic and supportive partner or community, into a woman who might just be able to form the affective links with children which would enable her meaningfully to exercise her procreative capacities. And yet the evidence surveyed by the House of Lords indicates that she has already developed from the age of four, when she was first received into care, from being a 'wild animal' to someone who will in a short time be going to an adult training centre ... To arrest Jeanette's metamorphosis at the age of 17 and to treat her as though she will never become 27, 37, or 40, abandons 25 years of potential reproductive capacity, affinitive development, and emotional maturing to expert evidence which is necessarily speculative in nature, imprecise, and heavily opinionated. It is used to justify a procedure which is certain in its consequences, definite, and irreversible.

De Cruz suggests that the decision may have been made in something approaching indecent haste:

De Cruz, SP, 'Sterilisation, wardship and human rights' (1988) 18 Fam Law 6:

Should the Law Lords have deferred the decision, pending further investigation and observation? The Canadian courts took nearly seven years to decide Eve's case, and it took 16 months for the Supreme Court to produce its judgment, after studying a very wide range of expert opinions and the exhaustive research of the Canadian Law Commission. In their desire not to be faced with a jurisdictional problem once Jeanette reached the age of 18, the English Law Lords only took 28 days to decide the case, but their assumptions about her future conduct may well have led them to discount other possibilities too readily.

As far as adult patients are concerned, the leading case is *Re F (Mental Patient: Sterilisation)* [1990] 2 AC 1. The facts of that case concerned a female mental patient, a woman in her thirties, who had been assessed as having a mental age of a four to five. She was a voluntary in-patient in a mental hospital where she had formed what was described as a sexual relationship with a male patient. Both hospital staff, and the patient's mother, felt that she would not be able to cope with childbirth, nor with the subsequent rearing of a child, and that it would, therefore, be in her best interests to be sterilised. A declaration was sought from the court that the proposed sterilisation would be lawful. The unanimous decision of the Court of Appeal and the House of Lords was that the operation was in her best interests.

In both this case and the case of Jeanette the mental age of the women concerned was a crucial factor. The crude application of intelligence assessments to social and emotional development is questionable:

Lee, R and Morgan, D, 'Sterilisation and mental handicap: sapping the strength of the State?' (1988) 15 JLS 229:

The problem of mental age

If the Law Lords appear to have been woefully uninformed as to the reality of the present life for mentally handicapped women, they are also less than convincing in showing an understanding of their capacities. One of the most persistent criticisms of the decision in the professional press concerned the emphasis ascribed to the criteria of mental age, and the use to which this was put. Having stated that Jeanette had a mental age of five or six, the judgments in *Re B* seem to treat Jeanette as if she were simply a child of that age. Jeanette, like all other handicapped people, would be expected to demonstrate different functional abilities across a whole range of skills. Intelligence testing offers little information as to many of these abilities, and in so far as it leads to labels such as 'mental age of five', it misdescribes the mentally handicapped person in a discriminatory fashion. Jeanette may not read at all, unlike many six year olds, but she may consistently outperform most children of that age in terms of socialisation or self-help. In addition, the criterion of 'mental age' was treated as static. Yet, as Woolrych has observed ... the use of the discredited concept of 'mental age' is disturbing, since current experiences indicate learning potential is dependent on the quality and variety of services available in developing an understanding of issues such as the connection between sex and having babies.

Nor will the concept of mental age shed much light upon Jeanette's biological and emotional state as a 17 year old woman. While it may be difficult to grapple with the concept of a physically mature woman manifesting childlike intelligence in some respects, we must be careful that we do not discount and become repulsed by the notion that this person manifests adult sexual desires. This is a problem facing many parents of mentally handicapped young women.

Can we expect judges to be aware of the controversy which surrounds the notion of mental age? It is used, in part, to justify an irreversible surgical procedure. This procedure eliminates reproductive capacities, infringing what some would claim to be a basic human right. If the courts are to be used to channel issues of controversial ethical dilemmas, and if they are to legitimate their authority to resolve them, then informed judgment is a starting point.

It was stated in *Re B* that the case was about removing the 'right to reproduce'. Is there such a right? It is often stated that there is: for example, Art 12 of the European Convention on Human Rights enshrines the 'right to marry and found a family'.

Freeman, MD (ed), *Medicine, Ethics and the Law*, 1988, London: Stevens, p 72:

Why do we have the rights we have and do we have the right to reproduce? One common answer links rights with interests. Such a view was implicit in Bentham and Ihering and is found in such contemporary writers as Feinberg and McCloskey. Thus, Feinberg writes that 'the sort of beings who can have rights are precisely those who have (or can have) interests'. It is an argument often employed by those who believe that animals have rights. It is also one of the arguments employed by Carby-Hall to demonstrate the Jeanette did not have the right to reproduce. She writes: 'A being can truly be said to have an interest in x, the subject of a potential right, if and only if x will benefit him in the sense of furthering some or all of his present or future desires.' She argues that a necessary condition of possession of a right is at least the capacity to possess the relevant concepts and a desire for that right. Jeanette clearly lacked the former and almost certainly the latter. But is this association of rights and interests justifiable? I think not. What this does not answer is how the having of interests establishes the grounds for having rights. Animals have interests. I have an interest in Middlesex winning the County Cricket Championship. In neither would it make sense to talk of rights. Human beings do not have the same interests. Surely this does not justify an unequal distribution of human rights. I agree with Alan White that 'no valid argument can be given either for including or for excluding children, imbeciles (*inter alia*) ... as holders of rights on the ground that being capable of having a right ensures or necessitates being capable either of having something in one's interest or of being interested in something. Hence, he concludes, 'the question whether animals, etc ... can or cannot have interests, either in the sense of something being in their interest or in the sense of their being interested in something, is irrelevant to the question whether they can have rights ...

Before we pursue the justifying principle any further it may be as well to ponder the Carby-Hall claim. Can it be right that a necessary condition for the possession of a right is the capacity to possess relevant concepts and a desire for the right in question? Carby-Hall is far from being alone in thinking that it is. In *Causing Death and Saving Lives*, Glover puts the case as follows:

> Desires do not presuppose words, but they do presuppose concepts. A baby can want to be fed, or be changed, or go to his mother, although he does not speak. Innumerable signs of recognition and pleasure show us that he has these concepts. But a baby cannot want to escape from death any more than he can want to escape the fate of being a chartered accountant when grown up. He has no idea of either.

Glover goes on to argue that the autonomy argument is no objection to infanticide. 'In killing a baby, someone is overriding the baby's autonomy to no greater extent than he would be if he prevented the mother from coming home that day.' Or, in the language of *Re B*: 'In sterilising Jeanette, we are overriding her autonomy to no greater extent than we would be doing if we prevented her seeing her boyfriend this evening (by, for example, arranging for him to be elsewhere).' I do not find this very convincing. The fact that a baby has no awareness of, or desire for, life cannot mean that it does not have a right to life. It may be difficult, if not impossible, to exercise a right if one is unaware of its existence or one lacks the concepts or the desire, but this cannot mean that one lacks the right in question.

Freeman is trying to resist the argument that Jeanette had no right to reproduce as long as she was unaware of that so called right. Is awareness of such a right relevant to its existence? If you are deliberately locked in a room and are unaware of this, does it mean that up until the point that you wish to leave you have no right to leave the room? Of course, in the cases of Jeanette and F, it was assumed that they would never wish to leave the room, but it is questionable whether that assumption is justified. Further, the assertion that the right to reproduce meant nothing to her belongs to a dangerous species of argument, ie, 'you have no rights because you are incapable of exercising them, or incapable of exercising them in your own best interests'.

It could be said that there is no *right* to reproduce because such a right is unenforceable. It might be better to say that one has a right to *attempt* to reproduce. However, viewed in this language, would it make sense to say that in the cases of Jeanette and F, they had no right to attempt, because that presupposes a decision making capacity which they may not have had? It is doubtful whether this is correct. Many children are produced unintentionally. If one was only endorsing a right to attempt to reproduce, it may be argued that such an unintentional pregnancy was less valuable than others. Might the better view be that of Raanan Gillon who argues that there is a *prima facie* right not to be prevented? (See 'On sterilising severely mentally handicapped people' (1987) 13 JME 59.) The right may not be absolute, but it is arguable that it should only be overridden, in the words of Brennan J, 'to avoid a tragedy that is imminent and certain'.

Is it even necessary to consider the issue in the language of rights? It must be the case that a woman, even if mentally impaired, is entitled to the same amount of respect for her human dignity and physical integrity as any other person. There is a strong argument that subjecting her to invasive surgery on the off-chance that she may become pregnant and 'pregnancy does not mean anything to her', is flouting respect for her dignity as a human being.

The cases of Jeanette and F are very different in at least one important respect. In the case of Jeanette, there was no suggestion that she was sexually active, or indeed, that she wished to be (it does not necessarily follow that she did, despite the so called provocative gestures – again consider her in comparison with a competent woman). In the case of F, however, it was said that she was having a sexual relationship (in the Court of Appeal, p 9):

Lord Donaldson MR: The particular problem in this case arises out of a relationship F has formed with another patient, P. This is of a sexual nature and probably involves sexual intercourse or something close to it on about two occasions a month ... There is no evidence of distress or distaste on the part of F. It is probable that she obtains some physical enjoyment. When asked what has happened she replies, 'Nice'. Dr McDonald does not regard P as having the state of mind to make him criminally liable and Dr McDonald certainly does not regard what is happening as sexual molestation. Professor Bicknell made the point that F is quite strong willed and if she does not want something she will not have it. Therefore, whilst there is no direct evidence whether F is a purely passive participant or obtains active enjoyment, I incline to the latter view. There is also evidence that F enjoys a cuddle with those with whom she has some bond. The attitude of F's carers to her relationship with P has been neither to encourage nor discourage it. Although there has been some criticism that this is equivocal, it is, in my judgment, entirely understandable and appropriate.

Some may argue that F needed protecting from this just as much as Jeanette may have needed protecting from sexual exploitation. However, too much 'protection' may interfere with the right to a private life, which, for example, is protected by the European Convention on Human Rights, Art 8. Many legal mechanisms and social conventions allow competent individuals a considerable measure of privacy. It is generally accepted that mentally impaired people should be afforded similar access to privacy and the means to enjoy pleasurable intimate activities as far as is possible (see, for example, O'Brien, J and Tyne, A, *The Principle of Normalisation*, 1981, London: Campaign for Mentally Handicapped People). At least this is accepted in principle, the practical considerations of providing the necessary facilities are less well worked out.) This was acknowledged in *Re F* by Lord Donaldson MR, p 9:

> There has been a shift from the paternalistic to a much freer approach. Mentally handicapped people have the same needs, feelings and longings as other people, and this is much more frequently acknowledged nowadays than years ago.

It was argued by the Official Solicitor that the proper course of action was to put an end to the relationship with P, but surely it would have been wrong to deny F the opportunity of sexual enjoyment simply as a contraceptive measure, as this would have been treating her differently from people deemed to have capacity. The desirability of sterilisation as opposed to other forms of contraception, however, does not follow from the desirability of allowing this woman a degree of sexual freedom. What does follow from the case of *Re F* is that there was a real risk of pregnancy from a sexual relationship which, it appeared, was pleasurable and non-exploitative. The question of obtaining the consent of P (on the assumption that he may have been able to give consent) to the use of contraception, or even vasectomy, was not raised. If P was not capable of consenting, it is highly questionable whether sterilisation of him would ever have been in his best interests (see Douglas, G, *Law, Fertility and Reproduction*, 1991, London: Sweet & Maxwell), but it is, perhaps, significant that the issue was never considered.

A difficulty which does arise in this context is that under s 7 of the Sexual Offences Act 1956, it is an offence to have sexual intercourse with a mental defective (defined as someone with severe impairment of intelligence and social functioning). This may well place obstacles in the way of the sexual liberation of mentally impaired people. It is suggested that the offence, codified over 40 years ago, does not reflect the changes in attitude towards the 'normalisation' of impaired people alluded to above.

Two other sterilisation cases merit attention. In *Re W (Mental Patient) (Sterilisation)* [1993] 1 FLR 381 Hollis J authorised a sterilisation operation in circumstances where there was no evidence that the woman was involved in any sexual activity. In *Re P (A Minor) (Wardship: Sterilisation)* [1989] 1 FLR 182, the application was in respect of a 17 year old girl, who was described as having the intellectual development of a six year old, but with 'normal' sexual libido. Evidence suggested that she was likely to improve in the development of her 'social' skills. It was also said that pregnancy would be disastrous for her because she would be unlikely agree to an abortion, and to take the child away from her would cause her great distress as she had some maternal feelings. In *B*, it will be recalled, the fact that Jeanette had *no* maternal feelings was of some importance. We are now faced with a situation where the *presence* of maternal feelings is still disastrous. The question again arises: was this girl being treated in the same way as a 17 year old with capacity? An important factor in the case of *P* was that the type of operation proposed was considered to be reversible. If it was clear that pregnancy would be a disaster, what was the significance of reversibility, if it was not to regard the surgical procedure in the same light as contraceptive measures?

In *Re F*, Lord Bridge had suggested (p 52) that doctors may be under a *duty* to carry out a sterilisation operation, even for what we have described as 'non-therapeutic' reasons, if it was in the best interests of the patient. What is to be made of this suggestion? It is arguable that this could never be the case in respect of non-therapeutic sterilisations, in that the doctor's duty arises from the therapeutic context only.

However, *Re F* brings us face to face with the *Bolam* test in interpreting 'best interests'. In the Canadian case of *Re Eberhardy's Guardianship* (1981) 307 NW 2d 881 it was stated:

Heffernan J: While courts are always dependent upon the opinions of expert witnesses, it would appear that the exercise of judicial discretion unguided by well thought out policy determination reflecting the interests of society, as well as of the person to be sterilised, are hazardous indeed. Moreover, all seriously mentally retarded persons may not *ipso facto* be incapable of giving birth without serious trauma, and some may be good parents. Also there has been a discernible and laudable tendency to 'mainstream' the developmentally disabled and retarded. A properly thought out public policy on sterilisation or alternative contraceptive methods could well facilitate the entry of these persons into a more nearly normal relationship with society.

The 'interests of society' can be interpreted in two ways. First, these interests can be used to legitimise eugenic sterilisations. The second interpretation, and it is submitted that this is preferred in the light of Heffernan J's other remarks, is that the 'ad hoc' approach to best interests is open to substantial criticism. If there is a need to take on wider policy issues, then does this seriously undermine the *Bolam* test, relying as it does on the primacy of *medical* opinion?

Although there is no legal obligation to bring these cases before the court (although it may be a matter of 'good practice', see *Re F* above), the Official Solicitor has issued a Practice Note stating that the sanction of a High Court judge will be required in 'almost all circumstances'. There is also some guidance as to what should be evidenced before the court:

Practice Note (Sterilisation: Minors and Mental Health Patients) **[1993] 3 All ER 222:**

8 (1) (a) the patient is incapable of making his or her own decision about sterilisation; and

   (b) the patient is unlikely to develop sufficiently to make an informed judgment about sterilisation in the foreseeable future (in this connection it must be borne in mind;

      (i) that the fact that a person is legally incompetent for some purposes does not mean that he or she necessarily lacks the capacity to make a decision about sterilisation; and

      (ii) that in the case of a minor his or her youth and potential for development may make it difficult or impossible to make the relevant finding of incapacity);

 (2) that the condition which it is sought to avoid will in fact occur, for example, in the case of a contraceptive sterilisation that there is a need for contraception because:

   (a) the patient is physically capable of procreation; and

   (b) the patient is likely to engage in sexual activity, at the present or in the near future, under circumstances where there is a real danger as opposed to mere chance that pregnancy is likely to result;

 (3) that the patient will experience substantial trauma or psychological damage if the condition which it is sought to avoid should arise, for example, in the case of a contraceptive sterilisation that:

   (a) the patient (if a woman) is likely if she becomes pregnant or gives birth to experience substantial trauma or psychological damage greater than that resulting from the sterilisation itself; and

   (b) the patient is permanently incapable of caring for a child even with reasonable assistance, for example, from a future spouse in a case where the patient has or may have the capacity to marry;

 (4) that there is no practicable less intrusive alternative means of solving the anticipated problem than immediate sterilisation, in other words that:

(a) sterilisation is advisable at the time of the application rather than in the future;

(b) the proposed method of sterilisation entails the least invasion of the patient's body;

(c) sterilisation will not itself cause physical or psychological damage greater than the intended beneficial effects;

(d) the current state of scientific and medical knowledge does not suggest either (i) that a reversible sterilisation procedure or other less drastic solution to the problem ought to be avoided, for example, some other contraceptive method will shortly be available or (ii) that science is on the threshold of an advance in the treatment of the patient's disability; and

(e) in the case of contraceptive sterilisation all less drastic contraceptive methods, including supervision, education and training, have proved unworkable or inapplicable.

The Law Commission has recommended that any treatment or procedure intended or reasonably likely to render the person permanently infertile should required court authorisation unless it is to treat a disease of the reproductive organs or relieve existing detrimental effects of menstruation (Law Commission, *Report on Mental Incapacity*, Report No 231, 1995, London: HMSO, para 6.4). This brings us to consideration of the latter justification of sterilisation.

Sterilisation to manage menstruation – therapeutic or non-therapeutic?

In *Re Eve* it was said:

> **La Forest J**: ... I should perhaps add ... that sterilisation may, on occasion, be necessary as an adjunct to treatment of a serious malady, but I would underline that this, of course, does not allow for subterfuge or for treatment of some marginal medical problem ... The recent British Columbia case of *Re K* (1985) 19 DLR (4th) 255, is at best dangerously close to the limits of the permissible.

The case of *Re K* concerned the authorisation of a sterilisation operation on a child to prevent menstruation occurring because the child had an aversion to blood. There have been several other cases where sterilisation has been advocated as a suitable way of managing menstruation. For example in *Re E (A Minor) (Medical Treatment)* [1991] 2 FLR 585 and *Re GF (Medical Treatment)* [1992] 1 FLR 293 hysterectomies were authorised in both cases where the women, described as severely handicapped, suffered from excessively heavy periods. In *Re E* the proposed sterilisation was in respect of a 17 year old girl. Sir Stephen Brown P held that since it was for therapeutic reasons and not to achieve sterilisation, the parents could consent to the operation, and there was no need for the intervention of the court. In *Re GF* the woman was an adult.

Again, Sir Stephen Brown referred to the therapeutic nature of the procedure, stating that, because of this, there was no need for a declaration as to its lawfulness. It is submitted that the removal of court protection in this way is wrong. It was suggested earlier in this chapter that the therapeutic/non-therapeutic distinction may not always protect the person lacking capacity. Sterilisations carried out for the purposes of 'menstrual management' do achieve sterilisation, even if this was not the purpose. To remove the need for an order of the court is to deny the person valuable protection from non-therapeutic sterilisations being carried out under the guise of 'therapeutic' purposes.

The dangers of such operations being used for non-medical reasons have been considered by Natasha Cica:

Cica, N, 'Sterilising the intellectually disabled' (1993) 1 Med L Rev 186, p 198:

Care must ... be taken in defining when performing a hysterectomy to prevent menstruation may be considered to be 'therapeutic'. It is submitted that four broad principles should govern this category of sterilisation.

1 The procedure should only be described as therapeutic if performed to alleviate or prevent a recognised clinical condition. Merely 'hygienic' purposes should, for the reasons discussed above, be classified as non-therapeutic. The recognised clinical condition may be a physical condition such as a disorder whose symptoms include excessively heavy or painful periods. Or it may be a psychiatric or psychological condition, in which case 'mere' distress or embarrassment would seem to be insufficient. The distress or disturbance suffered by the woman must be sufficiently serious to pose an identifiable danger to her mental health. Again this is necessary to ensure that the woman's best social interests are not confused with, her best medical interests. This requirement that a clinically recognised psychiatric or psychological condition be present was imposed by Brennan J in *Department of Health v JWB and SMB* (1992) 66 ALJR 300 when he referred to the need for 'a psychiatric disorder' of sufficient severity before suppression of menstruation via hysterectomy may be justified. The requirement was arguably also implicit in Deane J's description of his second category of permissible sterilisations [in *Department of Health v JWB and SMB*]. As described above, this category was based upon the facts of the New Zealand case of *Re X* (1992), in which the intellectually disabled 15 year old's reaction to menstrual pain would have been fits of uncomprehending irritability, violence towards others and self-mutilation. For a case to fall within Deane J's second category, menstruation must entail 'grave and unusual problems and suffering ... pain and extraordinary behavioural and personal problems'. Deane J specified that these grave, unusual and extraordinary problems may arise from, *inter alia*, an inability to comprehend or cope with pain; a phobic aversion to blood; or a complete inability to cope with problems of hygiene with *psychiatric or psychological consequences*.

2 Such a procedure will only be 'therapeutic' if the clinically recognised condition is already present or is virtually certain to arise in the near

future. There must be a 'real possibility' that the condition will arise. The less imminent the clinical condition whose treatment is sought by hysterectomy, the more likely the physical, psychiatric or psychological state of the intellectually disabled woman will change and that hysterectomy will not be required.

3   A hysterectomy will only be 'therapeutic' if it is *necessary* for the above purposes, in that it is a treatment of 'last resort'. There must be no alternative, less invasive treatment which would effectively alleviate the condition. The harm done must be proportionate to the risk of harm avoided. Brennan J's notion of 'proportionality' is clearly the guiding principle here.

4   There must be advice from appropriately qualified medical experts that the above conditions are satisfied. Where the health-threatening condition is psychiatric or psychological, expert advice must be given by an appropriately qualified psychiatrist or psychologist. The expert opinions of general practitioners and gynaecologists alone would be insufficient in such cases.

The Law Commission (see above, p 217) has not thought it necessary to require court authorisation for such procedures, but the report goes on to say:

Law Commission, *Report on Mental Incapacity*, Report No 231, 1995, London: HMSO, para 6.9:

... many of our respondents expressed concern about operations being labelled 'for menstrual management', with the result that no independent supervision at all is required. A consultant in developmental psychiatry who has made a special study of sterilisation of people with learning disabilities suggested that the level of menstrual distress is often misrepresented, and that further investigation can reveal less drastic means of coping with the problem than a sterilisation operation.

The Commission goes on to recommend that such procedures should require a certificate from an independent medical practitioner where it is for relieving the existing detrimental effects of menstruation. Is this a safeguard? It is submitted that it is not. There is no suggestion that the certificate should specify whether the 'detrimental' effects are medical or social; it does not impose a requirement as to the gravity of the detrimental effects, and no mention is made of alternative measures that could be taken.

Abortion

It was stated in *Re SG (A Patient)* [1993] 4 Med LR 75 (see above, p 183) that the provisions of the Abortion Act are an adequate safeguard for an incompetent woman, and there is no need of court authorisation. It is submitted that they are not (see Chapter 8). In addition, assuming that the woman (although incompetent) has expressed a wish to have the child, there is something highly distasteful about forcing her to submit to an abortion.

Whilst there may be many occasions when an abortion will be the best course of action for an incompetent woman, it is suggested that the vigilance necessary in cases of sterilisation should be present when considering the performance of an abortion (see, for example, the remarks of Lord Donaldson MR in the Court of Appeal in *Re F*, p 19).

CHAPTER FIVE

CONFIDENTIALITY AND ACCESS TO MEDICAL RECORDS

CONFIDENTIALITY – THE DUTY

The ethical obligation

It is not only of academic interest to look at the ethical justifications for the obligation of confidence, it is also important to keep them in mind when examining the circumstances in which the obligation can be lawfully breached, and to consider whether the breaches in question can also be justified on ethical grounds.

As we have seen, the doctrine of utilitarianism assesses the ethics of a course of action on the basis that it will result in the best consequences overall. In the context of confidentiality, therefore, the obligation is justified by the utility of doctors keeping medical information secret. The argument is that if there no assurance of secrecy, then patients would be reluctant to seek medical advice and treatment, or would be less than frank when doing so. This would, it is argued, have an adverse effect on the health of society. The argument is described by Raanan Gillon.

> **Gillon, R, *Philosophical Medical Ethics*, 1986, Chichester: John Wiley, p 108:**
>
> Why should doctors from the time of Hippocrates to the present have promised to keep their patients' secrets? If confidentiality is not a moral good in itself what moral good does it serve? The commonest justification for the duty, of medical confidentiality is undoubtedly consequentialist: people's better health, welfare, the general good, and overall happiness are more likely to be attained if doctors are fully informed by their patients, and this is more likely if doctors undertake not to disclose their patients' secrets. Conversely, if patients did not believe that doctors would keep their secrets then either they would not divulge embarrassing but potentially medically important information, thus reducing their chances of getting the best medical care, or they would disclose such information and feel anxious and unhappy at the prospect of their secrets being made known.

The utilitarian view is particularly appropriate to confidentiality as it will readily admit that the duty is not absolute and can be breached in certain circumstances. It would be argued that the breach is justified when the utility of disclosure outweighs the utility produced by keeping the confidences. As will be seen, the only legal justification at common law for disclosure is either that the patient has consented, or that it is in the public interest to disclose. The language of the public interest defence has a strong utilitarian flavour: *AG v Guardian Newspapers (No 2)* [1990] AC 109, p 282, *per* Lord Goff:

Lord Goff: although the basis of the law's protection of confidence is that there is a public interest that confidences should be preserved and protected by the law, nevertheless that public interest may be outweighed by some other countervailing public interest which favours disclosure.

Francis Gurry, *In Breach of Confidence*, 1984, Oxford: Clarendon Press, says (p 5):

The public interest is a reincarnation of the older common law principle of public policy, which was described by Winfield as 'a principle of judicial legislation or interpretation founded on the current needs of the community'. Its function in the enforcement of confidences is the same as the role played by public policy in the formulation of contract law. It provides a starting point for the courts' intervention and circumscribes the scope of that intervention.

As we have already seen, utilitarianism can be contrasted with deontological theories in which duty rather than purpose is the fundamental concept of ethics. Gillon states:

Gillon, R, *Philosophical Medical Ethics*, 1986, Chichester: John Wiley, p 108:

Deontologists ... are likely to base their arguments for confidentiality not just (if at all) on welfare considerations but also on the moral principle of respect for autonomy or sometimes on a putatively independent principle of respect for privacy, which is seen as a fundamental moral requirement in itself. Thus, while the principle of medical confidentiality is not defended as a moral end in itself, it is defended by utilitarians and deontologists alike as a means to some morally desirable end the general welfare, respect for people's autonomy, or respect for their privacy.

Beauchamp and Childress suggest an approach based upon autonomy:

Beauchamp, TL and Childress, JF, *Principles of Biomedical Ethics*, 4th edn, 1994, Oxford: OUP, p 423:

... A second approach to the justification of rules and rights of confidentiality does not ground them exclusively in goals or consequences, but looks to moral principles or rules such as respect for autonomy and privacy. The argument for privacy ... can here be extended to confidentiality, where breaches have often been viewed as primarily violations of privacy and personal integrity ...

These concerns are reflected in the various ethical codes referred to in Chapter 1. The Hippocratic Oath states: '... all that may come to my knowledge in the exercise of my profession or outside of my profession or in daily commerce with men, which ought not to be spread abroad, I will keep secret and will never reveal.' The Declaration of Geneva contains a similar statement.

The General Medical Council's guidance

It must be remembered that the following guidance issued by the General Medical Council does not have the force of law, and cannot be taken to be co-extensive with the law. However, there is no doubt that the guidance has persuasive authority (see the reference thereto in *W v Egdell* [1990] 1 All ER 835, p 843).

General Medical Council, *Confidentiality: Guidance from the General Medical Council*, 1995, London: GMC:

Disclosure within teams

3   Modern medical practice usually involves teams of doctors, other health care workers, and sometimes people from outside the health care professions. The importance of working in teams is explained in the GMC's booklet *Good Medical Practice*. To provide patients with the best possible care, it is often essential to pass confidential information between members of the team.

4   You should make sure – through the use of leaflets and posters as necessary – that patients understand why and when information may be shared between team members and any circumstances in which team members providing non-medical care may be required to disclose information to third parties.

5   Where the disclosure of relevant information between health care professionals is clearly required for treatment to which a patient has agreed, the patient's explicit consent would not be needed where a general practitioner discloses relevant information to a medical secretary to have a referral letter typed, or a physician makes relevant information available to a radiologist when requesting an X-ray.

6   There will also be circumstances where, because of a medical emergency, a patient's consent cannot be obtained, but relevant information must in the patient's interest be transferred between health care workers.

7   If a patient does not wish you to share particular information with other members of the team, you must respect those wishes. If you and a patient have established a relationship based on trust, the patient may choose to give you discretion to disclose information to other team members, as required.

8   All medical members of a team have a duty to make sure that other team members understand and observe confidentiality.

Disclosure to employers and insurance companies

9   When assessing a patient on behalf of a third party (for example, an employer or insurance company) you must make sure, at the outset, that the patient is aware of the purpose of the assessment, of the obligation that the doctor has towards the third parties concerned, and that this may necessitate the disclosure of personal information. You should undertake such assessments only with the patient's written consent.

Disclosure of information without the patient's consent

Disclosure in the patient's medical interests

10   Problems may arise if you consider that a patient is incapable of giving consent to treatment because of immaturity, illness or mental incapacity, and you have tried unsuccessfully to persuade the patient to allow an appropriate person to be involved in the consultation. If you are convinced that it is essential in the patient's medical interests, you may disclose relevant information to an appropriate person or authority. You must tell the patient before disclosing any information. You should remember that the judgment of whether patients are capable of giving or

withholding consent to treatment or disclosure must be based on an assessment of their ability to appreciate what the treatment or advice being sought may involved, and not solely on their age.

11   If you believe a patient to be a victim of neglect or physical or sexual abuse, and unable to give or withhold consent to disclosure, you should usually give information to an appropriate responsible person or statutory agency, in order to prevent further harm to the patient. In these and similar circumstances, you may release information without the patient's consent, but only if you consider that the patient is unable to give consent, and that the disclosure is in the patient's best medical interests.

12   Rarely you may judge that seeking consent to the disclosure of confidential information would be damaging to the patient, but that the disclosure would be in the patient's medical interests. For example, you may judge that it would be in a patient's interests that a close relative should know about the patient's terminal condition, but that the patient would be seriously harmed by the information. In such circumstances information may be disclosed without consent.

Disclosure after a patient's death

13   You still have an obligation to keep information confidential after a patient dies. The extent to which confidential information may be disclosed after a patient's death will depend on the circumstances. These include the nature of the information, whether that information is already public knowledge, and how long it is since the patient died. Particular difficulties may arise when there is a conflict of interest between parties affected by the patient's death. For example, if an insurance company seeks information about a deceased patient in order to decide whether to make a payment under a life assurance policy, you should not release information without the consent of the patient's executor, or a close relative, who has been fully informed of the consequences of disclosure.

14   You should be aware that the Access to Health Records Act 1990 gives third parties right of access, in certain circumstances, to the medical records of a deceased patient.

Disclosure for medical teaching, medical research and medical audit
Research

15   Where, for the purposes of medical research there is a need to disclose information which it is not possible to anonymise effectively, every reasonable effort must be made to inform the patients concerned, or those who may properly give permission on their behalf, that they may, at any stage withhold their consent to disclosure.

16   Where consent cannot be obtained, this fact should be drawn to the attention of a research ethics committee which should decide whether the public interest in the research outweighs patients' right to confidentiality. Disclosure to a researcher may otherwise be improper, even if the researcher is a registered medical practitioner.

Disclosure in the interests of others

18   Disclosures may be necessary in the public interest where a failure to disclose information may expose the patient or others to a risk of death or

serious harm. In such circumstances, you should disclose information promptly to an appropriate person or authority.

19 Such circumstances may arise, for example, where:

- a patient continues to drive, against medical advice, when unfit to do so. In such circumstances, you should disclose relevant information to the medical adviser of the Driver and Vehicle Licensing Agency without delay ...;

- a colleague, who is also a patient, is placing patients at risk as a result of illness or another medical condition. Guidance on this issue, and on the rights of doctors who are ill, is contained in the GMC's leaflet, [*Serious Communicable Diseases*];

- disclosure is necessary for the prevention or detection of a serious crime.

The guidance also deals with disclosure in connection with teaching, during the course of court proceedings and to tax inspectors.

Consider the suggestion here that disclosure within the family is acceptable (para 12). It is here that the interface between the law and the pragmatism exemplified by these sorts of guidelines reflects many of the essential difficulties of medical law. What is a doctor to do, say, when faced with a distressed spouse of a terminally ill patient? If the patient has informed the doctor that he does not wish any form of disclosure to the spouse, then although any subsequent conversations with that spouse may be difficult, it is quite clear that the doctor must refuse to discuss his patient's medical condition. However, in the absence of that express request on the part of the patient, under what principle does the doctor justify discussing the patient's medical condition with relatives of the patient? In the case of *Re S (Hospital Orders: Court's Jurisdiction)* [1995] 3 All ER 290, it was held that blood ties conferred no right to determine the course of treatment or care, and this would surely extend to the acquisition of confidential information. It seems that the law does not sanction such disclosure, unless one can argue that there is some form of implied or tacit consent.

Consider also that there is still an obligation of confidentiality after the death of the patient (para 13). Although the law lacks clarity on this point, it may be that the legal obligation of confidence will not remain after the death of the patient (see further below, p 261).

The issues raised by this guidance are considered under the appropriate headings below.

The legal obligation

A rights-based approach might regard the duty of keeping confidences as a respect for the right to privacy. There is no right to privacy in English law, although in practice much that is private can be protected in other ways, for example, the tort of trespass, nuisance and so on. Furthermore, the European

Convention on Human Rights, due to be incorporated into English law, protects the right to a 'private life' (Art 8).

What is the difference between a right to privacy and a right to have confidential information protected? The law imposes a number of requirements in order for a cause of action to arise for breach of confidence, and these criteria mean that, for example, press photographers owe no duty of confidence unless the photography takes place in 'confidential circumstances', or there had been a prior agreement not to publish. If neither of these applied, only a right to privacy could offer protection from publication. However, Richard Scott would like to see a more imaginative use of the law of confidence:

> **Scott, R, 'Introduction', in Clarke, L (ed), *Confidentiality and the Law*, 1990, London: LLP, p xxi:**
>
> [Referring to] the recent Court of Appeal decision in *Kaye v Robertson* ((1990) *The Times*, 21 March). The Court of Appeal held that a trespassing journalist who took unauthorised photographs of the plaintiff in his hospital bed, could not be restrained by injunction from publishing the photographs in a daily newspaper. One of the judges commented on '... the failure of ... the common law of England ... to protect in an effective way the personal privacy of individual citizens'. Another said that a right to privacy 'had so long been disregarded ... that it could be recognised now only by the legislature'. But nowhere, in the report of the judgments, was there any mention of the law of confidentiality. Why not? It is not essential to a cause of action based on the law of confidentiality that the information or material should have been specifically disclosed or confided by a confider. Lord Griffiths made that point in his speech in the *Spycatcher* case.

However, as far as medical information is concerned, this may, by its very nature, impose a duty of confidentiality upon the media. In other words, would the duty which would have originated in the context of the doctor-patient relationship pass down the line to whoever may acquire the information? Although Scott does not specifically allude to this point, might it have been arguable that the fact that Gorden Kaye was in a hospital bed was a piece of medical information, and the publication of a photograph affirming that was a breach of medical confidentiality, rather than an intrusion into privacy?

Identifying the nature of the obligation

The law of the obligation to keep confidences is not easy to categorise. It is sometimes regarded as an application of equitable principles, sometimes as belonging to the law of tort and/or contract. There is no doubt that the obligation may arise under the law of contract, either expressly or impliedly, but it is clear that it is wider than that. Certainly as far as medicine is concerned, if it were contract-based only, there would be no legal obligation to keep confidences within the context of National Health Service treatment (see *Pfizer Corporation v Ministry of Health* [1965] AC 512). There has been much academic debate on the subject:

Gurry, F, *In Breach of Confidence*, 1984, Oxford: Clarendon Press, p 25:

The jurisdictional basis of the action for breach of confidence has been a source of lingering uncertainty and controversy. Contract, equity and property have at different times each provided the basis on which the courts have granted relief. In some cases, a mixture of these bases has been relied on. Thus, in *Alperton Rubber Co v Manning* Peterson J referred to the defendant's conduct as 'a breach of trust or confidence, and ... a breach of the implied provision in all contracts of service that the employee will observe the rules of honesty'; and, in *Prince Albert v Strange*, the court founded the defendants' liability first on property, secondly on a 'breach of trust, confidence or contract'.

The lack of clarity in the law led to a Law Commission inquiry which reported in 1981 (Law Commission, *Breach of Confidence*, Report No 110, Cmnd 8388, 1981, London: HMSO). The Commission made a number of recommendations, the principal one being that there be a new statutory tort of breach of confidence. No government action has ever been taken on this.

The obligation of confidence, whatever its origin, although not absolute, is free standing, in that the preservation of confidence itself is in the public interest and therefore an end in itself. However, it can conflict with other matters of public interest. It is important to stress that when conflicts arise, they are conflicts between two competing *public* interests, not between private and public interests.

Scott, R, 'Introduction', in Clarke, L (ed), *Confidentiality and the Law*, 1990, London: LLP, p xxii:

The law of confidentiality, like the law of negligence and the law of nuisance, requires a balance to be struck. The balance will, on both sides, involve public and private interests. The newspapers that wanted to publish extracts from *Spycatcher* had private commercial interest in doing so. But there was also a public interest in freedom of speech. On the other side there was a public interest in the protection of the secrets of the security service (no private interest since the litigant was the Government). In the *Francome* case, the plaintiff had a private interest in maintaining the privacy of his telephone conversations but, ranged on the same side, there was a public interest that private telephone conversations should not be the subject of eavesdropping. On the other side, the *Daily Mirror* could rely, in aid of its own private interest, on the public interest in the disclosure of alleged wrongdoing. These are examples to make the point that every case where the law of confidentiality is invoked requires the judge to strike a balance between competing interests.

The elements of an action for breach of confidence

The essential elements of the law can be summarised by the statement in *AG v Guardian Newspapers (No 2)* [1990] AC 109, pp 281–82, *per* Lord Goff:

Lord Goff: I start with the broad general principle (which I do not intend in any way to be definitive) that a duty of confidence arises when confidential information comes to the knowledge of a person (the confidant) in circumstances where he has notice, or is held to have agreed, that the information is confidential, with the effect that it would be just in all the circumstances that he should be precluded from disclosing the information to others ...

[In addition to] this broad general principle, there are three limiting principles to which I wish to refer. The first limiting principle (which is rather an expression of the scope of the duty) is highly relevant to this appeal. It is that the principle of confidentiality only applies to information to the extent that it is confidential. In particular, once it has entered what is usually called the public domain (which means no more than that the information in question is so generally accessible that, in all the circumstances, it cannot be regarded as confidential) then, as a general rule, the principle of confidentiality can have no application to it ...

The second limiting principle is that the duty of confidence applies neither to useless information, nor to trivia ...

The third limiting principle is of far greater importance. It is that, although the basis of the law's protection of confidence is that there is a public interest that confidences should be preserved and protected by the law, nevertheless that public interest may be outweighed by some other countervailing public interest which favours disclosure.

There can be no doubt that the doctor-patient relationship gives rise to an obligation of confidence which fits clearly into the criteria applied generally in the law.

Hunter v Mann [1974] 1 QB 767 confirmed such an obligation which was reiterated in *AG v Guardian Newspapers (No 2)* [1990] AC 109, p 255, *per* Lord Keith:

Lord Keith: The law has long recognised that an obligation of confidence can arise out of particular relationships. Examples are the relationships of doctor and patient, priest and penitent, solicitor and client, banker and customer.

The uncontroversial nature of the obligation, therefore, means that generally problems will only arise when decisions have to be made which will breach the obligation and whether the breach can be justified. Indeed it may be said that the doctor's duty of confidence is over-determined in that it stems both from the quality of the information and from the circumstances in which it is acquired, each of which is independently sufficient. It follows that, although not usually the subject of litigation, there may be difficulties, first, if the information is not *medical* information, and secondly, if it has been imparted in circumstances other than a doctor-patient consultation.

The confidential information

The law on confidentiality will protect a variety of types of information, imparted in a variety of different situations. Information acquired in the confidential circumstances of an employment relationship, for example, will be protected, as will that acquired in the course of an intimate domestic relationship. The latter need not be a marriage, nor even a heterosexual relationship. This was examined in the case of *Stephens v Avery* [1988] 1 Ch 449, where it was held that information relating to sexual conduct (in that case, a lesbian relationship) could be the subject of a legally enforceable duty of confidentiality.

On this basis, therefore, information concerning the sexual conduct of a patient, if imparted to a doctor in circumstances of confidentiality, will be protected, even though it is not medical information. The Court of Appeal decision in *R v Wilson* [1996] 3 WLR 125 raises this issue. In that case, the defendant appealed against a conviction for actual bodily harm under s 47 of the Offences Against the Person Act 1861. He had been charged as a result of marking his wife's buttocks with his initials by use of a hot knife. This was done with her consent, and, it appeared from the case reports, at her specific request. Although the appeal was concerned with the applicability of the decision in *R v Brown* [1993] 2 All ER 75, the implications for medical confidentiality arise from the fact that the matter appears to have come to the attention of the police from a report made to them by her doctor, who became aware of the marks during the course of a medical examination (see (1996) *The Times*, 5 March and (1996) *The Guardian*, 1 March, p 5).

If the police were informed of this by the doctor, without the consent of the woman concerned, then here was a potential breach of confidentiality. The fact that the information was not strictly medical would not protect the doctor, because first, on the basis of *Stephens v Avery*, it has the necessary quality of confidence, and secondly, it was imparted in the circumstances of a medical consultation.

The circumstances in which the information is acquired

It may be that it is not clear that the circumstances are such as to amount to 'confidential' circumstances. The inadvertent acquisition of information which clearly has the necessary quality of confidence about it, binds the recipient, as was suggested by Lord Goff in *AG v Guardian Newspapers (No 2)* [1990] AC 109, p 282:

> **Lord Goff**: I realise that, in the vast majority of cases, in particular those concerned with trade secrets, the duty of confidence will arise from a transaction or relationship between the parties – often a contract, in which event the duty may arise by reason of either an express or an implied term of that contract. It is in such cases as these that the expressions 'confider' and

'confidant' are perhaps most aptly employed. But it is well settled that a duty of confidence may arise in equity, independently of such cases; and I have expressed the circumstances in which the duty arises in broad terms, not merely to embrace those cases where a third party receives information from a person who is under a duty of confidence in respect of it, knowing that it has been disclosed by that person to him in breach of his duty of confidence, but also to include certain situations, beloved of law teachers, where an obviously confidential document is wafted by an electric fan out of a window into a crowded street, or where an obviously confidential document, such as a private diary, is dropped in a public place, and is then picked up by a passer-by.

The case of *R v Wilson* is, again, interesting in relation to this point, as it raises the possibility of a doctor being obliged towards a third party when he acquires confidential information in the context of a medical consultation.

Wheat, K, 'Can paternalism ever justify a breach of confidence?' (1997) 3(3) Health Care Risk Report 12:

Extension of duty

Another difficult question raised to which there is no clear answer is the position of the husband of the patient in this case. Could it be argued that the doctor owed him a duty of confidence? Further, would it make any difference if he were also a patient of the doctor? To look at the latter question first, if the doctor-patient relationship is to make any difference, then it must be the case that the duty extends to any information obtained about a patient which has the necessary quality of confidence.

It cannot be said with any degree of certainty that this reflects the legal position. Gurry, for example, says that, although the duty is not limited to information acquired directly from the patient but extends to information from other sources, that further information must have been picked up by the doctor by way of his or her position as the patient's doctor. Kennedy and Grubb interpret this as extending to information obtained from third parties who know of the doctor-patient relationship, but pass no comment as to whether it would extend to non-medical information.

Here, the information would not have been obtained by the doctor by virtue of his status as the patient's doctor, but as another patient's doctor, and, although the third party here, namely the wife, would have known about the doctor-patient relationship, the information was not of a medical nature. Given the difficulties, therefore, in arguing that the duty owed is a duty owed *qua* doctor, perhaps it is open to the husband to rely upon the general law of confidentiality and a duty owed to him regardless of him being a patient of the doctor concerned.

...

Elements of a breach of confidence action

[Referring to the *Guardian* criteria] [t]here is no difficulty in satisfying the first limb of the test as the information concerned intimate details of a sexual relationship, which will possess the necessary quality of confidence. As to the second limb, although a consultation between doctor and patient will usually impart an obligation of confidence, it is arguable that the circumstances only impart the obligation by the doctor towards the patient ...

If it is clear from its nature that information is confidential, then a third party should be bound by it (see *Saltman Engineering v Campbell Engineering* [1963] 3 All ER 413), so it is hard to see how the fact that it is not acquired by chance, but in the context of another, different set of confidential circumstances should make any difference.

Statutory obligations of confidence

Good, utilitarian, public health arguments can sometimes justify a specific emphasis on confidentiality via statutory means. An example of this is contained within the National Health Service (Venereal Disease) Regulations 1974 SI 1974/29:

The National Health Service (Venereal Diseases) Regulations 1974 SI 1974/29

Confidentiality of information

2   Every Regional Health Authority and every District Health Authority shall take all necessary steps to secure that any information capable of identifying an individual obtained by officers of the Authority with respect to persons examined or treated for any sexually transmitted disease shall not be disclosed except:

(a) for the purpose of communicating that information to a medical practitioner or to a person employed under the direction of a medical practitioner in connection with the treatment of persons suffering from such disease or the prevention of the spread thereof; and

(b) for the purpose of such treatment or prevention.

Kennedy, I and Grubb, A, *Medical Law*, 2nd edn, 1994, London: Butterworths, p 646:

This regulation was introduced so as to give statutory emphasis to the obligation of confidence in this area of medical practice. The reasons are obvious: thus, the circumstances under which disclosure can be made are carefully circumscribed. Curiously, the Regulations have not been amended to apply to NHS trusts (but see NHS Trust (Venereal Disease) Directions 1991). It could be argued that the wording of the provision is such as to allow a patient's GP to be informed by those working in a genito-urinary clinic without the consent of, and even in the face of the refusal of, the patient. This has particular significance in the context of HIV infection where some have argued for the right of the GP to be informed of a patient's HIV status, allegedly in the interests of the patient so as to ensure any future care is medically optimal but, in the case of some doctors at least, in their own perceived interests.

A careful reading of the words of the Regulation suggests that it is only information relating to treatment for venereal disease and only when the GP himself is also treating for the disease that the exception comes into play. In essence it is merely an example of sharing information in the context of team care.

Even if this is wrong, a further point can be made. The notion of treatment entails the need for the patient's consent which itself entails agreement to share information about his condition. Arguably, Regulation 2(b) can have no application in the absence of the patient's agreement to the transfer of the information to his GP.

A small, but important, point to notice is that the obligation of confidence under the Regulations applies to any disease which is 'sexually transmitted'. If this is so, a patient who is HIV positive may need to look to the common law for protection of his confidence if he became infected by some other means as, for example, if he is a haemophiliac or has otherwise become HIV positive as a result of an infected blood donation. Alternatively a 'sexually transmitted disease' within the Regulations could be said to be one usually transmitted through sexual contact but which may be transmitted by other means. Blood, for example, may be infected with syphilis and transfused into someone who then develops the disease. The disease remains a 'sexually transmitted disease'. On this analysis HIV infection would be within the Regulations regardless of the means of infection. (See *X v Y* [1988] 2 All ER 648, in which Rose J assumes the latter to be the case.)

Incompetent patients and confidentiality

Are patients who lack capacity to make decisions about medical treatment owed the same duty of confidentiality?

Children

The ability of children to consent to medical treatment was dealt with in Chapters 3 and 4. The leading case is *Gillick v West Norfolk and Wisbech AHA* [1986] AC 112, and it is important to remember that this case was about confidentiality as well as consent. It will be recalled that Mrs Gillick objected to a DHSS circular which stated that a doctor, acting in good faith, would not be acting unlawfully if he prescribed contraceptives to a girl under the age of 16, and that, exceptionally, this could be done without informing the child's parents, as the principle of confidentiality applied between a doctor and a patient under the age of 16.

As we have seen, the *Gillick* case has been subject to a number of interpretations by the Court of Appeal which have sought to limit its application to one of protection for doctors acting in good faith, rather than an assertion of a child's right to self-determination when he has the necessary capacity. Although these later cases (*Re R (A Minor) (Wardship: Medical*

Treatment) [1991] 4 All ER 177 and *Re W (A Minor) (Medical Treatment)* [1992] 4 All ER 627) were not about confidentiality, they have implications for this area of medical law. In *Re R* Lord Donaldson said, p 186:

> **Lord Donaldson:** ... the judges treated *Gillick's* case as deciding that a *'Gillick* competent' child has a right to refuse treatment. In this I consider that they were in error. Such a child can consent, but if he or she declines to do so or refuses, consent can be given by someone else who has parental rights or responsibilities. The failure or refusal of the *'Gillick* competent' child is a very important factor in the doctor's decision whether or not to treat, but does not prevent the necessary consent being obtained from another competent source.

The clear implication of this interpretation is that a doctor, faced with a refusal of medical treatment by a child, is entitled to seek consent from a parent or someone *in loco parentis*. Suppose, however, the child consents to treatment, but requests that his parents are not informed? Two views can be taken of the implications for confidentiality of Lord Donaldson's interpretation of *Gillick*. The doctor is protected if, in good faith, he respects the child's confidence, and he cannot have a duty to disclose. If, however, the doctor discloses the matter to the child's parents (let us say, in the course of another consultation), then, one view of Lord Donaldson's interpretation is that he will not be in breach of any duty of confidence owed to the child, because the child's consent to treatment was not based on child autonomy, but on the provision of a 'flak jacket' of legal immunity for the doctor. In other words, the obligation of confidence would be modified in exactly the same way as is the requirement that there be a valid consent. The second view would be that the doctor should respect the child's request, as breaching confidentiality serves no purpose in relation to securing treatment. The latter view is to be preferred, being more consistent with the ethic of confidentiality.

However, if one takes a true autonomy view of *Gillick*, ie, that a child may be capable of making decisions about medical treatment so that he can refuse rather than consent, then it must be the case that he is entitled to respect of his medical confidences. It may be argued that the doctor is still under an obligation to inform his parents of what is happening because, although the parents will not be responsible for the consequences of medical treatment which they may have opposed if they had been given the opportunity, they will still have general parental responsibility for the child. On the other hand it was clear from *Gillick* that some duty of confidentiality was owed. It is no explanation to say, without more, that it depends on the nature of the treatment, because capacity to consent depends upon the understanding by the child of that particular treatment. However, the nature of the treatment may mean there are circumstances where a child is deemed to have sufficient understanding to, say, consent to an abortion. In consequence, even if this conflicts with parental opinion it may be necessary for the parents to be informed of the refusal, and the reasons for it, to enable them to continue to act as parents.

In the context of confidentiality, it is tempting to take the view that *Gillick* was special on its facts, ie, contraceptive advice, and that there was a strong element of policy in the decision, to avoid teenage pregnancies, and that the *Gillick* view on consent to other forms of medical treatment and advice would not usually involve a co-extensive view on confidentiality. Jonathan Montgomery comments on the situation in the USA:

Montgomery, J, 'Confidentiality and the immature minor' [1987] Fam Law 10:

The American position

American litigation in the field of birth control and abortion for minors proceeds by considering the extent of constitutional rights to privacy. In *Bellotti v Baird* 443 US 662 (1979) the court was asked to strike down a statute requiring parental consent before a minor was entitled to an abortion. Such a statute, said Powell J in giving the judgment of the court, could not be constitutional because it allowed an agency external to the minor herself to have a veto. A permissible system could be built around the 'mature minor rule'. Under that rule, a girl could go to court in order to have the abortion authorised. If she can prove herself sufficiently mature to take the decision herself, the court will automatically uphold her autonomy. If she cannot prove this, but can show that it would be in her best interests to have the abortion, the court must authorise the procedure. Otherwise the court has a discretion. In these latter circumstances the court may decide that it will be in the best interests of the child to inform her parents.

This position is similar to that which now prevails in English law. It differs in that the person who must decide whether the minor is sufficiently mature to take her own decision is, in this country, a doctor and not a judge. Powell J also considered the issue of confidentiality for the immature minor. He held that the Massachusetts statute before him was only constitutionally valid because under it 'every pregnant minor is entitled in the first instance to go directly to the court for a judicial determination without prior parental notice, consultation or consent' (443 US 662, p 649). Translated into the English context, this would mean that a minor is entitled to approach his or her doctor to have that person determine her capacity to consent to the medical procedures without her parents being informed. If she is found not to have that capacity, she must choose between not receiving the treatment or telling her parents, but that is 'her choice, not the doctor's'.

Incompetent adults

The unhappy state of affairs with regard to medical decision making on behalf of incompetent adults has been examined in Chapter 4. At present, decisions can be taken, and treatment administered if these are in the patient's best interests. It is arguable that it will always be in the patient's best interests to respect his confidences, unless one or more of the circumstances exist in which confidence can be breached lawfully in respect of a competent adult patient.

CONFIDENTIALITY – BREACHING CONFIDENCES

The duty of confidence is not absolute and there are circumstances in which medical information can be divulged. This part of the chapter will examine these circumstances.

Consent

It may seem trite to say that confidence can be breached with the consent of the patient, but this fell to be considered by the court in the case of *C v C* [1946] 1 All ER 562. A doctor had refused to disclose details of the respondent's venereal disease on the basis that it would have been in breach of his duty of confidentiality, despite the fact that both the divorcing petitioner *and* the respondent (ie, the patient) had requested this:

> **Lewis J:** The question which arises out of these circumstances is: is a doctor, when asked by his patient to give him or her particulars of his or her condition and illness to be used in a court of law, when those particulars are vital to the success or failure of the case, entitled to refuse and in effect to say, 'Go on with your case in the dark and I will tell you in court when I am subpoenaed what my conclusions are'? In the present case the patient asked the doctor to give her this information and asked him also to give the petitioner that same information, with the object of their being placed in a position which would enable them to know whether or not the petitioner had a case against the respondent, in other words, to assist the course of justice. It is, of course, of the greatest importance from every point of view that proper secrecy should be observed in connection with venereal disease clinics, and that nothing should be done to diminish their efficiency or to infringe the confidential relationship existing between doctor and patient. But, in my opinion, those considerations do not justify a doctor in refusing to divulge confidential information to a patient or to any named person or persons when asked by the patient so to do. In the circumstances of this case the information should have been given, and in all cases where the circumstances are similar the doctor is not guilty of any breach of confidence in giving the information asked for.

It is also important to remember that consent must be validly obtained. Given the powerful position of a doctor in the doctor-patient relationship, it is of considerable importance that the patient's consent is obtained scrupulously.

Public interest

Gurry, F, *In Breach of Confidence*, 1984, Oxford: Clarendon Press, p 324:

The influence of principles based on the public interest is predominant in the action for breach of confidence. The public interest has two principal roles in the action. In the first place, since it is the law of the land that confidences are enforceable obligations, it is, of course, 'in the public interest that when information is received in confidence – for a limited and restricted purpose, as it always is – it should not be used for other purposes'. The public interest requires that confidences, like contracts, 'be held sacrosanct'. In this role, the public interest operates not only in the private sector, to enforce a confider's right to preserve the confidentiality of information which he entrusts to another, but also in the public sphere, where the public interest in national security or joint ministerial responsibility may require a public official or a Cabinet minister to keep confidential information secret.

But the public interest also has an opposing role which sometimes requires that confidences be broken, and that information which the courts would otherwise protect from disclosure be released for various purposes. The opposing public interests which call for the release of confidential information may be the interests of justice itself, or the disclosure of iniquity, and, wherever such a judicially recognised opposing interest is identified it must 'be put into the scales against the public interest in preserving privacy and protecting confidential information'.

The philosopher, Richard Hare, sums up the picture as follows:

Hare, RM, 'The philosophical basis of psychiatric ethics', in *Essays on Bioethics*, 1993, Oxford: Clarendon Press, p 23:

If, for example, [a psychiatrist] has as a patient somebody who he knows will be a great deal of trouble to anybody who is so unwise as to employ him, has he any duty to reveal the fact when asked for a medical certificate? Here, as before, it is obviously no use treating the duty of confidentiality to the patient and the duty of candour to the employer as duties on the same level but ranked in order of priority; for it may depend on the case which duty should have precedence. If the patient is an airline pilot and his condition will cause him to lose control of the plane, we may think the public interest paramount; if he is a bank clerk and is merely going to turn up late to work from time to time, we may think that his condition should be concealed.

... At the critical level of moral thinking we are bound to be impartial between the interests of all those affected by our own actions. So at this level, we shall have to give no special edge to our patients, but simply ask, in each case we consider, what action would produce the best results for all those affected, treated impartially ...

The following are examples of public interests which may outweigh the competing public interest in maintaining confidences.

Disclosure to maintain the freedom of the press

There is a public interest in the freedom of the press and other forms of media to investigate and report on matters of legitimate public concern. This was examined in the case of *X v Y* [1988] 2 All ER 648, where the court was unsympathetic to the interests of press freedom, in the face of the protection of the anonymity of patients being treated for AIDS. A health authority sought an injunction restraining a newspaper from publishing the names of two practising doctors who were also being treated for AIDS. The names of the doctors had been given to the newspaper by an employee within the health authority. The issue of freedom of the press was dealt with by Rose J, p 661:

> **Rose J:** I keep in the forefront of my mind the very important public interest in freedom of the press. And I accept that there is some public interest in knowing that which the defendants seek to publish (in whichever version). But in my judgment those public interests are substantially outweighed when measured against the public interests in relation to loyalty and confidentiality both generally and with particular reference to AIDS patients' hospital records ... The deprivation of the public of the information sought to be published will be of minimal significance if the injunction is granted; for, without it, all the evidence before me shows that a wide ranging public debate about AIDS generally and about its effect on doctors is taking place among doctors of widely differing views, within and without the BMA, in medical journals and in many newspapers, including *The Observer*, *The Sunday Times* and the *Daily Express*. Indeed, the sterility of the defendants' argument is demonstrated by the edition of the second defendant's own newspaper dated 22 March 1987. It is there expressly stated, purportedly quoting a Mr Milligan, that three general practitioners, two of whom are practising (impliedly in Britain), have AIDS. Paraphrasing Templeman LJ in the *Schering* case, the facts, in the most limited version now sought to be published, have already been made available and may again be made available if they are known otherwise than through the medium of the informer. The risk of identification is only one factor in assessing whether to permit the use of confidential information. In my judgment, to allow publication in the recently suggested restricted form would be to enable both defendants to procure breaches of confidence and then to make their own selection for publication. This would make a mockery of the law's protection of confidentiality when no justifying public interest has been shown.

The authority succeeded on the basis that the doctors needed protection just as any other patient did. Rose J said, p 665:

> **Rose J:** The public in general and patients in particular are entitled to expect hospital records to be confidential and it is not for any individual to take it upon himself or herself to breach that confidence whether induced by a journalist or otherwise.

Disclosure to prevent crime

In the case of *X v Y*, the health authority unsuccessfully tried to obtain disclosure of the name of the person within the authority who had criminally sold the medical records of the doctors concerned (ie, contrary to the Public Bodies Corrupt Practices Act 1889 and the Prevention of Corruption Act 1906). The argument of the authority was based on its alleged duty to prevent crime. The court held that it had no public duty to prosecute crime, and that its real purpose had been to prevent publication which was prevented on other grounds. Rose J considered the wording of s 10 of the Contempt of Court Act 1981 which states that, *inter alia*, the information required must be *necessary* for the prevention of crime (p 664):

Rose J: I accept that it is right to stress that the word used in the section is 'necessary' and I am unable to accept the submission of counsel for the plaintiffs that the effect of Slade LJ's judgment is of general application in construing the word 'necessary' as 'likely to be of substantial assistance', for such an approach would not only be contrary to the word in the 1981 Act but would be at variance with what was said in the House of Lords in the *Guardian* case in the speeches of Lord Diplock, Lord Fraser and Lord Roskill to which I have earlier referred. What I understand Slade LJ to be saying is that, in the circumstances of that case (and necessity is a question of fact in each case: see *per* Lord Diplock in the *Guardian* case [1984] 3 All ER 601, p 607; [1985] 1 AC 339, p 350), disclosure was necessary if it was likely to be of substantial assistance to the inspectors. It was central to that decision that those seeking disclosure were specifically charged with investigating and hence preventing criminal offences.

The position of a health authority is entirely different and the question for me is whether the evidence proves necessity in this case on the balance of probability. I am unable to accept the submission of counsel for the second defendants based on *Gouriet v Union of Post Office Workers* [[1978] AC 435]; s 10 refers to prevention, not prosecution, and it is not, in my judgment, a prerequisite for success that the plaintiffs should adduce evidence from a prosecuting arm of the Crown, whether the Attorney General, police officers, investigating inspectors or otherwise. Every citizen has an interest in the prevention of crime and satisfaction as to necessity is, by the terms of the section, a matter for the court, not some other body. But there must, in my judgment, be clear evidence in relation to necessity ... I accept, contrary to the submission of counsel for the second defendants, that the plaintiffs' motive is not merely curiosity or a desire to punish or threaten the culprit. They do not want such a breach to happen again, whether for payment of money (which may be crucial to the occurrence of a criminal offence) or otherwise. But the prevention of crime is not one of their tasks and the physician neither said nor, in my view, implied that criminal investigation was the intended or likely consequence of disclosure. He did not suggest that the matter had been referred to the police and there was no evidence as to what security procedures existed or what inquiries had been made to identify the source. Appropriate deterrent action could take a variety of forms, from warning the culprit to dismissal, and might well not, for policy reasons, extend to criminal investigation. There was no clear evidence as to how few or how many of the plaintiffs' servants had access to the hospital records, but he said that security procedures had been improved since the breaches in question. The evidence in relation to the offer of money to a nurse was, in my judgment, too vague to support an inference of necessity. Accordingly, though I bear in mind that the plaintiffs do not have to show that there is no other means of identification available or that all other possible means of identification have been exhausted, the evidence in this case falls short of proving that disclosure of the source is necessary for the prevention of crime. The matter can be tested by the use of Lloyd LJ's two questions. As to the first, disclosure would no doubt be of real importance to the plaintiffs in carrying out their inquiry. But, as to the second, it cannot be said that the purpose of their inquiry is the prevention of crime.

The protection of the public from crime was considered in *W v Egdell* [1990] 1 All ER 835. The patient was a prisoner in a secure hospital following conviction for a number of killings and woundings, and had made an application to a mental health review tribunal with a view to being transferred to a regional unit. Such a step would be a step towards discharge, and, therefore, the question arose as to whether the patient was still a danger to the public. His legal advisers sought the opinion of an independent psychiatrist, which, it was hoped, could be produced in support of the application. Dr Egdell, however, formed the view that the patient was still dangerous. In the light of this, the patient's application was withdrawn. However, his case was due to be reviewed under the automatic review process, under s 79(1) of the Mental Health Act 1983, and Dr Egdell, realising that his report, commissioned confidentially and independently by the patient's legal advisers, would not be included in the notes, sent a copy to the medical director of the hospital and a further copy to the Home Office. The patient brought an action alleging breach of confidence, but the court upheld the breach on the grounds of the public interest, ie, the protection of the public from dangerous criminal acts. The patient failed in his action at first instance and appealed. The Court of Appeal stated (*per* Bingham LJ, p 851):

> **Bingham LJ**: The parties were agreed, as I think rightly, that the crucial question was how, on the special facts of the case, the balance should be struck between the public interest in maintaining professional confidences and the public interest in protecting the public against possible violence. Counsel for W submitted that on the facts here the public interest in maintaining confidences was shown to be clearly preponderant. In support of that submission he drew our attention to a number of features of the case, of which the most weighty were perhaps these:
>
> (1) Section 76 of the Mental Health Act 1983 shows a clear parliamentary intention that a restricted patient should be free to seek advice and evidence for the specified purposes from a medical source outside the prison and secure hospital system. Section 129 ensures that the independent doctor may make a full examination and see all relevant documents. The examination may be in private, so that the authorities do not learn what passes between doctor and patient.
>
> (2) The proper functioning of s 76 requires that a patient should feel free to bare his soul and open his mind without reserve to the independent doctor he has retained. This he will not do if a doctor is free, on forming an adverse opinion, to communicate it to those empowered to prevent the patient's release from hospital.
>
> (3) Although the present situation is not one in which W can assert legal professional privilege, and although tribunal proceedings are not strictly adversarial, the considerations which have given rise to legal professional

privilege underpin the public interest in preserving confidence in a situation such as the present. A party to a forthcoming application to a tribunal should be free to unburden himself to an adviser he has retained without fearing that any material damaging to his application will find its way without his consent into the hands of a party with interests adverse to his.

(4) Preservation of confidence would be conducive to the public safety: patients would be candid, so that problems such as those highlighted by Dr Egdell would become known, and steps could be taken to explore and if necessary treat the problems without disclosing the report.

(5) It is contrary to the public interest that patients such as W should enjoy rights less extensive than those enjoyed by other members of the public, a result of his judgment which the judge expressly accepted (see [1989] 1 All ER 1089, p 1105; and [1989] 2 WLR 689, p 714).

Of these considerations, I accept (1) as a powerful consideration in W's favour. A restricted patient who believes himself unnecessarily confined has, of all members of society, perhaps the greatest need for a professional adviser who is truly independent and reliably discreet. (2) I also, in some measure, accept, subject to the comment that if the patient is unforthcoming, the doctor is bound to be guarded in his opinion. If the patient wishes to enlist the doctor's wholehearted support for his application, he has little choice but to be (or at least convince an expert interviewer that he is being) frank. I see great force in (3). Only the most compelling circumstances could justify a doctor in acting in a way which would injure the immediate interests of his patient, as the patient perceived them, without obtaining his consent. Point (4), if I correctly understand it, did not impress me. Counsel's submissions appeared to suggest that the problems highlighted by Dr Egdell could be explored and if necessary treated without the hospital authorities being told what the problems were thought to be. I do not think this would be very satisfactory. As to (5), I agree that restricted patients should not enjoy rights of confidence less valuable than those enjoyed by other patients save in so far as any breach of confidence can be justified under the stringent terms of r 81(g).

Counsel for Dr Egdell justified his client's disclosure of his report by relying on the risk to the safety of the public if the report were not disclosed. The steps of his argument, briefly summarised, were these:

(1) As a result of his examination Dr Egdell believed that W had a long standing and abnormal interest in dangerous explosives dating from well before his period of acute illness.

(2) Dr Egdell believed that this interest had been overlooked or insufficiently appreciated by those with clinical responsibility for W.

(3) Dr Egdell believed that this interest could throw additional light on W's interest, also long standing and in this instance well documented, in guns and shooting.

(4) Dr Egdell believed that exploration of W's interest in explosives and further exploration of W's interest in guns and shooting might lead to a different and more sinister diagnosis of W's mental condition.

(5) Dr Egdell believed that these explorations could best be conducted in the secure hospital where W was.

(6) Dr Egdell believed that W might possibly be a future danger to members of the public if his interest in firearms and explosives continued after his discharge.

(7) Dr Egdell believed that these matters should be brought to the attention of those responsible for W's care and treatment and for making decisions concerning his transfer and release.

Dr Egdell's good faith was not in issue. Nor were his professional standing and competence. His opinions summarised in (1), (2), (3) and (4) (although not accepted) were not criticised as ill-founded or irrational. Dr Egdell deferred to the greater knowledge of another medical expert relied on by W concerning the regime in a regional secure unit but did not (as I understood) modify his view that the explorations he favoured should take place before transfer ...

There is one consideration which, in my judgment, as in that of the judge, weighs the balance of public interest decisively in favour of disclosure. It may be shortly put. Where a man has committed multiple killings under the disability of serious mental illness, decisions which may lead directly or indirectly to his release from hospital should not be made unless a responsible authority is properly able to make an informed judgment that the risk of repetition is so small as to be acceptable. A consultant psychiatrist who becomes aware, even in the course of a confidential relationship, of information which leads him, in the exercise of what the court considers a sound professional judgment, to fear that such decisions may be made on the basis of inadequate information and with a real risk of consequent danger to the public is entitled to take such steps as are reasonable in all the circumstances to communicate the grounds of his concern to the responsible authorities. I have no doubt that the judge's decision in favour of Dr Egdell was right on the facts of this case.

The question arises whether this case is different from a case where a dangerous criminal is *at large* and a doctor breaches medical confidentiality to enable him to be taken into custody. It is arguable that there is an important difference. After all, in the *Egdell* case the patient was already the subject of expert medical scrutiny by the doctors at the hospital where he was detained; if those doctors had formed the view that the patient was no longer dangerous (ie, a view contrary to that of Dr Egdell), does not this difference of professional opinion considerably weaken the public interest defence to disclosure? Kennedy and Grubb (*Medical Law*, 2nd edn, 1994, London: Butterworths, p 657), suggest that it may turn on whether the breaching doctor is basing his view on new facts of which he is aware, and which, without breaching confidence, are not known by the other doctor. If it is merely a difference of opinion based on the same set of facts, then there is a good argument against disclosure.

The public interest defence in the prevention of crime was upheld by the Court of Appeal in the case of *R v Crozier* (1990) *The Independent*, 11 May, where a psychiatrist, instructed by the defendant in an attempted murder case, disclosed his report to the prosecution when he realised that the defence had not produced it in court, when sentence was passed. As a result, the Crown informed the judge of the contents of the report, and the judge quashed the sentence of imprisonment and made a hospital order instead.

There is no doubt that the patient in *W v Egdell* had committed very grave criminal offences. Would fear of less serious offences justify disclosure? Although case law in non-medical areas of confidentiality appears to put all crimes in the same basket (see *Initial Services Ltd v Putterill* [1968] 1 QB 396, *Malone v Commissioner of Police of the Metropolis (No 2)* [1979] 2 All ER 620), in the Egdell case, the repeated references to the safety of the public – 'In this case the number and nature of the killings by W must inevitably give rise to the gravest concern for the safety of the public' (*per* Sir Stephen Brown P, p 846) – strongly suggests that the risk of minor crimes being committed would not sway the court in the same way. Furthermore, the non-medical cases generally concern issues of fraud upon the general public (see *British Steel Corporation v Granada Television Ltd* [1981] 1 All ER 417). The GMC guidance on this subject is illuminating:

18   Disclosures may be necessary in the public interest where a failure to disclose information may expose the patient or others to risk of death or *serious* harm. [Emphasis added.]

An example given is disclosure being necessary to prevent or detect a *serious* crime (again, emphasis added).

It should also be noted that in the *Egdell* case, it was said that the risk must be 'real, immediate and serious' (*per* Sir Stephen Brown P, p 845). This is important, as it must mean that a doctor acting in good faith and in the genuine belief that there is such a risk, will be in breach of confidence if it transpires that the risk did not amount to one that was real, immediate and serious. Should all three of these requirements be satisfied: what of a risk which is real and serious, but unlikely to materialise for some time?

What of past, undetected criminal offences? Again, the GMC guidance should be noted, and the implications of the judgments in *Egdell*. However, the *risk* of a crime being committed is different to a past crime gone unpunished, the former only a perceived likelihood of criminal activity, the latter a certainty (on the assumption that the doctor is certain). Nevertheless, clearly the GMC do not consider it desirable that non-serious crime should be reported to the police, and, it is submitted, that is the correct view on the basis that the counterveiling public interest in maintaining medical confidences outweighs disclosure, as, we suggest, was the case in *Wilson*.

Disclosure to prevent civil wrongs

Gurry, *In Breach of Confidence*, 1984, Oxford: Clarendon Press, p 334, reviews the case law, and concludes that disclosure of a *proposed* civil wrong would be in the public interest, but doubts whether the disclosure of a past civil wrong would satisfy this, as 'this would serve only to raise quibbling enmities and thus destroy, rather than advance, the public welfare', whilst in the context of commercial confidences it may be the case that proposed civil wrongs may justify a breach. However, it is hard to envisage the circumstances in which past or future civil wrongs would justify a breach of medical confidences. Medical confidentiality would always override the prevention of civil wrongs because of weightier public interest arguments. In any event, what might be an example of a situation where a doctor would consider breaching confidence to prevent a proposed civil wrong? Perhaps a doctor may consider reporting a patient to his employer, if, for example, he has failed to disclose a medical condition on a job application form, for example, psychiatric history (see *O'Brien v Prudential Assurance Co* [1979] IRLR 140). It is submitted that this sort of medical busybodying would be swiftly condemned by the courts and the General Medical Council. Although para 19 of the GMC's guidance gives the example of disclosure to the DVLC in the case of a patient who is driving against medical advice as a justification for breach of confidentiality, it is submitted that this would not be an example of a civil wrong justifying disclosure, but a case in which the protection of third parties would be at issue.

Disclosure for the public good

It might be argued that if no wrong, criminal or civil, has been, or is likely to be committed, then disclosure could not possibly be justified. However, there is clear authority for the fact that 'the public good' can be sufficient. The Court of Appeal in *Lion Laboratories v Evans and Express Newspapers* [1985] QB 526, authorised the publication of internal documents from the manufacturer of the intoximeter that cast doubt upon the accuracy of the machine, which was widely used in the convictions for drink-driving offences. The court held that the possibility of future wrongful convictions raised a matter of legitimate public interest despite the fact that no wrongdoing was involved.

It is possible to envisage countless examples of revelation of medical information for the public good, for example, the publication of information about new drugs and treatments and breakthroughs in medical research may be in the public good. Release of information about the dangers to public health, for example, an outbreak of illness caused by contaminated materials, would, of course, always be in the public good (indeed, the public health authorities would be under a positive duty to do this). However, in most of these cases, there would be no need to name identifiable individuals, so there would be no breach of confidentiality. Nevertheless, if circumstances were such that individuals had to be named, for example, a patient at large suffering from a highly dangerous and contagious disease, identification may be necessary.

Consider the facts of the case of *Distillers Co (Biochemicals) Ltd v Times Newspapers Ltd* [1975] QB 613, below, p 249, and whether similar facts, giving rise to a breach of medical confidentiality, would be justified for the public good.

Disclosure for the protection of third parties

It might be thought that the protection of third parties would come within the ambit of preventing either a criminal or a civil wrong. However, it may be necessary to disclose medical information when neither of these apply. The case of *Re C (A Minor) (Evidence: Confidential Information)* (1991) 7 BMLR 138, concerned the proposed adoption of a one year old baby. A day before the hearing, the mother withdrew her consent to the adoption. At an adjourned hearing, the adopting parents' solicitor produced an affidavit sworn voluntarily by the mother's GP, containing evidence of her medical condition and fitness to bring up a child. The mother objected to the admissibility of this evidence as it was a breach of medical confidentiality. She was unsuccessful at first instance, and the case went to the Court of Appeal. Sir Stephen Brown said, p 143:

> **Sir Stephen Brown**: It is in fact an unusual case. There is no previous authority which is directly in point, and all the cases which have been cited to the court refer to very different situations. The court is concerned with the proposed adoption of a little child. That is, of course, a very serious matter for the child, as well as being a serious decision for the court to have to make when the mother is withholding her consent. The court should have before it all relevant and significant information which will assist it to make a right decision.
>
> In this case, it is clear that the doctor's affidavit is highly relevant. If it can properly be placed before the judge, then it should be admitted. I consider that this case rests on its own very special facts. Moreover, I have considerable hesitation in reaching a conclusion that there was, in fact, any breach of confidence by the doctor in this case. I observe that it was apparently conceded before the judge that, *prima facie*, there was a breach of confidence. However that may be, in my judgment in this case the doctor was justified in making available her evidence. It may be that it could have been made available to the mother's advisers at an earlier stage, or in some other way, but that is not the issue before this court. In any event, I believe that a judge, if carrying out any balancing exercise, would be fully justified in coming down clearly in favour of admitting this evidence.
>
> It should also be recognised that the disclosure of the material contained in this affidavit was the subject of a restricted disclosure. It was not being made available to the public at large. It was being made available only to the judge who had to decide the application, and to those who were also bound by the confidentiality of the hearing in chambers.

Accordingly, I have no hesitation in reaching the conclusion that the judge was correct to rule that this evidence was admissible and that it should be admitted.

What is of particular interest is the suggestion that the finding at first instance that there had been a breach of confidence, albeit a justified breach, may not have been correct. This was a view supported by both the other appeal judges. This was on the basis that the child was also (or had been) a patient of the doctor. However, in our view this is the wrong approach. To hold that there is no breach is tantamount to saying there was no duty in the first place.

Of course, in all these cases we are looking at *competing* public interests, and the protection of children will frequently justify a refusal of disclosure. In *D v National Society for the Prevention of Cruelty to Children* [1977] 1 All ER 589, the mother of a child who, it had been alleged, had been abused by her, brought proceedings in negligence against the NSPCC, following the shock-induced illness she had suffered as a result of the society's inspector's call to her home. She alleged that the society had failed to investigate properly the complaint made against her. The society denied negligence and made an application to the court for an order that there should be no discovery of documents which might reveal the identity of the complainant. The House of Lords held that in the interests of the proper functioning of a body such as the NSPCC, charged with the duty of protecting children against ill-treatment, they should have immunity from disclosure, analogously to the guaranteed anonymity of police informers. The case also upheld the principle of disclosure in the interests of the administration of justice.

Confidentiality and HIV and AIDS

It will be recalled that the case of *X v Y* concerned the difficulties that can arise in relation to information relating to HIV and AIDS. Such is the concern about this sensitive area that the GMC have issued special guidance to doctors on dealing with such patients. A patient who is HIV positive is not, of course, ill. The patient is merely carrying the virus, which, it is thought, will almost always develop into the Acquired Immunity Deficiency Syndrome, a condition characterised by an extremely distressing variety of symptoms.

Both HIV and AIDS attract huge stigma. This is partly because there is no cure for AIDS, and although it is too soon to say with any certainty, it is still assumed that an HIV positive person will become ill with AIDS sooner or later. However, many other incurable conditions exist, with prognoses far worse than that of someone recently discovered to be HIV positive, who could well live for over 10 years with no sign of AIDS, with the prospect of a cure becoming available in the meantime. It is suggested that the stigma is as a result of two things: first, the fact that it may be transmitted through sexual activity, and secondly, the fact that someone with no outward manifestations of illness may nevertheless be carrying a lethal virus about which very little is known. It also carries some stigma because of the erroneous belief, amongst some, that it is exclusive to, or caused by homosexual activities and/or drug use. Commenting upon the stigmatisation, Robert Lee states:

Lee, R, 'Disclosure of medical records: a confidence trick?', in Clarke, L (ed), *Confidentiality and the Law*, 1990, London: LLP, p 40:

Even though the law seems to give relatively limited rights to patients regarding information about themselves, that body of law nonetheless proceeds from the basis that information relating to health and health status generally is a private matter. However, in one field this is particularly true, as the regulations governing disclosure of information relating to communicable diseases tend to illustrate. The rationale is presumably that persons can be stigmatised by the fact that they are suffering from a communicable disease. Often this has to do with methods of contraction of that disease. In the case of AIDS, methods of contraction may include homosexual practices and intravenous drug usage so that those suffering from AIDS may also be members of social groups who already suffer from various forms of stigma or engage in criminal activities. On the other hand, it seems relatively clear that the virus is unlikely to be spread by most forms of casual or everyday contact. Nonetheless we have seen that persons who are HIV positive are shunned in schools, hospitals and work places.

In this context confidentiality has a clear public health purpose. Medical confidence will encourage persons to come forward for testing, education, counselling, examination and treatment. Indeed co-operation in relation to medical practices may depend on confidentiality. If it is to be made widely known that certain persons who have volunteered for blood transfusions have been rejected for unspecified reasons, then people may draw their own (perhaps wrong) conclusions. This may lead to persons refusing to volunteer blood or come forward for blood testing.

This problem has been identified for some time, as the practices in relation to venereal diseases show. The National Health Service (Venereal Diseases) Regulations 1974 confine the communication of information on this subject to medical practitioners alone and for the treatment and prevention of the diseases in question. However AIDS is not included within the 1974 Regulations notwithstanding the fact that it is primarily sexually transmitted. The AIDS (Control) Act 1987, on the other hand, requires a mass of statistical information, but to no stated or obvious purpose. Finally AIDS is not a notifiable disease under the Public Health (Control of Disease) Act 1984, but the Secretary of State does have the power to hospitalise, and if necessary detain persons under the Public Health (Infectious Diseases) Regulations 1988.

Insurance problems are also thought to be one of the special aspects of HIV and AIDS disclosure. Lee goes on to consider this:

Lee, R, 'Disclosure of medical records: a confidence trick?', in Clarke, L (ed), *Confidentiality and the Law*, 1990, London: LLP, p 40:

The other area in which AIDS-related information creates difficulties of medical confidence is insurance. The problem here, from the perspective of the life insurance company, is that younger males are usually a low premium group, but if HIV positive, will undergo prolonged illness which will prove fatal. On the other hand the risk to the insurance companies may be over-emphasised, given that the persons most likely to become HIV positive are not likely to be strong purchasers of life insurance, being either homosexuals with a lack of dependants, or young drug users who have perhaps not given much thought to life insurance purchase. Insurance companies might counter that, given the long latency period of HIV, it is not always possible to look at the present lifestyle of an individual in order to assess that individual for insurance purposes.

Nonetheless, one option for insurance companies in this area is to isolate a target population for whom life insurance is regularly refused. This would include perhaps single males aged between 20 years and 50 years with no insurable interests and whose lifestyle might be indicated by such questions as residence, or leisure activity. The alternative is simply to use AIDS antibody testing. The problem here is that false positive results run at something like one in every 20,000 tests. The stigmatisation which may result from a false positive, in addition to the difficulties that will then face that person in relation to obtaining insurance and employment, are of sufficient concern that a number of the States legislatures have banned or restricted the use of blood tests in order to determine insurability.

The GMC has provided specific guidance on serious communicable diseases:

General Medical Council, *Serious Communicable Diseases*, 1998, London: GMC:

Informing other health care professionals

18 If you diagnose a patient as having a serious communicable disease, you should explain to the patient:

- the nature of the disease and its medical, social and occupational implications, as appropriate;

- ways of protecting others from infection;

- the importance of giving the professionals who will be providing care information which they need to know about the patient's disease or condition. In particular, you must make sure the patient understands that general practitioners cannot provide adequate clinical management and care without knowledge of their patients' conditions.

19 If patients still refuse to allow other health care workers to be informed, you must respect the patients' wishes except where you judge that failure to disclose the information would put a health care worker or other patient at serious risk of death or serious harm. Such situations may arise, for example, when dealing with violent patients with severe mental illness or disbility. If you are in doubt about whether disclosure is appropriate, you should seek advice from an experienced colleague. You should inform patients before disclosing information. Such occasions are likely to arise rarely and you must be prepared to justify a decision to disclose information against a patient's wishes.

Disclosures to others

20 You must disclose information about serious communicable diseases in accordance with the law. For example, the appropriate authority must be informed where a notifiable disease is diagnosed. Where a communicable disease has contributed to the cause of death, this must be recorded on the death certificate. You should also pass information about serious communicable diseases to the relevant authorities for the purpose of communicable disease control and surveillance.

21 As the GMC booklet *Confidentiality* [see above, p 223] makes clear, a patient's death does not, of itself, release a doctor from the obligation to maintain confidentiality. But in some circumstances disclosures can be justified because they protect other people from serious harm or because they are required by law.

Giving information to close contacts

22 You may disclose information about a patient, whether living or dead, in order to protect a person from risk of death or serious harm. For example, you may disclose information to a known sexual contact of a patient with HIV where you have reason to think that the patient has not informed that person, and cannot be persuaded to do so. In such circumstances you should tell the patient before you make the disclosure, and you must be prepared to justify a decision to disclose information.

23 You must not disclose information to others, for example relatives, who have not been, and are not, at risk of infection.

It will be seen, therefore, that if there is a serious and identifiable risk to a specific individual, such as a spouse or other sexual partner, then disclosure can be made. Recalling the case of *Re C (A Minor) (Evidence: Confidential Information)* (1991) 7 BMLR 138, if the partner is also the patient of the doctor, the Court of Appeal suggested there may be no breach (see above, p 244).

The administration of justice

Francis Gurry has commented upon this:

Gurry, F, *In Breach of Confidence*, 1984, Oxford: Clarendon Press, p 346:

In litigation, two competing aspects of the public interest often come into conflict: the administration of justice, which requires the full disclosure of all relevant evidence to assist the courts in their judicial functions; and the maintenance of the privacy of confidential communications, which militates against the disclosure of information which has been received under an obligation of confidence. Where a party or witness is required to give evidence which relates to information received in confidence, the conflict arises. In general, the administration of justice has been regarded as paramount ...

Generally speaking litigants have a right to obtain and present evidence in the course of court proceedings. For a very detailed account of this, see McHale, J, *Medical Confidentiality and Legal Privilege*, 1993, London: Routledge.

In the course of civil proceedings, ss 33 and 34 of the Supreme Court Act 1981 provide for the discovery of documents during the course of a court action (s 34), and, where appropriate, prior to the commencement of proceedings (s 33). The question as to how far documents discovered in the course of legal proceedings may subsequently be published was considered in *Distillers (Biochemicals) Ltd v Times Newspapers Ltd* [1975] QB 613. The case concerned the drug thalidomide, and in proceedings brought by those injured by the drug, certain documents were ordered to be disclosed. One of the claimants' expert advisers entered into an agreement with the defendants to sell them the documentary information. The plaintiff company sought an injunction to prevent publication. The injunction was granted on the basis that those who disclosed documents were entitled to the court's protection against any use of the documents otherwise than in the action in which they were disclosed. Talbot J said, p 625:

> **Talbot J**: Whilst, as I have said, the public have a great interest in the thalidomide story (and it is a matter of public interest), and any light thrown onto this matter to obviate any such thing happening again is welcome, nevertheless the defendants have not persuaded me that such use as they proposed to make of the documents which they possess is of greater advantage to the public than the public's interest in the need for the proper administration of justice, to protect the confidentiality of discovery of documents. I would go further and say that I doubt very much whether there is sufficient in the use which the defendants have proposed to raise a public interest which overcomes the plaintiffs' private right to the confidentiality of their documents. In any event I consider that the plaintiffs have established their right (this is not really disputed) and have an arguable case for its protection by an injunction.

To refer back to the 'public good' justification, it is clear from this case that the court found that the proper administration of justice outweighed any public interest in knowing about the history of the drug thalidomide. Although it is clear that doctors have no immunity from the normal processes of disclosure in court proceedings, in *Hunter v Mann* [1974] 1 QB 767 it was said by Lord Widgery that a doctor who did not wish to answer a question in court because it would involve confidential issues, may point this out to the judge, who should advise as to whether it is necessary to answer the question.

Disclosure in the interests of national security

It is highly unlikely that this could apply to medical information. It is enough to note it as a legitimate area of public interest.

Medical research

It might be thought that there are no special considerations in the case of disclosure in research, but it is different, in that it could be argued that by consenting to take part in research, particularly non-therapeutic research, there was an altruistic motive on the part of the research subject which changes the nature of confidentiality.

However, the GMC guidance (see paras 15–16 reproduced above, p 225) stresses the importance of consent, so it appears that the only special aspect of research and confidentiality is that information may well be disclosed, but anonymously.

Exchange of information amongst health care workers

This is a grey area. Although it is included here as a particular example of the way in which confidences may be breached, unauthorised exchange of information amongst health care workers may fall foul of the law unless it can be argued that the patient has impliedly consented to this because he knows that he is being cared for by a team of people. This is reflected in the GMC guidance (see paras 3–8 reproduced above, p 223).

The Department of Health publication *The Protection and Use of Patient Information* (March 1996) stresses that all NHS staff, and non-NHS staff working in health care settings, such as hospital social workers, are subject to the same 'common law' duty of confidence.

It is instructive, however, to consider into how many pairs of hands medical information may fall. Gillon, referring to the investigation by a doctor of a patient's complaint:

Gillon, R, *Philosophical Medical Ethics*, 1986, Chichester: John Wiley, p 109:

... Dr Siegler was 'astonished to learn that at least 25 and possibly as many as 100 health professionals and administrative personnel at our university hospital had access to the patient's record and that all of them had a legitimate need, indeed a professional responsibility, to open and use that chart'.

Is it arguable that the larger these numbers become, the less significant the concept of medical confidentiality becomes?

Breaches of confidence justified by statute law

A number of statutory provisions provide for the disclosure of information, and doctors generally are not exempt.

The Prevention of Terrorism Act 1989:

18 Information about acts of terrorism

(1) A person is guilty of an offence if he has information which he knows or believes might be of material assistance–

(a) in preventing the commission by any other person of an act of terrorism connected with the affairs of Northern Ireland; or

(b) in securing the apprehension, prosecution or conviction of any other person for an offence involving the commission, preparation or instigation of such an act, and fails without reasonable excuse to disclose that information as soon as reasonably practicable:

(i) in England and Wales, to a constable;

(ii) in Scotland, to a constable or the procurator fiscal; or

(iii) in Northern Ireland, to a constable or a member of Her Majesty's Forces ...

Note also the provisions of the Road Traffic Act 1988:

172 (2) Where the driver of a vehicle is alleged to be guilty of an offence to which this section applies–

(a) the person keeping the vehicle shall give such information as to the identity of the driver as he may be required to give by or on behalf of a chief officer of police; and

(b) any other person shall if required as stated above give any information which it is in his power to give and may lead to identification of the driver.

In this sub-section references to the driver of a vehicle include references to the person riding a cycle.

(3) A person who fails to comply with the requirement of sub-s (2)(a) above is guilty of an offence unless he shows to the satisfaction of the court that he did not know and could not with reasonable diligence have ascertained who the driver of the vehicle or, as the case may be, the rider of the cycle was.

(4) A person who fails to comply with the requirement of sub-s (2)(b) above is guilty of an offence.

The case of *Hunter v Mann* [1974] 1 QB 766 examined the extent to which this requirement was applicable to doctors in relation to the forerunner of the 1988 provision, s 168 of the Road Traffic Act 1972. The relevant part of the provision is identical to the 1988 Act. The question to be answered by the Divisional Court was whether a doctor who failed to comply with the provision under s 172(2)(b) above, in respect of information brought to his knowledge in the course of his professional relationship with a patient, was guilty of an offence under s 172(3). The argument on the part of the doctor was that the relevant words should be given a restricted meaning, so as to exclude confidential information, and those in a special position of confidence such as doctors. Boreham J, p 774:

Boreham J: For my part I cannot find any ground for saying that a restricted meaning should be given. I find the words clear and unequivocal. I accept, as Mr Bingham has suggested, that one should assume that Parliament has passed this Act, and this section in particular, with the existing law in mind. Accepting that, then it seems to me that Parliament must have been conscious of the use of very wide words here and if it had been intended to create exceptions, why then it would have been easy enough to do so. It has not been done. Moreover I ask myself the question: if there is to be a restriction how far is it to go? Where is it to stop? I find it impossible to provide an answer to that question.

In these circumstances I am driven to the conclusion that a doctor acting within his professional capacity, and carrying out his professional duties and responsibilities, is within the words 'any other person' in s 168(2)(b).

The next limb of Mr Bingham's argument was directed at the words in the expression 'information which it is in his power to give'. He contends that power must include a legal right, that there is no legal right or power to disclose so far as a doctor is concerned and, therefore, that he is not caught by those words.

I am not going to attempt to define 'power'. It seems to me a word of fairly common understanding and reading it in its ordinary way I have no difficulty in coming to the conclusion that a doctor in the circumstances in which the defendant found himself had the power. It may be that but for the section in the Act he would not have exercised that power because of his duty to his patient, but that seems to me to beg the question, for that would have been in accordance with his duty not to make voluntary disclosure. Once it is decided that the defendant is a person to whom the statutory duty imposed by s 168(2)(b) applies, then I have no doubt that he had the power. I think that it would be no injustice to Mr Bingham to say that this is the least strenuously argued of his points and I find it a point without substance ...

In my view it is important when one is considering this section to have in mind that on many occasions serious accidents are caused by people who take away, without consent, other people's motor cars and who have no hesitation in leaving the scene as quickly as they possibly can so as to avoid detection. I, therefore, find it a comfort to think that the section gives the police a wide power for the purpose of detecting people who may cause damage to others.

May I say, before leaving this case, that I appreciate the concern of a responsible medical practitioner who feels that he is faced with a conflict of duty. That the defendant was conscious of a conflict and realised his duty, both to society and to his patient, is clear from the finding of the justices, but he may find comfort, although the decision goes against him, from the following. First, that he has only to disclose information which may lead to identification and not other confidential matters; secondly, that the result, in my judgment, is entirely consistent with the rules that the British Medical Association have laid down and from which I have quoted in the course of this judgment.

In the result I have come to the conclusion that the justices were correct and that this appeal, therefore, must be dismissed.

Information must also be disclosed pursuant to the Abortion Regulations 1991 SI 1991/499:

5   (a) for the purposes of carrying out their duties–

       (i)   to an officer of the Department of Health authorised by the Chief Medical Officer of that Department, or to an officer of the Welsh Office authorised by the Chief Medical Officer of that Office, as the case may be, or

      (ii) to the Registrar General or a member of his staff authorised by him; or

   (b) for the purposes of carrying out his duties in relation to offences under the Act or the law relating to abortion, to the Director of Public Prosecutions or a member of his staff authorised by him; or

   (c) for the purposes of investigating whether an offence has been committed under the Act or the law relating to abortion, to a police officer not below the rank of superintendent or a person authorised by him; or

   (d) pursuant to a court order, for the purposes of proceedings which have begun; or

   (e) for the purposes of *bona fide* scientific research; or

   (f) to the practitioner who terminated the pregnancy; or

   (g) to a practitioner, with the consent in writing of the woman whose pregnancy was terminated; or

   (h) when requested by the President of the General Medical Council for the purpose of investigating whether there has been serious professional misconduct by a practitioner, to the President of the General Medical Council or a member of its staff authorised by him.

In the interests of public health, disclosure of serious infectious diseases can be made pursuant to the Public Health (Control of Disease) Act 1984.

Public Health (Control of Disease) Act 1984:

10 Notifiable diseases

In this Act, 'notifiable disease' means any of the following diseases–

   (a) cholera;

   (b) plague;

   (c) relapsing fever;

   (d) smallpox; and

   (e) typhus.

11 Cases of notifiable disease and food poisoning to be reported

(1) If a registered medical practitioner becomes aware, or suspects, that a patient whom he is attending within the district of a local authority is suffering from a notifiable disease or from food poisoning, he shall, unless he believes, and has reasonable grounds for believing, that some other registered medical practitioner has complied with this sub-section with respect to the patient, forthwith send to the proper officer of the local authority for that district a certificate stating–

(a) the name, age and sex of the patient and the address of the premises where the patient is;

(b) the disease or, as the case may be, particulars of the poisoning from which the patient is, or is suspected to be, suffering and the date, or approximate date, of its onset ...

Under s 31 of the Human Fertilisation and Embryology Act 1990 there is provision for regulations to be made to allow children conceived as a result of infertility treatment to obtain certain genetic information about their origins. At the moment there are no such regulations.

Although the Police and Criminal Evidence Act 1984 empowers the police to search for and seize materials, these do not include 'excluded material', and medical records and human tissue or tissue fluid would normally fall within the definition of 'excluded material' under ss 11 and 12 of the Act.

Note the provisions of ss 33 and 34 of the Supreme Court Act 1981, which provide for disclosure of documents during the course of litigation considered above.

Might there be a common law duty to disclose?

As we have seen in *Hunter v Mann* [1974] 1 QB 766, a doctor may have a statutory duty to disclose certain information about a patient. However, might there be circumstances in which a common law duty may arise, as opposed to the common law defence which gives a doctor a *discretion* to disclose? This is illustrated by the case of *Tarasoff v Regents of the University of California* 17 Cal 3d 425 (1976). A patient of a psychologist confided that he intended to kill a girl. The psychologist informed the campus police who briefly detained the man, releasing him on the basis that he appeared to be rational. He subsequently killed the girl, and her parents sued the University for failing to warn them that their daughter was in danger. By a majority the California Supreme Court upheld their claim:

> **Tobriner J**: We shall explain that defendant therapists cannot escape liability merely because Tatiana herself was not their patient. When a therapist determines, or pursuant to the standards of his profession should determine, that his patient presents a serious danger of violence to another, he incurs an obligation to use reasonable care to protect the intended victim against such

danger. The discharge of this duty may require the therapist to take one or more of various steps, depending upon the nature of the case. Thus it may call for him to warn the intended victim or others likely to apprise the victim of the danger, to notify the police, or to take whatever other steps are reasonably necessary under the circumstances ...

In each instance the adequacy of the therapist's conduct must be measured against the traditional negligence standard of the rendition of reasonable care under the circumstances ... In sum, the therapist owes a legal duty not only to his patient, but also to his patient's would-be victim and is subject in both respects to scrutiny by judge and jury ... Some of the alternatives open to the therapist, such as warning the victim, will not result in the drastic consequences of depriving the patient of his liberty. Weighing the uncertain and conjectural character of the alleged damage done to the patient by such a warning against the peril to the victim's life, we conclude that professional inaccuracy in predicting violence cannot negate the therapist's duty to protect the threatened victim ...

Justice Clark, dissenting, stated:

Clark J: Until today's majority opinion, both legal and medical authorities have agreed that confidentiality is essential to effectively treat the mentally ill, and that imposing a duty on doctors to disclose patient threats to potential victims would greatly impair treatment ... Policy generally determines duty. Principal policy considerations include foreseeability of harm, certainty of the plaintiff's injury, proximity of the defendant's conduct to the plaintiff's injury, moral blame attributable to defendant's conduct, prevention of future harm, burden on the defendant, and consequences to the community.

Overwhelming policy considerations weigh against imposing a duty on psychotherapists to warn a potential victim against harm. While offering virtually no benefit to society, such a duty will frustrate psychiatric treatment, invade fundamental patient rights and increase violence. The importance of psychiatric treatment and its need for confidentiality have been recognised by this court. It is clearly recognised that the very practice of psychiatry vitally depends upon the reputation in the community that the psychiatrist will not tell ... Assurance of confidentiality is important for three reasons:

Deterrence from treatment

First, without substantial assurance of confidentiality, those requiring treatment will be deterred from seeking assistance. It remains an unfortunate fact in our society that people seeking psychiatric guidance tend to become stigmatised. Apprehension of such stigma apparently increased by the propensity of people considering treatment to see themselves in the worst possible light creates a well recognised reluctance to seek aid. This reluctance is alleviated by the psychiatrist's assurance of confidentiality.

Full disclosure

Second, the guarantee of confidentiality is essential in eliciting the full disclosure necessary for effective treatment. The psychiatric patient approaches treatment with conscious and unconscious inhibitions against revealing his innermost thoughts ...

Successful treatment

Third, even if the patient fully discloses his thoughts, assurance that the confidential relationship will not be breached is necessary to maintain his trust in his psychiatrist – the very means by which treatment is effected ...

Given the importance of confidentiality to the practice of psychiatry, it becomes clear that the duty to warn imposed by the majority will cripple the use and effectiveness of psychiatry. Many people, potentially violent – yet susceptible to treatment – will be deterred from seeking it; those seeking it will be inhibited from making revelations necessary to effective treatment; and, forcing the psychiatrist to violate the patient's trust will destroy the interpersonal relationship by which treatment is effected.

Violence and civil commitment

By imposing a duty to warn, the majority contributes to the danger to society of violence by the mentally ill and greatly increases the risk of civil commitment – the total deprivation of liberty – of those who should not be confined. The impairment of treatment and risk of improper commitment resulting from the new duty to warn will not be limited to a few patients but will extend to a large number of the mentally ill. Although under existing psychiatric procedures only a relatively few receiving treatment will ever present a risk of violence, the number making threats is huge, and it is the latter group – not just the former – whose treatment will be impaired and whose risk of commitment will be increased.

Michael Jones examines the issue in relation to the case of *W v Egdell* (see above, p 239):

> **Jones, M, 'Medical confidentiality and the public interest' (1990) 6 Professional Negligence 16:**
>
> The question arises whether, if Dr Egdell had not disclosed his report and W had been released and had shot someone else, the psychiatrist would have owed a duty of care to the victim? W had made no specific threats, though Dr Egdell clearly regarded him as a potential danger 'to the public'. In these circumstances the courts would probably not impose a duty of care, on the basis that the victim was merely a member of a large unascertained class. Although, in the final analysis, the public is comprised of individuals, in *Hill v Chief Constable of West Yorkshire* the House of Lords held that the police owed no duty of care to the victim of a notorious serial murderer for allegedly negligently failing to apprehend him, partly on the ground that the victim 'was one of a vast number of the female general public who might be at risk from his activities but was at no special distinctive risk ...'. This would be consistent with the approach of the American courts.
>
> On the other hand, in *Holgate v Lancashire Mental Hospitals Board* (1937) a hospital was held liable for negligently releasing on licence a dangerous patient who had been compulsorily detained following convictions for violent offences. The patient entered the plaintiff's home and assaulted her. The judge seemed

to assume that a duty of care existed and the report deals largely with the question of whether there had been negligence. The case may be justified on the basis of the degree of control exercised by the defendants over the dangerous patient, a control analogous to the relationship between gaoler and prisoner which may give rise to a duty of care. The independent psychiatrist does not exercise this degree of control, and so some alternative basis for a duty of care would have to be established. It has been argued that this is to be found in the doctor's unique capacity to influence the patient's behaviour, whether through treatment or advice. But this is questionable, given that the doctor's ability to influence the patient may be limited, and in the circumstances which arose in *W v Egdell* it may be virtually non-existent. The basis of any potential duty of care, it is submitted, is the foreseeability of harm to the victim. It is unfashionable these days to rest a duty of care on foreseeability alone. There must also be a sufficiently proximate relationship between plaintiff and defendant, and it must be just and reasonable in the circumstances to impose a duty. But the more foreseeable the harm, the more likely it is that a court will find the relationship between the parties to be proximate. Thus, if a patient made genuine threats of serious injury to an identified third person and there was a real risk that the threats would be carried out, it is arguable that a doctor would come under a duty of care to the potential victim. It is difficult, however, to see how this duty can be based on the doctor-patient relationship *per se*. If, for example, the patient had made the same statement to a friend, there would be no obvious reason for distinguishing between the obligations of the friend and the doctor to the potential victim, apart from the purely practical point that the doctor may be in a better position to assess whether the threats are genuine. The duty, if any, arises from the defendant's knowledge of the foreseeable danger of serious physical harm to the third party.

There are difficulties, however, with imposing such a duty. The first is conceptual, and stems from the 'mere omissions' rule, namely that there is no general obligation in tort to take positive steps to confer a benefit on others by preventing harm befalling them. So, for example, there is no obligation to rescue someone in danger, even if rescue would involve little or no effort and involves no danger to the rescuer (for example, shouting a warning to a blind man about to walk over the edge of a cliff). The rule has been criticised, but it will be applied in the absence of special circumstances giving rise to a duty to intervene, such as a special relationship between the plaintiff and defendant or some degree of control by the defendant over the conduct of a third party who caused damage to the plaintiff. If, it might be argued, the doctor's relationship with the patient is not sufficient to give him 'control' over the patient's conduct, then there is nothing (other than mere foreseeability of harm) on which to base a duty to intervene. Possession of knowledge, which, if not passed on in the form of a warning, may result in harm to the 'victim', does not in itself constitute control, otherwise the observer of the blind man walking off the cliff would owe a duty of care.

A further difficulty which might militate against the imposition of a duty of care (probably as part of the assessment of whether it was just and reasonable) is that the doctor could be placed on the horns of a dilemma. If he overestimates the danger presented by the patient he is open to an action for breach of confidence by the patient. On the other hand, if he underestimates the danger and the patient harms a third party, the doctor may be liable in negligence. Moreover, although the risk of an action for breach of confidence exists in any event where the doctor has miscalculated the 'public interest', a duty of care to potential victims would tend to push the balance towards disclosure rather than non-disclosure. This problem may be more apparent than real, given that a doctor need only act with reasonable care to avoid liability for negligence, and the *Bolam* test gives the profession considerable discretion in setting the boundaries of what is reasonable. It is true that where the imposition of a duty of care might lead to a defendant being subject to conflicting duties the courts may be reluctant to find a duty of care, but where the public interest defence applies there is no duty to maintain confidentiality and so no conflict with a possible duty of care. Indeed, in Scott J's view in *W v Egdell* the public interest may require a doctor to disclose the information ... a situation which can hardly involve a conflict with a potential duty of care. Thus if, as seems likely, the circumstances in which a duty of care would be imposed are narrower (or at least, not broader) than the circumstances in which the public interest defence applies there could never be such a conflict ...

This discussion of the doctor's possible duty of care to third parties has concentrated on the position of the psychiatrist and his patient. Another obvious situation in which, arguably, a duty of care would arise is that of the patient with AIDS. Would a practitioner owe a duty to the patient's sexual partner(s) to inform them of the patient's condition and the potential risk to their health if the patient refused consent to the disclosure? If the sexual partner was also the doctor's patient there would probably be little difficulty in finding a duty of care, since a 'duty to inform' could be seen as part and parcel of the doctor's more general duty to exercise reasonable care to safeguard the health of his patient. It might be thought somewhat arbitrary, however, if the doctor's liability in this situation turned upon whether the sexual partner happened also to be one of his patients. Arguably, the duty would arise irrespective of the sexual partner's status, on the basis that serious physical harm was foreseeable as a real risk.

An analogy could be drawn here with cases where it is alleged that a doctor has negligently permitted a person to come into contact with a contagious disease. For example, in *Lindsey County Council v Marshall* the House of Lords held the defendants liable for negligently failing to warn the plaintiff of the risk of infection by puerperal fever when she was admitted to their maternity home, following a recent outbreak of the disease. In this case the plaintiff was a patient, but the result should not differ if she were not. If, for example, a doctor was negligent in discharging an infectious patient from hospital, and as a result a third party contracted the disease, the third party would surely have a claim against the doctor.

This view was confirmed in the Californian case of *Reisner v Regents of the University of California* (see (1997) Med L Rev 250), where a doctor was found to have been in breach of a duty of care owed to the sexual partner of a patient who had contracted HIV after receiving a contaminated blood transfusion, which information had been concealed by the doctor concerned. It was said that the patient would have been likely to have warned her sexual partner. However, it was said that third parties who might have become infected by contact with the sexual partner would not be owed a duty of care on remoteness principles.

To whom should disclosure be made and what should be the extent of that disclosure?

It is well established that even if a breach of confidence may be justified, it may still be actionable if the disclosure goes further than that which is necessary. If, for example, as was alluded to by Bingham LJ, p 848, in *W v Egdell* [1990] 1 All ER 835, Dr Egdell had disclosed his report to a newspaper, or commented upon it in a journal article, then this would have been going further than was necessary in the public interest of prevention of crime. The defence of public interest was only available to him in the disclosure to the hospital treating the patient, and the Home Office. Similarly, a doctor who is justified in revealing one aspect of the patient's condition is not thereby justified in revealing other medical information. For example, the revelation that a woman is HIV positive, as we have seen, may occasionally be justified. A doctor who, at the same time, points out that this was discovered in the course of an abortion procedure will be in breach of confidence. However, additional information may be revealed if it is necessary by way of explanation. This point was dealt with in *Egdell*, p 853.

> **Bingham LJ**: Counsel for W argued that even if Dr Egdell was entitled to make some disclosure he should have disclosed only the crucial paragraph of his report and his opinion. I do not agree. An opinion, even from an eminent source, cannot be evaluated unless its factual premise is known, and a detailed 10-page report cannot be reliably assessed by perusing a brief extract.

CONFIDENTIALITY – REMEDIES

Detriment

In *AG v Guardian Newspapers (No 2)* [1990] AC 109, there was no clear stance as to whether there is a need for detriment to be shown in private actions for breach of confidence. Lord Goff, for example, left the question open (pp 281–82). Although there are instances where a patient would suffer pecuniary loss as a result of that breach (for example, disclosure of a medical condition to an employer which results in dismissal), in many cases no quantifiable loss would result. It is arguable that breach of confidence should be actionable *per se*, or that, if detriment is required, the breach itself is a detriment to the patient in the sense that he has been betrayed.

An interesting point arises if we consider inadvertent disclosure. Up until now we have assumed that the act of disclosure has been deliberate. However, if a confidential medical report were to be carelessly lost in a public place, does the patient have to show that damage has resulted from this? In other words would the negligence criterion be applied, ie, that damage must have resulted from the non-deliberate act? This will be examined further in relation to damages.

Damages

The rather curious New Zealand case of *Furniss v Fitchett* [1958] NZLR 396 was decided on negligence principles. The facts were as follows. The marriage of a Mr and Mrs Furniss was under a great deal of strain. Both were patients of Dr Fitchett. Mr Furniss asked the doctor to provide him with a letter detailing his wife's psychiatric problems, which he did. It was not marked 'confidential' and the doctor did not know how it was to be used. Just over a year later, it was produced in the course of a court hearing – the first time Mrs Furniss had heard of it. She suffered what is oddly described in the law report as 'shock to the injury of her health'. Leaving aside the difficult issue of what sort of injury this is (the judge referred to it as 'physical' injury), the general negligence criteria were applied. Barrowclough CJ said, p 404:

> **Barrowclough CJ**: ... I find that the defendant doctor was aware that the opinion which he expressed ... would, if it should come to the knowledge of his patient, be likely to injure her in her health. I find also that in the circumstances in which he issued that certificate – handing it to the patient's husband to be given to his solicitor, knowing that the husband and wife were then estranged, and without marking it as confidential or otherwise restricting its use – he ought reasonably to have foreseen that the certificate or its contents would be likely to come to the knowledge of his patient. I conclude, therefore, that in the circumstances to which I have referred, the doctor owed to his patient at common law a duty to take reasonable care to ensure that no expression of his opinion as to her mental condition should come to her knowledge. The doctor did not take any precautions in that respect ...

The last point is an odd one. If this letter had been disclosed to a number of people, but in circumstances which Mrs Furniss would not know about, the implication is that the doctor would be off the hook. Indeed, the judge seemed to doubt whether the ethical duty of confidentiality was reflected in the law at all. However, the case resulted in the award to Mrs Furniss the sum of A\$3,250 in damages.

Although it is probably the case that actual loss does not have to be shown, as a general principle, damages should reflect the degree of loss suffered. Unjustifiable disclosure of HIV or AIDS may well result in considerable and long standing distress. Given that we are not here considering a strict application of negligence criteria, it is submitted that, ordinary distress as opposed to psychiatric illness, would attract damages. The Law Commission, *Breach of Confidence*, Report No 110, Cmnd 8388, 1981, London: HMSO, paras 4.79–4.82, examined the issue of damages for mental distress, and concluded that there is no basis for the award of damages for mental distress for a non-contractual breach of confidence, ie, for our purposes, when we are considering NHS treatment. However, they recommend that damages should be awarded for mental distress, if a person of reasonable fortitude would so suffer.

The Law Commission also considered whether punitive damages might be available for breach of confidence, but decided it was wrong to look at the issue in isolation. Under the present criteria set down by *Rookes v Barnard* [1964] AC 1129, and *AB v South West Water Services Ltd* [1992] 4 All ER 574, punitive damages would not be available.

Injunctions

It is important to remember that the injunction is a discretionary remedy, and, in the context of breach of confidence, if the information is already in the public domain, there will be no purpose served by an order preventing further publication: see *AG v Guardian Newspapers (No 2)* [1990] AC 109.

An injunction at the final trial of the action will rarely be granted if there has been no interim injunction when the proceedings are first issued, because if there has been no prior prevention of publication, then by the time of trial, the information will either be well and truly in the public domain, or no longer worth suppressing.

The interim injunction, therefore, is the key weapon in a breach of confidence action. It means that publication will be prevented for what may be a long time before trial. The basis upon which such relief would be granted was set out in *American Cyanamid Co v Ethicon Ltd* [1975] AC 396, and is generally known as 'the balance of convenience test', where the court has to decide whether either party will suffer irreparable harm and, if both will suffer, who will suffer the most.

The dead

As we have seen, the Hippocratic Oath binds a doctor to keep medical confidences after death, and the GMC guidance reflects this. However, it is not clear whether there is any legal obligation to keep confidences after the death of the person to whom the duty is owed, ie, in medicine, after the death of the patient.

Kennedy, I and Grubb, A, *Medical Law*, 2nd edn, 1994, London: Butterworths, p 643:

What effect does the death of a patient have on the obligation of confidence? The traditional ethical principle is stated by the GMC in the 'Blue Book' in para 91: 'The fact of a patient's death does not of itself release a doctor from the obligation to maintain confidentiality.' Is this the legal position? We are not considering here the separate and equally difficult question of whether an action for a breach of confidence which occurred during the life of a patient survives his death. Instead, we are concerned with an action by a patient's estate for disclosures after the death of the patient. Such a claim could only be brought if the estate had itself suffered a legal wrong. Arguably, the estate can only be legally wronged in this context if it inherits a right of the deceased which is unlawfully interfered with after death. So, for example, the right to sue on a contract passes to the estate. Similarly, where property passes to the estate on death any unlawful dealing with it by others will give the estate a right of action. Thus the crucial question is whether the right to have confidences observed is a right which passes as a chose in action to the estate. There is no clear answer. It could be argued that since what is at stake is the deceased's feelings and reputation, the analogy with the law of defamation is persuasive (ie, the cause of action does not survive death). Of course, in relation to defamation, the position is governed by statute. In our view the courts would reflect this policy in the case of breach of medical confidence. Even if this view were wrong, the law may require the estate to show detriment as a condition of the claim. This would, of course, be difficult.

Davies, M, *Medical Law*, 1996, London: Blackstone Press, pp 45–46:

2.10 Confidence and death

A brief mention should be made of confidences that endure after death. Why? Simply because of the ethical notion of respecting the memory of the deceased but also because medical revelations can harm the living. The declaration of Geneva, it will be recalled, could not be clearer on the matter. Strangely, there is little confidential about the death itself because the death certificate itself is a public document. Mason and McCall Smith pertinently note the stigma of AIDS following victims to the grave. To be strictly accurate on the death certificate, the doctor should correctly indicate the cause of death. If 'AIDS' is placed on the certificate, then ill-informed rumour might well attach to living partners, friends and relatives. The key to the issue of death and confidentiality in medical law takes one back to the beginning: upon what is it based? If it is the reciprocity of the doctor-patient relationship, then that has ceased to exist. If it is the doctor's duty to society as a whole, then this 'public' duty might include an enduring duty of overall medical confidence.

ACCESS TO MEDICAL RECORDS – ETHICAL CONSIDERATIONS

As a corollary to the duty of confidentiality owed by a doctor to a patient, one could be forgiven for assuming that a patient should have an unfettered right to see his medical records. After all, if a doctor is to be privy to intimate medical information which he has a duty to keep quiet about, but not an absolute duty, then the accuracy of that information should be verifiable at least by the patient concerned. At first sight, it might seem that here there are two discrete patient rights, ie, the right to respect for privacy and the right to know what the doctor is placing in the medical records. However, in practice they are intertwined. The patient's right to protection of confidences must surely extend to the right to know that the information concerned is accurate. Further, the utilitarian argument that the patient will be more candid if confidentiality is protected and that such candour is necessary for the patient's health and that of society generally, also sustains the proposition that a patient should have a right to check the accuracy of that information. (Interestingly, it has been argued that, in order to preserve confidentiality, patients should keep their own medical records. See 'Editorial' (1991) 17 JME 115, and the article in the same edition by Gilhooly, M and McGhee, S, 'Medical records: practicalities and principles of patient possession'.)

On the other hand, if the patient has only a discretionary right (or, indeed, no right at all), then this would usually be justified on paternalistic principles. The types of arguments that are advanced in the cause of paternalism, are, for example, that the patient would not understand the records, that they may frighten or confuse him, the doctor would not be able to make 'frank' comments about the patient and so on. However, are paternalistic principles justifiable in certain circumstances where revelation of the contents of records may damage the patient or others? It will be seen that both common law and statute favour the paternalistic approach.

ACCESS TO MEDICAL RECORDS – THE LAW

Statutory provisions

Access to Health Records Act 1990

This legislation was passed as a result of the case of *Gaskin v United Kingdom* [1990] 12 EHRR 36, where the European Court of Human Rights held that the UK's refusal to grant a right of access by a patient to his health records was in breach of Art 8 of the European Convention.

3   **Right of access to health records**

(1)   An application for access to a health record, or to any part of a health record, may be made to the holder of the record by any of the following, namely–

(a)   the patient;

(b)   a person authorised in writing to make the application on the patient's behalf;

(c) where the record is held in England and Wales and the patient is a child, a person having parental responsibility for the patient;

(d) where the record is held in Scotland and the patient is a pupil, a parent or guardian of the patient;

(e) where the patient is incapable of managing his own affairs, any person appointed by a court to manage those affairs; and

(f) where the patient has died, the patient's personal representative and any person who may have a claim arising out of the patient's death.

(2) Subject to s 4 below, where an application is made under sub-s (1) above the holder shall, within the requisite period, give access to the record, or the part of a record, to which the application relates–

(a) in the case of a record, by allowing the applicant to inspect the record or, where s 5 below applies, an extract setting out so much of the record as is not excluded by that section;

(b) in the case of a part of a record, by allowing the applicant to inspect an extract setting out that part or, where that section applies, so much of that part as is not so excluded; or

(c) in either case, if the applicant so requires, by supplying him with a copy of the record or extract.

(3) Where any information contained in a record or extract which is so allowed to be inspected, or a copy of which is so supplied, is expressed in terms which are not intelligible without explanation, an explanation of those terms shall be provided with the record or extract, or supplied with the copy.

As indicated above, however, the Act does provide only a qualified right of access.

4   Cases where right of access may be wholly excluded

(1) Where an application is made under sub-s (1)(a) or (b) of s 3 above and–

(a) in the case of a record held in England and Wales, the patient is a child; or

(b) in the case of a record held in Scotland, the patient is a pupil,

access shall not be given under sub-s (2) of that section unless the holder of the record is satisfied that the patient is capable of understanding the nature of the application.

(2) Where an application is made under sub-s (1)(c) or (d) of s 3 above, access shall not be given under sub-s (2) of that section unless the holder of the record is satisfied either–

(a) that the patient has consented to the making of the application; or

(b) that the patient is incapable of understanding the nature of the application;

and the giving of access would be in his best interests.

(3) Where an application is made under sub-s (1)(f) of s 3 above, access shall not be given under sub-s (2) of that section if the record includes a note, made at the patient's request, that he did not wish access to be given on such an application.

5 **Cases where right of access may be partially excluded**

(1) Access shall not be given under s 3(2) above to any part of a health record–

    (a) which, in the opinion of the holder of the record, would disclose:

        (i) information likely to cause serious harm to the physical or mental health of the patient or of any other individual; or

        (ii) information relating to or provided by an individual, other than the patient, who could be identified from that information; or

    (b) which was made before the commencement of this Act.

(2) Sub-section (1)(a)(ii) above shall not apply–

    (a) where the individual concerned has consented to the application; or

    (b) where that individual is a health professional who has been involved in the care of the patient;

    and sub-s (1)(b) above shall not apply where and to the extent that, in the opinion of the holder of the record, the giving of access is necessary in order to make intelligible any part of the record to which access is required to be given under s 3(2) above.

(3) Where an application is made under sub-s (1)(c), (d), (e) or (f) of s 3 above, access shall not be given under sub-s (2) of that section to any part of the record which, in the opinion of the holder of the record, would disclose–

    (a) information provided by the patient in the expectation that it would not be disclosed to the applicant; or

    (b) information obtained as a result of any examination or investigation to which the patient consented in the expectation that the information would not be so disclosed ...

If the record holder forms the opinion that the information may cause serious harm to the health of the patient or another, access may be excluded to the relevant part of the records. Yet again, this reflects medical paternalism. Further, it is makes no sense that access should be refused because it may seriously harm the patient. If the patient is refused access on this ground, is not the refusal itself likely to cause harm? Speculation as to what the records may contain could, and probably would, cause considerable anxiety. Even if one accepts the argument that many patients do not want to know about risks of treatment before consent is given, the same argument cannot apply to access. Patients of sound mind, who have gone to the trouble of making an application, should have their requests respected. Harm caused to third parties raises different issues, which would depend upon the identity of the third party, the type and magnitude of the harm and so on.

It will be seen that it is envisaged that a child may be capable of understanding 'the nature of the application' and may therefore apply for access (sub-s 4(1)). The Act does not state that the child must be capable of understanding the records, nor indeed is it implied anywhere that an adult applicant must be capable. It is arguable that such a requirement would defeat the purpose of the Act, providing, as it would, many opportunities for denial of access.

Further, the Act also protects the child patient by allowing the record holder to refuse to disclose 'information provided by the patient in the expectation that it would not be disclosed to the applicant' (sub-s 5(3)(a)). However, given that a doctor's duty of confidentiality towards a child is qualified (see above, p 233), this adds little to the common law position.

The Act does not apply to records made before 1 November 1991. However, see s 5(2), where the commencement date restriction does not apply if, in the opinion of the record holder, it is necessary to give further access to make intelligible the later records. As it would be possible for the holder to give voluntary access to the earlier records if it was thought desirable, this adds nothing to patient rights, but seems to be there merely as an assurance for the record holder.

Data Protection Act 1984

Before the 1990 Act came into force, computerised medical records could be accessed under the Data Protection Act 1984, which gives 'data subjects' the right to know what information about them is electronically stored and the right to inspect it. However, as far as medical records are concerned, the Act was modified by statutory instrument in 1987.

The Data Protection (Subject Access Modification) (Health) Order 1987 SI 1987/1903:

4 (1) The subject access provisions shall not have effect in relation to any personal data to which this Order applies in any case where either of the requirements specified in para (2) below is satisfied with respect to the information constituting the data and the obligations contained in para (5) below are complied with by the data user.

(2) The requirements referred to in para (1) above are that the application of the subject access provisions–

(a) would be likely to cause serious harm to the physical or mental health of the data subject; or

(b) would be likely to disclose to the data subject the identity of another individual (who has not consented to the disclosure of the information) either as a person to whom the information or part of it relates or as the source of the information or enable that identity to be deduced by the data subject either from the information itself or from a combination of that information and other information which the data subject has or is likely to have.

Kennedy and Grubb (*Medical Law*, 2nd edn, 1994, London: Butterworths, p 632), point out that 'the balance seems more favourable to the patient's right of access since the criteria for excluding access are expressed in more objective language in that no reference is made to the formula "in the opinion of the holder of the record"'.

Access to Medical Reports Act 1988

This Act confers a right of access to medical reports obtained for employment or insurance purposes:

3 Consent to applications for medical reports for employment or insurance purposes

(1) A person shall not apply to a medical practitioner for a medical report relating to any individual to be supplied to him for employment or insurance purposes unless–

   (a) that person ('the applicant') has notified the individual that he proposes to make the application; and

   (b) the individual has notified the applicant that he consents to the making of the application.

(2) Any notification given under sub-s (1)(a) above must inform the individual of his right to withhold his consent to the making of the application, and of the following rights under this Act, namely–

   (a) the rights arising under sub-ss 4(1)–(3) and 6(2) below with respect to access to the report before or after it is supplied;

   (b) the right to withhold consent under sub-s (1) of sub-s 5 below; and

   (c) the right to request the amendment of the report under sub-s (2) of that section, as well as of the effect of sub-s 7 below.

The Act also gives a right for the individual to have access to the report before it is supplied, and provides for the correction by the patient of matters contained in the report.

It is interesting to note the provision of s 3(1). Clearly, this adds nothing to the common law, as a doctor could not provide a medical report to a third party without consent if he is the patient's own doctor, and it is important to note that the Act only applies to reports prepared by a medical practitioner who is, or has been, responsible for the clinical care of the individual (s 2(1)). What of the situation where the doctor is nominated by an insurance company or employer, to whom the Act does not apply? Would an obligation of confidence arise? It is submitted that, once the doctor had examined the patient and obtained medical information, without express or implied consent that it would be disclosed, the doctor would owe a duty of confidence. However, would it be easier to conclude that implied consent had been given by attending the medical appointment in the first place?

The right under the Act is qualified in the same way as it is under the Access to Health Records Act and the Data Protection Act.

There is a right to apply to the court if access is refused (sub-s (8)).

Common law

As has been seen above, there is now a qualified, statutory right of access to medical records, but this does not apply to non-computerised records made prior to 1 November 1991. The common law is still, therefore, of considerable importance. The issue was examined by the Court of Appeal in the case of *R v Mid Glamorgan Family Health Services Authority and Another ex p Martin* [1995] 1 WLR 110. The facts were as follows. As a young man, the applicant had received psychiatric treatment from doctors employed by the respondents. He had also received assistance from a female social worker, with whom he became infatuated. She was taken off his case, and for some years he had sought access to his medical records, to find out why the social worker had been removed and why he had subsequently been committed under the 1959 Mental Health Act. Access had been refused, on the basis that they were the property of the relevant authority and that disclosure would be damaging to the applicant and to third parties. The applicant's lawyers had responded to the effect that these doctors were in no position to judge whether the applicant would be damaged. Clearly, this was a forceful argument, and it resulted in a compromise offer: the respondents would agree to disclose the records to a medical adviser nominated by him, for that person to decide whether they may be damaging. The offer was refused. The judge at first instance dismissed the application for unmediated disclosure. In the Court of Appeal, the appeal was dismissed.

> **Nourse LJ**, p 116: ... a public body, in fulfilment of its duty to administer its property in accordance with its public purposes, is bound to deal with medical records in the same way as a private doctor. In that regard the observations of Lord Templeman in *Sidaway* [1985] 1 AC 871, p 904, are pertinent:
>
>> I do not subscribe to the theory that the patient is entitled to know everything nor to the theory that the doctor is entitled to decide everything. The relationship between doctor and patient is contractual in origin, the doctor performing services in consideration for fees payable by the patient. The doctor, obedient to the high standards set by the medical profession, impliedly contracts to act at all times in the best interests of the patient. No doctor in his senses would impliedly contract at the same time to give to the patient all the information available to the doctor as a result of the doctor's training and experience and as a result of the doctor's diagnosis of the patient. An obligation to give a patient all the information available to the doctor would often be inconsistent with the doctor's

contractual obligation to have regard to the patient's best interests. Some information might confuse, other information might alarm a particular patient. Whenever the occasion arises for the doctor to tell the patient the results of the doctor's diagnosis, the possible methods of treatment and the advantages and disadvantages of the recommended treatment, the doctor must decide in the light of his training and experience and in the light of his knowledge of the patient what should be said and how it should be said.

These observations provide a sensible basis for holding that a doctor, likewise a health authority, as the owner of a patient's medical records, may deny the patient access to them if it is in his best interests to do so, for example if their disclosure would be detrimental to his health. In the light of the offer made in the respondents' solicitor's letter of 24 March 1993, that is a complete answer to the applicant's application. I agree with Popplewell J that the respondents have offered all that is necessary to comply with their duty to the applicant. The judge was entitled, in the exercise of his discretion, to refuse the applicant the relief that he sought and I would affirm his decision on that ground. Although the respondents have not taken this point, it might also, as a matter of discretion, have been affirmed on the ground that the applicant did nothing effective to pursue his rights against either of the respondents between 1981 and 1990.

It is inherent in the views above expressed that I do not accept that a health authority, any more than a private doctor, has an absolute right to deal with medical records in any way that it chooses. As Lord Templeman makes clear, the doctor's general duty, likewise the health authority's, is to act at all times in the best interests of the patient. Those interests would usually require that a patient's medical records should not be disclosed to third parties; conversely, that they should usually, for example, be handed on by one doctor to the next or made available to the patient's legal advisers if they are reasonably required for the purposes of legal proceedings in which he is involved. The respondents' position seems to be that no practical difficulty could arise in such circumstances, but that they would act voluntarily and not because they were under a legal duty to do so. If it ever became necessary for the legal position to be tested, it is inconceivable that this extreme position would be vindicated. On all the other points taken by the applicant I agree with Popplewell J. I would dismiss this appeal.

The court also relied on the fact that, although there were a number of statutory rights to access, these were not absolute, and could be wholly or partially excluded in appropriate circumstances. Some commentators, such as Dermot Feenan, have found this an unsatisfactory decision:

Feenan, D, 'Common law access to medical records' [1996] 59 MLR 101:

Detriment to patient – insufficient

The framing of the exception in terms only of detriment to the patient seems insufficient protection of a patient's interests in personal health information. The sufficiency of the exception may be tested by reference to analogous law, comprising persuasive Commonwealth and American *dicta* and British legislation. In the leading American authority on informed consent, *Canterbury v Spence*, the court held that a doctor is not obliged to disclose where disclosure poses *such a threat of detriment* to the patient as to become unfeasible or contraindicated from a medical point of view. It is recognised that patients may become *so emotionally distraught* on disclosure as to *foreclose a rational decision*, or complicate or hinder the treatment, or perhaps even pose psychological damage to the patient. Where that is so, the cases have generally held that the physician is armed with a privilege to keep the information from the patient, and we think it clear that portents of that type may justify the physician in action he deems medically warranted.

Here harm alone was insufficient. There had to be harm of the type envisaged by the court. Similarly, in the South Australian Supreme Court, King CJ approved his *dictum* in a previous case to the effect that a doctor is justified in withholding information 'when he judges *on reasonable grounds* that the patient's physical or mental, might be seriously harmed by the information'. Here, the court imposes two qualifications on the prospect of harm. First, that there must be reasonable grounds for establishing such a prospect, and, second, that the harm must be serious.

It is easy to understand why these courts require more than simply the doctor's view of potential detriment. There appears to be an implicit acknowledgment by them of the danger of paternalistic bias by the doctor regarding information disclosure. Aside from judicial precedent, mounting empirical evidence undermines doctors' assertions designed to restrict or obstruct information disclosure on the basis that patients would be unable to deal with harmful information. In 1982 the United States President's Commission for the Study of Ethical Problems in Medicine and Biomedical and Behavioral Research stated:

> Despite all the anecdotes about patients who committed suicide, suffered heart attacks, or plunged into prolonged depression upon being told 'bad news', little documentation exists for claims that informing patients is more dangerous to their health than not informing them, particularly when the informing is done in a sensitive and tactful fashion.

Similar findings exist in relation to medical records. It is also acknowledged that unless the exception is carefully circumscribed it may swallow up the primary principle of information disclosure. Arguably, similar considerations apply to access to medical records.

The exception in *Martin* also falls short of similar policy encapsulated in British freedom of information legislation. In the Access to Health Records Act 1990, which gives a statutory right of access to health records, sub-s 5(1)(a) provides that access shall not be given where in the opinion of the holder of the record ... information is '*likely* to cause *serious harm* to the physical or mental health of the patient ...'. This section makes clear the gravity of harm and its likelihood. These criteria reflect the fact that the purpose of the legislation, which was to establish a right of access to health records, was not to be circumscribed too easily. Identical wording, and similar policy considerations, are found in the relevant legislative provisions exempting disclosure made under the Data Protection Act 1984 and in the Access to Medical Reports Act 1988.

It seems that the Court of Appeal in *Martin* simply accepted the opinion of the consultant psychiatrist and, thence, the respondents' solicitors, that disclosure would be detrimental to the patient. As the above common law dicta and legislation show, detriment alone ought to be insufficient.

Is it not the case that the 'serious harm' exception in relation to *the patient*, however stringently applied, is contrary to patient autonomy? Surely if the patient is competent and suitably warned, he should be entitled to run the risk?

A paternalistic approach was taken by the Australian Supreme Court of New South Wales in the case of *Breen v Williams* [1995] 6 Med LR 385, where the doctor's right to decide what it would be good for a patient to know was upheld:

> **Mahoney JA**, p 427: Subject to what I shall say, the documents are created for the purpose of such diagnosis and treatment and they are merely what the doctor uses to achieve those purposes. Accordingly, in my opinion, *prima facie*, a medical file kept by a doctor is the property of the doctor.
>
> However, the position is, of course, more complicated. It is necessary to examine the circumstances surrounding the creation of each document. Documents created merely for the purposes of the doctor, for example, as records of his practice, as material from which to assess charges and the like, will be the property of the doctor. On the other hand, some documents created for the purpose of enabling the doctor to diagnose and to determine the treatment to be recommended may be the property of the patient. Thus, a document, though held by the doctor, may be the property of the patient because it was procured by or for the patient and has been paid for by her. X-rays, pathology reports and some reports by consultant specialists may be such: cf as to the case of a solicitor *Wentworth v de Montfort*, p 356B. Correspondence with consultant specialists or with treating hospitals may, if of this kind, be the property of the patient.
>
> More difficult questions arise in relation to matters such as those particularly referred to by Dr Cashman in the present case, namely, notes taken by the doctor to record the patient's medical history and her signs and symptoms. In one sense such records are made for the purposes of the patient, the making of them is one of the things which the doctor, by his engagement, may undertake to do. In this sense, the document is created so that there may be a record of what the patient has told the doctor and her signs and symptoms at the time. The record may not merely help in the instant diagnosis and a selection of treatment, it may provide a valuable resource for future purposes. Considered in isolation, a record of this kind, if it were contained in a separate document, would, I think, be the property of the patient.
>
> On the other hand, the doctor may – as Dr Williams has said he ordinarily will – include with the record of the history and the signs and symptoms of the patient, comments and observations which are made and recorded for the purpose of helping the doctor form the diagnosis and the opinion to be formed as to treatment. There may be observations – Dr Williams used the term

'musings' – which, if standing alone, would ordinarily be the property of the doctor and not of the patient. It is the fact that these things are combined in the documents which illustrates the nature of the problem in a case such as this.

The combination of such things: the history, signs and symptoms on the one hand and the 'musings' and other things on the other hand, may be accidental in the sense that the combination of the two in the one record is not inherent in the process of medical knowledge. But the thrust of Dr Williams' evidence is, I think, that such a combination is not accidental. His evidence suggests that the combination of these two things is inherent in the way medical practice is conducted or, at least in the way he conducts his practice. The trial judge accepted this portion of the doctor's evidence.

If the records kept by the doctor be in this form, then, in my opinion, the records remain the property of the doctor ...

This decision does not deny that a patient has a right to know the main contents of his records, what it denies to him is the right to look through them and discover his doctor's comments. The reason given for this is that the doctor will be inhibited when making his notes, and that may not be in the patient's interest. It is easy to see that a doctor may feel restrained from making adverse comments relating to, say, genuineness of symptoms, when, for example, referring a patient to another doctor, if he thought that the patient may see this. However, the suspicions must be based upon factual matters such as an inconsistent history of symptoms, and physical examination failing to accord with alleged symptoms, and surely these are matters which the doctor should discuss openly with his patient. Or is it arguable that there is a risk of losing the patient's trust?

However, in *Breen v Williams*, there was a dissenting judgment, by Kirby P, in favour of disclosure, which relied on there being a fiduciary duty owed to the patient. This was following the Canadian Supreme Court decision of *McInerney v MacDonald* (1992) 93 DLR (4th) 415. In this case comment was made as follows:

La Forest J, p 421: Information about oneself revealed to a doctor acting in a professional capacity remains, in a fundamental sense, one's own. The doctor's position is one of trust and confidence. The information conveyed is held in a fashion somewhat akin to a trust. While the doctor is the owner of the actual record, the information is to be used by the physician for the benefit of the patient. The confiding of the information to the physician for medical purposes gives rise to an expectation that the patient's interest in and control of the information will continue. The trust-like 'beneficial interest' of the patient in the information indicates that, as a general rule, he or she should have a right of access to the information and that the physician should have a corresponding obligation to provide it.

How might the fiduciary duty argument have changed the decision of the Court of Appeal in *Martin*?

Supreme Court Act 1981

As mentioned previously, ss 33 and 34 of the Supreme Court Act permit disclosure of documents, both prior to commencement of proceedings, and during the course of those legal proceedings. Not only is this an exception to the principle of confidentiality; it may also provide an opportunity for a patient to acquire knowledge of his medical records. The provisions of the Act permit disclosure to the applicant's *legal* and *medical* advisers only. However, does this prevent the adviser disclosing the contents of the documents to the patient? It is submitted that it does not. If the adviser, either medical or legal, is to advise, then a discussion of the medical history is inevitable, and for this purpose the contents of the notes will be revealed. However, this perhaps may not extend to giving the patient photocopies of the notes, as it could be interpreted as a circumvention of the provisions of ss 33 and 34.

CHAPTER SIX

MEDICAL MALPRACTICE

INTRODUCTION

Medical malpractice may be defined, broadly, as any unjustified act or failure to act upon the part of a doctor or other health care worker which results in harm to the patient. In this chapter we shall be considering the means, under the civil law, by which a victim of such malpractice may pursue a claim for redress, and the difficulties that lie in his way. (The rare instances in which the doctor may also be the subject of criminal liability have been noted already, in Chapter 2.)

First, what form might the patient's claim take? On the face of it, there would seem to be three possibilities – to sue in tort, either in battery or negligence, or to mount an action for breach of contract. In practice, however, it is the second of these, a negligence action, which offers the only appropriate channel for the vast majority of malpractice claims. The first option, battery, which forms the civil analogue to the crime of assault, generally only arises as a possibility in those rare cases where treatment is carried out without any consent at all (see above, Chapter 3). It is no use to the patient who, having given such consent, suffers injury, however poor the execution of the treatment subsequently turns out to be.

As for the third option, breach of contract, the first thing to note is that this will not assist patients treated under the NHS scheme (ie, the majority of patients in this country), who provide no consideration in return for the services they receive: see *Appleby v Sleep* [1968] 2 All ER 265. What, though, of the growing numbers of patients treated in the private sector? Whilst it is true that the latter may sue for breach of contract instead of (or as well as) in negligence, in proving a breach they have exactly the same task as their NHS counterparts. This is because, in implying the terms which govern such contracts, the courts have held the standard of skill and care warranted by the private doctor to be identical to the standard of care required to avoid a claim in negligence. In *Thake v Maurice* [1986] QB 644, a case in which a patient treated privately sued following the failure of his vasectomy, Neill LJ in the Court of Appeal commented:

> **Neill LJ**: I do not consider that a reasonable person would have expected a responsible medical man to be intending to give a guarantee. Medicine, though a highly skilled profession, is not, and is not generally regarded as being, an exact science. The reasonable man would have expected the defendant to exercise all the special care and skill of a surgeon in that

speciality; he would not in my view have expected the defendant to give a guarantee of 100% success.

This common law standard of care is also echoed in s 13 of the Supply of Goods and Services Act 1982, which provides that a person who supplies services in the course of a business must carry them out with reasonable care and skill.

Accordingly, in the remainder of this chapter we shall be focusing upon actions in medical negligence. In order for such actions to succeed, a number of basic elements (familiar from the general tort of negligence) must be made out, ie, the existence of a duty of care, the fact of its breach, and that legally recognised damage was thereby caused, and we shall consider these various requirements in turn. It is, of course, notorious that medical negligence claims are, by their nature, often very hard to prove (as well as being costly, time consuming and traumatic for those involved), and we shall conclude by considering the case for legal reforms in this area.

THE DUTY OF CARE

The duty to the patient

The patient must establish that the defendant, who may be a doctor, nurse, NHS trust, or a health authority, owed him a legal duty of care. This is probably the easiest element to show. As Michael Jones comments:

> **Jones, M, *Medical Negligence*, 1996, London: Sweet & Maxwell, p 29:**
>
> Normally, there will be no difficulty in finding a duty of care owed by the doctor to his patient, at least where the claim is in respect of personal injuries, and this is true even where there is a contractual relationship. The practitioner may also owe a duty of care to the patient in respect of pure financial loss. In addition, there are a number of circumstances where a doctor may also owe a duty of care to a third party arising out of the treatment given to the patient, but the incident and extent of such duties is more problematic.

The well known case of *Barnett v Chelsea and Kensington Hospital Management Committee* [1968] 1 All ER 1068 is authority for the proposition that an open accident and emergency unit has a duty to treat or at least assess the patient. The facts arose after three nightwatchmen, who were taken ill after drinking some tea, went to their local hospital's casualty department, but were sent away without being seen by a doctor. Nield J stated:

> **Nield J:** I turn to consider the nature of the duty which the law imposes on persons in the position of the defendants and their servants and agents. The authorities deal in the main with the duties of doctors, surgeons, consultants, nurses and staff when a person is treated either by a doctor at his surgery or the patient's home or when the patient is treated in or at a hospital. In *Cassidy*

v Ministry of Health [1951] 2 KB 343, Denning LJ dealt with the duties of hospital authorities and said:

> In my opinion, authorities who run a hospital, be they local authorities, government boards, or any other corporation, are in law under the self-same duty as the humblest doctor. Whenever they accept a patient for treatment, they must use reasonable care and skill to cure him of his ailment. The hospital authorities cannot, of course, do it by themselves. They have no ears to listen through the stethoscope, and no hands to hold the knife. They must do it by the staff which they employ, and, if their staff are negligent in giving the treatment, they are just as liable for that negligence as is anyone else who employs others to do his duties for him. Is there any possible difference in law, I ask, can there be, between hospital authorities who accept a patient for treatment and railway or shipping authorities who accept a passenger for carriage? None whatever. Once they undertake the task, they come under a duty to use care in the doing of it, and that is so whether they do it for reward or not.

Here the problem is different and no authority bearing directly on it has been cited to me. It is to determine the duty of those who provide and run a casualty department when a person presents himself at that department complaining of illness or injury and before he is treated and received into the hospital wards. This is not a case of a casualty department which closes its doors and says that no patients can be received. The three watchmen entered the defendants' hospital without hindrance, they made complaints to the nurse who received them and she in turn passed those complaints on to the medical casualty officer, and he sent a message through the nurse purporting to advise the three men. Is there, on these facts, shown to be created a relationship between the three watchmen and the hospital staff such as gives rise to a duty of care in the defendants which they owe to the three men?

... In my judgment, there was here such a close and direct relationship between the hospital and the watchmen that there was imposed on the hospital a duty of care which they owed to the watchmen. Thus, I have no doubt that Nurse Corbett and Dr Banerjee were under a duty to the deceased to exercise that skill and care which is to be expected of persons in such positions acting reasonably, or, as it is, I think very helpfully, put by the learned author of *Winfield on Torts*, 7th edn, 1963, p 183:

> Where one is engaged in a transaction in which he holds himself out as having professional skill, the law expects him to show the average amount of competence associated with the proper discharge of the duties of that profession or trade or calling, and if he falls short of that and injures someone in consequence, he is not behaving reasonably.

In relation to general practitioners, who operate outside hospitals, these clearly owe a duty of care to their own patients, ie, those who are registered with them. Moreover, by virtue of the National Health Service (General Medical Services) Regulations 1992 SI 1992/635, Sched 2, para 4(1)(h), such a practitioner is required, pursuant to his statutory contract with the area family health services authority, to treat:

(h) persons to whom he may be requested to give treatment which is immediately required owing to an accident or other emergency at any place in his practice area, provided that–

  (i)   he is not, at time of the request, relieved of liability to give treatment under para 5; and

  (ii) he is not, at the time of the request, relieved, under para 19(2), of his obligation to give treatment personally; and

  (iii) he is available to provide such treatment;

  and any persons by whom he is requested, and agrees, to give treatment which is immediately required owing to an accident or other emergency at any place in the locality of any FHSA in whose medical list he is included, provided there is no doctor who, at the time of the request, is under an obligation otherwise than under this head to give treatment to that person, or there is such a doctor but, after being requested to attend, he is unable to attend and give treatment immediately required ...

(Paragraphs 5 and 19(2) of the Schedule relieve the doctor of liability to treat, respectively, in cases where he is elderly or infirm, or another doctor is already present.)

Recently, the nature of the duty of care owed in such cases by the practitioner to the *patient* was considered *obiter* by Stuart-Smith LJ in *Capital and Counties v Hants* CC [1997] 2 All ER 865:

> **Stuart-Smith LJ**: As a general rule a sufficient relationship of proximity will exist when someone possessed of special skill undertakes to apply that skill for the assistance of another person who relies upon such skill and there is direct and substantial reliance by the plaintiff on the defendant's skill (see *Hedley Byrne and Co Ltd v Heller and Partners* and *Henderson v Merrett Syndicates Ltd*). There are many instances of this. The plaintiffs submit that that which is most closely analogous is that of doctor and patient or health authority and patient. There is no doubt that once the relationship of doctor and patient or hospital authority and admitted patient exists, the doctor or the hospital owe a duty to take reasonable care to effect a cure, not merely to prevent further harm. The undertaking is to use the special skills which the doctor and hospital authorities have to treat the patient. In *Cassidy v Ministry of Health (Fahrni, Third Party)* [1951] 1 All ER 574, p 588, Denning LJ said:
>
> > In my opinion, authorities who run a hospital, be they local authorities, government boards, or any other corporation, are in law under the self-same duty as the humblest doctor. Whenever they accept a patient for treatment, they must use reasonable care and skill to cure him of his ailment.
>
> In *Barnett v Chelsea and Kensington Hospital Management Committee* [1968] 1 All ER 1068, Nield J drew a distinction between a casualty department of a hospital that closes its doors and says no patients can be received, in which case he would by inference have held there was no duty of care, and the case before him where the three watchmen who had taken poison entered the hospital and were given erroneous advice, where a duty of care arose.

Likewise, a doctor who happened to witness a road accident will very likely go to the assistance of anyone injured, but he is not under any legal obligation to do so (save in certain limited circumstances which are not relevant) and the relationship of doctor and patient does not arise. If he volunteers his assistance, his only duty as a matter of law is not to make the victim's condition worse.

There is a clear difficulty with this last assertion by Stuart-Smith LJ (repeated in *Powell v Boldaz* (1997) 39 BMLR 35). By stopping and assisting, the doctor is treating the injured person and has voluntarily assumed a responsibility for him; the victim has become the doctor's patient and the *Bolam* standard of care (see below, p 289) will govern his actions. The latter standard will, of course, be situation specific and equate to whatever the reasonable Good Samaritan doctor would do in the circumstances. Surely a reasonable doctor would try to stabilise and improve the accident victim's condition and hence (save for the most pressing reasons) is not entitled in law simply to 'wash his hands' of the patient. (See also in this regard the decision of the Supreme Court of South Australia in *Goode v Nash* (1979) 21 SASR 419.)

The duty to third parties

Interesting questions arise as to how far a doctor will owe a duty to third parties with whom he personally has no dealings, but who are injured in a foreseeable way through contact with one of the doctor's patients. For example, if the doctor fails to spot that one of his patients is carrying a contagious disease, and the latter subsequently passes on the infection, does someone he infects have any right of action against the doctor? As a general rule, and in accordance with established principles of tort, a person (A)'s liability for injury caused by another (B) to a third party (C) has tended to depend upon two factors: first, the extent to which B is an involuntary agent in the events which lead to C's injury; and secondly, the ability on A's part to foresee C's presence in relation to B. The second of these factors appears to have led the Court of Appeal to reject the plaintiff's claim in the case of *Goodwill v British Pregnancy Advisory Service*.

Goodwill v British Pregnancy Advisory Service [1996] 2 All ER 161, CA (Peter Gibson and Thorpe LJJ)

M had a vasectomy operation organised by the defendants and was told that that the operation had been successful, and that he would not need contraception in the future. He later had sexual intercourse with the plaintiff, whom he told of his vasectomy. The plaintiff also consulted her own doctor who assured her that there was little chance of her becoming pregnant with M. Subsequently the plaintiff became pregnant by M and had a daughter. In her action against the defendants, she claimed damages for the expense of the birth, costs of bringing up her child and loss of working income. Peter Gibson LJ, dismissing her claim, stated:

Peter Gibson LJ: In my judgment, for the plaintiff to have a sustainable case in negligence against the defendants in respect of a financial loss arising from reliance on advice given by the defendants, it must appear that arguably the governing principles laid down in the *Hedley Byrne* case [1963] 2 All ER 575, [1964] AC 465, are satisfied. The words of Lord Oliver in *Caparo Industries plc v Dickman* [1990] 1 All ER 568, p 589; [1990] 2 AC 605, p 638, have been taken by this court to be a clear statement of the guidance to be obtained from *Hedley Byrne* on the proximity or relationship which must exist between the giver of the advice and the person who acts on it if there is to be a cause of action in negligence. Lord Oliver said:

> What can be deduced from the *Hedley Byrne* case, therefore, is that the necessary relationship between the maker of a statement or giver of advice (the adviser) and the recipient who acts in reliance on it (the advisee) may typically be held to exist where: (1) the advice is required for a purpose, whether particularly specified or generally described, which is made known, either actually or inferentially, to the adviser at the time when the advice is given; (2) the adviser knows, either actually or inferentially, that his advice will be communicated to the advisee, either specifically or as a member of an ascertainable class, in order that it should be used by the advisee for that purpose; (3) it is known, either actually or inferentially, that the advice so communicated is likely to be acted on by the advisee for that purpose without independent inquiry; and (4) it is so acted on by the advisee to his detriment. That is not, of course, to suggest that these conditions are either conclusive or exclusive, but merely that the actual decision in the case does not warrant any broader propositions.

Of these conditions, I need only fasten on (3), although I am extremely dubious on the plaintiff's pleadings as to the satisfaction of conditions (2) and (4). How the defendants knew or should have known that their advice would be communicated to the plaintiff and relied upon by her as (according to the pleadings) a warranty of permanent infertility when she did not meet, or commence a sexual relationship with, Mr MacKinlay until three years later, it is not apparent. It is not pleaded that the advice was in a form showing that the defendants expected or intended its communication to Mr MacKinlay's sexual partners, nor is it pleaded that Mr MacKinlay alerted the defendants that he would be passing on the advice to his sexual partners ... But in any event I do not see how condition (3) is satisfied. It is not alleged, nor could it reasonably be alleged, that the defendants knew that their advice when communicated to the plaintiff was likely to be acted upon by her without independent inquiry. The defendants could know nothing about the likely course of action of future sexual partners of Mr MacKinlay.

In my judgment on the plaintiff's pleadings the defendants were not in a sufficient or any special relationship with the plaintiff such as gives rise to a duty of care. I cannot see that it can properly be said of the defendants that they voluntarily assumed responsibility to the plaintiff when giving advice to Mr MacKinlay. At that time they had no knowledge of her, she was not an existing sexual partner of Mr MacKinlay but was merely, like any other woman in the world, a potential future sexual partner of his, that is to say a member of an indeterminately large class of females who might have sexual relations with Mr MacKinlay during his lifetime. I find it impossible to believe that the policy of the law is or should be to treat so tenuous a relationship between the adviser and the advisee as giving rise to a duty of care, and there is no analogous situation recognised as giving rise to that duty.

By contrast, in the case of *Thake v Maurice* [1986] QB 644, a vasectomist, who failed to warn his patient of the risk of the operation spontaneously reversing, was held to owe a duty to the latter's wife when she conceived as a result.

Somewhat different issues are raised by the sad necessity on occasion for doctors to break bad news to a patient's next of kin. The question of the duty of care in this context was one of the issues considered recently by the Court of Appeal in *Powell and Another v Boldaz and Others* (1997) 39 BMLR 35, in which a young boy died after a failure to diagnose Addison's disease:

Stuart Smith LJ: I turn then to consider whether the pleaded post-death matters can give rise to an action for negligence ... Mr Powers submits that the duty of care arises under the principles enunciated by Lord Bridge of Harwich in *Caparo Industries plc v Dickman* [1990] 2 AC 605, pp 616E–18F, namely where the following three elements are present:

(a) foreseeability of damage arising from the relevant act or omission;

(b) a sufficient relationship of proximity between the parties;

(c) as a matter of legal policy it is fair, just and reasonable that a duty of care should exist.

I propose to consider first whether a sufficient relationship of proximity existed. It must be appreciated that prior to 17 April 1990, although the plaintiffs were patients of the defendants in the sense that they were on their register, the only patient who was seeking medical advice and treatment was Robert. It was to him that the defendants owed a duty of care. The discharge of that duty in the case of a young child will often involve giving advice and instruction to the parents so that they can administer the appropriate medication, observe relevant symptoms and seek further medical assistance if need be. In giving such advice, the doctor obviously owes a duty to be careful. But the duty is owed to the child, not to the parents. As Lord Diplock said in *Sidaway v Governors of Bethlem Royal Hospital* [1985] AC 871, p 890:

... a doctor's duty of care, whether he be a general practitioner or consulting surgeon or physician, is owed to that patient and none other, idiosyncrasies and all.

After the death the defendants may owe the plaintiffs a duty of care; but this depends upon whether they are called upon or undertake to treat them as patients. There are many situations where a doctor will have close contact with another person, without the relationship of doctor-patient arising so as to involve the duty of care. Two examples are to be found in the speech of Lord Browne-Wilkinson in *X (Minors) v Bedfordshire County Council* [1995] 2 AC 633, pp 752D–53A, one being a psychiatrist examining a child and interviewing a parent for the purposes of discharging the local authority's care responsibilities, the second is the examination of a claimant or plaintiff by a doctor on behalf of an insurance company. In neither of these cases does the doctor undertake to treat the person as a patient and his only duty is not to damage him in the course of the examination.

These are cases where the doctor's obligations are to the local authority or insurance company and there may well be a conflict of interest between them and the person examined. Another example can be found in the case of a doctor who goes to the assistance of a stranger injured in an accident. He does not as a rule undertake the doctor-patient relationship so as to make him liable for lack of care, but only a duty not to make the condition of the victim worse (see *Capital and Counties v Hants County Council* [1997] 2 All ER 865, p 883).

I do not think that a doctor who has been treating a patient who has died, who tells relatives what has happened, thereby undertakes the doctor-patient relationship towards the relatives. It is a situation that calls for sensitivity, tact and discretion, but the mere fact that the communicator is a doctor, does not, without more, mean that he undertakes the doctor-patient relationship. It is of course possible that the doctor in such a situation may realise that the shock has been so great that some immediate therapy is needed, but even so this situation is probably more akin to the doctor giving emergency treatment to an accident victim, though no doubt it will be a question of fact and degree in each case whether doctor-patient relationships came into existence by the doctor undertaking to treat and heal the person as a patient.

If the relatives concerned happen to be on the doctor's register as patients, the position in my judgment is no different, though if the doctor perceives that counselling or medicinal treatment is required and it is given by the doctor or is sought by the patient, then the doctor-patient relationship will exist in relation to the advice and treatment given and the duty of care will arise.

Who to sue?

Individual doctors (with the exception of GPs) and nurses are unlikely to be sued directly by the injured patient. A legal claim will normally be made against the health professional's employer, who will be vicariously liable. This assumes that the negligent doctor or nurse was an employee and was acting in the course of their employment. The Department of Health has produced special guidance on handling clinical negligence claims against NHS staff:

> **Department of Health, *NHS Indemnity – Arrangements for Negligence Claims in the NHS*, October 1996, Catalogue No 96 HR 0024, London: DoH:**
>
> **Purpose of this document**
>
> This document describes the arrangements which apply to handling clinical negligence claims against NHS staff (NHS Indemnity). It updates the guidance given in Health Circular HC (89) 34 ...
>
> **Clinical negligence**
>
> Clinical negligence is defined as:
>
>> ... a breach of duty of care by members of the health care professions employed by NHS bodies or by others consequent on decisions or

judgments made by members of those professions acting in their professional capacity in the course of their employment, and which are admitted as negligent by the employer or are determined as such through the legal process.

The term health care professional includes hospital doctors, dentists, nurses, midwives, health visitors, pharmacy practitioners, registered ophthalmic or dispensing opticians (working in a hospital setting), members of professions allied to medicine and dentistry, ambulance personnel, laboratory staff and relevant technicians.

Main principles

NHS bodies are vicariously liable for the negligent acts and omissions of their employees and should have arrangements for meeting this liability.

NHS Indemnity applies where:

(a) the negligent health care professional was:

    (i) working under a contract of employment and the negligence occurred in the course of that employment;

    (ii) not working under a contract of employment but was contracted to an NHS body to provide services to persons to whom that NHS body owed a duty of care;

    (iii) neither of the above but otherwise owed a duty of care to the persons injured;

(b) persons, not employed under a contract of employment and who may or may not be a health care professional, who owe a duty of care to the persons injured. These include locums; medical academic staff with honorary contracts; students; those conducting clinical trials; charitable volunteers; persons undergoing further professional education, training and examinations; students and staff working on income generation projects.

Where these principles apply, NHS bodies should accept full financial liability where negligent harm has occurred, and not seek to recover their costs from the health care professional involved.

Who is not covered

NHS Indemnity does not apply to family health service practitioners working under contracts for services, for example: GPs (including fundholders), general dental practitioners, family dentists, pharmacists or optometrists; other self-employed health care professionals, for example, independent midwives; employees of FHS practices; employees of private hospitals; local education authorities; voluntary agencies ...

Circumstances covered

NHS Indemnity covers negligent harm caused to patients or healthy volunteers in the following circumstances: whenever they are receiving an established treatment, whether or not in accordance with an agreed guideline or protocol; whenever they are receiving a novel or unusual treatment which, in the judgment of the health care professional, is appropriate for that particular patient; whenever they are subjects as patients or healthy volunteers of clinical research aimed at benefiting patients now or in the future.

In certain circumstances the hospital or health authority may be directly liable to the patient in negligence; in *Wilsher v Essex AHA* [1986] 3 All ER 801 the Court of Appeal suggested that such liability would arise if it were shown that the hospital authorities had filled treatment positions with staff who were unable (through inexperience or otherwise) to cope with the demands made upon them. Direct liability will also arise where the plaintiff's injury is attributable to some overall failure, of an organisational nature, to provide a safe environment for carrying out treatment. In *Bull v Devon AHA* [1993] 4 Med LR 117, one of the plaintiff's twins was born brain damaged due to the delay in getting the registrar to attend her. The defendants maintained maternity services on two sites and the system for calling him over to effect delivery had broken down.

Liability of the Department of Health

Could the Department of Health and the Secretary of State be held to owe a duty of care to an injured plaintiff, in so far as the injury is alleged to be the consequence of some failure at the level of national policy making? Clearly, given the nature of the discretion given to the Secretary of State in fulfilling his duties under s 3 of the National Health Services Act 1977, it will be very hard to sustain an action in negligence. Indeed, if any action is to lie, it might be thought to do so only in judicial review (on the latter, see above, Chapter 2). Nevertheless, in the case of *Re HIV Haemophiliac Litigation* [1990] NLJR 1349, the Court of Appeal was not prepared to reject the possibility of a negligence action out of hand. The plaintiffs were a group of haemophiliacs who were infected with the HIV virus after being treated with infected blood products from the USA. They claimed that the failure by the Secretary of State to provide for UK self-sufficiency in blood supplies had been negligent. The action only concerned the preliminary question of whether discovery (requiring the Department of Health to make its internal documents available to the plaintiffs) should be ordered:

> **Bingham LJ**: Mr Andrew Collins QC for the Department ... pointed out, relying on recent authority, that there is no close precedent for such a claim as the present, which differs in nature and scale from the negligence actions with which the courts customarily deal. Furthermore, he argued, the plaintiffs' complaints relate to matters within areas of political and administrative discretion which the courts are incompetent to evaluate (save, where *vires* are in issue, on applications for judicial review). There were, he said, by analogy with *Hill v Chief Constable of West Yorkshire* [1989] AC 53, strong reasons of public policy (or justice and reasonableness) for not holding a minister and department exercising public functions for the benefit of the community as a whole to owe a duty of care towards individual members of the public.

These are points properly and responsibly argued and they may ultimately prevail, but on the necessarily brief arguments which we have heard at this stage I am not at present satisfied that they must do so.

Latterly, in *Danns and Another v Department of Health,* unreported; (1997) LEXIS Transcript, 5 March, the Department of Health was sued for not passing on the risks of late recanalisation of the vas in male sterilisation to a patient whose partner became pregnant after the operation. The Department was aware of this risk after a reported academic study but decided not to publicise the findings generally in the media. The plaintiff alleged that it was negligent in not doing so. However, the action failed *inter alia* on the ground that there was in fact no duty of care owed by the Department:

> **Leggatt LJ**: Mr Cartwright sought to support his submission that the Department was negligent, by looking to the component parts of the tort and contending that there was foreseeability, because it must have been obvious that there could be health consequences from an unexpected pregnancy, as well as proximity on the basis that the reliance of the general public on the Department was also obvious. He sought to reinforce that aspect by inviting attention to the recent case of *Munroe Ltd v London Fire Authority* [1996] 4 All ER 318 ... in which (p 329) Rougier J was contrasting the position of the London Fire Authority with a hospital. He said, p 329D:
>
>> I consider that against the background of the highly personal element involved in 'adequate medical care', proximity has effectively been imposed upon hospital authorities by the statute. In obedience to that statute, they hold themselves out as being prepared to assume responsibility for the sick and injured. Patients are invited in, whether to the ward or the casualty department, and are entitled to rely upon the hospital assuming responsibility for them.
>
> It seems to me that that kind of proximity is itself to be contrasted in the present context with the position of the Department, which is, indisputably, incomparably more remote from the patient than is the casualty department of a hospital.

THE BREACH OF DUTY

The standard of care

The ordinary professional

The first point to note is that the standard of care against which the doctor will be judged is not going to be that of the ordinary reasonable man who enjoys no medical expertise. Instead, in holding himself out as possessing the special skills of his profession, the doctor is under a duty to conform to the ordinary standards of that profession. In *Bolam v Friern Hospital Management Committee* [1957] 1 WLR 582 McNair J put this point as follows:

McNair J: How do you test whether [an] act or failure is negligent? In an ordinary case it is generally said that you judge that by the action of the man in the street. He is the ordinary man. In one case it has been said that you judge it by the conduct of the man on the top of a Clapham omnibus. He is the ordinary man. But where you get a situation which involves the use of some special skill or competence, then the test whether there has been negligence or not is not the test of the man on the top of the Clapham omnibus, because he has not got this special skill. The test is the standard of the ordinary skilled man exercising and professing to have that special skill. A man need not possess the highest expert skill at the risk of being found negligent. It is well established law that it is sufficient if he exercises the ordinary skill of an ordinary competent man exercising that particular art.

It is further apparent, however, that doctors will not be treated as an homogenous group in this context. Referring to the case of *Hunter v Hanley* (1955) SC 200 Lord Bridge stated in *Sidaway*:

> The language of the *Bolam* test clearly requires a different degree of skill from a specialist in his own special field than from a general practitioner. In the field of neuro-surgery it would be necessary to substitute for Lord President Clyde's phrase 'no doctor of ordinary skill', the phrase 'no neuro-surgeon of ordinary skill'.

What does 'ordinary skill' mean here? Might the case be difficult, so that a neuro-surgeon of special skill might be needed? If so, would there be negligence if such a neuro-surgeon were not used, and, would the negligence be in breach of the health authority's primary duty of care, or would the 'ordinary' neuro-surgeon be in breach?

Junior doctors

A particular difficulty arises in relation to the level of skill expected of junior medical staff who, *ex hypothesi*, will lack the experience of the ordinary competent doctor. Here, the courts have felt obliged to follow the reasoning in *Nettleship v Weston* [1971] 3 All ER 581, in which a learner driver was held to be subject to the same standard of care as the reasonably competent and experienced driver. This principle had been stated in the early medical negligence case of *Jones v Manchester Corporation* [1952] 2 All ER 125, where a patient died after the maladministration of anaesthetic by a doctor qualified for only five months. It was said that 'errors due to inexperience are no defence'.

There is an understandably pragmatic aspect to this approach. Courts do not want to apply a sliding scale of standards of care depending upon the subjective attributes of the particular defendant. The liability of junior doctors was one of the issues that fell to be considered by the Court of Appeal in *Wilsher v Essex AHA*.

Wilsher v Essex AHA **[1987] QB 730, CA (Sir Nicolas Browne-Wilkinson VC, Glidewell and Mustill LJJ)**

The plaintiff was a premature baby who was treated in the defendant's antenatal unit. He was given oxygen by two doctors, both inexperienced. They inserted the catheter through which the oxygen was to be administered, into a vein rather than an artery. This is, apparently, a common mistake and was not due to negligence. The position of the catheter can be checked by use of an x-ray. The doctors, however, failed to notice the mistake, and the senior registrar checking their work also failed to notice. The majority of the Court of Appeal confirmed that there should be a uniform standard of care:

> **Glidewell LJ**: In my view, the law requires the trainee or learner to be judged by the same standard as his more experienced colleagues. If it did not, inexperience would frequently be urged as a defence to an action for professional negligence.
>
> If this test appears unduly harsh in relation to the inexperienced, I should add that, in my view, the inexperienced doctor called upon to exercise a specialist skill will, as part of that skill, seek the advice and help of his superiors when he does or may need it. If he does seek such help, he will often have satisfied the test, even though he may himself have made a mistake. It is for this reason that I agree that Dr Wiles was not negligent. He made a mistake in inserting the catheter into a vein, and a second mistake in not recognising the signs that he had done so on the x-ray. But, having done what he thought right, he asked Dr Kawa, the senior registrar, to check what he had done, and Dr Kawa did so. Dr Kawa failed to recognise the indication on the x-ray ...

As this makes clear, junior doctors are entitled to expect their work to be checked, and, on the facts of the case, were found not to be liable (although the registrar was); indeed, the court suggested that a hospital could be primarily liable if it failed to have a proper system for inspecting the work of junior staff (see above, p 284).

Mustill LJ commented as follows on the argument that there should be a subjective standard of care dependent upon the doctor's experience:

> **Mustill LJ**: To my mind, this notion of a duty tailored to the actor, rather than to the act which he elects to perform, has no place in the law of tort. Indeed, the defendants did not contend that it could be justified by any reported authority on the general law of tort. Instead, it was suggested that the medical profession is a special case. Public hospital medicine has always been organised so that young doctors and nurses learn on the job. If the hospitals abstained from using inexperienced people, they could not staff their wards and theatres, and the junior staff could never learn. The longer term interests of patients as a whole are best served by maintaining the present system, even if this may diminish the legal rights of the individual patient: for, after all, medicine is about curing, not litigation.
>
> I acknowledge the appeal of this argument, and recognise that a young hospital doctor, who must get on to the wards in order to qualify without necessarily being able to decide what kind of patient he is going to meet, is not

in the same position as another professional man who has a real choice whether or not to practise in a particular field. Nevertheless, I cannot accept that there should be a special rule for doctors in public hospitals – I emphasise public, since presumably those employed in private hospitals would be in a different category. Doctors are not the only people who gain their experience, not only from lectures or from watching others perform, but from tackling live clients or customers, and no case was cited to us which suggested that any such variable duty of care was imposed on others in a similar position. To my mind, it would be a false step to subordinate the legitimate expectation of the patient that he will receive from each person concerned with his care a degree of skill appropriate to the task which he undertakes, to an understandable wish to minimise the psychological and financial pressures on hard-pressed young doctors.

However, his Lordship arguably muddied the waters by introducing the notion that one could ascertain the standard of care by reference to the 'post' that the doctor held:

Mustill LJ: For my part, I prefer [the proposition which] relates the duty of care not to the individual, but to the post which he occupies. I would differentiate 'post' from 'rank' or 'status'. In a case such as the present, the standard is not just that of the averagely competent and well informed junior houseman (or whatever the position of the doctor) but of such a person who fills a post in a unit offering a highly specialised service. But, even so, it must be recognised that different posts make different demands. If it is borne in mind that the structure of hospital medicine envisages that the lower ranks will be occupied by those of whom it would be wrong to expect too much, the risk of abuse by litigious patients can be mitigated, if not entirely eliminated.

What is the difference between this and the assessment (which the court will refuse to undertake) of junior doctors by reference to reasonable doctors with the same limited experience? The answer would seem to lie in the existence of a minimum standard attaching to each 'post', below which no doctor, however new to the job, can fall. For his part, Sir Nicolas Browne-Wilkinson VC, who dissented from the majority view, stated:

... one of the chief hazards of inexperience is that one does not always know the risks which exist. In my judgment, so long as the English law rests liability on personal fault, a doctor who has properly accepted a post in a hospital in order to gain necessary experience should only be held liable for acts or omissions which a careful doctor with his qualifications and experience would not have done or omitted.

(The case subsequently went to the House of Lords on the issue of causation, see further below, p 313.)

Emergencies

An exception to the principle, that a doctor will be judged according to the standard of reasonably experienced doctors in their field, is provided by emergency treatment. Michael Jones has commented as follows on the level of experience expected in the latter context:

Jones, M, *Medical Negligence*, **1996, London: Sweet & Maxwell, p 135:**

In an emergency it may well be reasonable for a practitioner inexperienced in a particular treatment to intervene, or indeed for someone lacking medical qualifications to undertake some forms of treatment. For example, a bystander who renders assistance at a road accident does not necessarily hold himself out as qualified to do so. He would be expected to achieve only the standard that could reasonably be expected in the circumstances, which would probably be very low. This approach is clearly borne of the emergency since if there was no urgency, the unqualified person who undertakes treatment which is beyond his competence would be held to the standard to be expected of the reasonably competent and experienced practitioner. A person who holds himself out as trained in first aid must conform to the standards of 'the ordinary skilled first aider exercising and professing to have that special skill of a first aider'.

Secondly, in relation to treatment decisions taken in an emergency, a doctor will not be found negligent simply because the reasonably competent doctor would have made a different decision, given more time and information. In the case of *Wilson v Swanson* (1956) 5 DLR (2d) 113, the Supreme Court of Canada held that there was no negligence when a surgeon had to make an immediate decision whether to operate, when the operation was subsequently found to have been unnecessary. Moreover, the skill itself required in the execution of treatment may be somewhat lower. As Mustill LJ commented in the *Wilsher* case:

Mustill LJ: An emergency may overburden the available resources, and, if an individual is forced by circumstances to do too many things at once, the fact that he does one of them incorrectly should not lightly be taken as negligence.

Accepted practice – the *Bolam* test

Development and rationale

In determining whether, in a particular case, a doctor has satisfied the appropriate standard of care, the courts will look in the first place to accepted practice within the profession: has the doctor conducted himself in the manner in which other doctors would have conducted themselves in the same circumstances? Of course, medicine is a developing science and new schools of thought as to how best to carry out treatments are constantly emerging. For this reason, the courts do not expect to find uniformity of standard medical practice in any given case. Rather, they ask whether the doctor has conformed with an (note the use of the indefinite article) accepted practice within the profession. This approach informed McNair J's direction to the jury in the famous (or infamous) case of *Bolam v Friern Hospital Management Committee* [1957] 1 WLR 582.

Bolam v Friern Hospital Management Committee [1957] 1 WLR 582 (McNair J)

The plaintiff suffered from clinical depression and it was decided to treat him with electro-convulsive therapy (ECT), which involves passing an electric current through the patient's brain to induce a fit. In the 1950s this was fairly novel treatment and doctors differed as to how best to minimise the risk of the patient suffering bone fractures during the fit. At the hospital where Mr Bolam was treated, a system of manual restraint in which nurses held the patient down, but only by the chin, was in use (two other practices adopted elsewhere involved the use of rigid restraint, and relaxant drugs administered following a general anaesthetic, respectively). Unfortunately, in the plaintiff's case the manual restraint was ineffective and he suffered serious pelvic injuries during treatment:

> **McNair J**: Counsel for the plaintiff put it in this way, that in the case of a medical man, negligence means failure to act in accordance with the standards of reasonably competent medical men at the time. That is a perfectly accurate statement, as long as it is remembered that there may be one or more perfectly proper standards; and if a medical man confirms with one of those proper standards then he is not negligent. Counsel for the plaintiff was also right, in my judgment, in saying that a mere personal belief that a particular technique is best is no defence unless that belief is based on reasonable grounds. That again is unexceptional. But the emphasis which is laid by counsel for the defendants is on this aspect of negligence: he submitted to you that the real question on which you have to make up your mind on each of the three major points to be considered is whether the defendants, in acting in the way in which they did, were acting in accordance with a practice of competent respected professional opinion ... I myself would ... put it this way: a doctor is not guilty of negligence if he has acted in accordance with a practice accepted as proper by a responsible body of medical men skilled in that particular art.

Although this is a first instance jury direction, it has been approved at appellate level on many occasions since. Of particular interest is the judgment of Lord Scarman in a leading case from the 1980s, *Maynard v West Midlands RHA*.

Maynard v West Midlands RHA [1984] 1 WLR 634, HL (Fraser, Elwyn-Jones, Scarman, Roskill, Templeman LL)

The plaintiff was being treated for a chest complaint. Her consultants believed her probably to be suffering from tuberculosis, but, given also the slight chance that she might have Hodgkin's disease, decided to carry out an exploratory operation, to reach a concluded diagnosis. This confirmed that the plaintiff had tuberculosis, but also (through an inevitable risk materialising without fault on the defendants' part) left her paralysed in one of her vocal chords. At trial, the expert witnesses were divided over whether the decision to perform the operation had been an appropriate one in the circumstances. The trial judge preferred the view of the plaintiff's experts that the risk inherent in it had not been worth taking, and awarded damages. The defendants' appeal was allowed by the Court of Appeal and the matter reached the House of Lords:

> **Lord Scarman**: The present case may be classifiable as one of clinical judgment. Two distinguished consultants, a physician and a surgeon experienced in the treatment of chest diseases, formed a judgment as to what was, in their opinion, in the best interests of their patient. They recommended that tuberculosis was the most likely diagnosis. But in their opinion, there was an unusual factor, viz, swollen glands in the mediastinum unaccompanied by any evidence of lesion in the lungs. Hodgkin's disease, carcinoma, and sarcoidosis were, therefore, possibilities. The danger they thought was Hodgkin's disease; though unlikely, it was, if present, a killer (as treatment was understood in 1970) unless remedial steps were taken in its early stage. They therefore decided on mediastinoscopy, an operative procedure which would provide them with a biopsy from the swollen gland which could be subjected to immediate microscopic examination. It is said that the evidence of tuberculosis was so strong that it was unreasonable and wrong to defer diagnosis and to put their patient to the risks of the operation. The case against them is not mistake or carelessness in performing the operation which is admitted was properly carried out, but an error of judgment in requiring the operation to be undertaken.
>
> A case which is based on an allegation that a fully considered decision of two consultants in the field of their special skill was negligent clearly presents certain difficulties of proof. It is not enough to show that there is a body of competent professional opinion which considered that theirs was a wrong decision, if there also exists a body of professional opinion, equally competent, which supports the decision as reasonable in the circumstances. It is not enough to show that subsequent events show that the operation need never have been performed, if at the time the decision to operate was taken it was reasonable in the sense that a responsible body of medical opinion would have accepted it as proper.

It may well be wondered if there was not an easier way in which the doctors in *Maynard* could have avoided litigation. In particular, what did they *tell* the patient before they decided to operate? This is not known, because the patient's medical notes were missing for the period during which the doctors made their decision. However, there was no argument advanced that the doctors had discussed the treatment with the patient in terms of risks and alternatives, which would perhaps have resulted in the patient deciding against undergoing what might well prove to be unnecessary surgery.

Subsequently, in *Sidaway v Governors of Bethlem Royal Hospital* [1985] 1 All ER 1018, a case which dealt squarely with the issue of disclosing risks of treatment to the patient (a topic addressed fully above, Chapter 3), the same Law Lord articulated the *Bolam* test in the following terms:

> **Lord Scarman**: The *Bolam* principle may be formulated as a rule that a doctor is not negligent if he acts in accordance with a practice accepted at the time as proper by a responsible body of medical opinion even though other doctors

adopt a different practice. In short, the law imposes the duty of care, but the standard of care is a matter of medical judgment.

It should be recalled, however, that this came within the context of Lord Scarman's (minority) opinion that the *Bolam* test was *not* an appropriate basis for deciding if the doctor was in breach of his duty to advise of risks. It is therefore strictly *obiter*. (We address how far this formulation of *Bolam*, which has nevertheless been influential, was, and is, an accurate one, below, p 297.)

What are the main reasons that the courts have for using the *Bolam* test in cases of medical negligence? One has already been mentioned: medicine is recognised as not being an exact science; there may, at any given moment, be two or more perfectly respectable ways of dealing with a particular problem. Indeed one could go further and cite the possibility of competition between different accepted practices as a key element in allowing progress in treatment to be made. *Bolam* itself provides an illustration of this: in the 1950s only one of three schools of thought administered ECT following a general anaesthetic, but nowadays it is invariably done this way. Despite the risks associated with anaesthesia itself, experience ultimately has shown this to be preferable to running the risks of bone fracture associated with either rigid or manual restraint.

An altogether more contentious feature of the test is the great weight that it attaches to medical opinion. Why, it might be asked, do the courts concern themselves with the question of whether what the defendant did accorded with such opinion, rather than simply pronounce the conduct in question either negligent or not, as the case may be? The answer lies partly in the often highly technical nature of some of the information. In the Court of Appeal case of *Dwyer v Roderick* (1983) 127 SJ 805, May LJ stated:

> **May LJ**: It would be to shut one's eyes to the obvious if one denied that the burden of achieving something more than the mere balance of probabilities was greater when one was investigating the complicated and sophisticated actions of a qualified and experienced doctor than when one was inquiring into the inattention of the driver in a simple running down action.

However, it could be argued here that the courts have fallen into the habit of too readily mystifying medical matters. As Michael Jones comments:

> **Jones, M, *Medical Negligence*, 1996, London: Sweet & Maxwell, p 106:**
>
> Where the case does not involve difficult or uncertain questions of medical or surgical treatment, or abstruse or highly technical scientific issues, but is concerned with whether obvious and simple precautions could have been taken, the question of the practice of experts should be largely irrelevant. The courts do not rely on expert rally drivers, for example, to say whether a motorist was negligent.
>
> Moreover, before any question of complying with accepted practice can arise the court must be satisfied on the evidence presented to it that there is a responsible body of professional opinion which supports the practice. It is

always open to the court to reject expert evidence applying the ordinary principles of credibility that would be applied in any courtroom, for example, that the evidence is internally contradictory, or that the witness was acting as an advocate rather than an impartial and objective expert.

Jones comments upon the disparity here with non-medical cases as follows:

Jones, M, *Medical Negligence*, 1996, London: Sweet & Maxwell, p 101:

It is clear that outside the context of medical negligence the courts have had no difficulty with the notion that commonly adopted practices may themselves be negligent. This has been most apparent in cases of employers' liability, but it is also evident in some cases involving professional liability. In *Lloyds Bank v Savory and Co* [1933] AC 201, for example, Lord Wright rejected the proposition that a bank is not negligent if it takes all the precautions usually taken by bankers 'in cases where the ordinary practice of bankers fails in making due provision for a risk fully known to those experienced in the business of banking'. More recently, in *Edward Wong Finance Co Ltd v Johnson, Stokes and Masters* [1984] AC 296, the Privy Council held that a particular conveyancing practice widely followed in Hong Kong was negligent because the practice had an inherent risk which would have been foreseen by a person of reasonable prudence, and there was no need to take this risk. The fact that virtually all other solicitors adopted the same practice was not conclusive evidence that it was prudent, nor did it make the risk less apparent or unreal.

A key factor which appears to have influenced the courts in their, at times, excessively deferential attitude towards medical opinion is the fear of otherwise encouraging an explosion of malpractice litigation and an uncongenial climate for doctors to go about their business of treating patients: as Mustill LJ commented in *Wilsher v Essex AHA* [1987] QB 730, 'medicine is about curing, not litigation'. This attitude found its most notorious expression in Lord Denning's suggestion (repeated in a number of cases over the years), that an 'error of clinical judgment' could not amount to negligence, a view finally laid to rest in 1981 in the case of *Whitehouse v Jordan*.

Whitehouse v Jordan [1981] 1 All ER 267, HL (Wilberforce, Edmund-Davies, Fraser, Russell, Bridge LL)

The plaintiff was born brain damaged, allegedly as a result of the defendant obstetrician's negligence. The latter had made prolonged attempts at normal delivery using forceps before realising this was impossible. The plaintiff, suing by his mother as next friend, argued that the defendant should have moved more quickly to delivery by Caesarean section:

Lord Edmund Davies: ... [T]he principal questions calling for decision are: (a) in what manner did Mr Jordan use the forceps? And (b) was that manner consistent with the degree of care which a member of his profession is required by law to exercise? Surprising though it is at this late stage in the development of the law of negligence, counsel for Mr Jordan persisted in submitting that his client should be completely exculpated were the answer to question (b), 'Well, at worst he was guilty of an error of clinical judgment'. My

Lords, it is high time that the unacceptability of such an answer be fully exposed. To say that a surgeon committed an error of clinical judgment is wholly ambiguous, for, while some such errors may be completely consistent with the due exercise of professional skill, other acts or omissions in the course of exercising 'clinical judgment' may be so glaringly below proper standards as to make a finding of negligence inevitable. Indeed, I should have regarded this as a truism were it not that, despite the exposure of the 'false antithesis' by Donaldson LJ in his dissenting judgment in the Court of Appeal, counsel for the defendants adhered to it before your Lordships.

But doctors and surgeons fall into no special category, and, to avoid any future disputation of a similar kind, I would have it accepted that the true doctrine was enunciated, and by no means for the first time, by McNair J in *Bolam v Friern Hospital Management Committee* in the following words, which were applied by the Privy Council in *Chin Keow v Government of Malaysia* [1967] 1 WLR 813:

> ... where you get a situation which involves the use of some special skill or competence, then the test as to whether there has been negligence or not is not the test of the man on the top of a Clapham omnibus because he has not got this special skill. The test is the standard of the ordinary skilled man exercising and professing to have that special skill.

If a surgeon fails to measure up to that standard in any respect ('clinical judgment' or otherwise), he has been negligent and should be so adjudged.

Gerald Robertson commented upon wider implications of this case as follows:

Robertson, G, '*Whitehouse v Jordan* – medical negligence retried' (1981) 44 MLR 457:

Three of their Lordships expressly rejected the view put forward by Lord Denning that 'we must say, and say firmly, that, in a professional man, an error of judgment is not negligence'. In the words of Lord Edmund-Davies:

> To say that a surgeon committed an error of clinical judgment is wholly ambiguous, for, while some such errors may be completely consistent with the due exercise of professional skill, other acts or omissions in the course of exercising 'clinical judgment' may be so glaringly below proper standards as to make a finding of negligence inevitable.

However, Lord Fraser, in line with some commentators, placed a more charitable interpretation on Lord Denning's words, concluding that the Master of the Rolls had really meant to say that an error of judgment is not *necessarily* negligent. This interpretation is, however, clearly incorrect, as the unambiguous nature of Lord Denning's *dictum* would suggest. If Lord Denning had truly intended to say that an error of judgment is not necessarily negligent, his advance reading of the draft of Donaldson LJ's dissenting judgment would have indicated that his words were capable of an entirely different interpretation and would therefore have to be revised. The strongest evidence for suggesting that Lord Denning intended to say that an error of clinical judgment is not negligence lies in the fact that *Whitehouse* is not the first case in which he has made this unequivocal statement. In *Hucks v Cole* in 1968 Lord Denning observed that:

So a doctor is not to be held negligent simply because something goes wrong. It is not right to invoke against him the maxim *res ipsa loquitur* save in an extreme case. He is not liable for mischance or misadventure. Nor is he liable for an error of judgment.

A similar, albeit less unequivocal, statement can be found in *Hatcher v Black* in 1954. Surely it cannot be that on these three separate occasions Lord Denning has been unable to find the right words to express his true opinion on this issue.

In these circumstances one must ask why it is that Lord Denning should have repeatedly expressed a statement of law which is patently untenable, particularly in the face of Donaldson LJ's dissenting judgment which clearly exposes it as such. It is submitted that the explanation lies in Lord Denning's view, underlying many of his judgments in such cases, that, as a matter of policy, medical negligence claims ought to be discouraged ... This policy has been based primarily on the need to protect the professional reputation of the doctor, which it is said, is 'as dear to him as his body, perhaps more so, and an action for negligence can wound his reputation as severely as a dagger can his body'. In *Whitehouse* a second justification was added, namely, the prospect of an American-style medical malpractice crisis arising in this country. No mention, however, was made of the fact that the Pearson Commission recently considered this question and concluded that there was no cause to fear that a crisis of American proportions would develop in this country.

The disturbing feature of this aspect of the *Whitehouse* case is not simply that a strong pro-defendant policy is discernible – such is true of many medical negligence cases. However, when the desire to implement a particular policy, such as discouraging medical negligence claims, reaches such an extent as to conflict with the dispassionate consideration of an individual case on its own merits, then there is genuine cause for concern. It is submitted that such is true of the Court of Appeal's decision in *Whitehouse*. Lord Denning's comment, following on from a detailed account of the plaintiff's physical and mental retardation, that 'the saddest part of it is that she [the mother] blames it all on the hospital and particularly on Mr Jordan', gives a revealing insight into the Master of the Rolls' view of the case. The policy considerations implicit in this, and similar comments, go a long way to explain the existence of the myth that 'an error of clinical judgment is not negligent'.

Clearly, the approach of Lord Denning accorded insufficient weight to the interests of the patient, but, whilst exposing it as wrong, the House of Lords nevertheless affirmed the majority of the Court of Appeal in *Whitehouse* that the defendant had not been negligent. This was in contrast to the trial judge's finding of fact that he had been so.

Application and scope

As we have seen, in deciding whether a particular doctor has been negligent, the *Bolam* test looks first to medical opinion as to what amounts to accepted medical practice. Clearly, it is vital in this context that the courts should be able to distinguish respectable schools of thought from the idiosyncratic views of maverick practitioners. The case of *Hills v Potter* [1984] 1 WLR 641, suggested a rigorous test, *per* Hirst J:

> **Hirst J**: I do not accept the argument that by adopting the Bolam principle, the court in effect abdicates its power of decision to the doctors. In every case the court must be satisfied that the standard contended for on their behalf accords with that upheld by a substantial body of medical opinion, and that this body of medical opinion is both respectable and responsible, and experienced in this particular field of medicine.

However, subsequent developments have not borne out this earlier view. In *DeFreitas v O'Brien* [1995] 6 Med LR 128, the view taken by the Court of Appeal was that the key word was 'responsible', not 'substantial'. In that case the court held that, out of a dozen specialists in the UK, three of those specialists (and the three included the defendant) could constitute a responsible body of opinion. Otton LJ took the view that the issue could not be decided by counting heads. The court held that given the evidence of these three specialists, the burden of proof had not been satisfied by the plaintiff, that is, it was up to her to show 'that the decision to operate on that basis was a decision that no reasonable doctor working within their specialism would take'. Khan and Robson comment on the decision as follows:

> **Khan, M and Robson, M, 'What is a responsible group of medical opinion?' (1995) 11 Professional Negligence 4:**
>
> ... we would take issue with the view that the matter of whether a practice is accepted and responsible cannot be determined by 'counting heads'. Numbers must play a part in determining whether the practice is accepted and therefore responsible. In examining the practice the first matter the court must consider is to see who has adopted the practice – thus the court counts heads. It therefore follows that the greater the number adopting the practice, the more likely the practice is to be regarded as not only being accepted but also of being responsible. Surely it implies that the greater the number of followers the practice has, the higher the degree of respectability it attracts. What is not being suggested is that the matter of whether a practice is accepted or responsible can be determined by solely looking at numbers alone; it is and should be determined by looking at the risk caused by following the practice. If, by following the accepted practice, there is a situation which gives rise to a high risk that injury could result and the accepted practice does not take on board a rather obvious precaution, then it is submitted that this is the time where it may be appropriate to count heads and query whether the practice is still responsible or, at the very least, ask fellow practitioners in a related field whether they would, for instance, consider a body of three a responsible group. Numbers may only have a limited part to play but they should not be dismissed out of hand. *DeFreitas* sets a worrying precedent: now perhaps a small fringe group practising experimental techniques can legitimately constitute a responsible body.

Another question which arises concerns the extent to which accepted practices must keep pace with advances in medical knowledge, if practitioners abiding by them are to avoid falling below the requisite standard of care. The case of *Crawford v Board of Governors of Charing Cross Hospital* (1953) *The Times*, 8 December, found that there had been no breach of duty when an operative procedure was performed resulting in paralysis, which some months previously had been the subject of a report in *The Lancet* suggesting that the procedure was likely to produce such paralysis. The Court of Appeal rejected the claim on the basis that doctors cannot be expected to read every article in the medical press. However, this does not get to the heart of the issue. It is correct that doctors cannot be expected to read *every* article, but they should surely be expected to keep abreast of developments in their field. (See also *Gascoigne v Ian Sheridan and Co and Latham* [1994] 5 Med LR 437).

Whilst initially confined to assessing matters of diagnosis and treatment, the *Bolam* test has since become ubiquitous in defining the courts' approach to allegations of malpractice against medical professionals. It will be recalled from Chapter 3 that, in *Sidaway v Governors of Royal Bethlem and Maudsley Hospital* [1985] 1 All ER 1018, the majority of the House of Lords used it as the starting point for determining the standard of care owed by doctor to patient in respect of disclosing risks. Moreover, in *Gold v Haringey HA*, the Court of Appeal held that it made no difference whether such risks were attendant upon treatment of a therapeutic or non-therapeutic nature. It can be strongly argued, as it indeed was by Lord Scarman in his dissenting speech in *Sidaway*, that such a protective attitude towards doctors (at the expense of the patient's right to make an informed choice as to treatment) is inappropriate: see above, Chapter 3. In particular, there appears to be nothing here of a highly complex technical nature that judges need to understand if they are to pass judgment. Just as controversial has been the extension of *Bolam* into areas in which the nature of decision making by doctors is predominantly ethical rather than medico-technical. These include, in particular, determinations as to when treatment is and is not in the best interests of patients who are incompetent. The use of the test for resolving such issues is the subject of further discussion elsewhere (see above, Chapter 4 and below, Chapters 10–12).

Impugning accepted practice – 'new Bolam'

In Lord Scarman's judgments in the cases of *Maynard* and *Sidaway* (see above, p 291), the *Bolam* test appeared to be framed in such a way as to make compliance with an accepted practice a complete defence: that is to say, provided a doctor could show that what he had done complied with such a practice, he could never be found negligent. However, this was never regarded universally as the correct interpretation of the test, and it was one rejected especially vociferously by Commonwealth courts. In the case of *F v R*

(1983) SASR 189, Bollen J, in the Supreme Court of South Australia, commented as follows:

> **Bollen J**: Many cases require the calling of expert evidence. These experts frequently express opinions on matters within their field. Sometimes they speak of what is usually done in any activity within that field. Why is the evidence received? It is received to guide or help the court. A court cannot be expected to know the correct procedure for performing a surgical operation. The court cannot be expected to know why a manufacturer should guard against metal fatigue. A court cannot be expected to know how to mix chemicals. And so on. Expert evidence will assist the court. But in the end it is the court which must say whether there was a duty owed and a breach of it. The court will have been guided and assisted by the expert evidence. It will not produce an answer merely at the dictation of the expert evidence. It will afford great weight to the expert evidence ... But the court does not merely follow expert evidence slavishly to a decision ... If the court did merely follow the path apparently pointed by expert evidence with no critical consideration of it and the other evidence, it would abdicate its duty to decide, on the evidence, whether in law a duty existed and had not been discharged ...
>
> ... I can find nothing in *Bolam v Friern Hospital Management Committee* which justifies any suggestion that evidence of the practice obtaining in the medical profession is automatically decisive of any issue in an action against a surgeon for damages in negligence ...
>
> ... I respectfully think that some of the cases in England have concentrated rather too heavily on the practice of the medical profession.

Note what is said here about deciding on the evidence whether the duty had been breached. It is pointing up what has always been the case: that courts *evaluate* the evidence they hear. The uncritical acceptance of the defendant's evidence *alone*, even when it is given by the appropriate experts, is the unacceptable interpretation of the *Bolam* test which denies that there is an obligation to evaluate. That English courts, too, ultimately reserved the right to review an accepted practice and on occasion found it wanting, is apparent from the decision of the Court of Appeal in *Hucks v Cole*.

Hucks v Cole (1968) *The Times*, 9 May, CA (Lord Denning MR, Diplock and Sachs LJJ)

The plaintiff was pregnant and under the care of Dr Cole, her general practitioner. On 4 October 1963 her ring finger became swollen and a sore developed. Dr Cole told her that it was nothing to worry about. Nor did he inform the maternity hospital, where she gave birth on 10 October. The day after the birth the hospital, concerned about the finger and the fact that one of her toes was also affected, carried out tests which revealed that she was suffering from fulminating septicaemia. She was given antibiotic treatment, but when this ended and she was placed back in the care of Dr Coles, he failed to give penicillin treatment:

Sachs LJ: When the evidence shows that a lacuna in professional practice exists by which risks of grave danger are knowingly taken, then, however small the risks, the courts must anxiously examine that lacuna – particularly if the risks can be easily and inexpensively avoided. If the court finds, on an analysis of the reasons given for not taking those precautions, that, in the light of current professional knowledge, there is no proper basis for the lacuna, and that it is definitely not reasonable that those risks should have been taken, its function is to state that fact and where necessary to state that it constitutes negligence. In such a case the practice will no doubt thereafter be altered to the benefit of patients.

On such occasions the fact that other practitioners would have done the same thing as the defendant practitioner is a very weighty matter to be put in the scales on his behalf; but it is not, as Mr Webster readily conceded, conclusive. The court must be vigilant to see whether the reasons given for putting the patient at risk are valid in the light of any well known advance in medical knowledge, or whether they stem from a residual adherence to out of date ideas ...

Despite the fact that the risk could have been avoided by adopting a course that was easy, efficient, and inexpensive, and which would have entailed only minimal chances of disadvantages to the patient, the evidence of the four defence experts to the effect that they and other responsible members of the profession would have taken the same risk in the same circumstances has naturally caused me to hesitate considerably on two points. First, whether the failure of the defendant to turn over to penicillin treatment during the relevant period was unreasonable. On this, however, I was in the end fully satisfied that in the light of the admissions made by the defendant himself and by his witnesses – quite apart from Dr May's very cogent evidence – that failure to do this was not merely wrong but clearly unreasonable. The reasons given by the four experts do not to my mind stand up to analysis ...

Secondly, as to whether in the light of such as to what other responsible medical practitioners would have done, it can be said that even if the defendant's error was unreasonable, it was negligent in relation to the position as regards practice at that particular date. On this second point it is to be noted that this is not apparently a case of 'two schools of thought' (see the speech of Lord Goddard in *Chapman v Rix*, on 21 December 1960, p 11): it appears to be more a case of doctors who said in one form or another that they would have acted or might have acted in the same way as the defendant did, for reasons which on examination do not really stand up to analysis.

Hucks v Cole was not properly reported at the time and was not referred to in any of the key medical negligence cases of the 1980s, which addressed the standard of care (*Whitehouse v Jordan*, *Maynard v W Midlands RHA*, *Sidaway v Governors of Bethlem Hospital*, and *Wilsher v Essex AHA*). However, it resurfaced in 1993 as an Appendix to the Law Report on the Court of Appeal's judgment in *Bolitho v City and Hackney HA* (1992) at [1993] 4 Med LR 393. *Bolitho* itself subsequently went to the House of Lords and can now be regarded as the leading modern authority on the application of the *Bolam* test in relation to medical negligence in this country.

Bolitho v City and Hackney HA **[1997] 4 All ER 771, HL (Browne-Wilkinson, Slynn, Nolan, Hoffmann, and Clyde LL)**

The plaintiff two year old was re-admitted to hospital on 16 January 1984 after suffering a serious bout of the croup. He had been experiencing breathing difficulties following his earlier discharge on 15 January but, following further treatment, appeared to be progressing satisfactorily. On 17 January he suffered two acute episodes in which his breathing appeared to be temporarily obstructed, and on both occasions the nurse observing him summoned the senior paediatric registrar. However, neither the latter nor her senior house officer responded to the calls and the plaintiff subsequently suffered a third episode, which led to cardiac arrest and brain damage.

It was accepted for the defendant that the failure of its doctors to attend the plaintiff amounted to a breach of duty. However, it claimed that, even if they had attended, they would not have instigated the one procedure – intubation – which would have saved him. Although this was a defence based essentially on lack of causation (see further the discussion below, p 322), to succeed it required the court to accept that the hypothetical failure to intubate in such a case would not itself have been a breach of duty. In this regard, the defendant adduced evidence from a number of expert witnesses to the effect that, faced with a patient exhibiting the plaintiff's history and symptoms, they too would not intubate:

> **Lord Browne-Wilkinson:** ... [I]n my view, the court is not bound to hold that a defendant doctor escapes liability for negligent treatment or diagnosis just because he leads evidence from a number of medical experts who are genuinely of the opinion that the defendant's treatment or diagnosis accorded with sound medical practice. In the *Bolam* case itself, McNair J stated ... that the defendant had to have acted in accordance with the practice accepted as proper by a 'responsible body of medical men'. Later ... he referred to 'a standard of practice recognised as proper by a competent *reasonable* body of opinion'. Again, in the passage which I have cited from *Maynard*'s case, Lord Scarman refers to a 'respectable' body of professional opinion. The use of these adjectives – responsible, reasonable and respectable – all show that the court has to be satisfied that the exponents of the body of opinion relied upon can demonstrate that such opinion has a logical basis. In particular in cases involving, as they so often do, the weighing of risks against benefits, the judge before accepting a body of opinion as being responsible, reasonable or respectable, will need to be satisfied that, in forming their views, the experts have directed their minds to the question of comparative risks and benefits and have reached a defensible conclusion on the matter.
>
> There are decisions which demonstrate that the judge is entitled to approach expert professional opinion on this basis. For example, in *Hucks v Cole* ... [a] number of distinguished doctors gave evidence that they would not, in the circumstances, have treated with penicillin. The Court of Appeal found the defendant to have been negligent ...

Again in *Edward Wong Finance Co Ltd v Johnson Stokes and Master* [1984] 1 AC 296, the defendant's solicitors had conducted the completion of a mortgage transaction in 'Hong Kong style' rather than in the old fashioned English style. Completion in Hong Kong style provides for money to be paid over against an undertaking by the solicitors for the borrowers subsequently to hand over the executed documents. This practice opened the gateway through which a dishonest solicitor for the borrower absconded with the loan money without providing the security for such loan. The Privy Council held that even though completion in Hong Kong style was almost universally adopted in Hong Kong and was therefore in accordance with a body of professional opinion there, the defendant's solicitors were liable for negligence because there was an obvious risk that could be guarded against. Thus, the body of professional opinion, though almost universally held, was not reasonable or responsible.

These decisions demonstrate that in cases of diagnosis or treatment there are cases where, despite a body of professional opinion sanctioning the defendant's conduct, the defendant can properly be held liable for negligence (I am not here considering questions of disclosure of risk). In my judgment that is because, in some cases, it cannot be demonstrated to the judge's satisfaction that the body of opinion relied upon is reasonable or responsible. In the vast majority of cases the fact that distinguished experts in the field are of a particular opinion will demonstrate the reasonableness of that opinion. In particular, where there are questions of assessment of the relative risks and benefits of adopting a particular medical practice, a reasonable view necessarily presupposes that the relative risks and benefits have been weighed by the experts in forming their opinions. But if, in a rare case, it can be demonstrated that the professional opinion is not capable of withstanding logical analysis, the judge is entitled to hold that the body of opinion is not reasonable or responsible.

On the facts, his Lordship (with whose judgment the rest of the House of Lords agreed) held that the hypothetical decision not to intubate the plaintiff would have been in accord with responsible medical practice:

Lord Browne-Wilkinson: According to the accounts of Sister Sallabank and Nurse Newbold, although Patrick had had two severe respiratory crises, he had recovered quickly from both and for the rest presented as a child who was active and running about. Dr Dinwiddie's view was that these symptoms did not show a progressive respiratory collapse and that there was only a small risk of total respiratory failure. Intubation is not a routine, risk-free process. Dr Roberton described it as 'a major undertaking – an invasive procedure with mortality and morbidity attached – it was an assault'. It involves anaesthetising and ventilating the child. A young child does not tolerate a tube easily 'at any rate for a day or two' and the child unless sedated tends to remove it. In those circumstances it cannot be suggested that it was illogical for Dr Dinwiddie, a most distinguished expert, to favour running what, in his view, was a very small risk of total respiratory collapse rather than to submit Patrick to the invasive procedure of intubation.

It is apparent that, in requiring 'responsible practice' to stand up to logical analysis, Lord Browne-Wilkinson has in mind some form of risk-benefit analysis: the risks inherent in a given procedure must be justified by the benefit it may bring (including the amelioration of any greater risk). However, whilst this may lead to rejection of practices, which entail quite unnecessary risks (ie, those where negligible or no benefit is to be gained from running them, as in *Hucks v Cole* and *Edward Wong*), it remains unclear what a judge is to do when faced with evidence of a practice which, say, exposes the patient to a 1% risk of total paralysis but carries a 90% chance of curing the patient's stiff neck. Is such a practice 'illogical'?

In the Court of Appeal in *Bolitho*, Dillon LJ had suggested that before impugning an accepted practice, the court should be satisfied that it was *'Wednesbury* unreasonable'. As we saw in Chapter 2, this test is employed in judicial review proceedings and requires a very high degree of unreasonableness (the practice in question must be perverse or irrational). In so doing, it reflects the courts' reluctance to second-guess the decisions of public bodies, which are entrusted with a discretion over how to best to implement policy (often involving considerations of finite resources). Such a test would seem an inappropriate basis on which to assess the individual treatment decisions made by doctors, and indeed it finds no place in Lord Browne-Wilkinson's judgment. Nevertheless, arguably the latter's approach is scarcely more favourable to the plaintiff:

> **Lord Browne-Wilkinson:** I emphasise that in my view it will very seldom be right for a judge to reach the conclusion that views genuinely held by a competent medical expert are unreasonable. The assessment of medical risks and benefits is a matter of clinical judgment which a judge would not normally be able to make without expert evidence. As the quotation from Lord Scarman [from *Maynard v W Midlands RHA*] makes clear, it would be wrong to allow such assessment to deteriorate into seeking to persuade the judge to prefer one of two views, both of which are capable of being logically supported. It is only where a judge can be satisfied that the body of expert opinion cannot be logically supported at all that such opinion will not provide the bench mark by reference to which the defendant's conduct falls to be assessed.

It will be recalled that the *Maynard* case concerned a patient who, in undergoing a diagnostic operation to eliminate the possibility that she had Hodgkin's disease, was exposed to the risk of damage to her vocal chords. The doctors who carried out the operation were held (by the appellate courts) to have acted responsibly. As suggested earlier, to the extent that doctors do engage, as they often must, in trading off such risks and benefits on behalf of their patients, it is plausible to suppose that the latter should normally be consulted in the matter. Although this is a question of the doctor obtaining properly informed consent (and as such is addressed in Chapter 3, above), this, rather than the search for some elusive standard of 'logic' to govern his calculations, might be a preferable means of resolving a negligence claim here.

Such an approach can already be seen in the High Court judgment of Morland J in *McAllister v Lewisham and N Southwark HA* [1994] 5 Med LR 343.

Interestingly, the doctor's duty to disclose risks of treatment to the patient was the one area that Lord Browne-Wilkinson in *Bolitho* excepted from his general principle that a doctor acting in accordance with a body of professional opinion can still be negligent if the judge is not satisfied that such opinion is reasonable or responsible. Unfortunately, the reason for such an exception remains unclear: it may be that his Lordship took the view that this aspect of the law was already sufficiently settled by the majority judgments in *Sidaway v Governors of Bethlem Hospital*. Applying these, it could be argued that, prior to *Bolitho*, the courts were already more prepared to impugn accepted practice in relation to non-disclosure of risks (see further the discussion above, Chapter 3). However, this way of understanding the exception is not an entirely natural one, in the context of his Lordship's surrounding phraseology. Moreover, given *Sidaway*'s dubious reworking by the Court of Appeal in both *Gold v Haringey HA* [1988] 2 All ER 888 and *Blyth v Bloomsbury HA* [1993] 4 Med LR 151 (in which Lord Diplock's minority speech – with its unqualified adoption of *Bolam* – was followed), it would be surprising for Lord Browne-Wilkinson not to take the opportunity expressly to endorse the application of the majority view, if that was his intent. Two other possibilities remain: either his Lordship himself belongs to Lord Diplock's camp or, more optimistically, he wishes to signal that, in the future, the other minority view in *Sidaway*, that of Lord Scarman advocating the use of the doctrine of informed consent, may be preferred by the courts.

Departures from approved practice

Where there is only a single course of treatment recognised by the medical profession, it will be practically impossible to demonstrate that it is illogical and hence not truly responsible. (Arguably, it could be said, even then, that judges might consider practices in other jurisdictions and find that these were superior and should have been adopted by the medical profession here, but this approach was rejected in *Whiteford v Hunter* (1950) 94 SJ 758.) However, how far does the converse apply? That is, will deviation from such practice automatically be regarded as negligent? This issue was addressed in the case of *Clark v MacLennan*.

Clark v MacLennan [1983] 1 All ER 416, HC (Peter Pain J)

The plaintiff was a woman who had recently given birth and was suffering from stress incontinence. The gynaecologist performed a corrective operation one month after the birth of the child. The normal practice was not to perform such operations until at least three months after birth, as the condition often spontaneously resolved itself and there would be less likelihood of haemorrhage. A haemorrhage did in fact take place, and despite further surgery, the plaintiff's condition became permanent. Although evidence was that in very special circumstances the operation might be performed early, this was not an exceptional case. In fact, none of the witnesses knew of a case where the operation had taken place earlier than three months. Contrasting this situation where there is more than one approved practice, Peter Pain J stated:

> **Peter Pain J**: Where ... there is but one orthodox course of treatment and the doctor chooses to depart from that, his position is different. It is not enough for him to say as to his decision simply that it was based on his clinical judgment. One has to inquire whether he took all proper factors into account which he knew or should have known, and whether his departure from the orthodox course can be justified on the basis of these factors.
>
> The burden of proof lies on the plaintiff. To succeed she must show, first, that there was a breach of duty and, second, that her damages flowed from that breach ...
>
> ... [C]ounsel for the plaintiff contended that, if the plaintiff could show: (1) that there was a general practice not to perform an anterior colporrhaphy until at least three months after birth; (2) that one of the reasons for this practice was to protect the patient from the risk of haemorrhage and a breakdown of the repair; (3) that an operation was performed within four weeks; and (4) that haemorrhage occurred and the repair broke down, then the burden of showing that he was not in breach of duty shifted to the defendants.
>
> It must be correct on the basis of *McGhee* [*v National Coal Board* [1973] 1 WLR 1] to say that the burden shifts so far as damages are concerned. But does the burden shift so far as the duty is concerned? Must the medical practitioner justify his departure from the usual practice?
>
> It is very difficult to draw a distinction between the damage and the duty where the duty arises only because of a need to guard against the damage. In *McGhee's* case it was accepted that there was a breach of duty. In the present case the question of whether there was a breach remains in issue.
>
> It seems to me that it follows from *McGhee* that where there is a situation in which a general duty of care arises and there is a failure to take a precaution, and that very damage occurs against which the precaution is designed to be a protection, then the burden lies on the defendant to show that he was not in breach of duty as well as to show that the damage did not result from his breach of duty.

Peter Pain J's view that, in cases of departure from approved practice, the burden shifts to the defence to prove absence of negligence was subsequently doubted, however, by Mustill LJ in the Court of Appeal in *Wilsher v Essex AHA* [1986] 3 All ER 801:

> **Mustill LJ**: ... [A]lthough the judge [in *Clark v MacLennan*] indicated that he proposed to decide the case on burden of proof ... this could be understood as an example of the forensic commonplace that, where one party has, in the course of the trial, hit the ball into the other's court, it is for that other to return it. But the prominence given in the judgment to *McGhee* and the citation from

Clark in the present case suggest that the judge may have set out to assert a wider proposition, to the effect that in certain kinds of case of which *Clark* and the present action form examples, there is a general burden of proof on the defendant. If this is so, then I must respectfully say that I find nothing in ... general principle to support it.

In the light of this, it may be more accurate to speak in terms of evidential presumptions: the fact, if it is established, that the defendant failed to act in accordance with accepted practice supports a *prima facie* inference of negligence, which it is then up to the defendant to rebut. Such rebuttal will be more difficult if the accepted practice is universal and is specifically directed against the risk that the defendant, in failing to comply, allowed to materialise. A case in point is that of *Chin Keow v Government of Malaysia* [1967] 1 WLR 813 in which a patient died after the doctor gave her penicillin without checking for the possibility of an allergic reaction. The doctor was unable to give any satisfactory explanation of his failure to observe accepted practice in this regard.

On other occasions, however, the doctor may be able to provide cogent reasons for departing from normal practice. In fact, the importance of giving doctors a certain degree of latitude to try out 'innovative' forms of treatment was noted by Lord Clyde in the pre-*Bolam*, Scottish decision of *Hunter v Hanley* (1955) SC 200:

> **Lord President Clyde**: ... [I]n regard to allegations of deviation from ordinary professional practice ... such a deviation is not necessarily evidence of negligence. Indeed it would be disastrous if this were so, for all inducement to progress in medical science would then be destroyed. Even a substantial deviation from normal practice may be warranted by the particular circumstances. To establish liability by a doctor where deviation from normal practice is alleged, three facts require to be established. First of all it must be proved that there is a usual and normal practice; secondly it must be proved that the defender has not adopted that practice; and thirdly (and this is of crucial importance) it must be established that the course the doctor adopted is one which no professional man of ordinary skill would have taken if he had been acting with ordinary care.

It is important to distinguish here between medical research, which is a planned exercise designed specifically to test a new form of treatment, using control groups and almost always approved by a local ethics committee (see further below, Chapter 10), and a 'one off' treatment for a particular patient. We are only concerned at present with the latter situation. There is no doubt that there would be no *automatic* finding of negligence, if the treatment was innovative. In *Sidaway* Lord Diplock stated:

> **Lord Diplock**: Those members of the public who seek medical or surgical aid would be badly served by the adoption of any legal principle that would confine the doctor to some long-established, well tried method of treatment only, although its past record of success might be small, if he wanted to be

confident that he would not run the risk of being held liable in negligence simply because he tried some more modern treatment, and by some unavoidable mischance it failed to heal but did some harm to the patient. This would encourage 'defensive medicine' with a vengeance.

It must be right that doctors should not be afraid to try new treatments when existing ones are not working. Such a constraint would inhibit the development of better treatments, contrary to important utilitarian considerations, and would be contrary to trying to do the best for the individual patient (both of these limbs must be satisfied as utility without more would involve using the patient merely as a means to an end).

There are two important issues here. First (subject to a possible defence of therapeutic privilege), it is suggested that the patient should be fully apprised of the fact that the treatment is innovative, and, accordingly, that there may be side effects or other risks that the doctor does not know about. Secondly, the context in which the treatment is given must be considered. In some cases, established treatments may not have been successful, and the patient will, perhaps, agree to accept a 'long shot' chance of success as a last resort. However, what of the situation where other conventional treatments exist and have not been tried? Certainly in such a case the patient should be fully informed about these alternatives, associated risks, likely outcomes and so on, but the question must be raised as to whether novel treatment should be given at all. When would such treatment be in the best interests of *this* patient?

A case in which unjustified 'experimentation' on the part of a doctor was at issue is that of *Hepworth v Kerr* [1995] 6 Med LR 139. The plaintiff was admitted to hospital in 1979 for a mastoid operation. During the course of the operation the anaesthetist reduced the patient's blood pressure to a very low level for a period of one and a half hours. The purpose was to create a relatively blood-free operating field in the middle ear. The anaesthetist had been using this technique for some years and had used it in around 1,500 cases. However, in the case of this patient the level to which he reduced the blood pressure was 40 mm Hg, when a minimum of 60 mm Hg was strongly indicated in the medical literature. McKinnon J described the defendant as 'plainly negligent'.

> **McKinnon J**: As I find, the defendant adopted a new hypotensive anaesthetic technique which, as he knew, had never been attempted routinely before. Other anaesthetists had never gone to such low levels over such long periods. The defendant, as he accepted, was to begin with, at least, plainly experimenting. He expected serious complications such as cerebral or cardiac thrombosis to occur. He was surprised when they did not. He never, however, attempted to embark upon any proper scientific validation of his technique in some 1,500 patients by the time of the plaintiff's operation ...
>
> I simply cannot, and do not, accept that the defendant was justified in doing what he did without proper scientific validation of his technique.

Proving the breach

In every case it is for the plaintiff to demonstrate that the defendant was negligent *on the balance of probabilities* (ie, according to the usual civil burden of proof). As we have seen, this makes things very awkward for plaintiffs in cases where medical opinion is divided as to whether the defendant's conduct accorded with responsible medical practice: see *Maynard v W Midlands RHA* [1984] 1 WLR 634, and *Ashcroft v Mersey RHA* [1983] 2 All ER 245. Following *Bolitho*, it may be said that the onus is squarely on the plaintiff to show that the conduct in question 'cannot be logically supported at all'.

On other occasions, though, where, as a matter of evidence, it is not clear what such conduct actually consisted of, a plaintiff may be able to bypass these difficulties by entering a plea of *res ipsa loquitur*. A plaintiff who enters such a plea (literally 'the thing speaks for itself') alleges that the injury could not have happened *without* negligence, and therefore throws the ball into the doctor's court to show otherwise. To get this far, he must establish three elements: first, the defendant (either primarily or vicariously) must be in control of the situation prior to injury; secondly, in the ordinary course of events such injury does not occur; and finally, the plaintiff does not have all the facts to show what actually happened. (It is the latter aspect which gave rise to the principle in the first place so as to allow a plaintiff to sue in circumstances where he cannot properly plead specific allegations of negligence.) Tort lawyers have long debated whether the principle means, in effect, that the burden of proof is reversed. The favoured view is that it does not. In the Privy Council decision of *Ng Chun Pui v Lee Chuen Tat* [1988] RTR 298, it was said that *res ipsa loquitur* is no more than the use of a Latin maxim to describe the state of the evidence from which it is proper to draw an inference of negligence. In other words, if the plaintiff asserts that such an accident would not normally happen without negligence, he is merely inviting a finding of negligence earlier in the proceedings than usual.

Two relatively early medical negligence cases in which the principle was invoked are *Roe v Minister of Health* [1954] 2 QB 66 and *Cassidy v Ministry of Health* [1951] 2 KB 343. In *Roe* the plaintiffs were paralysed during the course of surgery due to the contamination of their anaesthetic by phenol: the latter had seeped through invisible fissures in the glass storage vessels in which the anaesthetic was stored.

> **Denning LJ**: The judge [at first instance] has said that those facts do not speak for themselves, but I think that they do. They certainly call for an explanation. Each of these men is entitled to say to the hospital: 'While I was in your hands something has been done to me which has wrecked my life. Please explain how this has come to pass.' ... I approach this case, therefore, on the footing that the hospital authorities and Dr Graham were called on to give an explanation of what has happened.

(The defendant was eventually able to establish that, at that time, the danger of such contamination was unknown to science.) In *Cassidy*, the plaintiff was admitted for surgery to correct Dupuytren's syndrome which had resulted in the contraction of the third and fourth fingers of his left hand. After surgery the contraction had spread to his two other fingers. The Court of Appeal held that *res ipsa loquitur* applied. It was Denning LJ again who stated:

> If the plaintiff had to prove that some particular doctor or nurse was negligent, he would not be able to do it. But he was not put to that impossible task: he says:
>
> > I went into the hospital to be cured of two stiff fingers. I have come out with four stiff fingers, and my hand is useless. That should not have happened if due care had been used. Explain it, if you can.

It may be thought that, in the context of medical treatment, it may in fact be quite difficult to say of any given adverse outcome that this could not have occurred without negligence. This was a point which was taken in the Canadian case of *Girard v Royal Columbian Hospital* (1976) 66 DLR (3d) 676:

> **Andrews J**: The human body is not a container filled with a material whose performance can be predictably charted and analysed ... [M]edical science has not yet reached the stage where the law ought to presume that a patient must come out of an operation as well or better than he went into it.

Michael Jones has commented on this problem as follows:

> **Jones, M, *Medical Negligence*, 1996, London: Sweet & Maxwell, p 150:**
>
> It is widely accepted that medical treatment carries risks, and that the occurrence of injury is not necessarily evidence of a lack of reasonable care ... There is a distinction, however, between saying, on the one hand, that 'things can go wrong in medicine', or 'it is not an exact science and an untoward occurrence is not evidence of negligence', and, on the other hand, saying that this particular procedure carries a specific risk of a particular complication and that complication has occurred. The former statement makes a vague appeal to 'risk' in general to deny the applicability of *res ipsa loquitur*. Such a claim would not necessarily be confined to medical treatment, and seeks in effect to deny the validity of the principle entirely. The latter approach identifies a particular feature of the circumstances, an inherent and specific risk, which provides a reasonable explanation of how the injury could have occurred without negligence.

In both *Delaney v Southmead HA* [1995] 6 Med LR 355 and *Bouchta v Swindon HA* [1996] 7 Med LR 62, the courts were doubtful that the principle had much application in medical negligence cases. On the other hand, there have been a number of cases where the principle has been successfully argued. In *Saunders v Leeds Western HA* (1985) 129 SJ 225, the plaintiff, a young child, underwent cardiac arrest during a hip operation. She pleaded *res ipsa loquitur* on the basis of medical evidence that the heart of a fit child does not suddenly stop under anaesthetic if proper care is taken. The defendant responded by stating that the arrest had been caused by a blood clot travelling from the site of the operation to the heart. However, the court found that proper monitoring would have disclosed a forewarning of the arrest which could have been prevented. Similarly, in *Glass v Cambridge HA* [1995] 6 Med LR 91, in which cardiac arrest also occurred during anaesthesia, the defendant's explanation that a gas embolism had occurred when the plaintiff's wound was being cleaned with hydrogen peroxide was rejected as being inconsistent with the medical evidence of the plaintiff's injury.

Ultimately, though, in the light of the third element of *res ipsa loquitur* – that it should be unclear on the evidence what really happened, the advent of careful record keeping in respect of medical mishaps has probably made reliance upon the plea redundant in most situations. In *Bull v Devon AHA* [1993] 4 Med LR 22, a case in which there was a significant lapse of time before the matter was brought to trial, Mustill LJ stated:

> **Mustill LJ**: The plaintiff's advisers were able to put in evidence from the records as part of their case the outlines of what actually happened. They called expert testimony to establish what should have happened, and could point to a disconformity between what the witnesses said should have happened and what actually happened ... I do not see that the present situation calls for recourse to an evidentiary presumption applicable where the defendant does, and the plaintiff does not, have within his grasp the means of knowing how the accident took place. Here all the facts that are ever going to be known are before the court.

CAUSATION

Assuming that the plaintiff manages to establish that the defendant doctor was 'negligent' (in the sense of having breached his duty of care), it does not follow that he will succeed in his claim in *negligence*. A further, and in this context often very troublesome, hurdle remains for him to negotiate in the form of proving causation.

A framework for analysis

Causation constitutes the link between the defendant's breach of duty and the damage suffered by the plaintiff. In some cases this may appear straightforward: for example, if a surgeon's knife slips during delicate spinal surgery and severs the spinal cord, we would not hesitate to cite this as the cause of the patient's subsequent paralysis. However, in other instances, especially where a complex and unpredictable disease holds sway, it may be much harder to separate out the various contributing factors and say that it was a breach of duty by the doctor, and not one of those other factors, that caused the patient's injury.

As Hart and Honoré have pointed out (*Causation in the Law*, 2nd edn, 1985, Oxford: Clarendon Press), establishing factual causation consists of two stages (though the earlier tends to pass unnoticed). First, in identifying an event, 'C', as a candidate for the label 'the cause' of another event, 'E', we normally alight, from the total set of antecedent conditions necessary and sufficient to produce E, upon just one member of the set: that which, from our perspective, strikes us as the deviation from the norm. For example, in saying that the cause of fire damage to a given building was someone carelessly throwing a lighted cigarette into a wastepaper basket, we ignore the many other background conditions – the presence of paper in the basket, the lack of a sprinkler system, the presence indeed of oxygen in the air, etc – all necessary and together sufficient for the result. Since the latter are normal features of the situation, mentioning them has no point: it does not explain why *on this occasion* fire occurred.

Secondly, then to confirm, for the purposes of the tort of negligence, that the 'candidate condition', the discarded cigarette, is indeed the cause of the fire damage, the familiar 'but for' test is usually applied. The test poses the following hypothetical question: 'But for (ie 'in the absence of') the discarded cigarette, would the damage have occurred?' If the answer is 'no', then the cigarette's presence *made the difference*. It can be regarded as the cause in the sense of a *'conditio sine qua non'* (necessary condition) for the damage. A good illustration of the test's application, in the context of medical negligence, is provided by the case of *Barnett v Chelsea and Kensington Hospital Management Committee* [1968] 3 All ER 1068. Here, three nightwatchmen attended the defendant's casualty department complaining of being violently sick after drinking some tea. The casualty doctor on duty negligently failed to see the men and they were sent away untreated. One of them later died from what it transpired were the effects of arsenic poisoning. However, in her subsequent action against the authority, the man's widow failed to establish causation: the court was satisfied, on the basis of expert testimony, that, even had the deceased been treated promptly, his condition (given its rarity) would have been diagnosed too late to save him.

On other occasions, however, the 'but for' test may fail to produce a result:

Stauch, M, 'Causation, risk and loss of chance in medical negligence' (1997) 17 OJLS 205:

Although the 'but for' test, with its emphasis on causal necessity ... provides a good starting point for the legal inquiry into causation, there are, as is well known, a number of situations in which the test fails to do its job. Suppose, in [the fire-damage] example, that, at the very moment that the cigarette was carelessly thrown into the wastepaper basket, a short-circuit had occurred elsewhere in the building starting a separate fire. If, asked once again to identify the cause of the damage to the building, we attempted to apply the 'but for' test here, we should be disappointed; it cannot be said of either fire that 'but for' its presence, no damage would have occurred. In so far as each fire would have spread unchecked, then, taken individually, neither was necessary for such damage. We have in fact now uncovered a key assumption made by the 'but for' test; that of a neutral causal backdrop rather than one charged in such a way that the same outcome is independently in motion anyway. More specifically, the test is premised upon the presence, at any one time, of no more than a single causal set sufficient for a given outcome.

The more accurate 'NESS test', developed by Richard Wright in North America following suggestions by JL Mackie and Hart and Honoré, expressly allows for the contrary possibility. In such cases, it holds that our candidate condition may still be termed 'a cause' where it is shown to be a necessary element in just one of several co-present causal sets each independently sufficient for the effect. There are in fact two ways that such co-presence can manifest itself, and Wright terms these, respectively, 'duplicative' and 'pre-emptive' causation. The first occurs when two (or more) such sets operate simultaneously to produce the effect; in other words, the effect is over-determined. This was the case in our previous example of the damage to a building by fire: the conflagration began in two places at once, through the carelessly discarded cigarette and the short-circuit, respectively. It is apparent that, in contrast to the 'but for' test (whose counter-intuitive result is that neither was a cause), the NESS test allows us to regard both the cigarette and short-circuit as causative of the damage.

Pre-emptive causation, by contrast, occurs when, through coming about first in time, one causal set 'trumps' another, potential set lurking in the background. The causal potency of the latter is frustrated for, as Wright states, 'a necessary condition for the sufficiency of any set of actual antecedent conditions is that the injury not have occurred already as a result of other actual conditions outside the set'. An example offered by Wright of causal pre-emption is where D shoots and kills P as he is about to drink from a cup poisoned by C. Here, the NESS test makes it clear that it is D's act alone which is the cause of P's death (again, compare the unsatisfactory result produced by the 'but for' test, which would exculpate both C and D). C's act, on the other hand, does not satisfy the NESS test: poison does not feature in the list of necessary elements in any operative set of conditions sufficient for P's death; instead it is a necessary part of a potential but, as things turn out, inoperative, causal set.

Multiple causation cases

Causation cases involving the presence of more than one causal set not only show up the limitations of the 'but for' test; they are also instances of a broader concept, namely 'multiple causation'. The latter arises where, in addition to mere background conditions, we are aware of more than one candidate condition competing for the title 'cause' of an event. In the case of co-present causal sets, the phenomenon occurs because each of the sets will crystallise around at least one candidate condition.

On the other hand, multiple causation can also occur within the confines of a single causal set. This will be the case if there are a number of candidate conditions (deviations from the norm), which, taken one at a time, would not in fact have been sufficient to complete the set in conjunction only with the background conditions. Wright mentions the example of a corpulent man who slips while running down some poorly lit stairs: here there are three possible candidates for causing the fall and it may be that the accident came about only through the cumulative working of all three.

Evidential uncertainties

Cases of multiple causation remain extremely problematic from an *evidential* point of view. It is often just not possible, given the incomplete state of our scientific knowledge, to disentangle the causal sets at play and be sure that the candidate condition we are interested in (a breach of duty by the defendant) was a necessary element in any one of them. (Perhaps the set containing the breach was pre-empted by another causal set containing a rival candidate condition, etc.) In such cases, at least where it is clear that the defendant's conduct has exposed the plaintiff to an added risk of harm, the courts have on occasion been prepared to allow recovery without the latter having to show that it actually materialised and caused the harm.

In *McGhee v National Coal Board* [1972] 3 All ER 1008, an employee of the defendant brought an action alleging that his dermatitis had come about due to the coal board's failure to provide him with proper washing facilities. This meant that he had to cycle home with the brick dust, to which his work unavoidably exposed him, still caked to his skin. Here there was no doubt that brick dust caused the plaintiff's injury. The difficulty lay in determining whether the 'guilty' dust (ie, that which continued to adhere to the plaintiff on his journey home) had played any causative role. The House of Lords' solution was to assert that, in this type of case, it was open to a court simply to infer, as a question of fact, that the defendant's breach had materially contributed to the injury. Indeed, in one of the judgments, Lord Wilberforce appeared to go further and suggest that once the plaintiff has shown that the defendant's breach of duty created a risk of harm, the burden of proving that it did *not* materialise and materially contribute to the harm passed to the defendant.

Medical negligence cases

Medical negligence cases stemming from therapeutic treatment raise problems of multiple causation as a matter of course. Two candidate conditions (the doctor's breach of duty *and* the patient's underlying illness) are present in the circumstances leading to injury. The question of how far the plaintiff-friendly approach to resolving such difficulties in *McGhee* should continue to apply in the field of medical negligence was faced by the House of Lords in *Wilsher v Essex AHA*.

Wilsher v Essex AHA [1988] 1 All ER 871, HL (Bridge, Fraser, Lowry, Griffiths, and Ackner LL)

The plaintiff baby was found to be suffering from retrolental fibroplasia (RLF), rendering him virtually blind, following treatment in the defendant's post-natal unit. Owing to a breach of duty by hospital staff, the baby had been over-saturated with oxygen in the first weeks of his life (see above, p 287). However, whilst this might, according to some of the evidence, have caused or contributed to the RLF, there were four other natural conditions, all of which had afflicted the baby, and which could equally have had the same effect. The majority of the Court of Appeal found for the plaintiff on causation on the basis of Lord Wilberforce's speech in *McGhee*; the defendant appealed:

Lord Bridge: The Court of Appeal, although it felt unable to resolve the primary conflict in the expert evidence as to the causation of Martin's RLF, did make a finding that the levels of PO2 which Martin experienced in consequence of the misplacement of the catheter were of a kind capable of causing RLF. Mustill LJ expressed his anxiety whether 'by making a further finding on an issue where there was a sharp conflict between the expert witnesses, we are going too far in the effort to avoid a retrial' (see [1986] 3 All ER 801, p 825). But he concluded that it was 'legitimate, after rereading the evidence', to make this finding based on 'the weight of the expert evidence'. This finding by the Court of Appeal is challenged by counsel for the authority as one which it was not open to it to make ... But assuming, as I do for the present, that the finding was properly made, it carried the plaintiff's case no further than to establish that oxygen administered to Martin as a consequence of the negligent failure to detect the misplacement of the catheter was one of a number of possible causes of Martin's RLF.

Mustill LJ subjected the speeches in *McGhee v National Coal Board* [1972] 3 All ER 1008 ... to a careful scrutiny and analysis and concluded that they established a principle of law which he expressed in the following terms:

> If it is an established fact that conduct of a particular kind creates a risk that injury will be caused to another or increases an existing risk that injury will ensue, and if the two parties stand in such a relationship that the one party owes a duty not to conduct himself in that way, and if the first party does conduct himself in that way, and if the other party does suffer injury of the kind to which the risk related, then the first party is taken to have caused the injury by his breach of duty, even though the existence and extent of the contribution made by the breach cannot be ascertained.

Applying this principle to the finding that the authority's negligence was one of the possible causes of Martin's RLF, he held that this was sufficient to enable the court to conclude that the negligence was 'taken to have caused the injury'. Glidewell LJ reached the same conclusion by substantially the same process of reasoning. Sir Nicolas Browne-Wilkinson VC took the opposite view ...

Much of the academic discussion to which [*McGhee*] has given rise has focused on the speech of Lord Wilberforce, particularly on two paragraphs. He said:

... First, it is a sound principle that where a person has, by breach of duty of care, created a risk, and injury occurs within the area of that risk, the loss should be borne by him *unless he shows that it had some other cause*. Secondly, from the evidential point of view, one may ask, why should a man who is able to show that his employer should have taken certain precautions, because without them there is a risk, or an added risk, of injury or disease, and who in fact sustains exactly that injury or disease, have to assume the burden of proving more: namely, that it was the addition to the risk, caused by the breach of duty, which caused or materially contributed to the injury? In many cases of which the present is typical, this is impossible to prove, just because honest medical opinion cannot segregate the causes of an illness between compound causes. And if one asks which of the parties, the workman or the employers should suffer from this inherent evidential difficulty, the answer as a matter in policy or justice should be that it is the creator of the risk who, *ex hypothesi*, must be taken to have foreseen the possibility of damage, who should bear its consequences. (My emphasis.)

He then referred to *Bonnington Castings Ltd v Wardlaw* and *Nicholson v Atlas Steel Foundry and Engineering Co Ltd* and added:

... I must say that, at least in the present case, to bridge the evidential gap by inference seems to me something of a fiction, since it was precisely this inference which the medical expert declined to make. But I find in the cases quoted an analogy which suggests the conclusion that, *in the absence of proof that the culpable condition had, in the result, no effect*, the employers should be liable for an injury, squarely within the risk which they created and that they, not the pursuer, should suffer the consequence of the impossibility, foreseeably inherent in the nature of his injury, of segregating the precise consequence of their default. (My emphasis.)

My Lords, it seems to me that both these paragraphs, particularly in the words I have emphasised, amount to saying that, in the circumstances, the burden of proof of causation is reversed and thereby to run counter to the unanimous and emphatic opinions expressed in *Bonnington Castings Ltd v Wardlaw* [1956] 1 All ER 615 ... to the contrary effect. I find no support in any of the other speeches for the view that the burden of proof is reversed and, in this respect, I think Lord Wilberforce's reasoning must be regarded as expressing a minority opinion.

The conclusion I draw ... is that *McGhee v National Coal Board* laid down no new principle of law whatever. On the contrary, it affirmed the principle that the onus of proving causation lies on the pursuer or plaintiff. Adopting a robust and pragmatic approach to the undisputed primary facts of the case, the majority concluded that it was a legitimate inference of fact that the defenders' negligence had materially contributed to the pursuer's injury. The decision, in my opinion, is of no greater significance than that and the attempt to extract from it some esoteric principle which in some way modifies, as a matter of law, the nature of the burden of proof of causation which a plaintiff or pursuer must discharge once he has established a relevant breach of duty is a fruitless one.

In the Court of Appeal in the instant case Sir Nicolas Browne-Wilkinson VC, being in a minority, expressed his view on causation with understandable caution. But I am quite unable to find any fault with the following passage in his dissenting judgment:

> ... To my mind, the occurrence of RLF following a failure to take a necessary precaution to prevent excess oxygen causing RLF provides no evidence and raises no presumption that it was excess oxygen rather than one or more of the four other possible agents which caused or contributed to RLF in this case. The position, to my mind, is wholly different from that in *McGhee*, where there was only one candidate (brick dust) which could have caused the dermatitis, and the failure to take a precaution against brick dust causing dermatitis was followed by dermatitis caused by brick dust. In such a case, I can see the common sense, if not the logic, of holding that, in the absence of any other evidence, the failure to take the precaution caused or contributed to the dermatitis. To the extent that certain members of the House of Lords decided the question on inferences from evidence or presumptions, I do not consider that the present case falls within their reasoning. A failure to take preventive measures against one out of five possible causes is no evidence as to which of those five caused the injury.

Arguably, following *Wilsher*, the courts will be reluctant to 'bridge the evidential gap' and infer that the defendant's breach was causative of injury unless the overall risk of such injury was produced in the first place by the defendant. After all, in *McGhee*, all of the brick dust emanated from the coal board's brick kiln, even though only some of it represented a breach of duty and here it may well be thought acceptable as a matter of policy to impose liability. By contrast, in an action for medical negligence, the original risk of harm to the patient is generally not of the doctor's making, but stems from the patient's illness.

Claims for loss of chance

In *Wilsher* we saw that, due to the over-complexity and lack of clarity of the available evidence, the plaintiff was unable to show that the defendant's breach of duty had played a causative role in his injury. However, in many instances, notably where a doctor's failure to make a prompt or proper diagnosis of a given illness is at issue, the plaintiff *will* have evidence as to the effect this has had upon him. Such evidence takes the form of class statistics which record the chances of recovery for patients who *are* diagnosed with the relevant condition at a similar stage of progression.

The courts were required to decide whether a claim founded upon such statistical evidence was admissible in the case of *Hotson v East Berkshire HA*.

Hotson v East Berkshire HA [1987] 1 AC 750, HL (Bridge, Brandon, Mackay, Goff and Ackner LL)

The plaintiff schoolboy attended the defendant's casualty department after falling from a tree and injuring his hip. The defendant failed, in breach of duty, to carry out an x-ray of the hip and by the time the true extent of the injury was discovered (when the boy returned to hospital several days later) permanent disability was unavoidable. However, the medical evidence was to the effect that, even with immediate diagnosis, 75% of patients with such an injury went on to develop the same disability anyway.

Rather than suing on the basis that the defendant had caused the disability itself (clearly an impossible task, given the need to satisfy the civil standard of proof by showing *on the balance of probabilities* that the failed diagnosis had played a necessary part in it), the plaintiff restricted his claim to the loss of the residual 25% chance that proper diagnosis would have resulted in successful treatment. At first instance, Simon Brown J accepted that the loss of a substantial chance of this kind was actionable and awarded damages assessed at 25% of the full quantum in respect of such an injury. The Court of Appeal (Sir John Donaldson MR, Dillon and Croom-Johnson LJJ) unanimously affirmed this approach:

> **Sir John Donaldson MR**: ... Mr Whitfield, for the defendants, submits that no causal connection between the negligence and the development of avascular necrosis and consequent disability has been established, since a 25% likelihood fails to achieve the requisite standard of proof. Without that causal connection, there can be no liability in damages based upon that development. In more concrete terms, it is all, ie, £46,000, or nothing – £46,000 if the likelihood of the connection exceeds 50% and otherwise nothing. In the instant case it is nothing.
>
> In Mr Whitfield's submission, damages in respect of a lost chance are recoverable only where the defendant breaks a contract under which the plaintiff was entitled to a chance or where chances are relevant to valuing an injury proved to result from the defendant's breach of duty. An example of a successful contractual claim for damages for the loss of a chance is provided by *Chaplin v Hicks* [1911] 2 KB 786, where an entrant in a beauty competition was not notified of the date of the final and so lost the chance of a prize ...
>
> As a matter of common sense, it is unjust that there should be no liability for failure to treat a patient, simply because the chances of a successful cure by that treatment were less than 50%. Nor, by the same token, can it be just that if the chances of a successful cure only marginally exceed 50%, the doctor or his employer should be liable to the same extent as if the treatment could be guaranteed to cure. If this is the law, it is high time that it was changed, assuming that this court has power to do so.
>
> Equally I am quite unable to detect any rational basis for a state of the law, if such it be, whereby in identical circumstances Dr A who treats a patient under the National Health Service, and whose liability therefore falls to be determined in accordance with the law of tort, should be in a different position from Dr B who treats a patient outside the service, and whose liability

therefore falls to be determined in accordance with the law of contract, assuming, of course, that the contract is in terms which impose upon him neither more nor less than the tortious duty ...

It has been said times without number that the categories of negligence are never closed and, subject to the rules relating to remoteness of damage which are not material in the instant case, I can see no reason why the categories of loss should be closed either ...

The health authority appealed to the House of Lords:

Lord Bridge: The plaintiff's claim was for damages for physical injury and consequential loss alleged to have been caused by the authority's breach of their duty of care. In some cases, perhaps particularly medical negligence cases, causation may be so shrouded in mystery that the court can only measure statistical chances. But that was not so here. On the evidence there was a clear conflict as to what had caused the avascular necrosis. The authority's evidence was that the sole cause was the original traumatic injury to the hip. The plaintiff's evidence, at its highest, was that the delay in treatment was a material contributory cause. This was a conflict, like any other about some relevant past event, which the judge could not avoid resolving on a balance of probabilities. Unless the plaintiff proved on a balance of probabilities that the delayed treatment was at least a material contributory cause of the avascular necrosis he failed on the issue of causation and no question of quantification could arise. But the judge's findings of fact ... are unmistakably to the effect that on a balance of probabilities the injury caused by the plaintiff's fall left insufficient blood vessels intact to keep the epiphysis alive. This amounts to a finding of fact that the fall was the sole cause of the avascular necrosis.

The upshot is that the appeal must be allowed on the narrow ground that the plaintiff failed to establish a cause of action in respect of the avascular necrosis and its consequences. Your Lordships were invited to approach the appeal more broadly and to decide whether, in a claim for damages for personal injury, it can ever be appropriate, where the cause of the injury is unascertainable and all the plaintiff can show is a statistical chance which is less than even that, but for the defendant's breach of duty, he would not have suffered the injury, to award him a proportionate fraction of the full damages appropriate to compensate for the injury as the measure of damages for the lost chance.

There is a superficially attractive analogy between the principle applied in such cases as *Chaplin v Hicks* [1911] 2 KB 786 (award of damages for breach of contract assessed by reference to the lost chance of securing valuable employment if the contract had been performed) and *Kitchen v Royal Air Force Association* [1958] 1 WLR 563 (damages for solicitors' negligence assessed by reference to the lost chance of prosecuting a successful civil action) and the principle of awarding damages for the lost chance of avoiding personal injury or, in medical negligence cases, for the lost chance of a better medical result which might have been achieved by prompt diagnosis and correct treatment. I think there are formidable difficulties in the way of accepting the analogy. But I do not see this appeal as a suitable occasion for reaching a settled conclusion as to whether the analogy can ever be applied.

As I have said, there was in this case an inescapable issue of causation first to be resolved. But if the plaintiff had proved on a balance of probabilities that the authority's negligent failure to diagnose and treat his injury promptly had materially contributed to the development of avascular necrosis, I know of no principle of English law which would have entitled the authority to a discount from the full measure of damage to reflect the chance that, even given prompt treatment, avascular necrosis might well still have developed ...

Although their Lordships stopped short of saying that there could never be recovery in medical negligence for loss of chance, they gave little clue as to when it might be allowed. From Lord Mackay's judgment, it appears that they may have been thinking of the *McGhee* type of case where, as a matter of policy, it is desirable that a defendant should be penalised for failure to mitigate a risk of his own making: liability should not be excused on the basis of statistics showing that injury to the plaintiff was likely, even had such mitigation occurred. However, as already noted, *McGhee* offers little analogy with the standard medical negligence scenario. Subsequently, in *Tahir v Haringey HA* (1995, unreported), Otton LJ, speaking obiter, was content to regard *Hotson* as straightforwardly disallowing such claims in the context of medical negligence.

The House of Lords' decision in *Hotson* is open to strong criticism. Once again, the evidential uncertainty at issue derived from the presence of multiple causation. However, in contrast to a case where the doctors' breach of duty has taken a positive form (as, for example, in *Wilsher*), the analysis here is concerned with the contents of a *single* causal set. (The reason is that non-treatment cannot suffice to complete such a set in conjunction with mere background conditions: the patient's original illness must necessarily also be a member.) While even here it may never be known if the individual plaintiff would have benefited from treatment he was negligently denied, it is submitted that empirically derived statistics (where available) serve to bring us significantly closer to the truth than adherence to the balance of probabilities standard of proof:

Stauch, M, 'Causation, risk and loss of chance in medical negligence' (1997) 17 OJLS 205:

... the causal laws by reference to which particular assertions of cause and effect are justified are typically incomplete in form. Given both the state of our knowledge and the nature of our motivation we are rarely either able or willing to specify every member of the antecedent causal set upon which a given result invariably follows. Instead, we generally make do with causal generalisations which make reference to just a few of the set's elements. Such generalisations take the form of 'If (C, B, ??), then E', where 'C' is a candidate condition, 'B' a bundle of more obvious background conditions, and '??' stands for the presence of further, unknown conditions. The corollary of the incompleteness in such causal statements is that, given the antecedent, C, alone, we cannot predict for certain that E will follow: it may be that on this particular occasion, the '??' are absent. What we can do, however, by employing statistics which record the previous occasions when E has been observed to follow C, is state with a high degree of accuracy the probability that E will follow this time ...

Such matters seem at first sight to be remote from the concerns of the lawyer. As already noted, the latter conducts his causal inquiry from a point in time when the effect is known to have come about. Accordingly, when on a given occasion E follows upon C and B, the presence of other unknown conditions can normally be taken on trust. Nevertheless, it is precisely the incompleteness in our causal laws which is the basis of the peculiar evidentiary difficulties created by multiple causation cases. In such cases, our inability to specify fully the relevant causal sets means that, even where a given candidate condition, C1, is followed by E, we cannot be sure whether C1 featured in an operative set: it may be that, on this occasion, the unknown further conditions required to complete the set were absent, and that E instead came about through the working of a different set containing a rival candidate condition, C2. Even in the simpler causal scenario in *Hotson*, where only a single causal set was present, it was impossible to say on the evidence whether the patient's non-treatment had featured in it. ... [I]t might simply have contained the original fall, background conditions, plus further unknown conditions. The use of statistics, however, minimises such uncertainty by telling us over a range of similar cases how frequently the unknown conditions appear: in *Hotson*, 75% of the time (or on 75 out of every 100 occasions). Conversely, on the other 25% of occasions, when the unknown conditions are absent, non-treatment does feature in the set (ie, treatment will benefit the patient).

Statistics and the balance of probabilities

Given the *prima facie* interest and utility of these statistics, why was the House of Lords in fact so hostile to their use in Hotson? A number of reasons may be suggested.

First, their Lordships almost certainly distrusted the fact that, as just noted, statistical statements assert a connection between types of event over a range or 'class' rather than in respect of an individual case. Paradoxically this misgiving was best expressed in Croom-Johnson LJ's judgment in the Court of Appeal (which was ultimately favourable to the plaintiff):

> If it is proved statistically that 25% of the population have a chance of recovery from a certain injury and 75% do not, it does not mean that someone who suffers that injury and does not recover from it has lost a 25% chance. He may have lost nothing at all. What he has to do is prove that he was one of the 25% and his loss was caused by the defendant's negligence. To be a figure in a statistic does not itself give him a cause of action.

Instead, the House of Lords felt that, in line with established authority, the question of causation that the case raised was to be determined, like any other issue of past (as opposed to hypothetical) fact, on the balance of probabilities ...

[However], the idea that in a case of 'past fact' the balance of probabilities standard of proof could provide a more satisfactory means of resolving the issue of causal uncertainty than the use of statistics, shows a general failure to understand the epistemological relationship between the two approaches. As already noted, in multiple causation cases, the inherent incompleteness of our causal laws means that we are often unable to allocate causal responsibility between rival candidate conditions. However, whereas statistics derived systematically from our previous experience of similar cases, provide us with a very accurate probability-weighting for each candidate, the balance of probabilities test attempts to perform the same operation by appealing crudely to what we *feel* the likely cause to have been. The relevant feeling must, once again, derive from our previous experience of similar cases, but this time in its rawest form.

Human agency in the causal chain

Complications of a different kind arise in cases in which resolving the causal inquiry requires us to decide how a human agent would have behaved in the hypothetical circumstances of no original breach of duty. In contrast to the cases considered previously, in which the causal chain consists only of physiological events, such as the progress of an untreated disease, it may well be felt that the balance of probabilities standard of proof remains the most acceptable one here. (To assert that because, in a given situation, X% of persons are observed to do A, a particular individual, P, is X% likely to do A, would be to take an unduly mechanistic view of human agency.) Nevertheless, problems remain in applying the standard.

Non-disclosure cases

A common type of case, in the context of medical negligence, which requires us to assess the impact of human agency in the causal chain, is where the doctor fails to advise the patient of a given risk attached to treatment. Here (assuming both that such failure is a breach of duty and that the risk subsequently materialises) the patient, in order to succeed in his claim, must show that, on the balance of probabilities, he would not have agreed to the treatment had he been properly advised. The question of how far a court will be guided by what an objective 'reasonable patient' would have chosen to do in similar circumstances was addressed in *Smith v Barking, Havering and Brentwood HA*.

Smith v Barking, Havering and Brentwood HA [1994] 5 Med LR 285, QB (Hutchison J)

The plaintiff was a young woman with a serious spinal condition. Without surgery forthwith she would inevitably develop tetraplegia within a matter of months. However, the surgeon who treated her failed to warn her of the 25% risk of immediate tetraplegia attendant on the operation, which indeed materialised.

Hutchison J: There was some discussion as to whether the issue of causation should be approached on what was called the objective or the subjective basis – ie, was the question to be resolved by deciding what a reasonable person in the plaintiff's position would have chosen to do, or by deciding what the plaintiff herself would have chosen to do. In support of the former approach I was referred to the Canadian authority of *Reibl v Robert A Hughes* [1980] 2 SCR 880 and in support of the latter to the decision of Hirst J in *Hills v Potter* [1984] 1 WLR 641. Both counsel invited me to accept that in the end the matter must be one for decision on a subjective basis. This must plainly as a matter of principle be right, because the question must be: 'If this plaintiff had been given the advice that she should have been given, would she have decided to undergo the operation or not?'

However, there is a peculiar difficulty involved in this sort of case – not least for the plaintiff herself – in giving, after the adverse outcome of the operation is known, reliable answers as to what she would have decided before the operation had she been given proper advice as to the risks inherent in it. Accordingly, it would, in my judgment, be right in the ordinary case to give particular weight to the objective assessment. If everything points to the fact that a reasonable plaintiff, properly informed, would have assented to the operation, the assertion from the witness box, made after the adverse outcome is known, in a wholly artificial situation and in the knowledge that the outcome of the case depends upon that assertion being maintained, does not carry great weight unless there are extraneous or additional factors to substantiate it. By extraneous or additional factors I mean, and I am not doing more than giving examples, religious or some other firmly held convictions; particular social or domestic considerations justifying a decision not in accordance with what, objectively, seems the right one; assertions in the immediate aftermath of the operation made in a context other than that of a possible claim for damages; in other words, some particular factor which suggests that the plaintiff had grounds for not doing what a reasonable person in her situation might be expected to have done. Of course, the less confidently the judge reaches the conclusion as to what objectively the reasonable patient might be expected to have decided, the more readily will he be persuaded by her subjective evidence.

I should make it clear that nothing I have said is intended to reflect adversely on the plaintiff or to suggest that I have any doubts as to her honesty; but, as I listened to her grappling with the different hypothetical questions which were put to her, I felt the greatest sympathy for her and reflected that one would need almost to be a saint to answer such questions objectively – ie, without allowing one's reaction to be influenced by the knowledge of what had, in fact, happened and appreciation of the vital significance of the question. Hence the importance of giving proper weight to an objective assessment of what a reasonable patient could be expected to decide in the light of such proper advice as should have been given.

This subjective approach, which nevertheless takes account of objective 'reasonableness' for evidential purposes, is in our view clearly correct.

Failure to attend

Another type of case where the courts must attempt to 'second-guess' how an agent would have behaved in hypothetical circumstances of no earlier breach of duty is where a doctor negligently fails to attend the patient. Assuming that treatment is available which would benefit the patient (cf *Barnett v Kensington and Chelsea HA*), would the doctor have administered it? Recently, in the important House of Lords decision of *Bolitho v City and Hackney HA* [1997] 4 All ER 771 (see above, p 300), the plaintiff's claim turned on this issue. As we have seen, the doctor in that case claimed that, even had she attended the patient, she would not have instigated the one procedure – intubation – capable of saving him. In the Court of Appeal, Simon Brown LJ, in a dissenting judgment, had suggested that the court should in such a case simply presume that the procedure in question would have been used:

> **Simon Brown LJ**: I have no doubt that the resultant issue, the issue of causation, was correctly formulated by the judge ... applying the test of probability. More particularly, in the light of his subsequent medical findings, it could have been formulated thus: had Dr Horn or a suitable substitute attended when called, would Patrick on the balance of probabilities have been intubated? I see no reason why the position here should be any different to that arising if a nurse's call is not responded to and no evidence exists as to which of several doctors might have attended. The question surely is: what would an attending doctor probably have done? And given that the doctor would probably do that which she or he should do, the question becomes: what should a doctor do in such circumstances? How then should that question be approached? ...
>
> When it comes to deciding what inferences here may legitimately be drawn from the established primary facts, prominent amongst the factors to be borne in mind are surely these. First, the literature in this field of medicine, and not least the generally accepted statements (as found by the judge) that 'respiratory failure ... is a common complication in many disease processes and should always be readily suspected, especially if there are unexplained signs and symptoms', and 'any child who reaches the hospital alive should not ... die from upper airway obstruction'. Second, that the very purpose of Sister Sallabank calling for the senior paediatric registrar was to ensure that whatever needed to be done for Patrick was done. The initial assumption must surely be that the doctor's attendance would have been of some use. Third is the indisputable fact that intubation alone would have benefited the child. Given all that, and given, fourth, the entire history of this case as it would have presented itself to an attending doctor – the background to Patrick's readmission on 16 January, his being 'specialled' that day, Sister Sallabank's view at the time of the first episode that something was so acutely wrong that she wanted Patrick seen by the senior paediatric registrar and not merely the senior houseman, her decision that a nurse should then remain permanently with him, and, when the second episode occurred, her renewed worry and decision again to call the senior paediatric registrar – I have no difficulty in inferring that whichever doctor had attended would have acted in the one

way which would have been effective. In so deciding, I do not overlook Nurse Newbold's evidence nor Dr Dinwiddie's school of thought. But it is all very well for the specialists now to theorise over what would or would not have appeared to be indicated by second hand descriptions of the child's developing condition; the reality is that no one will ever know quite how that condition would have presented itself to a competent doctor, learning the history as he would have done and examining the patient for himself. In my judgment, therefore, the case called for the 'robust and pragmatic approach' endorsed by *Wilsher*, and the assumption of causation suggested by the speeches in *Cumming (or McWilliams) v Sir William Arrol and Co* [1962] 1 All ER 623. So at least it strikes me, although not, as I recognise, my Lords.

However, this approach did not commend itself to the majority (Dillon and Farquharson LJJ) and it was repudiated by Lord Browne-Wilkinson in the House of Lords:

> **Lord Browne-Wilkinson**: Where, as in the present case, a breach of a duty of care is proved or admitted, the burden still lies on the plaintiff to prove that such breach caused the injury suffered: *Bonnington Castings Ltd v Wardlaw* [1956] AC 613; *Wilsher v Essex AHA* [1988] AC 1074. In all cases the primary question is one of fact: did the wrongful act cause the injury? ... In a case of non-attendance by a doctor, there may be cases in which there is a doubt as to which doctor would have attended if the duty had been fulfilled. But in this case there was no doubt: if the duty had been carried out it would have either been Dr Horn or Dr Rodger, the only two doctors at St Bartholomew's who had responsibility for Patrick and were on duty. Therefore in the present case, the first relevant question is 'what would Dr Horn or Dr Rodger have done if they had attended?' As to Dr Horn, the judge accepted her evidence that she would not have intubated. By inference, although not expressly, the judge must have accepted that Dr Rodger also would not have intubated: as a senior house officer she would not have intubated without the approval of her senior registrar, Dr Horn ...
>
> However in the present case the answer to the question 'what would have happened?' is not determinative of the issue of causation. At the trial the defendants accepted that if the professional standard of care required any doctor who attended to intubate Patrick, Patrick's claim must succeed. Dr Horn could not escape liability by proving that she would have failed to take the course which any competent doctor would have adopted. A defendant cannot escape liability by saying that the damage would have occurred in any event because he would have committed some other breach of duty thereafter. I have no doubt that this concession was rightly made by the defendants. But there is some difficulty in analysing why it was correct. I adopt the analysis of Hobhouse LJ in *Joyce v Merton, Sutton and Wandsworth HA* [1996] 7 Med LR 1. In commenting on the decision of the Court of Appeal in the present case, he said, p 20:
>
> > Thus a plaintiff can discharge the burden of proof on causation by satisfying the court *either* that the relevant person would in fact have taken the requisite action (although she would not have been at fault if she had not), *or* that the proper discharge of the relevant person's duty towards

the plaintiff required that she take that action. The former alternative calls for no explanation since it is simply the factual proof of the causative effect of the original fault. The latter is slightly more sophisticated: it involves the factual situation that the original fault did not itself cause the injury but that this was because there would have been some further fault on the part of the defendants; the plaintiff proves his case by proving that his injuries would have been avoided if proper care had continued to be taken. In the *Bolitho* case the plaintiff had to prove that the continuing exercise of proper care would have resulted in his being intubated.

There were, therefore, two questions for the judge to decide on causation: (1) 'What would Dr Horn have done, or authorised to be done, if she had attended Patrick?' And: (2) 'If she would not have intubated, would that have been negligent?' The *Bolam* test has no relevance to the first of those questions but is central to the second.

There can be no doubt that, as the majority of the Court of Appeal held, the judge directed himself correctly in accordance with that approach ... The dissenting judgment of Simon Brown LJ in the Court of Appeal is based on a misreading of the judge's judgment. He treats the judge as having only asked himself one question, namely, the second question. To the extent that the Lord Justice noticed the first question – would Dr Horn have intubated? – he said that the judge was wrong to accept Dr Horn's evidence that she would not have intubated. In my judgment it was for the judge to assess the truth of her evidence on this issue.

Importantly, as this judgment makes clear, where the agent whose hypothetical conduct is called into question is the defendant, such conduct – if it is to be accepted as negating causation – must in any event fall within the bounds of the non-negligent.

However, though Lord Browne-Wilkinson's approach is attractive as a matter of logic, and appears to give the plaintiff 'two bites at the causation cherry', misgivings may be felt as to how it will be applied in practice. In particular, there is perhaps a danger that judges will henceforth be less ready to scrutinise the doctor's evidence on the 'would' question (evidence, which as Simon Brown LJ noted, is likely, if anything, to be less reliable than that of the *plaintiff* in an analogous non-disclosure case). Whereas, in the latter type of case – where there is only the 'would' question – the courts assess the cogency of the plaintiff's evidence by reference to the objective 'reasonable man' standard, here they may be tempted to defer questions of 'reasonableness' to the second 'should' question stage. To do so, however, would make life significantly more difficult for the plaintiff. This is because 'reasonableness' undergoes a shift in meaning between the two stages, from a *quantitative* standard (is this the way doctors generally respond in this type of situation?) to a *qualitative* one (is this a not demonstrably illogical way for them to respond?). The latter is, of course, an easier standard for the defendant's hypothetical conduct to satisfy.

Remoteness of damage

In so far as causation is established as a question of fact, it does not follow automatically that liability will be imposed on the defendant: sometimes the damage resulting from his breach of duty will be regarded as too remote. (In such a case, it is sometimes stated, albeit rather misleadingly, that the plaintiff has failed to establish *legal* causation.) Generally this involves a determination on the part of the court that (as a matter of policy) it would be inefficient or unjust to burden the defendant with liability. An example is where the plaintiff's injury occurs through a freakish concatenation of conditions, whether present at the time of the defendant's negligent act or supervening later in the causal chain; here a court might well hold that such injury was not 'reasonably foreseeable'.

As a perusal of the leading authorities in the general area of negligence will reveal, the concepts of remoteness and reasonable foreseeability are susceptible to extensive manipulation by the courts on policy grounds (see, for example, the two *Wagon Mound* cases [1961] AC 388 and [1967] 1 AC 617). Fortunately, in the context of medical negligence, it is enough to observe that injury to a patient, as a consequence of a doctor's breach of duty, will rarely, if ever, be treated as unforeseeable. A case in point is that of *Hepworth v Kerr* [1995] 6 Med LR 139, in which a doctor was held liable for using an experimental anaesthetic technique on a patient which resulted in a spinal stroke. The risk of inducing a spinal stroke was in fact not known about, but the risk of a cerebral stroke (thus making the procedure's use negligent) was. One possible exception arises in the context of a non-disclosure case. In the Scottish case of *Moyes v Lothian Health Board* [1990] 1 Med LR 463, a doctor warned the patient of the standard risk of an angiography causing a stroke, but failed (in breach of duty) to warn her that, in her case, there was an extra risk of this due to her hypersensitivity to the dye. In the event, a stroke occurred, but this was due to the standard risk materialising. Assuming that the patient could prove that, had she been told of the extra risk, she would not have consented to the procedure, should she recover on causation? The question was not directly addressed, however Kennedy and Grubb suggest (*Medical Law*, 2nd edn, 1994, London: Butterworths, p 230) that it may have been open to the court to hold that her injury was too remote.

DAMAGES

Principles governing awards

The general principles applying to damages apply to all personal injury cases, and there is no special body of law which applies to medical malpractice cases. In view of this, readers are referred to the specialist personal injury texts for a detailed analysis (for example, Kemp and Kemp, *The Quantum of Damages in Personal Injury and Fatal Accident Claims*, 1975, London: Sweet & Maxwell). However, general principles and heads of damage are here considered in outline.

The general compensatory principle underlying tort is that a successful plaintiff should receive damages to restore him to the position he would have been in, had the tort never occurred. The law distinguishes here between general damages (non-pecuniary loss) and special damages (pecuniary loss). Plaintiffs are entitled to receive interest on damages, from the date of issue of proceedings (not the date the cause of action accrued) until the end of the trial, and depending upon the type of damages, they are calculated by a statutory formula (RSC Ord 6 r 2).

Damages for non-pecuniary loss

Damages in battery

Even if the plaintiff has sustained no loss, damages, albeit of a nominal amount, can be recovered. The other important point to note is that, in battery, there is no place for the concept of foreseeability; damages can be recovered for all direct consequences of the battery. For example, in *Allan v New Mount Sinai Hospital* (1980) 109 DLR (3d) 634, an anaesthetist, though not negligent, was liable for a highly unusual and unforeseeable reaction, when the action was brought in battery.

Pain and suffering and loss of amenity

According to McGregor (*McGregor on Damages*, 15th edn, 1988, London: Sweet & Maxwell), 'pain' is the immediately felt effect on the nerves and brain, while 'suffering' is distress not directly connected with any bodily condition, and would include fear of future incapacity (in relation to health, sanity or the ability to make a living), and humiliation, sadness and embarrassment caused by disfigurement. This may also include a sum for the anguish caused by reduced life expectancy (s 1(1)(b) of the Administration of Justice Act 1982). It must be stressed that there are no damages for ordinary mental distress such as shock or fear, but if, say, shock or grief has exacerbated the plaintiff's physical injury, then damages may be increased accordingly: *Kralj v McGrath* [1986] 1 All ER 54.

It is clear also that pure psychiatric injury may be compensatable in medical negligence cases, in so far as the limiting criteria imposed by the law of negligence are satisfied. In *Allin v City and Hackney HA* [1996] 7 Med LR 167, a woman recovered damages for post-traumatic stress disorder caused by being told (falsely) that her baby was dead. She suffered the 'shock' which is necessary in such cases. In contrast, recovery was not allowed in *Sion v Hampstead HA* [1994] 5 Med LR 170, where the cause of the psychiatric injury was watching someone die over a long period of time.

Damages for loss of amenity are to compensate for things like injuries to the senses, sexual dysfunction, loss of marriage prospects, loss of enjoyment of family life and loss of enjoyment of work. An interesting question arises as to whether the plaintiff who is unconscious should receive damages for these losses when he is not aware of them. The House of Lords had to consider this in the medical negligence case of *Lim Poh Choo v Camden and Islington AHA* [1980] AC 174, where, following an anaesthetic error, the patient was rendered almost completely unconscious so as to be unaware of her condition. It was argued by the defendant that her lack of awareness precluded an award of damages for loss of amenity. The court rejected this argument, relying upon the case of *H West and Son Ltd v Shepherd* [1964] AC 326, where it was said (*per* Lord Morris):

> **Lord Morris**: Certain particular questions have been raised. How are general damages affected, if at all, by the fact that the sufferer is unconscious? How are they affected, if at all, if it be the fact that the sufferer will not be able to make use of any money which is awarded?
>
> The first of these questions may be largely answered if it is remembered that damages are designed to compensate for such results as have actually been caused. If someone has been caused pain, then damages to compensate for the enduring of it may be awarded. If, however, by reason of an injury, someone is made unconscious either for a short or for a prolonged period with the result that he does not feel pain, then he needs no monetary compensation in respect of pain because he will not have suffered it ... An unconscious person will be spared pain and suffering ... The fact of unconsciousness is therefore relevant in respect of and will eliminate those heads or elements of damage which can only exist by being felt or thought or experienced. The fact of unconsciousness does not, however, eliminate the actuality of the deprivations of the ordinary experiences and amenities of life which may be the inevitable result of some physical injury.

In other words, damages for pain and suffering have to relate to actual experiences, whereas damages for loss of amenity can be assessed without reference to the plaintiff's experience.

Damages for pecuniary loss

Such damages include loss of earnings, medical expenses and the cost of care. There is also the possibility of the plaintiff recovering what is known as a 'Smith v Manchester' award to compensate for disadvantage on the labour market, ie, the plaintiff has been able to return to work but, due to the injury, would be disadvantaged in finding another job in the event of the present one ending (*Smith v Manchester Corporation* [1974] 17 KIR 1).

We consider below a number of situations in which special considerations apply.

Loss of a chance

At present, as we have seen, such claims are not regarded as valid in medical negligence under English law: see *Hotson v East Berkshire AHA* [1987] AC 750 discussed above, p 316. In so far as the House of Lords comes to review this area of law (as we believe it should), then it is clear that damages in such cases are readily quantifiable on the basis adopted by the lower courts in *Hotson* itself, ie, the full award for the relevant disability is divided by the statistical chance of avoiding it lost as a result of the defendant's negligence. What is perhaps not so obvious is that, equally, in cases in which the plaintiff currently receives the full quantum (under the 'all or nothing' balance of probabilities approach), a discount should be made where empirical statistics show that the plaintiff's chance of avoiding injury would in any event have been less than 100%. Though disapproved in *Hotson*, this approach (representing the *quid pro quo* from the defendant's point of view) was taken at first instance in *Clark v MacLennan* [1983] 1 All ER 416 and in *Bagley v North Herts HA* (1986) 136 NLJ 1014.

Fatal accidents

Section 1(1) of the Fatal Accidents Act 1976 gives a right to certain dependants to recover for their loss of dependency. In addition to this a fixed sum of 'bereavement' damages is recoverable (s 1A) by the spouse of the deceased or the parents of a deceased unmarried minor child.

Damages for congenital disability

There is a certain amount of linguistic confusion in this area, and often the expression 'wrongful birth' is used to mean very different things. The classification used here is adopted from Kennedy and Grubb (*Medical Law*, 2nd edn, 1994, London: Butterworths), where they classify wrongful life claims as those brought by the child alleging that it would have been better if he had never been born, and wrongful birth claims as those brought by parents for compensation for the birth of a damaged baby. It is apparent that damages can lie for the latter, but (probably) not for the former: see further the discussion below, Chapter 8.

Wrongful conception

Damages can, under English law, be awarded for the birth of a healthy child if the child had been born as a result of a failed sterilisation which was either performed negligently, or the patient was not warned about the possibility of the operation spontaneously reversing itself. This type of claim raises some interesting issues on policy and quantum.

In *Udale v Bloomsbury AHA* [1983] 2 All ER 522, the plaintiff, who became pregnant after a negligently performed sterilisation, claimed damages for the inconvenience and anxiety of pregnancy, the pain of childbirth, and the future costs of bringing up the child. In dismissing her action Jupp J stated:

Jupp J: The considerations that particularly impress me are the following: (1) it is highly undesirable that any child should learn that a court has publicly declared his life or birth to be a mistake, a disaster even, and he or she is unwanted or rejected. Such pronouncements would disrupt families and weaken the structure of society; (2) a plaintiff such as Mrs Udale would get little or no damages because her love and care for her child and her joy, ultimately, at his birth would be set off against and might cancel out the inconvenience and financial disadvantages which naturally accompany parenthood. By contrast, a plaintiff who nurtures bitterness in her heart and refused to let her maternal instinct take over would be entitled to large damages. In short, virtue would go unrewarded; unnatural rejection of womanhood and motherhood would be generously compensated. This, in my judgment, cannot be just; (3) medical men would be under subconscious pressure to encourage abortions in order to avoid claims for medical negligence which would arise if the child were allowed to be born; (4) it has been the assumption of our culture for time immemorial that a child coming into the world, even if, as some say, 'the world is a vale of tears', is a blessing and an occasion for rejoicing.

Subsequently, however, Peter Pain J took a different view in *Thake v Maurice* [1984] 2 All ER 513:

Peter Pain J: A healthy baby is so lovely a creature that I can well understand the reaction of one who asks: how could its birth possibly give rise to an action for damages? But every baby has a belly to be filled and a body to be clothed. The law relating to damages is concerned with reparation in money terms and this is what is needed for the maintenance of a baby...

The policy of the State, as I see it, is to provide the widest freedom of choice. It makes available to the public the means of planning their families or planning to have no family. If plans go awry, it provides for the possibility of abortion ...

Against that background I ask myself whether the reasons advanced by Jupp J [in *Udale*] are so compelling that I ought to follow his decision. I do not think they are and, in deference to his careful reasoning, I will consider them one by one.

I do not think that if I award damages here it will lead little Samantha to feel rejection. She is surrounded by a happy, albeit somewhat poverty-stricken, family life. It is this that must make her feel wanted and not rejected. She may learn in years to come that her conception was unwanted. But there is nothing exceptional about this. What matters to a child is how it is received when it enters life ...

Next I have to consider the difficulty in setting off the joy of Samantha against the financial disadvantages that her parents would undergo. If I adopt the public policy which Jupp J favours then virtue will indeed go unrewarded. Every credit is due to the plaintiffs for the way in which they have welcomed Samantha into the family. The method of set off presents difficulties but, once again, I think it can be solved by looking at the hard cash flow and ignoring the intangibles. Mrs Thake underwent pain and discomfort in the course of her labour, although it was not particularly difficult. As a result of these sufferings they had a healthy child. But the fact that she has been such a joy to them is largely of their own making. If they had been reluctant to accept her and grudging in the sacrifices they had to make for her support, then they might have had little joy. As I see it, the birth of a healthy child should be set off against their disappointment and the labour pains so that they cancel each other out. The joy they have for Samantha is largely of their own making in the way they have met their difficulties. The claim for Samantha's support and for the costs of the birth remain.

Peter Pain J, therefore, dismissed the application for damages for the pregnancy and childbirth as being intangible and offset by the joy of the child, but when it came to actual pecuniary loss, he repudiated the approach of Jupp J as unduly policy-oriented:

> **Peter Pain J**: I do not see the logical basis of this approach ... I entirely accept that the reasons put forward by Jupp J may be valid considerations in assessment of damages in a particular case. But I feel that to erect them into a rule of public policy application to all cases would work great injustice, as it would here.

The Court of Appeal in *Emeh v Kensington, Chelsea and Westminster AHA* [1985] QB 1012 preferred to adopt Peter Pain J's approach (as it indeed did when *Thake* itself subsequently came before it: see [1986] QB 644). Recently, the Scottish Inner House (Second Division) took the same view in *McFarlane v Tayside Health Board* 1998 SLT 307, in reversing a decision by the Outer House of the Court of Session that the recovery of damages in such cases was wrong on grounds of policy.

Limitation of actions

There are good pragmatic reasons for imposing time limits upon litigants, beyond which they cannot pursue their cause of action. These include the evidential difficulties which may arise when relevant documentation may have been destroyed, and memories have faded, and the fact that both plaintiffs and defendants need to know when an action is no longer possible. However, the common law imposes no limitation. This is governed entirely by statute law, the most recent statute being the Limitation Act 1980 (as amended).

The Act imposes time limits for different causes of action. The provisions which concern us in medical malpractice are those relating to contract where the limitation period is six years from the date on which the cause of action accrued (s 5), and personal injury claims, dealt with in s 11:

11 Special time limit for actions in respect of personal injuries

    (1) This section applies to any action for damages for negligence, nuisance or breach of duty (whether the duty exists by virtue of a contract or of provision made by or under a statute or independently of any contract or any such provision) where the damages claimed by

    the plaintiff for the negligence, nuisance or breach of duty consist of or include damages in respect of personal injuries to the plaintiff or any other person.

    ...

(3) An action to which this section applies shall not be brought after the expiration of the period applicable in accordance with sub-s (4) or (5) below.

(4) Except where sub-s (5) below applies, the period applicable is three years from–

    (a) the date on which the cause of action accrued; or

    (b) the date of knowledge (if later) of the person injured.

(5) If the injured person dies before the expiration of the period mentioned in sub-s (4) above, the period applicable as respects the cause of action surviving for the benefit of his estate by virtue of s 1 of the Law Reform (Miscellaneous Provisions) Act 1934 shall be three years from–

    (a) the date of death; or

    (b) the date of the personal representative's knowledge; whichever is the later.

The time limit of three years (in the case of medical negligence) is calculated from the date the damage occurred. This will usually be the date on which the breach occurred, but if the damage did not develop until a later date, then the provision of s 11(4)(b) will apply, ie, the date of the knowledge. This is important in the case of private medical treatment because, under s 5 of the Act, there is an absolute time limit of six years for bringing an action in contract. The plaintiff who is outside that time period can bring an action in tort instead if he can argue that the date of knowledge still brings it within the limitation period. Moreover, a discretion is vested in the court under s 33 of the Act to allow out-of-time claims if, in all the circumstances, it appears to it equitable to do so.

    In relation to persons under a disability (minors, or adults who are of unsound mind so as to be incapable of managing their own affairs) s 28 provides that time will not start to run until the disability ends or the person dies. In consequence, if the action accrued when the patient was a child, he will have until the age of 21 to bring proceedings. A person of unsound mind, who never achieves mental competency, will not be subject to any limitation period. In such a case a very long delay makes no difference to his right to issue proceedings at any time. In *Headford v Bristol and District HA* [1995] 6 Med LR 1, the plaintiff issued proceedings 28 years after the event. The defendant sought to deal with this by an application to have the proceedings struck out as being an abuse of legal process. The defendant was unsuccessful. The Court of Appeal held that, if the proceedings were within the open ended time limit envisaged by Parliament in s 28, then they could hardly be said to be an abuse of legal process.

Defences

It must be said that the usual tortious defences are rarely used in medical cases, and, for that reason, are dealt with briefly.

Contributory negligence

This could arise in a situation where a patient has not disclosed information and as a result of not knowing this, the doctor has prescribed treatment which damages the patient. The success of the defence would depend upon the requests made by the doctor, whether it was reasonable for the patient to know that that particular information was covered by the request and so on. The Canadian case of *Robitaille v Vancouver Hockey Club Ltd* (1979) 19 BCLR 158 is one of the rare examples of the success of this defence in medical negligence. A hockey player was found to have contributed to the damage caused by negligent treatment by not seeking further medical advice when his symptoms became more serious.

Volenti non fit injuria

This is where the defence argue that the patient had consented to the risk. It is arguable that this would never arise in the context of medical treatment, and there would appear to be no cases where this has been argued, at least successfully.

Necessity

This, as we have seen, can be a defence to treatment given without consent in an emergency. Could it ever be a defence to medical negligence? It may be arguable that it arises when a doctor is careless in giving treatment under very demanding and difficult circumstances. However, the better view would be to say that he simply had not fallen below the applicable standard of care.

Liability for defective medicines

Frequently patients may allege that they were injured, not through negligence on a doctor's part, but by medicinal drugs that they were (properly) given during treatment.

Before they are made available for prescription, medicines are subject to comprehensive licensing requirements pursuant to the Medicines Act 1968. However, the fact that such drugs may sometimes give rise to unpredictable and harmful metabolic reactions was brought poignantly to the public consciousness by the Thalidomide tragedy of the late 1960s and, given the difficulty in proving fault on the part of manufacturers (even the most thorough testing may fail to reveal a particular reaction in advance), provoked calls from both the Law Commission (Report No 82, Cmnd 6831, 1977) and the Pearson Committee (Cmnd 7054, 1978) for 'no fault' compensation to be introduced for such injury.

In the event, the emergence of a no fault scheme had to await initiatives at EC level in relation to defective consumer products generally. As a result of Directive 85/374/EEC, the Government passed Part I of the Consumer Protection Act 1987, which imposes strict liability upon manufacturers in respect of products put into circulation after 1 March 1988:

Product liability

1 Purpose and construction of Part I

This Part shall have effect for the purpose of making such provision as is necessary in order to comply with the product liability Directive and shall be construed accordingly.

...

2 Liability for defective products

(1) Subject to the following provisions of this Part, where any damage is caused wholly or partly by a defect in a product, every person to whom sub-s (2) below applies shall be liable for the damage.

(2) This sub-section applies to–

(a) the producer of the product;

(b) any person who, by putting his name on the product or using a trade mark or other distinguishing mark in relation to the product, has held himself out to be the producer of the product;

(c) any person who has imported the product into a Member State from a place outside the Member States in order, in the course of any business of his, to supply it to another.

...

(5) Where two or more persons are liable by virtue of this Part for the same damage, their liability shall be joint and several.

(6) This section shall be without prejudice to any liability arising otherwise than by virtue of this Part.

3 Meaning of 'defect'

(1) Subject to the following provisions of this section, there is a defect in a product for the purposes of this Part if the safety of the product is not such as persons generally are entitled to expect, and for those purposes 'safety', in relation to a product, shall include safety with respect to products comprised in that product and safety in the context of risks of damage to property, as well as in the context of risks of death or personal injury.

(2) In determining for the purposes of sub-s (1) above what persons generally are entitled to expect in relation to a product, all the circumstances shall be taken into account, including–

(a) the manner in which, and purposes for which, the product has been marketed, its get-up, the use of any mark in relation to the product and any instructions for, or warnings with respect to, doing or refraining from doing anything with or in relation to the product;

(b) what might reasonably be expected to be done with or in relation to the product; and

(c) the time when the product was supplied by its producer to another;

and nothing in this section shall require a defect to be inferred from the fact alone that the safety of a product which is supplied after that time is greater than the safety of the product in question.

4   Defences

(1) In any civil proceedings by virtue of this Part against any person ('the person proceeded against') in respect of a defect in a product it shall be a defence for him to show–

(a) that the defect is attributable to compliance with any requirement imposed by or under any enactment or with any Community obligation; or

(b) that the person proceeded against did not at any time supply the product to another; or

(c) that the following conditions are satisfied, that is to say–

(i) that the only supply of the product to another by the person proceeded against was otherwise than in the course of a business of that person's; and

(ii) that s 2(2) above does not apply to that person or applies to him by virtue only of things done otherwise than with a view to profit; or

(d) that the defect did not exist in the product at the relevant time; or

(e) that the state of scientific and technical knowledge at the relevant time was not such that a producer of products of the same description as the product in question might be expected to have discovered the defect if it had existed in his products while they were under his control; or

(f) that the defect–

(i) constituted a defect in a product ('the subsequent product') in which the product in question had been comprised; and

(ii) was wholly attributable to the design of the subsequent product or to compliance by the producer of the product in question with instructions given by the producer of the subsequent product ...

It will be seen that s 4(1)(e) gives manufacturers a defence in so far as the defect which caused injury was not one which was reasonably discoverable in the light of prevailing scientific and technical knowledge. This so called 'development risk' defence is clearly of great significance with regard to pharmaceutical products where research and development of new drugs occurs at the frontiers of medical science. Indeed, it was lobbying from the pharmaceutical industry (who argued that, without such a defence, drugs companies would be deterred from developing new products for fear of crippling liabilities if unforeseeable defects were to manifest themselves) that led to the inclusion of the defence in the EC Directive in the first place. Nevertheless, until recently it was thought by many that the UK Government, in drafting the defence in wider terms than those countenanced on the face of the Directive, had failed properly to discharge its obligations under EC law. As Patrick Milne explains:

Milne, P, 'Hope for manufacturers of defective products' (1997) NLJ 1437:

The Pearson Commission, Cmnd 7054, 1978, in recommending the introduction of a system of strict product liability, opposed the inclusion of what is commonly called a 'state of the art' or 'development risks' defence on the ground that 'to exclude development risks from a regime of strict liability would be to leave a gap through which, for example, the victims of another Thalidomide disaster might easily slip' (para 1259). The joint report of the Law Commission and Scottish Law Commission, *Liability for Defective Products*, Law Com No 82, 1977, took essentially the same approach. However, various defences are laid down in Part I of the Act and, in particular, s 4(1)(e) provides that any person proceeded against will have a defence if he can show:

(e) that the state of scientific and technical knowledge at the relevant time [ie, when the product was put into circulation] was not such that a producer of products of the same description as the product in question might be expected to have discovered the defect if it had existed in his products while they were under his control ...

This has always been the most controversial aspect of the Act. The effect of the defence is to subject some producers of goods to no more than a fault-based liability: if they can show that their failure to discover the defect through ignorance of certain scientific or technical knowledge was despite their having acted at all times with reasonable care, then they will escape liability not only in the tort of negligence but also under the Act. While the Directive does allow for a state of the art defence, s 4(1)(e) looks at first sight to be significantly more favourable to the producer (and own-brander and importer) than the defence in the Directive.

Article 7 of the Directive provides that the producer shall not be liable if he proves:

(e) that the state of scientific and technical knowledge at the time when he put the product into circulation was not such as to enable the existence of the defect to be discovered ...

This defence seems concerned not with whether a similar producer might be expected to have discovered the defect but simply with whether the relevant technical knowledge was in existence.

The possibility that the domestic legislation did not properly implement the Directive led to infringement proceedings in the European Court of Justice being instituted by the Commission against the UK. The court has recently given its judgment on the issue (Case C-300/95). It concluded that there was nothing to suggest that the UK courts, in interpreting s 4(1)(e), would not be able to achieve the result the Directive had in mind. Of probably greater interest, however, is what the court stated after acknowledging that the state of scientific and technical knowledge included 'the most advanced level of such knowledge':

> ... in order for the relevant scientific and technical knowledge to be successfully pleaded as against the producer, that knowledge must have been accessible at the time when the product in question was put into circulation.

The court conceded that this was bound to give rise to difficulties in the interpretation of Art 7(e) which would need to be resolved in future litigation, the national courts having recourse if necessary to Art 177 of the EC Treaty. Nonetheless, it is now clear that the Art 7(e) defence is more easily satisfied than its wording suggests. Since it is necessary to ask whether the relevant knowledge existed and was accessible, the mere fact that someone, somewhere, had the knowledge is not enough to prevent reliance on the defence.

Following the unsuccessful enforcement proceedings referred to (see *Commission v UK* (1997) *The Times*, 23 June), it would appear that the Government's interpretation of the defence, as defined in 1987 Act, was correct. The upshot is, as a prescient article by Christopher Newdick suggested at the time, that the regime of strict liability under the Act amounts to little more than a codification of the standard of care in negligence, albeit with the burden of proof reversed (see Newdick, C, 'The development risk defence of the Consumer Protection Act 1987' (1988) 47 CLJ 455). An additional problem, which may well confront claimants for drug injuries, is establishing that the product is defective in the first place. This is because many drugs have the propensity, while benefiting the vast majority of users, to produce 'idiosyncratic' reactions in a minority. Even where the potential existence of such reactions in a few persons (though not their identity) is suspected in advance – and comprises serious injury or even death – it may be that s 3 permits such trade-offs to take place. This is because the safety of the product must only be that which 'persons generally' are entitled to expect (in this respect, it may be queried once again whether the Act embodies the intent of the EC Directive which refers (in Art 6) to the expectations of 'a person').

Finally, the payment of compensation under the Act remains contingent upon causation being shown between the taking of the drug and injury. Given the frequently opaque nature of causal processes in this area (with plausible causal chains between phenomena often hard to find) it scarcely needs to be said that this remains a serious obstacle for many claimants. This is especially so in respect of idiosyncratic reactions to a drug on the part of a small minority of users where, *ex hypothesi*, the degree of regularity between cause (ingesting the drug) and effect (injury) which generally ground causal inferences will be absent. In two cases brought in negligence at common law, the courts indeed held that the plaintiffs had failed to show that the drugs they were given (an overdose of penicillin and the pertussis vaccine, respectively) were even capable of causing their injuries: see *Kay v Ayrshire and Arran Health Board* [1987] 2 All ER 417 and *Loveday v Renton* [1990] 1 Med LR 117. (Interestingly, with regard to the latter case, compensation has nevertheless been paid to the same claimants by the statutory tribunal established by the Vaccine Damage Payments Act 1976: see further below, Chapter 10.)

REFORMING THE LAW

Problems with the medical litigation system

Medical negligence cases are often very expensive to bring, because of the technical and complex nature of the litigation. Moreover, statistically, far fewer such claims succeed – 17% – than the average for negligence actions generally (around 80%). Nevertheless, this has not prevented a major upsurge in such claims over the last 20 years or so, with the public generally appearing less deferential, more aware of their rights, and holding higher expectations of what can and should be achieved on their behalf.

The Woolf Report, July 1996, London: HMSO, looked critically at medical negligence litigation and found some major problems:

Lord Woolf MR, *Access to Justice: The Final Report to the Lord Chancellor on the Civil Justice System in England and Wales,* **1996, London: HMSO:**

Chapter 15: Medical Negligence

Reasons for looking at medical negligence

1   Why have I singled out medical negligence for the most intensive examination during Stage 2 of my Inquiry? (I am using the term 'medical negligence' in this report to refer to any litigation involving allegations of negligence in the delivery of health care, whether by doctors, nurses or other health professionals.) It may appear a surprising choice, because medical negligence cases have no special procedures or rules of court. They are a sub-species of professional negligence actions, and they also belong to what is numerically the largest category of cases proceeding to trial, personal injury. Neither of these is singled out for special attention.

2   The answer is that early in the Inquiry it became increasingly obvious that it was in the area of medical negligence that the civil justice system was failing most conspicuously to meet the needs of litigants in a number of respects:

(a) The disproportion between costs and damages in medical negligence is particularly excessive, especially in lower value cases.

(b) The delay in resolving claims is more often unacceptable.

(c) Unmeritorious cases are often pursued, and clear-cut claims defended, for too long.

(d) The success rate is lower than in other personal injury litigation.

(e) The suspicion between the parties is more intense and the lack of co-operation frequently greater than in many other areas of litigation.

3   The cost of medical negligence litigation is now so high that smaller claims can rarely be litigated because of the disproportionate cost. It is difficult for patients to pursue a claim of any value unless they are eligible for legal aid. In the Supreme Court Taxing Office survey ... 92% of successful parties in medical negligence cases were legally aided. An analysis by the Law Society of a survey by Action for Victims of Medical Accidents (AVMA) of 376 cases conducted by solicitors' firms on its specialist panel indicates that 90% of cases which reached the stage of litigation were legally aided. If these figures are representative of medical negligence litigation generally, then in the vast majority of cases both sides are funded from the public purse. Here the cause for concern is the amount of money spent by NHS trusts and other defendants on legal costs: money which would be much better devoted to compensating victims or, better still, to improving standards of care so that future mistakes are avoided.

4   The new system of case management by the courts which I proposed in my interim report could do much to reduce cost and delay in medical negligence, and to encourage a more co-operative approach, enabling cases to settle on appropriate terms at an earlier stage. In particular:

(a) Clearer statements of claim and fully pleaded defences should speed up the progress of cases by helping to establish a factual matrix and define the real issues at an earlier stage.

(b) Claimants' offers will encourage earlier settlements on realistic terms.

(c) Extended summary judgment may help to weed out weak claims or defences at an earlier stage.

(d) Improved training and greater specialisation should help judges to identify weak cases, narrow and determine issues and limit the scope of evidence.

(e) More use of split trials will limit unnecessary work on quantum of damages in cases where liability is in issue (although this should not inhibit early work on quantum in cases where a valuation of the claim is possible).

Greater emphasis on early definition of issues between experts should encourage a more co-operative approach and reduce cost and delay.

5   The difficulty of proving both causation and negligence, which arises more acutely in medical negligence than in other personal injury cases, accounts for much of the excessive cost. The root of the problem, however, lies less in the complexity of the law or procedure than in the climate of mutual suspicion and defensiveness which is still all too prevalent in this area of litigation. Patients feel let down when treatment goes wrong,

sometimes because of unrealistic expectations as to what could be achieved. Doctors feel they are under attack from aggrieved patients and react defensively. The patients' disappointment is then heightened by what they perceive to be a refusal to acknowledge fault and an attempt to cover up.

6   Case management alone cannot provide the answer to this. A key requirement for achieving the necessary change is designing procedures for handling these cases, both at the pre-litigation stage and by the courts, so that a more co-operative and conciliatory approach to dispute resolution is achieved.

... blueprint for reform

16   A system for resolving disputes about medical treatment must be designed to meet the needs of doctors and other health professionals as well as patients. It should not be designed to suit the interests or convenience of lawyers, except in so far as this is necessary to ensure that the work is done properly.

17   Many people involved in medical negligence litigation have justifiably pointed out to me the importance of establishing at the outset what an injured patient wants. Proceedings often start because the claimant cannot get the information he is seeking, or an explanation or apology, from the doctor or hospital. Historically, solicitors have had no alternative but to advise legal action, which is unlikely to be appropriate in all cases unless the client's main or only objective is to obtain financial compensation.

18   Patients' needs and wishes may not be the same in all cases, and are not always compatible with those of health professionals. An obvious point is that both sides want to win, and for some individuals this may override considerations of speed, economy, or even fairness. Some patients want financial compensation, but they may also want to prevent a repetition of the mistreatment or misdiagnosis which occurred, or to get an apology or explanation for what went wrong. Sometimes, especially in cases where the physical injury was less serious, these non-monetary factors are the most important. Whatever form of redress they are seeking, most patients probably want:

(a)   impartial information and advice, including an independent medical assessment;

(b)   fair compensation for losses suffered;

(c)   a limited financial commitment;

(d)   a speedy resolution of the dispute;

(e)   a fair and independent adjudication; and (sometimes) a day in court.

19   Doctors and other health care professionals agree with patients in wanting a speedy resolution of any disputes, but this is not always compatible with their understandable wish for a fair assessment of their conduct, with a right of comment and hearing. Doctors in particular also want:

(a)   a discreet, private adjudication, which some would prefer to be by a medical rather than a legal tribunal;

(b) an expert of their own or their solicitor's choice; and

(c) an economical system, which does not encourage NHS trusts to settle cases over their heads, regardless of liability.

... change of culture

21 The extent of patients' mistrust of doctors and other hospital staff is illustrated by the submission I have received from Action for Victims of Medical Accidents (AVMA). They argue that the real reason for defendants' reluctance to investigate complaints where there is a possibility of legal action is a concern that such an investigation might indeed disclose negligence:

> [The defendants] do not in fact want a relatively simple and cheap way of investigating a complaint which might expose that there has been negligence.

22 If that mistrust is to be removed, the medical profession and the NHS administration must demonstrate their commitment to patients' well being by adopting a constructive approach to claims handling. It must be clearly accepted that injured patients are entitled to redress, and that professional solidarity or individual self-esteem are not sufficient reasons for resisting or obstructing valid claims.

23 Patients and their representatives, for their part, must recognise that some degree of risk is inherent in all medical treatment, and that even the best practitioners do sometimes make mistakes. They should not pursue unrealistic claims, and should make every effort to resolve disputes without recourse to litigation.

24 It is fundamental to my approach to civil litigation in general that legal proceedings should be treated as a last resort, to be used only when other means of resolving a dispute are inappropriate or have failed. When someone has a potential negligence claim against a doctor or hospital, the first essential step is to find out what the patient wants to achieve. If his or her main need is for substantial financial compensation to cover future loss of earnings or the cost of continuing care, then litigation may be (but is not always) the best way to proceed. If the patient is chiefly concerned to get an explanation or apology for what went wrong, or to ensure that procedures are changed so that future accidents can be avoided, then litigation is less likely to be the best course. Recourse to the NHS complaints procedures and, if necessary, the Health Service Ombudsman, may offer a more appropriate means of redress.

...

28 ... Effective communication ... needs to start before things go wrong. All patients who are about to undergo treatment should understand that the outcome of medical treatment can be uncertain, and should be told about the range of possible outcomes in their particular case. Wherever practicable, the advice should be confirmed in writing. Doctors and hospitals should encourage patients to report any unsatisfactory outcome as soon as possible, and to seek an explanation direct from the individual doctor or hospital before going to a solicitor.

29 Every patient who has suffered an adverse outcome is entitled to an explanation, and, where appropriate, an apology. In appropriate cases, there is no reason why an offer of compensation should not be made before any legal claim is notified, provided the patient is encouraged to seek independent advice on the offer. I understand that some hospitals offer to pay for such advice, to ensure that patients are not deterred from seeking it through fear of the cost.

The Woolf reforms, along with the reduction proposed by the Lord Chancellor in civil legal aid (though for the time being medical negligence cases will remain exempt), have attracted a great deal of controversy. However, it is generally accepted that reform to medical negligence litigation is inevitable. The possibility, adverted to by Lord Woolf of greater use of mediation, as an alternative to recourse to the courts, is indeed already being piloted in a number of regions:

Lovell, J, 'Mediation for clinical negligence cases' (1995) 1(8) Health Care Risk Report 1:

I write as a member of the Department of Health's mediation working party and leader of a pilot mediation scheme in Yorkshire for clinical negligence cases. The scheme is running in parallel with a pilot in the Anglia and Oxford region and is expected to run for a period of two years.

It is likely that up to 16 cases will be taken to mediation in Yorkshire under the pilot. It is considered appropriate, at least initially, to focus on baby bereavement cases and those cases where it is considered that there is some chance of success at trial, where discovery and exchange of witness statements and experts' reports have been completed and where there are significant costs to be saved by avoiding trial.

The mediator functions rather like a shuttle diplomat seeking common ground and probing in private the true intent and 'bottom line' of each party. Nothing said to the mediator in these private discussions can be passed on by the mediator to the other side, save with the consent of the party speaking to the mediator in confidence. By probing the strengths and weaknesses of each side, the mediator can facilitate settlement or, failing resolution, can help to narrow the issues in dispute.

In practice, a party can be surprised at how little his opposing party will settle for, following intervention by a mediator. On the other hand, where a party has a strong case, the strength of the evidence can be brought to the attention of the other side at an early stage, prompting withdrawal.

Of course, if settlement can be effected there are substantial costs and expenses to be saved, particularly if claims have the benefit of legal aid support.

Other advantages include the fact that mediation can serve as a safety valve 'day in court' exercise, giving the claimant an opportunity for all his concerns to be expressed to hospital representatives. It can also provide an early opportunity for patients' care needs to be reviewed and addressed in a positive light.

The principal advantage of mediation, however, is that it is a win/win situation, unlike arbitration or court litigation. This is because no resolution can be reached save by the consent of the parties and the mediator's decision is not binding. All discussions are without prejudice and either party can walk away at any stage.

On the other hand, there are caveats. There remains the risk that inappropriate use of mediation could increase the number of claims lodged against the health service. Also, the use of mediation may discourage the commissioning or use of appropriate expert advice, which is, of course, the key to all professional negligence actions. Furthermore, any mandatory mediation could lead to pressure to settle in respect of cases which should be fought in the interests of the health service as a whole.

One fear that has been expressed is that some parties, particularly those with legal aid support, may enter into mediation with no intention of settling and only to be better armed for trial. Such an objective should be quickly evident from questions put and questions unanswered in the mediation and of course, the other side can simply withdraw.

Views differ as to who should be present at mediations. One view is that the presence of experts cuts across the mediation process and positively inhibits settlement. Another view is that their presence is helpful, and another option is to appoint a single expert with the agreement of both sides to help by performing an independent advisory role.

Of fundamental importance is the presence of an individual who has the authority to agree a settlement on behalf of the party concerned. Also, the presence of the consultant involved in the matter may help in many cases to facilitate the 'day in court' satisfaction for an aggrieved party.

To consider mediation as an option is currently fashionable. Lawyers will be aware of the Practice Direction dated January 1995 relating to High Court cases, which provides that in the absence of specific directions to the contrary, solicitors for each party must lodge with the listing officer a completed checklist at least two months before trial which includes questions along the following lines:

- Has alternative dispute resolution been discussed with the client to resolve the dispute or particular issues?
- Might alternative dispute resolution resolve or narrow the issues?
- Has alternative dispute resolution been explored with other parties to resolve or narrow the issues?

The outcome of the pilot schemes and the evaluation are awaited with interest. Currently, I support mediation, given due professionalism, with particular regard to preparation for the mediation day and careful choice of case.

Moving to a 'no fault' system?

A more radical solution, which has been proposed by some commentators, is that we should move away from common law altogether towards a statutory 'no fault'-based system of liability for medical negligence. However, though the present adversarial system certainly has its share of faults, a number of its benefits should not be overlooked. Published medical negligence cases provide an educational function to both the public and the medical and other health care professions. Moreover, the adversarial court system may also act as a deterrent to bad practice. Whilst health care professionals have their own statutory professional bodies (including, for doctors, the General Medical Council (GMC), and the United Kingdom Central Council for nursing, midwifery, and health visiting), which can discipline and regulate their members (see Chapter 2), the courts remain the ultimate channel of accountability. The courts are very public, and that fact alone makes it the final and the most effective mechanism of health provider accountability.

Adrian Desmond, a solicitor working in the field, sets out the main arguments for and against introducing no fault compensation as follows:

Desmond, A, 'No fault compensation' (1996) 2(9) Health Care Risk Report 1

The May 1996 edition of the Consumers' Association magazine, *Which?*, includes a report on medical negligence. The Consumers' Association believes that the present system of redress for medical accidents would be improved by the introduction of a no fault compensation scheme. The policy statement will bring a wry smile to the faces of many solicitors, plaintiff and defendant, who specialise in medical negligence work. Little has changed since Rosie Barnes' private member's Bill (which sought to introduce no fault compensation in the UK) failed in 1991 in the face of government opposition. Is the Consumers' Association tilting at windmills and advocating a system that would harm the interests of patients and doctors alike? Surely the answer is 'yes'.

The arguments in support of a no fault system are attractive, but emotive. The State has assumed responsibility for providing a health care system. With that responsibility should come an obligation to compensate victims of failures in that system. Such a scheme should, however, only be implemented first, if a genuine and priority need had been identified, secondly, if such a system addressed that need and thirdly, if the proposal was practicable.

What need has been established? It is generally accepted that only a tiny proportion of victims of medical accidents obtain financial redress. One reason for that might be a conviction that suing medical staff who are doing their best, with resources that are often inadequate, is not always appropriate when a mistake is made. Leaving aside cases of profound injury, often individuals are motivated more by anger (for example, in the face of high handedness or deceit) than by a pressing need for compensation.

According to the Consumers' Association, there are around 30,000 reported accidents a year, most of which go uncompensated. Many more accidents must go unreported. Is it a health care priority for the nation to ensure that all of those accident victims receive financial compensation? Would the payment of compensation alone properly address the State's responsibilities?

Medical negligence litigation costs the UK about £200 million per annum in damages and costs. The argument is that savings on legal costs would help fund a no fault scheme, but even if all of that sum could be distributed to the 30,000 known accident victims each year, the average payment would be just

£6,667. That compares with Legal Aid Board figures suggesting that average damages in legally aided medical negligence cases which closed in 1993–94 were £25,000, although that included a tiny minority of cases resulting in damages of more than £50,000. If that average £25,000 was multiplied by the 30,000 reported accidents, the cost would amount to £750 million. That does not take into account the inevitably greater number of accidents which would be reported, nor the likely cost of the scheme.

The cost of such a scheme would probably mean that payments to victims would have to be capped and would not bear a proper relationship to compensation currently awarded by the courts. How fair would such a system of distribution seem? How would the existing tort system be affected, and would it remain in force for that minority of catastrophic cases where a capped payment would not be appropriate? If so, again, where are the savings?

Then there is the issue of causation. The patient would still have to prove that their injury results from negligence rather than a pre-existing or other condition or a recognised complication. Applicants would still need legal and medical assistance to do so. Where again are the savings?

No fault compensation schemes do not encourage analysis and prevention of accidents, nor do they provide for disciplinary steps against negligent staff, all of which can be important to the victim.

It is argued that such a scheme would compensate victims more quickly than the present system, but experience of the length of investigative time taken by the Criminal Injuries Compensation Board and the NHS Ombudsman suggests otherwise.

It is surprising that the no fault debate should recur now when there is greater optimism than ever that the ills of the current system can effectively be addressed by innovations such as specialist solicitors' panels, the Access to Health Records Act 1990, protocols relating to the recovery of medical records, the introduction of conditional fee arrangements, the new complaints system, initiatives such as mediation in medical negligence and the thorough overhaul of the civil justice system undertaken by Lord Woolf.

The New Zealand experience of no fault compensation is sometimes cited as a way forward for the UK. However, on close examination, significant problems in the implementation of such schemes reveal themselves. As Ken Oliphant notes:

Oliphant, K, 'Defining "medical misadventures" – lessons from New Zealand' (1996) 4 Med L Rev 1:

The New Zealand experience of no fault compensation for medical accidents provides cause for alarm for tort law reformers in the UK. New Zealand's Accident Compensation Scheme encompasses claims arising out of accidental injuries of all sorts, not just those which can be attributable to 'medical misadventure'. The latter, in fact, represent only a tiny fraction of the scheme's case-load, yet they have given rise to difficulties disproportionate to their frequency. These difficulties raise doubts as to the practicality of developing and maintaining a scheme of no fault compensation that deals exclusively with medical accidents, as some have urged for the UK. Had compensation for 'medical misadventure' in New Zealand been free standing – had it not been possible to draw on the credit earned by the successes of the Accident Compensation Scheme as a whole – then it is no exaggeration to suggest that the no fault experiment in that country might have failed.

This is not to say that ideas of a no fault compensation scheme for medical accidents should be consigned to the scrap heap. It may be possible to learn from the New Zealand experience and thereby to avoid certain of the difficulties that have afflicted the operation of the 'medical misadventure' provisions of that country's Accident Compensation Scheme. But no fault reformers will have to pay more attention to the definition of the core concept of 'medical accident' or 'medical misadventure' than they have hitherto. To date, there has been a wholly unwarranted complacency on this matter, most notably in two recent private members' Bills which sought to introduce no fault compensation for medical accidents. As Margaret Brazier comments, 'both Bills were flawed. Neither proposal adequately tackled the task of defining medical accident, and so patient eligibility for compensation' ... Absent a clearly defined set of qualifying conditions, it will be impossible to adhere to the sound accounting practices which are essential to the scheme's long term survival.

The need for clarity and precision on this matter is intensified by the special problems of causal attribution raised by the concept of 'medical misadventure'. The patient who suffers an adverse outcome of medical treatment has undergone that treatment for a reason: as a result of disease or personal injury, perhaps, or of some other condition such as pregnancy. The outcome of treatment may be viewed as adverse in that a pre-existing condition has been allowed to run its course, or in that the treatment has had certain harmful effects of its own. In both types of case, the question arises: on what basis is the adverse outcome to be attributed to 'medical misadventure' rather than to the pre-existing condition? Where tort law can rely upon the notion of 'fault', and the New Zealand Accident Compensation Scheme – by and large – on that of 'accident', those who advocate a no fault compensation scheme for 'medical misadventure' cannot draw upon common parlance and generally accepted standards to determine the boundaries of their proposed scheme. Yet these boundaries must be clearly drawn, lest the scheme be inundated, and overwhelmed, by claims more properly analysed as flowing from disease, personal injury by accident, and so on.

As these last two extracts suggest, the difficulties for the plaintiff associated with proving causation will in any event remain, and his ability to overcome them will determine whether he comes within the no fault scheme at all. Moreover, it may well be asked just what the moral basis of such a scheme is supposed to be. Once we abandon the restorative principle associated, however imperfectly, with the tort system (the idea that it is right for the injurer to compensate his victim), why pay out only to those injured by 'misadventure' rather than to everyone who becomes ill according to need? At any event, it seems unlikely that 'no fault' compensation for medical negligence will be adopted in the UK in the foreseeable future.

PART TWO

CHAPTER SEVEN

ASSISTED REPRODUCTION

INTRODUCTION

In the last 20 or so years, medical science has made significant strides in an area previously considered 'off limits', that of human reproduction. The law, in attempting to regulate these developments, has had to balance many competing interests and viewpoints in an area of particular ethical sensitivity. Four years after the birth, in Britain, of the world's first 'test tube baby', the Government established a Committee of Inquiry led by the moral philosopher, Dame Mary Warnock, to recommend an appropriate legislative response. The Warnock Committee, which reported in 1984, was well aware of the unprecedented and controversial nature of its remit:

Warnock Committee, *Report of the Committee of Inquiry into Human Fertilisation and Embryology,* **Cmnd 9314, 1984, London: HMSO (the Warnock Report):**

1.1 The birth of the first child resulting from the technique of *in vitro* fertilisation in July 1978 was a considerable achievement. The technique, long sought, at last successful, opened up new horizons in the alleviation of infertility and in the science of embryology. It was now possible to observe the very earliest stages of human development, and with these discoveries came the hope of remedying defects at this very early stage. However, there were also anxieties. There was a sense that events were moving too fast for their implications to be assimilated. Society's views on the new techniques were divided between pride in the technological achievement, pleasure at the new-found means to relieve, at least for some, the unhappiness of infertility, and unease at the apparently uncontrolled advance of science, bringing with it new possibilities for manipulating the early stages of human development.

1.2 Against this background of public excitement and concern, this Inquiry was established in July 1982, with the following terms of reference:

> To consider recent and potential developments in medicine and science related to human fertilisation and embryology; to consider what policies and safeguards should be applied, including consideration of the social, ethical and legal implications of these developments; and to make recommendations.

In the introduction to her 1985 book, *A Question of Life* (incorporating the report), Mary Warnock noted the stormy reception accorded to the report, and a key problem faced by the Committee:

Warnock, M, *A Question of Life,* **1985, Oxford: Blackwells, p viii:**

The Times, on 15 December 1984, carried a dramatic headline. It read 'Warnock: Ethics Undermined'. What followed was a denunciation of the Report of the Committee of Inquiry into Human Embryology ascribed to the Chief Rabbi which was, in fact, moderate in tone compared with some of the abuse to which members of the Inquiry had been, and are still, subjected both collectively and individually, since the publication of our report in July 1984. None of the members of the Inquiry had any doubt that they were concerned with moral issues. But we were not perhaps all of us certain how such issues ought to be approached, and especially how they should be approached by a body set up by Parliament to make recommendations which might lead to legislation. Many of our critics (including, I believe, the Chief Rabbi) have not really addressed themselves to this problem either: the problem of legislation, and its relation to morality, in such controversial fields.

The question of how far, and in what manner, legal regulation of human procreation should occur is undoubtedly one of great complexity. In what follows we shall first consider the principal parties whose interests stand to be affected, before looking at broader considerations which bear upon the issue.

The key interests at stake

Potential parents

People who wish to be parents and would otherwise be infertile are the most obvious beneficiaries of infertility treatment. As the Warnock Committee commented:

Warnock Committee, *Report of the Committee of Inquiry into Human Fertilisation and Embryology,* **Cmnd 9314, 1984, London: HMSO:**

2.1 In the past, there was considerable public ignorance of the causes and extent of infertility, as well as ignorance of possible remedies. At one time, if a couple were childless, there was very little they could do about it. Generally the cause of infertility was thought to be something in the woman which made her childless; only occasionally was it thought that there might be something wrong with the man. Even today, there is very little factual information about the prevalence of infertility. A commonly quoted figure is that one couple in 10 is childless, but accurate statistics are not available, nor is it known what proportion of this figure relates to couples who choose not to have children. In certain religious and cultural traditions, infertility was, and still is, considered sufficient grounds for divorce. In our own society, childless couples used to be advised to adopt a child. Now, as a result of improved contraception, the wider availability of legal abortion and changed attitudes towards the single mother, far fewer babies are placed for adoption.

2.2 Childlessness can be a source of stress even to those who have deliberately chosen it. Family and friends often expect a couple to start a family, and express their expectations, either openly or by implication. The family is a valued institution within our present society: within it the human infant receives nurture and protection during its prolonged period of dependence. It is also the place where social behaviour is learnt and where the child develops its own identity and feeling of self-value. Parents likewise feel their identity in society enhanced and confirmed by their role in the family unit. For those who long for children, the realisation that they are unable to found a family can be shattering. It can disrupt their picture of the whole of their future lives. They may feel that they will be unable to fulfil their own and other people's expectations. They may feel themselves excluded from a whole range of human activity and particularly the activities of their child-rearing contemporaries. In addition to social pressures to have children there is, for many, a powerful urge to perpetuate their genes through a new generation. This desire cannot be assuaged by adoption.

Gamete providers/surrogates

The success of many infertility treatments depends upon the use of gametes (sperm and eggs) and embryos or, in the case of surrogacy, gestational capacity, provided by third parties, ie, persons who, it is envisaged, will not subsequently be responsible for rearing the children born as a result of treatment. A key problem for the law in such cases is to determine how best to regulate the involvement of such third parties. Should such third parties (who are the genetic or gestational parents) receive money in return for their services? Should they be screened? How should they be counselled? In addition, in so far as a child results, what sort of claims should it have on such third parties? Should the latter be protected, for example, by absolute anonymity?

Potential children

The answers we give to these last questions clearly have a direct impact on the interests of children who result from infertility treatment involving third party providers. For example, giving gamete providers anonymity will be to deny the child's interest in knowing who one (at least) of its genetic or gestational parents is. In other cases, there may be a conflict between the interests of the potential child and its potential rearing parent(s). A more recent inquiry into reproductive technologies, led by the moral philosopher, Jonathan Glover, and sponsored by the European Commission, commented as follows:

> **Glover, J et al, Report to the European Commission on Reproductive Technologies, Fertility and the Family, 1989, London: Fourth Estate (the Glover Report), p 48:**
>
> The children are those most deeply affected. Their family circumstances may be unusually complicated: like adopted children, they may have to get used to

the fact that at least one of their social parents is not their biological parent. Much more importantly, their very existence results from reproductive help. If they are glad to be alive, they are perhaps the greatest beneficiaries. They are the people who have no say at the time the decisions are taken, and their needs and interests have to be given great weight. Their central need is for a certain kind of home and family ...

Embryos

So far we have been assuming that a child is born following treatment. The position is complicated when we introduce the human embryo (as a separate entity) into the equation. The procedure of IVF, in particular, involves the manipulation of the early human embryo. To work effectively, the procedure habitually requires the creation of more embryos than can ever be implanted in the uterus of the woman receiving treatment. There is therefore the question of what to do with such 'spare' embryos; must we simply let them perish? This in itself may be seen as a bad thing. Alternatively should we store them (there are techniques available for freezing both male sperm and early embryos) and, if so, for how long? Alternatively, is it permissible to use them for research purposes? Indeed, is there any reason not to employ IVF technology specifically to create embryos for research?

These last questions are hugely contentious because they turn partly on a debate of a metaphysical character, viz, do early embryos have any interests in the first place? We shall return to this question below, pp 362 *et seq*.

The response of the law

In the light of the interests and putative interests just outlined, how should the law respond? In a liberal democratic state, such as the UK, the autonomous activity of individual citizens, each pursuing their own ends, is regarded as of central importance, and this gives rise to a strong presumption in favour of respecting procreative liberty. In *A Question of Life* Mary Warnock had the following to say about the extent to which the law may intrude into the area of assisted reproduction:

> **Warnock, M, *A Question of Life*, 1985, Oxford: Blackwells, pp x–xii:**
>
> The relation between morality and the law has been a central issue in jurisprudence for very many years ... If the question is what measures to remedy infertility should be permitted in this country, the problem may be put in the following form: why should the law intervene to prevent people using whatever methods are possible to enable them to have children? Why should not everybody be entitled to whatever is currently the best and most efficient treatment for infertility? The issues here are quite closely parallel to the issues raised in the 1960s by the Wolfenden Report on homosexuality between consenting males. Ought the law to intervene to make such conduct criminal

or ought it not? The famous view of Lord Devlin (*The Enforcement of Morals*, 1959) was that where there is a consensus of opinion against a certain practice among members of the general public (exemplified by the notorious 'man on the Clapham omnibus') then the law must intervene to prevent conduct which is repellent to that public. A shared moral view, Lord Devlin argued, was the cement that bound society together. If such shared views were not reflected in law, if law did not enforce what society held to be morally right and wrong, then society itself would disintegrate. A society is characterised by a shared moral view; without it there would be no society. Therefore to act against such a shared view would be tantamount to treason. The law could no more permit acts contrary to the shared morality than it could permit treason.

The drawback with Devlin's view is that, increasingly, we are compelled to accept that 'common morality' is a myth. There is no agreed set of principles which everyone, or the majority, or any representative person, believes to be absolutely binding, and especially is this so in areas of moral concern which are radically and genuinely new. We saw that the concept of a 'rule' breaks down, in novel and hitherto unthought-of cases, and the notion that there is a consensus morality in such cases is equally untenable. The question must be recast: In situations where people disagree with each other as to the rights and wrongs of a specific form of behaviour, how do we decide whether or not the law is to intervene?

HLA Hart (*Law, Liberty and Morality*, 1963) identified two moral problems, one 'primary' and the other 'critical'. At the first level the question is whether a certain practice (homosexual acts between consenting males, or AID) is morally right or wrong; at the second level the question is whether, if the law intervened on this matter, the infringement of liberty involved would itself be morally right or wrong. If we consider a case that concerned the Inquiry, the case of AID, it is plain that moral opinions about it vary through the whole spectrum, from those who think it absolutely wrong (like members of the Jewish community, who think that it is 'bringing orphans into the world', and therefore necessarily wrong) through those who are doubtful, because of the possible risks to AID children, to those who regard it as an absolute right that anyone should have access to AID, whether they are married or single, hetero- or homosexual.

Furthermore, any law enacted to render AID a criminal offence, besides going against the moral views of a fair number of the community, would involve, in itself, a disagreeable intrusiveness, for AID is something that can relatively easily be carried out at home, without any medical intervention. For a law to be enforceable, there would need to be a band of snoopers or people ready to pry into the private lives of others, which might well itself constitute a moral wrong ...

The Human Fertilisation and Embryology Act Scheme

In 1990, Parliament enacted the Human Fertilisation and Embryology Act (HFEA). The Act followed many of the recommendations of the Warnock Report; perhaps most importantly, it accepted the need to establish a statutory regulatory authority to oversee continuing developments in this area. Some barriers in the form of absolute prohibitions – backed by criminal sanctions – were established. However, the Act is more notable for its flexibility and its willingness to entrust the new regulatory authority, the Human Fertilisation and Embryology Authority, with large amounts of discretion. Jonathan Montgomery, in assessing the impact of the 1990 Act and the tasks entrusted to the new Authority, has noted the way in which 'pragmatism' rather than 'principle' seems to have been the driving force behind the new legal regime:

Montgomery, J, 'Rights, restraints and pragmatism' (1991) 54 MLR 524:

The nature of the forum in which the debates about infertility treatment and embryo research are to be carried out is structured by a complex web of discretion, restraints control and accountability. The Human Fertilisation and Embryology Authority is to be given powers to oversee the activities of individual health practitioners, and will not be limited to applying standards established by parliament or government. It will be able, indeed required, to develop its own standards of what is acceptable and proper. The authority will thus have considerable autonomy. It will not be left entirely to its own devices, however, and a series of checks will exist to supervise the exercise of its power ...

Having conferred this considerable flexibility upon the licensing authority, the Government has also reserved a number of powers to reduce it. The boundaries of the power to license may be contracted and expanded by regulations. By requiring annual reports to the Secretary of State, detailing both past activities and those projected for the following 12 months, the Act seeks to ensure that the Authority's practice can be monitored (s 7). The reports are to be laid before parliament by the minister. Nevertheless, pending the exercise of the power to make regulations, considerable trust is placed in the members of the Authority.

The Act permits the Authority to exercise a high degree of control over practitioners. In addition to the power to grant or withhold licences, the Authority will be able to issue mandatory directions (ss 23 and 24). Failure to comply with these directions will sometimes constitute an offence (s 41(2)), but will always empower the Authority to revoke a licence (s 18(1)(c)). Secondly, a code of practice is to be drawn up to provide guidance as to the proper conduct of licensees. This is less coercive than the power to give directions in that disobedience will not in itself constitute an offence, but it may be taken into account by the Authority when considering revocation (s 25).

In practice, this will make it difficult for practitioners to resist the power of the Authority to make policy on controversial matters ... This will represent a considerable inroad into such people's clinical autonomy ...

... The final issue in relation to the Authority concerns its membership. Very different conclusions could be drawn about the framework which the Act establishes depending on the composition of the licensing body. On one model the purpose of the Authority might be to provide a forum for the resolution of the fundamental ethical disagreements. In this case one would expect the membership to reflect a range of views. This would leave fundamental issues open and make the creation of the Authority an exercise in democratic accountability. Such an authority would be intended to provide a forum for informed discussion and compromise. On the other hand, the aim of the selection process might be to facilitate the collective exercise of responsibility by the medical profession. This would be the model provided by the voluntary Licensing Authority set up by the profession following the Warnock Report. It would make the involvement of non-doctors a way of informing the profession of the views of the public rather than an exercise in external scrutiny. A glance at the membership list seems to reveal that the latter model is the more accurate.

The statute ensures that between one-third and half of the members will be drawn from medical professions and interested researchers ... Some 'non-professionals' will also be on the Authority: a television producer, a well known actress, and a senior bank official. There will be a nearly exact equal representation of the sexes.

In summary, the Human Fertilisation and Embryology Authority has been entrusted with considerable powers to determine what embryo research and infertility treatment will be carried out. A system of checks and balances has been created which will allow for the Authority to be accountable to parliament, but many of the normative principles to be applied will be established neither by the law nor by democratic discussion. In essence, the creation of the Authority is a pragmatic exercise in facilitating medical advances rather than a principled approach to the vindication of rights.

It is important to note that not all types of infertility treatment are regulated by the 1990 Act. In fact, to fall within the statutory licensing scheme, such treatment must either involve the creation of an embryo *ex vivo* (ie, outside the woman's body), or the use of genetic material which has been donated and/or stored: see ss 3 and 4 of the Act. The principal treatments that thus remain unlicensed are Artificial Insemination by Husband (AIH), provided that the woman is inseminated with sperm *freshly* obtained from her husband/partner; Gamete Intra-Fallopian Transfer (GIFT), in which fertilisation occurs *in vivo* and the product is then removed and placed directly in the woman's womb (to bypass blocked or damaged fallopian tubes); and the use of 'fertility drugs' to increase ovulation.

In the rest of this chapter, we shall be exploring in more detail the specific solutions adopted in relation to the key areas of licensed infertility treatment. We shall focus next upon IVF treatment involving the creation of an embryo *ex vivo*. Although IVF obviously has wide potential applications (it may be used in conjunction with forms of collaborative reproduction involving donated gametes and surrogacy), at this stage the assumption will be that the recipient couple are also the gamete providers. We will then address the additional complexities that arise when third party gamete providers are introduced into the picture by procedures such as Artificial Insemination by Donor (AID – often also termed 'DI') and egg donation. Here, the law must regulate not only the conditions subject to which donation occurs, but provide for the legitimacy of any resultant children. Finally, we look at one area where such third party involvement in reproduction has aroused particular controversy, namely surrogacy.

IN VITRO FERTILISATION

Background

In its report, the Warnock Committee explained the process of *in vitro* fertilisation (IVF) in the following terms:

> **Warnock Committee,** *Report of the Committee of Inquiry into Human Fertilisation and Embryology,* **Cmnd 9314, 1984, London: HMSO:**
>
> 5.2 The concept of IVF is simple. A ripe human egg is extracted from the ovary, shortly before it would have been released naturally. Next, the egg is mixed with the semen of the husband or partner, so that fertilisation can occur. The fertilised egg, once it has started to divide, is then transferred back to the mother's uterus. In practice the technique for recovery of the eggs, their culture outside the mother's body, and the transfer of the developing embryo to the uterus has to be carried out under very carefully controlled conditions. The development of laparoscopic techniques during the 1960s made the collection of the egg, in cases where the ovaries were accessible, relatively easy. (Another technique for egg recovery based on ultrasound identification has now been developed.) It was not particularly difficult to fertilise the human egg *in vitro*. The real difficulty related to the implantation of the embryo in the uterus after transfer. A pregnancy achieved in this way must not only survive the normal hazards of implantation of *in vivo* conception, but also the additional problems of IVF and embryo transfer. More is now known about how best to replicate the natural sequence of events, but undoubtedly achieving a successful implantation is still the most uncertain part of the procedure.

Pursuant to s 3(1) of the HFEA 1990, IVF is a treatment which may only be carried out under licence from the HFE Authority:

> **3   Prohibitions in connection with embryos**
>
> (1) No person shall–
>
> > (a) bring about the creation of an embryo; or
> >
> > (b) keep or use an embryo, except in pursuance of a licence.

The conditions that the Authority may attach to such a licence are elaborated upon in Sched 2, para 1 of the Act:

> **Schedule 2**
>
> **Activities for which licences may be granted**
>
> **Licences for treatment**
>
> > (1) A licence under this paragraph may authorise any of the following in the course of providing treatment services–

(a) bringing about the creation of embryos *in vitro*;

(b) keeping embryos;

(c) using gametes;

(d) practices designed to secure that embryos are in a suitable condition to be placed in a woman or to determine whether embryos are suitable for that purpose;

(e) placing any embryo in a woman;

(f) mixing sperm with the egg of a hamster, or other animal specified in directions, for the purpose of testing the fertility or normality of the sperm, but only where anything which forms is destroyed when the test is complete and, in any event, not later than the two cell stage; and

(g) such other practices as may be specified in, or determined in accordance with, regulations.

(2) Subject to the provisions of this Act, a licence under this paragraph may be granted subject to such conditions as may be specified in the licence and may authorise the performance of any of the activities referred to in sub-para (1) above in such manner as may be so specified.

(3) A licence under this paragraph cannot authorise any activity unless it appears to the Authority to be necessary or desirable for the purpose of providing treatment services.

(4) A licence under this paragraph cannot authorise altering the genetic structure of any cell while it forms part of an embryo.

(5) A licence under this paragraph shall be granted for such period not exceeding five years as may be specified in the licence.

Broadly, there are, in relation to IVF treatment services, two principal matters that the 1990 legislation has been required to determine. First, what rights, in respect of obtaining treatment, receiving adequate information in relation to such treatment, and controlling the use/disposition of their gametes and any *ex vivo* embryos created with them, are enjoyed by a couple seeking parenthood by such means? Secondly, what is the legal status of genetic material deriving from them, including gametes and *ex vivo* embryos?

The potential parents

Access to treatment

In so far as a heterosexual couple seeks treatment with IVF, matters are left very much up to the discretion of individual fertility clinics acting pursuant to the Code of Practice promulgated by the HFE Authority. Where a couple are refused treatment, para 3.31 of the Code (2nd Revision, December 1995) makes it clear that reasons should be given.

There are two main reasons why treatment might be refused. First, the couple may be medically unsuitable. Secondly, and far more controversially, they may be deemed socially unsuitable as parents. In the latter case, the decision essentially turns on the potential welfare of any child born as a result of treatment. The Glover Report addressed the key arguments in this regard, as follows:

Glover, J et al, Report to the European Commission on Reproductive Technologies, Fertility and the Family, 1989, London: Fourth Estate, pp 48–50:

It is hard to know who will be a good or bad parent. But children need warmth and love. Some of the worst cases of cruelty to children would make any humane person wish that those parents stayed childless. It is surely unthinkable that anyone would have wished to help them have children. Of course we cannot easily predict such disasters. But, where there seems a risk, there is a strong reason not to help.

Some other cases are much more controversial. Is it a disadvantage for a child to grow up with only one parent? (This often happens through death or separation, but should it be seen as a situation we ought deliberately to bring about for a child?) Is it a disadvantage to be brought up by a lesbian couple rather than by a mother and father? What about parents with severe psychological problems, say where one parent is an alcoholic or a drug addict? What about parents who are severely mentally handicapped?

... But a distinction has to be drawn between two very different types of case. If it is a question of giving a child to people who will behave with horrifying cruelty, it may be 'a mercy if the child is not born'. On the other hand, perhaps a child with only one parent suffers some disadvantage relative to other children, but few such children would feel life was anywhere near so bad as to wish they had not been born.

A parallel can be drawn with handicap. Some handicaps are so terrible that death can seem a mercy, and it is possible to think it would have been better if the person had not been born. But many handicaps are mild or only moderately severe. No one would think that colour blindness made it better for someone not to have been born. No one would think it wrong to help a couple have a child who would be at risk of colour blindness.

Just as there are degrees of handicap, so there are degrees of social disadvantage, and having only one parent perhaps comes towards the mild end of the spectrum. In the case of mild or only moderately severe social disadvantage, it may be misleading to say there is a conflict of interest between the future child and its potential parents. If the disadvantage is only relative, and the child will come nowhere near regretting having been born, it is hard to see how it can be in the interests of the future child for the potential parents to be denied help.

Although, as Glover notes, it seems far fetched (save in the most extreme cases) to suppose that the interests of the child could dictate that it never exist at all, the 1990 Act clearly requires such an assessment to be made. Section 13(5) provides as follows:

13 (5) A woman shall not be provided with treatment services unless account has been taken of the welfare of any child who may be born as a result of the treatment (including the need of that child for a father), and of any other child who may be affected by the birth.

In so far as infertility treatment is denied to a heterosexual couple, what, if any, form of legal redress is available to them? In respect of IVF provided by an NHS funded clinic, a case predating the 1990 Act, that of *R v Ethical Committee of St Mary's Hospital (Manchester) ex p Harriott*, suggests that an action may lie in judicial review:

R v Ethical Committee of St Mary's Hospital (Manchester) ex p Harriott [1988] 1 FLR 512, HC (Schiemann J)

The applicant applied for judicial review after being refused IVF treatment as a result of advice given to her consultant by the hospital's ethical committee. The committee was unhappy with the fact that she and her husband had already been rejected as foster parents on the basis of her past convictions for offences relating to prostitution.

Schiemann J: The applicant wishes to have a child. Unfortunately she has difficulty in conceiving one. She has applied a number of times to Manchester City's social services department to be allowed to foster or adopt children. These applications have been uniformly unsuccessful, the authority taking the view that the applicant's criminal record (which includes allowing premises to be used as a brothel and soliciting for prostitution), and her allegedly poor understanding of the role of a foster parent and the social services department, precluded them from approving her applications.

Frustrated in her desire to foster and adopt and to conceive by normal means, the applicant wishes to be considered for *in vitro* fertilisation ... under the National Health Service. The Health Service – to use an imprecise term for the moment – decided to refuse to give her this treatment. In this application for judicial review she complains of that decision essentially alleging that it was reached by the wrong body: alternatively that she was not given an adequate opportunity to make representations to the decision maker before the decision was taken.

This, I believe, is the first occasion when a decision to refuse treatment for an illness – and for present purposes infertility may be regarded as an illness – has been the subject of an application for judicial review. The respondents submit that the courts will not investigate the reasons behind a decision by the Health Service to refuse treatment nor, submit the respondents, will the courts investigate the procedures which have been followed in the decision making process. It will be obvious that this case potentially raises issues of the widest social and legal significance ...

Mr Bell, for the committee, submitted that judicial review does not lie to review any advice given by the committee. As at present advised, I would be doubtful about accepting that submission in its full breadth. If the committee had advised, for instance, that the IVF unit should in principle refuse all such treatment to anyone who was a Jew or coloured, then I think the courts might well grant a declaration that such a policy was illegal: see in this context, *R v Takeover Panel ex p Datafin plc* [1977] 2 WLR 699 in the Court of Appeal and *Gillick v W Norfolk and Wisbech Area HA and Another* [1986] 1 FLR 224 in the House of Lords. But I do not need to consider that situation in this case. Here the complaint is that the committee's advice was that the consultant must make up her own mind as to whether the treatment should be given. That advice was, in my judgment, unobjectionable.

So far as private clinics are concerned, a couple who could prove that the refusal of treatment for them stemmed from a blanket policy of the sort alluded to by Schiemann J would presumably have a remedy under the provisions of the Race Relations Act 1976.

More recently, a 37 year old woman failed to persuade the High Court to quash a health authority's decision to exclude her from its IVF programme on the basis of her age. The judge held that, in view of its limited resources and the lower success rates achieved with older women, the Authority's policy only to treat women below the age of 35 was not irrational: see *R v Sheffield HA ex p Seale* [1994] 25 BMLR 1.

Protection through counselling and informed consent

A problem which can be underestimated is the need for adequate counselling on treatment to be given to the couple being treated with IVF. This is necessary so that they can make an informed decision regarding ethically sensitive aspects of the procedure, such as the creation of surplus embryos with little chance of ever developing into fully fledged human beings, and the potential need for 'selective reduction' (see below, Chapter 8). Equally, they should be warned of the substantial risk that the treatment will fail: it has been estimated that only 14% of IVF procedures will result in a successful live birth.

Such counselling requirements are outlined in s 13(6) of the HFEA 1990:

13 (6) A woman shall not be provided with any treatment services involving–

  (a) the use of any gametes of any person, if that person's consent is required under para 5 of Sched 3 to this Act for the use in question;

  (b) the use of any embryo the creation of which was brought about *in vitro*; or

  (c) the use of any embryo taken from a woman, if the consent of the woman from whom it was taken is required under para 7 of that Schedule for the use in question,

  unless the woman being treated and, where she is being treated together with a man, the man have been given a suitable opportunity to receive proper counselling about the implications of taking the proposed steps, and have been provided with such relevant information as is proper.

Control over the use/disposition of embryos/gametes

One of the cornerstones of the 1990 Act consists in the great weight accorded to the consents of the gamete providers in determining what may be done with those gametes and/or any embryos created with them. In establishing a regime in which the providers are invited, following proper counselling, to specify the uses to which the material may be put, including in a range of hypothetical circumstances (eg, in the event of the death of a provider or the dissolution of the relationship between a pair of providers) the Act reflects a commitment to the autonomy of such providers. The key consent provisions are contained in Sched 3 to the Act:

Consents to use of gametes or embyos

Consent

1   A consent under this Schedule must be given in writing and, in this Schedule, 'effective consent' means a consent under this Schedule which has not been withdrawn.

2   (1)   A consent to the use of any embryo must specify one or more of the following purposes–

   (a)   use in providing treatment services to the person giving consent, or that person and another specified person together;

   (b)   use in providing treatment services to persons not including the person giving consent; or

   (c)   use for the purposes of any project of research,

   and may specify conditions subject to which the embryo may be so used.

   (2)   A consent to the storage of any gametes or any embryo must–

   (a)   specify the maximum period of storage (if less than the statutory storage period); and

   (b)   state what is to be done with the gametes or embryo if the person who gave the consent dies or is unable because of incapacity to vary the terms of the consent or to revoke it,

   and may specify conditions subject to which the gametes or embryo may remain in storage.

   (3)   A consent under this Schedule must provide for such other matters as the Authority may specify in directions.

   (4)   A consent under this Schedule may apply–

   (a)   to the use or storage of a particular embryo; or

   (b)   in the case of a person providing gametes, to the use or storage of any embryo whose creation may be brought about using those gametes;

   and in the para (b) case the terms of the consent may be varied, or the consent may be withdrawn, in accordance with this Schedule either generally or in relation to a particular embryo or particular embryos

   ...

In vitro fertilisation and subsequent use of embryo

6 (1) A person's gametes must not be used to bring about the creation of any embryo *in vitro* unless there is an effective consent by that person to any embryo the creation of which may be brought about with the use of those gametes being used for one or more of the purposes mentioned in para 2(1) above.

(2) An embryo the creation of which was brought about *in vitro* must not be received by any person unless there is an effective consent by each person whose gametes were used to bring about the creation of the embryo to the use for one or more of the purposes mentioned in para 2(1) above of the embryo.

(3) An embryo the creation of which was brought about *in vitro* must not be used for any purpose unless there is an effective consent by each person whose gametes were used to bring about the creation of the embryo to the use for that purpose of the embryo and the embryo is used in accordance with those consents ...

Storage of gametes and embryos

8 (1) A person's gametes must not be kept in storage unless there is an effective consent by that person to their storage and they are stored in accordance with the consent.

(2) An embryo the creation of which was brought about *in vitro* must not be kept in storage unless there is an effective consent, by each person whose gametes were used to bring about the creation of the embryo, to the storage of the embryo and the embryo is stored in accordance with those consents.

(3) An embryo taken from a woman must not be kept in storage unless there is an effective consent by her to its storage and it is stored in accordance with the consent.

In the case of consent to storage of embryos it is apparent that, by virtue of para 2(4) of the Schedule, such consents remain inherently revocable. Thus, notwithstanding the terms of any previous consent in relation to the disposition of an embryo in a given contingency, either gamete provider remains at liberty to vary those terms. This has the advantage of pre-empting troubling custody battles over stored embryos, such as have occurred in a number of US States. In this country, the withdrawal of the consent of either provider to the continued storage of any embryo formed with their gametes, for example following a divorce, would entail that further storage (and *a fortiori* use in IVF treatment) would be impermissible. Instead the clinic storing any such embryo would have to 'allow it to perish'.

The issue of the lawfulness of storing gametes, in this case sperm taken from an incompetent patient shortly before his death, was the subject of the recent decision of the Court of Appeal in *R v Human Fertilisation and Embryology Authority ex p Blood*:

R v Human Fertilisation and Embryology Authority ex p Blood [1997] 2 WLR 806, CA (Lord Woolf MR, Henry and Waite LJJ)

Mrs Blood sought judicial review of the HFE Authority's refusal to license infertility treatment of her with her dead husband's sperm. The sperm had been taken from Mr Blood as he lay in a coma shortly before his death from meningitis and consequently none of the written consents to its storage or use (stipulated in the 1990 Act) had been obtained.

> **Lord Woolf MR**: As to storage, s 4(1) makes it clear that it must always be pursuant to a licence. That means that storage can only take place lawfully in accordance with the requirements of the licence which for the present purposes are those contained in Sched 3. This means that there must be a consent in writing (para 1 and para 8) which complies with para 2(2) and para 3 before the storage can lawfully take place.

> **The position as to storage**

> Sperm can be used fresh or after it has been preserved. Its life, if not preserved, is extremely limited, a matter of a few hours. If it is preserved then it is being stored for the purposes of the Act and therefore is subject to the requirements of a licence. This is made clear by the definition of keeping or preserving sperm contained in s 2(2). The Act therefore takes the preservation process as the beginning of storage. This is understandable, since preservation involves the processing of gametes, and parliament has required that this should be done subject to the control of the licensing process. The result is that in the ordinary way no preservation can take place unless the required written consents exist. This would also apply in the case of the preservation of sperm intended for export unless a particular direction was obtained prior to preservation which permitted the storage to take place notwithstanding that there were not the requisite consents.

> It follows that Mr Blood's sperm should not in fact have been preserved and stored. Technically therefore an offence was committed by the licence holder as a result of the storage under s 41(2)(b) of the 1990 Act by the licensee. There is however no question of any prosecution being brought in the circumstances of this case and no possible criticism can be made of the fact that storage has taken place because Professor Cook of IRT was acting throughout in close consultation with the Authority in a perfectly *bona fide* manner, in an unexplored legal situation where humanity dictated that the sperm was taken and preserved first, and the legal argument followed. From now on, however, the position will be different, as these proceedings will clarify the legal position. Because this judgment makes it clear that the sperm of Mr Blood has been preserved and stored when it should not have been, this case raises issues as to the lawfulness of the use and export of sperm which should never arise again.

In the circumstances, it was held that, although Mrs Blood could not be lawfully treated with the semen in this country, she was entitled to export it and receive treatment in Belgium pursuant to her rights under Art 59 of the EC Treaty. In September 1997, the Government commissioned an inquiry, led by Professor Sheila McLean, into whether the consent provisions in the 1990 Act should be modified in the light of this case.

The embryo

What is its status?

From what has been said above, in relation to the primacy granted to the wishes of gamete providers in determining what may be done with resulting embryos, it might appear that the embryo's own status is an entirely subordinate one. This is partly true; as we have seen, the consequence of a gamete provider withdrawing consent to storage of an embryo is the latter's inevitable destruction. Nevertheless, there are important limits on the freedom of action of both gamete providers and others (ie, researchers) so far as their treatment of embryos is concerned. The ambivalence of the law on the early embryo was foreshadowed in the Warnock Report. After describing the initial stages of embryonic development, the report notoriously ducked the question of what moral inferences were to be drawn:

> **Warnock Committee,** *Report of the Committee of Inquiry into Human Fertilisation and Embryology,* **Cmnd 9314, 1984, London: HMSO:**
>
> 11.6 Once fertilisation has occurred, the subsequent developmental processes follow one another in a systematic and structured order, leading in turn through cleavage, to the morula, the blastocyst, development of the embryonic disc, and then to identifiable features within the embryonic disc such as the primitive streak, neural folds and neural tube. Until the blastocyst stage has been reached the embryo in vivo is unattached, floating first in the fallopian tube and then in the uterine cavity. From the sixth to the 12th or 13th day, internal development proceeds within the blastocyst while during the same period implantation is taking place. Both the internal and external processes of development are crucial to the future of the embryo. If the inner cell mass does not form within the blastocyst, there is no further embryonic development; while if implantation does not occur, the blastocyst is lost at or before the next menstrual period ...
>
> **The starting point for discussion**
>
> 11.8 It was the development of IVF that, for the first time, gave rise to the possibility that human embryos might be brought into existence which might have no chance to implant because they were not transferred to a uterus and hence no chance to be born as human beings. This inevitably led to an examination of the moral rights of the embryo.
>
> 11.9 Some people hold that if an embryo is human and alive, it follows that it should not be deprived of a chance for development, and therefore it should not be used for research. They would give moral approval to IVF if, and only if, each embryo produced were to be transferred to a uterus. Others, while in no way denying that human embryos are alive (and they

would concede that eggs and sperm are also alive), hold that embryos are not yet human persons and that if it could be decided when an embryo becomes a person, it could also be decided when it might, or might not, be permissible for research to be undertaken. Although the questions of when life or personhood begin appear to be questions of fact susceptible of straightforward answers, we hold that the answers to such questions in fact are complex amalgams of factual and moral judgments. Instead of trying to answer these questions directly we have therefore gone straight to the question of how it is right to treat the human embryo. We have considered what status ought to be accorded to the human embryo, and the answer we give must necessarily be in terms of ethical or moral principles.

The Warnock Committee nevertheless took the view that 'the status of the embryo is a matter of fundamental principle which should be enshrined in legislation' (para 11.17). This recommendation was largely followed in the HFEA 1990; although the Act omits mention of embryos enjoying any particular status, it does establish a number of restrictions and prohibitions in respect of them:

Activities governed by the Act

3   Prohibitions in connection with embryos

(1)   No person shall–

(a)   bring about the creation of an embryo; or

(b)   keep or use an embryo, except in pursuance of a licence.

(2)   No person shall place in a woman–

(a)   a live embryo other than a human embryo; or

(b)   any live gametes other than human gametes.

(3)   A licence cannot authorise–

(a)   keeping or using an embryo after the appearance of the primitive streak;

(b)   placing an embryo in any animal;

(c)   keeping or using an embryo in any circumstances in which regulations prohibit its keeping or use; or

(d)   replacing a nucleus of a cell of an embryo with a nucleus taken from a cell of any person, embryo or subsequent development of an embryo.

(4)   For the purposes of sub-s (3)(a) above, the primitive streak is to be taken to have appeared in an embryo not later than the end of the period of 14 days beginning with the day when the gametes are mixed, not counting any time during which the embryo is stored.

The Act thus adopts a 'two tier' approach to protecting the *ex vivo* embryo: in relation to the embryo's creation and use, either for IVF treatment of persons or for research prior to the formation of the primitive streak, this is sanctioned by licence with the additional proviso that the consents of the gamete providers be obtained. Activities falling outside this sphere of the permissible (eg, research after the primitive streak forms, placing embryos in animals, and cloning) are straightforwardly prohibited. Indeed such activities are, by virtue of s 41 of the Act, punishable by imprisonment of up to 10 years.

As the Warnock Report notes, the formation of the primitive streak marks that stage in embryonic development when a new individual entity is first discernible:

Warnock Committee, *Report of the Committee of Inquiry into Human Fertilisation and Embryology*, Cmnd 9314, 1984, London: HMSO:

11.5 The first of these features is the primitive streak, which appears as a heaping up of cells at one end of the embryonic disc on the 14th or 15th day after fertilisation. Two primitive streaks may form in a single embryonic disc. This is the latest stage at which identical twins can occur. The primitive streak is the first of several identifiable features which develop in and from the embryonic disc during the succeeding days, a period of very rapid change in the embryonic configuration. By the 17th day the neural groove appears and by the 22nd to 23rd day this has developed to become the neural folds, which in turn start to fuse and form the recognisable antecedent of the spinal cord.

The storage of embryos and gametes

As we have already seen, the consent of gamete providers must be obtained in order to continue to store their gametes/embryos in accordance with the Act. Such storage, in relation to embryos and semen (but not at present eggs) is possible by means of 'cryopreservation' (freezing). Nevertheless, two distinct legal problems are created. First (assuming always that valid consents have been obtained), should there be any absolute time limit beyond which the material in question may in any event not be kept? Secondly, are embryos and semen in storage *ex vivo* to be regarded as property? In other words, do they belong to anyone?

In relation to the first issue, the Warnock Committee recommended the need for an upper time limit to storage, on grounds both of the possible (albeit speculative) risk of physical harm to children born from embryos after extended storage, and the increased risk of gamete providers dying or falling into disagreement over the period in question. The 1990 Act reflected these concerns in stipulating in s 14(4)) maximum storage periods of 10 years for gametes and five years for embryos. More recently, however, following a report by the Human Fertilisation and Embryology Authority, it was felt desirable to relax this limit in respect of embryos. This was especially so in cases where gametes were taken from a female provider prior to therapy for cancer, where it is medically preferable to wait for as long as possible after such therapy before implanting her with any embryo formed with them.

The Government accordingly passed the Human Fertilisation and Embryology (Statutory Storage Period for Embryos) Regulations 1996 SI

1996/375. The Regulations replace the absolute limit on storage of embryos for longer than five years with a weak *presumption* that normally embryos will not be kept longer than this; in nearly every case this can be rebutted in favour of a 10 year limit (reg 2(4)(b)). Exceptionally the latter limit, itself, may be exceeded, notably in cases where a woman is due to undergo some other treatment, eg, radiotherapy, interfering with her fertility (see reg 2(2)(c)). Here, the only limit still operative is that implantation must be carried out on the woman in question before she attains the age of 55 (reg 2(1)).

In relation to embryos whose storage had begun prior to the passing of the Regulations, an obligation was imposed on the clinics storing them to obtain confirmation in writing from the providers that they had no objection to extending storage beyond five years. Whilst this ensured respect for the autonomy of such providers (the legal matrix in which their original consents had been given had changed), it had the unfortunate consequence that, in cases where the providers could not be traced, their embryos had to be allowed to perish.

The second problem alluded to above is whether there is property in the human embryo when it is stored *ex vivo*. The context in which such an issue is most likely to arise is when there is a dispute between the gamete providers over disposition. As we have seen, the joint consent requirement in Sched 3 to the Act forestalls the need in this country to pose the question in such a case. By contrast, in the USA, courts have had to grapple with it head on:

Davis v Davis 842 SW 2d 588 (1992), Tenn Sup Ct (Daughtrey J)

Mary Sue and Junior Lewis Davis were a married couple who, in the course of IVF treatment, allowed seven of their embryos to be cryopreserved. The couple were not asked to give advance directions on what should be done with the embryos in the event of their marriage breaking up, and when this subsequently occurred, they were unable to agree on the issue. Junior Lewis was adamant that he did not wish to reproduce outside wedlock and wanted the embryos destroyed. Mary Sue, for her part, initially wanted an attempt to be made to implant them in her. However, by the time the case reached the Tennessee Supreme Court she had changed her mind and wanted them to be given to another infertile couple.

> **Daughtrey J**: To our way of thinking, the most helpful discussion on this point is found not in the minuscule number of legal opinions that have involved 'frozen embryos', but in the ethical standards set by the American Fertility Society, as follows:
>
>> Three major ethical positions have been articulated in the debate over pre-embryo status. At one extreme is the view of the pre-embryo as a human subject after fertilisation, which requires that it be accorded the rights of a person. This position entails an obligation to provide an opportunity for implantation to occur and tends to ban any action before transfer that might harm the pre-embryo or that is not immediately therapeutic, such as freezing and some pre-embryo research.

At the opposite extreme is the view that the pre-embryo has a status no different from any other human tissue. With the consent of those who have decision making authority over the pre-embryo, no limits should be imposed on actions taken with pre-embryos.

A third view – one that is most widely held – takes an intermediate position between the other two. It holds that the pre-embryo deserves respect greater than that accorded to human tissue but not the respect accorded to actual persons. The pre-embryo is due greater respect than other human tissue because of its potential to become a person and because of its symbolic meaning for many people. Yet, it should not be treated as a person, because it has not yet developed the features of personhood, is not yet established as developmentally individual, and may never realise its biologic potential ...

... In its report, the Ethics Committee then calls upon those in charge of IVF programs to establish policies in keeping with the 'special respect' due pre-embryos and suggests:

Within the limits set by institutional policies, decision making authority regarding pre-embryos should reside with the persons who have provided the gametes ... As a matter of law, it is reasonable to assume that the gamete providers have primary decision making authority regarding pre-embryos in the absence of specific legislation on the subject. A person's liberty to procreate or to avoid procreation is directly involved in most decisions involving pre-embryos.

We conclude that pre-embryos are not, strictly speaking, either 'persons' or 'property', but occupy an interim category that entitles them to special respect because of their potential for human life. It follows that any interest that Mary Sue Davis and Junior Davis have in the pre-embryos in this case is not a true property interest. However, they do have an interest in the nature of ownership, to the extent that they have decision making authority concerning disposition of the pre-embryos, within the scope of policy set by law.

In the circumstances, Junior Lewis's interest in not procreating was held to outweigh Mary Sue's desire that the pre-embryos (an alternative term for the early embryo prior to implantation) should be given to another couple.

In the UK, in so far as the question arose (as conceivably it might in the case of a dispute between a pair of gamete providers (acting jointly) and the clinic storing their embryo(s)) it is likely that a similar *sui generis* approach (in which the wishes of the two gamete providers nevertheless predominate) would be followed.

Embryo research

The creation of human embryos *ex vivo* opens up significant opportunities for the conduct of medical research. As we have seen, subject to licence and to the gamete providers' approval, such research is currently permitted until the formation of the embryo's primitive streak. Nevertheless, for many people the possibility of such research is undoubtedly the most troubling aspect of IVF treatment, significantly more so than, for example, simply allowing spare or unwanted embryos to perish. Why this should be so is a complex question, which is inextricably linked to our attitudes towards unborn human life in general. In *A Question of Life* Mary Warnock commented as follows:

Warnock, M, *A Question of Life*, 1985, Oxford: Blackwells, pp xii–xiii:

There was, however, a more testing kind of question [than the issue of regulating fertility treatment], infinitely more important, in my opinion.

This was the question of research using human embryos ... Utilitarianism could ... by itself, provide no solution, simply because the very question at issue was whether or not embryos count as those whose harms and benefits, pleasures and pains, have to be thrown into the balance to be weighed against the benefits or harms to society as a whole. But here we had, it seemed, an issue on which legislation must be foreseen, and must be enacted quickly. No one felt inclined to argue that the decision whether or not to embark on research with the use of human embryos was a matter of personal conscience, as they might in the case of AID, surrogacy, or, for that matter, homosexuality between adults. Everyone agreed that this was a matter on which there must be legislation, and that whether and to what extent embryos should be used must be a decision for the law.

It is certainly true that the moral permissibility of embryo research turns upon the issue of the embryo's moral status in a particularly direct way. This is because, unlike the cases of 'spare embryos' allowed to perish in the course of IVF or of embryos/foetuses destroyed through abortion (see below, Chapter 8), the rights/interests of identifiable, fully fledged individuals are not directly implicated. To the extent that the view of embryo-as-person is rejected, such research may appear acceptable in principle. On the other hand, as argued by John Robertson, other problems – notably the symbolic damage it may cause – remain:

Robertson, JA, *Children of Choice*, 1994, Ewing: New Jersey: Princeton University Press, p 201:

... creating embryos for research and then discard deserves protection only if other important interests are served that justify whatever symbolic costs deliberate creation and discard of embryos entails. The purpose here is to increase knowledge of how to treat infertility, improve contraception, and treat or prevent cancer or birth defects. With cryopreservation of extra embryos limiting the number donated for research, a policy against creating embryos solely for research and discard could greatly limit the amount of embryo research. Research with embryos would then occur only with spare embryos created as a byproduct of IVF treatment of infertility, which may be too few to meet all research needs, with the result that important research across a range of fields is lost. The symbolic benefits of protecting embryos from being created solely for research purposes does not appear to justify this loss. If the embryo is so rudimentary that research on excess, discarded embryos does not harm them and is permissible, there would appear to be no additional harm to embryos from creating them for this purpose only. In both cases research will occur at the same stage of development, and thus no added harm would occur from deliberate creation of embryos for research purposes.

Opponents, however, would argue that additional symbolic harm arises from creating embryos solely to be vehicles of research and then discarded. Additional symbolic harm results because creating embryos with the intent to discard them demonstrates a profound disrespect for the earliest stages of human life. This practice permits human life to be created, manipulated, and discarded for utilitarian purposes, without regard to the embryo's own interests or potential. The deliberateness of the act – creating new human life only to destroy it – is thus viewed as symbolically more offensive than research on excess embryos created as a byproduct of the IVF process of treating infertility.

The issue of embryo research split the Warnock Committee, with a bare majority (9:7) in favour of research on embryos deliberately created for that purpose. Of the dissenters, three opposed any research at all while the other four believed it should take place only upon 'spares' left over from IVF treatment. Subsequently, the 1987 Government White Paper, which preceded the Human Fertilisation and Embryology Bill, offered parliament a free vote on two alternative legislative approaches to embryo research. The thinking behind these alternatives was explored at the time by Margaret Brazier in the following article:

Brazier, M, 'The challenge for Parliament', in Dyson, A and Harris, J (eds), *Experiments on Embryos*, 1990, London: Routledge, pp 128–32:

The alternative draft clauses (Options A and B) outlined in the White Paper offer parliament something considerably less than freedom to determine fundamental principles relating to the legal and moral status of the human embryo. Option A does not affirm the full humanity of the embryo created *in vitro*. It protects the embryo only from interference via intrusive research procedures, and not from destruction. Option B is equally limited. The Statutory Licensing Authority is to be empowered only to license projects to research on embryos up to 14 days of development and statutory restrictions are to be imposed on the types of research to be permitted. There is no Option C to offer the prospect of research to any later date ... Nor, it seems, can the 14 day limit, if enacted, be extended other than by parliament itself. Options A and B are in themselves compromise proposals; the principles on which each option itself is based and the exclusion of any further options must now be examined.

Option A: prohibiting research

The basic intent of Option A is to attempt to prohibit embryo experimentation while limiting any consequent damage to the IVF programme. Necessarily then, procedures involving observation of the embryo in the Petri dish and aimed at preparing the embryo for transfer to the mother will not be prohibited. Nor will the legislation prohibit the storage of embryos, or impinge on the practice of inducing super-ovulation to create 'spare' embryos, not all of which will be implanted in the mother. Surplus embryos will be 'allowed to perish' either if unsuitable for implantation, or if the donors withhold their consent to storage of 'their' embryos, or, if unused before then, at the expiry of the five year storage period proposed by the White Paper.

Option A thus sanctions the creation of embryos 'doomed to die'. That accords the embryo *in vitro* less than fully human status, so can Option A itself be ethically acceptable to people who maintain that from the fusion of egg and sperm a genetically unique person is created who is as entitled to the law's protection as any born child or adult human being? I think that this can be achieved only at the cost of compromising to some extent any absolutist view of the humanity of the embryo from the conclusion of the fertilisation process. That compromise cannot be based on a preference for destruction over research *per se*. 'Killing' an embryo by washing it down the drain cannot in itself be morally preferable to researching on the embryo (at a time when it is certain that the embryo can feel no pain) before washing it down the drain. So other grounds for compromise must be sought.

There are perhaps at least three possible grounds. First, the creation of embryos 'doomed to die' could be prevented only by prohibiting the practice of super-ovulation of patients scheduled for IVF treatment and the consequent creation of 'spare' embryos. This would effectively stultify and maybe destroy the IVF programme itself. If doctors could harvest only one egg at a time, chances of establishing a successful pregnancy by implanting three or four embryos would be lost. Freezing embryos would necessarily have to be prohibited. This would mean women would have to submit to several interventions to secure eggs, at extra expense and stress to them. The arguments for not prohibiting the creation of spare embryos sounds forceful. But once it is conceded that damaging the prospects of successful IVF treatment justifies the inevitable destruction of some embryos, the case against research is significantly weakened. Is the IVF programme a greater moral imperative than the potential to reduce or eliminate genetic defects?

The two other grounds for the compromise in Option A are the inherent instability of all early embryos, and the contention that deliberate interference with embryos is of a different moral order to 'allowing embryos to perish'. In vivo, many fertilised eggs do not implant in the uterus, others implant briefly but are lost before the woman knows herself pregnant, in what may seem to be just a slightly late or heavy period. So is losing a few embryos *in vitro* morally very different? Again the argument confounds itself. If losing a few human lives is no big deal, why cannot they be lost usefully via research? Only if the contention can be upheld that deliberate interference is of a different order to incidental destruction, can Option A in its present form be justified. And that depends on accepting that the crucial issue is the *intent* of those dealing with the embryo. It would be permissible to create a human being, hoping and intending that it fulfil its potential as an embryo growing within a woman to become a child, albeit knowing that that intent might not be attained. It is not permissible to interfere with that embryo for purposes of no benefit for it. That is a derogation from the humanity of the embryo ...

Option B: permitting research

Option B, which if enacted would permit limited research on human embryos specifically licensed by the Statutory Licensing Authority, is once again a carefully designed compromise proposal intended maybe to maximise parliamentary support for permitting research. The time limit of 14 days from placing the egg and sperm together for fertilisation recommended by Warnock is adopted. Practices which raise the spectre of mad scientists tampering with the human race are specifically banned. Thus the Government seeks to avoid any claim that research, if permitted at all, takes us onto the 'slippery slope' towards science fiction nightmares.

Four categories of potential research projects will be banned by the draft Bill. The first two prohibited categories seek to allay fears of the creation of a master race and/or sub-categories of specially designed humans. Thus genetic manipulation of the embryo to create a being with 'certain predetermined characteristics through modification of the early embryo's genetic structure', and research into the production of clones are to be outlawed. The remaining prohibited categories deal with trans-species research. The Bill will prohibit transfer to a human uterus, or vice versa, of any hybrid embryo combining human and non-human gametes. Trans-species fertilisation *in vitro* will itself be forbidden except for the purpose of assessing sub-fertility. The 'hamster test' to investigate the quality of human sperm will thus remain lawful, but anyone permitting development of a trans-species fertilised egg beyond the two cell stage will commit a criminal offence.

The choice of prohibited categories of research occasions little comment. The procedures selected to ban unacceptable research are of more interest. The proposed legislation will be flexible. Provision is made both for parliament by affirmative regulation to make exceptions to the prohibited categories if new developments make such a measure appropriate, and also to extend the categories of prohibited research by regulation. This is in marked contrast to the decision to opt for an absolute time limit of 14 days from fertilisation, after which further research becomes a criminal offence. In the White Paper at least no provision is made for extension of that limit other than by repeal of the legislation and its replacement by a new governing statute.

The inflexibility of the 14 day time limit on research enforceable by criminal penalties raises the question of why the options before parliament were limited to two. Why is there no Option C? This could have embodied either a more flexible 14 day limit open to extension by regulation, or a fixed but much longer limit expiring 28–40 days after fertilisation. The selection of a 14 day limit by Warnock depended on their choice as a reference point of the formation of the primitive streak marking the beginning of the individual development of the embryo. This represents the latest stage at which identical twins can develop and by that time it is possible to tell whether the cells will continue to develop as an embryo or may constitute an abnormality such as hydatidiform mole. The key to a 14 day limit rests on individuality. No research should take place once the embryo has developed the markers that indicate that it could develop as a single individual ...

In the event, as we know, Parliament chose to adopt option B.

Concerns over future developments

Last, but by no means least, mention must be made of a number of miscellaneous concerns that arise in respect of technological advances in the area of assisted reproduction. Practices such as cloning, the implantation of animal embryos in women and human embryos in animals (see s 3 of the HFEA 1990) are prohibited not merely, or even primarily, to protect existing embryos, but rather to express society's disquiet over the possibility of such practices. The same is true in relation to possible genetic engineering, which arguably is actually *in the interests* of the embryos/children thus created. The Glover Report commented upon the latter issue as follows:

> **Glover, J *et al*, *Report to the European Commission on Reproductive Technologies, Fertility and the Family*, 1989, London: Fourth Estate, pp 138–41:**
>
> Safe gene therapy is not yet with us. But it is better to start thinking about the implications of likely technological developments before they arrive. The stage when a technology seems too remote to be worth thinking about has been followed so often by abrupt transition to the stage when it is already out of control. If ... 'negative' gene therapy [permitting diseases to be screened out] does come, one worry is that it may be part of a slide towards other, non-medical interventions of a 'positive' kind, designed to make 'improvements' in people. The technology for this is even further off. But the eventual mapping and sequencing of the human genome, together with knowledge of how genes affect characteristics, may one day make positive genetic engineering possible. One view is that, just as a child can benefit from an upbringing which makes him or her more intelligent, more musical, or better at making friends, so a child could equally benefit from genetic changes which are found to have the same effects.
>
> The other view is that it is in the interests of the child not to be genetically the product of other people's decisions. As the European Parliament put it (Recommendation 934/1982), there is a 'right to genetic inheritance which has not been artificially interfered with, except for therapeutic purposes'.
>
> Positive genetic engineering is in many ways an extremely disturbing prospect. But it is debatable whether the issue is best seen in terms of violating the rights of those whose genes would be altered ... [A] particular problem about this right is how far people would in fact feel that their interests had been overridden. Some people might greatly dislike the fact that their genes had been chosen for them; but others might feel that they had gained from having genes making them more intelligent or more amiable, and be glad that their genes were not left to the natural lottery.
>
> It might be hard to convince people in this second category that a right of theirs had been violated. Perhaps the fact that some might be glad of the intervention is not enough to justify it. But there are complex issues here, and there is a suspicion that the 'right' has been plucked out of the air to settle a difficult issue at great speed.

There are real causes for concern about positive genetic engineering, and it is worth bringing them into sharper focus.

One concern is perhaps obvious to any late 20th century European. This is the danger of giving new technological powers to a government with a programme of racist eugenics, or perhaps to one which had some other, not 'race' linked, category of people it regarded as less than fully human. In our countries there is nearly universal revulsion against this kind of outlook. But technology once developed is always available, and it is hard to be sure that such an outlook will never return.

Another cause for concern is not the deliberate use of genetic engineering for perverted ends, but the accidental side effects of well intentioned uses. One problem is that we may overlook some genetic linkage between different characteristics. In choosing, say, genes for high intelligence, we may find we have inadvertently also chosen genes for high levels of aggression or depression. All technology carries with it the risk of mistakes and unwanted side effects. Here the 'mistakes' will be human beings. There is also the risk of disasters which are irreversible: 'mistaken' genes would be passed on to future generations.

Another problem is that if certain characteristics were frequently selected, those who did not have them might come to be seen as inferior. It may be hard to keep the decent reluctance to see people in terms of some competitive rank ordering, when, in another part of our mind, we are ranking characteristics which may be available for our children.

There are also enormous problems about who would take the decisions. These problems are sometimes gestured at by describing the choice as 'playing God', with the implication that it would take a great deal of presumption to put oneself forward as qualified to choose the genes of another person.

Perhaps, if there were great benefits, we would overcome our reluctance to play God in this way. But there would remain the question of whose decision it should be. Many shudder at the idea of some central government committee taking such decisions. The alternative of parents choosing for their children is much more attractive. But that too has huge unsolved problems. Could parents not sometimes choose disastrously for their children? And suppose too many parents chose the same characteristics? What social limits to their choice would be set, and by what means?

... This adds up to a case for saying that positive human genetic engineering is unethical now (or when it becomes available) and will remain so at least until policies have been worked out to cope with the huge problems it raises.

Leaving the uncertain consequences of such practices to one side, many of the concerns surrounding them are arguably non-consequentialist in form. Moreover, they illustrate the point that, even in a liberal society, values other than individual autonomy are held to be of fundamental importance. As scientific advances in this field continue apace, the Government established a new body, the Human Genetics Advisory Commission, in December 1996, to assist in monitoring and advising upon developments. This is an important safeguard, as the 1990 Act's ability to control such matters is increasingly compromised by the emergence of new scientific techniques not foreseen by the parliamentary draftsman. For example, although the HFEA 1990 prohibits human cloning by replacing the nucleus of an embryonic cell (under s 3(3)(d)) it is silent about parthenogenetic cloning (in which the female egg is stimulated to develop without fertilisation, producing a genetic copy of the mother). In 1990 the latter technique was not believed to be a realistic possibility; however, in February 1997, it was successfully used to produce a sheep.

There is, on the other hand, one issue which has already caused unease for a number of years. This is the selection, in the course of IVF treatment, of embryos for implantation on the basis of their sex. How far should this be permitted for merely social (as opposed to medical) reasons? The Warnock Report had the following to say:

Warnock Committee, *Report of the Committee of Inquiry into Human Fertilisation and Embryology,* **Cmnd 9314, 1984, London: HMSO:**

Other reasons for sex selection

9.11 So far we have discussed the use of sex selection in a clinical context, where it would be practised solely for the purpose of avoiding hereditary sex-linked disorders. We see no reason why, if a method of selecting the sex of a child before fertilisation is developed, this should not be offered to couples who have good medical reasons for choosing the sex of their child. But if an efficient and easy method of ensuring the conception of a child of a particular sex became available, it is likely that some couples would wish to make use of it for purely social reasons. Such a practice would obviously affect the individual family and the children involved, and would also have implications for society as a whole. It is impossible to predict, either in the long or the short term, the likely effects of such a practice on the ratio of males to females within society. It is often suggested that a majority of couples would choose that their first child was male, and if this happened, it could have important social implications, since there is considerable evidence that the first born sibling may enjoy certain advantages over younger siblings. It would have particular implications for the role of women in society, although some would argue that these effects would today be less damaging than they might have been a hundred years ago. These important considerations make the Inquiry dubious about the use of sex selection techniques on a wide scale, but because of the difficulty of predicting the outcome of any such trend we have not found it possible to make any positive recommendations on this issue. Nevertheless, we consider that the whole question of the acceptability of sex selection should be kept under review.

These concerns are echoed in the HFE Authority's Code of Practice, which currently states that sex selection should not be carried out for social reasons (2nd Revision, December 1995, para 7.20).

COLLABORATIVE REPRODUCTION

Background

The term 'collaborative reproduction' (borrowed from JA Robertson) is used to describe situations in which a third party (who will have no parenting role once the child is born) assists in the production of the child. Such assistance may come either through the donation of gametes and embryos, or (in the case of a woman) the provision of her uterus to gestate the child. The latter practice, known as surrogacy, raises particular problems and will accordingly be dealt with separately below, p 390. For the time being we shall restrict our discussion to issues centring on gamete/embryo donation; useful summaries of the key techniques can be found in the Warnock Report:

Warnock Committee, *Report of the Committee of Inquiry into Human Fertilisation and Embryology,* **Cmnd 9314, 1984, London: HMSO:**

I   Artificial insemination

4.1   The term artificial insemination (AI) is used to refer to the placing of semen inside a woman's vagina or uterus by means other than sexual intercourse. The principle of this technique has been known for centuries in the veterinary context. The simplicity of artificial insemination contrasts sharply with the technical complexity of more recent developments such as *in vitro* fertilisation. It begins with the collection of semen from the husband or a donor, through masturbation. The semen is either placed in the upper part of the vagina next to the cervix or injected into the uterus through a fine catheter. Insemination is undertaken near the predicted time of ovulation, the time in a woman's menstrual cycle when she has the highest chance of conceiving. The semen used may be fresh or it may have been previously frozen and thawed before use ...

...

II   Artificial insemination by donor (AID)

4.6   Artificial insemination by donor (AID) may be used when investigations have shown the husband to be sterile or to have significantly reduced fertility, or it may be used for the avoidance of hereditary diseases when these are carried by the male ... In this procedure the woman is inseminated with semen from a donor.

...

III   Egg donation

6.1   Egg donation has been attempted in the United States of America and in Australia, where there has been one live birth. This procedure may help those women who cannot themselves produce an egg. It may also help those who would be candidates for IVF except that in their case egg collection is impossible because their ovaries are inaccessible. About 5% of infertile couples might benefit from the technique. A mature egg is recovered from a fertile woman donor, for example, during sterilisation, and is fertilised *in vitro*, using the semen of the husband of the infertile woman. The resulting embryo is then transferred to the patient's uterus. If it implants she may then carry the pregnancy to term. There are other situations where eggs might be donated. When a woman is herself undergoing infertility treatment and several eggs have been recovered from her, she may be prepared to donate one or more eggs to another woman whose infertility can be treated only by egg donation.

...

IV Embryo donation

7.1 Embryo donation would help the same groups of women who might benefit from egg donation and, more particularly, the even smaller number whose husbands are also infertile. Embryo donation may take two forms. One involves the donation of both egg and semen. The donated egg is fertilised *in vitro* with donated semen and the resulting embryo transferred to a woman who is unable to produce an egg herself and whose husband is infertile. The second method, known as lavage, does not involve removing the egg by surgical intervention. Instead the egg is released naturally from the ovary at the normal time in the donor's menstrual cycle. At the predicted time of ovulation she is artificially inseminated with semen from the husband of the infertile woman (or from a donor if the husband is also infertile). Some three to four days later, before the start of implantation, the donor's uterus is 'washed out' and any embryo retrieved is then transferred to the uterus of the infertile woman. If the embryo implants successfully the recipient carries the pregnancy to term. Embryo donation by lavage is, according to its advocates, much safer for the donor as it does not require general anaesthesia, and a simple and safer procedure is involved; moreover, for the embryo, there is the advantage of a shorter interval *in vitro* during which time it might deteriorate. When semen from the husband is used, the child is genetically his, though not his wife's.

The potential use of such techniques to assist single women, or those in lesbian relationships, to conceive has occasioned much political debate. More usually, the persons relying on them will be a heterosexual couple where one (or possibly both) of them is infertile, but even here difficulties may arise. As Robertson writes:

Robertson, JA, *Children of Choice*, 1994, Ewing: New Jersey: Princeton University Press, pp 119–20:

Resort to donor gametes or surrogates is not an easy choice for infertile couples. The decision arises after previous efforts at pregnancy have failed, thus confronting the couple with the fact of one or both partners' infertility. A collaborative technique is chosen because it offers an opportunity to have a child who is the biologic offspring of one or, in the case of egg donation and gestational surrogacy, both partners. Yet collaborative reproduction occurs in an uncertain ethical, legal, and social milieu, where social practices and legal rules are still largely unclear.

A basic commitment to procreative liberty – to the freedom to have and rear offspring – should presumptively protect most forms of collaborative reproduction. After all, collaborative reproduction occurs for the same reason as IVF: the couple is infertile and cannot produce offspring. They need donor or surrogate assistance if they are to have children. Even if both rearing partners are not reproducing in the strict genetic sense, at least one partner will have a genetic or gestational relationship with their child. The same techniques may also be sought by a single woman or a same-sex couple that wishes to have offspring. In a few cases, donor gametes are used to avoid genetic handicap in offspring.

Despite its clear link to procreative choice, collaborative reproduction often generates controversy and even calls for prohibition. Collaborative reproduction is problematic because it intrudes a third party a donor or surrogate – into the usual situation of two party parenthood, and separates or deconstructs the traditional genetic, gestational, and social unity of reproduction. A child could in theory end up with three different biologic parents (a genetic mother, a gestational mother, a genetic father) and two separate rearing parents, with various combinations among them. Such collaboration risks confusing offspring about who their 'true' parent is and creating conflict about parental rights and duties.

The Glover Report discusses the possible effects of widespread use of collaborative reproduction on society at large. Of particular concern to many is its perceived threat to traditional notions of the family.

Glover, J et al, _Report to the European Commission on Reproductive Technologies, Fertility and the Family_, 1989, London: Fourth Estate, pp 53–55:

Our ability to separate social from biological parenthood may create new patterns of relationship, such as families with two social parents of the same sex. Or one woman may be both aunt and mother to the same child. The family has for so long been the setting for our deepest relationships, both in childhood and in adult life, that any major changes need very careful thought. Even the possibility of changes may widely be seen as a threat. We believe that an unspoken general anxiety about the family often underlies the more specific disputes on the surface of the public debate on the new techniques of reproduction ...

1   The traditional family and some changes

Historical generalisations are usually simplifications, admitting of many exceptions. Aware of this, we tentatively offer a rough sketch of a traditional ideal of the family, perhaps with its roots in 19th century Europe, and of some ways in which the family nowadays often differs from it. The foundation of the traditional ideal family was a heterosexual couple embarking on a monogamous marriage for life. Adultery and prostitution existed, but were seen as a falling away from the ideal of the exclusive monogamous relationship. The rarity of contraception meant there were a lot of children.

The rarity of divorce meant that the stability of the family could be taken for granted as the children grew up and as the couple grew old. The father earned the money and had authority in the family, while the mother cared for the children and looked after the home. (Nineteenth century middle class families more often came close to this ideal than did working class families, where the woman often had to work.) The spread of contraception has helped to change the picture. Families have fewer children, and mothers more often go out to work. This, together with other changes of attitude, has weakened the traditional authority of the father, who is no longer the unique provider. Contraception has also diminished one of the dangers of extramarital sex. The longer expectation of life may have added to the pressures on the traditional family. When people marry now, their partnership has a longer time in which to survive or break up than would probably have been the case a century ago. The spread of divorce has made children (and their parents) less able to rely on the permanence of their family.

Marital breakdown can be devastating for an abandoned spouse, and also for the children. Security and stability are so important for both children and adults to flourish that the traditional family is often and understandably seen as something to defend against further erosion.

But the drawbacks of the traditional arrangements are also often pointed out. The absence of divorce could imprison people in unhappy marriages. Couples had no choice about the number of their children. The size of a family was limited only by the brutal method of high infant mortality. Women had few opportunities for fulfilled lives except in the single traditional role of wife and mother ... Men, tied to earning a living, were often effectively excluded from close relations with their children. Social pressures limited the children's role too. Parental domination over children could extend even to what job they took or whom they married. And a social structure based so much on the family left no recognised social place for homosexuals.

People of libertarian outlook, together with feminists and those who campaign for homosexual rights, see the loosening of the traditional family structure mainly as gain. Those more conservative about the family see the mounting divorce rate as a disaster. Disagreement about the relative gains and losses is not something this committee need try to resolve; we note that the changes have created a climate in which artificial reproductive techniques are more readily accepted ...

What, then, are the current legal implications of gamete/embryo donation for the immediate parties to such an enterprise? In addressing this issue, we may distinguish between the interests of the potential rearing parent(s), the gamete provider(s), and any child who is born as a result. In practice, however, the weight attached by the law to the interests of one party will inevitably affect those of the others.

The potential rearing parent(s)

Access to treatment

Pursuant to s 4(1) of HFEA 1990, infertility treatment involving the use of third party gametes may only be carried out under licence. (The same condition applies to donated embryos by virtue of s 3 of the Act.) The first major issue is who should be eligible for such treatment. In particular, should it be limited to those in a traditional heterosexual marriage who are unable to reproduce by reason of medical infertility, or may it be given also to single persons or homosexual couples whose 'infertility' is a product of their chosen lifestyle? We have already seen (from the Glover Report) how this may influence the future development of the family and, indirectly, society. The Warnock Committee, for its part, had the following to say on the matter:

Warnock Committee, *Report of the Committee of Inquiry into Human Fertilisation and Embryology*, Cmnd 9314, 1984, London: HMSO:

2.9 ... the various techniques for assisted reproduction offer not only a remedy for infertility, but also offer the fertile single woman or lesbian couple the chance of parenthood without the direct involvement of a male partner. To judge from the evidence, many believe that the interests of the child dictate that it should be born into a home where there is a loving, stable, heterosexual relationship and that, therefore, the *deliberate* creation of a child for a woman who is not a partner in such a relationship is morally wrong. On the other side some expressed the view that a single woman or lesbian couple have a right under the European Convention to have children even though those children may have no legal father. It is further argued that it is already accepted that a single person, whether man or woman, can in certain circumstances provide a suitable environment for a child, since the existence of single adoptive parents is specifically provided for in the Children Act 1975.

2.10 In the same way that a single woman may believe she has a right to motherhood, so a single man may feel he has a right to fatherhood. Though the feminist position is perhaps more frequently publicised, we were told of a group of single, mainly homosexual, men who were campaigning for the right to bring up a child. Their primary aim at present is to obtain in practice equal rights in the adoption field, but they are also well aware of the potential of surrogacy for providing a single man with a child that is genetically his. There have been cases in other countries of surrogacy in such circumstances. It can be argued that, as a matter of sex equality, if single women are not totally barred from parenthood, then neither should single men be so barred.

2.11 We have considered these arguments, but, nevertheless, we believe that as a general rule it is better for children to be born into a two-parent family, with both father and mother, although we recognise that it is impossible to predict with any certainty how lasting such a relationship will be.

Although the Warnock Committee stopped short of making specific recommendations on this point, its attitudes were reflected by the insertion into the HFEA 1990 of s 13(5). We have already discussed some of the difficulties of this provision (see above, p 357). In this context, the parenthetical clause in s 13(5), which directs the treatment provider to consider the child's need for a father, is of especial relevance.

As was suggested above, p 357, in respect of a couple seeking treatment, an action in judicial review may lie against refusal of treatment by an NHS clinic: *Ex p Harriott* (1988). However, on the face of it, no such action could be maintained in respect of a refusal to treat a single person or homosexual couple, since such a use of discretion is expressly legitimated by the Act. Might it be possible to challenge the validity of the Act itself, though, under anti-discrimination law at EC level? Some encouragement to do so may be found in the recent decision of the European Court of Justice in *P v S and Cornwall County Council* [1996] IRLR 347, an employment case involving the dismissal of an employee following a sex-change operation. The judgment suggested that the concept of 'sex discrimination' under EC law may be wider than discrimination based purely on biological sexual status. However, in the later case of *Grant v South West Trains* C-249/96; [1998] IRLR 206, the European Court of Justice, somewhat inconsistently, refused to extend the concept of sex discrimination to discrimination on the ground of sexual orientation. Nevertheless, in the light of the proposed incorporation of the European Convention on Human Rights into English law, a challenge could perhaps be mounted under Art 8 (the right to respect for family life).

Counselling requirements

As in the case of a couple seeking IVF treatment, those seeking treatment involving donated gametes are required to be offered counselling pursuant to s 13(6) of the 1990 Act (see above, p 358). Arguably, the need for potential rearing parents to receive counselling in such a case is particularly pressing. As noted by Robertson, they must of necessity accept the fact of their infertility as a couple and, where the infertility is specifically attributable to one partner, the latter's possible reaction to rearing a child not genetically his or her own must be canvassed. Infertility is still a problem attracting a significant degree of stigma in our society and how well the rearing parents adjust to it will clearly have an impact on the subsequent well being of any child.

Legal status vis à vis child

It is self-evident that a couple (or indeed a single person) who seek infertility treatment, involving the use of third party gametes/embryos, will be vitally concerned about the legitimacy of any child born as a result. Indeed, the attitude of the law towards this issue will probably be one of the most significant factors taken into account by would-be rearing parents when deciding whether to opt for treatment in the first place. The response of the legislature is found in ss 27–28 of the HFEA 1990:

27 Meaning of 'mother'

(1) The woman who is carrying or has carried a child as a result of the placing in her of an embryo or of sperm and eggs, and no other woman, is to be treated as the mother of the child.

(2) Sub-section (1) above does not apply to any child to the extent that the child is treated by virtue of adoption as not being the child of any person other than the adopter or adopters.

(3) Sub-section (1) above applies whether the woman was in the United Kingdom or elsewhere at the time of the placing in her of the embryo or the sperm and eggs.

28 Meaning of 'father'

(1) This section applies in the case of a child who is being or has been carried by a woman as the result of the placing in her of an embryo or of sperm and eggs or her artificial insemination.

(2) If–

(a) at the time of the placing in her of the embryo or the sperm and eggs or of her insemination, the woman was a party to a marriage; and

(b) the creation of the embryo carried by her was not brought about with the sperm of the other party to the marriage;

then, subject to sub-s (5) below, the other party to the marriage shall be treated as the father of the child unless it is shown that he did not consent to the placing in her of the embryo or the sperm and eggs or to her insemination (as the case may be).

(3) If no man is treated, by virtue of sub-s (2) above, as the father of the child but–

(a) the embryo or the sperm and eggs were placed in the woman, or she was artificially inseminated, in the course of treatment services provided for her and a man together by a person to whom a licence applies; and

(b) the creation of the embryo carried by her was not brought about with the sperm of that man, then, subject to sub-s (5) below, that man shall be treated as the father of the child.

(4) Where a person is treated as the father of the child by virtue of sub-s (2) or (3) above, no other person is to be treated as the father of the child.

(5) Sub-sections (2) and (3) above do not apply–

(a) in relation to England and Wales and Northern Ireland, to any child who, by virtue of the rules of common law, is treated as the legitimate child of the parties to marriage;

(b) in relation to Scotland, to any child who, by virtue of any enactment or other rule of law, is treated as the child of the parties to a marriage; or

(c) to any child to the extent that the child is treated by virtue of adoption as not being the child of any person other than the adopter or adopters.

(6) Where–

(a) the sperm of a man who had given such consent as is required by para 5 of Sched 3 to this Act was used for a purpose for which such consent was required; or

(b) the sperm of a man, or any embryo the creation of which was brought about with his sperm, was used after his death;

he is not to be treated as the father of the child ...

Briefly, the effect of these provisions is that in all cases, the woman who receives the donated gametes (sperm or eggs), or a donated embryo, and gestates the child to term, is the legal mother of that child. Conversely, in no case will a donor (either male or female) of genetic material be regarded as the legal parent. In the case of donated sperm, where the woman in receipt of it is married, the presumption of legitimacy will apply, so that her husband is regarded as the child's legal father. The only exception would be where he could positively demonstrate that he had not consented to his wife receiving such treatment. In respect of unmarried women, there is no similar presumption of legitimacy, but in so far as she received infertility treatment together with her partner, the latter will be treated as the child's father at law. The 1990 Act thus encourages couples who receive licensed treatment within its terms (in contrast to the case of unlicensed 'DIY' treatments where the legal father would remain the gamete provider). However, it is apparent that, as a consequence of this policy, situations will arise (eg, where a husband shows he did not consent to his wife's treatment or, perhaps more often, a single woman is given licensed treatment) where the child will be legally fatherless. In this context, it was confirmed in the case of *U v W (AG Intervening)* [1997] 2 FLR 282, that the partner of a woman who received IVF treatment (using donated embryos) in Italy was not the legal father of the resulting twins, even though he had been present with her at the clinic when it was administered.

The gamete providers

The ethical and legal issues in relation to the third party 'collaborators' who contribute their gametes in order for others to be treated may conveniently be divided into two parts. First, how should they be treated at the initial point of recruitment and screening; secondly, what role, if any, should they be accorded after the birth of any child which, genetically, is theirs?

Recruitment and screening issues

How should society go about finding gamete providers and how much care should be taken over their selection? Another question is whether they should receive counselling about the implications of donation for their own protection. At present, the recruitment of donors occurs under a shroud of secrecy, with the main source of donated semen continuing to be students in medical schools. Although Warnock disapproved of payment in return for such donations, s 12(e) of the 1990 Act contemplates that payment for gametes and embryos may occur pursuant to 'directions' issued individually to clinics by the HFE Authority. At present, a modest fee of £15 is standardly paid for semen, the fear being that otherwise the supply would diminish.

It might well be thought desirable to organise recruitment upon different lines: the Warnock Committee was clearly impressed with the system operative in France:

Warnock Committee, *Report of the Committee of Inquiry into Human Fertilisation and Embryology*, Cmnd 9314, 1984, London: HMSO:

4.27 We have heard from many sources about the difficulty of finding semen donors. It is our hope that this problem will diminish with growing public acceptance of AID, and with the legal changes we have recommended. We were however interested to hear of the way in which the French AID system recruits new donors. Prospective recipients of AID are asked to approach married couples among their friends with a view to persuading them to make a donation, not for the use of any particular recipient, to the semen bank. This approach seems to us to have several benefits: it spreads the appeal for donors to a broader section of the community; it emphasises the donation aspect, and couples rather than individuals are party to the donation. We heard of a strong dependence in some UK clinics on students for donations and we are concerned that a young man may in later years find the fact that he has made donations difficult to discuss with his wife and children. An argument has also been put to us that the only way to attract sufficient donors in this country is to offer a fee. The practice of the payment of donors varies considerably at the moment. It is something about which we are uneasy, given the atmosphere in which AID is practised. We are concerned that the offer of a fee may tempt some men to withhold from the doctor details that would, if known, make them unacceptable as donors.

However, the Committee recognised that for a French-style scheme to work, a general change in attitude toward male infertility would be required.

In contrast to sperm donation, payment for eggs from women is frowned upon and generally does not take place. Although this may appear *prima facie* to be an example of double standards, the principal reason is doubtless the far higher risks and discomfort attached to egg harvesting. In this sense it is akin to organ donations, for which payment is currently prohibited by criminal statute (see further below, Chapter 11).

The next issue concerns the need for the screening of donors. On the face of it, the desirability of doing so seems uncontroversial. However, though no one would seriously question the need to identify potential risks to the woman receiving treatment or to any resulting child (eg, where sperm is infected with the HIV virus), matters are more problematic when it comes to the screening/selection of donors for their *positive* attributes. This arguably enhances the autonomy of would-be parents. However, Warnock commented unfavourably upon the practice, in parts of the USA, of offering the latter a choice of donors:

Warnock Committee, *Report of the Committee of Inquiry into Human Fertilisation and Embryology*, Cmnd 9314, 1984, London: HMSO:

4.19 It is the practice of some clinics in the USA to provide detailed descriptions of donors, and to permit couples to exercise choice as to the donor they would prefer. In the evidence there was some support for the use of such descriptions. It is argued that they would provide information and reassurance for the parents and, at a later date, for the child. They might also be of benefit to the donor, as an indication that he is valued for his own sake. A detailed description also offers some choice to the woman who is to have the child, and lack of such choice can be said to diminish the importance of the woman's right to choose the father of her child.

4.20 The contrary view, also expressed in the evidence, is that detailed donor profiles would introduce the donor as a person in his own right. It is also argued that the use of profiles devalues the child who may seem to be wanted only if certain specifications are met, and this may become a source of disappointment to the parents if their expectations are unfulfilled.

Warnock instead felt that information provided to the rearing parent(s) should be limited to that needed for their reassurance, such as the donor's ethnic group and genetic health (para 4.21). In fact, the current Code of Practice operated by the HFE Authority appears to be rather more liberal: it suggests that donors should be 'encouraged to provide as much other non-identifying biographical information about themselves as they wish' for passing on to prospective parents (2nd Revision: December 1995, para 3.42). Nevertheless, the risk of 'runs' on attractive donors is largely pre-empted by para 7.18, which imposes a limit of 10 live births per gamete provider.

In relation to the need for counselling of donors, this is provided for under Sched 3 (paras 1, 3 and 5) of the 1990 Act, which makes it clear that the offer of such counselling is a precondition of valid consent to the disposition of one's gametes under the Act (see above, p 359).

A final issue requiring consideration under this head pertains to the obtaining of donor eggs. It has already been noted that payment (beyond nominal expenses) is not favoured in respect of eggs and also that the process of harvesting them is painful and not without risk. Unsurprisingly, then, there is (in contrast to semen) a general shortfall in the supply of such eggs, and nearly all egg donation, in so far as it occurs, comes from women close to the intended recipient. In 1993 a potential solution was mooted, namely the harvesting of aborted female foetuses for their eggs (the eggs, albeit in undeveloped form, are already present at this stage and technology might make their use possible in the future). The suggestion, predictably, excited controversy, not only because of the practice's dependency on abortion (see the discussion of the use foetal tissue transplants generally below, Chapter 11, p 605), but also because of anxieties over the psychological well being of any child that might be born as a result. Accordingly, the Government asked the HFE Authority to prepare a report on the practice. Nevertheless, by the time the Authority reported in July 1994 (against it), Parliament had already legislated on the matter: s 3A of the HFEA 1990 (as inserted by the Criminal Justice and Public Order Act 1994) provides that:

3A Prohibition in connection with germ cells

(1) No person shall, for the purpose of providing fertility services for any woman, use female germ cells taken or derived from an embryo or a foetus or use embryos created by using such cells.

(2) In this section 'female germ cells' means cells of the female germ line and includes such cells at any stage of maturity and accordingly includes eggs; and 'fertility services' means medical, surgical or obstetric services provided for the purpose of assisting women to carry children.

Two points are noteworthy here. First, the provision appears to leave open the possibility that such eggs could be used for the purpose of creating embryos solely for research purposes. Secondly, whilst one may agree in principle with parliament's conclusion, the manner in which it proceeded seems, in this case, significantly to have usurped the role of the HFE Authority as originally contemplated by the 1990 Act.

Status vis à vis resulting children

As we have already seen, the HFEA 1990 (ss 27–28) makes it clear that, in relation to children born through treatment involving gamete donation, all parental powers and obligations inhere in the recipient(s) of such gametes, not the donor(s). A difficult question arises, however, over how far the identity of donors (genetic parents) should be kept from such children. As the Glover Report notes:

Glover, J et al, Report to the European Commission on Reproductive Technologies, Fertility and the Family, 1989, London: Fourth Estate, p 37:

Our sense of who we are is bound up with the story we tell about ourselves. A life where the biological parents are unknown is like a novel with the first chapter missing. Also there are the marked similarities between children and their biological parents. The child may wonder who is the person, perhaps among those passed in the street, who has that degree of closeness.

On the other hand, for young children who know who the semen donor was, there may be problems about their identity. They may see neither person as being unambiguously their father. This suggests that it may not be in the children's interest to be told who the donor is at an early age, but is not a point against a system of the Swedish type, setting the right to know at the age of 18. And, since the legal right to know need not be exercised, no child loses anything by it. Since some people care so much about their origins, seeing them as an important part of their identity, the interests of the children count strongly in favour of the right to know ...

Some of us were inclined to see knowledge of one's origin as so central to identity as to be a right. We all accept that ignorance of it can be a severe psychological disadvantage, and we give this great weight in thinking about policy. But the claim that this knowledge is an absolute right suggests, for instance, that it should always outweigh any degree of unwillingness by donors to discard the protection of anonymity. Is this plausible?

As the report mentions, in Sweden, children born from donated gametes have the legal right, once they are 18, to discover the identity of the donor(s). The report continues by assessing the impact of such a scheme as follows:

Glover, J *et al, Report to the European Commission on Reproductive Technologies, Fertility and the Family,* **1989, London: Fourth Estate, pp 36–38:**

The effect of abolishing anonymity in Sweden seems to have been an initial decline in numbers of donors. This may suggest that many donors prefer to be anonymous, quite apart from fear of paternity suits. But this must be linked to two other effects of the new law. There was a decline in demand: couples felt less comfortable at the thought that the child might eventually wish to contact the donor. And physicians in some AID centres refused to continue offering AID under the new law. In the centres still continuing with AID, the numbers of donors have returned to normal, although they are now more often older and more often married ...

In a system without anonymity, donors need not themselves be hugely disadvantaged. As in Sweden, their legal position can be protected. There may be some disadvantages in later contact by their offspring. But no one need become a donor if they think this possibility is a terrible one. Perhaps the interests of the children count for more than the possible disadvantages to the donors.

But the case for anonymity does not here simply rest on a direct appeal to the interests of the donors. The fear is that, through putting off potential donors, abolition of anonymity will damage the whole programme. The losers will be infertile couples who will no longer be able to have this help in having children because potential donors have voted with their feet.

The extreme views are, on the one hand, that knowledge of the donor is an inviolable right, and, on the other hand, that anonymity should always be guaranteed. Perhaps a reasonable middle course can be found.

We suggest that the child's interests create a strong *presumption* in favour of openness, but with protection for the various parties involved. As in the Swedish model, the social parents should be protected from intrusion when the 'child' still is a child, and the donor should be protected from paternity claims. But, although we favour openness, this is a presumption rather than an absolute right. There is a case for adopting a Swedish-type law for an experimental period, and seeing what happens to donor recruitment. If it slumps disastrously, public appeals could be tried to counteract the effects of the new system. If none of this worked, there would then be a case for abandoning the experiment.

The Warnock Report was more cautious and recommended (para 4.22) that the anonymity of semen donors be guaranteed. Its position is that reflected in the 1990 Act. Though the latter requires the HFE Authority to maintain a register linking gamete providers so far as possible with resultant offspring, access to it is strictly controlled:

Human Fertilisation and Embryology Act 1990:

Information

31   The Authority's register of information

> (1)   The Authority shall keep a register which shall contain any information obtained by the Authority which falls within sub-s (2) below.

> (2)   Information falls within this subsection if it relates to—

>> (a)   the provision of treatment services for any identifiable individual; or

>> (b)   the keeping or use of the gametes of any identifiable individual or of an embryo taken from any identifiable woman, or if it shows that any identifiable individual was, or may have been, born in consequence of treatment services.

> (3)   A person who has attained the age of 18 ('the applicant') may by notice to the Authority require the Authority to comply with a request under sub-s (4) below, and the Authority shall do so if—

>> (a)   the information contained in the register shows that the applicant was, or may have been, born in consequence of treatment services; and

>> (b)   the applicant has been given a suitable opportunity to receive proper counselling about the implications of compliance with the request.

> (4)   The applicant may request the Authority to give the applicant notice stating whether or not the information contained in the register shows that a person other than a parent of the applicant would or might, but for ss 27–29 of this Act, be a parent of the applicant and, if it does show that—

>> (a)   giving the applicant so much of that information as relates to the person concerned as the Authority is required by regulations to give (but no other information); or

    (b) stating whether or not that information shows that, but for ss 27–29 of this Act, the applicant, and a person specified in the request as a person whom the applicant proposes to marry, would or might be related.

  (5) Regulations cannot require the Authority to give any information as to the identity of a person whose gametes have been used or from whom an embryo has been taken if a person to whom a licence applied was provided with the information at a time when the Authority could not have been required to give information of the kind in question ...

Whilst the section contemplates that, in the future, regulations may be passed requiring the Authority to divulge specified information about the donor to such offspring who have attained the age of 18 and been offered suitable counselling (s 31(3)–(4)), at present no such regulations have been enacted. Moreover, if and when they are, s 31(5) makes it clear that they will not be retrospective in effect. Thus a child born today would have no right of access to such information even if, by the time it reaches 18, regulations are in force which give children *born then* such a right.

Anonymity may be understood partly in terms of protecting the donor, but perhaps more salient are the interests of the recipient(s) of treatment who will rear the child. Such is the continued stigma surrounding infertility (of males in particular), that many such parents are unlikely to tell the child that it was produced by collaborative reproduction in the first place. Indeed in Sweden the evidence is that, whilst levels of donation may have returned to normal, would-be rearing parents are increasingly travelling abroad for treatment.

The child

It is apparent from the foregoing discussion that, while the law gives a nod to the interests of prospective children (in s 13(5) of the HFEA 1990), in practice these are largely subordinated to those of the other key players in the collaborative reproductive process, ie, the gamete providers and the rearing parents. The interests of the latter in preserving anonymity/confidentiality appear to prevail over any interest the child may have in knowledge as to its provenance. The philosophical justification for this is that, without such protection for these other parties, the child would perhaps never have existed at all, and that surely its existence, albeit with the marginal disadvantage of not knowing who one (or possibly both) of its genetic parents is, is preferable from its own point of view.

There are, on the other hand, two specific exceptions allowed for by the HFEA 1990 where a child may have some rights to discover information pertaining to its genetic antecedence. First, as is apparent from s 31 itself, partial disclosure is allowed for under sub-s (4)(b) where a person produced by fertility treatment is contemplating marriage. Indeed, given that a person may marry at 16, s 31(6)–(7) specifically extends this right to those aged between 16 and 18, as follows:

31 The Authority's register of information

(6) A person who has not attained the age of 18 ('the minor') may by notice to the Authority specifying another person ('the intended spouse') as a person whom the minor proposes to marry require the Authority to comply with a request under sub-s (7) below, and the Authority shall do so if–

(a) the information contained in the register shows that the minor was, or may have been, born in consequence of treatment services; and

(b) the minor has been given a suitable opportunity to receive proper counselling about the implications of compliance with the request.

(7) The minor may request the Authority to give the minor notice stating whether or not the information contained in the register shows that, but for ss 27–29 of this Act, the minor and the intended spouse would or might be related.

It is apparent that these provisions are designed to reduce the risk of children born from the same donated gametes from entering into an incestuous marriage with each other.

Secondly, full disclosure (ie, which identifies the individual gamete provider) may occur in accordance with s 35 of the Act:

35 Disclosure in interests of justice: congenital disabilities, etc

(1) Where for the purpose of instituting proceedings under s 1 of the Congenital Disabilities (Civil Liability) Act 1976 (civil liability to child born disabled) it is necessary to identify a person who would or might be the parent of a child but for ss 27–29 of this Act, the court may, on the application of the child, make an order requiring the Authority to disclose any information contained in the register kept in pursuance of s 31 of this Act identifying that person ...

Such disclosure is part of a cluster of provisions designed to afford remedies to children injured prenatally in the course of fertility treatment provided to one or both of their parents. Gillian Douglas explains the logic and potential effect of these provisions as follows:

Douglas, G, *Law, Fertility and Reproduction*, 1991, London: Sweet & Maxwell, pp 137–38:

English law does not usually permit a child to bring an action for 'wrongful life' which is a claim that he or she should never have been born. However, a handicapped child who claims that his or her birth resulted from defective gametes being used, or a defective embryo being wrongly transferred, has now been given a right of action under the Congenital Disabilities (Civil

Liability) Act 1976, which was originally enacted to deal with cases concerning prenatal injury.

That legislation was amended by the 1990 Act, to make clear that a child may sue under it where he or she is born disabled, and the disability results from an act or omission in course of the selection, or the keeping or use outside the body, of the embryo ... or of the gametes used to bring about the creation of the embryo.

While this will cover damage caused by cryopreservation, for example, it also encompasses selection of gametes or an embryo, and is therefore akin to the wrongful life action, because the plaintiff will be arguing that the particular gametes or embryo should never have been transferred and the plaintiff should therefore never have been born.

The new section is obviously directed towards the medical staff who carry out the treatment. Under s 1A(3), they are liable if, at the time of the embryo transfer, placement of the sperm and eggs in the woman, or insemination, either or both parents knew the risk of the child being born disabled as a result of the act or omission. This is an added incentive to ensure that patients are aware of the risks they run, and it also means that it will be rare that a child will be able to succeed under the Act.

Where the *donor* of the gametes fails to reveal infection or genetic disease, it will be more difficult for the child to bring a claim. Of course, in most cases, there would be no advantage to the child to sue the donor rather than the doctor, who will carry insurance. But where a condition cannot be revealed by testing, so that the doctor would not be at fault, the child might wish to seek redress from the donor. The anonymity of the donor may in such a case be overridden, by the child applying to the court for an order under s 35 of the 1990 Act requiring the Authority to disclose identifying information, so that the child may sue under the 1976 Act. The child would have to rely on s 1 of that Act, which requires that an 'occurrence' ... 'affected either parent of the child in his or her ability to have a normal healthy child ...'. Section 4(4A) now provides that 'parent' includes a person who would be a parent, but for the operation of ss 27–29 of the 1990 Act, so a child could claim where, for example, the sperm donor had been exposed to radiation, leading to genetic aberrations which may cause childhood leukaemia. However, where a donor carries a genetic disease such as cystic fibrosis, there would not seem to have been an 'occurrence' which has affected his ability to have a normal healthy child, for he was born with the gene. A child who suffers from the disease may not therefore be able to claim against him.

As Douglas notes, the need for 'an occurrence' makes the precise scope of s 35 somewhat uncertain. Moreover, it can be argued that the very extension of protection to a child who, but for the negligent conduct in question, would not have been conceived, is (unless the child's life is a truly awful one) vulnerable to philosophical objections of the type noted above by the Glover Report. It also appears to run counter to recent case law (see the discussion of 'wrongful life', below, Chapter 8).

SURROGACY

Background

The concept of surrogacy, the possible motivations behind its practice, and the variety of forms it may take, are described by Gillian Douglas:

Douglas, G, *Law, Fertility and Reproduction*, 1991, London: Sweet & Maxwell, pp 141–44:

Surrogacy has received more adverse criticism than any of the other 'new' reproductive techniques. It was the first to receive legislative attention, in 1985 ... The true incidence of surrogacy is unknown, though it seems likely that the amount of emotion expended upon it is out of all proportion to the extent to which people would and do resort to it in order to have children. But surrogacy, together with abortion, raises in perhaps starkest form the questions of (a) the extent to which women should be free to exploit and control their reproductive capacity, even when they have no wish to raise a child themselves, and (b) the degree to which others should be able to call upon that reproductive capacity to fulfil their own needs.

Our stereotyped images of motherhood and of the appropriate circumstances in which children should be born are particularly challenged here. Additionally, the conflict between the potential of surrogacy to enhance female reproductive freedom, and its potential to allow exploitation and control by others of women's bodies, has been responsible for considerably divided opinions among feminists on the desirability of its practice.

(a) Definition of surrogacy

Surrogacy was defined by the Warnock Committee as the 'practice whereby one woman carries a child for another with the intention that the child should be handed over after birth'. This implies that the carrying woman acts *at the request of another woman* who is usually unable to have a child herself. While this may be so in some cases, the impression gleaned from the few cases which have arisen in this country, and the greater number in the United States of America, suggests rather that the inspiration and driving force for the arrangement often comes from the husband or partner (the 'commissioning father') of the infertile woman. It is the man's desire to have a child genetically related to himself which appears the prime motivation for many surrogacy arrangements. However, it is certainly right to stress that the essence of surrogacy is that the woman who bears the child gives it to someone else to be raised.

Some confusion surrounds the definition of surrogate arrangements. The carrying woman may or may not be the genetic mother. In the more common type of surrogate arrangement at present, she provides the ovum, and the commissioning father provides the sperm. This type of arrangement has been called partial surrogate motherhood. As IVF and embryo technology become surer, and now that the Human Fertilisation and Embryology Act 1990 caters for, and perhaps encourages, such treatments, a different type of surrogacy can be expected to become more common. In this version, the commissioning mother provides the ovum, which is fertilised *in vitro* with her husband's sperm, then gestated in the surrogate's uterus. This full surrogacy may also be described as womb-leasing. The carrying woman is not genetically related to the child she carries.

Since the general aim of these reproductive techniques is to maximise the possibility of having a child who is genetically related to the intended parents, it is to be expected that womb-leasing would offer a 'better' bargain to the commissioning parents because the child would be genetically theirs.

In English law, the only statutory definition of surrogacy is contained in the Surrogacy Arrangements Act 1985. Under s 1(2), a surrogate mother:

> ... means a woman who carries a child in pursuance of an arrangement
>
> (a) made before she began to carry the child; and
>
> (b) made with a view to any child carried in pursuance of it being handed over to, and the parental rights being exercised (so far as practicable) by, another person or other persons.

By s 1(3):

> An arrangement is a surrogacy arrangement if, were a woman to whom the arrangement relates to carry a child in pursuance of it, she would be a surrogate mother.

It has been the prospect of a woman bearing a child for money which has generated most heat in the surrogacy debate, and indeed, evidence suggests that few women are likely to enter into surrogacy for altruistic reasons.

(b) When might surrogacy be used?

Partial surrogacy could be used where the commissioning mother is unable either to produce eggs or to gestate them. Full surrogacy could be utilised where the woman ovulates, but may lack a uterus, or where carrying a child could be dangerous for her health, or for that of the child. For example, the commissioning mother might have kidney disease or high blood pressure, or she might have a history of miscarriages or ectopic pregnancies ... Surrogacy could also be used as a less high-tech strategy where one or other of the commissioning parents carries a genetic disorder which might be passed on to offspring. The Warnock Committee noted that surrogacy could theoretically be used for 'convenience', where the commissioning mother is physically able to bear a child, but wishes to avoid doing so, perhaps in order not to interrupt her career, or not to affect her appearance. Surrogacy could also be utilised by lesbian women, and by single men and male homosexuals who want to bring up children.

Ethical considerations

As Douglas hints, the Warnock Report was generally hostile to surrogacy. Its principal objection seems to have taken a deontological form, viz, 'that people should treat others as a means to their own ends, however desirable the consequences, must always be liable to moral objection' (para 8.17). Glover, reporting to the EC Commission in 1989, summarised the main arguments for and against the practice as follows:

Glover, J et al, *Report to the European Commission on Reproductive Technologies, Fertility and the Family*, 1989, London: Fourth Estate, pp 74–76:

1 The case for surrogacy

Part of the case is straightforward. Surrogacy relieves childlessness. For women who have had repeated miscarriages, or who suffer from conditions making pregnancy dangerous, surrogacy may be the only hope of having a child.

Another, more problematic, argument appeals to the interests of the child who would not have existed without surrogacy.

Another argument appeals to liberty. Some strong justification is needed for preventing people from bearing children to help their sisters or friends. And a similar strong justification is needed for preventing people freely contracting to do this for someone for money. This argument relates to the legality of surrogacy, but does nothing to show that surrogacy is a good thing in itself. The central case for that has to rest on relieving the burden of childlessness.

2 The case against surrogacy

(a) *The children*: One line of thought appeals to the rights of the child. It appears in the Catholic document issued by the Congregation for the Doctrine of the Faith, which says that surrogacy 'offends the dignity and the right of the child to be conceived, carried in the womb, brought into the world and brought up by his own parents'.

This case seems to us not overwhelming. Even if the child has a strong interest in being created sexually, to call this a *right* is to claim that it trumps *any* interests of the childless couple. This requires that being the child of a surrogate is such an indignity that, by comparison, relieving any degree of the potential parents' misery is to count for nothing. We have not found the powerful supporting argument this would need.

The objection is made even weaker by a further problem. For the potential child, the alternative to surrogacy may be non-existence. It seems unlikely that the child will see surrogacy as so bad as to wish he or she had not been born at all. The 'right' looks like one the child will later be glad was not respected. It is hard to see the case for giving this supposed interest any weight at all, let alone for saying that it justifies leaving people unwillingly childless.

Another argument appeals to the psychological effects of surrogacy on the child. If the surrogacy is paid for there is a danger that the child will think he or she has been bought. Also, it is sometimes suggested that surrogacy breaks a bond formed by the time of birth. Dr John Marks, the chairman of the British Medical Association, has said: 'By the time a baby is born there is a bond between the mother and the child. With surrogacy you break that bond. You are depriving the child of one natural parent. We think that is wrong.' (*The Guardian* (1987) 8 May). It is reported that the General Medical Council may ban doctors from involvement in surrogacy. This step has already been taken in West Germany.

The surrogate mother may well feel a bond between herself and the child. But is there reason to believe in any bond in the other direction before birth? Or could this be an illusion created by projecting the mother's feelings on to the foetus? If the child's feelings are a reason against surrogacy, the baby has to have, by the time of birth, highly specific feelings towards the particular woman who bears him. The evidence for this can charitably be described as slight.

Suppose, for the sake of argument, that there is such a bond. It is then undesirable to break it. But, where it is broken, is the child so harmed that it would have been better if he or she had not been born? For this is what banning surrogacy on these grounds seems to imply. We do not have such drastic thoughts about people who are adopted. The British Medical Association's Board of Science is quoted as saying that while adoption may be 'the next best thing' for a child facing an uncertain future, any arrangement where a surrogate mother hands over the child 'dooms it to second best from the start' (*The Independent* (1987) 8 May). But is it obvious here that no life at all is preferable to 'second best'?

(b) *Conflicts*: The conflicts sometimes arising between the potential parents and the surrogate mother may harm the child, and this is part of the case against surrogacy.

(c) *Effects on the family*: Perhaps introducing a third party so intimately into the process of having children may weaken the institution of the family ...

(d) *The surrogate mother*: The position of the surrogate mother varies, according to whether she is bearing a child to help a sister or friend, or has made a commercial arrangement. There is the criticism that surrogacy is an invasion of her bodily integrity. This criticism may be weaker if she willingly agreed than if she was forced into it by money problems. Sometimes she may bitterly regret having agreed to give away the baby. As we have seen, there is a danger of her being exploited. Financial pressures may put her in a weak position to resist contractual conditions which give little weight to her interests.

Another important motive for volunteering to act as a surrogate seems to be the desire for friendship with the parents-to-be. As this is usually exactly what the parents-to-be do not want, it is an illusory objective. She wants friendship: she is treated as a provider of a service, and afterwards dismissed ...

The response of the law

It is important that the questions of the moral and legal permissibility of surrogacy are kept separate. In particular, the law must distinguish in its response between two different moments in time; it must first determine how far it is legitimate to discourage, or indeed prohibit, the formation of surrogacy arrangements in the first place. Secondly, however, in so far as its strictures at this earlier stage are ignored and a surrogacy arrangement results in pregnancy, the law must attribute rights and duties to the participants and, if they are in dispute, adjudicate between them. In doing so, of course, the position of any resulting child must be resolved. These two distinct stages were recognised by Latey J in one of the first surrogacy cases to reach the English courts.

Re C (A Minor) (Wardship: Surrogacy) [1985] FLR 846, HC (Latey J)

A partial surrogacy arrangement, negotiated by an agency, was entered into between an American commissioning couple and a British woman, Kim Cotton (who was married with three children of her own). Following the successful birth of a child, it was clear that Mrs Cotton was happy to relinquish all parental rights in respect of it. The commissioning father issued a wardship summons in order to obtain custody, which was duly granted.

> **Latey J**: First and foremost, and at the heart of the prerogative jurisdiction in wardship, is what is best for the child or children concerned. That and nothing else. Plainly the methods used to produce a child, as this baby has been, and the commercial aspects of it, raise difficult and delicate problems of ethics, morality and social desirability. These problems are under active consideration elsewhere.
>
> Are they relevant in arriving at a decision on what now and, so far as one can tell, in the future is best for this child? If they are relevant, it is incumbent on the court to do its best to evaluate and balance them.
>
> In my judgment, however, they are not relevant. The baby is here. All that matters is what is best for her now that she is here and not how she arrived. If it be said (though it has not been said during these hearings) that because the father and his wife entered into these arrangements it is some indication of their unsuitability as parents, I should reject any such suggestion. If what they did was wrong (and I am not saying that it was), they did it in total innocence.
>
> It follows that the moral, ethical and social considerations are for others and not for this court in its wardship jurisdiction.
>
> So, what is best for this baby? Her natural mother does not ask for her. Should she go into Mr and Mrs A's care and be brought up by them? Or should some other arrangement be made for her, such as long term fostering with or without adoption as an end?
>
> The factors can be briefly stated. Mr A is the baby's father and he wants her, as does his wife. The baby's mother does not want her. Mr and Mrs A are a couple in their 30s. They are devoted to each other. They are both professional people, highly qualified. They have a very nice home in the country and another in a town. Materially they can give the baby a very good upbringing. But, far more importantly, they are both excellently equipped to meet the baby's emotional needs. They are most warm, caring, sensible people, as well as highly intelligent. When the time comes to answer the child's questions, they will be able to do so with professional advice if they feel they need it. Looking at this child's well being, physical and emotional, who better to have her care? No one.

Clearly, the two stages are often not separate in practice: the anticipated response of the law at the second stage will almost certainly have an impact on the parties' decision to risk entering into the arrangement in the first place. Nevertheless, in conceptual terms, it is useful to look at each in turn.

Entering into the surrogacy arrangement

Following adverse media reaction to the *Re C* case, and in the light of the recommendations of the Warnock Committee, parliament enacted the Surrogacy Arrangements Act 1985 (SAA 1985). After defining such arrangements (see the extract from Douglas above, p 390), the Act went on, in s 2, to make the negotiation of surrogacy arrangements on a commercial basis a criminal offence:

2   Negotiating surrogacy arrangements on a commercial basis, etc

(1)   No person shall on a commercial basis do any of the following acts in the United Kingdom, that is–

(a)   initiate or take part in any negotiations with a view to the making of a surrogacy arrangement;

(b)   offer or agree to negotiate the making of a surrogacy arrangement; or

(c)   compile any information with a view to its use in making, or negotiating the making of, surrogacy arrangements;

and no person shall in the United Kingdom knowingly cause another to do any of those acts on a commercial basis.

(2)   A person who contravenes sub-s (1) above is guilty of an offence; but it is not a contravention of that sub-section–

(a)   for a woman, with a view to becoming a surrogate mother herself, to do any act mentioned in that sub-section or to cause such an act to he done; or

(b)   for any person, with a view to a surrogate mother carrying a child for him, to do such an act or to cause such an act to be done.

(3)   For the purposes of this section, a person does an act on a commercial basis (subject to sub-s (4) below) if–

(a)   any payment is at any time received by himself or another in respect of it; or

(b)   he does it with a view to any payment being received by himself or another in respect of making, or negotiating or facilitating the making of, any surrogacy arrangement.

In this sub-section 'payment' does not include payment to or for the benefit of a surrogate mother or prospective surrogate mother.

As is apparent, the thrust of the legislation is against the facilitators of commercial surrogacy arrangements, notably agencies which make a profit from mediating between a would-be commissioning couple and a potential surrogate. Similarly, s 3 of the SAA 1985 imposes criminal liability on those involved in the advertising of such arrangements. In respect of s 2, it is important to note that s 2(2) expressly confers an immunity from criminal liability upon the immediate participants: s 2(2)(a) protects the surrogate and s 2(2)(b) the commissioning couple (in accordance with established principles of statutory interpretation, the reference to 'him' in the latter clause includes 'her'). This reflected the view of the Warnock Committee that it would be undesirable for the birth of a child to a surrogate to be tainted with criminality.

Would a doctor (or his clinic) who received a fee for medically facilitating a surrogate pregnancy (eg, by carrying out IVF or AID treatment on the surrogate) be liable for any offence? The answer (assuming that he has the appropriate licence to carry out such treatment under the HFEA 1990) would appear to be 'no'. However, the BMA, in its recent guidelines, *Changing Conceptions of Motherhood: The Practice of Surrogacy in Britain*, 1996, London: BMA, continues to be cautious in its advice to doctors, suggesting that surrogacy be considered 'an option of last resort'.

Resolving surrogacy arrangements

We must now consider the second stage at which the law may need to become involved in surrogacy, namely when an arrangement results in pregnancy (and the birth of a child). Two possibilities need to be considered. First, the parties to a surrogacy arrangement may have fallen into dispute. Secondly, in so far as there is no dispute (ie, the surrogate is willing to hand over the child and the commissioning parents are happy to accept it and to pay the agreed fee), there remains the need to legitimate the child.

Where the parties are in dispute

Typically, the surrogate, during the course of her pregnancy, may decide that she is not, after all, prepared to go through with the agreement to hand the child over after birth. In an early case (from 1978, though only reported in 1985), the court had to consider what its response should be in precisely these circumstances.

A v C [1985] FLR 445, CA (Stamp, Cumming-Bruce and Ormrod LJJ)

Mr A wanted a child of his own before he married Mrs B, a divorcee who was no longer able to have children. They accordingly found a surrogate, Miss C, who agreed to bear Mr A's child in return for £3,000. Miss C was impregnated with Mr A's sperm by AID but later changed her mind about handing over the child. At first instance, Comyn J held that the agreement was void on grounds of public policy but that Mr A could continue to have access to the child. Miss C appealed:

Ormrod LJ: This is an appeal from an order which was made by Comyn J on 20 June 1978 under which he gave care and control to the mother of a child born about a year ago and made an order for access by the father to the child covering the next two years or until further order. He also made a supervision order in favour of the local authority.

The judge gave judgment in open court, asking that the press should take all the necessary steps to avoid identifying the parties and it is quite plainly a case in which that same course should be followed in any report of this appeal.

The fact that the judge gave judgment in open court makes it unnecessary and, in my view, undesirable to recapitulate the quite deplorable story which lies behind this case. It is only necessary to say in the barest outline what happened.

The father, who is in a position to know very well how to behave, found himself in a position of some difficulty, because he was living, unfortunately for him, with a lady who, through no fault of her own, could not have any more children. He appears to have become obsessed with the idea that it was essential to his future happiness that he should be able to be the father of a child himself and have the pleasure and the privilege of bringing that child up as his own child. It is a state of mind which is very easy to understand and sympathise with. It is very unfortunate for both men and women when they find themselves in a situation where they are unable to have that very natural satisfaction.

The only difference between this father and the others is that the others try to accept it, whereas this father embarked upon the most extraordinarily naive plan to achieve his object – simply to find a woman who was prepared to be artificially impregnated with his semen to produce a baby which would then be handed over to him and the lady with whom he was living (and to whom he is now married) for adoption. It is a simple, logical, but totally inhuman proceeding, and shows, in my view, very grave defects in his character and, indeed, in the characters of all three participants, because the lady with whom he was living was definitely involved in the plan, no doubt now to her great regret. One can feel very sorry for her in that she must feel that it was her fault in a sense that the father was in the position in which he was, so that she felt obliged to help him and take part in this most extraordinary and irresponsible arrangement. It is unnecessary to make any more comment on the irresponsibility shown by all three of the adults in this case, which is perhaps only rivalled by the irresponsibility of the person who performed the insemination on the mother. Having said that, so far as the background is concerned, I do not propose to say any more about it.

The judge gave, if I may say so with respect, a most careful and lucid judgment and one in which he has found all the necessary facts with great clarity. He has avoided none of the difficulties which arose on the disputed facts. Since we are only concerned here with an appeal against that part of the order which provides for access, I do not think that it will be useful to travel over this sad and miserable story any more. It is enough to say that the mother, at a fairly early stage in the pregnancy, began, quite naturally, to feel grave doubts about the course which she had embarked upon and by the time the child was born she had plainly made up her mind that she could not possibly go on with such a bizarre and unnatural arrangement and she forewent the substantial sum of money which she was to be paid in the event of her handing over the baby.

The judge has described the mother's situation and her background and the father's. It is quite apparent that there is a wide gulf socially and culturally between them and that the future contains nothing at all except bitterness for their future relationship. We are dealing here with two people who have never had any sort of relationship together at all, not even a relationship amounting to one single isolated act of intercourse taking place casually on some occasion and never to be repeated. Here we have nothing but the clinical fact that the father has contributed the necessary male sperm to the conception of this child. That is the sum total of his contribution to this child ...

In the circumstances Mr A was denied access.

This case is notable for the censorious comments of all three Lords Justices. Though attitudes towards the practice have softened somewhat in the years since that decision, Parliament subsequently chose (when enacting the HFEA 1990) to amend the SAA 1985 so as to reinforce the point that surrogacy contracts will be void and of no effect:

1A Surrogacy arrangements unenforceable

No surrogacy arrangement is enforceable by or against any of the persons making it ...

Nevertheless, the unenforceability of the arrangement will not, in itself, be determinative of the outcome in a surrogacy dispute. This is because what is generally at issue is the future of a child: is it to be brought up by the surrogate who gestated it or the couple who commissioned it (and to whom it may be partly or wholly genetically related)? Thus, in principle, and notwithstanding the voidness of their contractual rights, it might seem that the commissioning parents could win custody.

An analogy might be suggested here with cases of marital break-up in which the custody of a child is at issue. The courts, in dealing with such matters as residence and contact, will, in accordance with the provisions of the Children Act 1989, regard the welfare of the child as paramount. This approach can indeed already be seen at work in the pre-Children Act case of *Re P (Minors)*.

Re P (Minors) [1987] 2 FLR 421, HC (Sir John Arnold P)

Mrs P, a divorcee with one son of her own, entered into an arrangement with Mr B to bear his child and hand it over to him and his wife, Mrs B. As her pregnancy progressed, she began to have doubts about honouring the agreement and these hardened following the birth of twins. Although upset about disappointing Mr and Mrs B, she ultimately refused to hand the twins over. The latter were made wards of court.

Sir John Arnold P: In this, as in any other wardship dispute, the welfare of the children, or child, concerned is the first and paramount consideration which the court must, by statute, take into account, and that is what I do.

These children have been, up to their present age of approximately five months, with, quite consistently, their mother and in those circumstances there must necessarily have been some bonding of those children with their mother and that is undoubtedly coupled with the fact that she is their mother, a matter which weighs predominantly in the balance in favour of leaving the children with their mother, but there are other factors which weigh in the opposite balance and which, as is said by Mr B through his counsel, outweigh the advantages of leaving the children with their mother, and it is that balancing exercise which the court is required to perform ...

What then are the factors which the court should take into account? I have already mentioned on the side of Mrs P the matters which weigh heavily in the balance are the fact of her maternity, that she bore the children and carried them for the term of their gestation and that ever since she has conferred upon them the maternal care which they have enjoyed and has done so successfully. The key social worker in the case who has given evidence testifies to the satisfactory nature of the care which Mrs P has conferred upon the children and this assessment is specifically accepted by Mr B as being an accurate one. I start, therefore, from the position that these babies have bonded with their mother in a state of domestic care by her of a satisfactory nature and I now turn to the factors which are said to outweigh those advantages, so as to guide the court upon the proper exercise of the balancing function to the conclusion that the children ought to be taken away from Mrs P, and passed over, under suitable arrangements, to Mr and Mrs B. They are principally as follows. It is said, and said quite correctly, that the shape of the B family is the better shape of a family in which these children might be brought up, because it contains a father as well as a mother and that is undoubtedly true. Next, it is said that the material circumstances of the B family are such that they exhibit a far larger degree of affluence than can be demonstrated by Mrs P. That, also, is undoubtedly true. Then it is said that the intellectual quality of the environment of the B's home and the stimulus which would be afforded to these babies, if they were to grow up in that home, would be greater than the corresponding features in the home of Mrs P ... Then it is said that the religious comfort and support which the B's derive from their Church is greater than anything of that sort available to Mrs P. How far that is true, I simply do not know. I do know that the B's are practising Christians and do derive advantages from that circumstance, but nobody asked Mrs P about this and I am not disposed to assume that she lacks that sort of comfort and support in the absence of any investigation by way of cross-examination to lay the foundations for such a conclusion. Then it is said, and there is something in this, that the problems which might arise from the circumstance that these children who are, of course, congenitally derived from the semen of Mr B and bear traces of Mr B's Asiatic origin would be more easily understood and discussed and reconciled in the household of Mr and Mrs B, a household with an Asiatic ethnic background, than they would be if they arose in relation to these children while they were situated in the home of Mrs P, which is in an English village and which has no non-English connections ...

As regards [these] factors, they are, in the aggregate, weighty, but I do not think, having given my very best effort to the evaluation of the case dispassionately on both sides, that they ought to be taken to outweigh the advantages to these children of preserving the link with the mother to whom they are bonded and who has, as is amply testified, exercised over them a satisfactory level of maternal care, and accordingly it is, I think, the duty of the court to award the care and control of these babies to their mother.

This case suggests that there is a strong presumption that the welfare of the child is best served by leaving it with the surrogate mother. This is especially so, given the inevitable delay, following the birth of the child, in such disputes coming before the courts. The position might well be different where the surrogate initially surrenders custody of the child and subsequently tries to reclaim it from the commissioning couple. This is borne out by the decision of the New Jersey Supreme Court in the well known American case, *In the Matter of Baby M* 537 A 2d 1227 (1988). Whilst holding the agreement void, the court allowed custody to remain with the commissioning couple (with whom, by the time of the final hearing, the child had been living for 18 months).

Are there any other circumstances in which the commissioning couple might win out? In particular, might the fact of a particular surrogacy being 'total' in nature make a difference? (All the cases considered so far have been ones of partial surrogacy, ie, the surrogate has also been the genetic mother.) The first point to remember is that, whether the surrogacy is total or partial, the surrogate remains the mother at law: see s 27 of the HFEA 1990. Having said that, it might be felt that the commissioning couple should have more rights in cases where they both are the child's genetic parents and the surrogate 'merely' gestated it.

In a Californian case, *Anna J v Mark C et al* 12 Cal App 4th 977 (1991), the court, in awarding custody in a total surrogacy case to the genetic parents, saw genetic, rather than gestational, parenthood as the locus of parental rights. Significantly, however, the commissioning/genetic parents in that case (as in the *Baby M* case) were already caring for the child. Where this is not so, it is suggested that the courts – at least in the UK – may well prefer to allow the child to remain with the surrogate. For one thing, they would be reluctant to send out a signal to future surrogate mothers who, while pregnant, change their minds about handing over the child that, where it is not genetically their own, it could be taken from them against their will. As the Glover Report argues, this could be bad for the child. Instead, the report suggests that 'the possibility of the surrogate mother changing her mind should be accepted by the couple as one of the risks of this way of trying to overcome childlessness'.

Where the parties are agreed

Fewer problems arise where there is consensus between the surrogate and commissioning couple that the child be handed over.

Indeed, s 30 of the HFEA 1990 expressly allows for application to the court by the commissioning parents to obtain a parental order in respect of the child. This section, which was brought into effect on 1 November 1994 by the HFE (Parental Order) Regulations 1994, provides that:

30 Parental orders in favour of gamete donors

(1) The court may make an order providing for a child to be treated in law as the child of the parties to a marriage (referred to in this section as 'the husband' and 'the wife') if–

(a) the child has been carried by a woman other than the wife as the result of the placing in her of an embryo or sperm and eggs or her artificial insemination;

(b) the gametes of the husband or the wife, or both, were used to bring about the creation of the embryo; and

(c) the conditions in sub-ss (2)–(7) below are satisfied.

(2) The husband and the wife must apply for the order within six months of the birth of the child or, in the case of a child born before the coming into force of this Act, within six months of such coming into force.

(3) At the time of the application and of the making of the order–

(a) the child's home must be with the husband and the wife; and

(b) the husband or the wife, or both of them, must be domiciled in a part of the United Kingdom or in the Channel Islands or the Isle of Man.

(4) At the time of the making of the order both the husband and the wife must have attained the age of 18.

(5) The court must be satisfied that both the father of the child (including a person who is the father by virtue of s 28 of this Act), where he is not the husband, and the woman who carried the child have freely, and with full understanding of what is involved, agreed unconditionally to the making of the order.

(6) Sub-section (5) above does not require the agreement of a person who cannot be found or is incapable of giving agreement and the agreement of the woman who carried the child is ineffective for the purposes of that sub-section if given by her less than six weeks after the child's birth.

(7) The court must be satisfied that no money or other benefit (other than for expenses reasonably incurred) has been given or received by the husband or the wife for or in consideration of–

(a) the making of the order;

(b) any agreement required by sub-s (5) above;

(c) the handing over of the child to the husband and the wife; or

(d) the making of any arrangements with a view to the making of the order;

unless authorised by the court.

The requirement that the surrogate must consent to the order, and that such consent is not valid where given less than six weeks after the birth of the child, is clearly there to protect the surrogate's position. Less obviously defensible is the underlying condition that the commissioning parents should be married: it may plausibly be argued that this amounts to unjustified discrimination against couples in long term heterosexual relationships, who are unmarried. *A fortiori* it will also prevent those in homosexual relationships from utilising the section. Instead, such couples will be forced back to using other, less favourable methods of adoption under the Adoption Act 1976. It is also noteworthy that responsibility for registering a child's birth remains with the surrogate. Because the child will ultimately have access to the Register of Births, it is apparent that, in contrast to gamete donation, the surrogacy process cannot remain anonymous.

In so far as s 30 is used, the courts now have a precedent that they can follow in the decision of Johnson J in *Re Q (Parental Order)*.

Re Q (Parental Order) [1996] 1 FLR 369, HC (Johnson J)

Baby Q was born in the summer of 1995 as a result of a total surrogacy arrangement. The unmarried surrogate, who received IVF treatment at a licensed clinic, was paid £8,280 to cover her expenses and loss of earnings. The commissioning couple applied for a parental order under s 30:

Johnson J: ... Turning belatedly to the particular application made to me, I am satisfied that the statutory requirements are all complied with, but I mention three.

The first relates to the consent of the carrying mother. She had entered into the procedure with the best of intentions, but when the time came to relinquish the child that she had carried so devotedly, she was overcome with doubt and at first declined to give her consent. This reaction is natural and was contemplated by parliament in stipulating that the carrying mother is to be given at least six weeks after the birth to make her decision before she can give a binding consent. One of the duties of the guardian *ad litem* under the Family Proceedings Courts (Children Act 1989) (Amendment) Rules 1994 is to investigate the circumstance of the carrying mother's consent.

It may be of interest if I quote *verbatim* from the guardian's report:

I have visited Miss A twice in order to ascertain her wishes in this matter and to try and clarify the issues around her agreement to the order. Miss A explained how she came to offer herself as a surrogate mother due to seeing the anguish of infertile friends and how she had never thought she would have difficulty parting with the baby she bore. When she received details of Mr and Mrs B she immediately warmed to them and these first good impressions were confirmed when she met them. Miss A has two children of her own and they are both aware of this child's whereabouts. They met Mr and Mrs B numerous times prior to the child's birth, staying at the house both with their mother and alone. They have been told that Mrs B could not grow the baby in her own tummy so Miss A did it for her and they always knew that the baby would not be living with them. At about 28 weeks Miss A experienced some bleeding and was admitted to hospital. She questioned for the first time what she was doing and feels that it was only at this stage that the baby began to feel like a real person to her and that she began to bond with her. Notwithstanding this first period of questioning she decided to carry through handing over the baby to Mr and Mrs B and remained of this view until after the birth. She left hospital without the baby but unfortunately when she decided a few days later to go in and visit the baby the hospital refused her access. Miss A was very upset and although the refusal was due to a misunderstanding and she later saw the baby, she then visited her solicitor with a view to securing the baby's placement with her. This was the position until late July 1995, but Miss A then thought deeply about what she could give the baby versus Mr and Mrs B. At no time had her decision to withdraw her agreement had anything to do with dissatisfaction with Mr and Mrs B as parents and she gradually decided that it was right for the baby to remain with them. In talking to Miss A, it is clear that the depth of feeling she experienced towards her baby took her by surprise. She said that she felt no different toward this baby at her birth than she had felt towards her other children and had not really been prepared for this. It is clear that Miss A felt emotionally torn in half by the separation from the baby. With time, however, and as her own body settled after the birth, so she was able to think more clearly about the issues and this is why she decided to give her agreement. I prepared an agreement form for her to sign on my second visit and she did this willingly and in a positive and definite manner. She fully understands the effects of a parental order, understanding that she loses all parental responsibility, and wishes the order to be made as soon as possible. She does not now wish to attend court herself for the hearing.

This account of the feelings of this carrying mother shows the sensitivity and indeed difficulty of the task of the guardian *ad litem* in these cases. This is obviously a demanding role and I was greatly heartened by the obvious care, fairness and understanding with which this guardian had performed her function.

Secondly I had to consider whether or not I should authorise payments totalling £8,280 which had been made to Miss A by Mr and Mrs B.

I hold that such authorisation can be given retrospectively. In so doing I follow the decision of Latey J in *Re Adoption Application (Payment for Adoption)* [1987] Fam 81 ... which was concerned with a similar provision in the Adoption Act 1976.

The guardian told me that she had at first thought that this amount seemed rather high but on further inquiry she concluded that the payments were understandable. £3,280 was made up of payments to cover clothes, daily trips to the doctor for injections, child care provision of her own children during some of those visits and similar related expenses. A further £5,000 was a payment to compensate Miss A for loss of earnings. Given the circumstances of the pregnancy and her potential earnings of £15,000 [per annum], I joined with the guardian in concluding that the payment was reasonable and, retrospectively, I gave authority for it. Finally, in the course of the guardian's investigation, the consultant who had carried out the medical procedures insisted that in his view and in the view of his hospital, Mr B was to be treated as the legal father of the child. The guardian told me that in her experience this is a frequent misunderstanding of the legislation and it was for this reason that I was asked to give a formal ruling. Certainly on my application of the Act to the circumstances of this case, there was no man who was to be 'treated as the father' and whose consent was necessary to the making of the order. I hope that this judgment will draw attention to the working of this important new statutory provision and will help to resolve the problems that are raised by s 30 concerning who is to be treated as the father for the purpose of giving consent to the making of this new form of order.

This case is interesting for a number of reasons. First it shows the degree of attachment that the surrogate may develop towards the child she carries, even in the case of total surrogacy. Secondly, it confirms that, to qualify as a father under s 28 of the 1990 Act, the man must have an existing relationship with the woman *receiving treatment*. Here, despite Mr B's provision of the sperm and the intent that he would rear the child, his relationship was with the commissioning mother, not Miss A. Finally, the decision suggests that, at least where the sum is in no way extortionate, a court will be fairly relaxed about authorising payment retrospectively to the surrogate under s 30(7) of the 1990 Act.

In October 1997, following further adverse media publicity accorded to the practice of surrogacy, the Government commissioned an inquiry (headed by Professor Margaret Brazier) into the arrangements for payments and regulation under the 1985 Act.

CHAPTER EIGHT

PREGNANCY AND ABORTION

INTRODUCTION

By contrast with the issues looked at in Chapter 7, in which the law has had, in the main, to respond to novel problems created by recent advances in medical technology, abortion as a procedure has existed for centuries. Nevertheless, it remains one of the most intractable and emotive topics within the province of medical law. Broadly speaking, 'abortion' denotes the practice of terminating a pregnancy in such a way as to destroy the life of the foetus being carried by the pregnant woman. In the case of abortions carried out early in pregnancy on non-viable foetuses, the fact that the foetus is expelled from the womb is sufficient for its death. In other cases, where the foetus is more mature (and capable of surviving outside the womb), additional steps will be taken to ensure that it dies prior to delivery. Either way, it is apparent that the practice stands in direct opposition to the major forms of fertility treatment considered in the last chapter. There the intention is normally to produce a pregnancy resulting in a successful live birth. Here, the intention is to bring an existing pregnancy to an end without the birth of the child. In another sense, however, there is a close relationship between the practices in that they both implicate (albeit in opposing ways) reproductive freedom. As John Robertson notes:

Robertson, JA, *Children of Choice*, 1994, Ewing, New Jersey: Princeton University Press, p 26:

An essential distinction is between the freedom to avoid reproduction and the freedom to reproduce. When people talk of reproductive rights, they usually have one or the other aspect in mind. Because different interests and justifications underlie each, and countervailing interests for limiting each aspect vary, recognition of one aspect does not necessarily mean that the other will also be respected; nor does limitation of one mean that the other can also be denied.

However, there is a mirroring or reciprocal relationship here. Denial of one type of reproductive liberty necessarily implicates the other. If a woman is not able to avoid reproduction through contraception or abortion, she may end up reproducing, with all the burdens that unwanted reproduction entails. Similarly, if one is denied the liberty to reproduce ... one is forced to avoid reproduction, thus experiencing the loss that absence of progeny brings. By extending reproductive options, new reproductive technologies present challenges to both aspects of procreative choice.

Gillian Douglas has explored the background to the right to avoid reproduction claimed for individuals as follows:

Douglas, G, *Law, Fertility and Reproduction*, 1991, London: Sweet & Maxwell, p 15:

Methods, effective or not, for avoiding conception or childbirth are probably as old as civilisation itself, and various remedies to alleviate childlessness are probably of equal antiquity. To what extent have individuals been at liberty to make use of these? The former, certainly, have always been forthrightly condemned by the Roman Catholic Church, drawing originally upon the Jewish view that the duty to procreate through marriage is the first of all commandments. Sex became associated by St Augustine with sin, and could only be justified by procreation. Aquinas considered that to dissociate sex from procreation was to act against nature and therefore to sin.

The breaking down of this religious influence and the rise of a rights-based political philosophy in the West during the 18th and 19th centuries, utilised first by men and then by women, enabled individuals to challenge these old ideas and control of sexual behaviour. Since women are the central actors in reproduction, it is not surprising to find that the first wave of feminism in the 19th century was in part characterised by a desire to enable women to restrict their childbearing, albeit mainly to ensure that they could be better mothers to a few children, rather than poor mothers to too many. The possibility of a right to control one's reproductive capacity through contraception is more likely to be a female than a male concern because of the consequences for the woman where such a possibility is not permitted. In this century, the modern wave of feminism has demanded such a freedom directly, as an aspect of a general desire to gain autonomy and control over one's own body.

In this chapter, we shall first consider the principal moral arguments for and against abortion, together with the additional factors which influence the legal response to what many regard as an ethical impasse. Next, the present state of the law will be analysed, including the implications for the parties most directly affected by the practice. The final part of the chapter then takes the discussion beyond the question of abortion to address the legal position in relation to other forms of avoidable pre-natal harm.

The morality of abortion

Traditionally, the debate as to the rights and wrongs of abortion has been couched in terms of the 'right to life' of the foetus versus the pregnant woman's 'right to choose' whether or not to bear a child. In many cases, the position a person takes in this debate will depend upon the underlying moral status they accord to the human foetus. As Rosalind Hursthouse writes:

Hursthouse, R, *Beginning Lives*, Oxford: Blackwells, 1987, pp 27–28:

The simplest view on the issue of abortion, the one often expressed explicitly or implicitly by non-philosophers in letters to newspapers, discussions on the wireless and so on, is that the moral rights and wrongs of abortion can be unproblematically settled by determining the moral status of the foetus. Hence it is common to find people on the conservative side insisting that the foetus is an unborn baby and hence that abortion is infanticide or murder and absolutely wrong, while people on the opposite side insist that the foetus is just a clump of living cells and hence that abortion is merely an operation which removes some part of one's body and hence is morally innocuous.

Now it is certainly true that the question of the moral status of the foetus is important, for according to what its status is, different arguments will bear upon the rights and wrongs of abortion. If, as conservatives believe, the foetus has the same moral status as a baby, then the mother's moral right to abortion is, to say the least, problematic; if there were any such right, a quite particular case would have to be made out for it. If, on the other hand, the foetus has the same moral status as, say, a kidney, then the argument for the mother's moral right to abortion could proceed, quite generally, as an argument concerning the right, of both women and men, to decide what happens to their own bodies.

The physical attributes of the foetus and the developmental process that it undergoes during pregnancy are, as we saw in the previous chapter, agreed upon. What is controverted is the moral inferences as to its status that should be drawn from the physical facts. The two key contrasting views, the 'theological' and 'personhood' approaches, are discussed by Jane Fortin in the following extract, along with a middle position put forward by Michael Lockwood:

Fortin, J, 'Legal protection for the unborn child' (1988) 51 MLR 54:

1   The concept of 'personhood'

... most philosophers argue that the point in time when human life begins is quite distinct from and less relevant than when a human 'person' comes into existence. The advantage of this approach is that it avoids the 'speciesism' involved in maintaining that all human life automatically has a greater intrinsic value and right to protection than that of any other species. Instead, it concentrates on those aspects of human life that merit such preferment. Thus whilst few would claim that a human sperm or unfertilised egg merits greater protection than a 10 week old kitten, most would accept without question the automatic right to life of a 10 year old child. This is because the child has become a person and as such, his life has an intrinsic value both to himself and others. Arguably then, there is little reason for extending legal protection to human life until 'a person' comes into existence. If this argument is accepted, it becomes vital to establish a clear definition of 'personhood'; no easy matter when moral philosophers show little accord in their choice of essential attributes to be displayed by a 'person'.

Perhaps the most widely known to the general public is the traditional Roman Catholic approach to the question. This is a metaphysical one which, in its strictest form, maintains that a human person comes into existence at the moment of the ovum being fertilised. At this moment of 'ensoulment', the fertilised ovum becomes infused with a rational soul of its own and this theory of immediate animation is widely believed to embody the official teaching of the Roman Catholic Church ...

Some Roman Catholic philosophers adopt the less extreme theory of 'delayed animation'. This was developed by the theologian, Thomas Aquinas, who maintained that there were a number of stages in human generation and that ensoulment did not take place until a later stage, some time after conception. The more modern explanation is that a human soul can only infuse a human form which is sufficiently well developed to exhibit essentially human characteristics; clearly this does not occur until some time after conception.

Many moral philosophers reject the metaphysical approach to personhood which is so often associated with the Roman Catholic Church. In their view personhood is not defined by reference to the presence or otherwise of an immaterial human soul but by reference to a complicated combination of mental and or physical properties. There seems to be little agreement over which properties are essential, although many maintain that to be a person, a human being or entity must, *inter alia*, possess rationality and self-consciousness, be capable of action and be the subject of non-momentary goals or interests. Inevitably, many proponents of such a combination of properties, find it impossible to accept that a human foetus can be deemed a person and worthy of protection; consequently, in their view, there can be no moral objection to abortion, however late. Indeed, Michael Tooley lucidly presents the argument that since even a newly born child lacks these properties, infanticide is not morally objectionable.

2   Human organisms, human beings and persons

Although many would find Tooley's conclusion distasteful, its logic cannot be denied. A possible way of avoiding some, but not all, of these problems is to maintain three clear distinctions. Thus Michael Lockwood distinguishes between human organisms, human beings and persons. In this way, depending on the definition of 'human being', a newly born infant might be classified as such, with certain consequential rights, despite its not having attained the status of personhood. Lockwood uses the term 'human being' to describe what 'you and I are essentially, what we can neither become nor cease to be, without ceasing to exist'. Thus, in his view, this concept revolves round that of personal identity, which underlies 'certain discernible continuities' such as memory and personality – those unchanging elements in a human being which establishes his own unique blueprint. Accordingly, the concept of identity is established not by the continuities themselves but by those elements underlying them ...

In his view, it is only when the brain develops to this extent, that a human embryo can be said to have become a human being. Only then does it become able to sustain distinctively mental processes, thereby justifying certain protection. Lockwood himself feels that it is impossible to be precise over the point in time when this occurs. Nevertheless, on the basis of the existing, albeit sparse, scientific evidence, he suggests that an appropriate marker might be 10 weeks' gestation. Lockwood's analysis is attractively clear and less cold blooded than that of Tooley. Moreover, it has the advantage of allowing both the unborn and the newly born child to have a measure of protection as human beings, without claiming either to be a fully fledged person.

However, it is apparent that all three views described by Fortin require some commitment to unprovable 'metaphysical' premises. As Margaret Brazier has noted:

Brazier, M, 'The challenge for Parliament', in Dyson, A and Harris, J (eds), *Experiments on Embryos*, 1990, London: Routledge, p 134:

The difficulty is that the dispute is itself incapable of any conclusive resolution. Perception of the status of the embryo derives in many cases from the presence or absence of religious belief. Most, but not all, proponents of the belief that the embryo is from fertilisation a genetically unique individual as fully human as you or I, rest that belief, at least in part, on the embryo's potential possession of an immortal, immaterial soul ... Many, but again by no means all, proponents of allowing research on embryos deny or doubt the existence of the soul.

Thus the argument on abortion becomes for opponents: 'How can the law permit the wanton destruction of human life?' And supporters of liberal abortion laws respond: 'By what right do you seek to impose your personal unprovable claims about God and the soul on others?' The dispute reaches stalemate ... The humanity of the embryo is unproven and unprovable. But that acts both ways. Just as I cannot prove that humanity was divinely created and that each and every one of us possesses an immortal soul, so it cannot be proved that it is not so. Admitting the possibility of the soul, the moment of ensoulment cannot be proved. Nothing more or less can be concluded about the full humanity of the embryo save to say that the cases for and against are, to borrow a Scottish term, not proven.

Rather than attempting to found the moral status of the foetus on any particular attribute it possesses as it now is, an increasingly popular approach is to stress the potential (understood in terms of how it would develop naturally, other things equal) that the foetus has to become a person in the future. However, this concept stands in need of significant clarification if it is to bear any real moral weight. As Glover notes:

Glover, J *et al*, *Report to the European Commission on Reproductive Technologies, Fertility and the Family*, 1989, London: Fourth Estate (the Glover Report), p 97:

Perhaps what matters is not some property an embryo now has, but what it has the potential to become. This claim seems to imply that disposing of an embryo is wrong because it prevents the existence of a particular developed person, namely the one the embryo would have become. But this argument rules out contraception. You are a particular developed person, and contraception would have prevented your existence. The apparently innocuous word 'potential' turns out to be very slippery.

To avoid ruling out contraception, potentiality has to be interpreted differently. Perhaps the destruction of potential is not just a matter of the loss of a future developed person, but also the loss of something that has got a certain distance on the way there: the programme is already in existence, as all the genes are present. But this leaves some unanswered questions. If the properties an embryo now has do not generate a right to life, and the argument about one less future person does not do so either, why should combining the two considerations give the desired result? Of course a compound can have properties not possessed by its individual ingredients, but in this case some account is needed of the moral chemistry involved ...

It is accordingly important to consider whether there may be alternative ways to understand the debate which allow conclusions about the morality of abortion which do not depend on views about the status of the foetus. Two very different, but equally bold, attempts to re-couch the abortion debate to precisely this end have been made, respectively, by Judith Jarvis Thomson and Ronald Dworkin. Taking Thomson's argument first, in a celebrated article 'A defense of abortion', she suggested that, even if, for the sake of argument, we were to grant the foetus equal moral status to adult human persons, abortion would remain morally permissible in a large number of circumstances, given the prior right of the pregnant woman to exercise control over her body:

Thomson, JJ, 'A defense of abortion' (1971) 1 Philosophy and Public Affairs 1:

Most opposition to abortion relies on the premise that the foetus is a human being, a person, from the moment of conception. The premise is argued for, but, as I think, not well. Take, for example, the most common argument. We are asked to notice that the development of a human being from conception through birth into childhood is continuous; then it is said that to draw a line, to choose a point in this development and say 'before this point the thing is not a person, after this point it is a person' is to make an arbitrary choice, a choice for which in the nature of things no good reason can be given. It is concluded that the foetus is, or anyway that we had better say it is, a person from the moment of conception. But this conclusion does not follow. Similar things might be said about the development of an acorn into an oak tree, and it does not follow that acorns are oak trees, or that we had better say they are. Arguments of this form are sometimes called 'slippery slope arguments' – the phrase is perhaps self-explanatory – and it is dismaying that opponents of abortion rely on them so heavily and uncritically.

I am inclined to agree, however, that the prospects for 'drawing a line' in the development of the foetus look dim. I am inclined to think also that we shall probably have to agree that the foetus has already become a human person well before birth. Indeed, it comes as a surprise when one first learns how early in its life it begins to acquire human characteristics. By the 10th week, for example, it already has a face, arms and legs, fingers and toes; it has internal organs, and brain activity is detectable. On the other hand, I think that the premise is false, that the foetus is not a person from the moment of conception. A newly fertilised ovum, a newly implanted clump of cells, is no more a person than an acorn is an oak tree. But I shall not discuss any of this. For it seems to me to be of great interest to ask what happens if, for the sake of argument, we allow the premise. How, precisely, are we supposed to get from there to the conclusion that abortion is morally impermissible? Opponents of abortion commonly spend most of their time establishing that the foetus is a person, and hardly any time explaining the step from there to the impermissibility of abortion. Perhaps they think the step too simple and obvious to require much comment. Or perhaps instead they are simply being economical in argument. Many of those who defend abortion rely on the premise that the foetus is not a person, but only a bit of tissue that will become a person at birth; and why pay out more arguments than you have to? Whatever the explanation, I suggest that the step they take is neither easy nor obvious, that it calls for closer examination than it is commonly given, and that when we do give it this closer examination we shall feel inclined to reject it.

I propose, then, that we grant that the foetus is a person from the moment of conception. How does the argument go from here? Something like this, I take it. Every person has a right to life. So the foetus has a right to life. No doubt the mother has a right to decide what shall happen in and to her body; everyone would grant that. But surely a person's right to life is stronger and more stringent than the mother's right to decide what happens in and to her body, and so outweighs it. So the foetus may not be killed; an abortion may not be performed.

It sounds plausible. But now let me ask you to imagine this. You wake up in the morning and find yourself back to back in bed with an unconscious violinist. A famous unconscious violinist. He has been found to have a fatal kidney ailment, and the Society of Music Lovers has canvassed all the available medical records and found that you alone have the right blood type to help. They have therefore kidnapped you, and last night the violinist's circulatory system was plugged into yours, so that your kidneys can be used to extract poisons from his blood as well as your own. The director of the hospital now tells you: 'Look, we're sorry the Society of Music Lovers did this to you – we would never have permitted it if we had known. But still, they did it, and the violinist now is plugged into you. To unplug you would be to kill him. But never mind, it's only for nine months. By then he will have recovered from his ailment, and can safely be unplugged from you.' Is it morally incumbent on you to accede to this situation? No doubt it would be very nice of you if you did, a great kindness. But do you have to accede to it? What if it were not nine months, but nine years? Or longer still? What if the director of the hospital says: 'Tough luck, I agree, but you've now got to stay in bed, with the violinist plugged into you, for the rest of your life. Because remember this. All persons have a right to life, and violinists are persons. Granted you have a right to decide what happens in and to your body, but a person's right to life outweighs your right to decide what happens in and to your body. So you cannot ever be unplugged from him.' I imagine you would regard this as outrageous, which suggests that something really is wrong with that plausible-sounding argument I mentioned a moment ago.

In this case, of course, you were kidnapped; you didn't volunteer for the operation that plugged the violinist into your kidneys. Can those who oppose abortion on the ground I mentioned make an exception for a pregnancy due to rape? Certainly. They can say that persons have a right to life only if they didn't come into existence because of rape; or they can say that all persons have a right to life, but that some have less of a right to life than others, in particular, that those who came into existence because of rape have less. But these statements have a rather unpleasant sound. Surely the question of whether you have a right to life at all, or how much of it you have, shouldn't turn on the question of whether or not you are the product of a rape. And in fact the people who oppose abortion on the ground I mentioned do not make this distinction, and hence do not make an exception in case of rape ...

Despite its ingenuity, there are a number of difficulties with Thomson's argument. First, whilst it may well permit abortion in cases of rape, (where the woman has not given the foetus a 'right' to the use of her body) it is not clear that it can be extended to pregnancy which results from consensual sex. As Hursthouse notes:

Hursthouse, R, *Beginning Lives,* **Oxford: Blackwells, 1987, pp 187–89:**

... Thomson asserts it as a premise that a woman cannot be said to have given the foetus the right to use her body if she is pregnant because of rape. Plausibly the pregnancy must result from voluntary intercourse ... However this still leaves a very large number of cases; does Thomson agree that in all cases of pregnancy due to voluntary intercourse in full knowledge of the facts of life the mother could be said to have given the foetus the right to use her body – that the intercourse, as it were, amounts to an offer to have one's body thus used?

She clearly does not, but her argument at this point depends on two rather unsatisfactory analogies. In one she imagines that children come about by people-seeds taking root in one's carpet; this may happen even if one has gone to great trouble to try to prevent it by putting fine mesh screens over one's windows. In the other analogy, she does not consider children, but how people might acquire a right to use my house, and says it would be absurd to suppose that someone had acquired it by just blundering in, through a window I had happened to open, behind bars I had installed to keep people out which happened to have a defect. In each case I go to some trouble to try to keep people-seeds or people out; in each case there is supposed to be a way that would guarantee keeping them out, say with sealed windows, but it cannot be said that I am responsible for their being in my house and that hence they have a right to it simply because I do not go in for this extreme measure.

These analogies are obviously supposed to be with contraception; despite the woman's efforts not to become pregnant, she does. Given that she was trying not to, her voluntary intercourse cannot count as an offer, conferring a right, to have her body used by the foetus. But the difficulty with the people-seed analogy is that, because it is so far-fetched, it lacks all the background that enables one (sometimes) to make up one's mind. Do these people-seeds just root for nine months? What are the available alternatives to uprooting and killing them – can they be transplanted, can you swap your house for nine months with someone who wants children ...? The difficulty with the other analogy is that it misses out the crucial aspect of the foetus being dependent on the use of the woman's body for its survival ...

Secondly, there remains the problem that abortions are typically carried out by a third party, the doctor, and it may be argued that conceiving of abortion in terms of a conflict of maternal-foetal rights cannot settle the question of what would be an appropriate moral response on the part of such a third party. Finally, and more generally, Thomson's narrow focus on rights may be felt to obscure other ways in which an action is morally problematic. In particular, it does not follow, from the mere fact that the foetus lacks a right to use the woman's body, that abortion is morally innocuous. This is apparently recognised by Thomson herself:

Thomson, JJ, 'A defense of abortion' (1971) 1 Philosophy and Public Affairs 1:

We surely must all grant that there may be cases in which it would be morally indecent to detach a person from your body at the cost of his life. Suppose you learn that what the violinist needs is not nine years of your life, but only one hour: all you need do to save his life is to spend one hour in that bed with him. Suppose also that letting him use your kidneys for that one hour would not affect your health in the slightest. Admittedly you were kidnapped. Admittedly you did not give anyone permission to plug him into you. Nevertheless it seems to me plain you *ought* to allow him to use your kidneys for that hour – it would be indecent to refuse.

Again, suppose pregnancy lasted only an hour, and constituted no threat to life or health. And suppose that a woman becomes pregnant as a result of rape. Admittedly she did not voluntarily do anything to bring about the existence of a child. Admittedly she did nothing at all which would give the unborn person a right to the use of her body. All the same it might well be said, as in the newly amended violinist story, that she *ought* to allow it to remain for that hour – that it would be indecent in her to refuse.

In a telling recent contribution to the abortion debate, Ronald Dworkin has attempted to bridge the gap between the 'pro-life' and 'pro-choice' positions by identifying an important piece of common ground between the two camps. In particular, he argues that both conservatives and liberals share a common commitment to the sanctity of human life:

Dworkin, R, *Life's Dominion: An Argument about Abortion and Euthanasia*, 1993, London: HarperCollins, pp 88–90:

Both conservatives and liberals assume that in some circumstances abortion is more serious and more likely to be unjustifiable than in others. Notably, both agree that a late term abortion is graver than an early term one. We cannot explain this shared conviction simply on the ground that foetuses more closely resemble infants as pregnancy continues. People believe that abortion is not just emotionally more difficult but morally worse the later in pregnancy it occurs, and increasing resemblance alone has no moral significance. Nor can we explain the shared conviction by noticing that at some point in pregnancy a foetus becomes sentient. Most people think that abortion is morally worse early in the second trimester – well before sentience is possible – than early in the first one ... Foetal development is a continuing creative process, a process that has barely begun at the instant of conception. Indeed, since genetic individuation is not yet complete at that point, we might say that the development of a unique human being has not started until approximately 14 days later, at implantation. But after implantation, as foetal growth continues, the natural investment that would be wasted in an abortion grows steadily larger and more significant.

Human and divine

So our sense that frustration rather than just loss compromises the inviolability of human life does seem helpful in explaining what unites most people about abortion. The more difficult question is whether it also helps in explaining what divides them ...

Suppose parents discover, early in the mother's pregnancy, that the foetus is genetically so deformed that the life it would lead after birth will inevitably be both short and sharply limited. They must decide whether it is a worse frustration of life if the gravely deformed foetus were to die at once – wasting the miracle of its creation and its development so far – or if it were to continue to grow in utero, to be born, and to live only a short and crippled life. We know that people divide about that question, and we now have a way to describe the division. On one view, immediate death of the foetus, even in a case like this one, is a more terrible frustration of the miracle of life than even a sharply diminished and brief infant life would be, for the latter would at least redeem some small part, however limited, of the natural investment. On the rival view, it would be a worse frustration of life to allow this foetal life to continue, because that would add, to the sad waste of a deformed human's biological creation, the further, heartbreaking waste of personal emotional investments made in that life by others, but principally by the child himself, before his inevitable early death.

We should therefore consider this hypothesis: though almost everyone accepts the abstract principle that it is intrinsically bad when human life, once begun, is frustrated, people disagree about the best answer to the question of whether avoidable premature death is always or invariably the most serious possible frustration of life. Very conservative opinion, on this hypothesis, is grounded in the conviction that immediate death is inevitably a more serious frustration than any option that postpones death, even at the cost of greater frustration in other respects. Liberal opinion, on the same hypothesis, is grounded in the opposite conviction: that in some cases, at least, a choice for premature death minimises the frustration of life and is therefore not a compromise of the principle that human life is sacred but, on the contrary, best respects that principle ...

Although enlightening, Dworkin's inclusive strategy is not likely to satisfy everybody. In particular, in the metaphysical assumptions he makes about the foetus he appears to be far closer to the liberal than the conservative position. Even if he is right that some conservatives oppose abortion on the 'detached' ground that it frustrates life in the abstract, there will inevitably remain others whose opposition is derived from specific beliefs about foetuses which are not amenable to any compromise. Equally, it is likely that some adherents of a liberal-feminist persuasion will not be convinced that the foetus is to be regarded as any more sacred than other parts of the woman's body tissue. Nevertheless, it is probable that Dworkin's view is one that, empirically speaking, accurately reflects a broad consensus of opinion in our society today.

Abortion and legislation

The point that questions as to the morality of a practice must be distinguished from the rightness of legislating against the same was noted in Chapter 7. In relation to abortion, the salient arguments are well put by Rosalind Hursthouse:

Hursthouse, R, *Beginning Lives*, Oxford: Blackwells, 1987, pp 15–16:

The confusion of questions about morality and legislation is particularly common in arguments about abortion ... One reason why the questions become readily confused in debate is because of the tactics of opposition. Many people, particularly women, do think there is something wrong about having an abortion, that it is not a morally innocuous matter, but also think that the current abortion laws are if anything still too restrictive, and find it difficult to articulate their position on the morality of abortion without, apparently betraying the feminist campaign concerning legislation. To give an inch on 'a woman's right to choose', to suggest even for a moment that having an abortion is not only 'exercising that right' (which sounds fine) but also 'ending a human life' (which sounds like homicide) or even 'ending a potential human life' (which sounds at least serious) is to play into the hands of the conservatives.

What happens to the conservative and the liberal sides of the debate once the distinction between questions of morality and questions of legislation is drawn? In theory, drawing the distinction opens up the possibility of four different positions.

Morality of abortion	Laws on abortion	Position
Wrong	Restrictive	Conservative
Innocuous	Restrictive	'Totalitarian'
Innocuous	Liberal	Liberal/radical
Wrong	Liberal	Liberal/moderate

The 'totalitarian' position is of merely theoretical interest. (It might be occupied by someone in an underpopulated country, indifferent both to women's rights and to appeals to the sanctity of life, who thought it was necessary to increase the population quickly.) The first position is a familiar one. It is well known that the conservative position on legislation about abortion is based on a corresponding conservative position about its morality. According to the conservative view, abortion is morally wrong because it is the taking of human life, and hence, like any other case of homicide, justifiable in only a restricted range of circumstances, which should be laid down by law.

It is the possibility of two distinct liberal positions, which for want of better labels I will henceforth distinguish as the 'radical' and the 'moderate', which is not so familiar, and much that is said on the liberal side about women's rights leaves it quite unclear which of two views about the morality of abortion its supporters hold. Do they hold that abortion is morally quite innocuous – and hence that to have laws restricting women's access is as absurd and punitive as having laws which decreed, say, that women (though not men) were forbidden to cut their hair or smoke? Or do they agree with the conservatives that it is a morally very serious matter but hold that nevertheless the suffering and lack of freedom that women must at present undergo when abortion is not legally available not only justify but require our having laws which permit this wrong to be done whenever the woman wishes it? Is abortion a necessary evil as things are at present, or not an evil at all?

As this suggests, at a pragmatic level any lawmaker must consider the likely *effect* of laws which (for whatever reason) straightforwardly prohibited abortion. Experience, in both this country as well as in many others, has indeed tended to show that, rather than curtailing the practice, abortion will simply be driven underground.

THE LEGAL POSITION

Criminal law provisions

Abortion in the UK remains *prima facie* a criminal offence. Historically, the influence of the canon law of the Christian Church played an important part in the emergent common law on the subject. John Keown has charted this influence as follows:

> **Keown, J, *Abortion, Doctors and the Law*, 1988, Cambridge: CUP, pp 3–4:**
>
> ... the weight of available authority supports the view that the common law prohibited abortion, at the latest, after the foetus had become 'quick' or 'animated'. Animation was believed to occur when the foetus 'quickened' in the womb. An incident of the second trimester of pregnancy, quickening marks the first maternal perception of foetal movement. In associating the origin of life with quickening, the law betrayed both pragmatic and metaphysical influences. The former concerned the need to prove, in any prosecution for abortion, that the woman had been pregnant and that the foetus had been killed by the abortifacient act. Evidence of quickening would clearly facilitate prosecution. The metaphysical influence upon the law was the popular theory, originated by Aristotle and perpetuated by Galen, that human life began at the point of 'animation'. This theory was espoused by the canon law of the Christian Church and thence it found its way into the developing common law.

The criminal law of abortion achieved its modern form only in the mid 19th century. As JK Mason has written:

Mason, JK, *Medico-legal Aspects of Reproduction and Parenthood,* **1990, Aldershot: Dartmouth, p 100:**

The recognition of variable foetal rights has fluctuated in British law. The influence of medieval teaching was still apparent in 1803 when procuring the miscarriage of a woman who was 'quick with child' was a statutory offence subject to capital punishment. Abortion at an earlier state of gestation carried a lesser penalty, although it is difficult now to see much advantage to the culprit of a sentence of up to 14 years' transportation; nevertheless, the distinction was clearly meaningful at the time. The law remained the same until 1861 when the Offences Against the Person Act came into being. This introduced two major changes – first, the death penalty was replaced by potential penal servitude for life and, secondly, any distinction as to foetal age was abolished. The 1861 Act remains the definitive law in England, Wales and Northern Ireland ...

Section 58 of the Offences Against the Person Act (OAPA) 1861 provides as follows:

Attempts to procure abortion

58   Administering drugs or using instruments to procure abortion

Every woman, being with child, who, with intent to procure her own miscarriage, shall administer to herself any poison or other noxious thing, or shall unlawfully use any instrument or other means whatsoever with the like intent, and whosoever, with intent to procure the miscarriage of any woman, whether she be or be not with child, shall unlawfully administer to her or cause to be taken by her any poison or other noxious thing, or shall unlawfully use any instrument or other means whatsoever with the like intent, shall be guilty of felony, and being convicted thereof shall be liable to be kept in penal servitude for life.

Furthermore, s 59 of the Act prohibits various ancillary acts designed to facilitate the commission of the offence:

59   Procuring drugs, etc, to cause abortion

Whosoever shall unlawfully supply or procure any poison or other noxious thing, or any instrument or thing whatsoever, knowing that the same is intended to be unlawfully used or employed with intent to procure the miscarriage of any woman, whether she be or be not with child, shall be guilty of a misdemeanour, and being convicted thereof shall be liable to be kept in penal servitude.

It will be noted that the Act does not speak in terms of 'carrying out an abortion', but rather of 'procuring a miscarriage'. This (though it remains undefined) is arguably a narrower concept, which would apparently leave certain forms of foetal killing lawful, namely those where the woman does not 'miscarry' as a result of the procedure. The most startling example would be a situation in which the foetus is destroyed once the woman is already in labour: no miscarriage occurs here, but equally the foetus, even one which has partially emerged from the womb, does not yet enjoy the protection of the criminal law against homicide. The existence of such a legal lacuna was deplored by Talbot J in charging a jury at Liverpool in 1928, and his comments led to the passing of a further piece of legislation, the Infant Life (Preservation) Act 1929 (ILPA). Section 1(1) of the 1929 Act created a new offence of 'child destruction':

1   Punishment for child destruction

(1) Subject as hereinafter in this sub-section provided, any person who, with intent to destroy the life of a child capable of being born alive, by any wilful act causes a child to die before it has an existence independent of its mother, shall be guilty of felony, to wit, of child destruction, and shall be liable on conviction thereof on indictment to penal servitude for life:

Provided that no person shall be found guilty of an offence under this section unless it is proved that the act which caused the death of the child was not done in good faith for the purpose only of preserving the life of the mother.

Although, as noted, the primary purpose of this provision was the protection of the foetus during the course of its birth, it is apparent that its effect goes further by extending such protection back in time to the point in the pregnancy at which the foetus became 'capable of being born alive'. By virtue of s 1(2) of the Act, this is rebuttably presumed to be at 28 weeks' gestation:

1   (2) For the purposes of this Act, evidence that a woman had at any material time been pregnant for a period of 28 weeks or more shall be prima facie proof that she was at that time pregnant of a child capable of being born alive.

Thus, the 1861 and 1929 Acts operate to some extent in overlap: a termination carried out on a foetus capable of being born alive will, in so far as it occurs by way of a miscarriage, be an offence under both statutes. By contrast only the 1861 Act applies to the younger, non-viable foetus, and, conversely, only the 1929 Act to a foetus already in the course of its birth.

Defences to abortion prior to 1967

Section 1(1) of the Infant Life (Preservation) Act contains an express proviso to the effect that no offence is committed by a person who causes the death of the foetus in order to save the life of the pregnant woman. This provision was included because, before the development of modern Caesarean sections, the craniotomy (crushing the foetus' skull) was a standard medical procedure to deal with cases where normal delivery was not medically possible. It is apparent, however, that no similar defence was provided for in the Offences Against the Person Act in relation to procuring a miscarriage. A question that long remained open, therefore, was whether a doctor who terminated a pregnancy at this earlier stage in order to save the pregnant woman's life was necessarily guilty of an offence under the 1861 Act. The issue finally came before a court in 1938 in the case of *R v Bourne*.

R v Bourne [1939] 1 KB 687 (Macnaghten J)

A 14 year old girl became pregnant as a result of a brutal rape. Mr Bourne, an eminent gynaecologist, made public his intention to perform an abortion on the girl and, having obtained the consent of her parents, duly did so. He was charged with procuring a miscarriage contrary to s 58 of the OAPA 1861. In his defence, could a similar proviso to that found in the ILPA be read into the section and, if so, what was its scope?

> **Macnaghten J**: No such proviso is in fact set out in s 58 of the Offences Against the Person Act 1861; but the words of that section are that any person who 'unlawfully' uses an instrument with intent to procure miscarriage shall be guilty of felony. In my opinion the word 'unlawfully' is not, in that section, a meaningless word. I think it imports the meaning expressed by the proviso in s 1, sub-s (1) of the Infant Life (Preservation) Act 1929, and that s 58 of the Offences Against the Person Act 1861 must be read as if the words making it an offence to use an instrument with intent to procure a miscarriage were qualified by a similar proviso.
>
> In this case, therefore, my direction to you in law is this – that the burden rests on the Crown to satisfy you beyond reasonable doubt that the defendant did not procure the miscarriage of the girl in good faith for the purpose only of preserving her life ...
>
> What then is the meaning to be given to the words 'for the purpose of preserving the life of the mother'? There has been much discussion in this case as to the difference between danger to life and danger to health. It may be that you are more fortunate than I am, but I confess that I have found it difficult to understand what the discussion really meant, since life depends upon health, and it may be that health is so gravely impaired that death results. A question was asked by the learned Attorney General in the course of his cross-examination of Mr Bourne. 'I suggest to you, Mr Bourne,' said the Attorney General, 'that there is a perfectly clear line – there may be border-line cases – there is a clear line of distinction between danger to health and danger to life'. The answer of Mr Bourne was: 'I cannot agree without qualifying it; I cannot say just yes or no. I can say there is a large group whose health may be damaged, but whose life almost certainly will not be sacrificed. There is another group at the other end whose life will be definitely in very great danger.' And then he adds:
>
>> There is a large body of material between those two extremes in which it is not really possible to say how far life will be in danger, but we find, of course, that the health is depressed to such an extent that life is shortened, such as in cardiac cases, so that you may say that their life is in danger, because death might occur within measurable distance of the time of their labour.
>
> If that view commends itself to you, you will not accept the suggestion that there is a clear line of distinction between danger to health and danger to life. Mr Oliver wanted you to give what he called a wide and liberal meaning to

the words 'for the purpose of preserving the life of the mother'. I should prefer the word 'reasonable' to the words 'wide and liberal'. I think you should take a reasonable view of those words.

It is not contended that those words mean merely for the purpose of saving the mother from instant death. There are cases, we are told, where it is reasonably certain that a pregnant woman will not be able to deliver the child which is in her womb and survive. In such a case where the doctor anticipates, basing his opinion upon the experience of the profession, that the child cannot be delivered without the death of the mother, it is obvious that the sooner the operation is performed the better. The law does not require the doctor to wait until the unfortunate woman is in peril of immediate death. In such a case he is not only entitled, but it is his duty to perform the operation with a view to saving her life.

Mr Bourne was acquitted by the jury. Nevertheless, though an important decision, the law continued to remain in a state of some uncertainty. Margaret Brazier has described how pressure gradually built up in favour of legislative reform, culminating in the passing of a new Act, the Abortion Act of 1967:

Brazier, M, *Medicine, Patients and the Law,* **2nd edn, 1992, Harmondsworth: Penguin, p 290:**

The law embodied in the 1861 Act was applied rigorously up to 1967. In one case in 1927, a girl of 13 was prosecuted for attempting to induce an abortion on herself by taking laxative tablets and sitting in a hot bath. The rigour of the law was tempered by a defence to a charge of criminal abortion by a doctor, that he acted to preserve the life or health of the mother. At no time in England was abortion absolutely prohibited so as to require the mother to be sacrificed for her unborn child ... But the extent of the defence available to doctors was unclear. Some doctors interpreted this defence liberally as including the mother's mental health and even happiness. Others would intervene only to prevent a life-threatening complication of pregnancy endangering the woman. Illegal abortion flourished. And several thousand women were admitted to hospital for treatment after backstreet abortions. The Abortion Act 1967 was introduced to bring uniformity into the law, to clarify the law for the doctors, and to stem the misery and injury resulting from unhygienic, risky illegal abortions.

The effect of the Abortion Act 1967 as originally enacted

It is important to state at the outset that the Abortion Act 1967 has not replaced the pre-existing criminal law statutes on abortion. Rather, its effect is to provide a medical practitioner who carries out an abortion within its terms with a statutory immunity. As originally passed in 1967, the relevant terms were set out in s 1 of the Act as follows:

1 **Medical termination of pregnancy**

    (1) Subject to the provisions of this section, a person shall not be guilty of an offence under the law relating to abortion when a pregnancy is

terminated by a registered medical practitioner if two registered medical practitioners are of the opinion, formed in good faith–

(a) that the continuance of the pregnancy would involve risk to the life of the pregnant woman, or of injury to the physical or mental health of the pregnant woman or any existing children of her family, greater than if the pregnancy were terminated; or

(b) that there is a substantial risk that if the child were born it would suffer from such physical or mental abnormalities as to be seriously handicapped.

(2) In determining whether the continuance of a pregnancy would involve such risk of injury to health as is mentioned in para (a) of sub-s (1) of this section, account may be taken of the pregnant woman's actual or reasonably foreseeable environment.

(3) Except as provided by sub-s (4) of this section, any treatment for the termination of pregnancy must be carried out in a hospital vested in the Secretary of State for the purposes of his functions under the National Health Service Act 1977 or the National Health Service (Scotland) Act 1978 or in a place approved for the purposes of this section by the Secretary of State.

(4) Sub-section (3) of this section, and so much of sub-s (1) as relates to the opinion of two registered medical practitioners, shall not apply to the termination of a pregnancy by a registered medical practitioner in a case where he is of the opinion, formed in good faith, that the termination is immediately necessary to save the life or to prevent grave permanent injury to the physical or mental health of the pregnant woman.

Importantly, the 1967 Act gave immunity only in relation to the offence of procuring a miscarriage under ss 58 and 59 of the OAPA 1861. So far as the offence of child destruction was concerned, s 5(1) of the Act expressly provided that:

5   Supplementary provisions

(1) Nothing in this Act shall affect the provisions of the Infant Life (Preservation) Act 1929 (protecting the life of the viable foetus).

This meant that the 1929 Act continued to impose an upper time limit beyond which terminations (apart from those necessary to preserve the pregnant woman's life) could not lawfully take place. Unfortunately, the precise position of this upper time limit remained uncertain. This is because, although the 1929 Act mentions a gestational age of 28 weeks as amounting to '*prima facie* proof' that a foetus is capable of being born alive, this is merely a presumption. Thus, in principle, evidence could be led that a particular foetus, even after 28 weeks, was not yet capable of being born alive, or conversely (and more likely, given advances in neonatal care since 1929) that one of under 28 weeks was so capable. In this regard, the Court of Appeal was required to define the concept 'capable of being born alive' in the case of *C v S*.

C v S [1988] 1 All ER 1230, CA (Sir John Donaldson MR, Stephen Brown and Russell LJJ)

Mr C, whose ex-girlfriend was pregnant with a 18–21 week old foetus, sought an injunction to restrain her from having an abortion on the ground, *inter alia*, that the foetus at this age was capable of being born alive and hence fell within the protection of the ILPA 1929.

> **Sir John Donaldson MR**: We have received affidavit evidence from three doctors, none of whom has examined the first defendant. Their evidence is thus necessarily directed at the stage in the development of a foetus which can normally be expected to have been reached by the 18th to 21st week. On this, as one would expect, they are in substantial agreement. At that stage the cardiac muscle is contracting and a primitive circulation is developing. Thus the foetus could be said to demonstrate real and discernible signs of life. On the other hand, the foetus, even if then delivered by hysterotomy, would be incapable ever of breathing either naturally or with the aid of a ventilator. It is not a case of the foetus requiring a stimulus or assistance. It cannot and will never be able to breathe. Where the doctors disagree is as to whether a foetus, at this stage of development, can properly be described as 'a child capable of being born alive' within the meaning of the Act of 1929. That essentially depends upon the interpretation of the statute and is a matter for the courts.
>
> We have no evidence of the state of the foetus being carried by the first defendant, but if it has reached the normal stage of development and so is incapable ever of breathing, it is not in our judgment 'a child capable of being born alive' within the meaning of the Act and accordingly the termination of this pregnancy would not constitute an offence under the Infant Life (Preservation) Act 1929.

The notion that an ability to draw breath is central to the capacity to be born alive was subsequently followed by the High Court in the case of *Rance v Mid-Downs HA* [1991] 1 QB 587. However, in holding that a 26 week old foetus was protected under ILPA (the case's facts arose in 1983), Brooke J rejected the plaintiff's contention that 'viability', in the sense of enjoying longer term survival prospects, was also a necessary part of the concept.

The Abortion Act 1967 as amended

Since 1990, concerns as to the precise scope of the protection that the ILPA affords to the older foetus have assumed much less importance. This is because, though the Act remains on the statute book, its effect upon abortions carried out within the terms of the 1967 Abortion Act has been removed. The major reason for this step seems to have been a desire to clarify the law. As the House of Lords Select Committee on the Infant Life (Preservation) Bill reported in 1988:

Report of the Select Committee on the Infant Life (Preservation) Bill, **HL Paper No 50, 1987–88, London: HMSO:**

58   The Committee also recommend that the 1967 Act should be totally disengaged from the 1929 Act and that the s 5 proviso should be removed from the 1967 Act, with the consequence that the existing 28-week gestational limit for lawful abortions derived from the 1929 Act will cease to apply; and that the 1967 Act should specifically enact that a medical practitioner, acting in good faith and in full compliance with the other provisions of the 1967 Act, should not be liable to prosecution under the 1929 Act ... One of the unfortunate effects of the s 5 proviso, as has already been mentioned, is that many practitioners, and possibly most practitioners, wishing to avoid the possibility of a prosecution under the 1929 Act, approach the request for an abortion on the basis that the woman is 2 weeks later in her pregnancy than she is estimated to be. The Committee consider that this example of defensive medicine, though understandable as the law now stands, is highly undesirable. Medical practitioners who act in good faith should not stand in fear of the criminal law.

Ultimately, the changes were achieved by inserting amendments into the 1967 Act during the course of enacting the Human Fertilisation and Embryology Act 1990 (HFEA). In particular s 5(1) of the Abortion Act (as amended by s 37 of the HFEA 1990) now reads as follows:

5   **Supplementary provisions**

(1)   No offence under the Infant Life (Preservation) Act 1929 shall be committed by a registered medical practitioner who terminates a pregnancy in accordance with the provisions of this Act.

At the same time, parliament inserted a new s 1(1) into the Abortion Act 1967. This sub-section now spells out the grounds on which a lawful termination may be carried out as follows:

1   **Medical termination of pregnancy**

(1)   Subject to the provisions of this section, a person shall not be guilty of an offence under the law relating to abortion when a pregnancy is terminated by a registered medical practitioner if two registered medical practitioners are of the opinion, formed in good faith–

(a)   that the pregnancy has not exceeded its 24th week and that the continuance of the pregnancy would involve risk, greater than if the pregnancy were terminated, of injury to the physical or mental health of the pregnant woman or any existing children of her family; or

(b)   that the termination is necessary to prevent grave permanent injury to the physical or mental health of the pregnant woman; or

(c)   that the continuance of the pregnancy would involve risk to the life of the pregnant woman, greater than if the pregnancy were terminated; or

(d) that there is a substantial risk that if the child were born it would suffer from such physical or mental abnormalities as to be seriously handicapped.

In terms purely of content, the changes to the s 1(1) grounds are largely cosmetic. Their true impact (which undoubtedly amounts to a liberalising of the law) consists in the new time limits – or absence thereof – within which abortion may now take place. We shall consider each of the four grounds for termination provided for in the amended s 1(1) in turn:

(a) ... risk ... of injury to the physical or mental health of the pregnant woman or any existing children of her family

This ground is used to justify the great majority of abortions carried out in Britain. It is widest in scope and the suggestion that it permits abortions on 'social' as well as strictly 'medical' grounds is given weight by the terms of s 1(2) of the Act, which provides:

> (2) In determining whether the continuance of a pregnancy would involve such risk of injury to health as is mentioned in para (a) or (b) of sub-s (1) of this section, account may be taken of the pregnant woman's actual or reasonably foreseeable environment.

It is apparent that the risk in question need not be a substantial one; it is enough that it exceeds the risk to the woman of carrying out the termination. This has led to an argument that since, statistically, an abortion carried out in the first 12 weeks of pregnancy poses fewer health risks to the woman than carrying the foetus to term, the Act will invariably permit such early terminations. Jonathan Montgomery has commented upon the operation of ground (a) as follows:

> **Montgomery, J, *Health Care Law*, 1997, Oxford: OUP, p 365:**
>
> The first ground for termination is only available up to the 25th week. It applies where the two doctors have formed the opinion, in good faith, that the pregnancy has not exceeded its 24th week and that the continuance of the pregnancy would involve risk, greater than if the pregnancy were terminated, of injury to the physical or mental health of the pregnant woman or any existing children of her family.
>
> While this ground clearly refers to health matters, it has been described as a 'social' ground, because doctors may take account of the woman's actual or foreseeable environment when they assess the risks involved. This means that the inconvenience of having a child may provide a basis for an abortion. It has been argued that this makes it lawful to terminate a pregnancy on the basis of the sex of the foetus where the social and cultural pressures upon a woman to produce a child of a particular sex are strong.
>
> The majority of induced abortions are performed under s 1(1)(a). In 1993 there were 157,846 abortions to women resident in England and Wales. Approximately 1.2% of these were performed on the basis of foetal abnormality. Just over 96% were recorded as justified on the 'social grounds'.

This overwhelming pattern of 'social' abortions has led to the 1967 Act being criticised for allowing abortion on demand. This assertion is based on the practice of some doctors who argue that there is statistical evidence that carrying a foetus to term is more dangerous to the woman than terminating the pregnancy in its early stages. This enables them to hold that s 1(1)(a) is made out whenever a woman is pregnant. This argument has never been tested in the courts, but it appears that doctors have given 'pregnancy' as the sole reason for believing that termination is less risky than continuing without being prosecuted.

However, it is apparent that the fact that proceeding to term poses some risk to the woman is *not*, in itself, a sufficient reason for termination. Rather, the doctor must perform a balancing operation in respect of the patient and determine that termination itself carries a *lower* risk: it is after all possible that, in a particular case, the risks of termination may in fact be greater than those attached to continuance, eg, where the woman may subsequently suffer some form of psychological reaction. This need to identify the risks running both ways suggests that the doctor's role requires him to engage in more than mere statistical 'rubber stamping'.

Importantly, unlike the other grounds under s 1(1), ground (a) contains a time limit: it may only be invoked in so far as the pregnancy has not exceeded its 24th week. This limit was introduced in the 1990 amendments to compensate for the fact that, as already noted, the same amendments removed the effect of the ILPA 1929, which had previously supplied a rough upper time limit to lawful abortions. The uncertainty over when, exactly, this limit used to apply has been commented on above: see *C v S* and *Rance*, p 422. Nevertheless, the introduction of a specific time period has brought with it its own difficulties. As Andrew Grubb has noted:

Grubb, A, 'The new law of abortion: clarification or ambiguity' (1991) Crim LR 659:

Section 1(1)(a) does not specify the point in time which starts the clock running in calculating the 24 weeks. There are four possibilities: (A) the first day of the woman's last period; (B) the date of conception (up to 14 days later); (C) the date of implantation (up to 10 days later); and (D) the first day of the woman's first missed period (about four weeks after (A)).

In England the medical profession calculates the length of gestation of a baby on the basis of (A) because it is the most certain date of any of these alternatives. Options (B) and (C), namely the date of conception and the date the fertilised egg implants into the woman, by contrast, cannot be known for certain. But there are difficulties with option (D), because although the first day of the woman's first missed period is certain, it may be quite misleading to indicate length of pregnancy where, for example, following conception during the last week of a cycle the woman does not miss the next period but only the one that follows. The date calculated on the basis of (D) could be about five weeks after conception has actually occurred.

Consequently, when does time start to run? The law might accept the medical profession's approach because of the certainty it would achieve. More importantly, however, it might be accepted because it is the basis upon which parliament introduced the 24 week time limit in s 1(1)(a). The 24 week limit (as calculated by the medical profession) represents parliament's view of the stage of development when a foetus is capable of surviving. At this point the legislative intent is that the foetus should not be aborted except under the more restrictive grounds set out in the remainder of s 1(1). If any of the other options for starting time to run were accepted, this premise would be nullified. On that basis, in order to conform to the underlying premise that a foetus which is capable of surviving should not be aborted on the ground in s 1(1)(a), the time limit should actually be 22 weeks or even less.

On the other hand, there are a number of arguments which suggest that options (B) or (C) are more appropriate interpretations of s 1(1)(a). First, it is wrong to adopt an interpretation which leads to the absurd conclusion that a woman is pregnant in the 14 days (approximately) between the first day of her last period and the time of conception when this is patently not the case. Secondly, the medical profession's approach exemplified in option (A) could act to the detriment of a defendant, since it results in the shortest possible time for the 24 week period to run. A pregnancy calculated on the basis of (A) at 25 weeks is likely, in fact, to be a case where conception and implantation will have occurred less than 24 weeks before the abortion. Ambiguities in criminal statutes should be construed in a defendant's favour and not against him, particularly when interpreting a section providing a defence to a criminal offence ...

(b) ... termination necessary to prevent grave permanent injury to the physical or mental health of the pregnant woman

This ground contains no time limit and, by virtue of s 1(4), may be invoked in an emergency by a single doctor without waiting for a second certificate. Arguably, it simply codifies the common law defence available to the doctor who performs a therapeutic abortion designed to avoid serious harm to the woman, as established in *R v Bourne*. There is however one oddity. In speaking of the termination being 'necessary', the ground appears to require foresight by the doctor of such harm as a practical certainty, yet s 1(2) (which applies to this ground as well as (a) above) implies that a mere 'risk' of such injury will be sufficient. Whilst, doubtless, at some point a high enough risk may be treated, analytically, as forming a practical certainty, the term usually denotes something rather less than this.

(c) ... risk to the life of the pregnant woman, greater than if the pregnancy were terminated

Like ground (b) above, this ground may be used in an emergency by a single doctor. Although ground (c) specifically refers to risk to 'life', in practice a large measure of overlap may be expected between the two grounds. This is because, as was apparent in *R v Bourne*, it may be difficult to say, as a matter of evidence, where grave injury to health ceases and risk to life begins.

Moreover, given that – as in the case of ground (a) – the doctor is required to conduct a simple balancing of risks to determine whether a termination is justified, ground (c) may actually be easier to employ: the risk to the woman's life in continuing to term need not be substantial provided that it exceeds the risk involved in abortion. Ironically, the risks at issue are likely to be more readily quantifiable than the somewhat diffuse harms contemplated under ground (a), so it may be here that a 'statistical argument' would have the greatest purchase. For example, suppose that a doctor assesses the risk to the life of the woman in giving birth at 1 in 8,000. Provided the risk attached to termination is even lower, say, 1 in 10,000, an abortion would apparently be justified here. Since, in contrast with ground (a), no time limit is placed on terminations under this ground, it appears that an abortion in the circumstances just described could, in theory, take place until birth.

(d) ... substantial risk that if the child were born it would suffer from such physical or mental abnormalities as to be seriously handicapped

In common with the first three grounds, there are significant difficulties in interpreting the precise application and scope of this ground. On the face of it, however, it differs from the others in being directed to the welfare of the foetus rather than that of the pregnant woman. Derek Morgan has argued for a strict interpretation of the ground, allowing its use only in cases of 'foetal euthanasia', that is to say where termination is in the foetus' best interests:

Morgan, D, 'Abortion: the unexamined ground' (1990) Crim LR 687:

Section 1(1)[(d)] requires that the physician decide that there is a 'substantial' risk that the physical or mental abnormalities are such that the child if born would be 'seriously' handicapped ...

One immediate analogy which could be drawn is that of the severely handicapped neonate who if its condition had been known, might have been aborted under s 1(1)[(d)]. In two recent cases, the Court of Appeal has had to consider in what, if any, circumstances a severely handicapped infant might be allowed to die. in *Re C* the court was concerned with a baby born with an unusually severe form of hydrocephalus and with a poorly formed brain structure. She was physically handicapped, including generalised spastic cerebral palsy of all limbs, probable blindness and deafness and an inability to absorb food. In the first judgment of its kind, the High Court acknowledged and condoned the paediatric practice of managing some neonates towards their death rather than striving with heroic interventions to save or treat at all costs...

Re C amplified the earlier judgment of the Court of Appeal in *Re B*. There, the court had established, first, that these cases could only proceed under a 'best interests' test (in that case of the ward). And secondly, the court held that only in a case where the prognosis established that the child's life was going to be 'demonstrably ... so awful', and where there was no lingering doubt about that future, could a non-treatment order be contemplated. Lords Justices Templeman and Dunn observed that this would include cases of severe proved damage such that the court would be driven to conclude that non-treatment was appropriate. This would not be the case, however, where the prognosis or information about the damage was 'still so imponderable' that it would be wrong for the baby to be allowed to die.

The attempt to invoke an analogy between the handicapped foetus (even at term) and the similarly afflicted neonate is weakened, however, by the fact that, in another crucial respect, the law clearly regards the two situations as very different. In particular, whereas the foetus remains vulnerable to active measures to destroy it, the most that is permitted in relation to the neonate is the passive withholding of measures that would otherwise prolong its life (see further below, Chapter 12). The view that this ground, like the others, in fact goes principally to the mother's interests, is supported by the history behind the 1990 amendments, which removed the time limits restricting the abortion of handicapped foetuses 'capable of being born alive'. The 1988 Select Committee of the House of Lords had the following to say on the issue:

> *Report of the Select Committee on the Infant Life (Preservation) Bill*, HL Paper No 50, 1987–88, London: HMSO:
>
> 41 Although abortions on ground 4, that is to say, a substantial risk that the child if born would suffer from such abnormalities as to be seriously handicapped, are only a small proportion of the total abortions, they comprise most of the abortions performed after 24 weeks ... It is these late abortions which would be made more difficult to obtain if an upper limit of 24 weeks were to be imposed, and they represent in the opinion of the Committee a highly important factor. Whether an abortion is desired or justified in such a case will depend to a large extent on the degree of abnormality which is diagnosed and the circumstances and attitude of the parents. Although a severely handicapped child is often the cause of crisis and disaster, there are other cases where even severe handicap has been the means of inspiring love and care within the family, and even the strengthening of character and family ties. At its worst, a child severely affected by spina bifida may be not only mentally retarded, but also severely paralysed so as to be unable to walk, doubly incontinent, deaf and blind. It is obvious that the birth of such a child will constitute an immediate crisis for parents and doctors. Although some women elect nevertheless to have severely handicapped children, the Committee have received evidence that the cumulative effect on families of years of caring for a totally dependent child can be devastating, and when the parents die the child must all too often be institutionalised, with traumatic effects. Ante-natal care is rightly directed to the detection of mothers who are subject to these risks, and counselling must always be available, though the choice will be the mother's.

As we have seen, s 1(1)(d) speaks of the foetus suffering from 'such mental or physical abnormalities as to be seriously handicapped'. This undoubted vagueness is compounded by the fact that the section requires only 'a substantial risk' of such abnormalities. Gillian Douglas has commented on the application of the latter concept as follows:

Douglas, G, *Law, Fertility and Reproduction,* **1991, London: Sweet & Maxwell, p 94:**

A further problem is in deciding what amounts to a 'substantial' risk. The Royal College of Physicians describe a risk of more than 10% of producing a seriously abnormal child as a 'high' risk. Presumably, where the abnormality is less severe, a greater degree of probability would be classed as high. A one in 10 chance of a foetus carrying spina bifida may indeed be regarded as a substantial risk, but a further complication is that it is not generally possible to determine from pre-natal screening the degree of handicap an affected foetus may suffer. Parents may therefore be faced with the possibility of aborting a normal, or mildly affected foetus.

It would be preferable if the ground were ... clearly expressed to be based on the consequences for the *parents*, or subsumed under s 1(1)(a) and s 1(2). This would be a more justifiable rationale for aborting a potentially handicapped foetus, and it would also avoid overt reliance on eugenic factors. In any case, it would only need to be resorted to in a small number of cases, if current practice is indicative. At present, the detection of abnormalities is rarely relied upon as the sole ground for termination. This may be due to the delay inherent in current screening procedures making abortion less safe, and also more complicated and distressing when eventually carried out. If a doctor suspects abnormality, perhaps from the woman's prior history of child-bearing, or exposure to rubella, it may be preferable to perform the abortion earlier than to wait for confirmation which might still prove in error. Reliance may then be placed on another ground, such as injury to the woman's mental health.

Douglas suggests here that the severity of abnormality is relevant in deciding when a risk is 'substantial'. Arguably, however, Kennedy and Grubb's view, that the latter term goes primarily to the *probability* of the risk materialising (and should be kept separate from the question of what the *magnitude* of harm will be in so far as it does materialise), is preferable.

IMPLICATIONS OF THE LAW

The interested parties

Given the legal framework sketched above, what rights are enjoyed by the key actors in the abortion process? We begin by considering the position of the foetus itself.

The foetus

Self-evidently, the existence of the regime under the 1967 Abortion Act, permitting legal abortion in a large number of circumstances, means that the foetus has no legal right to life. In this regard, Jane Fortin has written as follows:

Fortin, J, 'Legal protection for the unborn child' (1988) 51 MLR 54:

... the abortion legislation has contrived a situation whereby a decision to terminate the life of the foetus can be reached by two doctors in consultation only with the mother. There is thus no possibility of anyone intervening on behalf of the foetus, to ensure that adequate consideration has been given to its particular stage of physical and mental development, in order to assess the precise degree of its increasing 'humanness' and whether it warrants protection against its mother's desire for an abortion.

In this context, there is a stark contrast between the legal protection accorded to the unborn and to the newly born. In relation to the latter, however premature, the wardship jurisdiction can be used to cast an immediate cloak of protection over the child, thereby ensuring that fundamentally important decisions relating to the child's future can be considered dispassionately by the High Court. Thus, in the case of *Re B*, the Court of Appeal authorised a life-giving operation on a Down's syndrome child, against the wishes of its parents who had rejected it. By contrast, it is clear from the decisions in *Paton* and *C v S* that although an abortion has a fatal effect on the unborn child, intervention by a third party would be impossible even if in his view the abortion decision has been reached erroneously ...

Despite the heavy responsibility for interpreting the 1967 Act imposed on the medical profession, it is surprising that the Act contains no guidance to them as to the factors to consider when deciding whether to approve an abortion. The omission of any direction specifically requiring the doctors to consider the interests of the foetus itself, when deciding whether to approve the abortion, implies that the abortion is a purely medical matter relating only to the mother herself and devoid of any moral implications relating to the foetus.

As Fortin notes elsewhere, the perceived need to safeguard the interests of the pregnant woman has led the courts to deny that the foetus, in utero, enjoys any legal personality. This important point lay behind the decision of the High Court in the case of *Paton v Trustees of BPAS*.

Paton v Trustees of British Pregnancy Advisory Services [1979] QB 276, HC (Sir George Baker P)

The plaintiff sought an injunction restraining his wife from having an abortion under the Abortion Act 1967. Although she had obtained the required certificates from two doctors that she satisfied one of the statutory grounds, the plaintiff alleged that she was in fact acting in *male fides*. As a starting point, the plaintiff needed to establish *locus standi* to bring his action, either in his own right or as 'next friend' of the foetus:

Sir George Baker P: The first question is whether this plaintiff has a right at all. The foetus cannot, in English law, in my view, have a right of its own at least until it is born and has a separate existence from its mother. That permeates the whole of the civil law of this country (I except the criminal law, which is now irrelevant), and is, indeed, the basis of the decisions in those countries where law is founded on the common law, that is to say, in America, Canada, Australia and, I have no doubt, in others.

For a long time there was great controversy whether, after birth, a child could have a right of action in respect of pre-natal injury ... but it was universally accepted, and has since been accepted, that in order to have a right the foetus must be born and be a child. There was only one known possible exception ... an American case, *White v Yup* 458 P 2d 617 (1969), where a wrongful 'death' of an 8 month old viable foetus, stillborn as a consequence of injury, led an American court to allow a cause of action, but there can be no doubt, in my view, that in England and Wales the foetus has no right of action, no right at all, until birth. The succession cases have been mentioned. There is no difference. From conception the child may have succession rights by what has been called a 'fictional construction', but the child must be subsequently born alive: see per Lord Russell of Killowen in *Elliot v Lord Joicey* [1935] AC 209, p 233.

Subsequently, Mr Paton failed to persuade the European Commission on Human Rights that the foetus' right to life is protected under Art 2 of the European Convention on Human Rights (see *Paton v UK* (1980) 3 EHRR 408). The Commission's view was that, given the intimate connection between the foetus' life and that of the pregnant woman, any such right must in any event be limited in cases where the latter's life and health are at stake.

The approach of the High Court in *Paton* was subsequently endorsed by the Court of Appeal, outside the context of abortion, in the case of *Re F (In Utero)*.

Re F (In Utero) [1988] Fam 122, CA (May, Balcombe and Staughton LJJ)

A woman with a history of psychiatric problems was 38 weeks pregnant when she absconded from the residential care home in which she lived. Her local authority, which was responsible for her care, sought to make her unborn child a ward of court as a preliminary to further measures to protect its health at this late stage in the pregnancy:

May LJ: Even though this is a case in which, on its facts, I would exercise the [wardship] jurisdiction if I had it, in the absence of authority I am driven to the conclusion that the court does not have the jurisdiction contended for. I respectfully agree with the *dictum* from the judgment of Sir George Baker P in the *Paton* case ...

Secondly, I respectfully agree with the judge below in this case that to accept such jurisdiction and yet to apply the principle that it is the interest of the child which is to be predominant is bound to create conflict between the existing legal interests of the mother and those of the unborn child, and that it is most undesirable that this should occur ...

Staughton LJ: I agree that this appeal should be dismissed. In their notice of appeal the local authority seek orders as follows:

(1) The tipstaff do seek and detain in a suitable place the defendant and do report her whereabouts to the plaintiffs and the court.

(2)   The defendant do not leave the jurisdiction so long as she remains pregnant and further following the birth of the said child do not remove the said child from the jurisdiction.

(3)   The defendant do forthwith surrender her passport or other travel document to the court.

(4)   The defendant do attend forthwith such hospital suitable for the delivery of the said unborn child as the plaintiffs in their discretion direct.

It will be observed that all are orders directed at the mother, as in the nature of things they must be until the child is born.

When the wardship jurisdiction of the High Court is exercised, the rights, duties and powers of the natural parents are taken over or superseded by the orders of the court. Until a child is delivered it is not, in my judgment, possible for that to happen. The court cannot care for a child, or order that others should do so, until the child is born; only the mother can. The orders sought by the local authority are not by their nature such as the court can make in caring for the child; they are orders which seek directly to control the life of both mother and child. As was said by the European Commission of Human Rights in *Paton v United Kingdom* ... p 415, 'the 'life' of the foetus is intimately connected with, and cannot be regarded in isolation from, the life of the pregnant woman' ...

Despite this, it should not be concluded that a foetus enjoys no legal protection at all. It is simply that, in the context of abortion, where there is a conflict between its interests and those of the pregnant woman, the law accords priority to the latter. (The degree to which the foetus is protected in other circumstances is explored below, p 451.)

An opposing, and on the face of it rather fanciful, issue concerns the degree to which the foetus has a right to be aborted. This question, nevertheless, has lain behind actions for so called 'wrongful life'. The leading English authority in point is *Mackay v Essex AHA*.

Mackay v Essex AHA [1982] QB 1166, CA (Stephenson, Griffiths and Ackner LJJ)

The plaintiff's mother was infected with German measles while pregnant with the plaintiff. The latter claimed, inter alia, that the defendant doctor had negligently failed to advise her mother of the desirability of an abortion, and (given that her mother would have accepted such advice) she had consequently suffered damage by 'entry into a life in which her injuries are highly debilitating, and distress, loss and damage':

Stephenson LJ: There is no doubt that this child could legally have been deprived of life by the mother's undergoing an abortion with the doctor's advice and help. So the law recognises a difference between the life of a foetus and the life of those who have been born. But because a doctor can lawfully by statute do to a foetus what he cannot lawfully do to a person who has been born, it does not follow that he is under a legal obligation to a foetus to do it and terminate its life, or that the foetus has a legal right to die ...

To impose such a duty towards the child would, in my opinion, make a further inroad on the sanctity of human life which would be contrary to public policy. It would mean regarding the life of a handicapped child as not only less valuable than the life of a normal child, but so much less valuable that it was not worth preserving, and it would even mean that a doctor would be obliged to pay damages to a child infected with rubella before birth who was in fact born with some mercifully trivial abnormality. These are the consequences of the necessary basic assumption that a child has a right to be born whole or not at all, not to be born unless it can be born perfect or 'normal', whatever that may mean. Added to that objection must be the opening of the courts to claims by children born handicapped against their mothers for not having an abortion ...

Finally, there is the nature of the injury and damage which the court is being asked to ascertain and evaluate.

The only duty of care which courts of law can recognise and enforce are duties owed to those who can be compensated for loss by those who owe the duties, in most cases, including cases of personal injury, by money damages which will as far as possible put the injured party in the condition in which he or she was before being injured. The only way in which a child injured in the womb can be compensated in damages is by measuring what it has lost, which is the difference between the value of its life as a whole and healthy normal child and the value of its life as an injured child. But to make those who have not injured the child pay for that difference is to treat them as if they have injured the child, when all they have done is not having taken steps to prevent its being born injured by another cause.

The only loss for which those who have not injured the child can be held liable to compensate the child is the difference between its condition as a result of their allowing it to be born alive and injured and its condition if its embryonic life had been ended before its life in the world had begun. But how can a court of law evaluate that second condition and so measure the loss to the child? Even if a court were competent to decide between the conflicting views of theologians and philosophers and to assume an 'after life' or non-existence as the basis for the comparison, how can a judge put a value on the one or the other, compare either alternative with the injured child's life in this world and determine that the child has lost anything, without the means of knowing what, if anything, it has gained?

Griffiths LJ: To my mind, the most compelling reason to reject this cause of action is the intolerable and insoluble problem it would create in the assessment of damage. The basis of damages for personal injury is the comparison between the state of the plaintiff before he was injured and his condition after he was injured. This is often a hard enough task in all conscience and it has an element of artificiality about it, for who can say that there is any sensible correlation between pain and money? Nevertheless, the courts have been able to produce a broad tariff that appears at the moment to be acceptable to society as doing rough justice. But the whole exercise, difficult as it is, is anchored in the first place to the condition of the plaintiff before the injury which the court can comprehend and evaluate. In a claim for wrongful life how does the court begin to make an assessment? The plaintiff does not say, 'But for your negligence I would have been born uninjured'. The plaintiff says, 'But for your negligence I would never have been born'. The court then has to compare the state of the plaintiff with non-existence, of which the court can know nothing; this I regard as an impossible task.

The pregnant woman

The general view is that the 1967 Act gives the pregnant woman no right to demand an abortion. As Jonathan Montgomery notes:

Montgomery, J, *Health Care Law*, 1997, Oxford: OUP, pp 365–66:

... it does not follow from the fact that doctors are in practice usually immune from prosecution that the Abortion Act 1967 provides for abortion on demand. The Act does not provide women with rights to terminate their pregnancy. Instead, it leaves them dependent upon finding a doctor who will co-operate with their wishes. This means that women who can afford to go to private clinics will usually have little difficulty obtaining a legal abortion. Those reliant on NHS provision, however, are faced with considerable variation between the practice of different doctors. Consequently, there is considerable disparity in the degree to which abortions are readily available both between and within different areas of the country. Official statistics showed that in 1973 only 10% of those seeking an abortion in Walsall were able to get one through the NHS, while in Oxford the figure was 79%.

It is therefore doctors who control access to abortions. Women's access to abortions is dependent on the ethical position of individual doctors and is vulnerable to prejudices of an essentially white middle class profession. Norrie has pointed out that terminations sought because the child is the 'wrong' sex are as justifiable under the Act as those because the pregnancy is inconvenient for economic or career reasons. However, the former is far less likely to be accepted by the medical profession. The Abortion Act 1967 may allow doctors to offer abortion on demand in the early stages of pregnancy, but it does not secure it for women.

It is certainly true that nowhere in the Abortion Act is there to be found any express right to an abortion and, in this omission, it could be argued that it is a less liberal measure than similar laws in many other jurisdictions. In the USA, for example, the effect of the decisions of the Supreme Court in *Roe v Wade* 410 US 113 (1976) and *Planned Parenthood v Casey* 112 S Ct 2791 (1992) is that, until viability, State laws placing undue obstacles in the path of abortion will infringe the woman's constitutionally protected right to privacy. However, although English law thus inhibits (at least in symbolic terms) a woman's freedom to terminate her pregnancy, it could be asked whether abortion differs in this respect from any other form of medical treatment available in this country. After all, it is well established that a patient cannot insist upon a particular procedure if the doctor does not believe it to be medically indicated as in the patient's best interests: see *R v Cambridge HA ex p B* (1995). In similar fashion, the general remedy for the patient who can show that they were improperly denied treatment is to bring an *ex post facto* action in negligence, and in this regard, too, abortion arguably is no different. Indeed, a number of successful cases have been brought by women who have argued that they should have been given the opportunity to have an abortion on the ground of foetal handicap contained in the 1967 Act. A notable example is the case of *Mackay v Essex AHA* considered above, p 432. Although the child lost its claim for 'wrongful life', the mother's action in 'wrongful birth' was allowed to proceed. In his speech, Griffiths LJ expressly suggested that the medical profession are under a duty to advise the pregnant woman of 'her right to have an abortion and the pros and cons of doing so'.

By contrast, in so far as a pregnant woman, who is a competent adult, chooses not to abort her foetus, it is clear that the law will not make her do so. At first glance, this assertion may seem to be a straightforward application of the principle that competent adults must always consent to medical procedures carried out upon them. However, this is to ignore the possible use of indirect legal means to pressurise women to opt for terminations in certain cases. For example, in the context of an action for wrongful birth, might a woman be denied compensation for the costs of raising a handicapped child on the basis that her failure to have a termination was 'unreasonable'? This question was at the heart of the case of *Emeh v Kensington and Chelsea AHA*.

Emeh v Kensington and Chelsea AHA [1985] QB 1012, CA (Slade, Waller and Purchas LJJ)

The plaintiff, who already had four children, underwent a voluntary sterilisation at the defendant's hospital. The operation was negligently performed and the plaintiff subsequently became pregnant, only discovering this fact when her foetus was of 17–20 weeks' gestation. She refused the defendant's offer of an abortion and later gave birth to a handicapped child. At first instance, Park J denied her claim for the costs of raising the child, finding that her failure to have the abortion amounted to a *novus actus interveniens*, which eclipsed the defendant's earlier negligence and made her the author of her loss. The plaintiff appealed:

> **Waller LJ**: In my opinion, on the findings of the judge, even as they were, I would be disposed to say that this conduct on the part of the plaintiff was not so unreasonable as to eclipse the defendants' wrongdoing. But ... when one sees no reference was made by the judge to the difference between a 20 week pregnancy and an eight week pregnancy, it would seem that when the plaintiff decided to have the baby and, having made that decision, she then decided to sue the defendants, her conduct could not be described as utterly unreasonable. Especially when one bears in mind that she had an argument with her husband about it – he apparently wanted her to have an abortion; and the judge accepted that evidence – that makes her decision all the more understandable. I would therefore come to the conclusion that that finding of the judge, namely her failure to undergo an abortion was so unreasonable as

to eclipse the defendants' wrongdoing, is incorrect, and that the plea of *novus actus*, or the failure to take steps to minimise the damage – in whatever way the matter is put – fails.

Slade LJ: The judge, in saying that her failure to obtain an abortion was so unreasonable as to eclipse the defendants' wrongdoing, was, I think, really saying that the defendants had the right to expect that, if they had not performed the operation properly, she would procure an abortion, even if she did not become aware of its existence until nearly 20 weeks of her pregnancy had elapsed.

I do not, for my part, think that the defendants had the right to expect any such thing. By their own negligence, they faced her with the very dilemma which she had sought to avoid by having herself sterilised.

For the reasons which I have attempted to give, I think that they could and should have reasonably foreseen that if, as a consequence of the negligent performance of the operation she should find herself pregnant again, particularly after some months of pregnancy, she might well decide to keep the child. Indeed, for my part I would go even a little further. Save in the most exceptional circumstances, I cannot think it right that the court should ever declare it unreasonable for a woman to decline to have an abortion in a case where there is no evidence that there were any medical or psychiatric grounds for terminating the particular pregnancy. And no such evidence has been drawn to our attention relating to this particular pregnancy of the plaintiff in the present case.

The father

It is well established that, under English law, the father of a foetus cannot prevent a pregnant woman from having an abortion, and indeed has no right even to be consulted over her proposed course of action. As we have seen, this was made clear in *Paton v Trustees of BPAS* [1979] QB 276.

Sir George Baker P: The father's case must ... depend upon a right which he has himself. I would say a word about the illegitimate, usually called the putative, but I prefer myself to refer to the illegitimate father. Although American decisions to which I have been referred concern illegitimate fathers, and statutory provisions about them, it seems to me that in this country the illegitimate father can have no rights whatsoever except those given to him by statute. That was clearly the common law. One provision which makes an inroad into this is s 14 of the Guardianship of Minors Act 1971, s 9(1) and some other sections of that Act which apply to illegitimate children, giving the illegitimate father or mother the right to apply for the custody of or access to an illegitimate child. But the equality of parental rights provision in s 1(1) of the Guardianship Act 1973 expressly does not apply in relation to a minor who is illegitimate: see s 1(7).

... [T]his plaintiff must, in my opinion, bring his case, if he can, squarely within the framework of the fact that he is a husband. It is, of course, very common for spouses to seek injunctions for personal protection in the matrimonial courts during the pendency of or, indeed, after divorce actions, but the basic reason for the non-molestation injunction often granted in the family courts is to protect the other spouse or the living children, and to ensure that no undue pressure is put upon one or other of the spouses during the pendency of the case and during the breaking up of the marriage ...

The law is that the court cannot and would not seek to enforce or restrain by injunction matrimonial obligations, if they be obligations, such as sexual intercourse or contraception (a non-molestation injunction given during the pendency of divorce proceedings could, of course, cover attempted intercourse). No court would ever grant an injunction to stop sterilisation or vasectomy. Personal family relationships in marriage cannot be enforced by the order of a court. An injunction in such circumstances was described by Judge Mager in *Jones v Smith* (1973) 278 So 2d 339 in the District Court of Appeal of Florida as 'ludicrous'.

I ask the question, 'If an injunction were ordered, what could be the remedy?' and I do not think I need say any more than that no judge could even consider sending a husband or wife to prison for breaking such an order. That, of itself, seems to me to cover the application here; this husband cannot by law stop his wife by injunction from having what is now accepted to be a lawful abortion within the terms of the Abortion Act 1967.

In his action before the European Commission of Human Rights (see above, p 430), Mr Paton argued that his right to 'respect for family life' under Art 8 of the European Convention on Human Rights had been infringed. In dismissing this claim, however, the Commission noted that Art 8(2) specifically limits that right in so far as necessary to protect the rights of another person (here the pregnant woman). The view taken in *Paton* as to the father's status was endorsed by the Court of Appeal in *C v S* [1988] QB 135, and recently led a Scottish court to reject a husband's application for an injunction to restrain his wife from having an abortion: see *Kelly v Kelly* 1997 SLT 896.

The doctor/health care worker

As will have been apparent in the discussion of s 1(1) of the Abortion Act 1967 above, the Act gives doctors a very wide discretion in determining whether the one of the grounds for lawful termination has been met. Writing in *The Lancet* in 1971, IM Ingram suggested that the wording of the Act is indeed so wide as to be meaningless, and, though the 1990 amendments to the Act have moved the key provisions around, it is apparent that they have not introduced any greater precision. What safeguards are there, then, to prevent an unscrupulous doctor from abusing his discretion? John Keown has discussed this issue as follows:

Keown, J, *Abortion, Doctors and the Law*, 1988, Cambridge: CUP, pp 130–32:

During the parliamentary debates on his Bill, Mr Steel [the Act's sponsor] said that it was necessary for such a measure as his to contain 'safeguards' against abuse, and he pointed to three 'essential and new' safeguards in his Bill: the requirements of certification of opinions, notification of abortions, and approval of premises where the operations were to be performed. To what extent have these safeguards, which he said would prevent abuse of the Act, operated as a check on excessively permissive interpretation of s 1?

The Abortion Regulations 1968–80

The Abortion Regulations 1968 came into effect on the same day as the Abortion Act in discharge of the statutory duty placed on the minister by s 2(1) of the Act. Section 3 of the Regulations deals with the certification of the practitioner's opinions. Section 3(2) requires the two opinions to be certified on 'Certificate A' before treatment is begun.

This Regulation undoubtedly represents a restriction on the practitioner's freedom in that it introduces a formality which he must observe, on pain of a fine. However, certification hardly restricts the exercise of medical discretion, for although it ensures a second opinion it requires neither the second practitioner to be of a particular status nor limits the number of practitioners who may be approached for a second opinion. It does not even require the second practitioner to see the patient. Indeed, it was concern at the failure of some doctors to do just this that led to the amendment of the Regulations, at the recommendation of Lane, to require the certifying practitioners to state whether they had seen or examined the patient. However, the Regulations as amended do not require either of the practitioners to see the patient and it is difficult to see how they might do so without being *ultra vires*.

As a safeguard against abuse of medical discretion, therefore, certification is only of limited effectiveness. Its main virtue is in ensuring a second opinion, but this had been standard practice well before the enactment of the Regulations, among both reputable and disreputable practitioners. Although the ostensible function of certification is the protection of the patient, it also serves the interests of the practitioner by helping to protect him from suspicion of impropriety.

If certification is only a limited safeguard against abuse of the Act, what of notification? This safeguard was built into the Act in the form of s 2(1)(b), and its requirements are specified in s 4 of the Regulations. Section 4(1) requires the operating practitioner to notify the abortion to the C[hief] M[edical] O[fficer] within seven days, including in the notification form such information as is specified in Sched 2 to the Regulations.

Unlike certification, notification did represent a significant innovation in this area of medical practice, for whereas it had long been usual to obtain a second opinion, practitioners had not previously reported the operation to a third party. Moreover, failure to notify might, like failure to certify, involve the practitioner in liability under s 2(3) of the Act, and also in suspicion of illegal abortion.

However, the effectiveness of notification as a safeguard is also limited, for, just as a practitioner could certify an illegal abortion as falling within the terms of the Act, so too could he notify such an operation as having been performed within the Act, and it would be extremely difficult to prove the absence of good faith. Moreover, if a practitioner fails to notify, his offence will be difficult to detect for, *ex hypothesi*, the CMO will not have been informed that an abortion has been performed.

The procedure for certification under the Act as amended is now dealt with in the Abortion Regulations 1991, made under s 2 of the Act. The Regulations provide, in reg 3, as follows:

Certificate of opinion

3 (1) Any opinion to which s 1 of the Act refers shall be certified–

(a) in the case of a pregnancy terminated in accordance with s 1(1) of the Act, in the form set out in Part I of Sched 1 to these Regulations; and

(b) in the case of a pregnancy terminated in accordance with s 1(4) of the Act, in the form set out in Part II of that Schedule.

(2) Any certificate of an opinion referred to in s 1(1) of the Act shall be given before the commencement of the treatment for the termination of the pregnancy to which it relates.

(3) Any certificate of an opinion referred to in s 1(4) of the Act shall be given before the commencement of the treatment for the termination of the pregnancy to which it relates or, if that is not reasonably practicable, not later than 24 hours after such termination.

(4) Any such certificate as is referred to in paras (2) and (3) of this Regulation shall be preserved by the practitioner who terminated the pregnancy to which it relates for a period of not less than three years beginning with the date of the termination.

(5) A certificate which is no longer to be preserved shall be destroyed by the person in whose custody it then is.

A rare case in which a doctor's performance of an abortion was impugned, on the basis that he had not formed the view in good faith that the termination came within one of the grounds under the 1967 Act, was that of *R v Smith*.

R v Smith (John) [1974] 1 All ER 376, CA (Scarman LJ, Mackenna and Mocatta JJ)

Dr Smith performed an abortion on a young woman without, apparently, either satisfying himself that continuance of her pregnancy would involve a risk greater than termination to her mental or physical health, or obtaining the requisite second opinion. The matter came to light because, following the operation, the patient became ill, and it was she who subsequently acted as the main prosecution witness. After his conviction by a jury of procuring a miscarriage contrary to s 58 of the OAPA 1861, Dr Smith appealed:

Scarman LJ: The [1967] Act, though it renders lawful abortions that before its enactment would not have been lawful, does not depart from the basic principle of the common law as declared in *R v Bourne*, namely that the legality of an abortion depends on the opinion of a doctor. It has introduced the safeguard of two opinions: but, if they are formed in good faith by the time the operation is undertaken, the abortion is lawful. Thus, a great social responsibility is firmly placed by the law on the shoulders of the medical profession ...

On 28 April 1970 at the Hayward Nursing Home a Miss Rodgers underwent an operation performed by the appellant, the initial purpose of which was to terminate her pregnancy. The prosecution's case is that he was not acting in good faith; he had not formed a *bona fide* opinion as to the balance of risk between termination and continuation of her pregnancy, that is to say, that the continuance would involve risk to her physical or mental health greater than if it were terminated. The appellant's defence was twofold: he said that he formed an honest opinion as to the need for an abortion, but that when he had the girl on the operating table, he found she was starting an inevitable abortion. Thus according to him, his operation became not a termination, but a facilitating and tidying up of an inevitable abortion – a natural process which had already begun. If this be the truth, the prosecution concedes that the operation would be lawful without the need of recourse to the Abortion Act 1967.

In arguing the appeal, counsel for the appellant directed the greater part of his argument not to the issue of inevitable abortion but to that of his client's good faith in deciding to terminate Miss Rodgers' pregnancy. But the course of the trial was somewhat different. The presence of an inevitable abortion already beginning when he operated was at the forefront of the doctor's defence. Professor Fairweather, the specialist called for the Crown, directed most of his evidence to this issue. No doubt both the Crown and the defence appreciated – correctly, we think – that, if the appellant was disbelieved when he said he found an inevitable abortion, his credit would be so undermined that he was unlikely to be believed when he asserted that his decision to terminate was taken only after he had formed an opinion in good faith as to the balance of risk. Nevertheless the two lines of defence merited, as indeed at trial they received, separate attention ...

The case against the appellant relied on the evidence of Miss Rodgers and of police officers who interviewed the appellant in November and December 1970 and March 1971. Professor Fairweather, a distinguished gynaecologist, gave evidence on the question as to the likelihood of an inevitable abortion when there had been no history of pain or bleeding; he thought it unusual but possible. In reply to the recorder he emphasised the need for careful inquiry when the reason for abortion was injury to mental health and agreed that the 1967 Act could be abused. Both defendants and Dr Davis gave evidence. The trial was a long one and culminated in a lengthy summing up.

Was the verdict unsafe? Counsel for the appellant took a great number of detailed points in his attack on the trial and the summing up. But, as he put it, his central submission was that a finding of bad faith against a doctor, when it relates to the forming of a medical opinion, cannot be safe or satisfactory unless supported by medical evidence pointing overwhelmingly to the lack of good faith ...

The question of good faith is essentially one for the jury to determine on the totality of the evidence. A medical view put forward in evidence by one or more doctors as to the good faith of another doctor's opinion is no substitute for the verdict of the jury. An opinion may be absurd professionally and yet formed in good faith; conversely an opinion may be one which a doctor could have entertained and yet in the particular circumstances of a case may be found either to have been formed in bad faith or not to have been formed at all. Although the 1967 Act has imposed a great responsibility on doctors, it has not ousted the function of the jury. If a case is brought to trial which calls in question the *bona fides* of a doctor, the jury, not the medical profession, must decide the issue. The risk of abuse, by some, of the protection afforded by the Act was recognised as a genuine risk by Professor Fairweather. In the instant case it was for the jury to determine whether the appellant had or had not abused the protection afforded him by the Act. By leaving the ultimate question to a jury, the law retains its ability to protect society from an abuse of the Act.

This case, which is undoubtedly an unusual one, appears, on the face of it, to be at odds with subsequent judicial reluctance (evident in Sir George Baker P's comments in *Paton v BPAS*) to scrutinise the doctor's *bona fides* in applying the terms of the Abortion Act.

Sir George Baker P: The case which was first put forward to me a week ago, and indeed is to be found in the writ, is that the wife had no proper legal grounds for seeking a termination of her pregnancy and that, indeed, not to mince words, she was being spiteful, vindictive and utterly unreasonable in seeking so to do. It now appears I need not go into the evidence in the affidavits because it is accepted and common ground that the provisions of the Act have been complied with, the necessary certificate has been given by two doctors and everything is lawfully set for the abortion ...

The case put to me finally by Mr Rankin ... is that while he cannot say here that there is any suggestion of a criminal abortion, nevertheless if doctors did not hold their views, or come to their conclusions in good faith, which would be an issue triable by a jury (see *Reg v Smith (John)* [1973] 1 WLR 1510), then this plaintiff might recover an injunction. That is not accepted by Mr Denny. It is unnecessary for me to decide that academic question because it does not arise in this case. My own view is that it would be quite impossible for the courts in any event to supervise the operation of the Abortion Act 1967. The great social responsibility is firmly placed by the law upon the shoulders of the medical profession: see per Scarman LJ in *Reg v Smith (John)* [1973] 1 WLR 1510, p 1512.

... The two doctors have given a certificate. It is not and cannot be suggested that the certificate was given in other than good faith and it seems to me that there is the end of the matter in English law.

More recently, a doctor who continued with a hysterectomy upon a patient whose pregnancy only came to light during the operation, was similarly charged with an offence under s 58 of the OAPA 1861. On this occasion, the doctor's defence that he had acted in good faith to preserve the woman from grave permanent injury to her mental health (within s 1(1)(b) of the Abortion Act) was accepted by the jury: see *R v Dixon (Reginald)* ((1995), unreported). While the doctor's evidence may appear flimsy ('in view of this lady's age, her very recent history of deliberate suicide attempt by overdose ... and her express wish for hysterectomy, we felt an emergency termination of pregnancy would be justified'), the case undoubtedly highlights the reluctance of juries to criminalise the practice of the modern abortion doctor.

An opposing, and ironically perhaps more effective, brake upon a doctor's discretion under the 1967 Act may consist in the potential ability of the pregnant woman to sue in negligence in so far as the doctor *fails* to assist her in having an abortion. As we have seen above, a claim of this sort was allowed in relation to the foetal handicap ground in *Mackay v Essex AHA* (1982) and it is almost certain that, where continued pregnancy causes reasonably foreseeable harm of a serious nature to the pregnant woman, the doctor's failure to authorise and/or carry out a termination under s 1(1)(b) or (c) of the Act would likewise be actionable. On the other hand, it may be doubted that a similar claim could be maintained in respect of s 1(1)(a), since the harms contemplated under that ground are arguably too amorphous to form the basis of a legal remedy.

A final issue in relation to the doctor is how far he may in fact refuse to participate in an abortion. This question is dealt with in s 4 of the Abortion Act 1967:

4   **Conscientious objection to participation in treatment**

   (1)   Subject to sub-s (2) of this section, no person shall be under any duty, whether by contract or by any statutory or other legal requirement, to participate in any treatment authorised by this Act to which he has a conscientious objection;

   provided that in any legal proceedings the burden of proof of conscientious objection shall rest on the person claiming to rely on it.

   (2)   Nothing in sub-s (1) of this section shall affect any duty to participate in treatment which is necessary to save the life or to prevent grave permanent injury to the physical or mental health of a pregnant woman.

As is apparent from s 4(2) above, this provision cannot be relied upon by a doctor called upon to perform an abortion in an emergency. The question (in non-emergency situations) of who, apart from the treating doctor, may rely on the conscientious objection clause, came before the House of Lords in *Janaway v Salford HA*.

Janaway v Salford HA [1989] AC 537, HL (Keith, Brandon, Griffiths, Goff and Lowry LL)

The plaintiff, a Roman Catholic, lost her job working as a secretary for the defendant health authority after refusing to type a letter of referral in respect of an abortion patient. She brought an action for unfair dismissal on the basis that her refusal was protected under s 4(1) of the Abortion Act 1967:

Lord Keith: The applicant claims the protection of s 4(1). The issue in the case turns on the true construction of the words in that sub-section 'participate in any treatment authorised by this Act'. For the applicant it is maintained that the words cover taking part in any arrangements preliminary to and intended to bring about medical or surgical measures aimed at terminating a pregnancy, including the typing of letters referring a patient to a consultant. The health authority argues that the meaning of the words is limited to taking part in the actual procedures undertaken at the hospital or other approved place with a view to the termination of a pregnancy ...

The argument for the applicant proceeds on the lines that the acts attracting the protection afforded by s 4(1) are intended to be co-extensive with those which are authorised by s 1(1) and which in the absence of that provision would be criminal. The criminal law about accessories treats one who aids and abets, counsels or procures a criminal act as liable to the same extent as a principal actor. In the absence of s 1(1) the applicant by typing a letter of referral would be counselling or procuring an abortion, or at least helping to do so, and subject to a possible defence on the principle of *R v Bourne* [1939] 1 KB 687 would be criminally liable. Therefore any requirement to type such a letter is relieved, in the face of a conscientious objection, by s 4(1).

The majority of the Court of Appeal (Slade and Stocker LJJ) accepted the main thrust of the applicant's argument, to the effect that s 1(1) and s 4(1) are co-extensive, but decided against her on the ground that her intention in typing a letter of referral would not be to assist in procuring an abortion but merely to carry out the obligations of her employment. In their view the typing of such a letter by the applicant would not be a criminal offence in the absence of s 1(1).

Nolan J, however, and Balcombe LJ in the Court of Appeal rejected the applicant's main argument. They accepted the argument for the health authority that on a proper construction the word 'participate' in s 4(1) did not import the whole concept of principal and accessory residing in the criminal law, but in its ordinary and natural meaning referred to actually taking part in treatment administered in a hospital or other approved place in accordance with s 1(3), for the purpose of terminating a pregnancy.

In my opinion Nolan J and Balcombe LJ were right to reach the conclusion they did. I agree entirely with their view about the natural meaning of the word 'participate' in this context. Although the word is commonly used to describe the activities of accessories in the criminal law field, it is not a term of art there. It is in any event not being used in a criminal context in s 4(1). *Ex hypothesi* treatment for termination of a pregnancy under s 1 is not criminal. I do not consider that parliament can reasonably have intended by its use to import all the technicalities of the criminal law about principal and accessory, which can on occasion raise very nice questions about whether someone is guilty as an accessory. Such niceties would be very difficult of solution for an ordinary health authority. If parliament had intended the result contended for by the applicant, it could have procured it very clearly and easily by referring to participation 'in anything authorised by this Act' instead of 'in any treatment [so] authorised'. It is to be observed that s 4 appears to represent something of a compromise in relation to conscientious objection. One who believes all abortion to be morally wrong would conscientiously object even to such treatment as is mentioned in sub-s (2), yet the sub-section would not allow the objection to receive effect.

Whilst it was thus made clear that Mrs Janaway's actions were too ancillary to the abortion procedure to bring her within the scope of the conscientious objection clause, the position of other facilitative agents, in particular the GP who might be asked to provide a second certificate as to an abortion falling within one of the statutory grounds, was left open. As Lord Keith continued:

> **Lord Keith**: A certain amount of argument was addressed to the Abortion Regulations 1968 SI 1968/390, which, *inter alia*, set out the form of certificate, known as the 'Green Form', to be signed by two registered medical practitioners in pursuance of s 1(1)(a) of the Act, and to the position in relation to s 4(1) of practitioners who might be required to sign such a certificate. The Regulations do not appear to contemplate that the signing of the certificate would form part of treatment for the termination of pregnancy, since reg 3(2) provides:
>
> > Any certificate of an opinion referred to in s 1(1) of the Act shall be given before the commencement of the treatment for the termination of the pregnancy to which it relates.
>
> It does not appear whether or not there are any circumstances under which a doctor might be under any legal duty to sign a green form, so as to place in difficulties one who had a conscientious objection to doing so. The fact that during the 20 years that the Act of 1967 has been in force no problem seems to have surfaced in this connection may indicate that in practice none exists. So I do not think it appropriate to express any opinion on the matter.

Forms of termination raising special issues

We conclude our examination of abortion by considering a number of procedures, in relation to the practice, that have generated particular legal or ethical concern.

Pre-implantation terminations

What is the legality of a measure which prevents a newly formed embryo from implanting in the woman's uterus in the first place? In particular, is it the case here that a 'miscarriage' is procured contrary to the terms of the OAPA 1861? Margaret Brazier has commented on this question as follows:

> **Brazier, M,** *Medicine, Patients and the Law,* **2nd edn, 1992, Harmondsworth: Penguin, pp 293–94:**
>
> The 1967 Act envisaged that once a diagnosis of pregnancy had been made, the doctor faced with a request for an abortion would then consider and weigh any risk to the woman or the child. But there is a drug approved for general use which will, if taken by a woman within 72 hours of intercourse, ensure that any fertilised ovum will not implant in the womb. This, inaptly named, 'morning after' pill is not the only means by which a fertilised ovum (egg) may be disposed of at a stage before pregnancy can be confirmed. An intra-uterine

device (IUD) fitted within a similar time after intercourse will have the same effect. And finally, if more than 72 hours elapse after unprotected intercourse before the woman seeks help, menstrual extraction can be used at or just after the due date of her next period. By this technique, an instrument attached to a vacuum is used to remove the whole of a woman's monthly period within a few minutes, including, if it exists, the product of any unwanted conception.

Are such methods lawful? They raise the question of where the line is to be drawn between contraception and abortion. A distinction must be made between the 'morning after' pill and the IUD on the one hand, and menstrual extraction on the other. The first two operate at a time before the fertilised ovum can implant in the womb. By the time menstrual extraction is utilised, the ovum will have become an implanted embryo. The action taken to remove that embryo by the vacuum clearly constitutes an induced abortion. The crucial legal issue then, in relation to the use of the 'morning after' pill and the IUD, is whether a procedure which prevents implantation is an act done to procure a miscarriage so as to make the doctor liable for criminal abortion. The woman herself will not be able to be proved to be with child. She will thus not be guilty of an offence herself, but could, as we have seen, be prosecuted for conspiracy with her doctor. The argument that prevention of implantation is no offence runs thus. There is no carriage of a child by a woman before implantation takes place, and so to prevent that event even occurring cannot be an act done to procure a miscarriage. Many fertilised ova fail to implant naturally and no one then suggests that a miscarriage has occurred. The opponents of post-coital birth control reply that the fertilised ovum is present within the body of the woman; she carries it within her. Therefore there is carriage of a child, and any act removing that child from her womb is an act done to procure a miscarriage. Up to 40% of implanted embryos also abort spontaneously. Thus arguments based on spontaneous loss of fertilised ova are irrelevant.

No successful prosecution has ever been brought in respect of either the 'morning after' pill, or the use of an IUD, as means of post-coital birth control. In 1983 the Attorney General expressed his opinion that prior to implantation there is no pregnancy and so means used to prevent implantation do not constitute procuring miscarriage. In 1991 a judge dismissed a prosecution for criminal abortion based on the insertion of an IUD agreeing with the Attorney General that until implantation there is no pregnancy. The Attorney General's ruling is persuasive, but not binding on his successors. The matter remains unresolved by higher judicial authority. In practice, however, doctors are prescribing the 'morning after' pill without any pretence of applying the criteria laid down in the Abortion Act.

Selective reduction

As we saw above, in Chapter 7, certain forms of fertility treatment, IVF or (more often) the use of super-ovulatory drugs, may result in a multiple pregnancy in which the woman carries more foetuses than can safely be brought to term. The term 'selective reduction' refers to the practice, in such a pregnancy, of deliberately terminating the lives of some of the foetuses in order to improve the survival chances of those that remain. Andrew Grubb has discussed the legal problems posed by the practice as follows:

Grubb, A, 'The new law of abortion: clarification or ambiguity' (1991) Crim LR 659:

Modern medicine has developed techniques whereby a multiple pregnancy may be reduced by killing one or more foetuses *in utero*. This has become particularly important in cases where infertility treatment has led to a multiple pregnancy. The greater the number of foetuses carried by a woman, the greater is risk to her health during pregnancy and at delivery. Equally, in these circumstances there is the risk of foetal mortality and of foetal handicap, including cerebral palsy, blindness and mental retardation.

Consequently, it is often desirable out of the interests of the mother and/or the foetuses that the pregnancy should be reduced in number. This is usually done in the first 14 weeks of the pregnancy by either injecting potassium chloride into the amniotic sac or into the heart of the foetus or by aspiration. Foetus(es) will die and may be spontaneously expelled or, more likely, will remain in the mother, wither and what remains will be expelled at the time the remaining healthy foetuses are delivered. This procedure is known as selective reduction.

In addition, a similar procedure may be used later in pregnancy when one of a number of foetuses (usually twins) is discovered to be seriously handicapped. Because of the slightly differing circumstances when it is used, it is sometimes distinguished from selective reduction and is known as selective foeticide ...

Legal position pre-[HFEA 1990]

It was not clear under the law prior to 1 April 1991 whether selective reduction and selective foeticide were covered by the abortion legislation. It could be argued that in cases where the 'reduced' foetus(es) is not expelled there is not a 'miscarriage' within the terms of s 58 of the Offences Against the Person Act 1861. The better view is, however, that the term 'miscarriage' does not require expulsion of the contents of the womb but merely that some or all of the contents cease to be carried alive within it. This would bring both procedures within s 58 of the 1861 Act. In any event, the argument overlooks the fact that ultimately, the withered and dead products of the foetus will be expelled at the time the remaining foetuses are delivered.

A further complication was raised as to whether selective reduction was a 'termination of pregnancy' within the Abortion Act 1967 because the woman is still pregnant in the sense that one or more of the healthy foetuses remains after the procedure. If there was no termination of pregnancy, then the procedure could never be lawful, because what was being done would not fall within the wording of the Abortion Act. There would be a crime but no possible defence.

In the light of these uncertainties, when parliament came to amend the Abortion Act in 1990 a new s 5(2) was introduced specifically to deal with the practice:

5   (2)   For the purposes of the law relating to abortion, anything done with intent to procure a woman's miscarriage (or, in the case of a woman carrying more than one foetus, her miscarriage of any foetus) is unlawfully done unless authorised by s 1 of this Act and, in the case of a woman carrying more than one foetus, anything done with intent to procure her miscarriage of any foetus is authorised by that section if–

(a)   the ground for termination of the pregnancy specified in sub-s (1)(d) of that section applies in relation to any foetus and the thing is done for the purpose of procuring the miscarriage of that foetus, or

(b)   any of the other grounds for termination of the pregnancy specified in that section applies.

It is apparent that the effect of this provision is that selective reduction will be lawful either to protect the health or life of the pregnant woman (in which case the foetus(es) for destruction may be randomly chosen) or to terminate the life of a particular foetus on the s 1(1)(d) ground of foetal handicap.

Drug-induced abortions

When the Abortion Act 1967 was first enacted, medical abortion invariably necessitated the surgical removal of the foetus by a qualified doctor. For this reason, s 1(1) confers immunity from criminal liability only where abortion is carried out by 'a registered medical practitioner'. Developments in abortion techniques since then, particularly the availability of new 'abortifacient' drugs, now allow others, besides doctors, to take a much more direct role in terminating pregnancy. How far will they be protected by the terms of the 1967 Act? The issue, in relation to nursing staff, was considered by the House of Lords in the case of *Royal College of Nursing of UK v DHSS*.

Royal College of Nursing of UK v DHSS [1981] AC 800, HL (Wilberforce, Diplock, Edmund-Davies, Keith and Roskill LL)

The RCN became concerned over the potential liability of its members in relation to the practice of using the drug Prostaglandin to carry out many abortions. The drug acts by stimulating contractions in the uterus, leading to the expulsion of the foetus. Here, whilst a doctor will perform the initial insertion of a catheter into the pregnant woman's uterus, the drug itself is later fed through the catheter by a nurse. The College sought a declaration that a DHSS circular authorising the practice was wrong in law.

> **Lord Keith:** Section 1(1) of the Act of 1967 can operate to relieve a person from guilt of an offence under the law relating to abortion only 'when a pregnancy is terminated by a registered medical practitioner'. Certain other conditions must also be satisfied, but no question about these arises in the present case. The sole issue is whether the words I have quoted cover the situation where

abortion has been brought about as a result of the procedure under consideration.

The argument for the respondents is, in essence, that the words of the sub-section do not apply because the pregnancy has not been terminated by any registered medical practitioner, but by the nurse who did the act or acts which directly resulted in the administration to the pregnant woman of the abortifacient drugs.

In my opinion this argument involves placing an unduly restricted and unintended meaning on the words 'when a pregnancy is terminated'. It seems to me that these words, in their context, are not referring to the mere physical occurrence of termination. The sidenote to s 1 is 'Medical termination of pregnancy'. 'Termination of pregnancy' is an expression commonly used, perhaps rather more by medical people than by laymen, to describe in neutral and unemotive terms the bringing about of an abortion. So used, it is capable of covering the whole process designed to lead to that result, and in my view it does so in the present context. Other provisions of the Act make it clear that termination of pregnancy is envisaged as being a process of treatment. Section 1(3) provides that, subject to an exception for cases of emergency, 'treatment for the termination of pregnancy' must be carried out in a National Health Service hospital or a place for the time being approved by the minister. There are similar references to treatment for the termination of pregnancy in s 3, which governs the application of the Act to visiting forces. Then by s 4(1) it is provided that no person shall be under any duty 'to participate in any treatment authorised by this Act to which he has a conscientious objection'. This appears clearly to recognise that what is authorised by s 1(1) in relation to the termination of pregnancy is a process of treatment leading to that result. Section 5(2) is also of some importance. It provides that: 'For the purposes of the law relating to abortion, anything done with intent to procure the miscarriage of a woman is unlawfully done unless authorised by s 1 of this Act.' This indicates a contemplation that a wide range of acts done when a pregnancy is terminated under the given conditions are authorised by s 1, and leads to the inference that, since all that s 1 authorises is the termination of pregnancy by a registered medical practitioner, all such acts must be embraced in the termination.

Given that the termination of pregnancy under contemplation in s 1(1) includes the whole process of treatment involved therein, it remains to consider whether, on the facts of this case, the termination can properly be regarded as being 'by a registered medical practitioner'. In my opinion this question is to be answered affirmatively. The doctor has responsibility for the whole process and is in charge of it throughout. It is he who decides that it is to be carried out. He personally performs essential parts of it which are such as to necessitate the application of his particular skill. The nurse's actions are done under his direct written instructions. In the circumstances I find it impossible to hold that the doctor's role is other than that of a principal, and I think he would be very surprised to hear that the nurse was the principal and he himself only an accessory. It is true that it is the nurse's action which leads directly to the introduction of abortifacient drugs into the system of the patient, but that action is done in a ministerial capacity and on the doctor's orders. Even if it were right to regard the nurse as a principal, it seems to me inevitable that the doctor should also be so regarded. If both the doctor and the nurse were principals, the provisions of the sub-section would be still satisfied, because the pregnancy would have been terminated by the doctor notwithstanding that it had also been terminated by the nurse.

I therefore conclude that termination of pregnancy by means of the procedures under consideration is authorised by the terms of s 1(1). This conclusion is the more satisfactory as it appears to me to be fully in accordance with that part of the policy and purpose of the Act which was directed to securing that socially acceptable abortions should be carried out under the safest conditions attainable. One may also feel some relief that it is unnecessary to reach a decision involving that the very large numbers of medical practitioners and others who have participated in the relevant procedures over several years past should now be revealed as guilty of criminal offences.

Lord Roskill: Learned counsel for the respondents did not shrink from the anomalies which would necessarily flow from the acceptance of his submission and the construction adopted by the majority of the Court of Appeal. There was, he said, only a limited qualification engrafted upon an otherwise unchanged criminal law and in 1967 parliament had legislated by reference to the surgical techniques of abortion as they then were and not for other techniques of abortion as they might subsequently be evolved. Pressed to say whether a new method must not be adopted which involved less risk to the patient, he replied that any such new method would only be lawful if the doctor were present throughout, a view which would seemingly make unrealistic demands upon medical manpower since no one suggested that each of the seven steps taken by the nurse, to which I have already referred, was not well within the capacity of someone possessed of the qualifications and experience which such a nurse would necessarily possess.

Whilst the decision of the House of Lords (by a narrow 3:2 majority) means that nursing staff involved in abortions enjoy the same statutory protection as doctors, the problem of who else might benefit has now arisen following the development of a further abortifacient drug, RU-486 or Mifepristone. This drug is similar in its operation to Prostaglandin but is significantly easier to administer. Indeed, the drug could, in principle, be made available on prescription in tablet form to be taken by pregnant women who remain out-patients. A new s 1(3A) was specifically introduced into the Abortion Act in 1990 to allow for Mifepristone to be taken, in the future, at GPs' surgeries (previously, under s 1(3), treatment to terminate a pregnancy could only be given at NHS or other hospitals approved by the Secretary of State). Nevertheless, as Kennedy and Grubb point out, a real difficulty remains:

Kennedy, I and Grubb, A, *Medical Law,* **2nd edn, 1994, London: Butterworths, pp 916–17:**

[Mifepristone] is prescribed by a doctor, dispensed by a pharmacist, but administered to herself by the pregnant woman. In this situation who terminates the pregnancy?

There are two possible situations which might arise. First, the termination is only completed after the woman has returned to the hospital some 36 to 48 hours later after the Prostaglandin pessary has been inserted. Here, undoubtedly the termination would be by the doctor even if the Prostaglandin were given by a nurse under his supervision (*Royal College of Nursing* case). This is not problematic for the law. However, the alternative situation that might arise is.

Suppose, instead, the effects of Mifepristone occur before the woman returns to the hospital for the Prostaglandin pessary. In 55% of cases bleeding (and therefore, the potential for a 'miscarriage') occur within 48 hours of administering Mifepristone. In a proportion of cases (about 3%) termination will occur before re-admission. In our view, in this situation it must be the pregnant woman and not the doctor who terminates the pregnancy. It is she who does the last voluntary act necessary to effect the termination. Legally, the situation is analogous to a case where a doctor provides the means (eg, pills) for a patient to kill himself. It is the patient who commits suicide. The doctor is guilty of assisting suicide, if anything. It cannot be said that he is guilty of murder since the law regards the patient's actions as the cause of death. Mutatis mutandis, here the woman causes her own termination. The provisions of the Abortion Act 1967 would not be complied with. Clearly, Parliament overlooked this fundamental point when it sought to bring Mifepristone within the framework of the Abortion Act.

However, an argument which would challenge this view could be mounted on the basis of the *Royal College of Nursing* case. There, the House of Lords ... extended 'medical practitioner' to include all acts performed by the medical team for whom the doctor is responsible ...

Could this wider notion of 'termination by a registered medical practitioner covering all action for which the doctor takes responsibility' (or 'charge') help in the case of Mifepristone? In one sense, a doctor does have responsibility for the patient throughout the treatment. However, it is a different kind of responsibility from that contemplated in the *Royal College of Nursing* case. In that case the responsibility denoted the right to control those who acted on his behalf in a professional capacity. In the case of Mifepristone, the responsibility relates to the doctor's ethical and legal duty to his patient. The relationship is neither one of control nor one where the patient (in administering the drug to herself) can be said to act on the doctor's behalf or be in his charge. It is unlikely that a future court would further expand the meaning of the 1967 Act to cover the use of Mifepristone.

At present, the use of Mifepristone in this country is restricted, in any event, to its administration by nursing staff in hospitals, in the same manner as Prostaglandin.

Late abortion and the living abortus

As noted, the 1990 amendments to the Abortion Act permit termination of pregnancy right up until birth under grounds (b), (c) and (d). Such late terminations are extremely rare and, due to restrictions in the licences granted to private abortion clinics (imposed by the Secretary of State pursuant to s 1(3) of the Act), may only be carried out in NHS hospitals. In practice, it is the last of the grounds, foetal handicap, which is almost always invoked in such circumstances.

By contrast with early abortions, where abortifacient drugs may be used, late abortions invariably require surgical intervention. Of course, the intention of the doctor is that the foetus will not survive the abortion process; however, unless measures are taken to kill the foetus while still inside the womb, there is a real chance that it will be born alive. What is the legal position of the doctor, in such circumstances, where the foetus only dies some time after delivery? In *AG's Reference (No 3 of 1994)* [1997] 3 WLR 421 the House of Lords considered a reference in respect of the acquittal for murder (on the directions of the trial judge) of a man who had stabbed his pregnant girlfriend in the abdomen. (The woman went into labour soon after the attack and, although the child was delivered alive, it died 120 days later due to its severe prematurity.) In reversing the decision of the Court of Appeal that a murder charge could lie in such circumstances, their Lordships were nevertheless extremely cautious to limit their response to the facts in hand (involving an intention by the respondent to harm the pregnant woman). Lord Mustill commented that he 'would wish to proceed with particular care in relation to allegations of murder stemming from an injury to the foetus unaccompanied by any causative injury to the mother'. However, given this present lack of certainty in the law, the doctor responsible for a late abortion would be well advised to take the greatest care that the foetus dies while it is still inside the womb.

PRE-NATAL HARM BEYOND THE ABORTION CONTEXT

General principles

Beyond the context of abortion, it is readily apparent that injuries may be caused to a foetus in utero which subsequently lead to it being born disabled. The question of whether a child damaged in this way can, after it is born, bring an action against the person responsible has created a surprising amount of difficulty for the common law. Nevertheless, in respect of children born after 21 July 1976, such a child has been given a statutory right to recover damages under the Congenital Disabilities (Civil Liability) Act 1976. Section 1 of this Act provides as follows:

1   **Civil liability to child born disabled**

   (1)   If a child is born disabled as the result of such an occurrence before its birth as is mentioned in sub-s (2) below, and a person (other than the child's own mother) is under this section answerable to the child in respect of the occurrence, the child's disabilities are to be regarded as

damage resulting from the wrongful act of that person and actionable accordingly at the suit of the child.

(2) An occurrence to which this section applies is one which–

    (a) affected either parent of the child in his or her ability to have a normal, healthy child; or

    (b) affected the mother during her pregnancy, or affected her or the child in the course of its birth, so that the child is born with disabilities which would not otherwise have been present.

(3) Subject to the following sub-sections, a person (here referred to as 'the defendant') is answerable to the child if he was liable in tort to the parent or would, if sued in due time have been so; and it is no answer that there could not have been such liability because the parent suffered no actionable injury, if there was a breach of legal duty which, accompanied by injury, would have given rise to the liability.

(4) In the case of an occurrence preceding the time of conception, the defendant is not answerable to the child if at that time either or both of the parents knew the risk of their child being born disabled (that it to say, the particular risk created by the occurrence); but should it be the child's father who is the defendant, this sub-section does not apply if he knew of the risk and the mother did not.

(5) The defendant is not answerable to the child, for anything he did or omitted to do when responsible in a professional capacity for treating or advising the parent, if he took reasonable care having due regard to then received professional opinion applicable to the particular class of case; but this does not mean that he is answerable only because he departed from received opinion.

(6) Liability to the child under this section may be treated as having been excluded or limited by contract made with the parent affected, to the same extent and subject to the same restrictions as liability in the parent's own case; and a contract term which could have been set up by the defendant in an action by the parent, so as to exclude or limit his liability to him or her, operates in the defendant's favour to the same, but no greater, extent in an action under this section by the child.

(7) If in the child's action under this section it is shown that the parent affected shared the responsibility for the child being born disabled, the damages are to be reduced to such extent as the court thinks just and equitable having regard to the extent of the parent's responsibility.

The effect of s 1(3) above is to found the child's action upon the concept of 'derivative liability', ie, it may only bring a claim in so far as the occurrence which caused its injuries involved a breach of duty by the tortfeasor to one of its parents. More recently, in two cases whose facts arose prior to 1976, *Burton v Islington HA* and *De Martell v Merton and Sutton HA* [1992] 3 All ER 833, the Court of Appeal had to tackle head on the problem at common law of how it is that a duty in tort can be owed to an entity which has no legal personality. In finding for the plaintiffs, Dillon LJ relied extensively upon Commonwealth authority, in particular the decision of the Supreme Court of Victoria in *Watt v Rama* (1972) VR 353:

Burton v Islington HA [1992] 3 All ER 833:

Dillon LJ: The main Commonwealth case from a country with a common law jurisdiction is *Watt v Rama* ... which has since been accepted by other appellate courts in Australia as a correct statement of the law, that is to say the common law of Australia. That was a case which arose out of injuries in a motor accident. The leading judgment is that of Winneke CJ and Pape J. It is founded on an analysis – in my judgment, correct – of the tort of negligence by reference to decisions of the House of Lords and the Privy Council and certain Australian decisions, and it is founded also on the *Montreal Tramways* decision. I can take up that judgment, at pp 358–59:

> The real question posed for our decision is not whether an action lies in respect of pre-natal injuries but whether a plaintiff born with injuries caused by the pre-natal neglect of the defendant has a cause of action in negligence against him in respect of such injuries. To this question the defendant answers 'No', because at the time of his neglect the plaintiff was not in existence as a living person, had no separate existence apart from her mother, was not capable of suing to assert a legal right, and was not a legal person to whom he could be under a duty.

There is then reference to well known authorities like *Donoghue v Stevenson* [1932] AC 562; *Dorset Yacht Co Ltd v Home Office* [1970] AC 1004; *Bourhill (Hay) v Young* [1943] AC 92; *Watson v Fram Reinforced Concrete Co (Scotland) Ltd* (1960) SC (HL) 92 and *Grant v Australian Knitting Mills Ltd* [1936] AC 85, and then to a South African decision which followed *Montreal Tramways v Leveille* [1933] 4 DLR 337 and to the *Montreal Tramways* case itself. After the citations the judgment continues, at pp 360–61:

> Those circumstances, accordingly, constituted a potential relationship capable of imposing a duty on the defendant in relation to the child if and when born. On the birth the relationship crystallised and out of it arose a duty on the defendant in relation to the child. On the facts which for present purposes must be assumed, the child was born with injuries caused by the act or neglect of the defendant in the driving of his car. But as the child could not in the very nature of things acquire rights correlative to a duty until it became by birth a living person, and as it was not until then that it could sustain injuries as a living person, it was, we think, at that stage that the duty arising out of the relationship was attached to the defendant, and it was at that stage that the defendant was, on the assumption that his act or omission in the driving of the car constituted a failure to take reasonable care, in breach of the duty to take reasonable care to avoid injury to the child ...

With respect, the analysis endorsed by his Lordship appears to confuse breach of duty with the damage which is thereby caused. It might be simpler to accept that legal duties can be owed to the unborn child, as a potential person, even though the corresponding right of such an entity to bring a claim remains contingent upon its subsequent birth. Though this approach may violate strict Hohfeldian logic (see above, Chapter 1, p 13), it seems to have been an unspoken assumption in many medical negligence claims: see, for example, *Whitehouse v Jordan* [1981] 1 All ER 267.

Ultimately, all that is being allowed in these cases is that a damaged child may recover damages where, but for the defendant's negligence, it would have been born undamaged. A claim, on the other hand, by such a child who, but for the defendant's negligence would never have been born at all, would, at least if the judgment of the Court of Appeal in *Mackay v Essex AHA* is followed, form an inadmissible 'wrongful life' action. Recently, however, this area of law has been thrown into some confusion by changes made to the Congenital Disabilities (Civil Liability) Act by the Human Fertilisation and Embryology Act 1990 (see above, Chapter 7).

Harm caused by the child's mother

It is important to note that, except in the case of negligent driving (allowed for in s 2 of the Act) no action will lie under the 1976 Act where the pre-natal injuries arose through the negligence of the child's mother. The policy grounds underlying this immunity are discussed by Jane Fortin as follows:

Fortin, J, 'Legal protection for the unborn child' (1988) 51 MLR 54:

By making liability to the child depend on liability to the parent, th[e] formula [of derivative liability] excludes a wide range of negligent acts and omissions on the part of the mother. Some would say that circumstances like those arising in the *Berkshire* case indicate quite clearly that the existence of maternal tortious liability would be a useful means of controlling the mother's ante-natal behaviour. Nevertheless, the Law Commission rejected the proposition that a child might sue its mother for pre-natal injuries caused by her negligence, largely on the social policy grounds that the existence of such a right of action would have deleterious effects on family cohesion. In particular, the mother might become vulnerable to litigation brought on behalf of her child, claiming that it was her failure to give up cigarette smoking or alcohol or to follow the latest dietary ante-natal regime that had caused the child's disablement. Moreover, the existence of such a cause of action might well fuel a matrimonial or parental conflict. Despite the undoubted sense grounding these fears, the Law Commission's acceptance of this social policy argument is inconsistent with their earlier claim that the unborn child could have no legal existence; surely the answer to the question whether the child could sue his mother in respect of pre-natal negligence, should have been that she could not, in any event, owe a duty to a legal nonentity. Nevertheless, the Law Commission was satisfied that different considerations applied to cases of pre-natal injury caused by a road accident, where the existence of third party insurance would prevent any risk of a child's claim against its mother causing family conflicts. Consequently, despite the unborn child's lack of legal personality, the 1976 Act does impose on the pregnant mother a duty of care in relation to it, but only in the context of driving a motor vehicle. The illogicality of such a provision can hardly be justified by the existence of ample insurance funds to meet any liability.

Despite the inconsistency of the exception relating to maternal liability for negligent driving, the 1976 Act maintains the general principle of the civil law that the unborn child has no legal personality. It is arguable that this principle is acquiring an element of unreality, particularly when the 1976 Act itself and now the *Berkshire* case, clearly adhere to the proposition that a child's development is a continuing process that commences at conception not birth.

In the case of *D v Berkshire County Council* [1987] 1 All ER 20, referred to by Fortin, the House of Lords held that events prior to a child's birth (which led to it being born with drug withdrawal symptoms) could properly be taken into account by magistrates when making a care order.

In general, it might seem paradoxical, given the relative ease with which the pregnant woman may dispose of her foetus altogether through abortion, that the law should concern itself with 'lesser harms' it may suffer as a result of her behaviour while pregnant. However, the point is, of course, that in the latter case alone there will be an existing person whose interests have been adversely affected by her conduct. The highly contentious question of whether, in cases of this sort, the criminal law might be invoked to afford protection to the foetus, is addressed by John Robertson:

Robertson, JA, *Children of Choice*, 1994, Ewing, New Jersey: Princeton University Press, pp 180–85:

Given the foreseeable impact of certain pre-natal acts or omissions on the welfare of offspring, one cannot reasonably argue that women and men have no pre-natal obligation to avoid harm to children they choose to bring into the world. The more contested question is what public policies and legal options should be pursued to prevent pre-natal harm to offspring. The choice ranges from education and access to treatment to post-birth sanctions and pre-natal imposition of treatment on pregnant women. Because procreative liberty is not involved, and because the conduct in question poses serious harm to offspring, coercive sanctions are not in principle excluded. However, as we shall see, the better policy in most cases will be to rely on information, education, and access to treatment ...

Opponents of prosecution also see a grave threat to personal privacy and civil liberties. If illegal drug use during pregnancy is independently punishable, then anything with the slightest pre-natal risk to offspring could be punished as pre-natal child abuse. Women could be prosecuted for smoking or drinking even moderate amounts of alcohol at any time during pregnancy, because even a few drinks might lower IQ points, and smoking increases the risk of prematurity and low birth weight. In the worst-case scenario, special pregnancy police will be commissioned to monitor women for pregnancies, and then surveil their behaviour; if they err, they are then stigmatised, shamed, fined, or incarcerated. Margaret Atwood's *The Handmaid's Tale*, a chilling novel of women forced to serve the needs of a repressive dictatorship, starts sounding much less fanciful than it appears to be ...

All these points deserve considered attention. They explain why prosecutions have been largely unsuccessful, are widely opposed, and are unlikely to be a key factor in preventing pre-natal harm. They also show why education, treatment, and services are the more desirable and most effective avenue for public policy.

Despite the drawbacks of a criminal approach, however, these criticisms do not establish that criminal sanctions should never be imposed on persons who culpably harm offspring by pre-natal conduct. When culpability is established, criminal law theory easily includes pre-natal as well as post-natal conduct that harms offspring. For example, Lord Coke in the 17th century recognised criminal liability for pre-natal actions that caused post-natal death ...

But will criminal prosecution do any good? This is a pragmatic policy judgment over which reasonable people may well differ. At the very least, prosecution will fulfil the law's function of enunciating minimum acceptable standards of conduct to which all citizens of the State, regardless of cultural affiliation, must conform. In this case, the standards are enunciated for conduct during pregnancy that risks avoidable harm to offspring. In denouncing unacceptable conduct, legal proscription and prosecution might encourage women to refrain from harmful pre-natal conduct, or to seek help, if they know that they are at risk of causing harm to offspring. In any event, it will announce the community's condemnation of such conduct, deter some injuries to offspring and generally contribute to community norms of acceptable behaviour.

Refusals of obstetric intervention

Perhaps even more controversial are cases in which, rather than doing anything active to harm her foetus, the pregnant woman passively declines medical intervention which her doctors tell her is necessary to prevent serious harm occurring to it. What should the law's approach be here? In *Re T (Adult: Refusal of Treatment)* [1992] 4 All ER 649, Lord Donaldson MR expressly left the question open as to whether the presence of a viable foetus could oust the normal principle that a competent adult patient has a right to refuse treatment:

> **Lord Donaldson MR:** An adult patient who ... suffers from no mental incapacity has an absolute right to choose whether to consent to medical treatment, to refuse it or to choose one rather than another of the treatments being offered. The only possible qualification is where the choice may lead to the death of a viable foetus. That is not the case here and if and when it arises, the court will be presented with a novel problem of considerable legal and ethical complexity.

Then, very soon afterwards, the issue came squarely before the High Court in the case of *Re S (Adult: Refusal of Treatment)*.

Re S (Adult: Refusal of Treatment) [1992] 4 All ER 671, Fam Div (Sir Stephen Brown P)

Mrs S was a 30 year old 'born-again Christian' in labour with her third child. Her foetus was in a position of 'transverse lie' and it was a practical certainty that, unless an immediate Caesarean section was carried out, her uterus would rupture, killing the child and, very possibly, Mrs S herself. The latter refused the operation, however, on religious grounds.

> **Sir Stephen Brown P**: ... I have heard the evidence of P, a Fellow of the Royal College of Surgeons, who is in charge of this patient at the hospital. He has given, succinctly and graphically, a description of the condition of this patient. Her situation is desperately serious, as is also the situation of the as yet unborn child. The child is in what is described as a position of 'transverse lie', with the elbow projecting through the cervix and the head being on the right side. There is the gravest risk of a rupture of the uterus if the section is not carried out and the natural labour process is permitted to continue. The evidence of P is that we are concerned with 'minutes rather than hours' and that it is a 'life and death' situation. He has done his best, as have other surgeons and doctors at the hospital, to persuade the mother that the only means of saving her life, and also I emphasise the life of her unborn child, is to carry out a Caesarean section operation. P is emphatic. He says it is absolutely the case that the baby cannot be born alive if a Caesarean operation is not carried out. He has described the medical condition. I am not going to go into it in detail because of the pressure of time.
>
> I have been assisted by Mr Munby QC appearing for the Official Solicitor as *amicus curiae*. The Official Solicitor answered the call of the court within minutes and, although this application only came to the notice of the court officials at 1.30 pm, it has come on for hearing just before 2 o'clock and now at 2.18 pm I propose to make the declaration which is sought. I do so in the knowledge that the fundamental question appears to have been left open by Lord Donaldson MR in *Re T (Adult: Refusal of Medical Treatment)* [1992] 4 All ER 649, heard earlier this year in the Court of Appeal, and in the knowledge that there is no English authority which is directly in point. There is, however, some American authority which suggests that if this case were being heard in the American courts the answer would be likely to be in favour of granting a declaration in these circumstances: see *Re AC* (1990) 573 A 2d 1235, pp 1240, 1246–48, and 1252. I do not propose to say more at this stage, except that I wholly accept the evidence of P as to the desperate nature of this situation, and that I grant the declaration as sought.

The President referred in his judgment to the American decision of *Re AC*. This was undoubtedly an unfortunate choice of authority. Ian Kennedy has charted the history of that case as follows:

> **Kennedy, I, *Treat Me Right*, 2nd edn, 1992, Oxford: OUP, pp 367–68:**
>
> On 10 November 1987, the Court of Appeals of the District of Columbia, in the case of Angela C, approved the lower court's order that a Caesarean section be carried out on a terminally ill woman with hours or days to live, despite her

apparent refusal of permission. The child was in its 26th week of gestation. The mother was heavily sedated and in extremis suffering from a metastatic oxygenic carcinoma in her lung. The operation was performed. The child died two hours thereafter. The mother died two days later. The court in upholding the order held that 'the trial judge did not err in subordinating AC's right against bodily intrusion to the interests of the unborn, [but potentially viable] child'. This was particularly so, the court held, because 'Caesarean section would not significantly affect AC's condition because she had, at best, two days left of sedated life'.

Obviously, 'significantly' assumes great significance here ...

[Footnote:] *Re AC* was subsequently reheard *en banc* and the Court of Appeals issued a second judgment on 26 April 1990, No 87-609 ... The court vacated its prior order on the grounds that there had not been a proper finding of fact whether AC was competent, or, if she was not, how 'substituted judgment' was to be applied. The court did, however, decide that the decision of a competent patient or substituted judgment should prevail, even if surgery was refused, in 'virtually all cases' unless there are 'truly extraordinary or compelling reasons to override them', by taking account, for example, of the State's interest in protecting life. At the same time the court did not dissent from, or overrule, a previous decision (1986) of the Superior Court in *Re Madyun* (unreported: published as Appendix to *Re AC*). In *Madyun*, the court authorised surgery on a woman who objected for religious reasons. 'All that stood between the Madyun foetus and its independent existence was, put simply, a doctor's scalpel [*sic*]. In these circumstances, the life of the infant inside its mother's womb was entitled to be protected.'

The issue of whether a court should authorise a Caesarean section against the wishes of the pregnant woman gives rise to considerable ethical and legal dilemmas. On the one hand, a situation in which the doctors stood idly by and allowed a mature foetus to rupture its mother's womb would arguably do serious symbolic damage to the concept of the sanctity of life, which any society must maintain. On the other, the thought of doctors carrying out invasive, and potentially risky, therapy upon unwilling patients is deeply troubling to the concept of individual autonomy, another of liberal society's fundamental values. Moreover, the fact that the patients whose rights are infringed in this way are invariably women, opens up the spectre of gender inequality and domination, a problem exacerbated by the time constraints operating which often mean that the women in question lack adequate legal representation.

In 1996 a spate of further Caesarean cases came before the English courts. In every case, it was declared that the treatment would be lawful. Almost without exception, though, the judges involved based their decisions on a prior determination of fact that the women in question were incompetent and could accordingly be treated in their best interests. In the first such case, *Tameside and Glossop Acute Services Trust v CH* [1996] 1 FLR 762, Wall J declared that a Caesarean could be performed without consent as treatment 'for mental disorder' within the terms of the Mental Health Act 1983: see below, Chapter 9. Subsequently Johnson J granted a declaration authorising intervention at common law in *Norfolk and Norwich (NHS) Trust v W* [1996] 2 FLR 613:

> **Johnson J**: On Friday 21 June 1996 an application was made to me for an order relating to a proposed medical procedure upon a patient in a hospital in Norwich. The application began at 4.45 pm and was made by Mr John Grace QC. The patient was not represented, but the hospital's solicitors had communicated with the Official Solicitor and Mr James Munby QC was present with Mr Hinchcliffe of the Official Solicitor's office. Mr Munby made submissions as *amicus curiae*. No one else was present, there were no affidavits or statements and the information upon which I had to base my decision came from Mr Grace and Mr Hinchcliffe who had both spoken by telephone to the consultants in Norwich caring for the patient.
>
> **The information available to the court**
>
> Miss W, a woman aged 32, had arrived at the hospital's accident and emergency department at 9 am that day. She was in the last stages of pregnancy, apparently having had no ante-natal treatment. She was in labour, fully dilated and ready to deliver her baby. She was said to be in a state of arrested labour. Throughout the day, despite the obvious indications to the contrary, she continued to deny that she was even pregnant. The hospital was able to ascertain that she had a history of psychiatric treatment, marked by non-co-operation by her with those seeking to help her. She had had three previous pregnancies all terminating by Caesarean section. There were two risks to the patient. In layman's terms, the first was that unless the foetus was delivered by 6 pm, it would suffocate within the patient; and the presence of a dead foetus in the patient would have serious, and indeed life-threatening, consequences for the health of the patient herself. The second risk was that the patient's old Caesarean scars would reopen and this too would lead to the life of the foetus being at risk with consequent risk to the patient herself ...
>
> ... In the *Tameside* case ... Wall J specifically left open the question whether the court has the power at common law to authorise the use of reasonable force as a necessary incident of treatment or whether the power was limited to cases which fell within s 63 of the Mental Health Act 1983. That section reads:
>
>> The consent of a patient shall not be required for any medical treatment given to him for the mental disorder from which he is suffering ... if the treatment is given by or under the direction of the responsible medical officer.
>
> In the present case in the opinion of the psychiatrist the patient was not suffering from a mental disorder within the meaning of this section and so, if the power exists, it has to be found in the common law.
>
> I held that in circumstances such as the present the court does have a power at common law to authorise the use of reasonable force. I reject the line of argument which had been put to Wall J in the *Tameside* case (p 770–74), preferring the submissions made to me by Mr Munby QC. I seek to apply the

principle enunciated by Lord Goff of Chieveley in *Re F*, namely that there must be a necessity to act and:

> ... the action taken must be such as a reasonable person would in all the circumstances take, acting in the best interests of the assisted person.

Conclusion

In reliance upon the opinion of the consultant psychiatrist and taking account of the information I had about the statements made by the patient during the course of the day, I held that although she was not suffering from a mental disorder within the meaning of the statute, she lacked the mental competence to make a decision about the treatment that was proposed because she was incapable of weighing up the considerations that were involved. She was called upon to make that decision at a time of acute emotional stress and physical pain in the ordinary course of labour made even more difficult for her because of her own particular mental history.

I held that termination of this labour would be in the best interests of the patient. I was satisfied that unless the patient was delivered of the foetus which she was carrying, whether by way of forceps delivery or by Caesarean section, then her own physical health would be put at risk. This risk would arise if the foetus died because of rupture of the patient's old Caesarean scar or by suffocation in the birth canal. The death of the foetus would have immediate and increasing deleterious effects upon the patient herself leading to serious physical damage and possible death. Termination would end the stress and the pain of her labour, it would avoid the likelihood of damage to her physical health which might have potentially life-threatening consequences and, despite her present view about the foetus, would avoid her feeling any feeling of guilt in the future were she, by her refusal of consent, to cause the death of the foetus.

Throughout this judgment I have referred to 'the foetus' because I wish to emphasise that the focus of my judicial attention was upon the interests of the patient herself and not upon the interests of the foetus which she bore. However, the reality was that the foetus was a fully formed child, capable of normal life if only it could be delivered from the mother ...

In this case, the view that the patient was incompetent appears to have been fully justified (see generally, on the question of establishing competence, above, Chapter 3). However, as Johnson J was hearing it, another emergency *ex parte* application was brought before him by Rochdale Healthcare NHS Trust in respect of Mrs C, a woman in labour who was similarly refusing to undergo a Caesarean. In finding her incompetent (in the course of a two minute hearing) the judge held that she was unable to 'make any valid decision about anything of even the most trivial kind' owing to the emotional stress and pain of labour. This was despite the evidence from Mrs C's obstetrician that she was, in the latter's opinion, competent: see *Rochdale NHS Trust v C* [1997] 1 FCR 274.

The preference in these decisions for intervention to be authorised on grounds of the woman's incompetence left the principle in *Re S* isolated and doubtful. As we have seen, Sir Stephen Brown P in that case adverted to *dicta* in Lord Donaldson MR's judgment in *Re T* as to the effect the presence of a viable foetus could have upon refusals of treatment. However, when the House of Lords in *Airedale NHS Trust v Bland* came to restate the general treatment-refusal principle, they did not mention any qualification in such a case. The issue has now been addressed once again at appellate level by the Court of Appeal in *Re MB*.

Re MB (An Adult: Medical Treatment) [1997] 2 FLR 426, CA (Butler-Sloss, Saville and Ward LJJ)

Miss MB required a Caesarean section in order to save her foetus from death or serious handicap. However, although she agreed to the operation, her 'needle phobia' caused her to panic in the operating theatre and refuse the preliminary anaesthetic. Hollis J granted a declaration that, in these circumstances, it would be lawful to provide her with the treatment in her own best interests and this was upheld, the same evening, by the Court of Appeal. Five weeks later, their Lordships handed down a reserved judgment:

> **Butler-Sloss LJ** (delivering the judgment of the court): All the decisions made in the Caesarean section cases to which we have referred arose in circumstances of urgency or extreme urgency. The evidence was in general limited in scope and the mother was not always represented as a party. With the exception of *Re S* ... in all the cases the court decided that the mother did not have the capacity to make the decision. In these extremely worrying situations, it is important to keep in mind the basic principles we have outlined, and the court should approach the crucial question of competence bearing the following considerations in mind. They are not intended to be determinative in every case, for the decision must inevitably depend upon the particular facts before the court:
>
> (1) Every person is presumed to have the capacity to consent to or to refuse medical treatment unless and until that presumption is rebutted.
>
> (2) A competent woman who has the capacity to decide may, for religious reasons, other reasons, for rational or irrational reasons or for no reason at all, choose not to have medical intervention, even though the consequence may be the death or serious handicap of the child she bears, or her own death. In that event the courts do not have the jurisdiction to declare medical intervention lawful and the question of her own best interests, objectively considered, does not arise ...
>
> ... Applying these principles to the facts of this case we find:
>
> (1) Miss MB consented to a Caesarean section.
>
> (2) What she refused to accept was not the incision by the surgeon's scalpel but only the prick of the anaesthetist's needle. Capacity is commensurate with the gravity of the decision to be taken.
>
> (3) She could not bring herself to undergo the Caesarean section she desired because, as the evidence established:

... a fear of needles ... has got in the way of proceeding with the operation ... At the moment of panic ... her fear dominated all ... at the actual point she was not capable of making a decision at all ... at that moment the needle or mask dominated her thinking and made her quite unable to consider anything else.

On that evidence she was incapable of making a decision at all. She was at that moment suffering an impairment of her mental functioning which disabled her. She was temporarily incompetent. In the emergency the doctors would be free to administer the anaesthetic if that were in her best interests.

A feature of some of the cases to which we have referred has been the favourable reaction of the patient who refused treatment to the subsequent medical intervention and the successful outcome. Having noted that, we are none the less sure that however desirable it may be for the mother to be delivered of a live and healthy baby, on this aspect of the appeal it is not a strictly relevant consideration. If therefore the competent mother refuses to have the medical intervention, the doctors may not lawfully do more than attempt to persuade her. If that persuasion is unsuccessful, there are no further steps towards medical intervention to be taken. We recognise that the effect of these conclusions is that there will be situations in which the child may die or may be seriously handicapped because the mother said no and the obstetrician was not able to take the necessary steps to avoid the death or handicap. The mother may indeed later regret the outcome, but the alternative would be an unwarranted invasion of the right of the woman to make the decision.

It is apparent that, though couched in strong terms, the Court of Appeal's endorsement of the principle that, where competent, the woman's autonomy must prevail over her own best interests and those of the foetus, is only *obiter*. On the facts, as we have seen, the court accepted Hollis J's finding that MB herself was not competent and thus treatment had been lawful. However, their Lordships' decision to disapprove the decision in *Re S* on the basis that, where the woman is competent, the court has no jurisdiction to intervene, is open to criticism:

Stauch, M, 'Court-authorised Caesareans and the principle of patient autonomy' (1997) 6 Nott LJ 74:

As their Lordships noted, it is a well established principle of English law that the foetus, until born, lacks legal personality. One reason, quite simply, is that the foetus' physical location within the pregnant woman would, if such personality were granted, lead to insoluble conflicts in cases where the interests of the woman and foetus were opposed. In this regard, the court referred, *inter alia*, to its own previous judgment in *Re F (In Utero)* which concerned the attempt by a local authority to ward the foetus of a mentally unstable woman who had absconded from her place of care. It endorsed the concern of Balcombe LJ in that case, that '[s]ince an unborn child has, *ex hypothesi*, no existence independent of its mother, the only purpose of extending the [wardship] jurisdiction to include a foetus is to enable the mother's actions to be controlled'. This, he felt, should, if appropriate at all, be a matter for Parliament.

After considering statutes which deal with the protection of unborn life, together with a number of ECHR and US authorities, the Court of Appeal in *Re MB* concluded:

> The foetus up to the moment of birth does not have any separate interests capable of being taken into account when a court has to consider an application for a declaration in respect of a Caesarean section operation. The court does not have the jurisdiction to declare that such medical intervention is lawful *to protect the interests of the unborn child* even at the point of birth. [Emphasis added.]

This, it is submitted, is correct so far as it goes. However, at most it follows that the interests of the foetus *per se* are not a sufficient warrant for intervention. Where the court appears, with respect, to have erred is in assuming that a court will therefore never have jurisdiction to declare treatment lawful in such a case, ie, on other grounds. Such a narrow reading of its own powers is contrary to other recent authorities in which doubts over medical treatment have been at issue. In fact, as a judicial tool, declaratory relief has been developed precisely to provide assistance to those, such as doctors, who are faced with urgent ethical dilemmas in situations of legal uncertainty ... [I]n *Re S (Hospital Order: Court's Jurisdiction)* ... Sir Thomas Bingham MR suggested that for such relief to be invoked, it was enough that there was 'a serious justiciable issue' before the court. As his Lordship commented, '[t]his is pre-eminently an area in which the common law should respond to social needs as they are manifested, case by case'.

Overriding an autonomous refusal?

Assuming that a court does, in principle, have the requisite jurisdiction to authorise treatment, should it do so against the competent and autonomous refusal of a pregnant woman to permit obstetric intervention? One might think the answer should always be in the negative. After all, an autonomous choice represents a considered value-ordering by the woman of her interests, and recognition of her integrity as an individual implies that we should not second-guess them. This is the more so, given that imposing intervention, while advancing some of her interests, will inevitably set back others.

A good illustration is provided by the case of [*Baby Boy Doe (A Fetus) v Mother Doe* 510 US 1032 (1993); 114 S Ct 652] a ruling by the US Supreme Court on the legitimacy of court-authorised Caesarean sections. Tabita Bricci was a Pentecostal Christian, whose faith forbade surgical intervention which would bring her pregnancy to an end before full term. In fact, a few weeks prior to birth, doctors determined that her foetus was receiving an inadequate oxygen supply and advised her that, unless delivery were carried out by immediate Caesarean section, her foetus would almost certainly die or suffer severe brain damage. In upholding Mrs Bricci's right to refuse the operation, the Supreme Court endorsed the ruling of the Illinois Supreme Court in a previous case, where it had held:

> Even though we may consider appellant's beliefs unwise, foolish or ridiculous, in the absence of an overriding danger to society we may not permit interference therewith ... for the sole purpose of compelling her to

accept medical treatment forbidden by her religious principles and previously refused by her with full knowledge of the probable consequences.

Here, if compulsory intervention had been authorised, it would have advanced the patient's interests in having a healthy live birth (which she clearly desired). On the other hand, it would clearly have damaged both her relationship with her faith and her general sense of herself as an autonomous agent. Moreover, forced surgical intervention would also have exposed her to attendant physical harm and risk of harm.

It is important to note, however, that in this last case the patient's refusal did not carry implications for her own somatic well being. What of a situation where the refusal of intervention will lead not only to death or serious harm to the foetus but also to the pregnant woman? That, after all, was the situation confronting the English High Court in *Re S*. In general, the courts, while recognising the force of the sanctity of life principle, which is directly implicated here, have given the impression that it is ultimately subordinate to the principle of patient autonomy ...

Nevertheless, it does not follow that a person enjoys an unlimited choice over the *manner* of their death, in so far as additional insult to the sanctity of life principle will be entailed. It is, for instance, generally accepted ... that a doctor is entitled to override a patient's refusal of treatment following a suicide attempt ... Arguably, a case where a pregnant woman will die without obstetric intervention also possesses features which set it apart from other cases in which life-saving treatment is refused. Most obviously, not only the woman but also her foetus, which (whatever its other attributes) is a potent symbol of life, stands to die. (Indeed, in cases where, without intervention, the woman's womb will rupture there is a sense in which the foetus operates as the instrument of death.) There is, perhaps, also the consideration that such deaths, if allowed, would take place in the maternity wards of hospitals.

For further discussion of the issues arising from the refusal of life-saving treatment, see above, Chapter 3.

Despite the failure to address the important substantive issue identified in the last extract, the Court of Appeal did enunciate a number of useful procedural guidelines to be followed in Caesarean cases:

Butler-Sloss LJ: It might be helpful to make some comments on the practice to be followed when the medical profession feel it necessary to seek declarations from the courts:

(1) The court is unlikely to entertain an application for a declaration unless the capacity of the patient to consent to or refuse the medical intervention is in issue.

(2) For the time being, at least, the doctors ought to seek a ruling from the High Court on the issue of competence.

(3) Those in charge should identify a potential problem as early as possible so that both the hospital and the patient can obtain legal advice.

In this case, for instance, the problem was identified at the ante-natal clinic.

(4) It is highly desirable that, in any case where it is not an emergency, steps are taken to bring it before the court, before it becomes an emergency, to remove the extra pressure from the parties and the court and to enable proper instructions to be taken, particularly from the patient and where possible give the opportunity for the court to hear oral evidence, if appropriate.

(5) The hearing should be *inter partes*.

(6) The mother should be represented in all cases, unless, exceptionally, she does not wish to be. If she is unconscious she should have a guardian *ad litem*.

(7) The Official Solicitor should be notified of all applications to the High Court. It would be helpful if, at least for the time being, the Official Solicitor was prepared to continue to act as *amicus curiae*, in cases where he is not asked to be the guardian *ad litem*. He will build up a body of expertise which will be most helpful to the judge hearing the application.

(8) There should in general be some evidence, preferably but not necessarily from a psychiatrist, as to the competence of the patient, if competence is in issue.

(9) Where time permits, the person identified to give the evidence as to capacity to consent to or refuse treatment should be made aware of the observations we have made in this judgment.

(10) In order to be in a position to assess a patient's best interests the judge should be provided, where possible and if time allows, with information about the circumstances of and relevant background material about the patient.

These guidelines have since been incorporated in Department of Health Circular EL (97) 32, issued in June 1997.

CHAPTER NINE

MENTAL HEALTH LAW

BACKGROUND

Introduction

At first sight it may be thought that mental illness should be treated like any other form of medical disorder. However, there are special difficulties involved in deciding precisely what we mean when we say that someone is mentally ill. Perhaps this is inevitable, given the nebulous nature of mental illness and its overlap with antisocial behaviour, the holding of bizarre beliefs, and eccentric lifestyles. In addition, the mentally ill are often stigmatised and misunderstood. Furthermore, the Mental Health Act 1983 provides for the compulsory detention of both criminal offenders and non-offenders if they are mentally ill and satisfy a number of other conditions. It is clear, therefore, that mental health law raises distinct ethical and legal issues.

Leaving aside the special problems that can arise when dealing with the mentally ill criminal offender, it is generally accepted that compulsorily detaining someone who has committed no offence is probably the most serious interference with civil liberties that a state can impose. In consequence, its ethical underpinning must be beyond reproach, and the mechanism which allows this to be done should be open to the most searching scrutiny. We are concerned here with balancing, on the one hand, the rights of the individual, and, on the other hand, both the utilitarian desire to protect the community at large, and the paternalistic impulse to protect the individual from harming himself. This is reflected in the Mental Health Act 1983, by which compulsory civil detention, either for assessment or treatment, is permitted when the patient is suffering from certain forms of mental disorder and ought to be detained either to protect himself or others (the latter being a mixture of paternalism and community protection).

What is mental illness?

There have been a number of writers who have questioned the existence of mental illness, or at least, questioned whether it is a *medical* condition. Interestingly, these views have been harnessed to both right and left wing perspectives. The American doctor and writer, Thomas Szasz, is one of the most well known proponents and approaches it from a libertarian analysis. His view is that *all* illness has a *physical* pathology, and the psychiatrist must be either a malevolent meddler or a benevolent, but misguided healer, and as he sees psychiatry as a study of personal conduct, and maintains that psychiatric interventions are directed at moral, rather than medical problems, the view he takes is that of the psychiatrist as malevolent meddler. Szasz's pithy summary of his thesis is uncompromising:

Szasz, T, *The Myth of Mental Illness: Foundations of a Theory of Personal Conduct*, revised edition, 1974, New York: Harper and Row, p 267:

Summary

The principal arguments advanced in this book and their implications may be summarised as follows.

1   Strictly speaking, disease or illness can affect only the body; hence, there can be no mental illness.

2   'Mental illness' is a metaphor. Minds can be 'sick' only in the sense that jokes are 'sick' or economies are 'sick'.

3   Psychiatric diagnoses are stigmatising labels, phrased to resemble medical diagnoses and applied to persons whose behaviour annoys or offends others.

4   Those who suffer from and complain of their own behaviour are usually classified as 'neurotic'; those whose behaviour makes others suffer, and about whom others complain, are usually classified as 'psychotic'.

5   Mental illness is not something a person has, but is something he does or is.

6   If there is no mental illness there can be no hospitalisation, treatment, or cure for it. Of course, people may change their behaviour or personality, with or without psychiatric intervention. Such intervention is nowadays called 'treatment', and the change, if it proceeds in a direction approved by society, 'recovery' or 'cure'.

7   The introduction of psychiatric considerations into the administration of the criminal law – for example, the insanity plea and verdict, diagnoses of mental incompetence to stand trial, and so forth, corrupt the law and victimise the subject on whose behalf they are ostensibly employed.

8   Personal conduct is always rule-following, strategic, meaningful. Patterns of interpersonal and social relations may be regarded and analysed as if they were games, the behaviour of the players being governed by explicit or tacit game rules.

9   In most types of voluntary psychotherapy, the therapist tries to elucidate the inexplicit game rules by which the client conducts himself; and to help the client scrutinise the goals and values of the life games he plays.

10   There is no medical, moral, or legal justification for involuntary psychiatric interventions. They are crimes against humanity.

Szasz has continued to maintain his basic contentions:

Szasz, T, 'Psychiatric diagnosis, psychiatric power and psychiatric abuse' (1994) 20 JME 135–38:

Psychiatric practice, as the term implies, is a practical, not a theoretical, enterprise. Accordingly, so long as psychiatrists continue to assign the role of mental patient to persons against their will, that fact will remain a fundamental characteristic of psychiatric practice ...

Art historians, drama critics, musicologists, and many other scholars also make subjective classifications. However, lacking State-sanctioned power over persons, their classifications do not lead to anyone's being deprived of life, liberty, or property. Surely, the plastic surgeon's classification of beauty is subjective. But because the plastic surgeon cannot treat his or her patient without the patient's consent, there cannot be any political abuse of plastic surgery. It is as simple, and inconvenient, as that.

Whilst not doubting the sincerity of Szasz's views, it is easy to see how they might be attractive to those who wish to reduce public spending on the care of those diagnosed as being mentally ill.

The British psychoanalyst, the late RD Laing, whose most well known publication is *The Divided Self*, first published in 1959 (reissued 1990, Harmondsworth: Penguin), took a different approach, and did not deny the existence of mental 'illness', but saw it as the reaction of a normal person to abnormal social pressures, for example, oppressive family situations. He related the experience of mental illness very much to being out of kilter with the social norm. It is not difficult to see how this approach might be used in libertarian and even anarchistic arguments against traditional social organisations. It must, however, be said that, interesting though theories such as those of Szasz and Laing are, they were never brought into the mainstream of psychiatry.

However, although most people would not dispute the existence of mental illness, there is an inevitable difference between patients who are physically ill, and patients who are mentally ill, in that it is by no means agreed what is meant by *mental* illness. Although there may be some dispute about areas of physical illness, generally, it is acknowledged that one can point to examples of physical 'normality', but clearly it would be futile to attempt to define a psychologically normal person. Whilst it is accepted that there can be desirable deviations from the physical norm (for example, athletic prowess), we are used to thinking of most significant deviations from the physical 'norm' as being undesirable. However, significant deviations from the psychological 'norm' can be *much better* than the norm, for example, in intellectual ability or capacity for forgiveness and compassion. Furthermore, in the case of physical characteristics, it is easier to decide whether the deviation is desirable or not, not least because mental qualities are essentially part of personal identity.

Unfortunately, as will be seen from the following, the Mental Health Act, whilst referring to a number of 'mental' conditions, does nothing to clarify the difficulties in defining mental illness. There is no definition of mental illness in the Act, nor is there any guidance in the Code of Practice produced to assist those using the provisions of the Act; it is simply a matter of clinical judgment in each case. Similarly, there has been little in the way of judicial consideration of the concept. One of the few cases is *W v L* [1974] QB 711, in which the Court of Appeal considered whether a young man was mentally ill following a series of acts of violence and cruelty. He had hanged a puppy, strangled a terrier with wire, made a cat inhale ammonia and then cut its throat, and had put another cat in the gas oven. When he turned his attention away from family pets, and threatened his wife with a knife and offered other forms of violence towards her, he was admitted as an emergency under the provisions of the 1959 Mental Health Act. Both Denning MR and Orr LJ accepted the medical evidence that the patient was psychotic, and did not consider the meaning of the expression 'mentally ill'. However, Lawton LJ made these observations (pp 718–19):

> **Lawton LJ**: The facts of this case show how difficult the fitting of particular instances into the statutory classification can be. Lord Denning MR and Orr LJ have pointed out that there is no definition of 'mental illness'. The words are ordinary words of the English language. They have no particular medical significance. They have no particular legal significance. How should the court construe them? The answer in my judgment is to be found in the advice which Lord Reid recently gave in *Cozens v Brutus* [1973] AC 854, p 861 namely, that ordinary words of the English language should be construed in the way that ordinary sensible people would construe them. That being, in my judgment, the right test, then I ask myself, what would the ordinary sensible person have said about the patient's condition in this case if he had been informed of his behaviour to the dogs, the cat and his wife? In my judgment such a person would have said: 'Well, the fellow is obviously mentally ill'. If that be right, then, although the case may fall within the definition of 'psychopathic disorder' in s 4(4), it also falls within the classification of 'mental illness'; and there is the added medical fact that when the EEG was taken there were indications of a clinical character showing some abnormality of the brain. It is that application of the sensible person's assessment of the condition, plus the medical indication, which in my judgment brought the case within the classification of mental illness, and justified the finding of the county court judge.

If it is the case that the words 'mental illness' are ordinary words and *have no particular medical significance*, what are the implications of this? In some ways this is an extraordinary conclusion, because if it has no medical significance, what significance does it have? The 'any normal person can see he's ill' definition of mental illness is a worrying one, and it adds fuel to the arguments of people such as Szasz.

The DHSS Consultative Document on the Mental Health Act 1959 in 1976 considered a closed definition of mental illness which would have required one or more of the following characteristics:

DHSS, *DHSS Consultative Document*, 1976, London: HMSO, Appendix II:

(i) more than temporary impairment of intellectual functions shown by a failure of memory, orientation, comprehension and learning capacity;

(ii) more than temporary alteration of mood of such degree as to give rise to the patient having a delusional appraisal of his situation, his past or his future, or that of others, or to the lack of any appraisal;

(iii) delusional beliefs, persecutory, jealous or grandiose;

(iv) abnormal perceptions associated with delusional misinterpretations of events;

(v) thinking so disordered as to prevent the patient making a reasonable appraisal of his situation or having reasonable communication with others.

In the event, a closed definition was not adopted, for reasons stated in the 1978 Review of the Act:

Review of the 1959 Mental Health Act, **Cmnd 7320, 1978, London: HMSO, para 1.17:**

There have been a few suggestions as to how mental illness might be defined, but comments have underlined the difficulties of producing a definition which would be likely to stand the test of time. Nor has there been much evidence that the present lack of definition of mental illness leads to any particular problems; the Government therefore proposes to leave it undefined.

The objection based on 'standing the test of time' illustrates the curious nature of our concept of mental illness: the notion that it will change with the passage of time. Whilst it is doubtless true that attitudes change (homosexuality was, until 1974, classified by the American Psychiatric Association as a mental disorder (see Kennedy, I, *The Unmasking of Medicine*, 1981, London: Allen & Unwin, Chapter 1)), it is worrying that a less volatile attitude to mental illness cannot be reflected in a workable definition.

There are a number of different ways of attempting to define the essential ingredient(s) of mental illness. Some consider it helpful to use lack of insight into one's own condition, for example, as an essential element of mental illness for the purpose of compulsory detention. It may be thought that this would certainly be in accordance with traditional views that psychoses, which are the most serious psychiatric illnesses, are characterised by lack of insight, but some psychiatrists would argue that many psychotic patients have considerable insight, whilst many suffering from neurotic conditions have little (see, for example, Gelder *et al*, *Oxford Textbook of Psychiatry*, 1996, Oxford: OUP). Some commentators argue that by encouraging patients to have 'insight', psychiatrists are manipulating them into co-operating with treatment regimes, perhaps as voluntary patients. Michael Cavadino has summarised the process by which patients may become manipulated:

Cavadino, M, *Mental Health Law in Context*, 1989, Aldershot: Dartmouth, p 30:

It is usually thought in psychiatry that 'lack of insight' is a bad sign, while the acquisition of insight shows that the patient is on the road to recovery. Its social significance is this: patients with 'insight' conform to sick role etiquette by acknowledging that their present state is undesirable, that they are ill, and that they should try to get well, typically by co-operating with the doctor ...

(This, of course, can put some people who do not believe that they are mentally ill in a classic 'Catch 22' situation: if they deny that they are ill, this may not be seen as a sign of health, but as a sign that they are in a particularly bad way, and particularly in need of drastic, perhaps compulsory intervention.)

Another approach is to define the illness by the presence of suffering. However, as Gelder *et al* say, it cannot be applied to everyone who would usually be regarded as ill, so, for example, 'patients with mania may feel unusually well and not experience suffering, though most people would regard them as mentally ill'. Although some mental illness has an organic origin, this is not often possible to locate, so defining mental illness by reference to the pathological process will not do.

If one looks at the two main psychiatric diagnostic manuals published by the American Psychiatric Association and the World Health Organisation (*Diagnostic and Statistical Manual of Mental Disorders*, 4th edn, 1994, Washington DC: American Psychiatric Press and *The Classification of Mental and Behavioural Disorders*, 1992, Geneva: World Health Organisation, known as DSM IV and ICD-10, respectively), it will be seen that the symptoms of all known psychiatric disorders are described in some detail, but, not surprisingly, 'mental illness' as such is not considered.

It should be noted that the category for admission for assessment is much wider than that for treatment. Under previous legislation (Mental Health Act 1959), this was known as admission for observation, and there was doubt whether it included treating the patient (surprisingly, the Act made no provision for treatment, so it was left to the clinical judgment of the doctors concerned). However, under the 1983 Act it is possible to treat the patient admitted for assessment (s 56(1)). Of particular relevance in this regard is the fact that it has been held that there is power to admit a patient for assessment under s 2, if he appears to be suffering from mental disorder, even though it turns out on assessment that the patient is not: *R v Kirklees Metropolitan Borough Council ex p C* [1993] 2 FLR 187, p 190:

Lloyd LJ: In passing, I should say that I do not, as at present advised, accept Mr Spencer's argument that s 2 is also confined to cases where the patient is in fact suffering from mental disorder. Having regard to the definition of patient in s 145 there is, in my view, power to admit a patient for assessment under s 2, if he appears to be suffering from mental disorder, on the ground that he or she is so suffering, even though it turns out on assessment that she is not.

Any other construction would unnecessarily emasculate the beneficial power under s 2 and confine assessment to choice of treatment.

Given these conclusions, it can be argued that if it is really for assessment, then treatment should not be possible without a patient's genuine consent.

Justifying detention

The Percy Commission, which reported before the Mental Health Act 1959, stated that it was wrong to detain someone compulsorily, before they had committed any criminal offence.

> **Lord Percy of Newcastle, *Report of the Royal Commission on the Law relating to Mental Illness and Mental Deficiency*, Cmd 169, 1954–57, London: HMSO (the Percy Commission), para 348:**
>
> ... Preventive detention under the ordinary criminal law may only be applied to offenders over a certain age who have a definite criminal record of a certain number of convictions for serious offences; and even preventive detention lasts only for a fixed period, after which the prisoner must be released even if it is almost certain that he will then commit further crimes. If one is to apply preventive control to psychopathic patients under wider conditions than these, one is in effect applying to them preventive detention in hospital in circumstances which would not justify preventive detention in prison under the criminal law. Whether or not special forms of control are justified on these grounds depends on how accurate the diagnosis of the patient's condition and the prognosis of his future behaviour is likely to be, and on the extent to which it is fair to assume that the risks to society from persons suffering from these forms of mental abnormality are greater than the risks which society runs from criminals who are not considered to be mentally abnormal.

Apart from having to be suffering from some form of mental disorder, the person compulsorily detained under the Act for assessment 'ought to be so detained in the interests of his own health or safety or with a view to the protection of other persons' (s 2(2)(b)), and in the case of a person compulsorily detained for treatment, it must be *'necessary* for the health or safety of the patient or for the protection of other persons that he should receive such treatment and it cannot be provided unless he is detained under this section' (s 3(2)(c)). It will be seen that, as with the type of mental disorder concerned, the 'protection' condition is wider in the case of admission for assessment, being 'ought to be so detained in the interests of ...' as opposed to 'necessary for ...' and this is hardly surprising. However, it is not clear as to what sort of risks must be involved for patients and/or third parties.

The Code of Practice contains no guidance on the safety of the patient; perhaps it is thought to be self-evident, but the assessment of the risk and the probability of the risk turning into reality must surely be of central importance. There is guidance on health risk which states:

Department of Health and Welsh Office, Mental Health Act 1983, *Code of Practice*, **London: HMSO, para 2.9:**

... those assessing patients must consider any evidence suggesting that the patient's mental health will deteriorate if he does not receive treatment; the reliability of such evidence which may include the known history of the individual's mental disorder; the views of the patient and of any relatives or close friends, especially those living with the patient, about the likely course of his illness and the possibility of its improving; the impact that any future deterioration or lack of improvement would have on relatives or close friends, especially those living with the patient, including an assessment of his ability and willingness to cope; and whether there are other methods of coping with the expected deterioration or lack of improvement.

Is the desire to protect from self-harm paternalistic and unsustainable? It has been argued that there is no interference with the positive freedom of the individual because there is a competing right held by the patient himself. The argument states that a person in ill health has reduced capacities to act and therefore less ability to make effective choices. In other words the patient will be *more free* as a result of the paternalistic intervention. Cavadino gives a good account of the civil libertarian, and other issues raised by the treatment of the mentally ill.

Cavadino, M, *Mental Health Law in Context,* **1989, Aldershot: Dartmouth, pp 138–41:**

... liberal thinkers such as Isaiah Berlin (1969) have usually adopted the 'negative concept of freedom'. Negative freedom is defined as the absence of coercion or constraint imposed on the individual by other people. (I use the word 'liberty' to mean freedom in this negative sense.) In this sense, everyone who is not prevented from doing so by other people is equally free to run a mile in under four minutes or to dine at the Ritz Hotel, although only some people (those fast enough, or rich enough) actually can.

There is, however, a rival concept of freedom which also has its adherents. 'Freedom in the positive sense' may be defined as 'the ability to make effective choices about one's own life'. In this positive sense, I am not free to run a mile in under four minutes, or to dine at the Ritz in my present financial circumstances. For to be 'positively free' is to be actually able to perform the action in question, not simply to be unconstrained by other people or by the law. To be sure, negative freedom (absence of constraint) is necessary in order to have positive freedom; but to be positively free additionally requires, first, the physical and psychological capacities to carry out the action or course of action in question; and second, access to any material resources necessary to perform the action. So I am not free to dine at the Ritz if I cannot physically get there or cannot afford it.

Surely liberal theory of any kind – even those which emphasise the importance of 'negative freedom' – must presuppose that 'positive freedom' is of value. For what else is the point of valuing negative freedom (as liberalism does) if this negative freedom does not actually enable people to make real, effective choices? For all that some liberals vehemently insist on employing the negative definition of freedom, it must be 'positive freedom' which is the intrinsically valuable commodity to human beings, with 'negative freedom' only of instrumental value in so far as it is conducive to real ability to choose. In short, if negative freedom is to be valued, this can only be because positive freedom is of more fundamental value.

If we accept that positive freedom is of value, and necessarily is of value to every human being, then any defensible philosophy of morality must accept as a basic principle that every individual has an equal right to maximum positive freedom. This is the 'positive freedom principle' (PFP). I suggest that this principle provides a much more consistent and coherent approach than liberal theories typically do ...

The presumption in favour of liberty must be a strong one. For as is generally accepted over a wide spectrum of political views, States and other powerful authorities have a distressing tendency to restrict liberty excessively (thereby depriving people of the positive freedom to which they are entitled). Given this, there are good reasons for holding (as liberalism does) that people should not be deprived of substantial liberty without strong justification being adduced. Thus it is indeed right that laws should be framed to protect negative freedom with clear criteria and adequate procedural safeguards.

What should the criteria for deprivation of liberty be? First, it is clear that the protection of others can in principle be a valid justification for deprivation of liberty. The potential victims of violent assault have a right to personal safety which comes into competition with the right to liberty of the potential detainee, since the infliction of injury represents an unjustified diminution of the positive freedom of the victim. The injured person's real abilities to act are diminished by injury and totally extinguished by death, because injury and death reduce or remove a person's physical capacities.

This is not to say, however, that people may be justly deprived of liberty without further ado if there is any evidence or belief, however slight, that they might be dangerous to others. The nature of the risk to others must be assessed together with its likelihood of eventuating. As Dworkin has suggested, we 'should treat a man against his will only when the danger he presents is vivid' [Dworkin, R, *Taking Rights Seriously*, 1978, London: Duckworth, p 11]. It also follows from the strength of the presumption in favour of liberty that cogent evidence of the patient's dangerousness should normally be adduced under conditions of due process before detention can be justified. (And incidentally, as we saw in Chapter 8, a psychiatrist's assessment that a patient is dangerous is by no means always 'cogent evidence'; due process requires that such evidence should be carefully scrutinised to assess its validity.)

What about parentalism [paternalism]? Here again a case can be made for interfering with the individual's (negative) liberty on the ground that there is a more important competing right to be protected. In this case, however, the competing right is not one owned by some other individual, but by the patient, the same person who has the right to liberty. If the intervention results in the preservation or promotion of the health of the patient, this could result overall in the maximisation of the patient's positive freedom. For a person in ill health has reduced capacities to act, and consequently less ability to make effective choices ...

(Note that this argument is not a utilitarian one. It does not rest on the contention that the patient will be happier or will suffer less if the intervention occurs. It argues that the patient will be more free overall if parentalism is allowed.)

This is a persuasive justification, but it depends upon much sharper definitions of self-harm, and the possibility of accurate diagnoses which at present we do not have.

As to the protection of others, it may be accepted even on strong libertarian grounds that detention of someone who, for example violently assaults others, is consistent with the concept of the freedom of the individual as the patient will be seriously interfering with their liberty. However, there are grave difficulties in the concept of 'dangerousness'.

Price, DPT, 'Civil commitment of the mentally ill: compelling arguments for reform' (1994) 2 Med L Rev 321:

It would certainly be unfair to suppose that mentally disordered persons could be involuntarily admitted to hospital because they as a class are more likely to be dangerous to others than non-mentally disordered persons, as there is no convincing evidence to support this assumption ...

If dangerousness is to be a criteria [sic] justifying commitment, some individual assessment of dangerous is required in each case.

In the Act itself (see above, p 473), the requirement regarding harm to others is weak: there is no suggestion that the severity of the harm, and likelihood of the risk are relevant.

The Code of Practice deals with the protection of others, and it is clear from this that, whilst it includes the protection of others from psychological as well as physical harm, risk to property is not enough.

Department of Health and Welsh Office Mental Health Act 1983, *Code of Practice*, London: HMSO, para 2.8:

In considering 'the protection of other persons' (see ss 2(2)(b) and 3(2)(c)) it is essential to assess both the nature and likelihood of risk and the level of risk others are entitled to be protected from taking into account:

- reliable evidence of risk to others;
- any relevant details of the patient's medical history and past behaviour;
- the degree of risk and its nature. Too high a risk of physical harm, or serious persistent psychological harm to others, are indicators of the need for compulsory admission;
- the willingness and ability to cope with the risk, by those with whom the patient lives;
- the possibility of misunderstandings resulting from assumptions based on a person's sex, social and cultural background or ethnic origin and from other medical/health conditions including deafness.

Referring to the sort of individual assessment envisaged by the Code, Price goes on to say:

Price, DPT, 'Civil commitment of the mentally ill: compelling arguments for reform' (1994) 2 Med L Rev 321:

However, even allowing for this, the difficulties are just beginning. Dangerousness is a social construct, it is not a psychiatric phenomenon and thus not peculiarly within the competence of psychiatrists to assess in individual cases. In any event, the problems in predicting dangerousness are immense. Almost all studies of predictive accuracy show that there are likely to be more false positives than true positives in any defined population. This is hardly surprising in view of the (relative) rarity of violent conduct and the fact that violent or dangerous conduct is at least partly a product of a person's environment (in other words it is situation specific). Some studies have shown very substantial overpredictions of dangerousness by psychiatrists, which is partially due to the understandable tendency to err on what can be considered from on perspective as 'the safe side'. The potential for erosion of civil liberties through the unwarranted removal of liberty is then clear.

Statutory control

History

Brenda Hoggett sets out the development of the law relating to the control of mentally disordered people. After describing the provisions of the Lunacy Act 1890 and the Mental Treatment Act 1930, she goes on:

Hoggett, B, *Mental Health Law*, 4th edn, 1996, London: Sweet & Maxwell, pp 6–7:

Until the 1959 Act, then, there were three different types of patient in mental illness hospitals – voluntary and temporary patients under the 1930 Act and patients certified under the various procedures in the 1890 Act. For mental 'defectives' there was a totally different, if rather less complex, set of procedures under the Mental Deficiency Acts of 1913 and 1927. These did not include a voluntary status, but the institutions were not expressly prohibited from taking patients without formality. After 1952, this was officially encouraged for short stays, and the Percy Commission recommended that it could be extended to long stay patients without waiting for legislation. In the Commission's report, and in the 1959 Act which implemented it, a determined effort was made to break down the rigid legal boundaries and integrate the separate legal systems relating to 'lunacy' and 'mental deficiency'.

Two developments lay behind much of the Percy Commission's thinking. First was the introduction of the National Health Service in 1948. This had led to most hospitals of any type being vested in the then Ministry of Health, and to some rearrangement of the functions of the Board of Control, but nothing had been done to remove the rigid and antiquated categorisation of mental hospitals. The Commission believed that there was no longer any need for strict legal control over public hospitals. Further, as improvements depend upon the availability of resources, full responsibility should rest with the government department which controlled the allocation of resources within the health service as a whole. The Board of Control could safely be abolished, and with it the legal segregation of mental hospitals from the main stream of hospital development.

Second was the great optimism about the advances in medical treatment for the major mental illnesses, through psycho-surgery, electro-convulsive therapy and above all the new breed of psychotropic drugs, the major tranquillisers. These made it possible for increasing numbers of seriously disordered patients to be discharged into the community or treated on clinical wards in ordinary hospital conditions. It no longer seemed necessary for the law to assume that these patients were inevitably different from the physically sick or injured. For the most part, they could be admitted to hospital in just the same way. Compulsory procedures could be kept only for those for whom they were absolutely necessary. Once in hospital, their treatment and care could be left in the hands of the medical profession. As many as possible would be discharged back into the community just like other patients.

Hence, removing the legal controls over mental patients was inextricably linked with removing the legal controls over their doctors. The 1983 Act was mainly concerned to reimpose some of the latter.

It is interesting that there has been a steady decline in the number of compulsorily detained patients.

Hoggett, B, *Mental Health Law*, 4th edn, 1996, London: Sweet & Maxwell, p 8:

More significant still was the decline in the proportion of patients in hospital at any one time who were liable to be detained. In 1955, 7% of those in mental illness hospitals were certified, because most voluntary patients stayed for only a short time and compulsion was still used for the long stay chronically ill; and virtually all mentally handicapped patients were detained. By 1986, fewer than 5% of all resident patients in NHS mental illness or mental handicap hospitals were detained. Figures for resident patients are no longer published, perhaps because the aim is to phase out the use of hospital as a place of permanent residence, and so the turnover is such that it would be misleading to give a snapshot on one particular day. The total number of detained residents is now thought to be around 11,500.

Although, as Hoggett points out, the apparent reduction in the number of compulsorily detained patients, is largely because before the 1983 Act there was no statutory 'voluntary' status, but it can also be argued that during an admission for assessment, the patient can be 'stabilised' in such a way as they will remain as a voluntary patient, rather than be detained further for treatment. This raises the concerns expressed above in relation to the potential for manipulation of patients.

Current scheme under the Mental Health Act 1983

The current legislation is the Mental Health Act 1983 (the Act). This will be examined in some detail later in this chapter, but it may be helpful to summarise the main provisions here, as these will be referred to when considering some of the fundamental issues raised by the care and control of the mentally disordered.

Although some of the most contentious aspects of the Act have been considered above, the formal requirements for detention should also be noted. For a detailed and exhaustive examination of the statutory provisions, readers are advised to consult Richard Jones's excellent guide to the Act (*Mental Health Act Manual*, 5th edn, 1996, London: Sweet & Maxwell).

Detention

Admission for assessment is dealt with in s 2 of the Act, and provides for compulsory admission for a period of up to 28 days. The patient can be treated during this time.

Under s 3 of the Act, patients can be admitted for longer periods. Admission under this section is for six months and renewable. The requirements that must be satisfied are somewhat more stringent than under s 2.

Under both ss 2 and 3, two doctors must make the appropriate recommendations for admission; if, however, it is a case of urgent necessity, one doctor's recommendation will suffice to justify admission for up to 72 hours (s 4). Section 136 also empowers police officers to remove someone who appears to be suffering from a mental disorder to a place of safety for up to 72 hours. Compulsory detention of patients who entered hospital on a voluntary basis is dealt with in s 5 of the Act.

The Act also provides for patients to be received into the guardianship of the local social services authority or of a person approved by the authority (s 7). The guardian is empowered to impose residence and treatment requirements.

Treatment

Under s 63 of the Act, the consent of a compulsorily detained patient is not required for treatment for the mental disorder from which he is suffering. As we shall see below, this has given rise to conceptual and ethical difficulties. However, certain types of treatment, such as psychosurgery, have more stringent requirements attached to their administration, and ss 57 and 58 impose additional conditions upon such treatments being given.

Safeguards for the patient

Patients compulsorily admitted have a right to appeal to a Mental Health Review Tribunal, in addition to a number of common law rights.

DETENTION

Mental disorder

Brief and somewhat unhelpful definitions of mental disorder and the other conditions referred to in the Act are contained within s 1:

1   Application of Act: 'mental disorder'

(1) The provisions of this Act shall have effect with respect to the reception, care and treatment of mentally disordered patients, the management of their property and other related matters ...

(2) In this Act–

'mental disorder' means mental illness, arrested or incomplete development of mind, psychopathic disorder and any other disorder or disability of mind and 'mentally disordered' shall be construed accordingly ...

Under s 1(3) of the Act, definitions exclude promiscuity, immoral conduct, sexual deviancy, alcohol or drug dependency without more. The *Review of the Mental Health Act 1959*, carried out by the Department of Health and Social Security (Cmnd 7320, 1978, London: HMSO) concluded that it was inappropriate to regard such problems as mental disorders.

The issue of sexual deviancy was considered in *R v Mental Health Act Commission ex p W* (1988) *The Times*, 27 May. The case concerned the administration of a drug known as Goserelin, a synthesis of hormones designed to reduce the male sex drive, and was primarily concerned with whether there was a need for the patient's consent to treatment (see below, p 503), but the court also had to consider whether the treatment was for mental disorder at all, because of the provisions of s 1(3).

Stuart Smith LJ: Where the mental disorder was quite distinct from the sexual deviancy referred to in s 1(3) of the Act, and the proposed treatment was solely for the purpose of dealing with the sexual deviancy condition, it was difficult to see how that could be treatment for mental disorder, although in practice it seemed likely that the sexual problem would, as here, be inextricably linked with the mental disorder and the treatment for one would be the treatment for the other.

Mental impairment

1   ...

(2) ... 'Mental impairment' means a state of arrested or incomplete development of mind (not amounting to severe mental impairment) which includes significant impairment of intelligence and social functioning and is associated with abnormally aggressive or seriously irresponsible conduct on the part of the person concerned ...

Note that the arrested or incomplete development must be accompanied by the defined conduct. 'Severe mental impairment' is defined in the same way with the additional requirement that the intelligence and social functioning must be severely impaired. The mentally impaired are, therefore, those who would at one time have been described as mentally handicapped or mentally retarded, and who, in more politically correct parlance, are now often referred to as having learning difficulties. However, it must be noted that, in order to be compulsorily detained under the Act for anything longer than 28 days for assessment, the impairment must be associated with antisocial behaviour of an 'abnormal' nature.

Psychopathic disorder

1 ...

(2) ... 'psychopathic disorder' means a persistent disorder or disability of mind (whether or not including significant impairment of intelligence) which results in abnormally aggressive or seriously irresponsible conduct on the part of the person concerned ...

This is a difficult concept, and has caused a great deal of agonising by those who have considered mental health law reform. It causes difficulty for two main reasons. First, the expression 'psychopathic' has no place in the psychiatric diagnostic manuals. Secondly, it is defined in the Act by reference to behaviour only: 'a persistent disorder or disability of mind ... which results in abnormally aggressive or seriously irresponsible conduct ...' Clearly, this implies that there has to be a disorder or disability in the first place, otherwise all criminal offenders would fall into this category, but how, in practice, is the disorder distinguished from its behavioural manifestations?

The Butler Committee which reported on mentally abnormal offenders (Cmnd 6244, 1975, London: HMSO) considered replacing the term 'psychopathic disorder' with 'personality disorder', as the term 'psychopathic' stigmatised those concerned.

Personality disorders are dealt with in the diagnostic manuals. DSM IV, 301.7 and ICD-10, F60.2 deal with the types of personality disorder related to, for example, reckless disregard for safety of self or others, consistent irresponsibility, lack of remorse and so on. The diagnostic criteria in DSM IV are summarised as follows:

DSM IV

Diagnostic criteria for 301.7 – antisocial personality disorder

A   There is a pervasive pattern of disregard for and violation of the rights of others occurring since age 15 years, as indicated by three (or more) of the following:

(1) failure to conform to social norms with respect to lawful behaviours as indicated by repeatedly performing acts that are grounds for arrest;

(2) deceitfulness, as indicated by repeated use of aliases, or conning others for personal profit or pleasure;

(3) impulsivity, or failure to plan ahead;

(4) irritability and aggressiveness, as indicated by repeated physical fights or assaults;

(5) reckless disregard for safety of self or others;

(6) consistent irresponsibility, as indicated by repeated failure to sustain consistent work behaviour or honour financial obligations;

(7) lack of remorse, as indicated by being indifferent to or rationalising having hurt, mistreated or stolen from another ...

The difficulty, of course, is that whilst it is accepted that personality disorders have long been recognised by the medical profession, there is an uncomfortable blurring of distinction between those diagnosed as suffering from a psychopathic disorder and those persistent offenders who have not been so diagnosed.

The Butler Committee (*Report of the Committee on Mentally Abnormal Offenders*, Cmnd 6244, 1975, London: HMSO), whilst dissatisfied about the use of the term 'psychopathic', expressed some reservations about replacing this with 'personality disorder', because of its potentially wide interpretation (para 5.25).

Treatability

This is an interesting concept: in order to be admitted for treatment under s 3, if the patient is suffering from either non-severe mental impairment or a psychopathic disorder, then the treatability condition must also be satisfied, ie, such treatment is likely to alleviate or prevent a deterioration of his condition. What is the purpose behind the treatability test? The *Report of the Royal Commission on the Law relating to Mental Illness and Mental Deficiency* (Cmd 169, 1954–57, London: HMSO) chaired by Lord Percy (the Percy Commission), suggested that 'treatability' be applied to all categories of mental disorder, apart from cases where protection of other people required detention of the patient.

However, the treatability requirement has been restricted to those suffering from non-severe mental impairment and psychopathy. Given the definitions of these conditions, which both contain the requirement that the patient be unable to avoid abnormally aggressive or seriously irresponsible behaviour, it is not surprising that, if there is no treatment for the conditions, hospitals would prefer not to have them as patients. The concern of the Percy Commission, however, was that the potential for abuse of civil liberties should be avoided, ie, we are here considering *civil* detention, and it is undesirable that people with antisocial tendencies should be detained *before* committing any offence. As far as psychopathic disorder is concerned, it is generally thought not to be treatable, and detention of the psychopath under s 3 will not often be possible.

Gunn, J and Taylor, P, *Forensic Psychiatry: Clinical, Legal and Ethical Issues*, 1993, Oxford: Butterworth Heinemann, p 397:

Treatability is in England a crucial issue as far as the personality disordered patient is concerned. The MHA 1983 says that compulsory treatment can only be given to the psychopathically disordered if 'such treatment is likely to alleviate or prevent a deterioration of his condition'. At first sight a not unreasonable criterion, but then it will be noticed that such a barrier is not placed in the way of the 'mentally ill' or those suffering from severe mental impairment. Such blatant legal discrimination between categories of patients is unusual, but it is heuristic. It illustrates what the stigmatised patient is up against and, in practice, very few such patients get into hospital under compulsory arrangements unless they are sent there by courts or unless they are temporarily redesignated as 'ill', for example, after a suicide attempt.

A recent 23 year follow-up of mentally disordered offenders (Robertson, 1987) has shown that for the group as a whole, they have a very high risk of 'unnatural death', ie, death from accidents, suicide, or homicide. At the age of 40 years, when violent death accounts for about 12% of deaths in the general population, it accounts for 50% of deaths among the mentally disordered; suicide, for example, is five times more common than in the general population for the third decade of life. The point of considerable interest here is that these trends occur across all diagnostic groups, the personality disordered were just as vulnerable to premature death as those with schizophrenia, affective disorder, and mental handicap. This information is unlikely to impress those who wish to define and reject the personality disordered patient as 'not ill' or not suffering from 'formal mental illness' ... but it should impress the thoughtful psychiatrist.

How then should we deal with the treatability criterion? Quite simply on clinical grounds after as thorough an assessment as possible. Treatability is not synonymous with curability. If a patient has renal failure, the only effective treatment available may be renal dialysis – this has to be done frequently and will not cure him. Such treatment keeps the patient alive and ameliorates his distress. For the personality disordered patient, his lifeline may be weekly support, a group, or even in-patient care. The fact that he may relapse when the treatment is stopped is not a reason for not providing it. For a patient to be deemed 'untreatable', he would need to be so resistant to treatment as to be unaffected by nursing, or support, or counselling, so unaffected as to make these techniques completely irrelevant to his management; a rare case ...

The Butler Committee saw prison as the proper place for the psychopath (after all, the definition of psychopathic disorder is little more than the description of criminal, or potentially criminal, behaviour), but that would be after the commission of a non-trivial offence.

The issue of treatability had to be considered recently by the Court of Appeal in connection with the discharge of a s 3 patient. In *R v Canons Park Mental Health Review Tribunal ex p A*, the patient had been diagnosed as suffering from a psychopathic disorder, the treatment for which was, in her case, group therapy. The Mental Health Review Tribunal which considered her case found that as she was refusing to co-operate with the therapy, she was untreatable, but should nevertheless be detained in the interests of her own health and safety and for the protection of others. The patient applied for judicial review of the decision on the basis that she had an absolute right to be discharged.

R v Canons Park Mental Health Review Tribunal ex p A [1994] 2 All ER 659

Roch LJ, pp 678–80:

Scope of the treatability test

The final matter is the question of the scope of the treatability rest. This court heard submissions on that issue. Mr Gordon on behalf of the applicant pointed out that arguments on the scope and meaning of the treatability test had not been deployed by counsel for the Tribunal before the Divisional Court. Mr Gordon went on to submit that this was not a live issue in this case because both Dr James and Dr Frank agreed that the only form of treatment for the applicant which was likely to alleviate or prevent a deterioration of her psychopathic disorder was that of group therapy, and that treatment to be effective required the willing co-operation of the patient. Mr Gordon accepted that medical treatment was, by reason of the terms of s 145 of the 1983 Act, wider than drugs, therapies or other treatment prescribed by doctors. He said:

> I accept that nursing care could be a step in the treatment of a mental disorder. But that was not the Tribunal's finding in this case.

The Tribunal's finding had been that group therapy was the only form of treatment likely to alleviate or prevent deterioration of the applicant's condition; that it required the applicant's willing co-operation in order to be likely to alleviate or prevent deterioration of her condition and that the applicant was unwilling to co-operate. Mr Gordon pointed out that the applicant would have co-operated with one to one therapy, but that the doctors were agreed that such therapy would have lead to a worsening of the applicant's condition and made her more dangerous.

Mr Richards' submissions were that the treatability test is concerned with the likely effect of treatment if such treatment were given, and is not concerned with the likelihood of the patient refusing such treatment. In this case there was a known treatment which was likely to alleviate or prevent deterioration of the applicant's condition, namely group therapy. Parliament could not have intended that a patient should be deemed untreatable simply because the patient withheld co-operation. That would place the key to the patient's being detained in hospital in the patient's own hands, and this would apply to cases where the patient was in hospital pursuant to an order of the Crown Court as well as to cases where the patient had been admitted under s 3 of the 1983 Act; s 37 of the Act also containing the treatability test. Further, such an interpretation would place a hitherto unnoticed constraint on the Secretary of State's discretion to make a transfer direction in respect of a prisoner under s 47 of that Act. Mr Richards' further submission was that the Divisional Court's conclusion on the meaning of treatability was not in accordance with medical experience of the treatment of those with psychopathic disorders. Here Mr Richards, in addition to passages in the reports and evidence of Dr James, relied on para 4 of Dr Raymond's affidavit. In such cases there may be an initial deterioration in the patient's condition, but detention in a secure environment with nursing care and medical supervision (medical treatment within the 1983 Act) can lead to the patient gaining an insight into his condition and the overcoming of the patient's initial refusal to co-operate. One of the skills of nurses and doctors in hospitals for the mentally disordered is to persuade their patients to accept treatment. A period of detention with nursing care and medical supervision is frequently a necessary prelude to treatment by way of therapy. If during such a period the patient is likely to gain an insight into his problem or is likely to change to being co-operative then that in itself is an alleviation of the patient's condition.

The Divisional Court, in my judgment, no doubt for the reason it did not have the advantage of the submissions addressed to this court on this aspect of the case, took too narrow a view of what could constitute medical treatment in hospital likely to alleviate or prevent a deterioration of the applicant's condition. I would suggest the following principles. First, if a Tribunal were to be satisfied that the patient's detention in hospital was simply an attempt to coerce the patient into participating in group therapy, then the Tribunal would be under a duty to direct discharge. Second, treatment in hospital will satisfy the treatability test although it is unlikely to alleviate the patient's condition, provided that it is likely to prevent a deterioration. Third, treatment in hospital will satisfy the treatability test although it will not immediately alleviate or prevent deterioration in the patient's condition provided that alleviation or stabilisation is likely in due course. Fourth, the treatability test can still be met although initially there may be some deterioration in the patient's condition, due, for example, to the patient's initial anger at being detained. Fifth, it must be remembered that medical treatment in hospital covers nursing and also includes care, habilitation and rehabilitation under medical supervision. Sixth, the treatability test is satisfied if nursing care, etc, are likely to lead to an alleviation of the patient's condition in that the patient is likely to gain an insight into his problem or cease to be unco-operative in his attitude towards treatment which would potentially have a lasting benefit.

If the treatability test is given the wider scope which in my judgment it should be given, then it becomes clear that the Tribunal was deciding that their duty to direct the discharge of the applicant did not arise because they were not satisfied that medical treatment in hospital was likely to alleviate or prevent a deterioration of the applicant's condition. Such a finding is not surprising when it is appreciated that the applicant's detention in the secure unit for medical treatment had eliminated the symptoms in the diagnosis of her condition on her first admission to St Luke's Hospital of deliberate self-harm and alcohol abuse and reduced those of reactive depression and suicidal ideation.

The Court of Appeal finding that medical treatment should not be narrowly construed in this context, and that she was not to be considered untreatable because of her refusal to co-operate is fraught with difficulties. Whilst this might be reasonable in relation to, say, drug treatment, there is something ironic about holding that a disorder is still treatable when the treatment consists of participation in group therapy (an essential element of which must be co-operation), and the patient refuses to co-operate. It is hard not to conclude that this is an example of judicial sleight of hand: the clinicians wanted to detain the patient, and therefore the 'treatability' condition had to be satisfied one way or the other.

Key parties involved

The Act refers to a number of key personnel who are empowered to take action in respect of patients liable to be detained. Under s 11 of the Act, applications for compulsory admission may be made either by an approved social worker, or by the patient's nearest relative.

Approved social worker

Under s 114 of the Act, the local authority must appoint a 'sufficient number of approved social workers for the purpose of discharging the functions conferred upon them'. Under the 1959 Act the same functions were carried out by mental welfare officers. It will be seen from the following (s 13) that the approved social worker's duty is described as being personal to them and not as a functionary of the local authority which has appointed them:

13 Duties of approved social workers to make applications for admission or guardianship

(1) It shall be the duty of an approved social worker to make an application for admission to hospital or a guardianship application in respect of a patient within the area of the local social services authority by which that officer is appointed in any case where he is satisfied that such an application ought to be made and is of the opinion having regard to any wishes expressed by relatives of the patient or any other relevant circumstances, that it is necessary or proper for the application to be made by him.

(2) Before making an application for the admission of a patient to hospital an approved social worker shall interview the patient in a suitable manner and satisfy himself that detention in a hospital is in all the circumstances of the case the most appropriate way of providing the care and medical treatment of which the patient stands in need.

(3) An application under this section by an approved social worker may be made outside the area of the local social services authority by which he is appointed.

(4) It shall be the duty of a local social services authority, if so required by the nearest relative of a patient residing in their area, to direct an

approved social worker as soon as practicable to take the patient's case into consideration under sub-s (1) above with a view to making an application for his admission to hospital; and if in any such case that approved social worker decides not to make an application he shall inform the nearest relative of his reasons in writing.

Cavadino comments on the role of the approved social worker as follows:

Cavadino, M, *Mental Health Law in Context,* 1989, Aldershot: Dartmouth, pp 111–13:

Applications: social workers and relatives

The Percy Commission, whose recommendations were embodied in the Mental Health Act 1959, envisaged that the application for compulsory admission should 'ideally' be made by the patient's nearest relative, with a Mental Welfare Officer of the local authority on hand to explain the procedure, arrange the patient's transport to hospital, and so on. If the MWO did make the application, this would be a second-best procedure, for use in situations when the relative was not available, unreasonably refused to make the application, or preferred the MWO to do the 'dirty work' (Percy, 1957, para 403). Thus the MWO's role was basically to act as the relative's agent, or else as a surrogate for an absent or inadequate relative. Certainly, the MWO was not expected to assume a judicial role corresponding to the magistrate under the Lunacy Act.

In practice the vast majority of applications for compulsory admission to hospital under the 1959 and 1983 Acts have always been made by social workers (MWOs under the 1959 Act and Approved Social Workers since 1983). This was certainly true of admissions to Fardale: out of 50 compulsory admissions in surveys A and B, relatives made the application in only three cases (6%). Even in the three cases where the relative did make the application, a social worker (approved as an MWO) was involved in the admission.

There was one case in which the social worker had taken the highly dubious course of asking the nearest relative (the patient's daughter) to make the application 'as a safeguard for myself' because the social worker 'wasn't 100% happy about doing a section on her'. Probably more typical, however, was the following case. The social worker explained the meaning of compulsory admission to the patient's wife, who agreed that it was necessary. The social worker considered asking the wife to make the application, but decided it would not be fair on her, and so made the application himself. Many social workers believe that it could damage the relationship between relatives if one relative signs the application to 'put away' the other. (In cases of compulsory admission there can be a strong sense of betrayal and of collusion between relatives and professionals even if this does not happen.) They also feel that relatives are not appropriate people to make applications because they are not in a position to take a detached view on whether the admission is justified, and may indeed have self-interested reasons for wanting to have the patient detained. And doubtless there is also a less lofty motivation here; professionals do tend to try to aggregate power to themselves and resist sharing it with lay people. In any event it is the usual policy of social workers that they and not the patients' relatives should make any application for admission, and it seems to be rare even to inform relatives of their power to apply. This policy is not forbidden or discouraged by the Mental Health Act, but it is quite the opposite of that envisaged by the Percy Commission.

(The reference here to 'Fardale' is reference to a study carried out by Cavadino between 1976 and 1978 at an NHS psychiatric hospital, to which he gave the fictional name of 'Fardale'.)

Nearest relative

The nearest relative is defined by s 26 of the Act:

26 Definition of 'relative' and 'nearest relatives'

(1) In this Part of this Act 'relative' means any of the following persons–

(a) husband or wife;

(b) son or daughter;

(c) father or mother;

(d) brother or sister;

(e) grandparent;

(f) grandchild;

(g) uncle or aunt;

(h) nephew or niece.

(2) In deducing relationships for the purposes of this section, any relationship of the half-blood shall be treated as a relationship of the whole blood, and an illegitimate person shall be treated as the legitimate child of his mother ...

(3) In this Part of this Act, subject to the provisions of this section and to the following provisions of this Part of this Act, the 'nearest relative' means the person first described in sub-s (1) above who is for the time being surviving, relatives of the whole blood being preferred to relatives of the same description of the half-blood and the elder or eldest of two or more relatives described in any paragraph of that sub-section being preferred to the other or others of those relatives, regardless of sex.

(4) Subject to the provisions of this section and to the following provisions of this Part of this Act, where the patient ordinarily resides with or is cared for by one or more of his relatives (or, if he is for the time being an in-patient in a hospital, he last ordinarily resided with or was cared for by one or more of his relatives) his nearest relative shall be determined–

(a) by giving preference to that relative or those relatives over the other or others; and

(b) as between two or more such relatives, in accordance with sub-s (3) above.

The definition does not include spouses who are separated and provision is also made for cohabitees and other persons with whom the patient has been residing to be treated as relatives (sub-ss (5)–(7)). It is possible for persons who do not come within the ambit of s 26 nevertheless still to act in the capacity of a nearest relative. The nearest relative may forfeit status, and can authorise another person to act under reg 14 of the Mental Health (Hospital, Guardianship and Consent to Treatment) Regulations 1983, or that person can be appointed by the county court to be the patient's nearest relative, under s 29:

> **29** ...
>
> (2) An order under this section may be made on the application of–
>
>   (a) any relative of the patient;
>
>   (b) any other person with whom the patient is residing (or, if the patient is then an in-patient in a hospital, was last residing before he was admitted); or
>
>   (c) an approved social worker;
>
>   but in relation to an application made by such a social worker, sub-s (1) above shall have effect as if for the words 'the applicant' there were substituted the words 'the local social services authority'.
>
> (3) An application for an order under this section may be made upon any of the following grounds, that is to say–
>
>   (a) that the patient has no nearest relative within the meaning of this Act, or that it is not reasonably practicable to ascertain whether he has such a relative, or who that relative is;
>
>   (b) that the nearest relative of the patient is incapable of acting as such by reason of mental disorder or other illness;
>
>   (c) that the nearest relative of the patient unreasonably objects to the making of an application for admission for treatment or a guardianship application in respect of the patient; or
>
>   (d) that the nearest relative of the patient has exercised without due regard to the welfare of the patient or the interests of the public his power to discharge the patient from hospital or guardianship under this Part of this Act, or is likely to do so.

In *W v L* [1974] QB 711, the Court of Appeal had to consider the meaning of s 29(3)(c), ie, when does a nearest relative *unreasonably* object?

> **Lord Denning MR**, p 717: This brings me to the final question: is the wife unreasonable in objecting to the making of an application for the husband's detention? This is a difficult question. One can see that she is pulled both ways: on the one hand, she is devoted to her husband and wants him to be with her, on the other hand, she is devoted to her baby and wants the baby to be with her too. No doubt she feels that she can cope. She says she knows her husband better than anyone else does; she will see that he takes his tablets; she is quite satisfied that neither she nor the baby will be in danger. So if you look at it from her own point of view, she may not be unreasonable. But I do not

think it correct to look at it from her own point of view. The proper test is to ask what a reasonable woman in her place would do in all the circumstances of the case. It is similar to the test in adoption cases in which the House of Lords have approved this statement:

> ... in considering whether she is reasonable or unreasonable we must take into account the welfare of the child. A reasonable mother surely gives great weight to what is better for the child. Her anguish of mind is quite understandable; but still it may be unreasonable for her to withhold consent. (*In re W (An Infant)* [1971] AC 682, p 698.)

So we come to this: looking at it objectively, what would a reasonable woman in her place do when faced with this wife's problem? It seems to me that a reasonable woman would say: my husband ought to go in for treatment and he ought to be detained until he is cured. It is too great a risk to have him home whilst the baby is so small. Her objection is therefore unreasonable. I think that the county court judge was quite right in so holding.

This view is confirmed by what has happened since. It appears that the wife has made statements which have caused much concern to those in the case. So much so that a medical report says:

> ... it is becoming even clearer that the liability to compulsory detention is an essential factor in keeping any control over this harrowing situation.

The right course is therefore for the mental welfare officer to make an application for the detention of the husband on the ground that the wife unreasonably objects to doing so. I would dismiss the appeal accordingly.

Under s 14, in the case of admission by a nearest relative, the hospital managers may request a report on the patient from the local social services authority.

Doctors

Applications must, of course, be supported by medical recommendations. An application under s 2 (admission for assessment), s 3 (admission for treatment) and s 7 (reception into guardianship) require two medical recommendations. An application under s 4 (emergency) needs only one recommendation. When two are required, one of them must be an approved doctor under s 12(2) of the Act. Each Regional Health Authority must approve, on behalf of the Secretary of State, a number of medical practitioners 'having special experience in the diagnosis or treatment of mental disorder'. Some might argue that both doctors should be so approved, and some commentators have questioned the fact that, even within the requirement that only one doctor need be approved under s 12(2), not all those doctors are psychiatrists (see Hoggett, B, *Mental Health Law*, 4th edn, 1996, London: Sweet & Maxwell, p 67).

The doctors must each have personally examined the patient, and, if the examination is not joint, no more than five days must have elapsed between the two examinations.

The literature often makes reference to 'RMOs'. The RMO is the responsible medical officer, and is defined by s 34(1) as the doctor in charge of the patient's treatment.

The categories of admission

Admission for assessment – s 2

Section 2 of the Mental Health Act states as follows:

2   Admission for assessment

(2)   An application for admission for assessment may be made in respect of a patient on the grounds that–

(a)   he is suffering from mental disorder of a nature or degree which warrants the detention of the patient in a hospital for assessment (or for assessment followed by medical treatment) for at least a limited period; and

(b)   he ought to be so detained in the interests of his own health or safety or with a view to the protection of other persons.

...

(4)   Subject to the provisions of s 29(4) below, a patient admitted to hospital in pursuance of an application for admission for assessment may be detained for a period not exceeding 28 days beginning with the day on which he is admitted, but shall not be detained after the expiration of that period unless before it has expired he has become liable to be detained by virtue of a subsequent application, order or direction under the following provisions of this Act.

It should be noted that, under s 11(3) if the application is made by an approved social worker, he must inform the nearest relative that an application is to be made. There is no requirement in respect of a s 2 admission for the approved social worker to have *consulted* with the relative (see s 11(4)), but under s 13(1), the social worker must have regard to any wishes expressed by the relative when deciding whether to make the application.

It should also be noted that, under s 2 admissions, the definition of the patient's condition is wide. The patient need only be suffering from 'mental disorder', which means mental illness, arrested or incomplete development of mind, psychopathic disorder and *any other disorder or disability of mind*. It will also be recalled that there is no illegality if it subsequently transpires that the patient is not suffering from mental disorder at all (*R v Kirklees Metropolitan Borough Council ex p C* [1993] 2 FLR 187).

Admission under s 2 is for 28 days only, and sub-s (4) states that the patient 'shall not be detained after the expiration of that period unless before it has expired he has become liable to be detained by virtue of a subsequent application, order or direction under the following provisions of this Act'. Clearly this means that it is not renewable, and it may be argued that no subsequent s 2 application could be made. However, in *R v South Western Hospital Managers ex p M* [1994] 1 All ER 161, it was held that the discretion of an approved social worker could not be fettered by the earlier decision of a Mental Health Review Tribunal to discharge a s 2 patient, albeit in this case, to pursue a subsequent application under s 3 (admission for treatment). The case is doubtful to the extent that it was stated that an application for habeas corpus was inappropriate (see below, p 513, and the subsequent case of *Re S-C (Mental Patient: Habeas Corpus)* [1996] 1 FLR 548). However, Laws J did say that such decisions by the social workers, doctors and hospital managers would be amenable to applications for judicial review. It seems therefore that a further s 2 application, made immediately after the expiry of an earlier one, would be judicially reviewable, but, on the reasoning employed by Laws J would not be automatically regarded as unlawful on the face of the statute.

Admission for treatment – s 3

Long term admission is sanctioned under s 3 of the Act.

3   Admission for treatment

...

(2)   An application for admission for treatment may be made in respect of a patient on the grounds that–

(a)   he is suffering from mental illness, severe mental impairment, psychopathic disorder or mental impairment and his mental disorder is of a nature or degree which makes it appropriate for him to receive medical treatment in a hospital; and

(b)   in the case of psychopathic disorder or mental impairment, such treatment is likely to alleviate or prevent a deterioration of his condition; and

(c)   it is necessary for the health or safety of the patient or for the protection of other persons that he should receive such treatment and it cannot be provided unless he is detained under this section

...

It can be argued that applications under s 3 are, more often than not, unnecessary. Why should this be the case? Although there is no obligation to do so, an application in respect of a patient who has not been formally sectioned before, will be under s 2 of the Act. As has been acknowledged already, an application under s 2 can be in respect of someone who is suffering from 'mental disorder', a wide category of persons who need not be more specifically diagnosed, and who are not necessarily treatable. However, not only does this make a s 2 admission more attractive, it also means that for up to 28 days a patient can be observed, and, if necessary, treated. After the lapse of this period of time, therefore, the patient may be a lot 'better' than when first admitted, and therefore more amenable to remaining as a voluntary patient, rather than by invoking the provisions of s 3. This 'labelling' process is considered further below. Phil Fennell points out the dangers of sedation of patients:

Fennell, P, *Treatment without Consent*, 1996, London: Routledge, p 218:

In recent years concern has grown about the use of antipsychotic drugs as major tranquillisers for emergency sedation, and for behaviour control where patients have no psychotic symptoms. Some [doctors in a Mental Health Act Commission (MHAC) study] described antipsychotic medication for mentally impaired patients as being for 'behaviour control'. In January 1994 it was alleged that in Ashworth Hospital, patients diagnosed as personality disordered or mentally impaired were being given antipsychotic medication not as a treatment for illness but as a means of controlling behaviour by keeping them sedated. These cases were drawn to the attention of the authorities by a team of MHAC visitors to the hospital. An independent consultant forensic psychiatrist brought in by the hospital recommended reduction in the drug doses. Nursing staff said that the patients' behaviour on high doses of medication had been aggressive and violent. When the medication was reduced, patients suffered severe withdrawal symptoms and became even more aggressive, suggesting that these are drugs of dependence.

The use – or abuse – of the wording of s 3 was considered in the case of *R v Hallstrom and Another ex p W (No 2)* [1986] 2 All ER 306. In that case, an admission under s 3 was made, and almost immediately the patient was discharged under s 17 (a provision of the Act which enables the RMO to grant leave of absence to any patient liable to be detained). The purpose was to allow compulsory treatment within the community. McCullough J said (p 315):

McCullough J: It stretches the concept of 'admission for treatment' too far to say that it covers admission for only so long as it is necessary to enable leave of absence to be granted after which the necessary treatment will begin. 'Admission for treatment' under s 3 is intended for those whose condition is believed to require a period of treatment as an in-patient. It may be that such patients will also be thought to require a period of out-patient treatment thereafter, but the concept of 'admission for treatment' has no applicability to those whom it is intended to admit and detain for a purely nominal period, during which no necessary treatment will be given.

Admission for assessment in emergencies – s 4

Section 4 of the Act states as follows:

4 Admission for assessment in cases of emergency

(1) In any case of urgent necessity, an application for admission for assessment may be made in respect of a patient in accordance with the following provisions of this section, and any application so made is in this Act referred to as 'an emergency application'.

(2) An emergency application may be made either by an approved social worker or by the nearest relative of the patient; and every such application shall include a statement that it is of urgent necessity for the patient to be admitted and detained under s 2 above, and that compliance with the provisions of this Part of this Act relating to applications under that section would involve undesirable delay.

(3) An emergency application shall be sufficient in the first instance if founded on one of the medical recommendations required by s 2 above, given, if practicable, by a practitioner who has previous acquaintance with the patient and otherwise complying with the requirements of s 12 below so far as applicable to a single recommendation, and verifying the statement referred to in sub-s (2) above.

(4) An emergency application shall cease to have effect on the expiration of a period of 72 hours from the time when the patient is admitted to the hospital unless–

(a) the second medical recommendation required by s 2 above is given and received by the managers within that period; and

(b) that recommendation and the recommendation referred to in sub-s (3) above together comply with all the requirements of s 12 below (other than the requirement as to the time of signature of the second recommendation).

Although it may be accepted that there will be cases which are genuine emergencies and where a streamlined admission procedure is necessary, some may find cause for concern if such a procedure is used frequently. Further, it is important to keep in mind the wording of the section: it should not be used where it is simply more convenient to admit in this way, and obtain a second recommendation once the patient is in hospital so that the patient can then be admitted under s 2 or s 3. These concerns were considered in the 1978 *Review of the 1959 Mental Health Act*:

Review of the 1959 Mental Health Act, **Cmnd 7320, 1978, London: HMSO, para 1.17:**

Emergency admission for observation (s 29)

2.3 Section 29 provides, in a case of urgent necessity, for the compulsory admission to hospital of a patient for observation. Twelve thousand people were admitted in this way in 1976. An application can be made by any relative (as defined by the Act) or by a Mental Welfare Officer, on the basis of a recommendation by any doctor. The section authorises detention for up to 72 hours only, unless the second medical recommendation which is required ... is obtained within that period. The intention of the 1959 Act was that ... s 29 should be used only in emergencies when there was not enough time to obtain the second medical recommendation. Section 29 has however been invoked more frequently than originally envisaged, and it has become the most widely used form of compulsory admission. There is also wide regional variation in its use. The Government hopes that the increasing development of the

24 hour crisis intervention services envisaged in the White Paper 'Better Services for the Mentally Ill' will in time reduce the need for such admissions, by enabling some emergencies to be contained without the need for compulsory admission to hospital or alternatively for two medical assessments to be provided. However, given the present constraints on manpower and resources, it is accepted that there is a continuing need for a statutory emergency procedure. While there is a good deal of support in comments on the Consultative Document for developing 24 hour crisis intervention services and for the view that these would reduce the use of s 29, it was also argued that, however fully developed, crisis intervention services could never adequately replace s 29 powers, particularly in rural areas. Comments included the point that s 29 allows for a short assessment or 'cooling off' period which can often lead to discharge within 72 hours or to the person staying in hospital as an informal patient.

2.4 The extent of regional variation in the use of s 29 powers attracted a good deal of comment. Community Health Councils were particularly critical that the powers are sometimes used to suit administrative expediency. Cases were cited where hospitals had made a rule that no informal admission should be accepted after 5 pm with the result that any admission after this time had to be a compulsory admission, usually under s 29. Any such rule still in being should clearly be discontinued, and hospital managers should ensure that adequate arrangements exist for the emergency admission of both voluntary and compulsory patients.

It should also be noted that treatment cannot be given to a patient admitted under this section under Part IV of the Act (ie, without his consent) so the patient is in the same position as a voluntary patient.

Guardianship – s 7

The requirements of s 7 are such that a patient over the age of 16 can be made the subject of a guardianship order if he is suffering from mental illness, psychopathic disorder, severe mental impairment or mental impairment, of a nature or degree which warrants his reception into guardianship. There is no treatability requirement. It must also be necessary in the interests of the welfare of the patient, or for the protection of others, although, as Hoggett points out, the latter is unlikely to arise very often, as the guardian's powers are unlikely to be effective in this respect. The powers of the guardian are to require specified residence; to require attendance for medical treatment, education and training, and to require access to the patient.

Guardianship is used infrequently (see the House of Commons Health Committee, *Report on Community Supervision Orders*, 1992–93, London: HMSO), and, given that substantial resources would be necessary to 'police' the system successfully, there must be doubts as to its usefulness. Mike Fisher, referring to the Social Services Research Group Study, carried out 1985–86, notes that during that 12 month period, the 63 incidents of guardianship constituted less than 1% of all detentions under the Act. He goes on to comment as follows:

Fisher, M, 'Guardianship under the mental health legislation: a review' [1988] J Soc Wel L 316:

The study shows that guardianship was rarely used as an alternative to compulsory admission. Guardianship was used only twice in response to a request to use a compulsory admission under ss 2, 3 or 4, and just once in response to requests for informal admission. The most extensive diversion of people from compulsory admission took the form of persuasion to enter hospital voluntarily: some 13% of those referred for compulsory admission under ss 2, 3 or 4 were informally admitted. It is clear from this data that guardianship is not currently being considered as a primary means of diverting people from being admitted compulsorily to hospital.

The SSRG study also provides information on the socio-demographic characteristics of people referred for guardianship ... principal target group for guardianship is seen as people over the age of 65. While only 20% of all people referred were aged 65 or more, 47% of those referred for guardianship were in this age group. In 65% of the requests to use s 7 in this age group, the outcome was that the person was made subject to guardianship.

The implication that guardianship is seen as relevant to elderly people suffering senile dementia is confirmed by an examination of diagnosis. While senile dementia was mentioned in 6% of all requests, this diagnosis was found in 32% of requests for guardianship. This table also shows, however, that senile dementia is not the only diagnosis linked with guardianship: a diagnosis of mental handicap also is likely to be associated with guardianship, echoing the dominant tendency under the 1959 Act.

Thus the SSRG study confirms that guardianship is selectively applied to certain categories of mentally disordered people, rather than used as a power of wide relevance in the prevention of unnecessary compulsory admission.

A person received into guardianship is not a person who is 'liable to be detained' for the purposes of s 56, and therefore the Part IV provisions as to treatment do not apply, ie, the patient cannot be treated for the mental disorder against his will (see below, p 499).

Whilst it is outside the scope of this book, it should be mentioned that the provisions of the National Health Service and Community Care Act 1990 were implemented, following the Griffiths Report of 1988, to ensure the identification of individual community care needs, the construction of community care packages and the co-ordination of these services.

The detention of in-patients – s 5

5   **Application in respect of patient already in hospital**

(1) An application for the admission of a patient to a hospital may be made under this Part of this Act notwithstanding that the patient is already an in-patient in that hospital or, in the case of an application

for admission for treatment that the patient is for the time being liable to be detained in the hospital in pursuance of an application for admission for assessment; and where an application is so made the patient shall be treated for the purposes of this Part of this Act as if he had been admitted to the hospital at the time when that application was received by the managers.

(2) If, in the case of a patient who is an in-patient in a hospital, it appears to the registered medical practitioner in charge of the treatment of the patient that an application ought to be made under this Part of this Act for the admission of the patient to hospital, he may furnish to the managers a report in writing to that effect; and in any such case the patient may be detained in the hospital for a period of 72 hours from the time when the report is so furnished.

...

The purpose of s 5 is to enable a hospital to detain a voluntary patient who decides that he is going to leave the hospital. Hoggett summarises the provisions and concerns thus:

Hoggett, B, *Mental Health Law*, 4th edn, 1996, London: Sweet & Maxwell, p 10:

Section 5(1) makes it clear that an application for compulsory 'admission' may be made in respect of a patient who has already been informally admitted to hospital. Indeed, a substantial proportion of applications relate to patients in hospital, most of them informal (Barnes, Bowl and Fisher, 1990; Department of Health, 1995). An application cannot be made in respect of a patient already detained under an application, except that an application for long term admission for treatment may be made while a patient is detained short term for assessment (s 5(1) and (6)). But if the authorities are not immediately able to complete an application, perhaps because a relative or social worker is not available, s 5 provides two procedures for keeping an informal patient in the hospital for a short time. Neither can be used to prolong the detention of a patient whose 'section' is about to expire (s 5(6)), and neither gives any statutory power to impose treatment without consent (s 56(1)(b)).

Both powers apply only to someone who is already an 'in-patient,' a term which is not defined. In ordinary language, it is usual to distinguish between an out-patient, who attends for an appointment with a specialist or for emergency treatment in casualty, and an in-patient, who has been allocated a bed in a ward. The Code of Practice (Department of Health and Welsh Office, 1993) defines an informal in-patient as someone 'who has understood and accepted the offer of a bed, who has freely appeared on the ward and who has co-operated in the admission procedure' (para 8.4). Thus, these powers should not be used as a way of preventing a would-be suicide from leaving casualty when he comes round after having been 'washed out', or to convert a day patient into an in-patient.

Where the provisions of s 5(2) and 5(4) are used, the patient cannot be treated without consent, ie, the patient is specifically excluded from the provisions of Part IV by s 56 of the Act.

Informal admission – s 131

Patients can be informally admitted under the Act, ie, they are voluntary patients, and, as such are free to leave at any time. Informal admission fell to be considered by the House of Lords in the case of *R v Bournewood Community and Mental Health NHS Trust ex p L* [1998] 3 All ER 289. An autistic patient had been 'informally' admitted to a mental health unit. The psychiatrist felt that formal detention was unnecessary unless the patient resisted treatment. The Trust argued that he was an informal patient under s 131 because he had chosen not to leave the hospital. The House of Lords held that it had clearly been intended that patients lacking the capacity to consent could be admitted under s 131. Their Lordships relied heavily on the findings of the Percy Commission, which reported prior to the 1959 Mental Health Act and which had envisaged such admissions as avoiding the stigmatisation of such patients with the label of having been 'sectioned'. Such patients would be admitted for treatment 'in their own best interests' (see generally, above, Chapter 4). The House of Lords was therefore sugggesting that the doctrine of necessity would apply. This is a worrying decision, because of the important civil liberty issues it raises, and because, it is submitted, on its facts, this case involved an inappropriate use of s 131. Furthermore, as the judgment of Lord Steyn acknowledged, the effect of the decision is to leave the 'compliant' incapacitated patient (ie, the patient who does not vociferously complain) without the safeguards of the 1983 Act.

Miscellaneous powers

Finally it must be noted that there are a number of powers under the Act conferred upon the police and social workers. Under s 115, an approved social worker may enter and inspect any premises if he has reasonable cause to believe that a mentally disordered person living there is not under proper care. Under s 136, a police officer may remove a person to a place of safety if he finds, in a public place, a person who appears to be suffering from mental disorder and to be in immediate need of care or control. Such a person can be detained to a maximum period of 72 hours to enable him to be examined by a doctor and interviewed by an approved social worker. Section 135 provides for the issue of warrants to search for and remove patients to a place of safety, so that persons believed to be suffering from mental disorder can be removed from private premises too. The power given to approved social workers under s 115 does not enable them to force entry, and in such circumstances it would be necessary to obtain a warrant under s 135.

The criminally insane

A detailed examination of this area would involve consideration of criminological matters and penal policy which are outside the scope of this book. However, it is important to remember that many patients compulsorily detained have arrived in that state via criminal sentences. A good, brief summary of the provisions which govern them, can be found in Hoggett, B, *Mental Health Law*, 4th edn, 1996, London: Sweet & Maxwell, pp 14–16, which also contains a more detailed analysis.

TREATMENT

Consent to treatment

As we saw in Chapter 3, adult patients in possession of the necessary decision making capacity have the right to refuse even life-saving medical treatment for any physical condition from which they may be suffering. However, in the case of patients detained under the Act, treatment for the mental disorder itself requires neither their express nor their implied consent (s 63). This is subject to exceptions contained within ss 57 and 58, for certain types of treatment, and subject to s 62 which deals with urgent treatment. Consent, however, is required of voluntary patients (ss 56(1) and 56(2)). These exceptions are examined in detail below, p 503, but first, the nature of treatment for mental disorder must be considered.

Treatment not needing the patient's consent

63 Treatment not requiring consent

The consent of a patient shall not be required for any medical treatment given to him for the mental disorder from which he is suffering, not being treatment falling within ss 57 and 58 above, if the treatment is given by or under the direction of the responsible medical officer.

The implication is that treatment for other purposes, ie, the patient's physical disorders, remains governed by the common law. The interpretation of what constitutes the medical treatment for the mental disorder from which the patient is suffering has recently been given a very wide interpretation by the courts. The Act defines medical treatment as including 'nursing, and also includes care, habilitation and rehabilitation under medical supervision' (s 145(1)), but there is no guidance as to how this should relate to the mental disorder from which the patient is suffering, and in the case of *B v Croydon HA* [1994] 2 WLR 294, the Court of Appeal interpreted this so as to permit a wide range of acts ancillary to the core treatment. The case concerned a s 3 patient, suffering from a psychopathic disorder, which, it was found, was treatable only by psychoanalytical psychotherapy. The patient made various attempts to harm herself, and when these were discovered and prevented, she decided that she would refuse to eat. The health authority decided to force feed her without her consent, and she applied to the court for an injunction to restrain them. At first instance the court refused this on the basis that it was treatment for the mental disorder and therefore, by reason of s 63, did not require her consent. The Court of Appeal upheld this.

It was accepted that, because of the 'treatability' requirement in s 3 (see above, p 482), it would not have been lawful to detain her unless her condition was treatable. However, it was held that it did not follow that every act which formed part of treatment as defined by s 145(1) must, *in itself*, be likely to alleviate or prevent a deterioration of the disorder. The naso-gastric feeding would be a form of concurrent care. Hoffmann LJ said, p 297:

> **Hoffmann LJ**: Mr Gordon says that food is a medicine. He draws our attention to the fact that some special foods (for example, gluten-free rice cookies for coeliacs) may be obtained on prescription. In my view, however, this is not relevant to whether food is a medicine within the meaning of s 58. The section is concerned with medicines administered as treatment for mental disorder. The words 'by any means' in the opening phrase show that one identifies a medicine by its chemical composition and not by whether it is administered to the patient through a tube down his throat or by being put before him on a plate. Even gluten-free rice cookies are not administered for mental disorder and in my judgment ordinary food in liquid form, such as would be used in tube feeding, is not a medicine within the meaning of s 58.
>
> That brings one back to the question of whether tube feeding would have been treatment for the mental disorder from which Ms B was suffering. My initial reaction was that it could not be. Ms B suffers from a psychopathic disorder which, according to the evidence, is incapable of treatment except by psychoanalytical psychotherapy. How can giving her food be treatment for that disorder? Mr Gordon says that it cannot. It may be a prerequisite to a treatment for mental disorder or it may be treatment for a consequence of the mental disorder, but it is not treatment of the disorder itself. He draws attention to s 3 of the Act, which specifies the grounds upon which a person suffering from a psychopathic disorder may be detained. It is not enough that the disorder must be 'of a nature or degree which makes it appropriate for him to receive medical treatment in a hospital' (sub-s (2)(a)). The proposed treatment must be 'likely to alleviate or prevent a deterioration of his condition' (sub-s (2)(b)) and it must be 'necessary for the health or safety of the patient or for the protection of other persons that he should receive such treatment' (sub-s (2)(c)). So Mr Gordon says that the patient cannot lawfully be detained unless the proposed treatment will alleviate or prevent a deterioration of his condition. No less should be required of the treatment which can be given without his consent under s 63.
>
> This is a powerful submission. But I have come to the conclusion that it is too atomistic. It requires every individual element of the treatment being given to the patient to be directed to his mental condition. But in my view this test applies only to the treatment as a whole. Section 145(1) gives a wide definition to the term 'medical treatment'. It includes 'nursing, and also includes care, habilitation and rehabilitation under medical supervision'. So a range of acts ancillary to the core treatment fall within the definition. I accept that by virtue of s 3(2)(b) a patient with a psychopathic disorder cannot be detained unless

the proposed treatment, taken as a whole, is 'likely to alleviate or prevent a deterioration of his condition'. In my view, contrary to the submission of Mr Francis, 'condition' in this paragraph means the mental disorder on grounds of which the application for his admission and detention has been made. It follows that if there was no proposed treatment for Ms B's psychopathic disorder, s 63 could not have been invoked to justify feeding her by naso-gastric tube. Indeed, it would not be lawful to detain her at all.

It does not however follow that every act which forms part of that treatment within the wide definition in s 145(1) must in itself be likely to alleviate or prevent a deterioration of that disorder. Nursing and care concurrent with the core treatment or as a necessary prerequisite to such treatment or to prevent the patient from causing harm to himself or to alleviate the consequences of the disorder are in my view all capable of being ancillary to a treatment calculated to alleviate or prevent a deterioration of the psychopathic disorder. It would seem to me strange if a hospital could, without the patient's consent, give him treatment directed to alleviating a psychopathic disorder showing itself in suicidal tendencies, but not without such consent be able to treat the consequences of a suicide attempt. In my judgment the term 'medical treatment ... for the mental disorder' in s 63 includes such ancillary acts.

Mr Francis was, I think, right to draw our attention to s 62 as throwing some light upon the question. Sections 57 and 58 place special restrictions upon the use of particular 'forms of medical treatment for mental disorder', surgical operations for destroying brain tissue or implanting hormones (s 57), electro-convulsive therapy and drugs (s 58). There are special procedures which must be followed before these treatments can be given. But s 62(1) says that in certain specified cases of emergency, these special rules need not be complied with. They include:

> ... any treatment–
>
> (a) which is immediately necessary to save the patient's life; or
>
> (b) ...
>
> (c) which (not being irreversible or hazardous) is immediately necessary to alleviate serious suffering by the patient; or
>
> (d) which (not being irreversible or hazardous) is immediately necessary and represents the minimum interference necessary to prevent the patient from behaving violently or being a danger to himself or to others.

Mr Francis says, in my view rightly, that these emergency cases are not primarily concerned with a direct alleviation or the prevention of a deterioration of the mental disorder. The danger to the patient's life or the likelihood of serious suffering or the patient being a danger to himself or others are more likely to be the results of symptoms of the disorder. Nevertheless, the treatment of such symptoms is assumed by s 62 to be a 'form of medical treatment for mental disorder', since otherwise it would not have come within ss 57 or 58 in the first place.

I therefore agree with Ewbank J in *In re KB (Adult) (Mental Patient: Medical Treatment)* (1994) 19 BMLR 144, p 146 when he said of the tube feeding of an anorexic: '... relieving symptoms is just as much a part of treatment as relieving the underlying cause.' To similar effect is the judgment of Stuart-White J, quoted by Sir Stephen Brown P in *Riverside Mental Health NHS Trust v Fox* [1994] 1 FLR 614, p 619. The decision in *In re C (Adult: Refusal of Treatment)* [1994] 1 WLR 290, in which a schizophrenic was held entitled to refuse treatment for gangrene, is distinguishable. The gangrene was entirely unconnected with the mental disorder.

Mr Gordon said that if the meaning of 'medical treatment for mental disorder' was wide enough to include ancillary forms of treatment, s 63 would involve a breach of the Convention for the Protection of Human Rights and Fundamental Freedoms, Cmnd 8969, 1953. He referred us to *Herczegfalvy v Austria* (1992) 15 EHRR 437 in which the court said, p 485, that a measure constituting an interference with private life and therefore *prima facie* contrary to Art 8(1) (like involuntary tube feeding) can only be justified under Art 8(2) if, among the other requirements of that article, its terms are sufficiently precise to enable the individual 'to foresee its consequences for him'. This requirement is necessary to prevent such measures from being a source of arbitrary official power, contrary to the rule of law. In my judgment s 63 amply satisfies this test. There is no conceptual vagueness about the notion of treating the symptoms or consequences of a mental disorder, although naturally there will be borderline cases. But there is no question of an exercise of arbitrary power.

This is arguably a disturbing decision, widening as it does the ambit of non-consensual treatment. Note also that this case has been followed in *Re VS (Adult: Mental Disorder)* [1995] 3 Med LR 292, and, even more controversially, in the case of *Tameside and Glossop Acute Services Trust v CH* [1996] 1 FLR 762, where it was held that the performance of a Caesarean section was treatment for mental disorder under s 63 (p 773):

Wall J: Is the question of inducing the defendant's labour and/or causing her to be delivered of her child by Caesarean section 'entirely unconnected' with her mental disorder? At first blush, it might appear difficult to say that performance of a Caesarean section is medical treatment for the defendant's mental disorder: I am, however, satisfied that on the facts of this case so to hold would be 'too atomistic a view', to use Hoffmann LJ's phrase in the passage from *B v Croydon HA* which I have cited and the reasoning of which I respectfully adopt.

There are several strands in the evidence which, in my judgment, bring the proposed treatment within s 63 of the Act. First, there is the proposition that an ancillary reason for the induction and, if necessary, the birth by Caesarean section is to prevent a deterioration in the defendant's mental state. Secondly, there is the clear evidence of Dr M that in order for the treatment of her schizophrenia to be effective, it is necessary for her to give birth to a live baby. Thirdly, the overall structure of her treatment requires her to receive strong antipsychotic medication. The administration of that treatment has been necessarily interrupted by her pregnancy and cannot be resumed until her child is born. It is not, therefore, I think, stretching language unduly to say that achievement of a successful outcome of her pregnancy is a necessary part of the overall treatment of her mental disorder. Treatment of C's gangrene was not likely to affect his mental condition: the manner in which the delivery of the defendant's child is treated is likely to have a direct effect on her mental state.

Exceptional treatment not covered by s 63

Section 57 – consent and a second opinion

This section covers the most drastic forms of treatment for mental disorder. It covers psychosurgery and any other form of treatment specified by the Secretary of State. At present, the only other form is surgical implantation of hormones for the purposes of reducing the male sex drive (pursuant to reg 16 of the Mental Health (Hospital, Guardianship and Consent to Treatment) Regulations 1983).

The question of surgical implantation to reduce the male sex drive was considered in *R v Mental Health Act Commission ex p W* (1988) 9 BMLR 77:

> **Stuart-Smith LJ**: Mr Fitzgerald initially argued that the treatment in question was not 'treatment for mental disorder' within the opening words of s 57, but was treatment for sexual deviancy, which is expressly excluded by s 1(3) of the Act from the definition of mental disorder. But it became clear in the course of the hearing that Dr Silverman did consider that the treatment was for the applicant's mental disorder as well as for his sexual deviancy, and this point was therefore not pursued. It is not therefore necessary to decide the question of construction whether, as Mr Fitzgerald submits, in order to found their jurisdiction in a case involving reg 16 the commissioners have to be satisfied that the treatment is for the mental disorder and not merely excessive or deviant male drive. The alternative argument is that reg 16 has to be read into s 57(1) and that once a person is a mental patient and the treatment proposed is the surgical implantation of the hormones for the purpose of reducing male sexual drive, Parliament has in effect decreed the treatment to be for mental disorder. While I see the attraction of this argument, since Parliament no doubt intended to protect mental patients who may not be able to consent, where the mental disorder is quite distinct from the sexual deviancy or other matter referred to in s 1(3) of the Act, and the proposed treatment is solely for the purpose of dealing with the sexual deviancy or other s 1(3) condition, it is difficult to see how this can be treatment for mental disorder. In practice, however, it seems likely that the sexual problem will be inextricably linked with the mental disorder, so that the treatment for the one is treatment for the other, as in this case.

The Code of Practice's guidance on s 57 treatment states:

> **Treatments requiring consent and a second opinion (s 57)**
>
> 16.6 Section 57 reflects public and professional concern about particular forms of treatment; such treatments need to be considered very carefully in view of the possible long term effects and the ethical issues that arise.

Procedures for implementing this section must be agreed between the Mental Health Act Commission and the hospitals concerned.

16.7 Before the RMO or doctor in charge of treatment refers the case to the Mental Health Act Commission:

(a) the referring doctor should personally satisfy himself that the patient is capable of giving valid consent and has consented;

(b) the patient and (if the patient agrees) his family and others close to him should be told that the patient's willingness to undergo treatment does not necessarily mean that the decision to proceed has yet been taken. The patient should be made fully aware of the provisions of s 57;

(c) for psychosurgery, the consultant considering the patient's case should have fully assessed the patient as suitable for psychosurgery;

(d) for psychosurgery, the patient's case should be referred to the Commission prior to his transfer to the neuro-surgical centre for the operation. The Commission organises the attendance of two appointed persons and a doctor. The appointed persons and the doctor will usually visit and interview the patient at the referring hospital at an early stage in the procedure;

(e) for surgical implantation of hormones for the purpose of reducing male sexual drive, the relationship of the sexual disorder to mental disorder, the nature of treatment, the likely effects and benefits of treatment and knowledge about possible long term effects require considerable care and caution should be taken.

16.8 It should be remembered that s 57 only refers to the surgical implantation of hormones for the reduction of male sexual drive where it is administered as a medical treatment for mental disorder; and that, if there is any doubt as to whether it is a mental disorder which is being treated, independent legal and medical advice must be sought. The advice of the Mental Health Act Commission should also be obtained about arrangements for implementing s 57 where necessary.

Section 58 – consent or a second opinion

Section 58 specifies treatment which requires consent or a second opinion. The treatment covered by s 58 is the controversial electro-convulsive therapy (ECT), and medicines administered over a period of three months or more.

It must be noted that this section does little to protect the patient's right to refuse treatment; it merely adds a safeguard by requiring that, in so far as the patient refuses, two doctors must recommend a course of treatment rather than one. Phil Fennell reports the results of a survey of second opinions carried out in 1992 (note that SOAD means Second Opinion Appointed Doctor):

Fennell, P, *Treatment without Consent,* **1996, London: Routledge, pp 282–83:**

Concerns of the 1970s and early 1980s led to the introduction of express legal provision for treatment without consent, which had previously been so much taken for granted as part of clinical authority that mentioning it did not even occur to legislators. By the 1980s it was necessary to spell it out. Part IV upheld the position of the RMO as in charge of a detained patient's treatment, and defined powers to treat without consent, subject to a second opinion procedure. If the personnel with power to decide whether or not to treat without consent had changed, did Part IV result in a change in the substance of these decisions? One clear incursion on clinical authority was that psychosurgery would no longer be allowed without valid consent. Another was that the decision of the SOAD to refuse permission was binding on the RMO and there was no appeal to the MHAC. Set against this is the fact that the second opinion is medical. Although there is a duty on the SOAD to consult other professionals, on occasion these are staff in occupations with little to do with patient care, and often nurses and others were brought in to 'get to know' the patient before being consulted. The test for giving the treatment, likelihood of benefit or prevention of deterioration, used in combination with the *Bolam* test, creates a presumption in favour of the RMO's judgment. Not surprisingly, the concordance rate for s 58 opinions is high. The 1992 survey showed that the main cases where authority was withheld for clinical reasons involved ECT or the 'new' antipsychotic Clozaril, because it was felt that other less drastic treatments should be given time to work. There was even one case, the Pimozide case, where the second opinion may have been a life saver. The survey also shows the extent of psychiatry's continued reliance on ECT, and in particular the strikingly high numbers of middle aged and elderly women who have the treatment. In this the pattern of the past is being followed, for women have traditionally been in the majority of those receiving radical treatment, whether it be clitoridectomy, ovariotomy, lobotomy, chemical shock, comas or ECT.

Perhaps the most important indicator of the effect on the substance of clinical decisions, and of the resilience of the experimental spirit, is the extent to which SOADs authorised high dose medication. The BNF recommended dose levels, used loosely as a yardstick in the second opinion process, are viewed by some psychiatrists as too low, and resistance to central prescription remains strong. The fact that 12% of medicine second opinions involved doses above [British National Formulary – BNF] limits does not suggest a significant interference with clinical authority. A poignant reminder of psychiatry's limitations were the numbers of patients in the MHAC 1 survey who had been on high doses of medication for years and who showed no improvement, remaining totally inaccessible (61 out of 232). Could it be that their medication contributed to their poor mental state?

Since s 58 offers no real protection to the patient, no real purpose of this provision is discernible.

The Law Commission (*Mental Incapacity*, Report No 231, 1995) recommended that the treatments under s 58(1) should require a certificate from an independent medical practitioner, rather than requiring that the patient be formally detained under the Mental Health Act (informal patients are already protected from the provisions of s 57 (s 56(2)).

The Code of Practice states:

Treatments requiring consent or a second opinion (s 58)

...

16.10 Whenever practicable, staff should give a patient treated by ECT a leaflet which helps him to understand and remember, both during and after the course of ECT, the advice given about its nature, purpose and likely effects. This may help ensure that a valid consent is in force.

Medication before three months

16.11 This period starts on the occasion when medication for mental disorder was first administered by any means during any period of continuing detention (see para 16.13 below). The medication does not necessarily have to be administered continuously throughout the three month period. The patient's RMO must ensure that the patient's valid consent is sought prior to the administration of any medication. If such consent is not forthcoming or is withdrawn during this period, the RMO must consider, if he wishes to proceed in the absence of consent, alternative treatment or give no further treatment.

Medication after three months (s 58)

16.12 At the end of the three month period referred to above the patient's RMO should personally seek the patient's consent to continuing medication, and such consent should be sought for any subsequent administration of medication. If the patient consents the RMO most certify accordingly (Form 38). The RMO should indicate on the certificate the drugs proposed by the classes described in the British National Formulary (BNF), the method of their administration and the dose range (indicating the dosages if they are above BNF advisory maximum limits). If the patient's consent is not forthcoming the RMO must comply with the safeguard requirements of s 58 (although for urgent treatment s 62 may apply).

...

Withdrawal of consent

16.15 A patient subject to the provisions of Part IV of the Act may withdraw consent at any time. Fresh consent or the implementing of s 58 procedures is then required before further treatment can be carried out or reinstated. Where the patient withdraws consent he should receive a clear explanation (recorded in the patient's records) of:

• the likely consequences of not receiving the treatment;

• (where applicable) that a second medical opinion under Part IV of the Act may or will be sought in order to authorise treatment in the continuing absence of the patient's consent;

• (where applicable) the doctor's power to begin or continue treatment under s 62 until a second medical opinion has been obtained.

Urgent treatment under s 62

Under s 62 urgent treatment, normally subject to the additional requirements of ss 57 and 58, may be given without satisfying those conditions, and if it is a form of treatment for which consent was required and that consent is subsequently withdrawn, treatment can continue under these provisions if it is thought that discontinuance of the treatment would cause serious suffering to the patient:

62   Urgent treatment

    (1) Sections 57 and 58 above shall not apply to any treatment–

        (a) which is immediately necessary to save the patient's life; or

        (b) which (not being irreversible) is immediately necessary to prevent a serious deterioration of his condition; or

        (c) which (not being irreversible or hazardous) is immediately necessary to alleviate serious suffering by the patient; or

        (d) which (not being irreversible or hazardous) is immediately necessary and represents the minimum interference necessary to prevent the patient from behaving violently or being a danger to himself or to others.

    (2) Sections 60 and 61(3) above shall not preclude the continuation of any treatment or of treatment under any plan pending compliance with s 57 or 58 above if the responsible medical officer considers that the discontinuance of the treatment or of treatment under the plan would cause serious suffering to the patient.

    (3) For the purposes of this section treatment is irreversible if it has unfavourable irreversible physical or psychological consequences and hazardous if it entails significant physical hazard.

It must be noted that it is only to ss 57 and 58 that s 62 applies. In practice, it will only be treatment under s 58 to which this section will apply, as the nature of s 57 treatments (at present, psychosurgery and surgical implantation of hormones to reduce the male sex drive) are unlikely to comply with sub-s (1)(a)–(d) in terms of hazard and/or irreversibility. The section would therefore be most likely to be used in the administration of medicine under s 58, when the three month period was about to elapse, and a second opinion could not be obtained. These occasions should be rare, genuine emergencies. However, in practice the situation may be very different. Fennell points out (*Treatment without Consent*, 1996, London: Routledge, Chapter 13) that ECT is given under s 62 and 'urgent treatment' is given under the *common law* to, for example, s 4 patients (ie, emergency admissions where one medical opinion only is needed), and to whom s 62 does not apply. We have already seen above, Chapter 4, that the common law will permit treatment to be given without consent to a patient *lacking capacity* when that treatment is in his best interests. The assumption must be, therefore, that when treatment is given to a s 4 patient, lack of capacity is presumed. Fennell says:

Fennell, P, *Treatment without Consent,* **1996, London: Routledge, p 223:**

The limits on hazardous treatments in s 62 do not offer adequate protection for patients for three principal reasons. First, there appears to be a tendency on the part of doctors to see it as permissive rather than restrictive. Second, the section does not apply to patients who are detained under powers authorising detention for 72 hours or less, such as the doctor's holding power or the emergency admission for assessment under s 4. In such cases, the Code of Practice suggests that authority for emergency treatment may be found in common law: on rare occasions involving emergencies where it is not possible immediately to apply the provisions of the ... Act the common law authorises such treatment as represents the minimum necessary to avert behaviour by the patient that is an immediate serious danger to self or to other people. On this view, where patients are treated under common law, the prohibition on hazardous treatments does not appear to apply. The third weakness of s 62 in medicine cases is that, where patients are detained under longer term powers, medicines may be given without consent during the three month stabilising period at the direction of the RMO, and without the need for a second opinion. Only four of the 116 uses of s 62 in the MHAC 2 sample were for medicines; three by men and one by a woman. Two occurred because the three month stabilising period had elapsed and the RMO had not requested a second opinion in time, and in the other two the patients had withdrawn consent. Very often emergency sedation is given in the period immediately following admission. After three months, the MHAC view is that PRN medication for which the patient's consent cannot be anticipated should be included by the SOAD on the Form 39. Since Form 39 certificates are widely drafted to authorise treatment in terms of BNF categories of drug, this is not an effective safeguard. Once there has been a second opinion which includes the PRN medication, s 58 has been complied with and there is no need for recourse to s 62.

Is it right to give any form of treatment without consent?

Psychiatrists, as it has been seen, have very wide powers to treat without consent. The interests of the wider community may be able to justify detention, but can they justify treatment? It is arguable that most treatment will be consented to because after the initial treatment, the patient is compliant and will therefore consent to subsequent treatment. But in the case of a refusal, why should we make treatment compulsory?

Given that a patient can refuse life-sustaining treatment for physical illness if mentally competent, what is the argument for saying that the mentally ill patient cannot refuse treatment of mental illness? The 1959 Mental Health Act did not deal with the issue of consent to treatment, and it was thought that detention was sufficient to suspend the need to obtain a patient's consent.

During the passage of the 1983 Mental Health Act through Parliament, a justification for being able to treat without consent was given by the Minister of Health in the debate on the proposal in parliamentary committee:

Special Standing Committee on the Mental Health (Amendment) Bill (Parliamentary Session 1981–82), 29 June 1982

... those who looked after them (those forcibly detained) would have to gaze on them knowing perfectly well that some treatment could be given to alleviate their suffering and distress and enable them eventually to recover their liberty. Hospitals are places of treatment ...

This reasoning relies upon the fact that, by detaining someone against their will on the ground that they are ill, means that it is in the interests of them regaining their liberty that they receive treatment to enable them to do just this. It has to be admitted that this argument has a certain force. What is clear is that the reason cannot be that, *by definition*, the mental patient is incompetent because of the vagueness of the definition of mental illness, and indeed, case law confirms that a long term mental patient can refuse life-sustaining treatment for a physical condition (see above, Chapter 3, p 117). The question is whether the patient has the capacity to understand the particular form of treatment.

Is competence treated differently when the patient is suffering from a mental disorder?

The case of *Re C (Adult: Refusal of Treatment)* [1994] WLR 290, as was seen in Chapter 3, dealt with capacity to consent to medical treatment, and that case was about a mentally disordered patient. In that enlightened judgment, the patient's mental capacity was considered in an objective and unpatronising manner. Thorpe J said, p 294:

Thorpe J: C himself, throughout the hours that he spent in the proceedings, seemed ordinarily engaged and concerned. His answers to questions seemed measured and generally sensible. He was not always easy to understand and the grandiose delusions were manifest, but there was no sign of inappropriate emotional expression. His rejection of amputation seemed to result from sincerely held conviction. He had a certain dignity of manner that I respect.

We have already seen above from the case of *B v Croydon HA* [1994] 2 WLR 294 that a woman who refused to be fed by naso-gastric tube could not, in law, do so because it was treatment for the mental disorder from which she was suffering and therefore her consent was not necessary. There was a finding at first instance (questioned by the Court of Appeal) that she had the capacity to refuse medical treatment. If the court had decided that she lacked capacity then the case would not have been controversial because a decision to feed her could have been made in her 'best interests' (see above, Chapter 4). The consequence of that decision appears to be that incidental care which is not for the treatment of the disorder *per se* but which is part of the general management of the patient can be given without consent. Of course, in some ways this will, on a pragmatic level, be inevitable, despite civil libertarian objections: a disruptive patient may be subjected to some form of restraint which does nothing to treat his condition but merely to keep him quiet and make life better for other patients. It is perhaps the controversial nature of force feeding that focuses attention here, and gives rise to the question as to the precise nature of 'treatment'. Under the Act it includes nursing, care, habilitation and rehabilitation (s 145(1), and note that 'habilitation' is included for reasons of semantics, ie, a severely disabled child, say, may never have had skills, so cannot be said to be *rehabilitated*), and in the context of treatment for physical illness, treatment has been held to cover counselling and advice (see *Gillick v West Norfolk and Wisbech AHA* [1986] AC 112). The difficulty in the case of patients compulsorily detained under the Act is the fact that their consent is dispensed with, and therefore, this wide definition of 'treatment' means that the patient can be physically managed non-consensually in ways which have no effect whatsoever on their progress towards cure or amelioration of the mental disorder from which they are suffering. The justification for treating such patients without consent clearly does not address this point, nor, it is submitted, can it justify these peripheral forms of treatment.

It is generally acknowledged that, if possible, it is always preferable to obtain the consent of a patient, even if treatment can be given without it. The Code of Practice states (para 16.4):

> Detained status of itself does not imply inability to give consent. For all treatments proposed for a detained patient, and which may be lawfully given under the Act, it is necessary first to seek the patient's agreement and consent.

This clearly envisages that, regardless of the provisions of s 63, initially the consent of the patient to treatment for the mental disorder should be sought.

Options for reform

As we have seen, there is no structure in English law for decisions to be made as to medical treatment by one party on behalf of another. However, there is a mechanism for a mentally disordered person to have his financial affairs managed by another pursuant to Part IV of the Act. The question arises: should statutory procedures be devised for the appointment of proxies to make decisions on behalf of mental patients who are incapable of consenting to treatment? The issue has already been considered above in relation to incompetent patients generally. The special consideration here is whether the statutory licence, given to doctors to treat compulsorily detained patients without consent under s 63, should be abandoned, and whether, in the case of those patients who are incapable of consenting, a similar provision for the management of their medical affairs should be instituted.

The Law Commission's wide-ranging report in respect of mental incapacity (Report No 231, 1995) is disappointing in respect of its consideration of the Mental Health Act. It assumes that treatment would continue to be given without consent under the provisions of the Act if they had been compulsorily detained. However, those patients not compulsorily detained would be subject to the proposed 'incapacity scheme' recommended in that report, which has been considered above, p 184. It may have been thought that the safeguards of ss 57 and 58, plus the Mental Health Review Tribunal appeal system, are enough protection for the formally detained patient. However, given the nature of the decisions in *B v Croydon HA* [1994] 2 WLR 294 and *Tameside and Glossop Acute Services Trust v CH* [1996] 1 FLR 762, treatment not obviously connected with mental disorder can now be given to such a patient without consent, and it is arguable that further protection is necessary.

SAFEGUARDING THE PATIENT

There can be no doubt that the powers of civil detention under the Act have great potential for abuse. The importance of protective procedures, therefore, cannot be overestimated .

The Mental Health Act Commission

Section 120 of the Act deals with the general protection of detained patients:

120 General protection of detained patients

> (1) The Secretary of State shall keep under review the exercise of the powers and the discharge of the duties conferred or imposed by this Act so far as relating to the detention of patients or to patients liable to be detained under this Act and shall make arrangements for persons authorised by him in that behalf–
>
> (a) to visit and interview in private patients detained under this Act in hospitals and mental nursing homes; and
>
> (b) to investigate:
>
> > (i) any complaint made by a person in respect of a matter that occurred while he was detained under this Act in a hospital or mental nursing home and which he considers has not been satisfactorily dealt with by the managers of that hospital or mental nursing home; and
> >
> > (ii) any other complaint as to the exercise of the powers or the discharge of the duties conferred or imposed by this Act in respect of a person who is or has been so detained.

The Commission carries out the functions under s 120(1) and 120(4), together with functions under s 61 of the Act (review of treatment given under s 57(2) and s 58(3)(b)). The Commission was established under s 11 of the National

Health Service Act 1977, and s 121 of the Mental Health Act 1983 provides for its continuance. In addition to the above, the Commission appoints medical practitioners and other persons for the purposes of providing second opinions and verifying consent to treatment under Part IV of the Act and examines reports on that treatment; submits proposals for inclusion in the Code of Practice; submits proposals in relation to s 57 treatments, and produces a biennial report on its activities. There are about 90 Commissioners, made up of doctors, nurses, social workers and lawyers.

It is important to note that the Commission's powers do not extend to voluntary patients, but only to those who are formally detained under the Act. This is regrettable: as we have seen, a large number of in-patients are not formally detained and, in particular, note the decision in *R v Bournewood Community and Mental Health NHS Trust ex p L* [1998] 3 All ER 289.

Challenging detention

The powers of the Commission are not designed to provide a mechanism for challenging the validity of the compulsory admission itself. There are, however, a number of ways in which a compulsorily detained patient may gain his liberty, both under the Act itself, and by the use of the common law.

Discharge of the patient under s 23

Section 23 states:

23 Discharge of patients

...

(2) An order for discharge may be made in respect of a patient–

(a) where the patient is liable to be detained in a hospital in pursuance of an application for admission for assessment or for treatment by the responsible medical officer, by the managers or by the nearest relative of the patient;

(b) where the patient is subject to guardianship, by the responsible medical officer, by the responsible local social services authority or by the nearest relative of the patient.

It should be noted that, under s 23, these are powers, and not duties, and therefore a patient cannot claim that, for example, once he ceased to be a danger to self, or others, he should be discharged under s 23.

Mental Health Review Tribunals

A statutory framework for challenging compulsory admissions was first introduced by the 1959 Act following the recommendations made by the Royal Commission (the Percy Commission, see para 438). Under s 66, patients, including those admitted for assessment, can apply to a Tribunal for a review of their case. The nearest relative also has a right to apply. There is also an automatic review process, under s 68, whereby hospital managers must refer to a Tribunal any patient admitted for treatment who has not exercised his right to apply within the first six months. They must also refer any patient admitted for treatment if his detention is renewed and three years have gone by since the case was last considered by a Tribunal.

Mental Health Review Tribunals consist of at least one 'legal member', one 'medical member' and the third must be neither a legal nor a medical member. Procedures are governed by the Mental Health Review Tribunals Rules. A useful summary of the entitlement to apply to a Tribunal is contained in Gostin, L and Fennell, P, *Mental Health: Tribunal Procedure*, 1992, London: Longman.

Habeas corpus

It may be thought that, since the introduction of the right to apply to a Mental Health Review Tribunal, this ancient remedy would have little application. However, it has continued to be used, and was given approval as, in certain circumstances, *the* only remedy for an unlawfully detained patient (see *Re S-C (Mental Patient: Habeas Corpus)* [1996] 1 FLR 548).

An application is made to the High Court, and in the case of a patient incapable of making the application, it may be done by a relative or friend. The term 'habeas corpus' means that the body must be produced, or justification for detention must be shown. The writ was used with great effect in the pre-1959 Act case of *R v Board of Control and Others ex p Rutty* [1956] 2 QB 109. In that case, the lack of evidence that a patient (described in the case as a 'borderline high grade mental defective') was subject to the provisions of the then legislation (the Mental Deficiency Acts 1913–27) resulted in the grant of an application for habeas corpus. Hoggett (*Mental Health Law*, 4th edn, 1996, London: Sweet & Maxwell, p 175) reports that as a result of that case, over 3,000 other patients in mental deficiency institutions were released.

In *Re S-C (Mental Patient: Habeas Corpus)* [1996] 1 FLR 548, the patient had been admitted and detained under s 3 at a time when the approved social worker knew that the patient's father objected to such an application. On the application form, the social worker had stated that she had consulted with the patient's mother who was, to the best of her knowledge and belief, the nearest relative, and did not object to the application. Sir Thomas Bingham MR said, p 557:

> **Sir Thomas Bingham MR**: ... the present case is one in which, in principle, an application for habeas corpus is appropriate. There is no attempt being made to overturn any administrative decision. The object is simply to show that there was never jurisdiction to detain the appellant in the first place, a fact which on agreed evidence appears to be plainly made out.

The second case to which I should refer is a decision of Laws J, *R v Managers of South Western Hospital ex p M* [1993] QB 683. The facts of that case, so far as relevant to the present appeal, are that an application was made under s 3 of the 1983 Act by an approved social worker. The applicant's mother was interviewed as the nearest relative although, for reasons that need not be elaborated, she was not the applicant's nearest relative but an uncle was. Some contact was made with the uncle but not in the capacity of nearest relative. Neither the mother nor the uncle objected to the s 3 process and the managers of the hospital accepted an application for admission for treatment under s 3 made in a form filled out by the approved social worker. The applicant sought leave to move for judicial review of the decision of the hospital managers to accept her admission under s 3, and that application failed. The applicant then applied for habeas corpus addressed to the hospital managers and another party.

Having outlined the facts so far as the nearest relative and the role of the nearest relative are concerned, Laws J said, p 700A:

> How do these findings bear on the legality of the applicant's detention, given the terms of s 6? Sections 6(1) and (2) confer authority to convey or detain the patient in hospital where the application is 'duly completed in accordance with the provisions of this Part of this Act'. In my judgment that is an objective requirement and means that the application must not only state that the relevant provisions (which include the requirements of s 11(4)) have been fulfilled, but also that it be the case that they have actually been fulfilled. Here they were not: s 11(4) was not complied with. It follows, in my judgment, that the managers were not authorised to detain the applicant unless they were entitled to act upon Miss Stiller's application by virtue of s 6(3). The contrast between s 6(1) and s 6(3) is of course between the words 'duly completed' and 'appears to be duly made'.

In my judgment, where an application on its face sets out all the facts which, if true, constitute compliance with the relevant provisions of Part II of the Act (again, including s 11(4)) it is an application which appears to be 'duly made' within s 6(3). If any of the facts thus stated are not true, then although the application appears to be duly made, it is not duly completed for the purposes of s 6(1) and 6(2). Here, Miss Stiller's application did state all the facts which, if true, constituted compliance with the relevant statutory provisions. Accordingly it was an application which appeared to be duly made. It follows that, although the managers were not authorised to detain the patient by s 6(2) standing alone, they were entitled to act upon the application, and thus to detain the patient, by virtue of s 6(3). Accordingly, the applicant's detention is not unlawful.

Speaking for myself, I would accept almost everything in that passage as correct with the exception of the last sentence. The judge goes straight from a finding that the hospital managers were entitled to act upon an apparently valid application to the conclusion that the applicant's detention was therefore not unlawful. That is, in my judgment, a *non sequitur*. It is perfectly possible that the hospital managers were entitled to act on an apparently valid application, but that the detention was in fact unlawful. If that were not so the implications would, in my judgment, be horrifying. It would mean that an application which appeared to be in order would render the detention of a citizen lawful even though it was shown or admitted that the approved social worker purporting to make the application was not an approved social worker, that the registered medical practitioners whose recommendations founded the application were not registered medical practitioners or had not signed the recommendations, and that the approved social worker had not consulted the patient's nearest relative or had consulted the patient's nearest relative and that relative had objected. In other words, it would mean that the detention was lawful even though every statutory safeguard built into the procedure was shown to have been ignored or violated.

Bearing in mind what is at stake, I find that conclusion wholly unacceptable. I am, for my part, satisfied that on present facts an application for habeas corpus is an appropriate, and possibly even the appropriate, course to pursue.

As indicated in that case, this must now cast doubt on the validity of the refusal of a writ of habeas corpus in the case of *R v South Western Hospital Managers ex p M* [1994] 1 All ER 161.

Judicial review

The above case considered whether the application for habeas corpus was appropriate, as it had been argued that the mechanism of judicial review was preferable. This argument had been rejected on the basis that it did not concern an administrative decision. Judicial review was successfully used in the cases of *R v Hallstrom and Another ex p W*, and *R v Gardner and Another ex p L* [1986] 1 QB 1090, which was considered in the following article:

Gunn, M, 'Judicial review of hospital admissions and treatment in the community under the Mental Health Act 1983' [1986] J Soc Wel L 290:

Miss W

Miss W had been admitted to a hospital for treatment under s 3 of the Mental Health Act 1983 (hereafter, the Act) on the basis of medical recommendations provided by Dr Hallstrom, a consultant psychiatrist with 'special experience in the diagnosis and treatment of mental disorder' (s 12(2)), and Miss W's general practitioner. It would seem that the application was made by the hospital social worker, who was presumably an approved social worker. The day after being admitted to hospital, Miss W was given leave of absence, subject to treatment conditions, under s 17.

She applied to a Mental Health Review Tribunal, which refused to direct her discharge from the effects of s 3. Thereafter, Miss W did not request a case stated by the Tribunal for consideration by the High Court under s 78(8), which would have allowed the court to consider simply the role of the Tribunal. Instead she went to the High Court for leave to apply for judicial review of the admission to hospital, which would allow wider consideration of the relevant issues. She sought an order for certiorari so that the admission would be quashed and regarded as though it had never been, or, in the alternative, a declaration that the admission was unlawful in the sense that the doctors did not have the power to do what they had done: they had acted *ultra vires* ...

There are three heads under which decisions and actions of doctors, approved social workers and nearest relatives are subject to control by judicial review: 'illegality, irrationality and procedural impropriety'. The major concern in the instant cases is with 'illegality'. Before considering it, it is worth noting that the irrationality ground also could be important. For example, if a nearest relative used the power of application for an improper purpose, such as getting the patient out of the house in order to make it easier to obtain control of his/her premises, that application could be quashed by the court. Indeed damages might now have to be paid to the 'patient'. It is unlikely that the principles of procedural impropriety will have much of a role to play because an extensive procedure complying with these principles is clearly laid down in the Act and if it is not fulfilled, the admission is illegal.

The right to apply for judicial review forms, along with an application for a writ of habeas corpus, a vital way in which the patient can complain about the original admission. Indeed, they form the only way, if it is right that a Mental Health Review Tribunal cannot consider the validity of the initial admission to hospital, as one member of the Court of Appeal, Ackner LJ, said in passing. It is important, therefore, to emphasise that a Mental Health Review Tribunal apparently can only decide whether a person should continue to be detained in hospital by considering whether the conditions justifying detention exist at the time the Tribunal sees the patient. Although judicial review and habeas corpus do permit consideration of the original admission decision, neither provide a form of appeal on the merits of the decision: neither can question whether the decision was right or wrong. Instead they concentrate on whether the doctors, social workers and nearest relatives had the legal power to admit the patient; they consider whether the discretion that the professionals have was exercised in a proper manner; for example, did they take all relevant factors into account?

A right to treatment for mental disorder?

Because of the civil liberty issues that it raises, much of the concern surrounding patient rights is to do with the patient's right to liberty unless there are compelling reasons to the contrary. However, it can also be asked whether a mentally ill patient has a right to be treated.

In terms of medical treatment generally, there have been a number of attempts over the years to persuade courts to intervene when limited health care resources within the UK National Health Service have resulted in the denial of treatment to physically ill patients (see Chapter 2 and, for example, the cases of *R v Secretary of State for Social Services ex p Hincks* (1980) 1 BMLR 93; *R v Central Birmingham HA ex p Walker* (1987) 3 BMLR 32; and *R v*

Cambridge HA ex p B [1995] 2 All ER 129). The conclusion to be drawn from these cases is that unless there is irrationality or procedural impropriety, the courts will not intervene. There is, therefore, very limited scope in making a challenge, and none in respect of *clinical* judgment.

However, the element of public protection in mental health law means that treatment for physical illness and treatment for psychiatric illness are not exactly comparable. There have been a number of recent incidents when members of the public have been injured and even killed by ex-psychiatric patients, and there has been something of an outcry that the persons concerned were not receiving treatment, or not receiving in-patient treatment (see, for example, newspaper reports in (1994) *The Independent*, 16 September; and (1995) *The Guardian*, 28 July; and (1997) *The Guardian*, 30 May). However, in this regard, note the case of *Clunis v Camden and Islington HA* [1998] 2 WLR 902, where the Court of Appeal held that there was no liability of a discharging health authority towards a patient who subsequently killed a member of the public (the *Jonathan Zito* case).

A patient is unlikely to request to be compulsorily detained under the Act, but could request to be informally admitted (s 131). For the purposes of this, the patient would have no more rights than a patient who demanded to be admitted to hospital for the treatment of physical illness. The decision would be based upon clinical judgment, and in the absence of judicially reviewable procedural irregularity, the courts would not intervene.

After the discharge of a patient detained under s 3 (or under certain criminal provisions, under ss 37, 47 or 48 of the Act, for detention), there is a duty on both the local health authority and the local social services authority to provide, in co-operation with the relevant voluntary agencies, after-care services until both are satisfied that the patient no longer needs them (s 117):

117 After-care

(1) This section applies to persons who are detained under s 3 above, or admitted to a hospital in pursuance of a hospital order make under s 37 above, or transferred to a hospital in pursuance of a transfer direction made under ss 47 or 48 above, and then cease to be detained and leave hospital.

(2) It shall be the duty of the District Health Authority and of the local social services authority to provide, in co-operation with relevant voluntary agencies, after-care services for any person to whom this sub-section applies until such time as the District Health Authority and the local social services authority are satisfied that the person concerned is no longer in need of such services.

This is a duty in respect of the individual patient rather than to the mentally disordered generally who are owed a similar duty under the National Health Service Act 1977 (Sched 8, para 2(1)).

Given the concern about the discharge of potentially dangerous patients mentioned above, it is interesting to speculate on the nature of this duty and whether it does impose a heavier onus on health care providers in the field of mental health than on their counterparts who are providing treatment for physical illnesses. This was considered in the case of *R v Ealing District HA ex p Fox* [1993] 3 All ER 170, where a health authority refused to provide psychiatric supervision for a patient who had been conditionally discharged by a Mental Health Review Tribunal subject to receiving psychiatric supervision in the community. In this case, the judge held that the health authority had erred in law in not attempting with all reasonable expedition and diligence to make arrangements so as to enable the patient to comply with arrangements *'required by a Mental Health Review Tribunal'* (*per* Otton J) (emphasis added). However, does this mean that if Tribunals are prepared to attach such conditions to discharge orders that they will be enforceable? The answer to this is in the negative. In Fox it was said that there should have been a reference back to the Tribunal, presumably with a view to amendment, and that duties owed to the patient could only be enforced by alleging procedural defectiveness through the mechanism of judicial review, which, as we have seen, are important, but limited in scope.

In other words, as with treatment for physical illness, the courts will defer to clinical judgment and will not compel treatment to be given, as long as the decision to refuse to treat has been taken in a procedurally sound way. In this particular case the authority's consultant psychiatrist was doubtful that supervision in the community would work. However, the judge said that the health authority is bound to continue to seek to provide the necessary treatment, either from its own resources or from elsewhere, and if it cannot do so, then the matter should be referred back to the Mental Health Review Tribunal to reconsider the discharge condition. However, suppose there was not clinical doubt, but simply lack of the appropriate resources to provide the treatment? After all, the reason for the failure to provide medical treatment is more likely to be lack of financial resources than anything else (although in the case of *R v Cambridge HA ex p B* [1995] 2 All ER 129, resources were in issue, but the stress was upon the likelihood of success of the treatment). The question of resources was raised in the case of *R v Hertfordshire CC ex p Three Rivers DC* (1992) 90 LGR 526. This was about the level of provision in the community under the National Health Service and Community Care Act 1990, which imposes a duty upon the local social services authority to assess the needs of, *inter alia*, discharged mental patients. It was held in that case that identifying the level and nature of the service to be provided may be constrained by available resources and that these constraints could properly be taken into account when identifying the appropriate level of service provision.

It should also be noted that s 7 of the Disabled Persons (Services, Consultation and Representation) Act 1986, which would apply to anyone receiving hospital treatment for six months or more for mental disorder, and which would require joint assessment of such a patient by the appropriate health and social services authorities, is not yet in force.

The conclusion is, therefore, that ultimately there is no 'right' to treatment for the psychiatrically ill any more than there is for the physically ill. The only right is to be considered for treatment and given the appropriate clinical assessment.

Liability towards patients

Criminal liability

Although the commission of common law or statutory offences against mental patients is rare, mention should be made of the specific statutory provisions which create criminal liability in respect of health care workers.

First, anomalously, s 128 of the 1959 Act remains in force. This makes it a criminal offence for a man on the staff of a hospital or mental nursing home, to have sexual intercourse with a female mental patient. Interestingly, it makes no reference to female staff having sexual relationships with patients, nor to male staff and male patients engaging in such activities. There is, under s 127 of the 1983 Act, a specific statutory offence of ill-treatment or wilful neglect of a mental patient, and under s 126, the offence of falsification of documents for the purposes of the Act.

Civil liability

False imprisonment

In addition to the remedies discussed above, a patient unlawfully detained may pursue a civil claim for false imprisonment, and, if successful, obtain an award of damages. In the case of *Furber v Kratter* (1988) *The Times*, 21 July, the patient succeeded despite the fact that the original detention was lawful. It was held that the substitution of a harsher regime than at first prescribed could constitute false imprisonment.

Battery and negligence

The same principles of common law negligence apply to the treatment of psychiatric patients. If it can be shown that those treating a potentially suicidal patient failed to supervise and treat in accordance with the appropriate standard of care, then the plaintiff will succeed: see *Selfe v Ilford and District Hospital Management Committee* (1970) 114 SJ 935. *Kirkham v The Chief Constable of the Greater Manchester Police* [1990] 2 QB 283 concerned a successful suicide in police custody. The widow of the person concerned succeeded in her claim. The Court of Appeal rejected the argument that the defence of *volenti* could apply: it was held that, as the person was clinically depressed, his judgment was too impaired in order for this to succeed. The latter point is of some interest: it is accepted that mental disorder itself does not mean that a patient is incompetent as far as medical decision making is concerned. Refusal of life-saving treatment by such a patient, unless it can be shown that the treatment is for the mental disorder *itself* (see the case of *B v Croydon HA*, above, p 499), is acceptable. However, a positive act of suicide in *Kirkham* should have been prevented on the basis of clinical impairment of judgment. Is there an illogicality here, or are we simply back to the distinction between positive acts, and omissions to take certain courses of action?

The liability of doctors and nurses to supervise suicidal patients was considered in the case of *Selfe v Ilford Hospital Management Committee* (1970) 119 SJ 935, where damages were awarded when there was found to be an unacceptable level of supervision. The clinical judgment of a psychiatrist was examined by the Supreme Court of Canada in the case of *Villemure v l'Hopital Notre-Dame et al* [1972] 31 DLR (3d) 454, where a *'Bolam'* argument as to what other doctors would have done was rejected. The majority decision approved the following finding of the trial judge:

Villemure v l'Hopital Notre-Dame et al [1972] 31 DLR (3d) 454:

The court is unable to accept the opinion of Drs Fortin and Saucier. It may be that they would have done exactly what Dr Turcot did. Had they done so, in the opinion of the court they would have been wrong and negligent. It is no answer to say it is impossible absolutely to prevent a person from committing suicide unless he is placed in a straitjacket. This of course is obvious. But it is surely possible to prevent him from committing suicide for 30 hours and until a sufficient investigation has been made into his condition to be able more accurately to diagnose his true situation. The court also rejects Dr Saucier's view that there were many factors which indicated that the patient's condition was not nearly as serious as might at first have been thought. The facts as proven of what happened prior to the entry into the hospital, coupled with the incidents in the hospital, indicate to the court rather a situation which should have made both Dr Turcot and the nurses take particular care of the deceased.

In the context of civil liability, mention must be made of a form of statutory immunity contained within s 139(1) of the Act:

139 (1) No person shall be liable, whether on the ground of want of jurisdiction or on any other ground, to any civil or criminal proceedings to which he would have been liable apart from this section in respect of any act purporting to be done in pursuance of this Act or any regulations or rules made under this Act, or in, or in pursuance of anything done in, the discharge of functions conferred by any other enactment on the authority having jurisdiction under Part VII of this Act, unless the act was done in bad faith or without reasonable care.

It will be seen that the reference to 'without reasonable care' means that this section gives no immunity against an action in negligence. However, under s 139(2), leave of a High Court judge is required to bring an action in the first place. Gunn considered the effect of s 139 on an application for judicial review:

Gunn, M, 'Judicial review of hospital admissions and treatment in the community under the Mental Health Act 1983' [1986] J Soc Wel L 290:

Section 139 of the Mental Health Act 1983

The decision of the Court of Appeal on these preliminary issues is of major importance to people compulsorily admitted to hospital. The court decided that s 139 does not operate as an additional barrier that patients as applicants for judicial review have to overcome beyond the requirements of RSC Ord 53, which apply to applicants for judicial review whatever the circumstances.

As has been stated s 139(2) requires a patient to obtain the leave of the High Court before being able to take civil proceedings. In *Winch v Jones*, the Court of Appeal decided that this leave should be granted when the court decides that 'on the materials available ... the applicant's complaint appears to be such that it deserves the fuller investigation which will be possible if the intended applicant is allowed to proceed'. This is similar to the ground upon which leave will be granted for an application for judicial review. *Hallstrom (No 1)* avoids the unnecessary confusion that would have arisen if leave had been required to be obtained both under s 139 of the Act and RSC Ord 53.

Section 139 and judicial review

Section 139(1) provides care staff with a defence when civil or criminal proceedings are taken against them. The decision of the Court of Appeal also means that this defence does not apply to applications for judicial review. This is a very significant decision because hearing a case on judicial review will allow the High Court to question the legality of many decisions taken in relation to patients in hospital and otherwise affected by the Act. In particular, it permits the High Court to question whether, for example, all the relevant factors were taken into account when the decision to admit the patient to hospital was made.

The decision in *Hallstrom (No 1)* means that the applicant for judicial review does not have to allege either bad faith or lack of reasonable care on the part of the person, for example, a doctor, whose action is being considered. Indeed, no such allegation was made by Miss W. A requirement to establish bad faith or lack of reasonable care would have been a major, often insuperable, obstacle for a patient to overcome.

CHAPTER TEN

MEDICAL RESEARCH

INTRODUCTION

Background

It is self-evident that medical science is not standing still. New therapies are constantly being developed in an ongoing battle against sickness and disease, and advances are not merely desired, but expected by society at large. However, their achievement inevitably involves carrying out previously untried treatment upon human subjects, with attendant uncertainty as to the treatment's capacity to harm rather than benefit the subjects in question.

In this chapter we are concerned with the legal and ethical issues presented by medical research. To this end, we look first at the scientific methodology of research, and examine the key ethical dilemmas raised by such practices. The remaining sections then consider the legal and quasi-legal constraints that operate upon the researcher: the requirement that the subject consent to research; the various voluntary codes which seek to impose further safeguards in this field; and the issue of *ex post facto* compensation for those injured during the course of research.

Defining 'research'

Scientific research may be defined, very broadly, as any systematic inquiry aimed at discovering new facts about the way things in the world around us behave. In the case of medical research, the object of such inquiry is new methods of treatment: what effects do they have upon human subjects?

It is important to emphasise the deliberate and systematic nature of the research enterprise. Otherwise, one might be inclined to regard all medical treatment as constituting 'research', given that our store of knowledge will inevitably increase in the course of providing it. As John Marshall comments:

Marshall, J, 'The case against experimentation', in Dyson, A and Harris, J (eds), *Experiments on Embryos*, 1989, London: Routledge, pp 55–56:

... [In] one sense any medical intervention is research. Giving an aspirin to a patient, though done thousands and thousands of times, may on the thousand-and-oneth [sic] occasion produce some unexpected, unpredictable result because of idiosyncrasies in that patient. Therefore, when people talk on the one hand about certain orthodox procedures which they do without thinking and, on the other hand, about unorthodox procedures, it is clear that there is a difference in degree but never a difference in kind. Anything that is done, any intervention in another person, can have unexpected and unpredictable results. But it is not about that that we are really talking in this context.

The other area which ought to be distinguished is that of improving therapy. Again, people think that there is a certain standard way of doing appendectomies, or coronary bypass procedures, that there is a certain standard way of treating people with respiratory failure. But medicine is always engaged in the business of improving therapy, and improving therapy is often on a research basis. When you try to modify some procedure because you think it might work better in a different way, you are engaged in a form of research, a form of inquiry.

It is generally accepted that, in scientific terms, randomised clinical trials (RCTs) represent the ideal form of medical research. The basic idea is that subjects are randomly divided into different groups. One will be offered the treatment under research, and another (the 'control group') will not. As is evident from the following extract written by Charles Fried in 1974, many therapies that are considered standard today were once the subject of RCTs to establish their efficacy:

Fried, C, *Medical Experimentation – Personal Integrity and Social Policy*, 1974, Amsterdam: North-Holland Publishing, pp 146–47:

Coronary bypass surgery

In recent years techniques have been developed for bypassing regions of serious atherosclerotic blockage in the major coronary arteries, and thus permitting increased blood supply to the heart muscle below these blockages. There have, however, been serious questions raised regarding the efficacy of this technique in certain cases of coronary artery disease, and some responsible persons have questioned whether in certain situations the more traditional 'best' therapies and regimens might not be as good if not better. Moreover, the incidence of surgical mortality itself is far from negligible, and the operation is extremely costly in terms of time, technical resources and blood needed for transfusion. If the claims of the more enthusiastic proponents of this technique were valid there would be many hundreds of thousands of good candidates for this surgery each year at staggering social cost.

In order to evaluate the claims for coronary bypass surgery in various categories of disease, a number of hospitals throughout the country have instituted randomised clinical trials. In one trial, participants are referred by their physician to cardiologists in the participating hospital. The participants are told that a study is being conducted in which they are involved, that they will receive the best available treatment for their case, and that they are free not to join in or stay in the study. Although they know of the alternative therapies, only if they ask are they told that the choice is determined by a randomising scheme.

The scientific utility of RCTs is derived from the elimination, through the randomisation process, of potential bias (either on the part of researcher or research subject) in observing and interpreting the results of the treatment.

However, as Sarah Hewlett notes, from the point of view of participants, a measure of inconvenience, and indeed risk, will be entailed:

Hewlett, S, 'Consent to clinical research – adequately voluntary or substantially influenced?' (1996) 22 JME 232:

Clinical research is necessary to establish the safety and efficacy of a therapy. It may include, for example, the testing of nursing or physiotherapy techniques, as well as the testing of new drugs ...

Clinical testing of a new drug is required by the Medicines Control Agency (MCA) before a product licence for that drug can be given. As the drug is being tested for safety and efficacy, patients taking part will be put at risk of unknown side effects and may also be randomised to receive either the unproven drug or a placebo. When we enter a patient into such a clinical trial we are normally testing a drug appropriate to his or her condition. However, because of randomisation we may not always be selecting a particular drug for a particular patient's needs. If the comparator drug is a placebo then we may not be acting in that patient's best interests. In some cases the patient is being used as a means to an end: establishing the safety and efficacy of a new drug for the benefit of future patients. The justification for this is that the only way to establish the most effective and safe treatments to improve health (desired by most members of society) is by clinical research. By consenting, the patient knowingly agrees to this goal and makes it his own, becoming an active participant in the research so that it cannot then be said that the patient is being used as a means to an end. Clearly the quality of that consent is therefore vital.

What does clinical research mean for the patient?

The scientific gold standard for clinical research is the randomised controlled trial (RCT) which attempts to establish statistically the risk-benefit ratio of the drug by reducing bias and controlling for variables. This it does by controlling the selection of well characterised groups of patients, randomising them into treatment groups, using standardised outcome measurements performed by blinded assessors, and stipulating a population size powerful enough to answer the question being asked. Although not without criticisms the RCT is a credible test of safety and efficacy within the medical world and some would say it would be unethical to introduce a new drug without RCT data.

Patients participating in an RCT will usually need to attend hospital regularly for safety and efficacy assessments – perhaps clinical examination, blood and urine samples, and possibly x-rays. Such visits may take several hours and their frequency varies from every few days to every month, as does the duration of the RCT (from a few days to several years). Neither the safety nor the efficacy of the drug is yet proven and in addition the patient may receive a placebo during the course of the study. When taken together these are not inconsiderable inconveniences for the patient and although hopefully kept to minimum impact, there is sometimes an element of risk.

(The term 'placebo', used here, refers to an inert substance, such as a 'dummy' pill, which is given to a subject so that he is unaware that he is in the control group not receiving the therapy under research.) We shall consider further the particular ethical dilemmas generated by the use of RCTs as a research tool below, p 533.

Therapeutic and non-therapeutic research

The distinction between therapeutic and non-therapeutic research is central to any discussion of the ethical and legal issues surrounding medical research. This does not go to the methodology of the research process (RCTs may equally be used for both), but derives from the two main classes of research subject on whom research may be carried out, and to what end.

Therapeutic

This type of research is defined as that which is carried out on patients with the direct potential for beneficial results in respect of their illness. The researcher (who is in a doctor-patient relationship with the subject) will commonly be attempting to establish whether a new treatment is more effective than existing therapy available for that condition. It is significant here, that the doctor/researcher, has what is termed a 'dual-intention': he desires both the attainment of new knowledge *and* benefits for the individual patient/subject.

Non-therapeutic

In contrast to the therapeutic form, non-therapeutic research denotes that which is carried out on volunteers (either drawn from the public or, perhaps, those hospitalised with unrelated conditions) and offers no hope of benefiting them personally. It often takes place in relation to new drug treatments in order to establish toxicity levels or any side effects. Here, the researcher is in the position of scientist alone: he does not owe duties to the research subject *qua* patient, and intends only the gaining of knowledge.

Although these two categories may admit of some blurring, they have been recognised for legal and ethical purposes as distinct and are addressed separately in Codes such as the Declaration of Helsinki (see below, p 530).

Innovative therapy

Both of the above forms of research may usefully be distinguished from the concept of innovative therapy: the latter denotes the use of novel treatment on a 'one off' basis. Although it is true that experience with such treatment may subsequently form the 'jumping off point' for proper research (especially if it turns out to be highly effective), it lacks the necessary systematic and repetitive quality to count as such itself; equally its level of scientific probity remains fairly low.

Significantly, from the doctor's point of view, the desire in such cases is solely to benefit the individual patient being treated in this way. Of course, he may foresee the likelihood of gaining new knowledge in the process, but this merely equates to a wide intention on his part to have it (contrast therapeutic research where it is part of his desire). The upshot is that there is no conflict between the doctor *qua* doctor and *qua* scientist: he acts as the former alone. In such a case, it is also submitted that (subject to gaining proper consent) the doctor may also run higher risks on the patient's behalf than those permissible in the context of research. This is because the intended beneficiary of the treatment is the patient alone; he is not being used as a means to any further end.

The concept of risk

As already mentioned, medical research, at least where its focus is invasive forms of therapy, exposes the human research subject to a degree of *additional* risk. Additional, that is to say, to the risks attendant upon receiving treatment where no research is being carried out. Why is this, and what meaning may be ascribed to the concept of risk itself, in this context?

We may begin by recognising, with Marshall above, p 523, that there is always a residual uncertainty, when carrying out any invasive medical procedure, as to whether the patient may in fact be harmed in the process. Given the complexity of each individual human metabolism, we can never be 100% sure in advance that, say, a particular drug will not react with some feature (perhaps of a highly idiosyncratic order) in that metabolism, perhaps with disastrous consequences. Nevertheless, the more often we give the treatment in question, the better the picture we build up of the drug's causal properties, including any such propensity to do harm, and, if so, with what frequency and magnitude.

Clearly, in the case of research involving novel treatment, we will lack this (relative) certainty: the very fact that a particular treatment is untried means that we have no databank of experience as to how the treatment in question has acted upon patients in the past. Although, by the very nature of things, the precise degree of risk presented to a research subject through their participation is thus difficult to quantify, the following rough categories have been proposed:

Nicholson, RH (ed), *Research on Children*, 1986, Oxford: OUP, p 119:

Table 5.6   Risk equivalents

British definition	Negligible	Minimal	More than minimal
American definition	Minimal	Minor increase over minimal	Greater than minor increase over minimal
Risk of death	less than 1 per million	1 to 100 per million	Greater than 100 per million
Risk of major complication	less than 10 per million	10 to 1,000 per million	Greater than 1,000 per million
Risk of minor complication	less than 1 per thousand	1 to 100 per thousand	Greater than 100 per thousand

Despite their tentative character, as we shall see below, pp 552–53, these categories are often considered ethically significant in furnishing acceptable parameters within which research may take place.

THE ETHICS OF GOOD RESEARCH PRACTICE

Background

Although, as we have seen, nearly all medical research involves some extra degree of risk to the research subject, without it medical science would be unable to progress properly. This raises a classic dilemma (similar to that in relation to the use of body tissue and organs from live donors, see below, Chapter 11): under what conditions and to what extent is it permissible to treat a person (the research subject) as a means to an end (here greater medical knowledge)?

The need for some form of response, at an international level, to this question became dramatically apparent in the wake of the Second World War when, at the Nuremberg Trials, Nazi doctors were revealed to have performed a catalogue of horrific medical experiments on inmates of concentration camps causing terrible suffering and death.

In the course of their judgment, the judges at Nuremberg articulated a set of parameters within which they felt research might acceptably take place. This has become known as the Nuremberg Code:

Katz, J, *Experimentation with Human Beings*, 1972, Bognor Regis: Russell Sage Foundation, pp 305–06:

Judgment

Beals, Sebring, Crawford JJ: ... The great weight of the evidence before us is to the effect that certain types of medical experiments on human beings, when kept within reasonably well defined bounds, conform to the ethics of the medical profession generally. The protagonists of the practice of human experimentation justify their views on the basis that such experiments yield results for the good of society that are unprocurable by other methods or means of study. All agree, however, that certain basic principles must be observed in order to satisfy moral, ethical, and legal concepts:

(1) The voluntary consent of the human subject is absolutely essential.

This means that the person involved should have legal capacity to give consent; should be so situated as to be able to exercise free power of choice, without the intervention of any element of force, fraud, deceit, duress, over-reaching, or other ulterior form of constraint or coercion; and should have sufficient knowledge and comprehension of the element of the subject matter involved as to enable him to make an understanding and enlightened decision. This latter element requires that before the acceptance of an affirmative by the experimental subject there should be made known to him the nature, duration, and purpose of the experiment; the method and means by which it is to be conducted; all inconveniences and hazards reasonably to be expected; and the effects upon his health or person which may possibly come from his participation in the experiment.

The duty and responsibility for ascertaining the quality of the consent rests upon each individual who initiates, directs, or engages in the experiment. It is a personal duty and responsibility which may not be delegated to another with impunity.

(2) The experiment should be such as to yield fruitful results for the good of society, unprocurable by other methods or means of study, and not random and unnecessary in nature.

(3) The experiment should be so designed and based on the results of animal experimentation and a knowledge of the natural history of the disease or other problem under study that the anticipated results will justify the performance of the experiment.

(4) The experiment should be so conducted as to avoid all unnecessary physical and mental suffering and injury.

(5) No experiment should be conducted where there is an *a priori* reason to believe that death or disabling injury will occur; except, perhaps, in those experiments where the experimental physicians also serve as subjects.

(6) The degree of risk to be taken should never exceed that determined by the humanitarian importance of the problem to be solved by the experiment.

(7) Proper preparations should be made and adequate facilities provided to protect the experimental subject against even remote possibilities of injury, disability, or death.

(8) The experiment should be conducted only by scientifically qualified persons. The highest degree of skill and care should be required through all stages of the experiment of those who conduct or engage in the experiment.

(9) During the course of the experiment the human subject should be at liberty to bring the experiment to an end if he has reached the physical or mental state where continuation of the experiment seems to him to be impossible.

(10) During the course of the experiment the scientist in charge must be prepared to terminate the experiment at any stage, if he has probable cause to believe, in the exercise of the good faith, superior skill, and careful judgment required of him that a continuation of the experiment is likely to result in injury, disability, or death to the experimental subject.

This was followed, in 1964, by the Declaration of Helsinki, which deals with the issues in a lengthier and more systematic fashion. As will be seen, the Declaration consists of a preamble followed by three parts: Part I enunciates ethical considerations which apply to medical research generally; Part II applies specifically to therapeutic, and Part III to non-therapeutic research. Three themes dominate: the research must be scientifically sound, it must satisfy the proportionality test (ie, risks to the subject should be commensurate with the expected benefits of carrying the research out), and there must be the greatest possible respect at all times for the integrity of the research subject:

Declaration of Helsinki (1964) (as amended – most recently in South Africa, October 1996)

It is the mission of the medical doctor to safeguard the health of the people. His or her knowledge and conscience are dedicated to the fulfilment of this mission.

The Declaration of Geneva of the World Medical Association binds the physician with the words, 'The health of my patient will be my first consideration', and the International Code of Medical Ethics declares that 'A physician shall act only in the patient's interest when providing medical care which might have the effect of weakening the physical and mental condition of the patient'.

The purpose of biomedical research involving human subjects must be to improve diagnostic, therapeutic and prophylactic procedures and the understanding of the aetiology and pathogenesis of disease.

In current medical practice most diagnostic, therapeutic or prophylactic procedures involve hazards. This applies especially to biomedical research.

Medical progress is based on research which ultimately must rest in part on experimentation involving human subjects.

In the field of biomedical research a fundamental distinction must be recognised between medical research in which the aim is essentially diagnostic or therapeutic for a patient, and medical research, the essential object of which is purely scientific and without implying direct diagnostic or therapeutic value to the person subjected to the research.

Special caution must be exercised in the conduct of research which may affect the environment, and the welfare of animals used for research must be respected.

Because it is essential that the results of laboratory experiments be applied to human beings to further scientific knowledge and to help suffering humanity, the World Medical Association has prepared the following recommendations as a guide to every physician in biomedical research involving human subjects. They should be kept under review in the future. It must be stressed that the standards as drafted are only a guide to physicians all over the world. Physicians are not relieved from criminal, civil and ethical responsibilities under the laws of their own countries.

I   Basic principles

(1) Biomedical research involving human subjects must conform to generally accepted scientific principles and should be based on adequately performed laboratory and animal experimentation and on a thorough knowledge of the scientific literature.

(2) The design and performance of each experimental procedure involving human subjects should be clearly formulated in an experimental protocol which should be transmitted for consideration, comment and guidance to a specially appointed committee independent of the investigator and the sponsor provided that this independent committee is in conformity with the laws and regulations of the country in which the research experiment is performed.

(3) Biomedical research involving human subjects should be conducted only by scientifically qualified persons and under the supervision of a clinically competent medical person. The responsibility for the human subject must always rest with the medically qualified person and never rest on the subject of the research, even though the subject has given his or her consent.

(4) Biomedical research involving human subjects cannot legitimately be carried out unless the importance of the objective is in proportion to the inherent risk to the subject.

(5) Every biomedical research project involving human subjects should be preceded by careful assessment of predictable risks in comparison with foreseeable benefits to the subject or to others. Concern for the interests of the subject must always prevail over the interests of science and society.

(6) The right of the research subject to safeguard his or her integrity must always be respected. Every precaution should be taken to respect the privacy of the subject and to minimise the impact of the study on the subject's physical and mental integrity and on the personality of the subject.

(7) Physicians should abstain from engaging in research projects involving human subjects unless they are satisfied that the hazards involved are believed to be predictable. Physicians should cease any investigation if the hazards are found to outweigh the potential benefits.

(8) In publication of the results of his or her research, the physician is obliged to preserve the accuracy of the results. Reports of experimentation not in accordance with the principles laid down in this Declaration should not be accepted for publication.

(9) In any research on human beings, each potential subject must be adequately informed of the aims, methods, anticipated benefits and potential hazards of the study and the discomfort it may entail. He or she should be informed that he or she is at liberty to abstain from participation in the study and that he or she is free to withdraw his or her consent to participation at any time. The physician should then obtain the subject's freely given informed consent, preferably in writing.

(10) When obtaining informed consent for the research project the physician should be particularly cautious if the subject is in a dependent relationship to him or her or may consent under duress. In that case the informed consent should be obtained by a physician who is not engaged in the investigation and who is completely independent of this official relationship.

(11) In case of legal incompetence, informed consent should be obtained from the legal guardian in accordance with national legislation. Where physical or mental incapacity makes it impossible to obtain informed consent, or when the subject is a minor, permission from the responsible relative replaces that of the subject in accordance with national legislation.

Whenever the minor child is in fact able to give a consent, the minor's consent must be obtained in addition to the consent of the minor's legal guardian.

(12) The research protocol should always contain a statement of the ethical considerations involved and should indicate that the principles enunciated in the present Declaration are complied with.

II Medical research combined with professional care (clinical research)

(1) In the treatment of the sick person, the physician must be free to use a new diagnostic and therapeutic measure, if in his or her judgment it offers hope of saving life, re-establishing health or alleviating suffering.

(2) The potential benefits, hazards and discomfort of a new method should be weighed against the advantages of the best current diagnostic and therapeutic methods.

(3) In any medical study, every patient – including those of a control group, if any – should be assured of the best proven diagnostic and therapeutic method. This does not exclude the use of an inert placebo where no proven diagnostic or therapeutic method exists.

(4) The refusal of the patient to participate in a study must never interfere with the physician-patient relationship.

(5) If the physician considers it essential not to obtain informed consent, the specific reasons for this proposal should be stated in the experimental protocol for transmission to the independent committee (I(2)).

(6)   The physician can combine medical research with professional care, the objective being the acquisition of new medical knowledge, only to the extent that medical research is justified by its potential diagnostic or therapeutic value for the patient.

III   Non-therapeutic biomedical research involving human subjects (non-clinical biomedical research)

(1)   In the purely scientific application of medical research carried out on a human being, it is the duty of the physician to remain the protector of the life and health of that person on whom biomedical research is being carried out.

(2)   The subjects should be volunteers – either healthy persons or patients for whom the experimental design is not related to the patient's illness.

(3)   The investigator or the investigating team should discontinue the research if in his/her or their judgment it may, if continued, be harmful to the individual.

(4)   In research on man, the interest of science and society should never take precedence over considerations related to the well being of the subject.

As will be apparent below, pp 560 *et seq*, the Helsinki Declaration has acted as a template for the various domestic codes, which have subsequently been drafted in respect of particular areas of research practice in the UK.

The duty of doctor/researcher

Our concern in this section is the duties of an *ethical* nature that the doctor/researcher may be held to owe to the research subject. (Consideration of duties imposed by the law is left until later in this chapter, below, pp 540 *et seq*.) In accordance with the central distinction, outlined above, between therapeutic and non-therapeutic research, we shall deal separately with the duties which exist in each case.

Duties to patients

Can therapeutic research, and the additional risks it entails, be reconciled (and if so, how far) with the doctor's pledge under the Hippocratic Oath to do the best for each of his patients? In itself, this question admits of an affirmative answer: the higher risks can be balanced against the hope that a new therapy will bring increased benefits for the patients so treated. However, matters are complicated by the use, in RCTs, of randomisation to determine the treatment given to each patient. For here it might well be argued that the doctor has abdicated his duty to tailor the treatment he provides to the latter's individual needs. The ethical conflict here, and the question of how far the patient's fully informed consent could provide a justification, is analysed by Charles Fried:

Fried, C, *Medical Experimentation – Personal Integrity and Social Policy*, 1974, Amsterdam: North-Holland Publishing, pp 51–56:

In the RCT a physician (or group of physicians) determines each individual's precise therapy by considering not only that individual's need, but also by considering the needs of the experimental design, that is the needs of the wider social group that will be benefited by a more definitive evaluation of the therapies concerned. Concretely, the actual therapy the patient receives is determined by a randomising scheme. Does this not, then, clearly pose the dilemma of the physician's duty to the individual and his interest in serving a wider group that would be benefited by the results of the trial? Is this not a case in which that conflict is resolved at least in part by sacrificing the interests and claims of the individual to those of the wider group? Now some would seek to short-circuit this philosophical inquiry at the outset by denying that any conflict exists and that the individual's interests have in any way been sacrificed.

The argument is frequently made that where the balance of opinion is truly in equipoise, there is no sense to the accusation that the prescribing of one or the other of the equally eligible treatments can constitute a withholding of anything or can constitute doing less than one's best (the alternative being no better). And so no one sacrifices anybody to anything. Surely, this is the strongest defence that can be made in favour of the RCT. Yet, this defence is unsatisfactory at least in so far as it seeks to show that there is in fact not even any problem to be resolved, no difficulty of conscience, of ethics and philosophy.

First, one might admit to a certain scepticism about whether the facts often, if ever, correspond to those which are needed to dissolve so handily the dilemma. Is it ever likely to be the case that in a complex medical situation the balance of harms and benefits discounted by their appropriate probabilities really does appear on the then available evidence to be in equipoise? Or even approximately enough in equipoise to make the argument go through? I would concede that as to a particular medical condition, even quite carefully defined, viewed across a general population there might be a number of cases where the balance between treatments was equal; but I would suppose that in many of these situations this equipoise would not exist in respect to a particular patient. Consider, for instance, the choice between medical and surgical intervention for acute unstable angina pectoris. I would suppose that a group of patients could be so defined that the risks and benefits of the two available courses of action were quite evenly balanced. But, when a particular patient is involved, with a particular set of symptoms, a particular diagnostic picture and a particular set of values and preferences (this last is an issue on which more must be said later), then one may doubt how often a physician carefully going into all of these particularities would conclude that the risks and benefits are truly equal.

Perhaps, after all, this may happen, and may happen often enough to justify a significant number of RCTs. But before one concludes that the dilemma has really been dissolved in these cases, one must be quite careful to determine whether the condition of equipoise obtains just because it has been previously decided not to inquire too closely into the particular circumstances of the particular patient, proceeding rather on the balance of risks and benefits as they pertain to a larger group. One must be careful of this, because if the equipoise appears as a result of this failure of inquiry, then the sacrifice has indeed taken place, but only at another level, in a different way. One might say that the individual patient has perhaps not been sacrificed in the crude sense that the best available treatment has been withheld from him, but he has been sacrificed in that for the sake of the experimental design his interest in having his particular circumstances investigated has been sacrificed. But this amounts to the same thing.

The RCT raises a further conflict between the interest of the individual and that of the experiment: what should the patient be told? Should he be told that he is receiving that therapy which in the judgment of his physicians is the best available in his case, or should he be told more fully that his therapy is being determined by some randomising device in furtherance of a medical experiment? In the case where the choice between the two treatments is not in equipoise, the failure to disclose the existence of the RCT adds insult to injury since it plainly withholds information which any patient should find relevant and indeed the basis for considering a change of doctors. The non-disclosure is deceptive because it fails to reveal that the patient's interests are, to some extent, being sacrificed for the sake of the experimental design and thus, the wider social good. That sacrifice might be the overt one of exposing the patient to the risk of a treatment which in the present state of knowledge is somewhat less favoured, or the less overt one of not inquiring fully into his particular circumstances (including his particular value system) in order to determine whether the balance of probabilities is in equipoise in his particular case. There are two justifications for non-disclosure frequently offered: (1) that the distress this would cause the patient would be therapeutically undesirable; and (2) that the disclosure would endanger the experiment by introducing a disturbing element or even by causing the patient to withhold his consent. Both justifications are inadequate to show that non-disclosure does not sacrifice some interest of the subject. Both justifications beg this question, since they assume that the choice by randomisation is proper, and thus they assume that limiting disclosure in order to facilitate this kind of experimentation is proper.

Finally, the failure to make full disclosure is problematic even in the case where the two treatments are really in equipoise for the particular patient, with his particular life plan and physical characteristics. That there is a real problem even here is suggested by the high probability that many patients would surely want to know or would feel deceived if they had not been told ... I shall argue that the patient has an interest in knowing and thus participating in processes that touch some of his most vital interests, even if we are sure that there is only one rational choice for him to make. Thus, whatever the compensating benefits to the participant in the RCT or to society as a whole, it seems pretty clear that the experimental subject has something to lose, and it is his doctor who is imposing these burdens on him. This does seem to conflict with the conception of a physician as bearing an obligation of undivided loyalty to his patient.

Clearly, these problems are particularly acute in the context of serious life-saving therapy, where one group of patients may end up with inferior treatment (or possibly no treatment at all) and where doctors may stand upon their 'therapeutic privilege' to avoid disclosure. Nor, as Graham Thorpe notes, is this diminished merely because the patient's condition is thought to be incurable:

> **Thorpe G, 'Experiments on the dying', in Williams, CJ (ed), *Introducing New Treatments for Cancer: Practical, Ethical and Legal Problems*, 1992, Chichester: John Wiley, pp 217–19:**
>
> In 1967 the debate concerning the medical ethics of research on patients was fuelled dramatically by the publication in Britain of a book, *Human Guinea Pigs*, by MH Pappworth. He drew attention to the fact that the human being was the only animal that doctors could experiment upon without a licence, and demonstrated a wide gap between the doctor's care of the patient and his pursuit of knowledge. A chapter was devoted to each of the following vulnerable groups: infants and children, pregnant women, mental detectives and mentally sick, prison inmates, the dying and the old, and patients awaiting or undergoing operations.
>
> Looking back 25 years, much of the research cited involved puncture and catheterisation of blood and other vessels, an indication of the frontier of medical progress at that time. Numerous examples of exploitation and abuse were given. With respect to the dying and the old, Pappworth lists the new techniques of splenic puncture to measure blood pressure in the splenic vein in patients with liver disease and percutaneous splenoportography, percutaneous transhepatic cannulation of a hepatic or portal vein, arterial and cardiac catheterisation, and cannulation of the thoracic duct.
>
> Other research involved the production of temporary anuria by the injection of large volumes of water intravenously to induce haemolysis, the measurement of oxygen consumption in paralysed men exposed to cold, and rib puncture with the injection of contrast medium to outline the azygos veins.
>
> In some of the patients, many of whom had advanced cancer, there were complications ranging from minor to serious, and several died as a direct result of the experiments. In a number of instances a new investigational procedure was first practised on cadavers and then on an ill patient with a poor prognosis. If he should die in the course of perfecting the technique or improving the operator's technical skill, then that would be unfortunate, but a lesser loss than a fitter patient or normal subject.
>
> All this research was non-therapeutic and of no benefit to the persons concerned and Pappworth argued that patients seriously ill with advanced disease should not be treated as expendable, but they were entitled to the best possible palliative care. As for experiments and research, they should be regarded as prohibited subjects. To this end acknowledged and observed safeguards should be introduced, otherwise abuses would inevitably continue.
>
> **A secret trial**
>
> Fourteen years later in 1981 an anterior resection of a carcinoma of the rectum was performed on an 84 year old widow who had previously enjoyed good

health. She died 15 days later from acute bone marrow depression induced by 5-fluorouracil (5-FU). At the inquest it emerged that the patient had been an unwitting participant in a randomised controlled trial ...

Following earlier work which suggested that the infusion of 5-FU into the portal vein would reduce the incidence of liver metastasis, a new multi-centre study had been set up. After an operation to remove a primary carcinoma of rectum had been performed, patients with no evidence of metastatic disease were allocated randomly into three groups. In one there was no further treatment. In the second group, as heparin had been given with the 5-FU in the previous study to determine whether this drug alone had any effect, a heparin infusion was given via the portal vein twice daily for seven days. In the third group 500 mg of 5-FU was infused with heparin as in the second group.

Careful consideration had been given by ethical committees as to whether patients and their relatives should be informed of the existence and details of the trial, and it had been decided that they should not be informed and therefore their consent was not sought.

Writing about this case in *The Lancet*, the barrister Diana Brahams stated:

> I find the concept of secret random control trials wholly unacceptable, and the reasons offered to justify them both unconvincing and unsatisfactory. It is usual to tell patients and obtain their consent apparently, but where the end measure is death and cancer is involved, the doctor thinks he knows best.

At the inquest, evidence showed that the trial protocol which required blood counts every other day after operation had not been followed and therefore the bone marrow depression which had occurred was not detected at an early stage. The coroner brought in a verdict of misadventure and stated that the whole idea of concealed controlled trials should be brought to the public notice so that proper discussion could take place.

On the other hand, it may be felt that to insist upon fully informed consent in this context may be counterproductive, not only from the point of view of hindering medical progress (in so far as one were prepared to recognise utilitarian trade-offs here) but in terms of the individual patient's own interests. An argument to this effect is put forward by Tobias and Souhani:

Tobias, J and Souhani, R, 'Fully informed consent can be needlessly cruel' (1993) 307 BMJ 1199:

Cruelty to patients

After many years of experience as committed trialists and believers in the statistical and clinical value of the randomised clinical trial, we feel that uniform recommendation for full written informed consent, as outlined, for example, by the Royal College of Physicians, may be not only bad for clinical trials but, far more important, unnecessarily cruel to patients.

Consider for example the case of cancer of the cervix. Since we now have, for the first time, several cytotoxic agents with activity in patients with advanced disease, it is of critical importance to establish whether or not this new approach combined with the conventional treatment (radiotherapy), offers an improvement in overall cure rate. If it does, this would be the first step forward in this tumour since radiotherapy was introduced as standard treatment over 50 years ago. The issue can be settled only by clinical trials of sufficient size to quantify any possible benefit but the difficulty that many trialists have with the informed consent consultation with these patients has made this kind of study extremely problematic.

It is neither faintheartedness nor a disinclination to be questioned that discourages the clinician; rather, it is the overwhelming difficulty of describing the details of a potentially valuable (but as yet unproved) new remedy, gaining the patient's assent, and later having to inform her that she has been randomised to receive radiotherapy alone. However carefully the pros and cons of chemotherapy may have been explained, the result of the randomisation often leads the doctor towards a rather shabby display of back pedalling, in which the possible advantages of the chemotherapy are 'talked down' and perhaps the side effects 'talked up'. The patient may become extremely distressed, which is not only counterproductive (with refusal to participate) but also alarming for the doctor and by no means easily resolved.

It does not take many such consultations to change a well intentioned and committed trialist into a disgruntled clinician who no longer feels that the game is worth the candle. It can be extremely difficult to sustain the doctor-patient relationship through such a harrowing discussion, and particularly unfortunate for patients such as those in the example above whose treatment by radiotherapy (that is, the control group) would be regarded as entirely conventional and proper. Both the support and reassurance of the doctor, and the patient's trust and confidence in the medical advice, may have been irretrievably lost. Too frank an explanation, with patient overload from too much information, can have most serious consequences.

A way forward

The ethical double standard is obvious. If doctors are sure they know which is the correct general policy of management, and if they recommend treatment according to their judgment or preference, they are excused any ethical criticism on the grounds of freedom of clinical judgment. All would agree that a clinician must be able to advise according to the particular circumstances (medical, social, psychological) of the patient, but what if the doctor is ill informed or dogmatic? Why should the clinician who shares with expert colleagues a genuine doubt about the best treatment be subject to the difficulties outlined above? ...

In ordinary clinical practice (outside clinical trials) it is essential that doctors judge how quickly to impart information and to what degree they will spell out the medical facts, especially if they are frightening or unpalatable. The move towards full disclosure of all details of diagnosis, treatment, and prognosis is a major change in social perception in the United Kingdom and the United States – one by no means found in all countries to the same degree. However, no sensible doctor makes full disclosure to every patient. This would be a recipe for needless cruelty and distress. Although in most branches of medicine an honest and candid approach is generally desirable, one of the challenges of clinical medicine is to know how quickly to proceed and how to judge the amount of information which should be given at a particular moment. Informing a patient is a continuous process.

We suggest that the process of informed consent should be viewed as another straightforward instance in which the clinical judgment of the doctor is paramount. Clearly, for a patient who wishes to know what underlies all aspects of decision making, there is no doubt that full explanation should be given, together with all the necessary information about the trial. At the other extreme a distraught patient, possibly within days of diagnosis of a potentially lethal illness, may be unable to take in any but the most basic details. Often in desperate need of reassurance, patients such as this can hardly be expected to cope with a full discussion of options to be decided at random. In between there will be more complex judgments in which the outlines of alternative treatments must be explained and the patient reassured that the treatment policy decided on will always be in his or her best interests. The crucial point here may sometimes include the question of whether to disclose that this decision is based on a randomisation in which the physician plays no direct part. This may be very unnerving for patients, and in some situations – for example, in discussion with parents of a child with cancer (in which age group randomised trials are usual) – it may be extremely difficult.

Duties to volunteers

As previously noted, the researcher who carries out non-therapeutic research on volunteers has no doctor-patient relationship with his subject. Nevertheless, this does not entail the absence of ethical duties on his part towards the latter. In some ways, indeed, it may heighten his obligations. As Charles Fried writes:

Fried, C, *Medical Experimentation – Personal Integrity and Social Policy*, 1974, Amsterdam: North-Holland Publishing, pp 26–27:

Non-therapeutic experimentation

No special doctrines apply to non-therapeutic experimentation. Indeed, to the extent that the experimentation is non-therapeutic, the fact that it is being carried out by doctors should be entirely irrelevant. The usual privileges under which doctors work, and the usual special doctrines according to which the liabilities of doctors are judged, should not be applicable, since they proceed from the premise that the doctor must be given considerable latitude as he works in the presumed interests of his patient. But that is not the case in non-therapeutic research. The doctor confronts his subject simply as a scientist.

In general, the law imposes a strict duty of disclosure, wherever an individual with a great deal to lose is exposed to a risk or is asked to relinquish rights by someone with considerably greater knowledge. And this is true, whether the relation is one of buyer and seller or involves some public interest. Persons selling cosmetics, automobiles or pharmaceuticals are required to make full disclosures of all the hazards involved in the products they sell. But policemen seeking damaging admissions from suspects are also required to issue a warning of constitutional rights and to offer legal assistance before those rights are waived. There is no reason why the case should be any different where a researcher asks an experimental subject to risk his health.

The Declaration of Helsinki (see above, p 530) reflects this position: whereas (exceptionally) a doctor may rely on the doctrine of 'therapeutic privilege' – see above, Chapter 3 – to avoid informing a patient of his participation in therapeutic research, no such argument is admissible in relation to volunteers. (We shall consider below, p 550, how far this increased duty of candour in cases of non-therapeutic research forms part of English law.)

CONSENT TO RESEARCH

Whereas research upon embryos may only be carried out under licence pursuant to the Human Fertilisation and Embryology Act 1990 (see above, Chapter 7), and that upon animals is regulated by the Animals (Scientific Procedures) Act 1968, there are no similar statutory safeguards operative in respect of research upon (full) human beings. Perhaps the major reason for this is that the human research subject is thought able to protect himself adequately against abuse by the researcher through the mechanism of consent at common law. How far is this really so? Although we have examined consent to treatment in some detail (see above, Chapter 3), medical research gives rise to some special considerations. For example, in relation to general treatment, consent may sometimes simply be inferred from the surrounding circumstances, as when a patient submits to a medical examination. In the context of therapeutic research, the additional (and cloaked) intention of the doctor/researcher means that the subject's consent cannot be so inferred.

It will be recalled that the three elements to a valid consent are capacity, voluntariness and information, and each will be examined in relation to therapeutic and non-therapeutic research, respectively.

Therapeutic research

The competent patient

The first issue here is to determine whether the subject has genuine capacity to consent. In this regard, could it be argued that the latter must possess a more sophisticated understanding than someone who is receiving 'ordinary' medical treatment? In one sense, the answer is 'yes', because the issues in a research project may be quite complex, but there is no real difference of criteria. Consent to general treatment requires an ability to understand the nature of the treatment and this general principle applies equally to therapeutic research.

More problematic, however, may be the requirement for such consent to be free from coercion. This is because there is a danger that pressure (real or perceived) may be placed upon a patient to agree to participate in a clinical trial for fear of not receiving the best treatment in the face of a refusal. Sarah Hewlett comments on this problem as follows:

Hewlett, S, 'Consent to clinical research – adequately voluntary or substantially influenced?' (1996) 22 JME 232:

Influences or controlling influences?

Whilst circumstances and people will always influence any decision we make, it is the responsibility of the researcher to ensure that in clinical research, these are not so strong as to be controlling. Unlike healthy volunteers, many patients invited to participate in clinical research will have an illness and the experience of illness (which may at times include pain, disability, fear of deterioration or death, physical or emotional dependence) and the accompanying psychological response (possibly depression, mourning, denial, anger, anxiety, passivity and regression to an invalid role) may well reduce autonomy. In addition, a request to enter a research trial may of necessity come at the time of, or soon after, the shock of diagnosis. Furthermore, some patients in hospital feel vulnerable – unaware of the normal routine or what is expected of them, and reduced, as they are, to wearing night clothes. Is it possible to make a reflective decision, free of strong influences in such a situation?

The doctor-patient relationship is centred around patients' trust that doctors act in their best interests. Thus even though the doctor has explained that treatment in the research trial is randomised and according to a strict protocol, patients often still believe that the doctor will only act in their best interests. In a recent trial 41% of patients believed there were no risks in a Phase II trial of a new anti-inflammatory agent, despite being told it was unlicensed and being tested for safety. So strong is this trust that patients may agree to anything the doctor suggests and even the invitation to participate may be viewed as a recommendation rather than a request. Patients may feel flattered by the request and under an obligation to help because of past care received.

For many patients the relationship is an unequal one, with the doctor being perceived as a powerful figure on whom they depend, making it difficult for them to take an unnaturally dominant role and refuse the doctor's request. Patients may fear that if they do so, the doctor will be displeased and their future care will be jeopardised. Patients may view clinical research as a means of access to care (which may be true for patients in countries where many people do not have health care insurance) and may also equate the frequent safety visits with improved care.

External pressures may be brought to bear on the patient: the patient may be asked to decide immediately, without time to reflect; family and friends may suggest the patient 'ought' to participate; the facts we give the patient will be laden with our beliefs; we may use closed questions or statistics which are loaded in a persuasive fashion (for example 75% of patients do well rather than 25% do badly); doctors may be under pressure to reach target numbers, with academic and financial kudos resulting from a completed trial. Thus the influences on the patient are multiple and complex.

She proposes several practical strategies for dealing with these problems:

Hewlett, S, 'Consent to clinical research – adequately voluntary or substantially influenced?' (1996) 22 JME 232:

Reducing influences on consent to clinical research

Whilst it could be argued that the adequately autonomous patient is the best person to decide if his or her decision is adequately voluntary, as health care professionals we have a professional responsibility to try and promote adequately voluntary consent by the manner in which we obtain it. This is similar to our responsibilities in trying to ensure adequately informed consent by the manner in which we inform patients. Areas where influences could be reduced include the doctor-patient relationship, selection of patients, education of the researcher and information given during recruitment.

The doctor-patient relationship

Interventions here might allow the patient to step back from the relationship and consider the proposal in a more detached manner. This could be done by using a researcher/doctor as well as a carer/doctor, by using a patient advocate or by recruiting patients in groups. Separating the doctors into researcher/doctors and carer/doctors may allow patients to feel less anxious about future care if they refuse. However, the doctors are likely to be, or to become, close colleagues; the carer/doctor will have to be responsible for recruitment, which involves him in the research; the researcher/doctor will need to know about the patient's care; and both doctors will need to deal with clinical problems as they arise, thus causing practical problems as a result of creating this split. In therapeutic research, care and research are so closely interlinked that it is impractical and impossible not to mix the two.

A patient advocate might ask questions on the patient's behalf, act as an impartial sounding board, and deter the doctor from pressurising or hurrying the patient. A lay advocate (friend or relative) might not be able to interpret technical details any better than the patient, might also be in awe of the perceived power of the doctor, and might influence the patient by the strength of their own relationship. A non-doctor health care professional might be well suited to advocacy because of his or her familiarity with the health care system, rapport with patients and ability to interpret technical data. However, such a professional may be seen as part of the doctor's team and may well be employed by the doctor so that he or she has a vested interest in encouraging recruitment. However, a trained advocate, perhaps funded by the health authority or trust, could be specifically trained and supervised by the research ethics committee. Such posts, separate from any research or care team, have the potential to develop into an independent advocacy system.

Talking to patients about clinical research in groups rather than individually may reduce pressure on patients – more outspoken patients may ask questions which others are reluctant to voice. However, patients may also find it difficult to go against the group decision if they do not agree with it.

Selection of patients

It has been suggested that we should first approach patients who are best able to understand the research, and who are most highly motivated and least captive, such as health care professionals who have the particular disease in question. The numbers in this group are likely to be so small as to make research impractical and where there is a link between educational level and disease, selecting highly educated subjects might bias the study.

Education of researchers

Education of health care professionals in research ethics and obtaining consent should ease pressure on patients by increasing the researchers' awareness. This is gradually happening as nursing and medical schools include medical ethics in their curricula.

Information to patients

Specific trial information sheets are vital and patients must have time to read and discuss them. However, as they are written by the researchers who wish the patient to consent there is the real possibility that they will be biased. Consumers for Ethics in Research (CERES) produce a standard leaflet on medical research which is not written in relation to specific projects. Having seen this leaflet and following our own research into consent, we have developed a Patient's Guide to Medical Research ... which is given to all rheumatology patients as they are invited to participate in clinical research, alongside the specific trial information sheets. It is independent of any single researcher or research trial, is designed to cover many of the issues raised in this article and has an 'easy' readability level.

We have made other changes to the consent process, including giving the responsibility for information-giving and initial interview and consent to the research nurses, who are perhaps seen as less powerful figures than the doctor. We give patients at least 48 hours to reflect on the proposal and encourage them to discuss it with family, friends and GP, before telephoning them to discuss the trial, answer questions and take their decision, which is passed on to the doctor on their behalf. We believe that these strategies reduce the difficulty patients experience in deciding to take part in research and we will be assessing this in future trials.

The Royal College of Physicians confirms in its Guidance (*Research Involving Patients*, 1990, London: RCP) that patients must feel free to decline to participate and assured that the refusal will not put them at a disadvantage (paras 7.4 *et seq*).

There is concern that certain groups in particular may be vulnerable to exploitation in the field of research. It will be recalled that this was examined above, in Chapter 3 (see the cases of *Freeman v Home Office* [1984] 1 All ER 1036 and *Kaimowitz v Michigan Department of Mental Health* 42 USLW 2063 (1973)). In relation to prisoners, the Royal College of Physicians' guidelines state:

Royal College of Physicians, *Research Involving Patients*, 1990, London: RCP:

7.48 It has been suggested that involuntary detention of any sort invalidates consent and hence makes participation in research impossible. We reject this view and consider that research into medical and psychological disturbances affecting prisoners may be beneficial. Furthermore, there is evidence that prisoners may not wish to be excluded from participation in worthwhile research. For example, we see no reason to exclude those patients who are imprisoned from a study involving patients with hepatitis merely because of their imprisonment.

7.49 We recommend that research should not be undertaken solely in prisoners who are patients as defined in s 2.1 unless the fact of being imprisoned is itself an essential component of the research.

7.50 In the case of research in which it is considered that the participation of an independent informed individual or patient's friend is helpful (see 7.22), the prison officer may not always be appropriate and another person such as a prison visitor should then be considered.

Mason and McCall comment as follows:

Mason, JK and McCall Smith, RA, *Law and Medical Ethics*, 3rd edn, 1991, London: Butterworths, p 357:

... the use of prisoners exposes many ethical issues essentially based on the arguments that some advantage, even if only imagined, must accrue to the prisoner participating in a trial; that advantage may be so great as to induce the prisoner to volunteer for research which involves greater discomfort or risk than would be accepted by a free man and, in particular, it may compromise his inalienable right to withdraw from the experiment. The arguments are not, however, entirely one way – it is possible to be paternalistic in an attempt to preserve people's autonomy. Thus, prisoners could well resent protective attitudes on the grounds that it is their right to dispose of their bodies and to take such risks as they please that is being compromised. This could be the subject of lengthy debate, but we would suggest that the conditions in today's prisons are such that any process which provides some relief deserves, at least, a sympathetic evaluation and, secondly, that many prisoners might be therapeutically benefited through helping society. But it is also felt that experiments on prisoners should be particularly rigidly controlled by ethical committees which should always contain lay members with experience in criminology ...

However, given the concerns we address later about the lack of sanctions given to ethics committees, it may be doubted as to whether they really can 'rigidly control' such a situation.

A further major issue in respect of therapeutic research carried out upon competent patients concerns the amount of information to which they are legally entitled. We have seen that a battery will be committed if the patient is not informed of the broad nature of an intended medical procedure. Kennedy and Grubb comment as follows:

Kennedy, I and Grubb, A, *Medical Law*, 2nd edn, 1994, London: Butterworths, pp 1045–46:

One view, and it is ours, is that where there is a dual intention on the part of the doctor, ie, to treat and to conduct research, any failure to inform the patient concerning *both* of these intentions and their possible consequences would amount in law to a battery. This is because in the absence of such knowledge the patient will have assented to a procedure which is materially different in its nature from that which the doctor intends to carry out. To put it another way, research adds a further component to the quality of the consent that the law requires.

The law does not require people to volunteer and will provide a remedy to the patient against the doctor who conscripts him, the remedy being in battery to demonstrate the law's concern for the rights of the patient. Indeed, arguably the failure to disclose the intention to conduct research would amount to fraud sufficient to vitiate any consent which might otherwise be valid. If this is the law, that failure to inform is a battery, then what must the doctor do to act lawfully? In short, the answer must be that the doctor must make explicit his intention to carry out research. A court may insist on the patient being informed of three particular matters in addition to this generalised intention. Each of them is an aspect of those interests of the patient which the law of battery seeks to protect. The patient must be informed: (1) that he may refuse to take part in the research project or may at any time withdraw from the research and that in either case if he does so he will suffer no adverse consequences in terms of the treatment he will then receive; (2) that the nature of the research may be such that he may be a member of a control group in a trial which is intended to evaluate the efficacy of a new therapy; (3) that the trial is a randomised controlled trial (RCT) if it be such.

As regards (2), one consequence of being a member of a control group could be that the patient does not receive the form of treatment which subsequently proves to be the more efficacious. To meet this ethical difficulty researchers ordinarily would be expected to provide for periodic examination of the emerging data. It is our view that a patient's consent is not informed for the purpose of the tort of battery unless he is made aware of this periodic review.

As regards (3), randomisation means that a treatment regime is assigned to a patient randomly without regard to the particular circumstances of that patient, his needs, his preferences or the preferences of his doctor. Again, it is our view that a patient may volunteer for such a trial but his consent is only valid if he is given the opportunity of knowing it is randomised and he is aware of what this means.

If Kennedy and Grubb's argument is correct, it would seem that the law is stricter in this sphere than are the relevant ethical codes: it is apparent that the Declaration of Helsinki expressly recognises that there will be situations in which the doctor 'considers it essential not to obtain informed consent' (para II(5)). Equally, the Royal College of Physicians, in *Guidelines on the Practice of Ethics Committees in Medical Research Involving Human Subjects* (August 1996) cite the Tobias and Souhami article (extracted above, p 537), to support its view that, where it would cause more distress to reveal the nature of the investigation but it is in the clinical interest of the patient, information can be withheld in 'exceptional circumstances'. However, as Kennedy and Grubb point out (*Medical Law*, 2nd edn, 1994, London: Butterworths, p 1046), if the patient would be caused distress by the knowledge that he is in a clinical trial, this is an argument for excluding him from the trial, not for including him without his knowledge. As yet, however, the position has not been tested in the courts.

In so far as the patient is sufficiently informed to preclude an action in battery, he may still have an action in negligence. Although in differing judgments, the majority of the House of Lords in *Sidaway v Bethlem Royal Hospital Governors* [1985] 1 All ER 643 regarded information disclosure as being broadly governed by the *Bolam* test (see further above, Chapter 3). However, should the same considerations apply in relation to research? Even if the amount of information given is at the discretion of the doctor, does not the fact that there is an objective other than the well being of the patient, impose a duty of candour over and above the *Sidaway* duty? In fact as matters stand, because *Sidaway* and *Bolam* take responsible approved practice as their starting point, and the various ethical codes on research generally emphasise the need for full disclosure, it can be argued that 'informed consent' is here already effectively part of English law.

Nevertheless, in *Sidaway* even Lord Scarman acknowledged that the obligation to disclose could be tempered by therapeutic privilege. In the USA, where there is Federal law which regulates medical research, the doctrine of therapeutic privilege is acknowledged (see Myers, D, *The Human Body and the Law*, 1990, Edinburgh: Edinburgh University Press). Given that, at least in part, the purpose of therapeutic research is to offer some benefit to the patient, is it not inevitable that something akin to therapeutic privilege will exist? A recent report from Peter Hamilton, the Sheriff in Aberdeen, however, highlights a case, where the patient had been positively misled:

Hamilton, P (Sheriff), 'Sheriff's Report, Aberdeen' (1997) Bulletin of Medical Ethics (August) 22:

28 January 1997

In 1993, while recovering from a fractured hip, Mrs Phyllis Moffit was recruited into a clinical trial after receiving the following revised patient information sheet:

> Dear ...
>
> We are asking patients who have had a hip fracture in the past if they will take part in a research project. The aim is to try to prevent their unaffected hip from breaking at a later date.
>
> In order to do this, we would like to have the opportunity to inject your unaffected hip (the one you have not broken) with a material which we think would actually strengthen the bone. It is composed of crystals of calcium, very like bone, and a protein which is known to stimulate bone growth.
>
> We know there is a one in five chance that you might break the other hip within four years, and therefore there would be great benefits if the

injection were to be successful. We are not aware of any significant risks associated with this injection.

If you agree to this injection, you will be admitted to Woodend Hospital. It will be done under a local anaesthetic in the operating theatre. It will involve having a small cut (about half an inch) made in your unaffected hip and the material being injected into your hip bone. This is not a painful procedure and should not inconvenience or incapacitate you in any way. This will not affect your mobility ...

Mrs Moffit died in August 1994 of heart failure while under sedation for the experimental hip surgery. The heart failure was caused by an unsuspected aneurysm of the coronary artery.

In this case, the statistic quoted in the information sheet as to the likelihood of a second hip fracture was based upon inconclusive evidence and had indeed been changed from an earlier sheet in which the chance was described as 'one in 10 over two years'. The victim's daughter gave evidence that the alarm her mother had felt on reading this was the chief reason she had agreed to participate in the research. Moreover, the research proposal approved by the local research ethics committee (LREC) (see below, p 561) had not mentioned the need for sedation of subjects as initially it had not been thought that the procedure would be painful. Whilst the researchers had become aware that this would in fact be required some time prior to recruiting Mrs Moffit, they failed either to amend the information sheet or to inform the LREC. Finally, although the patient here was recovering from a fractured hip, it may be queried whether this was really *therapeutic* research at all.

The incompetent patient

Children

First, does s 8 of the Family Law Reform Act 1969 (see above, Chapter 3) apply to research? The section refers to 'any surgical, medical or dental treatment', and it has been argued (by, for example, Kennedy and Grubb in *Medical Law*, 2nd edn, 1994, London: Butterworths) that this does not cover treatment which includes a research component. This would mean that the age of 16 would have no significance as far as consent of the child is concerned, but presumably the concept of *Gillick* competence would apply. The guidelines issued by the professional bodies acknowledge that children can consent to therapeutic research.

Royal College of Physicians, *Research Involving Patients*, 1990, London: RCP:

7.32 We think it very important that children should be consulted when the question of their participation in research arises. Even if an investigator believes that a child is capable of giving legally valid consent we advise that the approval of a parent or guardian should still be obtained before any research procedure is proposed to a child under the age of 16 years. It may also be desirable to obtain parental consent in some older children.

7.33 Details of the research procedure, including any discomfort involved, should be explained in terms capable of being understood both by the parent or guardian and by the child. We advise that the older child, as well as the parent or guardian, should give written consent for more than trivial procedures. Objection to taking part in a research procedure either by such a child (whether oral or by behaviour) or his parents or guardian should always be respected.

7.34 The position of the child who does not have the understanding to make such a decision is less clear. The investigator must look to the parents or guardians for consent to proceed but the question arises as to whether parents can properly consent in law to their child being subjected to a procedure which carries no prospect of direct benefit and some (even if only minimal) risk. The law is unclear, but the prevailing view appears to be that the duty of the parent to act in the best interests of the child can reasonably be interpreted as an obligation not to do anything clearly against the interests of the child. This seems sensible to us and we believe that where the research is for the benefit of children generally, and the child is incapable of giving consent, the investigator can properly rely on the consent of a parent or guardian. If, when the parental approval has been obtained, a child were to object to the procedure itself, for example, taking a blood specimen, the investigator should reconsider whether it would be appropriate to proceed.

Though the last paragraph is perhaps directed principally to non-therapeutic research (see further below, p 550) it is interesting to note the comment that 'the duty of the parent to act in the best interests of the child can reasonably be interpreted as an obligation not to do anything clearly against the interests of the child', which, as we have seen (above, Chapter 4) is taken from the speech of Lord Reid in the House of Lords case of *S v S* [1970] 3 All ER 107. The implication for therapeutic research appears to be that the therapeutic aspect of the treatment means that it would not be contrary to the child's interests. However, if we consider randomised control tests, where the child may be getting no treatment at all, and where the choice as to whether the child is treated is not made on clinical grounds, can it still be argued that this is not contrary to the interests of the child?

Incompetent adults

As we have seen, there is no proxy system in English law which enables consent to be given on behalf of an incompetent adult. It is startling, therefore, to note the Neuberger Report (see below, p 561), which found that 25% of ethics committees allowed proxy consent. We are, therefore, driven back to the 'best interests' argument, and the test in *Re F (Mental Patient: Sterilisation)* [1990] 2 AC 1. The same considerations apply as to children, and the question again arises as to whether treatment determined on randomised, rather than clinical, grounds in an RCT can ever be in the patient's best interests.

Non-therapeutic research

The competent volunteer

Given that we are not considering *treatment* at all, should the test of capacity to consent be different in this context? The test, it is suggested, will be the same. The volunteer will still be required to understand the nature of the procedure and any risks involved, and weigh up the risks of the procedure with the advantage of participating (either financial, or psychological well being because of the potential benefits to others).

However, just as there may be a temptation for a doctor, who wishes to treat a refusing patient in the latter's own interests, to regard such a patient as *incompetent*, here, where a researcher needs healthy volunteers to assist in what he believes to be valuable research, the opposite temptation may arise: that is to say, the researcher may be over-ready to find an assenting volunteer competent. It is clear that vigilance is needed to protect individuals from physical interference in both cases.

Difficulties also arise in the context of ensuring that consent to participate is truly voluntary. This is especially true of volunteers, who are already in hospital for unrelated treatment, and who may feel unable to refuse 'secondment' into a trial if approached by their doctor. Another potential group of research subjects, vulnerable in a somewhat different way, are the poor. Although the financial inducements are relatively modest, the sums may tempt those on low incomes. For example, advertisements in *The Big Issue* (a publication sold on the streets by the homeless) invite volunteers for medical research (stating that they are 'all approved by ethics committees'), for £100. The Royal College of Physicians, albeit in the context of research on patients, state:

Royal College of Physicians, *Research Involving Patients*, 1990, London: RCP, p 27:

... many studies, particularly in pharmacology, are lengthy and tedious, and may involve urine collection, multiple venepunctures or other procedures associated with some discomfort. It is reasonable that volunteers in this type of research should be paid, over and above reimbursement of expenses incurred. These payments are for inconvenience or discomfort and increased payments may be reasonable for procedures requiring extra care on the part of the subject or involving more discomfort.

Payments should never be for undergoing risk

Payments should not be such as to persuade people to volunteer against their better judgment, nor to induce them to volunteer more frequently than is advisable for their own good. While appreciating that any given sum would be viewed differently by a student or person who is unemployed than by a person in full paid employment, we suggest that payment should range somewhere between rates equivalent to current student grants and a daily rate equivalent to the average wage, but time involved and inconvenience incurred should be taken into consideration. All payments to volunteers should be approved by the ethics committee.

The next requirement, once again, is that the research subject be properly informed of the risks attendant upon participating in the research. Clearly, therapeutic privilege can have no part to play in research on healthy volunteers. In the Canadian case of *Halushka v University of Saskatchewan* (1965) 52 WWR 608 it was stated:

> **Hall JA**: The example of risks being properly hidden from a patient when it is important that he should not worry can have no application in the field of research. The subject of medical experimentation is entitled to a full and frank disclosure of all the facts, probabilities and opinions which a reasonable man might be expected to consider before giving his consent.

To what extent would the English courts similarly distinguish non-therapeutic from therapeutic research in this context? In the post-*Sidaway* case of *Gold v Haringey HA* [1987] 2 All ER 888, the Court of Appeal held that disclosure, in the context of non-therapeutic *treatment*, was just as much governed by the *Bolam* test as advice given in the course of therapy. However, it is probable that this question is of theoretical interest only since, as noted earlier in our discussion of therapeutic research, the *Bolam* test itself would surely impose the duty to obtain fully informed consent upon the researcher (all guidance, including the Declaration of Helsinki, is unanimously to this effect).

The incompetent volunteer

The expression 'incompetent volunteer' is, of course, a contradiction in terms. If the person is incompetent, then, by definition, he is unable to volunteer. However, others may 'volunteer' on his behalf, and this undoubtedly generates some of the most contentious ethical and legal issues in medical research. Indeed it may be felt that there is an argument for prohibiting any form of non-therapeutic research on those who lack the capacity to consent.

Children

It is generally thought ethically acceptable, in certain circumstances, to carry out non-therapeutic research upon children. That is certainly the view taken by such bodies as the Royal College of Paediatricians and the Royal College of Physicians, whose guidelines offer very similar advice here to that covering therapeutic research on patients. In the case of mature minors, there is an assumption that *Gillick* competence will apply. (Clearly, s 8 of the Family Law Reform Act 1969 will not apply to 16 and 17 year olds in this context: see above, p 54.) However, should children really be able to consent at all to non-therapeutic measures on *Gillick* principles? It is suggested here that the answer is 'yes', at least where the risks involved are negligible or minimal. After all, mature minors are capable of giving consent to major medical interventions, such as surgery, which may require them to comprehend and balance much higher risks.

Interesting issues arise when the child is incapable of consenting, and the parent consents on the child's behalf. Robert Redmon tackles arguments which state that children in such research are being used merely as 'ends' and sees participation as part of the child's wider development as a moral being, even though the research is not for the benefit of the child's immediate health:

Redmon, R, 'How children can be respected as "ends" yet still be used as subjects in non-therapeutic research' (1986) 12 JME 77:

If the child is old enough, she may enjoy seeing how this aspect of science functions, and her participation may aid her education. Also, this participation can be seen as part of her moral education. We certainly encourage our children to perform acts of benevolence when there is little chance of harm (walking down the road to take an invalid some food), and if the purposes of the research are *understood* well enough by the child, her participation might be viewed in the same way.

But if a child is an infant and too young to assent, much less consent, to such an experiment, then none of these benefits are possible. And, more importantly, what is required is a Kantian solution to this problem. Otherwise, the weighing of benefits can lead very easily to the misuse of the child.

However, these particular benefits – scientific and moral education – are of a different nature from most others (money, health, prestige, etc). To aid in the development of intellectual and, especially, moral abilities (or sensitivities) is to aid in the development of the individual's autonomy. For Kant, a person was only free when she was doing the morally praiseworthy thing (acting from 'a good will'). A development of a 'good will' (notwithstanding Kant's view that such a will is 'non-empirical' and thus, in some sense, innate) is a step towards being an ultimate 'end'.

Citing a piece by Hans Jonas, 'Philosophical reflections on experimenting with human subjects' (1969) Daedalus (Spring) 219, Redmon favours the approach whereby, if the goals of the subject are the same as the researcher, then the subject is not being merely used. This he refers to as an 'identification of interests':

Redmon, R, 'How children can be respected as "ends" yet still be used as subjects in non-therapeutic research' (1986) 12 JME 77:

Thus in allowing such experiments with 'minimal risk' (no more risk than can be expected in the normal, protective environment of a child), we are wagering that the child will 'identify' and approve of such experiments. This 'hypothetical consent' cannot be judged on the 'reasonable person' hypothesis since, as has been shown, it is difficult to predict how altruistic the 'reasonable person' would be in a moral situation. It does make sense, however, to ask how a person with a particular moral outlook, particular values, virtues and vices, would act. Thus the prediction of how the child will later view his participation must be made by those in the child's family, in particular by his parents. Their consent should be based upon their own values and the expectation that the child will share, to some extent, in them. They might reasonably expect, for example, that their child may later, as an adult, have an interest in the welfare of children whom the research may benefit. Their child will probably be a parent himself. They should also, as the National Commission for the Protection of Human Subjects recommended, be present during all stages of the research, and be involved in it as much as possible. This will help confirm their judgment that their child will later 'identify' with the research project.

My 'Kantian deliberations' thus lead to a tentative conclusion: if we can reasonably expect this child to 'identify' (in Jonas' sense) with the goals of the research when she is an adult, and that the identification will be strong enough to outweigh the harm of the knowledge of being used by her parents, and if the child (if old enough) assents, and if the possibility of harm is slight ('minimal risk'), then such research is permissible.

Could it be argued, in the light of this (and echoing the approach taken in the case of *S v S* [1970] 3 All ER 107), that parental consent to enter their child into non-therapeutic research involving minimal risk is not contrary to the child's best interests? In the US case of *Curran v Bosze* 566 NE 2d 1319 (1990), it was suggested that 'individual altruism in an abstract theoretical sense' was an insufficient basis for regarding a non-therapeutic procedure as in a child's best interests (see below, Chapter 11). Significantly, in that case, however, the children's mother opposed the procedure in issue.

For their part, both the British Paediatric Association, in its 1992 Guidelines, *The Ethical Conduct of Research Involving Children*, and the Medical Research Council in similarly titled guidance from 1991, suggest that non-therapeutic research on young, incompetent children is permissible with parental consent, provided that this is the only means of procuring the knowledge in question, and that the child is exposed to no more than minimal risk.

Adults

It is arguable that non-therapeutic research on the incompetent adult is always wrong, both morally, and in law, as it constitutes a battery. (Contrast the position of children, where at least a parent may (and must) consent on their behalf.) At the very least, additional safeguards will be necessary. The Law Commission in its report, *Mental Incapacity*, comments as follows:

Law Commission, *Mental Incapacity*, Report No 231, 1995, London: HMSO:

6.29 'Non-therapeutic' research ... does not claim to offer any direct or immediate benefit to the participant. Such procedures may well be scientifically and ethically acceptable to those who are qualified to decide such matters. If, however, the participant lacks capacity to consent to his or her participation, and the procedure cannot be justified under the doctrine of necessity, then any person who touches or restrains that participant is committing an unlawful battery. The simple fact is that the researcher is making no claim to be acting in the best interests of that individual person and does not therefore come within the rules of law set out in *Re F*. It was made abundantly clear to us on consultation, however, that non-therapeutic research projects of this nature are regularly taking place. We were told of a research project into the organic manifestations of Alzheimer's disease which involves the administration of radioactive isotopes to sufferers, followed by extensive testing of blood and bodily functions. Another project was said to involve the examination of written patients' records, although they are unable to consent to this examination. In some cases relatives are asked to 'consent' to what is proposed, and do so. It appears that some funding bodies and ethics committees stipulate for consent by a relative where the research participant cannot consent. As a matter of law, such 'consent' is meaningless. It appears that the question of the legality of non-therapeutic research procedures is regularly misunderstood or ignored by those who design, fund and approve the projects.

6.30 A number of our respondents expressed concern about non-invasive research based on observations, photography or videoing of participants (sometimes covertly). We accept that questions of dignity and privacy arise in such situations where the project is not designed to benefit the research participant.

6.31 We suggested in our consultation paper that the balance of expert opinion favours the participation of people unable to consent in even non-therapeutic research projects, subject to strict criteria. The majority of our consultees argued that there is an ethical case for such participation. This case turns on the desirability of eradicating painful and distressing disabilities, where progress can be achieved without harming research subjects ...

We recommend that research which is unlikely to benefit a participant, or whose benefit is likely to be long delayed, should be lawful in relation to a person without capacity to consent if (1) the research is into an incapacitating condition with which the participant is or may be affected and (2) certain statutory procedures are complied with. (Draft Bill, cl 11(1).)

The Commission, therefore, takes the view that one of the essential conditions of non-therapeutic research taking place on an incompetent person is that the person suffers from the condition which the research is seeking to alleviate. Clearly the effect of this will be significantly to restrict the amount of research which can be carried out on incompetent persons. Further, the Commission recommends the establishment of a Mental Incapacity Research Committee, so that a non-therapeutic research procedure would only be lawful in relation to a person who lacks capacity if such a committee has approved it.

Currently, as the Law Commission's report notes, non-therapeutic research on incompetent patients does occur and, indeed, the Medical Research Council's guidelines, *The Ethical Conduct of Research on the Mentally Incapacitated*, 1991, in this respect mirror its Guidance on incompetent minors: such research may be carried out provided the hoped-for knowledge is unprocurable by other means and risk to the subject is no more than minimal. However, whilst this position may appear plausible in ethical terms, its juridical basis remains obscure. In particular, how is such research to satisfy the 'best interests' requirement laid down in *Re F*? Admittedly, the courts have been prepared to construe best interests quite widely in recent cases (see especially the discussion of *Re Y* (1996) BMLR 111 below, Chapter 11), but only to the extent that some form of benefit can be shown to accrue directly to the individual concerned.

THE REGULATION OF RESEARCH IN THE UK

As will have become apparent by now, although there are a number of guidelines which are likely to have persuasive legal authority, there is no statutory regulation of the way in which clinical trials are conducted in this country. (The testing of new pharmaceutical products, which forms a partial exception to this, is looked at separately below, p 556.) Protection of research subjects (and the circumstances in which they may pursue a claim for damages as a result of their participation in a clinical trial) is therefore governed by the common law. We have already seen that consent forms the cornerstone of such protection, and that, not only is it of dubious value on occasion (recall, for example, the case of Mrs Moffit (see above, p 546)) but it fails to allow for the practice of research upon incompetent patients.

In this section we consider how the bare requirement of the research subject's consent is bolstered, both at common law itself, and more particularly by the regime of quasi-statutory guidance already referred to.

Common law

Contract

There are two contractual relations that are relevant to medical research. First, there is the contract between the research subject and the researcher, and secondly, the contract between the sponsor of the research (usually a drug manufacturer), and the researcher, or investigator. Ian Dodds-Smith comments as follows:

> **Dodds-Smith, I, 'Clinical Research', in Dyer, C (ed), *Doctors, Patients and the Law*, 1992, Oxford: Blackwell Science, p 146:**
>
> **The sponsor's obligations to the investigator**
>
> The contract between the sponsor/manufacturer and the investigator will govern the legal relationship between them. Ideally, to avoid uncertainty and possible unnecessary dispute, the agreement should be in writing and clearly expressed. There is no model format for such contracts – they may be and often are contained in a letter. The overriding concern, however, is that they should be unambiguous and contain all the crucial details relating to the protocol to be adopted, information to be made available about the test product, reporting of adverse drug reactions, the duration of the study, the

maintenance of patient confidentiality, the publication of results, liability for injury to subjects and the fee for the study. Under English law, certain conditions are implied additionally into any contract for services. These include that the service will be performed with reasonable care and skill and in a reasonable period. There are also rules under statute which may restrict the ability of the parties to exclude their liability for damages for personal injury caused by negligence.

The sponsor's obligations to the research subject

Contract

The Declaration of Helsinki does not address the matter of how the subject/sponsor relationship might be structured or recorded. In general, the sponsor and a patient subject do not enter into a direct contractual arrangement. However, where studies are to be conducted upon healthy volunteers, a form of contract may and usually will exist. In 1970 the Association of the British Pharmaceutical Industry (ABPI) published a report to which a simple form of written contract was appended. In 1986 the Royal College of Physicians issued a report on healthy volunteer studies in which it advocated the use of a 'simple form of contract' mainly to ensure that the subject would be compensated for any injury occurring during a trial. In the appendix to the report the college provided a checklist of matters which should be considered when drawing up such a contract. In 1988, the ABPI published revised Guidelines for medical experiments in non-patient human volunteers which contained both a model patient information form and draft provisions for a volunteer agreement and consent form and stated that all volunteers 'must sign a simple form of agreement' (recording the basis upon which they agreed to participate and dealing with four other basic matters) with the sponsor or outside research establishment (depending upon who had the responsibility for recruitment and supervision).

As Dodds-Smith states, in relation to the contract between sponsor and investigator, certain terms are implied into the contract. These terms will also apply to any contract between sponsor and research subject. Although when the patient is receiving NHS treatment, there will not be a contract, a contractual situation must arise, within the NHS as well as elsewhere, in the case of healthy volunteers (in the context of non-therapeutic research), as they are not being treated pursuant to a statutory obligation. Clearly, the Unfair Contract Terms Act 1977 would prevent any such contract excluding liability for damages for negligently caused personal injury, and there would be an implied term that the research would be carried out with reasonable skill and care.

Although, for the purposes of the research subject bringing an action for injuries suffered, the contents of the contract may well be important, in the context of the research subject failing to participate, or withdrawing part way through the research, would a court enforce such a contract? The answer must surely be that it is unenforceable from the point of view of the researcher. Damages would be unquantifiable, and an order for specific performance repugnant.

Tort

The torts of battery and negligence will apply to those who participate in medical research. These have already been considered in relation to consent, and will be looked at again, in the context of recovering compensation for injuries, below, p 568.

Criminal law

It is important to recall (see above, Chapter 3) that battery is a crime as well as a tort, and that statutory criminal offences may apply in the appropriate circumstances. Whilst, in the normal course of medical research, the criminal law would be unlikely to be invoked, note the US case of *Hyman v Jewish Chronic Disease Hospital* 251 NYS 2d 818 (1964), where doctors injected live cancer cells into 22 patients, not only without their consent, but by leading them to believe that the injections were part of their normal treatment. The Medical Association Review Board found the doctors guilty of fraudulent and deceitful conduct, but no criminal proceedings were taken. There is some precedent in English law in the case of *R v Burdee* (1916) 25 Cox 598, where a doctor who had prescribed cold water foot baths and a three day fast for a sick patient who subsequently died, was convicted of manslaughter. (As has previously been noted, however, something which is experimentation at best, and quackery at worst, is not research in the accepted sense of the term.)

Statutory provisions in relation to drugs testing

One area in which, exceptionally, there is a certain amount of statutory regulation is where research involves the administration of new drugs. Ian Dodds-Smith summarises the position as follows:

Dodds-Smith, I, 'Clinical Research', in Dyer, C (ed), *Doctors, Patients and the Law*, 1992, Oxford: Blackwell Science, p 144:

Regulatory approval

While there is no specific legislation regulating how a clinical trial in the UK must be conducted, there is provision for notification or approval by the licensing authority (the UK Health Ministers and Agriculture Ministers) of clinical trials prior to their commencement. This is done through the Medicines Control Agency.

Phase II and Phase III trials and pharmaceutical companies

Under the terms of the Medicines Act 1968 a supplier of an unlicensed medicinal product intended to be used in a trial in the UK involving patients must (unless he is already the holder of a product licence which authorises the trial) first apply for a clinical trial certificate – a CTC. A CTC (effective for two years but renewable) may be granted only after detailed pharmaceutical and toxicological data regarding the drug in question have been provided and assessed by the licensing authority (often with advice from an expert advisory committee) as not likely to involve serious risk to trial subjects. This can be a rigorous and lengthy procedure. Fortunately since the passing of an order in 1981 it has not been necessary in every case to apply for a CTC. The order introduced a scheme under which suppliers may be exempted from the need to hold a CTC for a new product for three years, provided certain undertakings are given and the licensing authority finds no objection. This is a form of negative clearance involving no assessment of the data and cannot be taken therefore as an indication of positive approval or that the licensing authority considers the proposed trial safe.

Doctors and dentists

Doctors and dentists conducting their own trials are exempt in some circumstances from the requirements to hold licences and certificates. Where a clinical trial in patients is to be initiated and conducted by a doctor or dentist other than under arrangements made by or with the manufacturer or supplier, there is no requirement for a CTC provided that certain conditions are met. This exemption is generally referred to as the 'DDX' provision. In order to qualify the doctor or dentist must show:

(i)   that the seller or supplier of the product is selling or supplying it exclusively for the purposes of the trial, or if not, in so far as it is also sold or supplied for other purposes, these are covered by a product licence or certificate or under an exemption;

(ii) that the clinical trial is not to be carried out under arrangements made by or on behalf of the product's manufacturer, seller, supplier or the person responsible for its composition;

(iii) that the doctor or dentist has notified the licensing authority of the trial, specifying the product, its use and the supplier's details.

In such cases the company supplier or seller is not required to have a product licence or a CTC.

The order means, for example, that if a doctor wishes to carry out trials on a drug which is licensed for certain indications but the trial is designed to investigate the use of the product in different indications, he would need to apply for a DDX. The manufacturer of the product would be supplying the doctor for the purposes of the trial. However, the manufacturer may also be supplying quantities of the drug to the same practitioner for use in its licensed indications, in which case those supplies must be covered by a product licence or an exemption provided by the Act ...

It is not unusual for new drugs to be the subject of trials after licensing (Phase IV). A requirement for some form of subsequent monitoring of a newly licensed drug can often be made a term of the product licence. If a doctor is carrying out his own study with a licensed product and the study involves using the product for the indications for which it is licensed, the trial needs no regulatory approval provided that notification has been given to the licensing authority and proper arrangements made for reporting adverse reactions. This provision would cover trials instigated by doctors whether within general practice or working within hospitals or clinics.

Note the emphasis on patients here: the 1968 Act does not apply to healthy volunteers (see s 130(4)).

Although it is arguable that the statutory regulation in the UK (both here and, in relation to research generally) is lamentably inadequate, there is a converse argument which states that medical researchers should carry out their work with as little State intervention as possible, as unfettered research is the best research. Harvey Teff reviews the arguments:

Teff, H, 'Regulation under the Medicines Act 1968: a continuing prescription for health' (1984) 47 MLR 303:

In essence the free market argument runs as follows. As long as consumers are provided with adequate information about products and can obtain compensation when they have been wrongfully injured, mandatory controls are not needed to deter manufacturers from producing unsafe drugs. Market forces provide ample incentives – in the form of competition, concern for reputation and the fear of costly litigation on top of huge initial expenditure. Any benefits to be derived from controls are outweighed by the negative features of a governmentally imposed regulatory structure.

In the first place there is the danger of excessive bureaucracy. Regulators, intent on maximising budgets and extending their jurisdiction, begin to perceive regulation as an end in itself and to measure 'success' by the sheer extent to which the activity in question is regulated. The form of control is given primacy over substantive achievements in ensuring the welfare of consumers ... Once the bureaucratic agency has been established, human nature dictates a substantial element of self-interest in how it operates. Hence the regulator tends to be unduly risk averse. In the context of pharmaceuticals, he has little or nothing to lose by refusing, or at least delaying, the grant of a licence; everything to lose if he approves a Thalidomide. Thus where guidelines are bound to be arbitrary to some extent – how many species of animals should be tested, over what period of time, for what risks – the regulator is prone to err on the side of caution, to indulge in a kind of 'defensive licensing' ...

But there are also indirect costs of regulation which are said to have helped undermine innovation and demoralise the domestic industry, namely the increasing use of foreign locations for testing purposes and reluctance to risk expenditure on potentially valuable, innovative drugs which might fail to meet evaluation requirements. 'Close copy' products abound, and it is claimed that useful drugs that could reduce morbidity and mortality have either been prevented from reaching the market, or so long delayed that lives have been unnecessarily lost and many patients forced to endure needless suffering. When confronted with the criticism that their resources are excessively concentrated on marginal, but lucrative, variants of established drugs for a limited range of illnesses, the pharmaceutical companies routinely cite the costs of regulation as a justification. Lack of innovation is portrayed as an unfortunate by-product of stringent controls, not simply as reflecting conscious commercial choice.

Such unlooked-for consequences would be more tolerable if regulation did significantly improve safety. Its opponents claim, however, that it merely fosters exaggerated expectations and creates an illusion of safety in the minds of the public. Useful drugs often have adverse side effects and can never be fully tested before they are marketed, since serious, rare side effects may not come to light until a drug has been used by a far greater proportion of the population than is feasible at the pre-marketing stage ...

In short, the argument against existing drug approval arrangements is that a combination of excessive cost and delay both outweighs any presumed increase in patient welfare and undermines the innovation, productivity, and hence competitiveness on the world market of a research-intensive industry which is a major contributor to the UK economy. On this view, the requirements of the 1968 Medicines Act, and the spirit in which it has been operated, are ultimately contrary to the interests of both patients and the community at large.

The benefits of regulation

It ought not to be assumed that the pharmaceutical industry is implacably opposed to the existence of mandatory controls. Far from it: one of the more interesting findings of the Hartley and Maynard survey was that despite considerable dissatisfaction with the workings of the 1968 Act, none of the respondents, all major manufacturers, were in favour of its abolition. The primary explanation put forward by the authors is the continuing need to comply with foreign regulatory requirements for overseas sales. A further important consideration is the effect of statutory regulation in providing substantial protection against competition from smaller firms, while at the same time enabling established ones to reap the benefits of compliance with an independent external standard. All the larger firms now operate as multinationals and relatively few concerns are in a position to be truly innovative. Of the 83 major manufacturers in the United Kingdom industry, 37 are American owned, 31 European owned, and only 15 British. How far the community's interests are in fact served by an oligopoly which dictates the pattern of pharmaceutical innovation and can exert a measure of influence on government policy is open to question. At the very least it raises doubts as to the applicability of the free market model, just as mounting evidence of questionable commercial practices especially, but by no means exclusively, in the Third World, points to the dangers of under-regulation in this uniquely structured industry.

Several of these dangers were revealed in a most telling fashion in the development and marketing in Germany of Thalidomide in the mid 1950s. Hastily conducted research and unsystematic clinical trials, mainly carried out by doctors who had continuing commercial dealings with the company, were followed by sweeping assertions of non-toxicity, which were repeated in the promotional literature of distributors in other countries, such as Distillers in the United Kingdom. Even accepting that the methods of Chemie Grunenthal, the German manufacturers, were not representative of the industry as a whole, many countries drew the moral that health is too serious a matter to be left entirely to pharmaceutical companies. And this conclusion can be seen as a major justification for a regulatory approach. For Thalidomide was an extreme illustration of risks inherent in unregulated drug production – a company inexperienced in drug manufacture, conceiving it to be a commercial imperative both to market with a minimum of delay and to resist withdrawal until overwhelming evidence of injury has emerged, in order to recoup a large initial outlay and reap early profits.

The strength of the case for mandatory controls does not however rest solely on the need to discourage a few irresponsible firms, nor even on the value of having an independent body to scrutinise procedures and identify defects in manufacturing processes and in research and development generally, important though all these functions undoubtedly are. The case derives much of its force from the peculiarity of drugs as products and the unusual nature of the prescription drugs market.

The free enterprise model is most convincing when applied to commodities whose defects are readily apparent to consumers with access to relevant information, strongly conscious of the costs of a 'bad buy' and able to obtain compensation when things go wrong. In the case of prescription drugs, market behaviour is not so readily influenced. The effective 'consumer' is a doctor who, in practice, is often in no position to obtain all the relevant information about products whose defects may not be easily detectable. He is also to a large extent insulated from considerations of cost. Furthermore, compensation is notoriously difficult to obtain in cases of alleged drug-induced injury.

The position of the doctor as dispenser of information merits close attention, since the case for relaxing pre-market controls is intimately bound up with the amount of trust we can confidently repose in him. In crude terms, whom should we trust more, the doctor or the regulator? The evidence on prescribing habits does not augur well for moves towards a freer market. Many doctors are inadequately informed about prescribing. Medical education has traditionally included very little clinical pharmacology, and the problem has been accentuated by the proliferation of new – and not so new – drugs in the last 20 years or so. Busy practitioners have too often succumbed to patients' demands for antibiotics to treat relatively trivial viral infections, to the practice of signing repeat prescription forms filled in by a receptionist without seeing the patient.

Quasi-statutory guidance

A number of bodies have issued guidelines, not only for researchers, but also for local research ethics committees, which amount to what is often described as 'soft law', inasmuch as, in litigation, departure from such guidance may provide strong evidence of malpractice.

We have already encountered some of this guidance. Other examples include Royal College of Physicians, *Guidelines on the Practice of Ethics*

Committees in Research Involving Human Subjects, 2nd edn, 1989, London: RCP; the European Commission, *Guidelines for Good Clinical Practice for Trials on Medicinal Products in the European Community*, Committee for Proprietary Medicinal Products III/3976/88-EN; and Association of the British Pharmaceutical Industry, *Guidelines for Medical Experiments in Non-Patient Human Volunteers*, 1988, London: ABPI.

Local Research Ethics Committees

As we saw above, p 531, the Declaration of Helsinki states as one of its basic principles that the design and performance of all research trials should be subject to scrutiny by 'a specially appointed committee independent of the researcher and sponsor' (para I(2)). The Royal College of Physicians made recommendations to the same effect in both 1967 and 1973, and in 1975 the Department of Health issued instructions to health authorities to implement them. The current NHS guidelines were formulated in 1991.

The guidance deals with the composition of an LREC as follows:

Department of Health, *Guidelines on LRECs*, 1991, London: DoH:

2.4 An LREC should have eight to 12 members. This should allow for a sufficiently broad range of experience and expertise, so that the scientific and medical aspects of a research proposal can be reconciled with the welfare of research subjects, and broader ethical implications.

2.5 Members should be drawn from both sexes and from a wide range of age groups. They should include:

- hospital medical staff
- nursing staff
- general practitioners
- two or more lay persons

2.6 Despite being drawn from groups identified with particular interests or responsibilities in connection with health issues, LREC members are not in any way the representatives of those groups. They are appointed in their own right, to participate in the work of the LREC as individuals of sound judgment and relevant experience.

However, the lack of the relevant experience was highlighted in a review of the role of LRECs carried out in 1992:

Neuberger, J, *Ethics and Health Care: The Role of Research Ethics Committees in the United Kingdom*, 1992, London: King's Fund Institute (the Neuberger Report), p 28:

Vetting the research

The DoH guidelines say that the [L]REC will need to know whether the scientific merit of a proposal has been properly assessed. It is not clear whether this should extend to the REC satisfying itself that the research is well designed. Several of the RECs visited regarded it as part of their function to examine the protocol design, claiming that 'bad research is unethical research'. They have to assess whether the expected benefits from the research are likely to justify the demands made on the human subjects. It is debatable whether they can do this without making, some assessment of the research itself. The issue becomes particularly acute when the applicant may be motivated by other concerns than the advancement of medical knowledge, for example where he is receiving substantial funds for carrying out the research, or is carrying it out as part of his training.

Against this it can be argued that the RECs do not have the skills or expertise to make such an assessment. They may also reflect their own personal biases; a case in point is nursing research. Much nursing research concerns patients' attitudes and views rather than the objective evaluation of different treatments. Some RECs view such research very positively, while others feel it is non-scientific, as well as unduly intrusive for patients, and should not be permitted.

Scientific assessment of research

There was no objective definition of 'scientific' and 'non-scientific' research. The tendency was for any research involving the use of questionnaires, and submitted by whatever discipline, to be regarded as 'non-scientific'. Those RECs which were largely medically dominated thus tended to class as 'non-scientific' a great deal of research that was submitted by nurses, psychologists, medical students and psychiatrists. Discussion often focused on the delivery of 'soft data' and on the poor design of questionnaires. It was clear that those who took that view thought the research methods used by other disciplines were inadequate and that the data were not to be trusted. It was therefore remarkable to see other RECs welcome non-medical research, and, in two cases, discuss ways of encouraging more qualitative research on the effects of certain treatments on patients.

One possible solution to the unsatisfactory nature of debate about the quality of the research is to ensure a wider spread of interest on the committee, as the DoH and RCP guidelines both suggest. For the technically complex scientific and medical research there is also an argument for a separate research methods committee, as exists in many US institutions and is under active discussion at a few UK institutions as well, to ensure that the research is vetted properly for its scientific validity before the REC sees it. Alternatively, members could be co-opted to the REC as necessity arose to discuss the complex issues, though lengthy technical discussion of very specialist issues might be difficult for lay and other non-specialist members. The solution followed by each REC and DHS might depend on the quantity of such complex and technical research that takes place in the institution. It is, however, clear that a confusion of roles exists, so that the RECs often act as both research and research ethics committees, often beyond their capabilities.

It can be questioned as to exactly what sort of experience is required of an LREC member, as it raises the question of the very function of the committee. The Department of Health guidance states baldly that the purpose of the committee is 'to consider the ethics of proposed research projects within the NHS'. Matters that they should have regard to, as a minimum, in doing so are as follows:

(a) Has the scientific merit of the proposal been properly assessed?

(b) How will the health of the research subjects be affected?

(c) Are there possible hazards and, if so, adequate facilities to deal with them?

(d) What degree of discomfort or distress is foreseen?

(e) Is the investigation adequately supervised and is the supervisor responsible for the project adequately qualified and experienced?

(f) What monetary or other inducements are being offered to the NHS body, doctors, researchers, subjects or anyone else involved?

(g) Are there proper procedures for obtaining consent from the subjects or, where necessary, their parents or guardians?

(h) Has an appropriate information sheet for subjects been prepared?

(i) Do procedures exist for monitoring the research as it progresses?

(j) Are there any arrangements for *ex gratia* compensation to be paid in case of injury?

However, as suggested in the Neuberger Report, there is argument that the scientific and ethical aspects of a committee's work should be separated. Paul McNeill surveys the issues in the following extract:

McNeill, PM, *The Ethics and Politics of Human Experimentation*, 1993, Cambridge: Press Syndicate of the University of Cambridge, pp 185–87:

Research ethics committees fall between the interdisciplinary professional review model and the jury model in that they are composed of some members who are there because of their expertise and other members who are there as representatives of the community without special expertise. For Veatch, this mixture represented a conflict in the premises underlying these committees.

... Originally, committees were 'peer review' panels rather than interdisciplinary committees in that most of the members were medically trained or were biomedical researchers. In most countries the membership of peer review panels has been expanded to include members of other professions (notably lawyers and the clergy) and, in some cases, members of the community. It is in this broadening of the membership of committees to include both those with professional expertise and those who are representative of the community that Veatch identified a basic schism in the committee structure. In his view, this split reflects the lack of any clear rationale 'of what these committees are supposed to be able to do, of what purposes they are to serve, [and] of what skills their members ought to have'. He considered that there was a need for a theory to clarify the ambiguities and for structural changes to be made to committees to make them consistent with that theory. Without these changes he believed it would be impossible for research ethics committees to fulfil their task successfully, although he acknowledged that subjects were better protected by committees, even as presently constituted, than by reliance on a researcher's judgment alone.

In my view, the schism described by Veatch is still apparent in committees all over the world. Interviews with members of committees in Australia and the United States have indicated that it is not clear to members whether their committee should function as a panel of experts (as in the interdisciplinary professional review model) or as committees expressing a community morality on the desirability of particular research projects (as in a jury model). In the main, committees appear to function as panels of experts with some small input from the lay members. The only countries to give equal representation to lay and professional members are New Zealand and Denmark ...

Our study of Australian committees and a study in the United States ... together show that the medical and research members participate more actively on committees and are generally regarded by all members of committees as more important in the decision making process. The non-medical and non-professional members become marginal in a number of ways. The use of language and technical terms which presume medical (and other technical) knowledge is one of the factors edging them to the margins (Glantz, 1984). Lay members may feel comfortable in offering an opinion on matters within their comprehension (such as the understandability of the consent form) but seldom speak on other issues. I suggest that this is one of the reasons why invasive, high risk research may be passed without question while relatively harmless research may consume a great deal of the committee's time and be disapproved by a committee (Shannon and Ockene, 1985). For example, many committees spend time on the wording of questionnaires (which have relatively low risks of harm) and relatively little time on technical protocols that are difficult to understand by members without the relevant expertise. Yet the technical and difficult studies are more likely to involve invasive procedures or drug research which have a higher risk of harm ...

Veatch considered that a 'dominance of the committee by scientific professionals' would produce a risk shift in the direction of the researchers' values – normally in favour of research'. 'Risk shift' is based on the observation that groups make riskier decisions than individuals (Douglas, 1985). The presence of community members is not likely to overcome the shift toward accepting risky proposals – at best it can dilute it. Veatch goes further in suggesting that 'even a feisty member of a minority will find it extremely difficult to withstand the psychological pressure to co-operate in forming a consensus'. He argued that as long as one researcher was on the committee it would still be influenced in the direction of research values compared with a committee composed on a 'jury model' ...

Veatch's solution to the conflict between the 'professional review model' and the 'jury model' was to have two committees. One of these would be composed entirely of professional members and would consider the acceptability of research proposals on the basis of scientific and professional criteria. The other committee would be composed entirely of community representatives who would consider the acceptability of research proposals in terms of community morality ...

McNeill sets out the different experiences of lay members, and health care workers other than doctors:

McNeill, PM, *The Ethics and Politics of Human Experimentation*, 1993, Cambridge: Press Syndicate of the University of Cambridge, pp 93–94

Table 4.2   Typical quotes from interviews with committee members about their perception of their performance:

Lay person

Initially I found it very hard in the meetings. Being a lay person, you sit there and think all these other people know so much more than me about the protocols: the lawyers, and the ministers, and the doctors are from high up in medical things. But then you realise that you have to put your two cents worth in when it's there because they often forget how the little people feel ... The main problem in the meetings is thinking how to say what I want to say and make it sound important. Really, the best way is to say what you feel, but it often appears unimportant compared to the other issues.

Minister of religion

My role in the committee meetings is from the back seat. I would only speak if I had problems after the science and drug aspects were explained. The discussion is largely up to the medical people ... There have been protocols where I seriously questioned the infringement on patients, but I've never opposed them on these grounds. I've always been convinced by the medical argument that the research had to be done.

Lawyer

There's six medical type people as against myself, a minister of religion, a lay man and a lay woman. And then you find the lay man and the lay woman more often than not are intimidated by the doctors, so they won't disagree with them because there's not the knowledge, there's not the confidence in having a view ... to stand up to them. And without the confidence I suppose that you have from being a fellow professional ... it's a bit terrifying for them. I have the confidence to express my views, but the other people just sit there and say nothing.

Medical graduate

The routine protocol that has no problems about it, is presented, usually by a medical man, and the others understand it, and we all come to a very quick decision and there's no problem. When there's a problem, where ethical issues as opposed to scientific issues are at stake, then the other people come into it.

Administrator

The number one thing that concerns me is that they [research proposals] are properly presented, because many of our committee now don't have medical training and they don't necessarily have scientific training ... My prime concern is to get a protocol to the committee in a form in which it can be understood by almost everyone present. The second thing is to get it through and to see that there are no obvious gaps.

Nurse

The nurse is a subservient role, she's still calling all the doctors 'Doctor'. So even though she might be quite active it's never going to be an active that actually challenges what is going on.

A lawyer's comment about the nurse

The nurse is very much subservient to the specialist doctors in the hospital. And it's difficult to change that. Always I feel that it was a conditioned response on the nurse's part that one didn't challenge, or shouldn't challenge, the specialist view, which for medical things is fair enough but these were not necessarily just medical things. So, the area in which she was conditioned to do what she was told tended to spill over into the non-medical and ethical issues.

The lack of training of members was highlighted in the Neuberger Report, and, perhaps in a belated response to this, the Department of Health have issued a briefing pack for research ethics committee members, although it is stated that it is aimed mainly at new and prospective members of research ethics committees. The first part considers general ethical issues, and the second leads the reader through eight different types of research, such as epidemiological studies and psychological research. Whether provision will be made for the ongoing training of members remains to be seen.

The Neuberger Report also concluded that an LREC did not have sufficient power to impose sanctions on those researchers who ignored their advice:

Neuberger, J, *Ethics and Health Care: The Role of Research Ethics Committees in the United Kingdom*, 1992, London: King's Fund Institute, p 34:

Enforcement and sanctions

RECs do not have adequate sanctions against those who ignore their advice. In some DHAs, it would be a disciplinary offence to conduct research on human subjects without getting ethical approval first. But that would by no means be the majority ...

... If the committee has no teeth, however hard it works, however carefully it comes to its decisions, it cannot fulfil its alleged task of protecting the public. It can perform a variety of valuable tasks. It can educate the medical and nursing and other health care staff about how to submit a research proposal. It can teach people how to consider the issues which might raise ethical doubts. It can chew over various issues beyond strict research, but have no locus in the decision making. It can discuss the issues relating to IVF and to surrogacy. It can question the value of various trials and procedures. But it cannot enforce its decisions.

It must be noted that there is no strict legal obligation upon researchers to put research proposals before an LREC, although certainly as far as NHS patients are concerned, the 1991 Guidelines state as follows:

Department of Health, *Guidelines on LRECs,* **1991, London: DoH:**

1.3 An LREC must be consulted about any research proposal involving:

- NHS patients (ie, subjects recruited by virtue of their past or present treatment by the NHS) including those treated under contracts with private sector providers;
- foetal material and IVF involving NHS patients;
- the recently dead, in NHS premises;
- access to the records of past or present NHS patients;
- the use of, or potential access to, NHS premises or facilities.

What would be the legal consequences of a breach of the above guidelines? Certainly, any researcher employed by the NHS who was in breach would be liable to dismissal or other form of discipline, but would a patient or healthy volunteer have any right of redress? It is likely that the breach would be akin to a breach of statutory duty, in the sense that it would not necessarily give rise to a private law right in itself. However, if the patient suffered injury, then failure to obtain LREC approval might point towards negligence, although the problem of causation would remain. Another problem, highlighted by the case involving Mrs Moffit (see above, p 546), arises where, though initially obtaining approval in the proper way, a researcher fails to keep the Committee apprised of changes in the execution of a project.

So far as research outside the NHS is concerned, the Guidelines state:

1.6 By agreement an LREC may also advise on the ethics of studies not involving NHS patients, records or premises, carried out for example by private sector companies, the Medical Research Council or universities.

However, even if the private sector can, in theory, ignore LRECs, in practice, because of the effect upon insurance and legal liability generally (not to mention publication), researchers will want to obtain approval of their projects (see Institute of Medical Ethics Bulletin, 1986).

Multi-centre trials

There has been concern about consistency of approach when the same research protocol comes before a number of different LRECs (see, for example, Neuberger). In consequence, the Department of Health are to set up a system of multi-centre research ethics committees (MRECs), one in each of the English regions and one each in Wales, Scotland and Northern Ireland. The Department of Health paper of 1997 (Ethics Committee, *Review of Multi-Centre Research*) states as follows:

Ethics Committee, *Review of Multi-Centre Research,* **1997, London: DoH:**

5 Each multi-centre research protocol will be considered by one MREC only, usually the one in the region in which the principal researcher is based. That MREC's advice will be given to LRECs in every locality involved, not just those within its host part of the United Kingdom.

6 Once MREC approval has been obtained LRECs in every locality involved will have the opportunity to accept or reject the protocol for local reasons but will not be allowed to amend it. LRECs may occasionally need to seek purely locally applicable amendments which do not affect the integrity of the protocol, for example information sheets and consent forms in minority languages. They should only do so when essential. LRECs will be asked to notify their decisions to the designated MREC within a specified timescale, and in particular give reasons if they refuse a proposal. Thus the system will incorporate an additional safeguard which could bring to the attention of an MREC any major points that had possibly been missed in its consideration of the scientific and wider ethical aspects. The MREC will be obliged to consider any such points.

7 The system will involve rigorous scrutiny of each protocol by the relevant MREC, including, where necessary, detailed discussion with the principal researcher and/or expert advisers. It will allow LRECs scope to discuss local matters pertaining to MREC-approved protocols with the local and/or principal researcher (where the latter can help expedite clearance) ...

Definition of multi-centre research

10 For the purposes of the MREC system research will be regarded as 'multi-centre' if carried out within five or more LRECs' geographical boundaries. LRECs may still make arrangements for one to review research involving two to four centres on behalf of them all ...

COMPENSATION FOR INJURIES ARISING FROM RESEARCH

Compensation at common law

As we saw above, p 544, a patient who is entered in a clinical trial without giving his properly informed consent may arguably have an action against the doctor in battery; this would perhaps be most likely in the case of a volunteer involved in non-therapeutic research. Failing an action in battery, however, an action in negligence may lie and could arise in two main ways, albeit in both cases the subject must show some tangible injury. In the first case, the trial itself may be properly conducted, but the doctor/researcher (whilst providing enough basic facts to escape an action in battery) fall below his duty of care in the amount of information he divulges to his subject, and the latter is able to show that, if properly informed, he would not have participated in the trial.

In the second case, the trial itself, in terms of design or execution, may turn out to be defective in some way. An additional issue which arises here is whether, to the extent that the defect was something which the LREC, in approving the trial, should have noticed, the members of that Committee could be joined as defendants in any action. This matter was of sufficient concern to be addressed directly by Department of Health Guidelines in 1991:

Department of Health, *Guidelines on LRECs*, 1991, London: DoH:

2.11 Concern has been expressed by some LREC members that they may be legally liable for injury caused to patients participating in research projects. DHAs will wish to advise appointees on these matters. Legal advice available to the Department of Health is that there is little prospect of a successful claim against a LREC member for a mishap arising from research approved as ethical by the LREC. Any such claim would lie principally against the researcher concerned and against the NHS body under the auspices of which the research took place. The principal defendants should seek to have any claim against an LREC member struck out. Those members of an LREC who are employees of an NHS body are already covered by NHS indemnity arrangements. The DHA should also bear any costs in the case of other LREC members unless the member concerned is guilty of misconduct or gross lack of care in the performance of his or her duties and provided that, if any claim is threatened or made, the member notifies the DHA and assists it in all reasonable ways. If necessary the DHA may give the following undertaking to this effect to LREC members who are not employees of an NHS body:

> We confirm that the DHA will take full responsibility for all actions in the course of the performance of your duties as a member of the LREC other than those involving bad faith, wilful default or gross negligence; you should, however, notify the DHA if any action or claim is threatened or made, and in such an event be ready to assist the authority as required.

'No fault' compensation?

Whatever form his action takes, the injured research subject (like his 'pure' patient counterpart) will have substantial hurdles to overcome, both in relation to the breach of duty question and causation. However, an ethical argument for treating research subjects more favourably than other patients injured in the course of treatment is that, just as society at large stands to benefit from any advances in medical knowledge that the research may secure, so it should bear the costs of mishaps along the way. Accordingly, it has frequently been urged that those injured in the course of medical research should be compensated on a 'no fault' basis. A direct analogy can be invoked here with persons injured in the course of a community-wide vaccination programme, who are entitled to 'no fault' compensation (albeit of a relatively paltry nature) under the Vaccine Damage Payments Act 1979:

1   Payments to persons severely disabled by vaccination

    (1)   If, on consideration of a claim, the Secretary of State is satisfied–

        (a) that a person is, or was immediately before his death, severely disabled as a result of vaccination against any of the diseases to which this Act applies; and

        (b) that the conditions of entitlement which are applicable in accordance with s 2 below are fulfilled,

    he shall in accordance with this Act make a payment of the relevant statutory sum to or for the benefit of that person or to his personal representatives.

    (1A)In sub-s (1) above 'statutory sum' means £30,000 or such other sum as is specified by the Secretary of State for the purposes of this Act by order made by statutory instrument with the consent of the Treasury; and the relevant statutory sum for the purposes of that subsection is the statutory sum at the time when a claim for payment is first made.

    (2)   The diseases to which this Act applies are–

        (a) diphtheria;

        (b) tetanus;

        (c) whooping cough;

        (d) poliomyelitis;

        (e) measles;

        (f) mumps;

        (g) rubella;

        (h) tuberculosis;

        (i) smallpox; and

        (j) any other disease which is specified by the Secretary of State for the purposes of this Act by order made by statutory instrument.

    (3)   Subject to s 2(3) below, this Act has effect with respect to a person who is severely disabled as a result of a vaccination given to his mother before he was born as if the vaccination had been given directly to him and, in such circumstances as may be prescribed by regulations under this Act, this Act has effect with respect to a person who is severely disabled as a result of contracting a disease through contact with a third person who was vaccinated against it as if the vaccination had been given to him and the disablement resulted from it.

    (4)   For the purposes of this Act, a person is severely disabled if he suffers disablement to the extent of 80% or more, assessed as for the purposes of s 57 of the Social Security Act 1975 or the Social Security (Northern Ireland) Act 1975 (disablement gratuity and pension) ...

In its 1978 Report, the Royal Commission on Civil Liability and Compensation for Personal Injury (the Pearson Committee), recommended that a similar scheme of compensation be established for injuries in the course of medical research. Whilst this recommendation has not been acted upon by Parliament, the DoH's LREC Guidelines, as we have seen (above, p 563), mention the existence of provision for *ex gratia* compensation as a relevant factor in the sanctioning of trials.

In every case, of course, it remains necessary for the research subject to demonstrate that his injuries were caused by participation in the trial. This may be by no means easy to do: after all, as noted above, p 523, research will be taking place precisely because the causal properties of the new treatment (including its propensity to do harm) are unclear. Sometimes, to be sure, the plaintiff's case will be a strong one, for example where everyone in the trial is similarly affected. However, where the plaintiff's injury is a more isolated occurrence, a court may well take the view that some unknown, independent cause was, just as likely, at work. (Recall, in this regard, the case of *Loveday v Renton* discussed above, Chapter 6.)

Drug-induced injury

One area in which the use of research subjects has attracted particular attention is in relation to the testing of new drugs and pharmaceutical products. There is a heightened sense here (engendered both by the power imbalance between subject and drug company and by the latter's pre-eminently economic motivation), that volunteers and patients participating in such trials require protection. As Soutar and McLean write:

> **Soutar, D and McLean, S, 'Medical progress and the law', in McLean, S (ed),**
> ***Legal Issues in Medicine, 1981, Aldershot: Gower, pp 116–17:***
>
> There is available a wide variety of clinical trials, using healthy volunteers or patients, in both therapeutic and non-therapeutic clinical research programmes. Trials may be randomised, or controlled, and the most valid clinical results are obtained in 'blind' and 'double blind' trials. The most helpful information, when trying to justify a new treatment, comes from comparative trials where one method of therapy is evaluated against another, but unfortunately such trials are rarely, if ever, performed prior to marketing a new product.
>
> Further, most manufacturers retain control over publication of the results of their clinical trials. This protects them from competitors by preventing premature release of information and, in the event that the product proves of little or no value, avoids public and professional humiliation. Not surprisingly, there is considerable concern as to the advisability of permitting the manufacturing industry this freedom in controlling the only sources of clinical data concerning a new medical product, and the recent controversy over the clinical information presented by the company in the marketing of Debendox/Bendectin is a case in point. This is not to suggest that all, or even many, companies will deliberately disguise unfavourable information regarding a new product, and in recent times at least one major company has accepted significant financial loss rather than market a product concerning whose safety there were serious doubts.

However, as in any industry, economic factors are of prime importance to companies, which invest a considerable proportion of their substantial income in researching and developing new drugs ...

Direct or indirect financial assistance to those performing clinical trials, is an additional moral and ethical problem. Such assistance can be used to persuade doctors to carry out clinical trials or to 'try out' the product following market release and here society is totally dependent on the moral and ethical codes of the individual manufacturers and doctors concerned. It could be argued that it is immoral for a manufacturer to finance or 'buy' a clinical trial, but should analysis and investigation require expensive and sophisticated equipment or specialised technical help, then perhaps the manufacturing industry should be responsible for providing these, even although this may amount indirectly at least to financing the project. Since often, in such cases, the specialised knowledge and equipment remain available for the medical staff concerned and thus benefit the National Health Service, it may be felt that the overall benefits of this practice outweigh the potential disadvantages.

Certainly, if doctors apply their ethical codes to the expected high standard, then problems should be minimised, although it has been suggested that the pressures on doctors are such that ' ... events ... have diminished an honourable profession [medicine] to the level of a junior partner in an immensely powerful industrial-medical complex' ...

In fact, the Association of the British Pharmaceutical Industry, in its Guidelines, has recommended that *ex gratia* compensation should be paid in cases where injury results. As Christopher Hodges writes:

Hodges, C, 'Harmonisation of European controls over research: ethics committees, consent, compensation and indemnity', in Goldberg, A and Dodds-Smith, I (eds), *Pharmaceutical Medicine and the Law*, 1991, London: RCP, pp 80–82:

The [ABPI] ... guidelines were revised in 1991 in the light of developing considerations, especially the 1990 report of the RCP's working party, *Research Involving Patients*. The relationship between the sponsor and subject is, in the case of [therapeutic research], not contractual and the guidelines state that the sponsor's assurance to abide by them is 'without legal commitment':

1.2 Compensation should be paid when, on the balance of probabilities, the injury was attributable to the administration of a medicinal product under trial or any clinical intervention or procedure provided for by the protocol that would not have occurred but for the inclusion of the patient in the trial.

1.3 Compensation should be paid to a child injured in utero through the participation of the subject's mother in a clinical trial as if the child were a patient-volunteer with the full benefit of these guidelines.

1.4 Compensation should only be paid for the more serious injury of an enduring and disabling character (including exacerbation of an existing condition) and not for temporary pain or discomfort or less serious or curable complaints.

1.5 Where there is an adverse reaction to a medicinal product under trial and injury is caused by a procedure adopted to deal with that adverse reaction, compensation should be paid for such injury as if it were caused directly by the medicinal product under trial.

1.6 Neither the fact that the adverse reaction causing the injury was foreseeable or predictable, nor the fact that the patient has freely consented (whether in writing or otherwise) to participate in the trial, should exclude a patient from consideration for compensation under these guidelines, although compensation may be abated or excluded in the light of the factors described in para 4.2 below.

1.7 For the avoidance of doubt, compensation should be paid regardless of whether the patient is able to prove that the company has been negligent in relation to research or development of the medicinal product under trial or that the product is defective and therefore, as the producer, the company is subject to strict liability in respect of injuries caused by it ...

4.1 The amount of compensation paid should be appropriate to the nature, severity and persistence of the injury and should in general terms be consistent with the quantum of damages commonly awarded for similar injuries by an English court in cases where legal liability is admitted.

4.2 Compensation may be abated, or in certain circumstances excluded, in the light of the following factors (on which will depend the level of risk the patient can reasonably be expected to accept):

4.2.1 the seriousness of the disease being treated, the degree of probability that adverse reactions will occur and any warnings given;

4.2.2 the risks and benefits of established treatments relative to those known or suspected of the trial medicine.

This reflects the fact that flexibility is required given the particular patient's circumstances. As an extreme example, there may be a patient suffering from a serious or life-threatening disease who is warned of a certain defined risk of adverse reaction. Participation in the trial is then based on an expectation that the benefit-risk ratio associated with participation may be better than that associated with alternative treatment. It is, therefore, reasonable that the patient accepts the high risk and should not expect compensation for the occurrence of the adverse reaction of which he or she was told.

There is provision for arbitration by an independent expert in the event of any difference of opinion.

Compensation is excluded, however, where:

1 The product failed to have its intended effect.

2 The injury was caused by another licensed medicinal product which was administered as a comparison with the product under trial.

3 A placebo has failed to provide a therapeutic benefit.

Compensation should not be paid, or should be abated, to the extent that the injury has arisen through:

1   A significant departure from the agreed protocol.
2   The wrongful act or default of a third party, including a doctor's failure to deal adequately with an adverse reaction.
3   Contributory negligence by the patient.

These Guidelines are echoed by guidance at EC level (*Guidelines on Good Clinical Practice for Trials on Medicinal Products in the EC* (CPMP of the EC, 1990, Brussels: EC Commission), which further stresses the weight to be accorded to the research subject, including the need, at least in the context of non-therapeutic research upon healthy volunteers, for fully informed consent.

Finally, in cases of drug-induced injury, the subject may also wish to bring an action under the Consumer Protection Act 1987. The difficulties of relying on this Act, however (which can be expected to be particularly acute in this context), have been addressed above, Chapter 6.

CHAPTER ELEVEN

ORGAN TRANSPLANTATION

INTRODUCTION

Organ transplantation is undoubtedly one of the triumphs of modern medicine. The procedure has become increasingly routine as a means of saving, and improving the quality of, the lives of thousands of people each year. The history of this programme, and the manner in which it has expanded to encompass an increasing variety of organs and other body tissue, has been chronicled by David Lamb:

Lamb, D, *Organ Transplants and Ethics*, 1990, London: Routledge, pp 7–9:

The idea of taking bone, skin, or organs from one person and transplanting them into another has been a subject of fascination and intrigue since earliest times. Yet until the 20th century the dream of creating a healthy whole person by transplantation remained in the realm of mythology and the miraculous. Early attempts at blood transfusion met with no success until knowledge of different blood types and their mutual compatibility or incompatibility was discovered. This meant that many attempts at blood transfusion during the 18th century resulted in charges of homicide before several European courts outlawed the practice. However, blood transfusion was widely used in the 1914–18 war when blood banks were created to store blood. This, perhaps, was one of the most important features in the early stages of the history of transplantation.

But blood is self-replaceable, and although there have been considerable ethical discussions about the policies for collection and distribution of blood, they do not address the kind of ethical and philosophical problems associated with the transplantation of non-regenerating solid organs, such as kidneys, hearts, lungs, pancreases, and livers.

Transplantation of non-vital organs has steadily increased during the 20th century. Skin grafts began in the late 1920s. This procedure is usually applied as a temporary measure in cases of burns. Recent experiments with cultured skin, however, suggest that procurement from donors may one day be unnecessary. Under appropriate conditions skin can be stored and there are now skin and bone banks, where bone is stored for treatment of the skeletal system.

Corneal transplants actually began in 1905, although the operation did not become routine until the 1940s. In 1983 a corneal transplant service was set up in the UK to encourage corneal donation. Improvements in storage techniques now allow corneas to be stored for up to 30 days. The Corneal Tissue Act of 1986 greatly enhanced cadaveric procurement in the UK by allowing non-medical personnel to remove corneas. Since 1944, when the world's first eye bank was opened in the Manhattan Eye, Ear and Throat Hospital, eye banks have become an integral part of most countries' health care systems ...

The modern transplant era, however, began with the transplantation of non-regenerating vital organs in the 1950s, but its antecedents can be traced back to the turn of the century when Dr Alexis Carrel and Dr Charles C Guthrie developed the technique of suturing blood vessels. Then, in 1902, an Austrian surgeon, Dr Emmerick Ullman, removed a kidney from a dog and kept it functioning in the body of another dog for a few days. The eventual failure of this transplant revealed the problem of rejection, and it was discovered in further experiments that successful transplants depend on a close genetic resemblance between donor and recipient ...

The major breakthrough in understanding rejection had to wait until Dr Peter Medawar, winner of the 1960 Nobel Prize, explained how the body's immunisation system recognises foreign bodies that enter it by means of markers or antigens, and then rejects foreign matter by means of the production of antibodies. This knowledge led to the development of tissue-typing, where the donor's and recipient's tissues are examined with a view to compatibility, such that the antigens of both tissues are sufficiently similar to prevent recognition as alien bodies and thus avoid exciting the destructive immune system response. In recent years great efforts have been made to overcome the rejection problem, without which surgical technique would be insufficient. Throughout the 1960s and 1970s drugs were developed which lessened the organism's ability to develop antibodies. But many of these had the unfortunate effect of weakening the recipient's immune system. However, a major breakthrough occurred in 1983 when a Swiss pharmaceutical company produced Cyclosporin, which selectively inhibits the rejection of foreign tissues without damaging their ability to combat viruses and bacteria. The ability to control tissue rejection marks the transition from the era of transplantation as an experimental therapy to the era of organ transplantation as routine therapy.

However, despite compelling evidence that such transplants are not only of significant therapeutic benefit to the majority of recipients but highly cost effective (in allowing savings in other, more expensive forms of treatment, for example, dialysis), this is an area which remains fraught with ethical difficulty. This is especially so as the demand for donor organs continues markedly to outstrip supply. As New *et al* note:

New, B, Solomon, M, Dingwall, R and McHale, J, *A Question of Give and Take*, 1994, London: Kings Fund Institute, p 9:

The transplanting of organs from one human to another is a medical intervention which 50 years ago would have seemed a suitable topic for a science fiction novel. And yet, in the 1990s, kidney transplants are the treatment of choice for end-stage renal disease, and heart and liver transplants offer the only chance of life for thousands of people across the world with chronic heart or liver failure. It is an operation which attracts intense media attention, particularly when children's lives are at stake. However, the reason for such attention is often particularly poignant, involving a race against time for a suitable donor.

Transplant activity is increasingly constrained by the shortage of organs, a phenomenon affecting every country which has developed the ability to undertake this form of surgery. Quite possibly uniquely, doctors and surgeons are prevented from alleviating suffering and avoiding death by the shortage of a particular physical resource – a human organ. Until medical science learns to replicate human tissue or replace organs with those from animals, the problem will remain: how can we maximise the supply of these organs by organisational or legal reforms without offending ethical principles?

We shall examine next the different sources from which organs for transplantation may be obtained, and the legal and ethical issues raised in each case. We then consider the (novel) legal problem of what status to accord to extracted body parts, before addressing the rights of the donee of such material. The chapter concludes by analysing possible measures of law reform aimed to increase the number of organs available for transplantation.

EXTRACTION OF MATERIAL

The live donor

The world's first successful kidney transplant, which took place in Boston in 1954, involved a live donation between identical twins. Indeed, until the development of powerful new immuno-suppressant drugs in the early 1980s, live donation between close relatives was preferred in order to reduce the chance of organ rejection by the donee. Although, since then, live donations have decreased as a proportion of total organ transplants (1997 statistics, from the UK Transplants Support Service Authority, show that in the UK live donors accounted for some 11% of kidney donations), the numbers have been rising in actual terms. Moreover, certain tissues, namely bone marrow, skin and blood, are invariably obtained from live donors. (In what follows, unless the context indicates otherwise, the terms 'organ donor' and its correlates are used to encompass tissue donation as well.)

Ethical considerations

The major ethical issue here is similar to that considered in the last chapter in relation to medical research, viz, how far is it permissible to expose a person to harm, or the risk of harm, in order to benefit another? Just as in the case of research, the question exposes a conflict between two differing systems of moral philosophy. As Price and Garwood-Gowers note:

> **Price, DPT and Garwood-Gowers, A, 'Transplantation from minors: are children other people's medicine?' (1995) 1 Contemporary Issues in the Law 1:**
>
> By virtue of the fact that removal of the material from the donor is primarily for the prospective benefit of another individual, the whole issue of living donation of body materials for transplantation raises starkly the conflict

between the two fundamental philosophical theories, deontological theory and consequentialist theory. Few areas of law highlight this conflict as keenly as deontological theory, of which Immanuel Kant is the prime exponent, which seeks to guide our actions by reference to overriding moral imperatives and insists that as part of a respect for persons their intrinsic moral worth dictates that they should not be used merely as a means to another's ends. By contrast, consequentialist approaches, of which utilitarianism is the pre-eminent example, attempt to judge the rightness or wrongness of an action according to the consequences which flow from it. The action which maximises happiness and minimises suffering is the preferred one. Clearly, on a utilitarian calculus the pendulum swings further in favour of donation than on a deontological approach in so far as the risks from donating even a paired organ are generally fairly modest, whereas transplanting such an organ has the potential to improve the quality (and duration) of life of the recipient dramatically.

The Kantian approach, with its emphasis on the primacy of human autonomy, might well be preferred here. On the other hand, as suggested in Chapter 1, the conflict between the two systems largely disappears once it is realised that any plausible form of utilitarianism must also accord great weight to individual autonomy (albeit as an instrumental rather than intrinsic value): a society in which persons could have their organs forcibly extracted for the benefit of others would be a perilous and miserable one indeed.

That said, an interesting question concerns how far autonomy in this area should be completely unfettered. This is relevant where a person actively wishes to donate an organ even though the consequences to them will be serious harm or death. Recently, the Nuffield Council on Bioethics commented as follows:

Nuffield Council on Bioethics, *Human Tissue: Ethical and Legal Issues*, 1995, London: Nuffield Council on Bioethics:

6.4 We identify the avoidance and limitation of injury as a basic requirement for any type of use of human tissue to be ethically acceptable. Avoidance and limitation of injury can be seen as expressing a central element of the undefined, yet widely endorsed, demand for respect for the human body and for respect for human dignity. In paras 6.7–6.16 we identify and elaborate this basic requirement which makes types of use of human tissue ethically acceptable.

6.5 We note, however, that the avoidance and limitation of injury is a complex requirement, and that in certain circumstances, injury can be avoided or limited only by inflicting injury. In our view, the only circumstance in which inflicting injury is acceptable is when it is done to avoid greater injury. It is this that justifies much medical treatment, and action taken in self defence and in other situations. This principle is also useful in evaluating proposed uses of human tissue.

6.6 Although we identify the avoidance and limitation of injury as basic to acceptable use of human tissue, there are other important considerations.

For example, consent of those from whom tissue is taken (patient, donor) or of relatives (post mortem) is important. Consent, however, is not the primary consideration. In particular, consent cannot justify injury: for example, killing or maiming cannot be justified by the victim being willing ...

Avoidance and limitation of injury

6.7 It is not easy to state the underlying rationale for viewing these and other sorts of action as unacceptable. The difficulty is in part that many people see these actions as wrong, repugnant or repellent for multiple reasons, about some of which there is no agreement. The most widely accepted reasons, however, often stress that these sorts of action fail to respect others or to accord them dignity, that they injure human beings by treating them as things, as less than human, as objects for use. Although all these phrases are vague, there is considerable agreement about a central range of injurious activity that would constitute disrespect for human beings and for human dignity ...

A related issue, touched upon below, pp 592 and 630, is how far a person should be entitled to benefit financially from the provision of his or her body parts.

The legal position at common law

The competent donor and consent

As a minimum, the donor must, where adult and competent, always consent to the removal of an organ. This is simply an application of the general rule that the consent of such a person is needed to any medical procedure (see above, Chapter 3). In this context, however, there may well be doubts about one of the preconditions for valid consent being present, namely freedom from coercion or undue influence. This is especially so in the vast majority of cases where the donation is between two members of the same family. As we saw in relation to consent, the Court of Appeal was obliged to consider the effect of institutionalised power relationships upon the reality of consent in the case of *Freeman v Home Office (No 2)* (1984). Nevertheless, there is a suspicion that, in the case of related live transplants, the courts do not wish to get involved in determining such matters, and are instead leaving the question very much to the doctors.

The law of assault

A question long unresolved at judicial level was whether the removal of an organ for transplant by a surgeon would qualify as an assault *notwithstanding* the donor's consent. Writing in 1970, Gerald Dworkin commented on this issue as follows:

Dworkin, G, 'The law relating to organ transplantation in England' (1970) 33 MLR 353:

To determine the legality of live donor transplantations it is first necessary to examine the legal basis for surgical operations generally. Under medieval law, a person committed the crime of mayhem (maim) if he so injured another as to make him less able to fight or to defend himself or to annoy an adversary. To amputate a limb, even with the victim's consent was, on the face of it, an unlawful act, since it deprived the king of a fighting man. In early Victorian times when soldiers, as part of their training, had to bite cartridges, a soldier got a dentist to pull out his front teeth to enable him to avoid training and it was thought that both were guilty of a crime. The modern law is obscure but the crime, to some extent, turns on two interconnected factors. The first is the nature of the physical harm: one person does not have a licence to mutilate or cause bodily harm to another for any purpose merely because that person has consented. The degree of bodily harm is, of course, important: the test is no longer whether it impairs or may impair the victim's ability to fight for his country, but presumably the seriousness of the harm must be of that order ... The second factor involves questions of public policy. The law may permit some kinds of assault and battery but not others: the dividing line between the permissible and the impermissible is not clear but the courts have accepted and still accept the burden of safeguarding individuals even against themselves.

The relevance of this aspect of the criminal law is that it provides a basis for saying that many surgical operations are *prima facie* unlawful. Without further justification not only would operations be criminal acts, but they would also be unlawful in the civil law and surgeons might be liable to pay compensation for the consequences of their acts, even though they had exercised all reasonable care. What are the criteria, then, which convert unlawful acts into lawful surgical operations? In some countries the criminal codes absolve from responsibility persons who perform in good faith and with reasonable care and skill a surgical operation upon another person, with his consent and for his benefit, if the performance of the operation is reasonable in the circumstances. No such provision appears in any United Kingdom legislation but it is clear, of course, that surgery, within limits, is a perfectly legal activity. Sir James Fitzjames Stephen formulated the general proposition that 'everyone has a right to consent to the infliction of any bodily injury in the nature of a surgical operation upon himself' and stated that although he knew of no authority for this, the existence of surgery as a profession assumed its truth.

Dworkin suggested four conditions that would need to be satisfied for surgery in general, and donor-organ removal in particular, to be lawful:

    (i)   *The patient must give a full, free and informed consent.* The importance of consent cannot be overemphasised ... It is clear that, in any common law jurisdiction, the general principle is that a patient should be informed of all the material facts relating to the operation which would enable a reasonable person to weigh up the risks and benefits and arrive at a rational decision whether or not to undergo the operation. Also, there should be no unfair pressure upon the patient which induces him to give his consent in spite of all the risks.

(ii) *The operation must be therapeutic: it must be expressly for the patient's benefit.*
The major distinguishing feature between surgical operations and
unlawful mutilation is, of course, that all surgical operations are allegedly
in the medical interests of the patient. Coke refers to a case in 1603 where
'a young and lustie rogue prevailed upon a friend to cut off his left hand,
so that he might be better able to beg'. Both were found guilty of the crime
of maim; today, they would also be criminally liable. In the criminal codes
of some countries, the provisions concerning surgical operations expressly
state that they must be for the patient's benefit; in other countries this,
until recently, has been accepted as being obvious.

(iii) *There must be lawful justification.* This is a relatively unexplored and open
ended requirement. Ethical and social questions are more relevant here
and the courts may occasionally use this rubric to extend the law to meet
new circumstances. Most surgical operations are lawful ... There are other
surgical operations, only arguably of therapeutic benefit to the patient,
where the courts nevertheless may be tempted to emphasise their lawful
justification. It is unlikely that the courts would condemn circumcision as
unlawful. No doubt the ritual circumcision of Jewish infants could be
upheld on grounds of religious toleration, although circumcision for non-
religious reasons would have to be accepted on wider public policy
grounds.

(iv) *Generally, the operation must be performed by a person with appropriate medical
skills ...*

It is suggested that, rather than each being necessary in its own right,
condition (ii) would tend nowadays to be regarded as a particular application
of the more general principle contained in (iii). In the present context (as
opposed to therapeutic surgery), it is all-important to look at the reason why
the operation is taking place: removal for transplantation is a socially
recognised good and is lawfully justified; removal for other purposes, for
example, because the person whose organ it was wanted to taste it, would
remain a battery. A further requirement, given that no therapeutic benefit will
accrue to the donor, appears to be that such removal not expose the donor to
an unreasonable amount of harm (or a significant risk thereof). In this regard,
the media reported in February 1996 that doctors had refused the request of a
father that his remaining kidney be transplanted into his chronically ill son
and he be placed on dialysis instead. He had previously given up his first
kidney to his other son.

The law of homicide

It follows *a fortiori* from what has just been said that the law will not sanction
the removal of vital organs where the consequence for the donor will be
death. Gerald Dworkin ('The law relating to organ transplantation in England'
(1970) 33 MLR 353) cites the comment, made extra-judicially by Edmund
Davies LJ (as he then was) to the effect that he would:

> ... be surprised if a surgeon were successfully sued for trespass to the person or
> convicted of causing bodily harm to one of full age and intelligence who freely

consented to act as donor always provided that the operation did not present unreasonable risk to the donor's life or health. That proviso is essential. A man may declare himself ready to die for another, but the surgeon must not take him at his word.

In such a case, the surgeon would be guilty of murder (or, at the very least, manslaughter). For this reason, transplants involving live donors are generally limited to tissues such as bone marrow, blood, and (now) liver lobes (which are all capable of regenerating) or kidneys, of which most people have a 'spare'. The only exception relates to so called 'domino transplants' of hearts which may occur following the donor's own receipt of a heart-lung transplant.

The incompetent donor

Adults

The legal position, until recently, was less clear in relation to the lawfulness of using incompetent adults as donors. Such persons are by definition incapable of giving their consent; rather, as we saw from the House of Lords decision in *Re F (Mental Patient: Sterilisation)* (see above, Chapter 4), they may be subjected to medical intervention only in so far as the procedure is in their best interests. Can donating an organ be regarded as in the donor's (as opposed to the donee's) best interests? An important US case in point is *Strunk v Strunk* 445 SW 2d 145 (1969) (Kentucky CA), where an affirmative answer was given. The court authorised a kidney transplant from Jerry, a 27 year old man with a mental age of six, to his 28 year old brother after hearing psychiatric evidence of the 'extremely traumatic effect' that his brother's death would have upon him.

Recently, the question finally arose for determination by an English court in the case of *Re Y*.

Re Y (Adult Patient) (Transplant: Bone Marrow) (1996) 35 BMLR 111, Fam Div (Connell J)

Miss Y was 25 years old and had been severely mentally and physically disabled from birth. She had lived in care since the age of 10. Her sister, aged 36, who suffered from preleukaemic bone marrow disorder, sought a declaration that it would be lawful to perform blood tests and possible bone marrow extraction upon Miss Y, despite the latter's inability to consent.

> **Connell J:** The taking of blood tests and the harvesting of bone marrow from the defendant who is incapable of giving informed consent would amount to assaults upon the defendant and would therefore be illegal unless shown to be in the best interests of the defendant and therefore lawful.
>
> The test to be applied in a case such as this is to ask whether the evidence shows that it is in the best interests of the defendant for such procedures to take place. The fact that such a process would obviously benefit the plaintiff is not relevant unless, as a result of the defendant helping the plaintiff in that way, the best interests of the defendant are served.

The approach is as set out in the case of *Re F (Mental Patient: Sterilisation)* [19901 2 AC 1 ... a non-therapeutic sterilisation case. Thus, the giving of medical treatment to mentally disordered adult patients is, save as to treatment for their mental disorder under the Mental Health Act 1983, governed by common law. The lawfulness of the action depends upon whether the treatment is in the best interests of the patient ...

This case is different from the case of *Re F* because it involves the concept of donation of bone marrow by a donor who is incapable of giving consent where a significant benefit will flow to another person. There was no other person in Re F who would have benefited directly as a result of the declaration sought, the benefits of sterilisation attaching solely to the mentally incapacitated subject of the application.

Nonetheless, I am satisfied that the root question remains the same, namely, whether the procedures here envisaged will benefit the defendant and accordingly benefits which may flow to the plaintiff are relevant only in so far as they have a positive effect upon the best interests of the defendant ...

The information provided by those who now care for the defendant in the residential home make it apparent that the defendant benefits from the visits which she receives from her family and from her occasional involvement in family events, for example, the wedding of one of her sisters, particularly because these visits maintain for her a link with the outside world which is helpful to her and which would otherwise be lost to her.

In addition, the Official Solicitor's representative observed affection between mother and daughter during a recent visit which demonstrated that her mother holds a special place in the defendant's world even if the defendant does not appreciate that this lady is in fact her mother.

If this application is not successful, the chances that the plaintiff will not survive are materially increased. She might be able to receive bone marrow from one of the two unrelated donors but evidence to me shows that the recipient's chances of survival for 18 months following transplant from a sibling are at least 40%, whereas those chances after donation from a stranger in the case of the plaintiff s illness are at best 30%. The match from strangers is never quite as good as the match from a sibling.

Further, if the plaintiff survives the first six months post-transplant then the prospects for survival semi-indefinitely are good. On the other hand, without any transplant her prospects of survival are very poor and are deteriorating fast. If the plaintiff dies, this is bound to have an adverse effect upon her mother who already suffers from significant ill health. One lay witness took the gloomy view that this event would prove fatal to the mother, but in any event her ability to visit the defendant would be handicapped significantly, not only by a likely deterioration in her health, but also by the need which would then arise for her to look after her only grandchild, E.

In this situation, the defendant would clearly be harmed by the reduction in or loss of contact to her mother. Accordingly, it is to the benefit of the defendant that she should act as donor to her sister, because in this way her positive relationship with her mother is most likely to be prolonged. Further, if the transplant occurs, this is likely to improve the defendant's relationship with her mother who in her heart clearly wishes it to take place and also to improve her relationship with the plaintiff who will be eternally grateful to her.

This case shows the court adopting a wide interpretation of 'best interests'; it is not somatic health alone which is relevant, but the wider interests a person has as part of the social community. (This approach is also in line with decisions relating to sterilisation looked at above, Chapter 4.) Nevertheless, there are important limits on invoking the test in order to justify organ extraction, especially where the organ is non-regenerative. As Andrew Grubb has commented:

Grubb, A, 'Commentary on *Re Y*' (1996) 4 Med L Rev 204:

Of course, the judge recognised that it was insufficient for him merely to identify a 'benefit' to Miss Y without weighing against this any detriment that she might suffer by undergoing the procedures. However, the risks inherent in the procedures – the general anaesthetic and the removal of two pints of bone marrow – were regarded as 'very small' (one in 10,000 risk of death) and non-existent (as bone marrow is regenerative) respectively. Further any pain that might arise from the harvesting could be controlled by morphine. And, of course, there could be a detriment by not undergoing the procedure ... In *Re Y*, Connell J referred to the 'harm' Miss Y would suffer (directly and indirectly) from the death of her sister although the evidence never elevated this to the level of psychiatric injury.

Limitations in future cases. Given the weaknesses in the evidence which have been suggested above, *Re Y* could be seen as giving a 'green light' to support donations by incompetent adults and children in the future. This would, I think, be a misreading of the case and not Connell J's intention for a number of reasons.

First, the case is probably an unusual one in that it concerned a procedure which does have minimal risks for the donor. Given the need to weigh the benefits of the procedure against the risks of doing it, it is not likely that a court would contemplate donation of non-regenerative tissue such as a kidney. Connell J suggested as much when he remarked that his decision should not be considered 'a useful precedent in cases where the surgery involved is more intrusive'. While the long term risks of having one kidney are not great, they do exist and the nature of the procedure suggests that it would be difficult to satisfy the 'best interests' test ...

Secondly, the courts will undoubtedly look for evidence of a 'close relationship' which will be damaged if the donee patient dies. It is most unlikely, therefore, that the court would contemplate even a minimally risky procedure if the donor's mental disability or if the child's age prevented them forming such a relationship. Donations by babies and the severely mentally disabled may thus be out of court. Also, the court will look for immediate psychological benefit and would reject as too tenuous evidence of the long term future benefit of not 'living in a family under the shadow of avoidable, premature death' ...

Thirdly, the court might well as a rule-of-thumb look for the 'agreement' (though obviously not the consent) of the donor as a condition to allowing the donation. This would also exclude donations from the very young or severely disabled. Also, it is unthinkable that the 'best interests' test could be satisfied if the donor objected to the donation.

Fourthly, there is no suggestion in Connell J's judgment that purely altruistic benefit will satisfy the 'best interests' test. He restricted himself to situations of 'psychological benefit' ... There is no support, therefore, in his judgment for permitting non-therapeutic research upon incompetent adults or children even though this does have strong professional support in exceptional cases of 'minimal risk' ...

Fifthly, at the invitation of the Official Solicitor, Connell J indicated that cases involving donation by an incompetent adult fell into the 'special category' of case where it was desirable that the court should be involved ...

Children

In contrast to the position with incompetent adults, there is no English authority directly on the question of live organ donation by minors. Moreover, this issue raises a number of further complications. First, in the case of older children who satisfy the test of *'Gillick* competence', can they consent in their own right to act as donors? The answer, in principle, would appear to be yes. As Lord Donaldson MR noted, *obiter*, in *Re W (A Minor)* (1992):

> **Lord Donaldson MR**: [Section 8 of the Family Law Reform Act 1969 establishing the presumption that a minor of 16 years can consent to medical treatment] extends not only to treatment, but also to diagnostic procedures (see sub-s (2)). It does not, however, extend to the donation of organs or blood since, so far as the donor is concerned, these do not constitute either treatment or diagnosis. I cannot remember to what extent organ donation was common in 1967, but the Latey Committee expressly recommended that only 18 year olds and older should be authorised by statute to consent to giving blood (see paras 485–89). It seems that parliament accepted this recommendation, although I doubt whether blood donation will create any problem as a *'Gillick* competent' minor of any age would be able to give consent under the common law.
>
> Organ transplants are quite different and, as a matter of law, doctors would have to secure the consent of someone with the right to consent on behalf of a donor under the age of 18 or, if they relied upon the consent of the minor himself or herself, be satisfied that the minor was *'Gillick* competent' in the context of so serious a procedure which would not benefit the minor. This would be a highly improbable conclusion. But this is only to look at the question as a matter of law. Medical ethics also enter into the question. The doctor has a professional duty to act in the best interests of his patient and to advise accordingly. It is inconceivable that he should proceed in reliance solely upon the consent of an under-age patient, however *'Gillick* competent', in the absence of supporting parental consent and equally inconceivable that he should proceed in the absence of the patient's consent. In any event he will need to seek the opinions of other doctors and may be well advised to apply to the court for guidance, as recommended by Lord Templeman in a different context in *Re B (A Minor) (Wardship: Sterilisation)* [1987] 2 All ER 206, pp 214–15
>
> ...

Lord Donaldson suggests here that it would be 'inconceivable' both that extraction would go ahead without parental consent *and* that it could occur solely on the basis of the latter (a necessary caveat in the light of his Lordship's 'flak jacket' approach to consent in his decision in the case (see above, Chapter 3)).

In the case of children who lack capacity, it is apparent that the parents must normally give proxy consent to any form of medical intervention upon them. Indeed, in the American case of *Bonner v Moran* 126 F 2d 121 (1941) (USCA DC) a doctor who failed to obtain parental consent was held liable in battery after taking skin grafts from a 15 year old boy to treat the latter's badly burnt cousin. On the other hand, it is clear that parental authorisation of such an intervention will not guarantee that it is lawful. Rather, as Lord Scarman suggested in *Gillick v W Norfolk and Wisbech HA* [1986] 1 AC 112, the parent's power here is one that they should exercise exclusively for the child's protection.

In fact, it appears that bone marrow donation between minor siblings is widely practised. Indeed, there is substantial anecdotal evidence to the effect that parents are sometimes conceiving children with a view to them acting as marrow donors to sick siblings. In relation to more intrusive and risky procedures, such as organ donation, it is much less likely that parental consent alone would suffice. Rather, as in the case of non-therapeutic procedures upon incompetent adults, the matter would almost certainly come before the court for a declaration of lawfulness. In the USA, whilst such declarations have been granted in several cases (see, for example, *Hart v Brown* 289 A 2d 386 (1972) which concerned a kidney transplant between seven year old identical twins), the court refused to make one in a more recent case, *Curran v Bosze* (1990).

Curran v Bosze 566 NE 2d 1319 (1990), Illinois Sup Ct

The plaintiff was the former wife of the defendant and mother of three and a half year old twins by him. The defendant's 12 year old son from a previous marriage was dying from leukaemia and the defendant brought a petition requiring her to submit the twins to a blood test to establish compatibility with the 12 year old with a view to a subsequent bone marrow transplant:

> **Calvo J**: In each of the foregoing cases where consent to the kidney transplant was authorised, regardless whether the authority to consent was to be exercised by the court, a parent or a guardian, the key inquiry was the presence or absence of a benefit to the potential donor. Notwithstanding the language used by the courts in reaching their determination that a transplant may or may not occur, the standard by which the determination was made was whether the transplant would be in the best interest of the child or incompetent person.
>
> The primary benefit to the donor in these cases arises from the relationship existing between the donor and recipient. In *Strunk* [*v Strunk*], the donor lived in a State institution. The recipient was a brother who served as the donor's only connection with the outside world. In both *Hart* [*v Brown*] and *Little* [*v*

Little 576 SW 2d 493 (1979)], there was evidence that the sibling relationship between the donor and recipient was close. In each of these cases, both parents had given their consent ...

We hold that a parent or guardian may give consent on behalf of a minor daughter or son for the child to donate bone marrow to a sibling, only when to do so would be in the minor's best interest.

The evidence reveals three critical factors which are necessary to a determination that it will be in the best interests of a child to donate bone marrow to a sibling. First, the parent who consents on behalf of the child must be informed of the risks and benefits inherent in the bone marrow harvesting procedure to the child.

Second, there must be emotional support available to the child from the person or persons who take care of the child. The testimony reveals that a child who is to undergo general anaesthesia and the bone marrow harvesting procedure needs the emotional support of a person whom the child loves and trusts. A child who is to donate bone marrow is required to go to an unfamiliar place and meet with unfamiliar people. Depending upon the age of the child, he or she may or may not understand what is to happen. The evidence establishes that the presence and emotional support by the child's caretaker is important to ease the fears associated with such an unfamiliar procedure.

Third, there must be an existing, close relationship between the donor and recipient. The evidence clearly shows that there is no physical benefit to a donor child. If there is any benefit to a child who donates bone marrow to a sibling it will be a psychological benefit. According to the evidence, the psychological benefit is not simply one of personal, individual altruism in an abstract theoretical sense, although that may be a factor.

The psychological benefit is grounded firmly in the fact that the donor and recipient are known to each other as family. Only where there is an existing relationship between a healthy child and his or her ill sister or brother may a psychological benefit to the child from donating bone marrow to a sibling realistically be found to exist. The evidence establishes that it is the existing sibling relationship, as well as the potential for a continuing sibling relationship, which forms the context in which it may be determined that it will be in the best interests of the child to undergo a bone marrow harvesting procedure for a sibling ...

Ms Curran has refused consent on behalf of the twins to the bone marrow transplant because she does not think it is in their best interests to subject them to the risks and pains involved in undergoing general anaesthesia and the harvesting procedure. While Ms Curran is aware that the risks involved in donating bone marrow and undergoing general anaesthesia are small, she also is aware that when such risk occurs, it may be life-threatening ...

This court shares the opinion of the circuit court that Jean Pierre's situation evokes sympathy from all who've heard [it]. No matter how small the hope that a bone marrow transplant will cure Jean Pierre, the fact remains that without the transplant, Jean Pierre will almost certainly die. The sympathy felt by this court, the circuit court, and all those who have learned of Jean Pierre's tragic situation cannot, however, obscure the fact that, under the circumstances presented in the case at bar, it neither would be proper under existing law nor in the best interests of the three and a half year old twins for the twins to participate in the bone marrow harvesting procedure.

Actions by donors in negligence

Whilst no special issues arise in respect of the duty of care owed by extracting surgeon to donor, interesting questions are posed by the negligence of third parties. Suppose A requires a kidney transplant because of negligent conduct by B; if C comes forward and donates one of his kidneys to A, can he then claim compensation from B? A Canadian case in which recovery was allowed in these circumstances is analysed by Gerald Robertson:

Robertson, G, 'A new application of the rescue principle' (1980) 96 LQR 19:

The recent decision of the Manitoba Queen's Bench in *Urbanski v Patel* (1978) 84 DLR (3d) 650 is further evidence of the significant contribution which Canadian courts have made in relation to 'rescue' cases in the law of tort (see for example, *Linden* (1971) 34 MLR 241). In the instant case, the plaintiff's daughter underwent a sterilisation operation performed by the defendant surgeon. During the course of the operation, the defendant mistakenly removed the patient's only kidney, believing it to be an ovarian cyst. The patient was immediately linked to a dialysis machine and the long process of waiting for a suitable kidney donor began. After almost 12 months of fruitless search, the plaintiff volunteered to have one of his own kidneys removed for transplantation to his daughter. This was done (unfortunately the transplant proved to be unsuccessful) and thereafter the plaintiff raised an action against the defendant claiming damages for the loss of his kidney. The plaintiff's claim was successful and he was awarded $8,650 in damages.

Not surprisingly, the court tackled this fact situation from the standpoint of 'foreseeability'. It concluded that it was reasonably foreseeable that if the defendant's negligence resulted in the removal of the patient's only kidney, 'one of her family would be invited, and would agree, to donate a kidney for transplant'. Thus the plaintiff's altruistic act was to be regarded as a natural and probable consequence of the defendant's negligence and therefore did not constitute a *novus actus interveniens*.

The only other case to have considered this question was that of *Sirianni v Anna* 285 NYS 2d 709 (1967), in which a New York court, dealing with an identical fact situation, dismissed the plaintiff's action on the grounds that the kidney donation was not a foreseeable consequence of the defendant's negligence. The court in Urbanski distinguished this decision on the basis that in 1967 kidney transplantation was still in its infancy, whereas by 1976 it had become accepted medical practice and was therefore 'entirely foreseeable'.

This treatment of the foreseeability question is, however, open to criticism. In regarding the issue of foreseeability as being relevant only to the question of remoteness, the court failed to consider whether or not the defendant owed the plaintiff a duty of care. The defendant was unaware, until after the operation, that the patient had only one kidney, and thus he could not be expected to have foreseen, at the time of the operation, that removal of the patient's kidney would result in the need for transplantation. It follows, therefore, that since injury to the plaintiff was not reasonably foreseeable at the time of the negligent act, no duty of care was owed to him by the defendant.

However, *Urbanski* is far from unique in failing to consider this question. Indeed, the decision is consistent with the approach adopted in many other rescue cases, in which courts have tended to gloss over the question of duty of care by concentrating on the foreseeability of the initial injury to the rescuee, rather than on the foreseeability of the rescue attempt ...

The significance of *Urbanski* lies in the fact that it extends the basis for recovery in rescue cases to an entirely new type of situation. In previous cases, the rescue attempt has involved a risk of physical injury to the rescuer, which he has chosen, either consciously or instinctively, to ignore in going to the assistance of the person in danger. In the *Urbanski* situation, physical injury is inevitable, and it is the rescuer's conscious decision to submit to such injury that forms the basis of the rescue attempt.

Despite this distinction, the court regarded the plaintiff's claim as falling within the established 'rescue principle', and it is submitted that an English court would be likely to do the same. There is no reason why the plaintiff's claim should be prejudiced merely because the sustaining of physical injury is a necessary part, and not merely an incidental consequence, of the rescue attempt ...

The court also concluded that the defence of *volenti* should be rejected, and once again it is thought that an English court would reach a similar conclusion. Cases such as *Haynes v Harwood* [1935] 1 KB 146 and *Baker v Hopkins* [1959] 1 WLR 966 demonstrate a firm reluctance on the part of English courts to uphold the defence of *volenti* in rescue cases. The plaintiff in *Urbanski* can scarcely be said to have voluntarily assumed the risk of injury, notwithstanding that he realised that such injury was inevitable, given the dilemma in which he had been placed by the defendant's negligent act. The plaintiff's parental feelings towards his daughter, coupled with an understandable sense of moral obligation, left him without any real choice in the matter.

Subsequently, however, in the case of *Moore v Shah* 458 NYS 2d 33 (1982), a New York court refused to award compensation similar circumstances. Weiss J commented as follows:

Weiss J: In order to recover, a plaintiff must be one within the 'zone of danger' (*Tobin v Grossman* 24 NY 2d 609 (1969) ... *Palsgraf v Long Is RR Co* 248 NY 339 (1928) ...). It is difficult to charge a physician with the responsibility to foresee each and every person other than his patient who might conceivably be affected by his negligence ...

Our research has disclosed but one reported case in which the plaintiff was an actual organ donor. In *Sirianni v Anna* 55 Misc 2d 553 (1967) ... where a similar factual pattern to the instant case existed, Special Term granted defendant's motion to dismiss the complaint. While this court is not bound by *stare decisis* to follow that decision, we are persuaded by subsequent cases that it was correct. Only one year ago, the Court of Appeals held that where there is no allegation that the defendant was negligent with respect to the plaintiff as opposed to the patient, the case does not fall within recognised limits to the rescue doctrine and it declined to extend existing principles of law so as to include third parties who suffer (shock) as a result of direct injury to others. (*Tobin v Grossman*) ... There are serious policy considerations which militate against the recovery sought here. Our decision may best be summarised in the words of then Associate Judge Breitel in *Tobin v Grossman* ... 'Every injury has ramifying consequences, like the ripplings of the waters, without end. The problem for the law is to limit the legal consequences of wrongs to a controllable degree' ... We decline here to extend the common law to create a remedy for these plaintiffs.

It is submitted that an English court would be more likely to favour the cautious approach adopted in *Moore* to that in *Urbanski*.

Statutory limitations – the Human Organ Transplants Act 1989

Following a well publicised scandal in the late 1980s, in which it was revealed that a Harley Street clinic was paying impoverished Turkish donors up to £3,000 for their spare kidneys, Parliament enacted the Human Organ Transplants Act 1989. It is important to note at the outset that, by virtue of the definition of 'organ' found in s 7(2), the Act only applies to non-regenerative body parts such as kidneys and not to bone marrow or blood. Sections 1 and 2 of the Act provide as follows:

Human Organ Transplants Act 1989:

1   Prohibition of commercial dealings in human organs

(1) A person is guilty of an offence if in Great Britain he–

   (a) makes or receives any payment for the supply of, or for an offer to supply, an organ which has been or is to be removed from a dead or living person and is intended to be transplanted into another person whether in Great Britain or elsewhere;

   (b) seeks to find a person willing to supply for payment such an organ as is mentioned in para (a) above or offers to supply such an organ for payment;

   (c) initiates or negotiates any arrangement involving the making of any payment for the supply of, or for an offer to supply, such an organ; or

   (d) takes part in the management or control of a body of persons corporate or unincorporate whose activities consist of or include the initiation or negotiation of such arrangements.

(2) Without prejudice to para (b) of sub-s (1) above, a person is guilty of an offence if he causes to be published or distributed, or knowingly publishes or distributes, in Great Britain an advertisement–

    (a) inviting persons to supply for payment any such organs as are mentioned in para (a) of that sub-s or offering to supply any such organs for payment; or

    (b) indicating that the advertiser is willing to initiate or negotiate any such arrangement as is mentioned in para (c) of that sub-section.

(3) In this section 'payment' means payment in money or money's worth but does not include any payment for defraying or reimbursing–

    (a) the cost of removing, transporting or preserving the organ to be supplied; or

    (b) any expenses or loss of earnings incurred by a person so far as reasonably and directly attributable to his supplying an organ from his body.

(4) In this section 'advertisement' includes any form of advertising whether to the public generally, to any section of the public or individually to selected persons.

(5) A person guilty of an offence under sub-s (1) above is liable on summary conviction to imprisonment for a term not exceeding three months or a fine not exceeding level 5 on the standard scale or both; and a person guilty of an offence under sub-s (2) above is liable on summary conviction to a fine not exceeding level 5 on that scale.

2 Restriction on transplants between persons not genetically related

(1) Subject to sub-s (3) below, a person is guilty of an offence if in Great Britain he–

    (a) removes from a living person an organ intended to be transplanted into another person; or

    (b) transplants an organ removed from a living person into another person;

unless the person into whom the organ is to be or, as the case may be, is transplanted is genetically related to the person from whom the organ is removed.

(2) For the purposes of this section a person is genetically related to–

    (a) his natural parents and children;

    (b) his brothers and sisters of the whole or half blood;

    (c) the brothers and sisters of the whole or half blood of either of his natural parents; and

    (d) the natural children of his brothers and sisters of the whole or half blood or of the brothers and sisters of the whole or half blood of either of his natural parents;

but persons shall not in any particular case be treated as related in any of those ways unless the fact of the relationship has been established by such means as are specified by regulations made by the Secretary of State.

(3) The Secretary of State may by regulations provide that the prohibition in sub-s (1) above shall not apply in cases where–

(a) such authority as is specified in or constituted by the regulations is satisfied:

   (i) that no payment has been or is to be made in contravention of s 1 above; and

   (ii)that such other conditions as are specified in the regulations are satisfied; and

(b) such other requirements as may be specified in the regulations are complied with ...

For live organ transplants to remain lawful, it is apparent that the Act requires two main conditions to be fulfilled. First, in no case must any payment have been made in respect of the organ: s 1. Secondly, the transplant must either involve a donor and donee who are genetically related (ss 2(1)–(2)) or, where this is not the case, specifically be approved by the regulatory authority set up for that purpose by the Secretary of State: s 2(3). We shall look at these requirements in turn, before briefly considering the policy behind the 1989 Act.

Non-payment

The thrust of the legislation is to criminalise commercial dealings in organs. To this end, s 1(1) prohibits offers to buy or sell organs or act as broker, while s 1(2) strikes at advertising designed to elicit such offers. It is noteworthy that, unlike the case of the Surrogacy Arrangements Act 1985 (see above, Chapter 7), no immunity is conferred upon the principals, ie, the donor and donee themselves. On the other hand, by virtue of s 1(3)(b), 'payment' (and hence a commercial dealing) does not occur where the donor merely receives his reasonable expenses including loss of earnings.

Genetically related donor and donee

The relevant genetic relationships are set out in s 2(2) of the Act and are represented diagrammatically by Kennedy and Grubb, *Medical Law*, 2nd edn, 1994, London: Butterworths (p 1089) as follows:

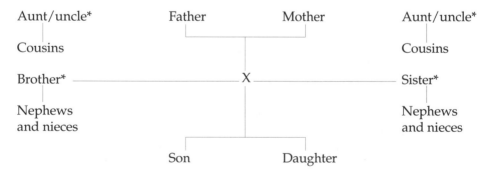

* includes 'of the half blood' (s 2(2)(c) and (d)).

The fact of any such relationship must be established prior to extraction in accordance with the terms of the Human Organ Transplants (Establishment of Relationship) Regulations 1989 SI 1989/2107. In some cases this may include the need for DNA testing.

Unrelated donor and donee – ULTRA

As already noted, in so far as the donor and donee do not fall within a specified genetic relationship, the transplant may only proceed with the sanction of the relevant regulatory authority. In this regard, the Unrelated Live Transplant Regulatory Authority (ULTRA) has been established pursuant to the Human Organ Transplants (Unrelated Persons) Regulations 1989 SI 1989/2480). Regulation 3 of the Statutory Instrument provides as follows:

3   **Transplants between persons who are not genetically related**

(1)   The prohibition in s 2(1) of the Act (restriction on transplants between persons not genetically related) shall not apply in cases where a registered medical practitioner has caused the matter to be referred to the Authority and where the Authority is satisfied–

(a)   that no payment has been, or is to be, made in contravention of s 1 of the Act;

(b)   that the registered medical practitioner who has caused the matter to be referred to the Authority has clinical responsibility for the donor; and

(c)   except in a case where the primary purpose of removal of an organ from a donor is the medical treatment of that donor, that the conditions specified in para (2) of this regulation are satisfied.

(2)   The conditions referred to in para (1)(c) of this regulation are–

(a)   that a registered medical practitioner has given the donor an explanation of the nature of the medical procedure for, and the risk involved in, the removal of the organ in question;

(b)   that the donor understands the nature of the medical procedure and the risks, as explained by the registered medical practitioner, and consents to the removal of the organ in question;

(c)   that the donor's consent to the removal of the organ in question was not obtained by coercion or the offer of an inducement;

(d)   that the donor understands that he is entitled to withdraw his consent if he wishes, but has not done so;

(e)   that the donor and the recipient have both been interviewed by a person who appears to the Authority to have been suitably qualified to conduct such interviews and who has reported to the Authority on the conditions contained in sub-paras (a)–(d) above and has included in his report an account of any difficulties of communication with the donor or the recipient and an explanation of how those difficulties were overcome.

Policy behind the Human Organ Transplants Act 1989

The background to the 1989 Act has already been mentioned. Hasty legislative response to a perceived public threat seldom makes for the best law and in this respect the Act may be criticised for providing exaggerated protection for the unrelated donor, while neglecting the related donor. Arguably, it is the latter who is ultimately more vulnerable to illicit pressure to donate. As Kennedy and Grubb comment:

Kennedy, I and Grubb, A, *Medical Law*, 2nd edn, 1994, London: Butterworths, p 1092:

... why did parliament distinguish between donations between genetically related persons and those who are not? The explanation offered by the then Parliamentary Under Secretary of State for Health, in the House of Commons (HC Deb, 6 July 1989) during the passage of the Bill was as follows:

> The Bill already excludes genetically related people from scrutiny by the authority. A reason for that is that the existence of a close genetic relationship can be verified with a high degree of accuracy by laboratory testing. In this country, the vast majority of live transplants would be covered by that exemption, as close family members are both more likely to come forward to offer themselves as donors and to prove compatible, in the medical sense.
>
> Under the Bill, the existence of a genetic relationship would be verified in each case in an objective way by such testing. Appropriate tests may have already been carried out in the process of trying to establish the compatibility of the donor and would-be recipient. In case of relatives 'in law' or people not related at all to the would-be recipient, the existence of some kind of relationship or personal tie is more difficult to establish. Unfortunately, we cannot rule out the possibility of non-genetic 'relationships' being formed solely for the purpose of the operation or of pressure – economic or otherwise – being brought to bear upon a donor to submit to a transplant operation.
>
> For those reasons, it is intended that the authority will consider the available evidence in each case where no genetic relationship has been established, before giving an independent decision on whether an offer of donation is altruistic. However, the fact that the authority will scrutinise all cases of live donation between non-related persons does not imply that unnecessary obstacles will be placed in the way of transplants between spouses or 'in-law' relations.

As this makes plain, parliament was concerned that the donation be entirely altruistic and presumes that this will be so in the case of those who are 'genetically related' whereas it may not be otherwise. It is fair to ask, however, if the key to altruism is close family ties, why should a spouse be treated as a stranger? Furthermore, grandparents and grandchildren are genetically related and may surely be presumed to act as altruistically as those included within the Act, yet they too are excluded as if they were strangers. It cannot be that a grandparent is necessarily too old to be a donor because someone may be a grandparent at 40!

By contrast, if altruism is the key, why should parliament restrict unregulated donation to the genetically related? It could be said that intrafamily donations may well be the product of severe social pressure ('coercion') rather than altruism ... In some jurisdictions, consequently, legislation prohibits the removal of non-regenerative tissue from a minor for the purpose of transplantation, recognising the danger of pressure within the family (see, for example, s 14(1) of the Human Tissue Act 1982 in Victoria, Australia).

The dead donor

As noted earlier, the development of new immuno-suppressant drugs within the last 15 years has diminished the importance of donor-donee compatibility and permitted the increased use of cadaveric transplants. Currently, nearly 90% of kidneys transplanted in the UK are obtained in this way and the practice enjoys a number of practical advantages. Most obviously, there is no difficulty in terms of exposing the dead donor to harm (or the risk of harm) and a total harvesting of organs is therefore possible, including the heart, lungs, pancreas, liver and eyes. On the other hand, some distinct problems are also created, notably the need for the organs to be removed fairly rapidly after death, if they are to be of any use. This raises the issue not only of who may authorise such removal, but also the larger question of how it is proper to treat the recently deceased human corpse. David Lamb has commented on this latter issue as follows:

Lamb, D, *Organ Transplants and Ethics*, 1990, London: Routledge, pp 122–24:

Although respect for the deceased takes different forms in different cultures, for the most part violation of the body's integrity for therapeutic purposes, such as organ transplantation, is not regarded as disrespect. At least no Western Church has adopted an unfavourable stance towards organ removal. Jewish, Christian, and Buddhist countries, despite prohibitions on the mutilation of corpses, permit cadaveric transplants provided prior consent of the deceased – or family consent – has been obtained.

The respect accorded to dead bodies in the Muslim faith rules out the study of anatomy on indigenous corpses. Post mortems are rare in Islamic countries. But in 1982 organ donation after death was declared *halal* (permissible) by the Senior 'Ulama' Commission, the highest religious authority in such matters, in Saudi Arabia ...

Nevertheless, there are sources of resistance to organ transplantation which deserve consideration. An important aspect of resistance to routine harvesting of cadaveric organs is the symbolic role which is assigned to the dead body. This role should not be underestimated, even though the interests of the living may outweigh those of the dead. Joel Feinberg ... cites a case which brings out the importance of such symbolism. In 1978 the Department of Transport in the USA contracted with several university laboratories to test designs for automobiles in actual crashes at varying velocities. Dummies had proven unsatisfactory. Some researchers – with the consent of the relatives – had substituted human cadavers. After a public outcry the tests were stopped, despite the Department of Transport's protest that such a decision would set back progress on safety protection for years. The grounds for the prohibition of these tests were that 'the use of human cadavers for vehicle safety research violated fundamental notions of morality and human dignity' ...

It should be stressed that no coercive measures were employed. Research workers were not coerced and the tests were conducted in private. Relatives had expressed consent and prior consent to donation for experimental purposes had been indicated by the deceased. What then, is the difference between this project, designed to save lives, and the use of cadavers for laboratory or transplantation purposes?

The only difference is the violent 'assault' on the cadavers during the car crashes. But the violence was not experienced violence. No pain or discomfort could possibly have been inflicted upon the 'victims'. The issue at stake appears to concern the symbolic role of the human cadaver. Violent assault on a cadaver is an assault on the important symbolic role assigned to the newly dead.

According to Feinberg, symbolic fears of this kind, though culturally significant, should not outweigh the imperative to save lives. Certainly objections to the routine salvaging of cadaveric organs based on symbolic fears should not impede research to improve life expectancy. To drive home this point Feinberg draws an analogy with William James' story of a Russian aristocrat who wept over a fictional tragedy in a theatre while her coachman froze to death outside in her carriage. In such cases the symbolic has outweighed the real.

There is merit in Feinberg's argument. But in reply it must be stressed that symbols are important to the very fabric of society. A society with no symbolic values for the dead is little short of savagery. Moreover, a body is not just a symbol. The newly dead continue as a presence, which is why they are referred to as deceased. The absence of the life that once existed has a very real presence ...

The position at common law

Establishing death

Traditionally, death was defined in terms of cessation of cardiovascular function, ie, the person had no pulse, was not breathing, etc. Advances in medical technology have rendered this approach obsolete: the features in question, though closely aligned with death, are no longer either sufficient or necessary for it (a person may be revived from the above state or, conversely, have the relevant functions sustained mechanically in the absence of all brain activity). Accordingly, a new definition of death was put forward in Guidelines issued by the Medical Royal Colleges in 1976 ((1976) 2 BMJ 1187). Death is now equated with irreversible loss of brainstem function: the brainstem, which is the last part of the brain to die off, is necessary both for any possibility of awareness (the upper brainstem) and for spontaneous reflexes such as respiration (lower brainstem).

Although this new concept of death (referred to interchangeably as 'brainstem death' or simply 'brain death') has not been incorporated into legislation, it is accepted by the courts. A leading case in point is that of *Re A*.

Re A [1992] 3 Med LR 303, Fam Div (Johnson J)

A was a 19 month old infant who was admitted to hospital with serious head injuries following a domestic incident. He was placed upon a ventilator but showed no signs of recovery. The hospital, after carrying out the diagnostic tests laid down by the MRC Guidelines, was satisfied that A was dead and applied for a declaration allowing his removal from the ventilator:

Johnson J: On 20 January – that is last Monday – the consultant removed A briefly from the ventilator to see whether he was capable of supporting himself without the ventilator. When she did so she heard slight gasping noises which led her to believe that A was not brainstem dead according to criteria now generally accepted in medical circles.

The precise definition of death has been the subject of recommendations by both the Royal College of Surgeons and the Royal College of Physicians and a working party of the British Paediatric Association. Applying the criteria laid down by her profession the consultant concluded on 20 January that A was not then brainstem dead. On the following day she again carried out the tests which are necessary to determine whether the necessary criteria are satisfied. The consultant described those tests to me and she explained to me that each one was satisfied. The tests lasted overall about half an hour.

Describing the criteria and her observations of A, and expressing myself in lay terms, her evidence was to the following effect. A's pupils were fixed and dilated. On movement of the head his eyes moved with his head. What is called the 'doll's eye response' was absent. On his eye being touched with a piece of cotton wool there was no response. On cold water being passed into his ear there was no eye movement in response. On steps being taken, in effect, to cause him to 'gag' there was no reflex reaction, neither was there reaction to pain being applied to his central nervous system. Finally, on his temporary removal from the ventilator to enable the carbon dioxide content of his body to increase there was no respiratory response. All in all, the consultant was satisfied that A was brainstem dead ...

On the same day the consultant had arranged for a colleague consultant paediatric neurologist to carry out the same tests that she had, herself, carried out the previous day with a view to confirming or otherwise the validity of her own professional conclusion. Under professional guidelines it was not necessary for her to seek a second opinion in that way, but she decided that in the particular circumstances of the case it would be a wise thing for her to do. Accordingly, the tests were carried out again on Wednesday of last week, 22 January, by this colleague who reached the same conclusion as had been reached by the first consultant. Both doctors were at pains to exclude other possibilities for A's state, including the possibility of his suffering from extreme hypothermia or some abnormality of his biochemistry. Moreover, they tested for drugs, lest his brainstem function should have been suppressed by the administration of some drug of which they had not been aware ...

Both doctors concluded that A was brainstem dead ...

It is now Monday 27 January. I have no hesitation at all in holding that A has been dead since Tuesday of last week, 21 January.

The ability to establish the fact of death swiftly, but nevertheless with an appropriate degree of certainty, is important in the context of transplanting organs where, to maximise the chances of success, removal should generally take place as soon as possible. In fact, in this regard the perceived need to satisfy the Code of Practice's diagnostic requirements has apparently halted a technique for organ retrieval previously deployed in the South West of England with some success. The background to the procedure in question, known as 'elective ventilation', and the debate it has aroused, are described by David Price:

Price, DPT, 'Organ transplant initiatives: the twilight zone' (1997) 23 JME 170:

In 1988 the Royal Devon and Exeter Hospital became the first British hospital to develop an E[lective] V[entilation] protocol. Patients in deep irreversible coma and believed to be dying imminently of intracranial haemorrhage were transferred to intensive care, with relatives' consent, so that artificial ventilation could be commenced immediately respiratory arrest occurred and until brain (stem) death tests could be satisfied. However, in October 1994, the Health Departments of England and Wales issued guidelines stating that EV for transplantation purposes constituted an unlawful battery – being non-therapeutic and not done in the best interests of the individual. This mirrored the conclusion of the 1994 King's Fund Institute Report (which none the less endorsed EV as an *ethically* acceptable practice, as incidentally have the BMA and the British Transplantation Society), and is probably an accurate perception of the present common law. Although an alternative 'not against the interests of the individual' test has been occasionally employed in relation to non-therapeutic procedures performed on minors, such a standard has yet to be legally employed in respect of a mentally incompetent adult person in a similar context ...

The meaning of death

... By contrast with the majority view across all disciplines, the clinicians who developed the Exeter protocol argue that the process of dying is not prolonged by EV, as the patient is already dead – one is ventilating a corpse ... Riad, from Exeter, has said, 'The procedure causes no harm to the patient as ventilation is instituted at the time of respiratory arrest *which is the consequence of brain death* ... Therefore it is important not to institute EV before respiratory arrest'. Such a sequence of events is explicitly referred to in the Memorandum on the Diagnosis of Death attached to *Cadaveric Organs for Transplantation* (1983) issued by the Conference of the Medical Royal Colleges:

In a minority of cases, brain death does not occur as a result of the failure of other organs or systems but as a direct result of severe damage to the brain itself from, perhaps, a head injury or a spontaneous intracranial haemorrhage. Here the order of events is reversed: instead of the failure of such vital functions as heart beat and respiration eventually resulting in brain death, brain death results in the cessation of spontaneous respiration: this is normally followed within minutes by cardiac arrest due to hypoxia. If, however, oxygenation is maintained by artificial ventilation, the heart beat can continue for some days, and haemoperfusion will for a time be adequate to maintain function in other organs, such as the liver and kidneys.

Supporters of the Exeter protocol argue that cessation of respiration is (necessary and sufficient) evidence that the patient has already succumbed to brain death – the question is whether this is so ...

Judicial acceptance

... although there is no definition of death in English law, brain stem death established in accordance with the agreed criteria incorporated in the code of practice of the medical royal colleges has been accepted as establishing legal as well as 'medical' death. However, whilst this constitutes judicial acceptance of these tests, it does not necessarily indicate that this is the *sole* criterion for the determination of death in law. But what, if any, other evidence of (brain) death would satisfy a court of law? In *Re A* ...two sets of tests were carried out to confirm [brain death], the first on 21 January and the second on 22 January. Johnson J stated: 'I have no hesitation at all in holding that A has been dead since Tuesday of last week, 21 January'. In other words, the *time* of death was *before* the second sets of tests were performed to confirm lack of brainstem responses. However, the code of practice states that the time of death should be recorded as the time when death was conclusively established and that 'Death is only conclusively established when the criteria have been satisfied on two successive occasions'. It appears therefore that the code was not fully adhered to in this instance, nor were the recommendations of the British Paediatric Association, which stipulate that in children older than two months, two sets of tests should be conducted separately by two experienced clinicians 12–24 hours apart. *Re A* illustrates that death can be legally declared to have occurred according to brain death criteria before two sets of tests have been completed and death has been confirmed ... Despite certain views to the contrary, it seems that there is no mandatory legal requirement at present that a person cannot be declared brain (stem) dead unless the recommendations of the report of the medical royal colleges – ie, the code of practice – have been complied with in their entirety. The code of practice, although highly influential, does not have the force of law ...

If, however, contrary to this analysis, the courts were not prepared to regard certain patients (viz, those who have received direct injury to the brainstem) as dead prior to ventilation, it does not automatically follow that ventilating them would be unlawful. That would only be the case if no responsible body of doctors could regard such a procedure as being in such a patient's best interests. At least where the patient had made a prior request to act as a donor, such a determination is by no means a foregone conclusion (in this context it is interesting to note the relaxed attitude of the Court of Appeal in *R v HFEA ex p Blood* [1997] 2 WLR 806 to the non-consensual extraction of sperm from a comatose and dying man).

In the light of these considerations, the advice contained in the 1994 DoH Circular, which led to the current moratorium on elective ventilation, may arguably have been premature.

Authorising removal of organs

Gerald Dworkin has commented upon the shortcomings in previous law in this area, and the consequent need for more recent statutory intervention, as follows:

Dworkin, G, 'The law relating to organ transplantation in England' (1970) 33 MLR 353:

The existing law

(a) *Common law.* The common law position concerning corpses is curious but relatively well established. A corpse cannot ordinarily be the subject of ownership. Usually the executor or next of kin will have lawful possession of the body and there is a duty to arrange for burial at the earliest opportunity. It follows that, at common law, a man cannot by his will, or otherwise, legally determine what shall happen with his body after his death, although in most cases his wishes concerning the disposal of his body will be observed. That does not, of itself, authorise organs to be taken from corpses for the purpose of transplantation.

(b) *Statute.* The need for human bodies for medical purposes is not new: bodies have always been required for anatomical teaching and research. But any attempt on the part of persons in possession of a body to sell it, even for the purpose of dissection, was unlawful; the bodies of persons convicted of murder were alone capable of being used for dissection. The scandals of body snatching and the publicity of the murder trial of Burke and Hare led to the passing of the Anatomy Act 1832, which enabled bodies to be supplied legally to medical schools for the purpose of anatomical examination. The demand for corpses was then successfully met for over a century.

It is only in recent times that the medical profession realised that the law relating to cadavers was far too restrictive. The successful development of the corneal graft operation focused attention on the lack of supply of eyes and the inability of potential donors to bequeath their eyes for such purposes. In a little debated, but carefully prepared, piece of legislation the Corneal Grafting Act 1952 (the wording of which to some extent followed the Anatomy Act 1832) was passed authorising the use of eyes of deceased persons for therapeutic purposes. This Act quickly proved to be too narrow, for it did not enable any other part of the body to be removed. However, once this kind of provision was on the statute book, it was much easier to extend it. The Human Tissue

Act 1961 replaced the 1952 Act and authorised, in certain circumstances, '*the use of the body or any specified part of the body after death for therapeutic purposes or for purposes of medical education or research*'. This Act, which provided a model for many other jurisdictions, at present governs the English law relating to cadaver transplantation.

The statutory position – the Human Tissue Act 1961

The Human Tissue Act (HTA) 1961 was designed to increase the ability of persons to donate their organs for therapeutic purposes after their death. Section 1 of the Act provides as follows:

1   **Removal of parts of bodies for medical purposes**

   (1) If any person, either in writing at any time or orally in the presence of two or more witnesses during his last illness, has expressed a request that his body or any specified part of his body be used after his death for therapeutic purposes or for purposes of medical education or research, the person lawfully in possession of his body after his death may, unless he has reason to believe that the request was subsequently withdrawn, authorise the removal from the body of any part or, as the case may be, the specified part, for use in accordance with the request.

   (2) Without prejudice to the foregoing sub-section, the person lawfully in possession of the body of a deceased person may authorise the removal of any part from the body for use for the said purposes if, having made such reasonable inquiry as may be practicable, he has no reason to believe–

      (a) that the deceased had expressed an objection to his body being so dealt with after his death, and had not withdrawn it; or

      (b) that the surviving spouse or any surviving relative of the deceased objects to the body being so dealt with.

   (3) Subject to sub-ss (4), (4A) and (5) of this section, the removal and use of any part of a body in accordance with an authority given in pursuance of this section shall be lawful.

   (4) No such removal, except of eyes or parts of eyes, shall be effected except by a registered medical practitioner, who must have satisfied himself by personal examination of the body that life is extinct.

   (4A) No such removal of an eye or part of an eye shall be effected except by–

      (a) a registered medical practitioner, who must have satisfied himself by personal examination of the body that life is extinct; or

      (b) a person in the employment of a health authority or NHS trust acting on the instructions of a registered medical practitioner who must, before giving those instructions, be satisfied that the person in question is sufficiently qualified and trained to perform the removal competently and must also either:

(i) have satisfied himself by personal examination of the body that life is extinct; or

(ii) be satisfied that life is extinct on the basis of a statement to that effect by a registered medical practitioner who has satisfied himself by personal examination of the body that life is extinct.

(5) Where a person has reason to believe that an inquest may be required to be held on any body or that a post mortem examination of any body may be required by the coroner, he shall not, except with the consent of the coroner–

(a) give an authority under this section in respect of the body; or

(b) act on such an authority given by any other person.

(6) No authority shall be given under this section in respect of any body by a person entrusted with the body for the purpose only of its interment or cremation.

(7) In the case of a body lying in a hospital, nursing home or other institution, any authority under this section may be given on behalf of the person having the control and management thereof by any officer or person designated for that purpose by the first-mentioned person.

(8) Nothing in this section shall be construed as rendering unlawful any dealing with, or with any part of, the body of a deceased person which is lawful apart from this Act.

Conditions for removal

The effect of this provision is to allow organs to be removed for transplant in two main situations: either where the deceased has made an express request to that effect (s 1(1)); or, in the absence of such a request, where reasonable inquiry reveals no objection to the same either by the deceased or by his spouse/surviving relatives (s 1(2)). In these circumstances, 'the person in lawful possession of the body' is empowered to authorise removal, and charged with making the relevant inquiries. This is generally thought to be the hospital where death occurs (an interpretation supported by the wording of s 1(7) of the Act). It is also important that the surgeon who does the removing should personally satisfy himself of the fact of death (s 1(4)) and that, where an inquest is a possibility, the consent of the coroner is obtained (s 1(5)).

Status of surviving relatives

As noted, the effect of s 1(2)(b) is to give the deceased's spouse and surviving relatives the opportunity to object to the transplant of the organs, in so far as the deceased has not expressed any wishes in the matter. It is apparent that this amounts to a conditional power of veto as opposed to a requirement that such persons must actively consent, since if they cannot be traced by reasonable inquiry, donation may simply proceed in their absence.

Nevertheless, significant vagaries in the provision remain both as to the meaning of 'any surviving relative' and with regard to what will amount to the making by the hospital of 'such reasonable inquiry as may be practicable'.

Gerald Dworkin has commented on these questions as follows:

Dworkin, G, 'The law relating to organ transplantation in England' (1970) 33 MLR 353:

Hospitals ... potentially have considerable powers to use bodies, subject only to the wishes of relatives. This section indicates that the surviving spouse or any other relatives may object, but no definition of surviving relatives is given. In other legislation where 'relative' is expressly defined, the word is given a very wide meaning and sometimes includes all relatives of the full blood or half blood, and adopted and illegitimate children; equally wide meanings have been given to the word in wills ...

The paradox of the section now becomes apparent. The hospital may have, and may wish to make immediate use of, a body, but whom do they consult? If the identity of the deceased is not known, can the body be used? If the surviving spouse or other close relatives expressly consent, must the hospital fear a more distant relative claiming that he would have objected had he been consulted in time? The only guidance given to the hospital is that it may act provided it has made such reasonable inquiry as may be practicable. Where the identity of the deceased cannot immediately be ascertained or the close relatives of a deceased immediately contacted, then it would be very dangerous for the hospital to deal with a body. Experience in other countries has shown that irate relatives are prepared to take proceedings against medical authorities who have not contacted them. The reply that it would not be practicable to spend too long trying to trace relatives since the body must be used within a short time after the death would not be decisive. The practicability of the inquiry must relate to the steps taken to trace the relatives, not to the practicability of using the body, since the basis of the provision is to allow the relative to object if he so wishes. Where a close relative is available and does not object, then the medical authorities are on slightly safer ground in proceeding in spite of the possibility that other relatives who were within the range of immediate contact and who were not consulted might object and claim that the use of the body was unlawful. It is clear, however, that a hospital will rarely be in a position to guarantee that it has made all reasonable inquiries if the body is used within a few hours of death.

A fairly relaxed approach to the problem can be found in the relevant DoH Guidance, reissued most recently in March 1998:

Department of Health, *Code of Practice for the Diagnosis of Brain Stem Death – Including Guidelines for the Identification and Management of Potential Organ and Tissue Donors*, HSC 1998/035, London: DoH:

8.8 ... the designated person's duty is only to 'make such reasonable enquiries as may be practicable'. In most instances it will be sufficient to discuss the matter with any one relative who had been in close contact with the deceased, determining whether there is reason to believe that any other relative would be likely to object. There is no need to establish a lack of objection from all relatives before authorising the removal of organs.

8.9 *Authorisation in the absence of relatives*. If a donor's relatives are unavailable it would be impracticable to ask them and if they were, for example, young children or very seriously ill it would generally be unreasonable to do so. In such circumstances the *designated person* can proceed to give authorisation if he has no reason to believe that there is a relevant objection, but a note of the enquiries made should be entered on the transplantation checklist. Cases when a potential donor's views about organ removal cannot be established and the relatives cannot be contacted are exceptional, but it is reasonable to assume in such cases that if a donor has belonged to a religious group which objects to the removal of organs from the body, he himself would have objected.

More generally, it should be noted that, under s 1 of the 1961 Act, the hospital is in any event left with a discretion as to whether or not to make use of the organs ('the person in lawful possession may ... authorise the removal ...', not 'shall'). Unsurprisingly perhaps, given the sensitivity of the issue, it appears that, as a matter of clinical practice, the hospital will not proceed in the face of objection by relatives, even where the deceased had expressed the desire to donate under s 1(1). As the Department of Health Circular notes:

> **Department of Health,** *Code of Practice for the Diagnosis of Brain Stem Death – Including Guidelines for the Identification and Management of Potential Organ and Tissue Donors,* **HSC 1998/035, London: DoH:**
>
> 8.2 *The donor card.* If a patient carries a signed donor card or has otherwise recorded his or her wishes, for example, by inclusion in the NHS Organ Donor Register, there is no legal requirement to establish lack of objection on the part of relatives, although it is good practice to take account of the views of close relatives. If a relative objects, despite the known request by the patient, staff will need to judge, according to the circumstances of the case, whether it is wise to proceed with organ removal. Staff need to consider the feelings of relatives, who may be under great stress, so that in practice any objections raised by relatives usually take priority over donor's wishes.

Effects of non-compliance with the Human Tissue Act 1961

Criminal

The Human Tissue Act does not on the face of it provide for any offence to be committed as a result of failure to comply with its terms. The question of whether a person who contravened those terms could nevertheless be indicted for the residual offence of breaching a statute was at issue in *R v Lennox-Wright* [1973] Crim LR 529 in which the defendant, who had forged his medical qualifications, removed eyes from cadavers for use in corneal transplants as part of his duties. He was charged, *inter alia*, with offences under s 1(4) of the Act which provided (prior to amendment by the Corneal Grafting Act 1986: see now s 1(4A)) that such removal could be effected only by a registered medical practitioner. However, it is unlikely that this decision would be followed in the light of the more recent Court of Appeal ruling in *R v Horseferry Road Justices ex p IBA* [1986] 2 All ER 666. There, it was stated that there is a general presumption, in modern statutory interpretation, that no offence will lie in a statute's contravention unless it expressly says so.

Tortious

Given the apparent lack of criminal sanction, is there any civil remedy available to those whose rights may be violated in the course of disobedience to the terms of the 1961 Act? The only plausible candidates for such rightholders are the deceased's spouse/surviving relatives in so far as they are not consulted pursuant to s 1(2)(b). The most obvious possibility might be for them to maintain an action in 'nervous shock'. However, as well as requiring that such persons suffer some recognised psychiatric illness, this must have been as a result of witnessing the traumatic event (ie, removal) or its aftermath with their own unaided senses: *Alcock v Chief Constable of South Yorkshire Police* [1991] 4 All ER 907.

Even assuming that, in order to plug a perceived lacuna in the law, a court took a more sympathetic view in the context of unauthorised organ removal, it is suggested that causation would remain a significant hurdle for any plaintiff. The presumption might well be that the plaintiff's sudden bereavement alone induced their illness, the effect of subsequent events being merely incidental.

Other sources of organs/tissue

Before leaving this area, a number of other possible sources of supply of organs and tissue need to be considered. As transplant technology continues to advance, some of these may be expected to assume increasing importance in the future.

Foetal tissue transplants

Recent developments in medical science have revealed the possibility of using live brain cells, harvested from aborted foetuses of 10–14 weeks' gestation, to treat certain degenerative brain disorders, notably Parkinson's and Alzheimer's disease. In the future, foetal pancreatic cells may also be used in the treatment of some forms of diabetes. In contrast to the issue of embryo research looked at above, Chapter 7, the focus here is on the usage of *in vivo* foetuses. The ethical difficulty that this gives rise to, and the entanglement of this issue with the abortion debate, is explored by David Lamb:

> **Lamb, D, *Organ Transplants and Ethics*, 1990, London: Routledge, pp 74–76:**
>
> What are the chief ethical objections to foetal tissue research and transplants? There are three closely related objections. First, it is argued that killing and then dissecting a foetus is an abuse to the developing human being. The second objection is that engaging in such practices will brutalise those who perform this work, and the third objection is that it will encourage abortions and even motivate conceptions with the express intention to abort ... In addition to these objections are ethical problems concerning the authorisation of embryo tissue research and transplantation.

The ... objections are so closely related that they can be dealt with together. The issue they relate to is the morality of voluntary termination of pregnancy. The morality of elected abortions has been widely discussed in learned journals, the popular media, and various legislative assemblies. Strong views have been expressed and the general standpoints are so familiar that they need not be repeated here. At present, however, voluntary termination of pregnancy, subject to certain conditions, is legally permissible in the USA, the UK, and several other European countries. If the opponents of voluntary termination are correct in stating that it is immoral, then it might be argued that performing an abortion is an abuse to the developing human being, and that those who perform this work are likely to become brutalised, and that any steps likely to increase the number of terminations should be resisted. In short, if voluntary termination is wrong, then so are actions which depend on it, and at least some degree of guilt by association is incurred by those who seek to benefit from the killing of a foetus. Moreover, an assurance that no foetus is ever dissected prior to death would be of no consequence. For on these terms the issue turns on the rightness or wrongness of killing the foetus in the first place ...

On these terms, it would seem that if the arguments against voluntary terminations are persuasive, then the only scope for ethical discussion on foetal tissue transplantation is whether it is morally acceptable to use material from spontaneous abortions. The problem is that material from the latter is less reliable than from voluntary abortions. This is because the possibility of foetal abnormality is too high, and because of various problems concerning the time lag between the actual death of the foetus and its expulsion from the uterus. In any case, most miscarriages occur too early for viable transplantation.

But given the obvious benefits of foetal cadaver research and transplantation, can these virtues be separated from what some people see as the immorality of elected abortion? According to the foregoing discussion the rights and wrongs of abortion and foetal tissue research and transplantation stand or fall together. Yet despite an obvious causal relationship between them, this is not necessarily the case. It could be argued that even if abortion is regarded as wrong, discussions concerning the ethical status of research on embryos and possible transplantation of foetal tissue are an independent issue. The UK Committee, chaired by John Polkinghorne (1989), outlined a 'separation principle' according to which there must be 'a separation of the supply of foetal tissue from its use'. This is to ensure that the need for foetal tissue does not influence decisions to have abortions. One consequence of this principle was the recommendation that whilst informed maternal consent is required for the use of foetal tissue, the woman concerned should have no knowledge of what happens to it.

What is the ethical basis of a separation principle? [John] Robertson, who maintains that the abortion issue and the ethics of foetal research can be treated separately, suggests an analogy with transplant organs taken from homicide victims. If consent is obtained, then the victim's organs can be retrieved and distributed to recipients without any suggestion that the surgeon who has received the heart, lung, or kidneys, was an accomplice to murder, even if he or she was aware of the source. By the same token medical students, who use cadavers of murder victims in anatomy, cannot be associated with a crime. Moreover, research on legally obtained cadavers of murder victims cannot, in any way, be said to be responsible for the brutalisation of the researchers or contribute to an increase in the homicide rate. 'One may benefit from another's evil act without applauding or approving of that evil', says Robertson ...

The Polkinghorne Report referred to here was presented in 1989 by a Committee of Inquiry, chaired by the Revd John Polkinghorne, into the research use of such foetuses. It set out its 'separation principle' as follows:

Polkinghorne Committee, *Review of Guidance on the Research Use of Foetuses and Foetal Tissue,* **Cm 762, 1989, London: HMSO (the Polkinghorne Report):**

4.1 We have taken the view that, whatever one's ethical opinion about abortion itself, it does not follow that morally there is an absolute prohibition on the ethical use of foetuses or foetal tissue from lawful abortion. We have argued that the termination of pregnancy and the subsequent use of foetal tissue should be recognised as separate moral questions and we regard it as of great importance that the separation of these moral issues should be reflected in the procedures employed. Accordingly, we have recommended that great care should be taken to separate the decisions relating to abortion and to the subsequent use of foetal material. The prior decision to carry out an abortion should be reached without consideration of the benefits of subsequent use. The generation or termination of pregnancy to produce material for research or therapy is unethical.

4.2 It has been argued that knowledge of the use of foetal tissue could influence mothers' decisions to have their pregnancies terminated. It has been suggested that the use of foetal tissue could place women under pressure when reaching a decision or result in more abortions taking place. It has even been put to us that someone could become pregnant in order to make a foetus available for medical use. In our view, pregnancy undertaken to such an end would be an ethically unacceptable use of the foetus as an instrument (treating it as a 'thing'). It is not possible fully to discern people's motivations, but it is possible to limit the degree to which morally dubious wishes can be implemented. To this end we recommend, not only the separation of the decisions relating to abortion and the subsequent use of foetal tissue, but also procedures which will make it impossible for a mother to specify that foetal tissue, which she makes available, should be used in a particular way.

A related question is whether the consent of the mother of the foetus should in fact be sought in these circumstances. David Lamb comments on this as follows:

Lamb, D, *Organ Transplants and Ethics,* **1990, London: Routledge, pp 78–79:**

It might be argued that having decided to terminate her pregnancy, she has foregone any rights concerning the foetal disposal. [John] Harris argues that there is no moral basis for seeking the mother's consent over what happens to an aborted foetus. 'Has she not already abdicated responsibility for the foetus by opting for abortion?' asks Harris ... Moreover, when the aborted foetus cannot live, or is already dead, Harris sees no moral requirement to seek maternal consent.

> If experimenters ask her for, and are given, permission to experiment on the foetus this permission will not absolve them from the responsibility of deciding for themselves whether such a course of action is ethically sound. And if she withholds permission, we must ask what gives her the right to decide that others should not benefit from the research or from transplantation ...

Harris is equally dismissive of the view that the mother has quasi property rights by virtue of the fact that the foetus is growing inside her. Deadly and infectious viruses may grow in someone's body without any claim that they are in some way 'owned' by the being who plays host to them. Furthermore, if it were established that a foetus were a person, then prohibitions against slavery would rule out property rights over the foetus ...

In contrast Robertson argues that the case for denying the mother's control is not persuasive: 'As a product of her body and potential heir that she has for her own compelling reasons chosen to abort, she may care deeply about whether foetal remains are contributed to research or therapy to help others' ... Thus, although:

> ... she cannot insist that foetal remains be used for transplant because no donor has the right to require that intended donees accept anatomical gifts, but she should retain the existing legal right to veto use of foetal remains for transplant research or therapy. Her consent to donation of foetal tissue should be routinely sought.

Now the case for giving the woman control, on Robertson's terms, seems to rest on the analogy with organ donation, such as live kidney donation. But this analogy is complicated by the suggestion that, by undergoing voluntary termination for family planning purposes, her interest in the foetus ceases with its removal. In electing an abortion, she is, on these terms, expressing an overriding interest in a premature separation from the foetus, consequently terminating any potential interest which could apply to the foetus. Having fulfilled her primary interest, further interest in the foetus would be foregone ...

For its part, the Polkinghorne Committee took the view that the woman's informed consent should always be obtained:

Polkinghorne Committee, *Review of Guidance on the Research Use of Foetuses and Foetal Tissue*, Cm 762, 1989, London: HMSO:

2.8 ... The use of foetal tissue from terminations of pregnancy has been justified by analogy with the use of human organs which have become available as a result of morally questionable circumstances, such as careless accident or even murder. However, it has been suggested that this analogy is imperfect, since in the case of abortions the one who consents to the use of the material (the mother) is also the one who has brought about its availability by her decision to seek the termination of the existence of her foetus. Some have argued that this decision abrogates the mother's subsequent rights in relation to her foetus. Again, this is an opinion to which the Committee has given careful consideration, but once more it is one that we are unable to accept. Because abortion is a decision of moral ambiguity and perplexity for many, reached only through a conflict of considerations, it seems too harsh a judgment of the mother's relation to her foetus to suppose that she is no longer in a special position with regard to it, following an abortion.

Xenotransplantation

Recently, much research effort has gone into the possibility of xenografting, literally the use of organs and tissue taken from non-human animals. Previously, though such transplants were occasionally tried (a well known case from 1984 concerned a Californian infant, baby Fae, who survived for three weeks with a baboon's heart) there was a formidable difficulty in the way of lasting success in the form of inevitable tissue rejection by the donee. However, there now seem real prospects of overcoming this problem by genetically engineering certain breeds of animals specifically for transplant purposes.

The Nuffield Council of Bioethics, in its recent report *Animal to Human Transplants: The Ethics of Xenotransplantation*, charted some of the obstacles that remain in the way of carrying out such transplants on a wide scale:

Nuffield Council on Bioethics, *Animal to Human Transplants: The Ethics of Xenotransplantation*, 1996, London: Nuffield Council on Bioethics:

10.9 Even if some use of animals for medical purposes can be justified in principle, their use for xenotransplantation raises specific issues that need further consideration. Particular concerns are raised by the use of primates, such as baboons ... The high degree of evolutionary relatedness between human beings and primates both suggests that xenotransplantation of primate organs and tissue might be successful and also raises questions about whether it is ethical to use primates in ways that it is not considered acceptable to use human beings. Certainly, any harm suffered by primates should be given great weight. This position is reflected in the principles underlying current practice in the UK. *The Working Party endorses the special protection afforded to primates used for medical and scientific purposes.*

10.10 The Working Party would accept the use of very small numbers of primates *as recipients of organs* during research to develop xenotransplantation of organs and tissue from non-primates. In this case, using a small number of primates for research, while undesirable, can be justified by the potential benefits if xenotransplantation were to become a successful procedure ...

10.11 The routine use of higher primates to supply organs for xenotransplantation on a scale sufficient to meet the organ shortage would represent a new use of primates in the UK. In addition to the special weight given to the harm suffered by primates, other concerns must be taken into account. The endangered status of chimpanzees rules out their use for xenotransplantation. The potential risk of extinction, even to a species like the baboon that is not currently endangered, must be taken seriously. Xenotransplantation using primate organs or tissue may pose particular risks of disease transmission ...

10.12 Given the ethical concerns raised by the use of primates for xenotransplantation, attention has turned to developing the pig as an alternative source of organs and tissue. As discussed below, in the view of the Working Party, the use of pigs for xenotransplantation raises fewer ethical concerns. To develop the use of primates for xenotransplantation, when there is an ethically acceptable alternative, would not be justifiable. *The Working Party recommends that non-primate species should be regarded as the source animals of choice for xenotransplantation.* However, possibilities for alleviating the organ shortage which do not involve the use of animals, such as increased donation of human organs, and the development of artificial organs and tissue, should be actively pursued ...

...

10.23 Important [animal] welfare implications are raised by the breeding of transgenic animals; producing animals free from infectious organisms; and removing organs and tissue from animals for xenotransplantation ... In view of [these] implications ... *the Working Party recommends that the Home Office should require that all animals use xenotransplantation are protected under the Animals (Scientific Procedures) Act 1986.* Any reputable company producing animals in order to supply organs and tissue for xenotransplantation would, in any case, wish to be licensed under the 1986 Act in order to reassure the public that their activities were meeting the highest standards of animal welfare. The Working Party recommends that the standards set by the 1986 Act become the minimum for the industry ...

Transmission of infectious diseases

10.24 Xenotransplantation of animal organs and tissue carries with it the potential risk that diseases will be transmitted from animals to xenograft recipients and to the wider human population ... It is difficult to assess this risk, since it is impossible to predict whether infectious organisms that are harmless in their animal host will cause disease in human xenograft recipients or whether the disease will spread into the wider human population. There are certain to be infectious organisms of both primates and pigs that are currently unknown, and some of these might cause disease in human beings. There is evidence that infectious organisms of primates, notably viruses, can pass into the human population and cause disease. This supports the recommendation that non-primate species should be regarded as the source animals of choice for xenotransplantation. The possible risk of disease transmission from pigs, however, also requires careful consideration ...

10.25 It is not possible to predict or quantify the risk that xenotransplantation will result in the emergence of new human diseases. But in the worst case, the consequences could be far-reaching and difficult to control. The principle of precaution requires that action is taken to avoid risks in advance of certainty about their nature. It suggests that the burden of proof should lie with those developing the technology to demonstrate that it will not cause serious harm. *The Working Party concluded that the risks associated with possible transmission of infectious diseases as a consequence of xenotransplantation have not been adequately dealt with. It would not be ethical therefore to begin clinical trials of xenotransplantation involving human beings ...*

In January 1997 a government inquiry, chaired by Professor Ian Kennedy, also took the view that, because of the unknown risks associated with infectious diseases passing from animal to human, clinical trials should be delayed. In the meantime, a new body, the Xenotransplantation Interim Regulatory Authority, has been set up to keep the situation under review.

Mechanical organs

Although artificial implants and other devices have long been a mainstay of modern medical science (for example, hip replacements, pacemakers, etc) in terms of organs, the only real candidate at present for such manufacture is the heart. David Lamb chronicles the history of such devices, and the ethical problems to which their use gives rise, as follows:

Lamb, D, *Organ Transplants and Ethics*, 1990, London: Routledge, pp 114–15:

The idea of a totally implantable artificial heart was first mooted in 1964, when the USA National Heart Institute drew up a plan for the construction of a prototype and obtained financial support from Congress for the project. The researchers were unrealistically optimistic, for they looked forward to the mass production and implantation of artificial hearts by 1970 ... Despite some limited success with animals, artificial implants into humans did not achieve any significant results. One major problem is the high incidence of strokes and chronic infections, which has not been overcome. The first human implantation of an artificial heart was performed in Texas in 1969 on a dying patient, Haskelle Karp, who survived for a further 65 hours with it before receiving a human heart. He died shortly after. In 1977 a woman in Zurich survived for two days with an artificial heart ... The initial belief that an artificial heart might function as a permanent replacement has given way to more realistic therapy. Artificial hearts are presently used, in a limited sense, as 'bridges' to assist survival until a donor becomes available. As of January 1987, some 17 US transplant centres were using artificial heart 'bridges', and 63 patients had been implanted with such a device ... The number of artificial hearts and ventricular assistance devices currently functioning as bridges is 200 worldwide ...

The deeper ethical and philosophical aspects of artificial heart implants surfaced in the widely discussed case of Dr Barney Clark, a retired American dentist who received an artificial heart in 1982. Dr Clark's own defective heart was replaced with a device made of polyurethane. The motor driving the heart was too large to be implanted, so it was placed in a cart which the patient had to push around. He lived for 112 days, and his death was caused by the failure of most of his other organs, but not by the failure of the heart, which went on pumping blood to a mass of dead organs, thus demonstrating the separability of the heart function from the mechanism of death. The longest survivor with an artificial heart was William Schroeder, who lived for 620 days, but during that time he suffered four strokes and developed chronic infections which sapped his strength ...

The suffering endured by Barney Clark and William Schroeder and their families certainly raises ethical problems concerning the extent to which doctors should strive to maintain life. But this limited success may bring hope for the future; hope that an artificial heart is not an impossible dream, and that with sufficient technological improvements artificial implants could reduce waiting lists for human organs.

Though they continue to be refined and developed, and in the long term may be expected to offer very real benefits, the use of artificial organs remains in its nascent stages.

THE STATUS OF EXTRACTED MATERIAL

The phenomenon of organ and tissue transplantation, and the practice of removing tissue for medical purposes including donation, give rise to interesting questions as to the status of such material. Is it susceptible of ownership, and, if so, who enjoys the relevant property rights? It is convenient to look at the position in relation to the whole body first, and then move on to look at ownership of body parts detached therefrom.

Rights in the whole body

Gerald Dworkin and Ian Kennedy have analysed this issue as follows:

Dworkin, G and Kennedy, I, 'Human tissue: rights in the body and its parts' (1993) 1 Med L Rev 291:

1   Rights in the whole body

A   During a person's life

One matter which is beyond question, whatever the position may have been when slavery flourished within the law, is that there are no longer any property rights over another living human being.

B   Rights of the deceased in his/her own body after death?

The common law position is the same after death. There are many dicta going back through the centuries proclaiming that there can be no property in a corpse. Thus, where a person by will had directed that his body should be cremated after death, it was held that such a request, though it might be honoured in practice, could not be imposed as a legal obligation upon his executors since he lacked any property rights in his body.

C   Rights of third parties in corpses

Nor do any third parties acquire any property interests in a corpse. At most, there are obligations on the next of kin or others in possession of a body to dispose of it decently and it may be a criminal offence at common law to neglect to carry out these duties or in any other way interfere with a corpse. Modern writers maintain that such well established rules survive and limit the modern law of theft (which involves the taking of property), at least to the extent that there could be no theft of a buried corpse.

D   Changing characteristics

The situation appears to change, however, after a period of time. If the law did not recognise any property rights in a cadaver, or in body parts, problems could arise at a later stage about the status of any physical material which remains. Thus, if the law is not prepared to recognise property rights in skeletons possessed by medical institutions or students, or in the embalmed body of Jeremy Bentham (which has been taken from University College London from time to time by enterprising students from other colleges), or in Egyptian mummies, then those who take them may not be committing any theft, nor, possibly, any legally redressible wrong against those from whom they have been taken.

The common law has occasionally grappled with this situation. If, after some time, the characteristics of the body, or the body parts, have changed in some way so that one is no longer concerned with a corpse awaiting burial, the law may look upon it as property and confer upon owners the usual rights to protect it from interference and to deal with it commercially. Thus, in *Doodeward v Spence* an Australian court appears to have held that a stillborn two-headed foetus, which had been preserved with spirits in a bottle by the doctor some 40 years earlier, was now an item of property in the hands of its present owner. In that case it was said that

> ... when a person has by the lawful exercise of work or skill so dealt with a human body or part of a human body in his lawful possession that it has acquired some attributes differentiating it from a mere corpse awaiting burial, he acquires a right to retain possession of it, at least as against any person not entitled to have it delivered to him for the purposes of burial ...

In this case it was said that work and skill had been bestowed by the plaintiff's predecessor in title upon the body and it had acquired actual pecuniary value.

Recently, this approach was endorsed, *obiter*, by the Court of Appeal in *Dobson v North Tyneside HA*.

Dobson and Another v North Tyneside HA and Another [1996] 4 All ER 474, CA (Butler-Sloss, Peter Gibson and Thorpe LJJ)

The family of a woman, who had died as a result of an undiagnosed brain tumour, brought a claim in conversion against the health authority for allowing the destruction of the woman's brain after it had been removed, and briefly stored in a jar of paraffin, for the purposes of a post mortem. The plaintiffs would have wished to use the same as evidence in their main action in medical negligence against the Authority.

> **Peter Gibson LJ**: Mr Hone ... submitted that the present case raises an important question of law ... whether it remains established law that there is no property in a dead body or part of a dead body so that personal representatives of a deceased cannot maintain a cause of action in respect of human tissue. That was modified before us ... and on the primary way in which he put his case, viz, in conversion, it is trite law that a person has title to sue if and only if he has at the time of conversion either actual possession or the immediate right to possession ...
>
> As the question of law as framed by Mr Hone indicates, in the present state of the English authorities there is no property in a corpse (see *Williams v Williams* (1880) 20 Ch D 659, p 662–63 and *Clerk and Lindsell on Torts*, 17th edn, 1995, para 13–50). However that bare statement needs some qualification. First, as is stated in *Clerk and Lindsell*, 'the executors or administrators or other persons charged by the law with the duty of interring the body have a right to the custody and possession of it until it is properly buried'. In the present case there were no executors and there was no administratrix until ... long after the body of the deceased was buried ... I am not aware that there is any authority that there is such a duty on the next of kin as such. If there is no duty, there is no legal right to possession of the corpse. However, even if that is wrong and the next of kin do have some right to possession of the body, there is no authority that right is otherwise than for the interment or other proper disposition of the body. The second qualification is also to be found in *Clerk and Lindsell* where it is said: 'Once a body has undergone a process or other application of human skill, such as stuffing or embalming, it seems it can be the subject of property in the ordinary way; hence it is submitted that conversion will lie for a skeleton or cadaver used for research or exhibition, and the same goes for parts of, and substances produced by, a living person.' Mr Hone relies on the tentatively expressed proposition in the first part of that statement, the authority for which is said to be *Doodeward v Spence* (1908) 6 CLR 406 ... *Doodeward v Spence* is ... not a decision establishing the proposition in *Clerk and Lindsell*. However I am prepared to accept that proposition is properly arguable, particularly in the light of the academic writings to which Mr Hone referred us (Matthews, P, 'Whose body? People as property' (1983) CLP 193, pp 193 *et seq*, *Palmer on Bailment*, 2nd edn, 1991, pp 9 *et seq* and Magnusson, R, in Palmer and McKendrick (eds), *Proprietary Rights in Human Tissue in Interests in Goods*, 1993, pp 237 *et seq*).
>
> Does this mean that it is arguable that when Dr Perry fixed the brain in paraffin, he thereby transformed it into an item the right to possession of which or the property in which belonged to the plaintiffs? For my part, I do not think so. The removal of the brain was lawfully performed in the course of the post mortem which at the coroner's request Dr Perry had undertaken to determine the cause of the deceased's death. Dr Perry was under an obligation imposed by r 9 of the Coroners Rules 1984 to make provision for the preservation of material which in his opinion bore upon the cause of death, but only for such period as the coroner thought fit ... I do not see how the fact

that the brain was so fixed rendered it an item to possession of which the plaintiffs ever became entitled for the purpose of interment or any other purpose, still less that the plaintiffs ever acquired the property in it ...

Rights in body parts

The effect of the decision in *Dobson* (which, after all, was primarily concerned with rights in the deceased's brain) is that, after death, the principles governing individual body parts are the same as those applying to the cadaver whole. That is to say, any ownership rights will be confined to third parties, normally medical personnel, who have some lawful business with such remains or have otherwise expended effort in the course of their preservation. We now need to consider the problem of body parts taken from a living person; the issue is complicated here by the fact that the latter, himself, may be felt to have a *prima facie* claim upon such material. The question, which is now of huge practical import given the scope for the commercial exploitation of DNA, was recently addressed by the Nuffield Council in its 1995 Report:

Nuffield Council on Bioethics, *Human Tissue: Ethical and Legal Issues*, 1995, London: Nuffield Council on Bioethics:

9.4 At common law the issue has not been tested in English law. It is instructive to inquire why the question of a claim over tissue once removed has not received legal attention. The answer seems simple. In the general run of things a person from whom tissue is removed has not the slightest interest in making any claim to it once it is removed. This is obviously the case as regards tissue removed as a consequence of treatment. It is equally true in the case of donation of tissue whether, for example, blood, bone marrow or an organ. The word donation clearly indicates that what is involved is a gift.

9.5 It is certainly true, of course, that an appendix or gallstone may be returned to a patient who may refer to it as her appendix or gallstone. But this says nothing about any legal claim that she may have to the appendix. In fact, in the case of the returned appendix, one view of the legal position may be as follows: the patient consents to the operation which involves the removal of her appendix: by her consent to the operation she *abandons* any claims to the appendix, on removal the appendix acquires the status of a *res* (a thing) and comes into the possession of the hospital authority prior to disposal; in response by a request of the patient that it can be returned the hospital gives the appendix to the patient as a gift; the appendix then becomes the property of the patient.

...

9.7 But there are other circumstances in which ... it could be argued, and has been by a number of commentators, that tissue once removed becomes the property of the person from whom it is removed. This is to say that consent to removal does not *entail* an intent to abandon. The tissue may well, in fact, be abandoned or donated, but these imply a prior coming into existence of a *res* and the exercise of rights over it. Indeed, such an analysis is logically essential, it is argued, even if the resulting property (ie, a person's assertion of a property right over the new *res*) exists merely for the moment (a *scintilla temporis*). On this view the person from whom tissue is removed must have a property right in the tissue which expressly or by implication he could waive on the removal so that the property passes to another. The consequence is, of course, that if the property right were not waived, it would be retained. To return to the example in para 9.5, the appendix would have become (and remained) the patient's property had she not by implication waived any right to it.

9.8 The case of *Venner v State of Maryland* decided by the Court of Special Appeals in Maryland, USA, may be of assistance. Powers J held that, 'By the force of social custom ... when a person does nothing and says nothing to indicate an intent to assert his rights of ownership, possession and control over [bodily] material, the only rational inference is that he intends to abandon the material'. The emphasis of this approach is clear:

1　The legal presumption is in favour of abandonment.

2　Abandonment may be prospective.

3　Where, however, the circumstances are such that abandonment may not be presumed, it must follow that if no consent were given, or a consent expressed to be 'on terms' were given, property rights over the tissue *would not necessarily pass* but would be retained by the person from whom the property was removed.

9.9 It is fair to say that some support for this approach can be derived from various statutes already referred to ... While the Human Tissue Act 1961 is of no assistance, both the Human Organ Transplants Act 1989 and the Human Fertilisation and Embryology Act 1990 appear to endorse a property approach. Indeed the latter, though relying upon a scheme of consents so as to avoid the need to decide the issue of property, contemplates that the control and disposal of gametes and embryos rests with the donor(s) and allows for the transfer of the reproductive material between those with a licence to deal with them. A final statutory provision, s 25 of the National Health Service Act 1977, also seems implicitly to adopt a property approach. The section provides that:

... where the Secretary of State has acquired:

(a)　supplies of human blood; ... or

(b)　any part of a human body; ...

he may arrange to make such supplies or that part available (on such terms, including terms as to charges as he thinks fit) to any person ...

...

9.11 ... A further legal approach is to argue that tissue once removed becomes property, but at the time of its removal it is *res nullis*, ie, that it belongs to no one until it is brought under dominion (the traditional legal example is the wild animal or plant). This would reflect the traditional view of 'no property in the body'. It would also mean that a person could not prospectively donate 'his' tissue once removed from the body. All he could do would be to consent to the removal. If this analysis were adopted, the tissue would be the property of the person who removed it or subsequently came into possession of it. The person from whom it was removed would not, however, have any property claim to it.

9.12 The current state of English law makes it unclear (at best) which of these approaches (or another) represents the law. Interest in the validity of property claims over removed tissue has, however, been rekindled because of the awareness of circumstances in which tissue has been removed and then developed in some way so as to serve as the basis for a commercial product. The *locus classicus* is the well known *Moore* case. In *Moore* the Supreme Court of California, trying a preliminary point of law, decided that Moore had no property right over the tissue taken from his body. Although not expressed in such a way, if we impose the language that we have employed, the court appears to have found that Moore's consent to the operation entailed an abandonment of any claim to the removed tissue. Thus, he could not assert a claim in property as the basis either for objecting to the removal of his tissue or for having a share in whatever profit was gained through its use. The issue of the validity of the consent he gave to the operation and subsequent procedures then becomes the focus of the case.

The case of *Moore v Regents of University of California* 793 Pd 479 (1990), referred to in the last paragraph, arose after the plaintiff had his spleen removed during treatment for leukaemia. Unknown to him, the doctors used the spleen to generate a cell line from which a highly lucrative drug was produced. Paul Matthews ('The man of property' (1995) 3 Med LR 251) has in fact criticised the Nuffield Report for suggesting that Moore, in consenting to the operation, was held to have 'abandoned' any property claims over the spleen; the majority of court instead appears to have taken the view that Moore never had any such claims in the first place.

Would an English court perhaps take a more favourable view of the property rights enjoyed by a plaintiff in such a case? There would seem to be two related reasons why someone might wish to assert the existence of such rights. First, the living donor would acquire the ability to exclude or restrict use or dealings by others with the tissue in question. However, it was precisely this possibility (potentially allowing the donor to hamper research of great value to medical science) which provided the decisive policy argument *against* such rights in *Moore*. Secondly, possessing rights of this nature could at least allow the donor to share in any commercial profits arising from the exploitation of his tissue. However, even if such apportionment were practicable, we may legitimately ask *why* individual donors should be entitled to benefit in this way. It could be argued that a fundamental aim of any equitable system of health care is to even out, not encourage, inequalities which arise from the 'natural lottery'.

Intellectual property rights

If the above arguments are accepted for not conferring property rights in body parts upon the donor, it does not follow that such rights should not be enjoyed by third parties. Indeed, the ability of researchers to safeguard discoveries and inventions achieved with human tissue through patenting may provide an important incentive for such research. This was acknowledged implicitly in the *Moore* case, where the doctors' right to patent the cell line created with Moore's tissue was left unchallenged. Nevertheless, as Bently and Sherman note, the issue of patenting in this area is not free from difficulty:

> **Bently, L and Sherman, B, 'The ethics of patenting: towards a transgenic patent system' (1995) 3 Med L Rev 275:**
>
> Article 53(a) [of the European Patent Convention] states that patents are not to be granted for inventions, the publication or exploitation of which would be contrary to *ordre public* or morality. Section 1(3)(a) of the Patents Act (UK) 1977 is in similar terms, stating that a patent will not be granted for 'an invention the publication or exploitation of which would be generally expected to encourage offensive, immoral or antisocial behaviour'.
>
> The first occasion on which Art 53(a) was discussed at the [European Patent Office] was in the *Onco Mouse* case. In this case, the Technical Board of Appeal was asked to consider whether it was necessary to apply Art 53(a) when deciding the patentability of a mouse which had been genetically modified so that the mouse would suffer from cancer. The applicant hoped that such altered mice would be useful in cancer research. Reversing the findings of the Examining Division, the Technical Board of Appeal stated that ethical concerns needed to be taken into account in deciding issues of patentability. In particular, it held that:
>
> > The genetic manipulation of mammalian animals is undeniably problematical in various respects, particularly where activated onco genes are inserted to make an animal abnormally sensitive to carcinogenic substances and stimuli and consequently prone to develop tumours, which necessarily cause suffering. There is also a danger that genetically manipulated animals, if released into the environment, might entail unforeseeable and irreversible adverse effects ... The decision as to whether or not Art 53(a) EPC is a bar to patenting the present invention would seem to depend mainly on a careful weighing up of the suffering of animals and possible risks to the environment on the one hand, and the invention's usefulness to mankind on the other.
>
> On reconsideration by the Examining Division, it was held that the usefulness of the invention in cancer research outweighed any suffering that might be caused to the animal and, as such, that it was not an immoral invention and therefore was *prima facie* patentable.
>
> The utilitarian approach adopted in *Onco Mouse* was applied in 1991, when the EPO warned the pharmaceutical company, Upjohn, that it would not accept an application to patent a mouse into which a gene had been introduced such

that the mouse would lose its hair. In considering the benefit which flowed from the invention (the usefulness of the mice in experiments to cure hair loss), as against the harm suffered by the mice, the EPO asserted that the invention was immoral and thus would not be patentable.

The next occasion on which the application of Art 53(a) was considered was in *Greenpeace UK v Plant Genetic Systems NV*. In this case, the opponents objected to the patent, which had been granted for a genetically engineered plant, on the grounds that it was inherently immoral and that it created environmental risks. Following the cost-benefit test suggested in *Onco Mouse*, the opponents argued that these concerns and risks should be balanced against the benefits likely to accrue from the invention. The Opposition Division refused to apply the utilitarian test, on the basis that it was only necessary to consider the exclusion where the invention would be universally regarded as outrageous, and an overwhelming consensus would exist to the effect that no patent should be granted. The upshot of this was that in most cases it would not be necessary to consider the morality of particular patents ...

The approach advocated in *Greenpeace* was adopted by the Opposition Division in the *Relaxin* case. This decision concerned an opposition by the Green Party to the Howard Florey Institute's patent for the DNA sequences of a naturally occurring substance, which relaxes the uterus during childbirth, and which had been obtained from the human ovary. There were three grounds of objection: first, that the use of pregnancy for profit was offensive to human dignity; secondly, that the applicant was involved in 'patenting life', an activity that was intrinsically immoral; thirdly, that such patenting was equivalent to slavery. In rejecting the Green Party's objections, the EPO noted that the tissue used in the research was donated during the course of necessary gynaecological operations and thus the procedures had not offended 'human dignity'. Moreover, the Opposition Division characterised DNA not as 'life' but rather as a 'chemical substance which carries genetic code'. The argument that the applicant was 'patenting life' was thus misconceived. Finally, it rejected the Green Party's assertion that such patenting was equivalent to slavery on the grounds that such an assertion misunderstood the nature of a patent. This was because, according to the Opposition Division, a patent does not give the proprietor any rights over a human being: all a patent monopoly provides is the right to prevent someone from practising the same invention *outside the human body*.

As with the *Greenpeace* decision, the Opposition Division's decision in *Relaxin* further highlights the problems that confront patent law in accommodating ethical considerations. This fact was explicitly acknowledged by the Opposition Division in *Relaxin* when it commented that '[w]hether or not human genes should be patented is a controversial issue on which many persons have strong opinions ... the EPO is not the right institution to decide on fundamental ethical questions'. Furthermore, the case reveals the difficulty involved in translating the ethical concerns of the objectors into the language of patent law. Faced with a choice between a scientific understanding of DNA as chemicals, and the social understanding of DNA as life, the former interpretation was preferred by the Opposition Division. This prioritisation of the scientific view of genetic process over the Green Party's approach illustrates the depth of the conflict between the logic of ethical objections and those of patenting, at least as currently understood.

Recently, the European Parliament has approved the terms of an EC Directive on the legal protection of biotechnological inventions, and this is likely to become law throughout the EC Member States by the year 2001.

IMPLANTATION OF MATERIAL

The interests of the would-be donee

Could someone, desperately in need of a transplant, legally compel another person to submit to the extraction of the necessary material if the latter is found to be a suitable donor? The answer, unsurprisingly in the light of what has been noted above, p 579, in respect of the need for the donor's consent, is a clear 'no'.

A well known case in point is that of *McFall v Shimp* 10 Pa D & C (3d) 90 (1978), in which an American court refused to compel a man to undergo a bone-marrow transplant in order to save his dying cousin. While Flaherty J took the view that the man's refusal to submit voluntarily to the extraction was *morally* indefensible, he was not prepared to recognise a legal duty to donate, which would fly in the face of the stress placed by liberal society on the inviolability of the individual (see further, the extract from his judgment cited above, Chapter 3, p 104). It is virtually certain that an English court, faced with a similar predicament, would come to the same conclusion.

The rights of the actual donee

Against the surgeon

As we have seen, much organ transplant therapy (especially that involving animal or artificial implants) remains highly experimental in nature. It has been suggested by JK Mason (in Dyer, C (ed), *Doctors, Patients and the Law*, 1992, Oxford: Blackwells, p 122) that, just as the donor cannot consent to the extraction of an organ if it is likely to cause them serious harm, 'it is equally unlawful to consent to accept an organ in the certainty or near certainty that it would be fatal to do so'. We respectfully doubt whether, so far as a 'near certainty' is involved, this is correct: a one in a thousand chance of life is surely better – other things equal – than no chance at all.

More generally, it is clear that if a transplant surgeon performs the operation without due care and, in so doing causes harm to the donee, the standard principles of negligence will apply to afford the latter a remedy (see above, Chapter 6).

Against the procurement agency

An allegation of negligence may also be framed against the agency or authority which procured the organ for transplantation. This will be so if the organ itself turns out to be defective in some way, notably if the donee is exposed to a virus, such as HIV or hepatitis, that the donor was carrying. The Nuffield Council on Bioethics considered some of the special problems that might face a donee plaintiff in such a case in its 1995 report as follows:

Nuffield Council on Bioethics, *Human Tissue: Ethical and Legal Issues,* **1995, London: Nuffield Council on Bioethics:**

12.53 Standards of care change from time to time: what was not negligence in 1990 may well be negligence in 1995. As knowledge, and the perception of risks and their avoidance, improve, so too do the obligations imposed upon those who work in these areas. For example, at one time far less was known than today about the various contaminants in blood products: HIV, hepatitis, syphilis, malaria and toxoplasmosis; and methods of screening or heat treating blood products were not so prevalent. There may have been no negligence liability on the supplier of defective blood had a person then been contaminated with an HIV virus. The situation would be different today, when the norm is to test for such viruses. But what of other viruses? Does an obligation to screen for all known viruses arise as soon as the risk of their presence becomes known? The view has been expressed that as:

> ... more and more minor contaminants of recombinant DNA derived human growth hormone are being identified which are biologically active and pose no safety problem ... the effort and expense in identifying them and then measuring them on a batch-to-batch basis may be out of proportion to the public health risk.

As long as no adverse consequences follow, that argument may appear to be sound. But what happens if a virus which is deliberately neglected turns out to be far more potent than was anticipated? This has been an issue with hepatitis C: could it be said to be negligent to take a professional, and considered, decision not to screen for this virus even when its presence but not its full potency were known? And what of such bodies as the Committee on the Safety of Medicines and the Licensing Authority ... should they be liable for failure to act earlier to impose higher standards of care? In the last resort, it will be for the courts to weigh up all the factors and decide whether the balance struck was reasonable ...

12.57 A product is 'defective' when it does not provide the safety which a person is entitled to expect, taking all the circumstances into account. Thus, instructions for use, contraindications and warnings and supplied information in one form or another may in some cases assist in determining whether the product was 'defective'. Contaminated blood supplied to patients, or a defective organ used for transplantation, are likely to be regarded as 'defective products' regardless of the information which is given to patients.

12.58 Liability is imposed upon producers, including manufacturers, importers and suppliers of such products. It is likely that human tissue would be regarded as 'products' for these purposes. This was recommended by the Pearson Royal Commission in 1978. Human tissue used for medical purposes, although not strictly manufactured, would possess the 'essential characteristics attributable to an industrial or other process'.

12.59 Although these strict liability provisions are an improvement on the negligence action, there are still many difficult hurdles which an injured person has to face before liability can be established. The two most difficult are the so called 'development-risk' defence and, once again, causation.

The residual hurdles mentioned in 12.59 are considered in connection with liability for defective medicinal products generally, see above, Chapter 6. Returning to the specific problem of contaminated supplies of human tissue, one case in which a class of plaintiffs did enjoy a certain amount of success under the common law was *Re HIV Haemophiliac Litigation*.

Re HIV Haemophiliac Litigation (1990) NLJR 1349, CA (Ralph Gibson and Bingham LJJ, Megaw J)

A group of nearly 1,000 haemophiliacs, who contracted the HIV virus following treatment with infected blood products imported from the USA, brought an action in negligence against, *inter alia*, the Department of Health. They argued that the failure by the Secretary of State to ensure that Britain was self-sufficient in the supply of such products had been a negligent breach of the statutory duty imposed by virtue of the National Health Service Act 1977 (see further on this above, Chapter 6). As a preliminary issue, the Court of Appeal was required to determine whether the plaintiffs had a sufficient *prima facie* case to justify making an order for discovery against the defendants.

> **Ralph Gibson LJ**: For my part ... I agree with Rougier J that the plaintiffs have made out at least an arguable case. It is obvious that it would be rare for a case on negligence to be proved having regard to the nature of the duties under the 1977 Act, and to the fact that, in the law of negligence, it is difficult to prove a negligent breach of duty when the party charged with negligence is required to exercise discretion and to form judgments upon the allocation of public resources. That, however, is not sufficient, in my judgment, to make it clear for the purposes of these proceedings, that there can in law be no claim in negligence. Nor, on the allegations of fact, can it be said that the plaintiffs have not alleged a case which could be upheld if in law the claim is viable ...
>
> These plaintiffs have suffered personal injury. It is possible, in my judgment, that the court, after full consideration, may in this case be driven to hold that in the circumstances of these claims, and notwithstanding the difficulties of proof of negligence for the reasons stated above, yet a duty of care is imposed by the law upon the central defendants in the discharge of their functions under the 1977 Act. Those difficulties of proof will, of course, include the matter of exercise of discretion, policy making, allocation of resources and the

distinction between failing to confer a benefit as contrasted with the infliction of harm.

In the wake of this ruling, the government settled the plaintiffs' main action out of court. It is likely, however, that the decision to do so was politically rather than legally motivated. Significantly, a class action currently being run by a group of haemophiliacs who, in similar circumstances, were infected with the hepatitis C virus, continues to be firmly opposed.

Lastly, it should be noted that other forms of action, besides those just mentioned, may be available against the procurement agency in appropriate cases. In *Ashcraft v King* 278 Cal Rptr 900 (1991), an American case, the plaintiff recovered in battery after receiving HIV infected blood from an anonymous donor; she had stipulated that she wanted blood obtained only from members of her immediate family. Equally, in France the director of a procurement agency was charged with manslaughter after a patient, who had received an infected corneal graft, died of rabies.

Against the donor

Because of limitations in current screening techniques, it is possible for infected tissue to fail to be identified even though the procurement agency took all reasonable precautions. In such a case a donee, injured through the use of such tissue, would have an action, if at all, only against the original donor of the material: it may be that the latter was (or should have been) aware of their infected status and/or failed to reply honestly to the inquiries of the procurement agency.

In a number of US and Commonwealth cases, the courts have been unsympathetic to the donee's cause. In *Rasmussen v South Florida Blood Service* 500 So 2d 533 (1987), a case in which the plaintiff became infected with HIV following a blood transfusion, public policy in favour of the preservation of donor anonymity was said to outweigh the donee's rights in the matter:

Barkett J: As the district court recognised, petitioner needs more than just the names and addresses of the donors. His interest is in establishing that one or more of the donors has AIDS or is in a high risk group. Petitioner argues that his inquiry may never go beyond comparing the donors' names against a list of known AIDS victims, or against other public records (for example, conviction records in order to determine whether any of the donors is a known drug user). He contends that because a limited inquiry may reveal the information he seeks, with no invasion of privacy, the donors' privacy rights are not yet at issue. We find this argument disingenuous. As we have already noted, the discovery rules allow a trial judge upon good cause shown to set conditions under which discovery will be given. Some method could be formulated to verify the Blood Service's report that none of the donors is a known AIDS victim while preserving the confidentiality of the donors' identities. However, the subpoena in question gives petitioner access to the names and addresses of the blood donors with no restrictions on their use.

There is nothing to prohibit petitioner from conducting an investigation without the knowledge of the persons in question. We cannot ignore, therefore, the consequences of disclosure to non-parties, including the possibility that a donor's co-workers, friends, employers, and others may be queried as to the donor's sexual preferences, drug use, or general lifestyle.

The threat posed by the disclosure of the donors' identities goes far beyond the immediate discomfort occasioned by a third party probing into sensitive areas of the donors' lives. Disclosure of donor identities in any context involving AIDS could be extremely disruptive and even devastating to the individual donor. If the requested information is released, and petitioner queries the donors' friends and fellow employees, it will be functionally impossible to prevent occasional references to AIDS ...

We wish to emphasise that although the importance of protecting the privacy of donor information does not depend on the special stigma associated with AIDS, public response to the disease does make this a more critical matter. By the very nature of this case, disclosure of donor identities is disclosure in a damaging context. We conclude, therefore, that the disclosure sought here implicates constitutionally protected privacy interests.

Our analysis of the interests to be served by denying discovery does not end with the effects of disclosure on the private lives of the 51 donors implicated in this case. Society has a vital interest in maintaining a strong volunteer blood supply, a task that has become more difficult with the emergence of AIDS. The donor population has been reduced by the necessary exclusion of potential blood donors through AIDS screening and testing procedures as well as by the unnecessary reduction in the donor population as a result of the widespread fear that donation itself can transmit the disease. In light of this, it is clearly 'in the public interest to discourage any serious disincentive to volunteer blood donation'. Because there is little doubt that the prospect of inquiry into one's private life and potential association with AIDS will deter blood donation, we conclude that society's interest in a strong and healthy blood supply will be furthered by the denial of discovery in this case.

More recently, some relaxation of this strict anonymity requirement has been allowed in favour of a rule of 'cloaked disclosure': see *Snyder v Mekhjian* (1991) 593 A 2d 318, and *PD v Australian Red Cross Society (NSW Div)* (1993) 30 NSWLR 376. Nevertheless, the point of doing this is to assist a plaintiff where there is a suspicion that the procurement agency may have been negligent in allowing the blood through. Indeed, as one of the conditions for receiving such information, the plaintiff has had to undertake not to sue the donor directly.

REFORMING THE LAW

As noted earlier, the whole area of organ transplantation is beset by the problem of an excess of demand for human organs over their supply. As at the end of 1997, there were, for example, a total of 5,539 persons awaiting kidney transplants in the UK, an increase of 169 over the previous year. Given the poignant consequence of a significant number of avoidable deaths, often of quite young people, it is natural that much attention has been focused on the possibility of remedying this shortfall through legal reform. In terms of the possible sources of organs and tissue identified above, cadaveric transplants seem prima facie to be the type where such reform may have the greatest chance of achieving positive results.

Addressing the shortfall in cadaveric organs

The current system for procuring cadaveric organs under the Human Tissue Act 1961, with its emphasis on the deceased's desire to donate (usually expressed in the form of a donor card) is sometimes described as an 'opting in' scheme. Such a description is somewhat misleading; as we have seen, failure to express such a desire does not automatically preclude the use of one's organs, it merely means that one's relatives – in so far as they can be located – gain the legal right to object to such use. (Conversely, doctors will not in practice stand on their strict right to take the organs in the face of objection by relatives even where there is a valid donor card.) Nevertheless, it is certainly true that possessing a donor card increases the likelihood that one's organs will be retrieved: at the very least, the presence of the card will ease the task psychologically for the doctors of asking for, and the relatives of agreeing to, donation.

The possibility of changing the law so as to downgrade the role of the relatives has been explored by New *et al* by reference to experience in other jurisdictions:

New, B, Solomon, M, Dingwall, R and McHale, J, *A Question of Give and Take*, **1994, London: Kings Fund Institute, pp 56–58:**

Changing the law on gaining consent

Of particular interest to policy makers has been the various legal frameworks within which procurement takes place. The UK, along with Germany, the Netherlands, Italy, Canada, Australia and New Zealand, have what might broadly be termed 'opting in' legal systems. Two other systems have generated much interest in the literature: presumed consent – also known as opting out – and required request.

Presumed consent

Presumed consent schemes have been introduced into many countries, although attempts to enact such legislation in the UK have always failed, the latest being the Transplantation of Human Organs Bill 1993. The international legislation falls into several categories. The purest version of the law allows automatic removal except in a situation in which the deceased has expressed an objection during his or her lifetime. This 'strict' type of presumed consent procedure applies in Austria where organs can be removed provided in his or her life, the person concerned has not expressed an objection. The views of close relatives are not taken into account ...

A slightly less strict version of presumed consent operates in Belgium where, if there is no explicit objection by the deceased, the relatives are allowed to object but the medical profession are under no obligation to seek their views. The relatives must initiate the process under these circumstances ...

Other, still weaker, schemes allow removal unless the deceased has made an explicit or informal objection at any time. Such a formulation of the law effectively requires that the relatives are consulted in order to glean the wishes of the deceased. Although it is formally the views of the deceased whilst alive which are being sought, such schemes allow the relatives to object on the deceased's behalf. France and Spain operate presumed consent legislation of this kind ...

Finally, a scheme in operation in Singapore provides for the automatic exclusion of certain categories of potential donor, including non-citizens and Muslims ... Muslims can, however, donate their organs if they wish, by pledging their organs whilst alive or if their relatives consent ...

Does presumed consent work? Belgium

Belgium enacted presumed consent legislation in June 1986 in the middle of a period of sustained and steady growth in kidney transplantation across Europe ...

Belgium did increase the number of available kidneys by a significant margin during 1987 – a rise of 37% over the year before – and this does not seem to be simply the continuation of an earlier trend. Furthermore, neither the UK, Germany nor the Netherlands experienced a similar increase in the same year. On the other hand, Austria did experience a similar increase, drawing attention to the fact that the effect experienced in Belgium could have been as a result of other factors (Austria did not introduce similar legislation in the same year, having done so in 1982, formalising a 200 year tradition of routinely utilising the corpse for medical purposes). For instance, the publicity devoted to the organ donation issue whilst the law was being debated could itself have promoted a greater willingness to donate on the part of the public and a more informed attitude on behalf of ICU staff. It has also been noted that the number of transplant co-ordinators increased at around this time, and that the law formalised systems of reimbursement so that donating hospitals could be sure that they would receive the appropriate payment for managing the donor.

These objections are inconclusive, however. One would expect a 'publicity effect' to subside. The increase in the number of co-ordinators was likely to be as much a result of the increased number of donors as the cause of it. And the law merely formalised payment systems which operated successfully for the majority of hospitals beforehand. But perhaps the best evidence is provided by ... [comparing] the difference between centres which always asked permission, and the centre which 'followed the law'. It is clear that the influence of publicity, co-ordinators and payment systems had no effect in those centres where relatives' permission is always sought. It certainly seems as though the law had an independent effect on kidney retrieval where its provisions were adopted ...

Another option may be to introduce a system of 'required request' as is operated in the USA. As the King's Fund Institute Report continues:

New, B, Solomon, M, Dingwall, R and McHale, J, *A Question of Give and Take,* **1994, London: Kings Fund Institute, pp 59–60:**

Required request

Required request and routine inquiry are used extensively in the United States with the aim of increasing the supply of organs. The Uniform Anatomical Gift Act 1987, which forms the model for many State statutes, makes provision for required request and routine inquiry. The development of required request policies by hospitals was encouraged by the Omnibus (Budget) Reconciliation Act 1986. This Act provides that failure on the part of hospitals to adopt routine inquiry or required request policies will lead to the denial of Medicare and Medicaid reimbursements from the Health Care Finance Authority.

Required request is a procedure in which inquiries must be made of the families of potential donors to see whether they would allow their relatives' organs to be used. Twenty six US States have this type of policy. The legislation in some States incorporates exceptions to the general duty of inquiry where, for example, the wishes of the deceased are already known, or the medical staff are unable to locate the family in a timely manner, or where inquiry would exacerbate mental or emotional distress.

Routine inquiry is the procedure of informing individuals and families of the option of organ donation. Eighteen States have legislation of this kind. Some States do not require hospitals to approach families directly but stipulate that they must establish organ and tissue donation committees to design policies which would result in prompt identification of donors and prompt referral to the Organ Procurement Agency.

How successful have the required request and routine inquiry schemes been? While there was an initial increase in the availability of organs, over time the schemes do not appear to have had a major impact ... One reason for this, it is suggested, is the lack of institutional commitment to ensuring that the required request procedures are followed. The United States experience illustrates that simply to enact required request legislation is not enough. It is vital to have adequately trained and qualified personnel.

As one organ procurement official observed: 'if you simply ask relatives about organ donation by simply citing the law the consent rate is zero ...'

Another reason suggested for the lack of dramatic impact of required request is that doctors find organ procurement time consuming and emotionally demanding. It is questionable whether statutory enactment of required request would have a significant impact. The national audit found that only 6% of relatives in the UK are not approached when an otherwise potential donor is on a ventilator, and many of these would probably have communicated their unwillingness to consider donation by other means.

Arguably, in this area, legal change unaccompanied by any corresponding change in cultural values (notably the pre-eminence accorded to the views of relatives), or commitment of greater technical resources to organ retrieval, is unlikely to decrease appreciably the shortfall in donor organs. As Bernard Teo has observed:

Teo, B, 'Strategies of organ procurement' (1992) 6 Bioethics 113:

What strategy of organ procurement a society ought to adopt depends on its willingness to expend resources for its transplant programme(s), ie, after the requirements of social priorities have been considered. If it chooses to ration resources for these programme(s), then it is arguably wiser to adopt a less efficient but ethically preferable strategy of expressed consent or its variants. The system would most likely yield a limited quantity of organs which would probably remain comfortably within the resources allocated for the programme(s). What would be the purpose of adopting a more efficient organ procurement policy when the number of procedures capable of being performed would be constrained by limitations in other resources? Furthermore, would those involved with the procurement of organs be as eager to procure organs?

Perhaps France is a case in point. In his report on the French organ transplant and procurement programmes, Arthur Caplan noted that concerns for the rising costs of health care have created a less than enthusiastic commitment of its scarce medical resources to its transplant programmes. Restrictions in the availability of resources for transplants have placed '... severe limits both in terms of personnel and hospital space on the number of transplants of all types that can now be performed'. Its effect on medical professionals is to dampen their enthusiasm in seeking out potential organ donors. Thus, it is arguable that France ought not to have adopted presumed consent without prior consideration of the extent to which it is prepared to support its transplant programmes. Furthermore, the policy creates ethical problems that are more difficult to overcome than would be the case if it had adopted ethically preferable, but less efficient, policies.

Of course, it might be argued that a more efficient system of organ procurement would create better chances for patients to find matching tissues since the chances would increase in proportion to the number of organs the system yields. The counter-argument to this is that a more efficient system of organ procurement could also increase the possibility of a fiscal overload, and subsequently distort a society's medical priorities if it is forced to spend more resources on its transplant program than it is willing. Thus it may be legitimate to question whether every State in the USA ought to adopt the policy of required request when some States have clearly indicated that transplants are not priorities in their health delivery, and have chosen to restrict resources for their programmes.

Even if there is a commitment to meet all its transplant needs, a society should first try out such ethically preferable strategies as expressed consent or, in the event of its failure, the system of required request ...

Even as a society contemplates the adoption of presumed consent, it ought to consider another important factor: political feasibility. It seems unwise for

France to have adopted the legislation without consideration of political feasibility. The French people hold a strong belief in the rights of families relative to cadaver disposal. French doctors find it '... psychologically intolerable to remove tissues from a body without obtaining the permission of the next of kin' which explains their customary practice of always asking familial consent for organ removal. In practice, France's presumed consent policy, ie, of not requiring familial consent, exists only on paper. It is the policy of required request that is being carried out. Thus it seems that France could have adopted the policy of required request which would have been more in tune with the French custom of familial consultation.

Elective ventilation – clarifying the law

The meaning of this practice and the background to the debate surrounding its legality have been described at p 598 above. Prior to the practice's suspension, the King's Fund Institute Report was optimistic about its potential to generate a significant number of additional donor organs:

> **New, B, Solomon, M, Dingwall, R and McHale, J, *A Question of Give and Take*, 1994, London: Kings Fund Institute, p 56:**
>
> ... what difference would a national policy of elective ventilation make? At Exeter – and this is likely to be an over-estimate – the team found on average three donors per year from the protocol from a population of 303,000. This translates into 10 donors pmp per year. The 277 ICUs in England ... serve a population of 47.8 million, which means that, at best, there would be 478 extra donors to be found nationwide, an average of just under two per unit. Let us assume an upper limit of three per unit for the purposes of this discussion.
>
> How long would these donors spend in an ICU bed? No electively ventilated donors should spend more than 48 hours in the ICU according to the Exeter experience, and this can be written into the protocol. Thus if donors turn out not to be suitable or do not continue to respiratory arrest, then they should be removed from the ICU. One donor in Exeter spent 127 hours in the ICU, but personal communication with staff from the hospital has confirmed that this would not be normal practice and only occurred because there was no pressure on ICU beds at the time. Indeed, all but two of the donors in the initial report of the protocol were in the ICU for less than 24 hours ... Let us estimate two bed days per donor as the highest likely average length of stay.
>
> Thus, on the most extreme estimate, units will, on average, have to accommodate three electively ventilated donors per year spending a total of six bed days in the unit. This would be in addition to the current mean occupancy rate of 1,314 bed days – an increase of 0.46%. 478 extra donors constitutes an increase of 66% on the English donor rate for 1991, but is likely to increase ICU workload by less than one hundredth of that proportion. Whilst it is acknowledged that these average figures hide the fact that some units will be at full capacity, and therefore entirely unable to contribute to the policy, this analysis draws attention to the relatively small impact such a policy would have on the intensive care community, whilst having a potentially enormous impact on transplant activity.

If this assessment is correct, the clarification of the law in this area should arguably be undertaken as a matter of some priority.

Creating a market in organs

The shortfall in organs could probably be eradicated at one stroke if we were prepared to sanction commercial dealings in them. However, such a possibility undoubtedly arouses widespread repugnance. The main arguments for and against permitting a market in organs are explored by Wilkinson and Garrard:

> **Wilkinson, S and Garrard, E, 'Bodily integrity and the sale of human organs' (1996) 22 JME 334:**
>
> ### The case in favour of permitting organ sale
>
> There's plenty to be said in favour of permitting a trade in human organs. Most obviously, it would generate an increased supply of a scarce and life-saving resource, as well as providing some much needed income for those who have little else to sell. Furthermore, it seems inconsistent to allow bomb disposal experts, firefighters and deep-sea divers to be paid for their dangerous (and sometimes painful) work, while preventing other people from being paid for the equally valuable contribution their kidneys would make to the well being of others. Finally, libertarian thoughts might incline us to permit people to dispose of their own body parts in whatever way they wish (we're talking about *their* body parts, after all, and so they should be allowed to do what they want with them).
>
> In spite of these considerations, though, many still find the idea of paying a healthy person for one of her organs deeply repugnant. Given the apparent advantages of permitting organ sale, what justification might there be for this reaction?
>
> ### The case against permitting organ sale
>
> There seem to us to be four standard objections to permitting organ sale, each of which we regard as ultimately unconvincing:
>
> **Pain and risk**
>
> The first is simply that the organ seller is subjected to an extremely high level of pain and risk. This in itself, though, can't be sufficient to justify a ban on organ sale, since we don't in general think that it's wrong to pay people for doing dangerous things. (There are numerous examples of this: firefighters, astronauts, miners and divers, to name but a few.) Common forms of 'risky labour' are often more dangerous than organ sale, but are regarded as heroic, rather than condemned; it is seen as quite proper to reward those who do them. And this difference in attitude can't be justified in terms of the good consequences that 'risky labour' produces, since the consequences of an organ sale (typically, saving a life) may be just as good or better.

Exploitation and commodification

The second worry is that the relationship between the buyer and seller is likely to be exploitative and to either cause or constitute an unacceptable *commodification* of the seller and/or her body. Brecher, for example, describes trading in human kidneys (along with many other practices) as 'exploitation based on making a commodity of human beings'.

There are two problems with this objection. First, although organ sale does necessarily involve treating a human body part as a commodity, there is no reason to suppose that this is *necessarily exploitative*. Would we really regard it as exploitative if the organ seller were wealthy, educated, rational and well informed and got paid £1,000,000 for her organ? Second, we do, in fact, permit many practices which are at least as exploitative and 'commodifying' as organ sale (for example, poorly paid labour). Of course, this doesn't show that exploitation and commodification are acceptable. But it *does* show that they aren't a special problem for organ sale and that they alone can't explain why organ sale is seen as more offensive than (say) low wages. (It may, of course, be argued that the thought that organ sale is worse than low wages is simply irrational and/or false. This is, roughly, Bob Brecher's view.)

It is sometimes claimed, however, that there is an important difference between banning a proposed new practice and banning an established one, since banning an established one will be more disruptive, unpopular and costly. This might provide a reason for banning organ sale, even if it were morally no worse than other permitted exploitative practices. For we could hold that although, as an ideal, we should ban all exploitative practices, in the real world we must settle for banning just those which we can ban, or can ban without excessive disruption and cost. However, although the distinction between banning new and banning existing practices is an important one, it is not sufficient to show that organ sale is morally worse than these other exploitative practices and so won't serve to explain or justify the widespread moral intuition that there is something especially objectionable about the sale of body parts. In short, it seems that the moral difference between organ sale and poorly paid labour is not merely that one is easier to ban than the other.

Undermining the practice of free donation

Another objection to permitting organ sale is that to do so would undermine the practice of free donation. Abouna *et al*, for example, claim that there is 'considerable evidence to indicate that marketing in human organs will eventually deprecate and destroy the present willingness of members of the public to donate their organs out of altruism'. There are two distinct worries here. The first is a purely practical one. If payment is allowed, then virtually all donors will begin to expect payment and so voluntary donations will cease. The second is that allowing payment for organs would deprive people of an opportunity to participate in 'giving' relationships with one another: relationships which have some ethical or social value, independently of their practical consequences.

Taking the second worry first, it is sufficient to point out that the mere permissibility of sale doesn't itself prevent people from donating (although it might, of course, encourage them to sell rather than donate). Organ givers are at liberty to waive their fee and, in a sense, the possibility of sale allows the (free) donor to be even more generous than she could otherwise have been; for not only does she give up her organ, but she gives up her fee as well.

As regards the first worry, it seems that there's no compelling reason to believe that organ sale would undermine the practice of free donation. After all, professional social work and charitable social work co-exist. Also, if organ sale led to a significant overall increase in the supply of organs, this would more than compensate for the reduced number of free organs. But in any case, it is far from clear that there is a significant practice of free donation to be undermined. As Harvey points out, 'it is doubtful that there is a great number of willing, non-related potential organ donors who will give without payment'. Given the high level of pain and risk involved, free donation (except by relatives, who might well waive the fee, if it were offered) is very unlikely to take place anyway.

Concerns about autonomy and consent

It is generally agreed that the absence of coercion and manipulation is required for genuine consent. And the final objection we consider is that no one could ever be in a position autonomously to consent to selling an organ such as a kidney, since the process would be so unpleasant and/or dangerous that only someone who was coerced or manipulated would agree to it. One virtue of this objection is that it would explain why we're more concerned about organ selling than the selling of blood and certain other body products. In the case of the latter, the level of pain and/or risk is very low, and so the need for coercion and manipulation is much less.

This objection does, indeed, raise a serious practical worry about the possibility of organ sellers being coerced, and it is certainly true that, were organ sale to be permitted, rigorous safeguards aimed at ensuring fully informed consent in every case would be required. But does organ sale necessarily involve coercion or manipulation? It seems not, since even a wealthy, informed and rational agent might consent to it (without coercion or manipulation) if the price were high enough. Would we want to say, in such a case, that the person hadn't really consented? (Of course, with a broad enough conception of manipulation, the answer to this question might be 'yes', but we would question whether so broad a conception would be able to do any ethical work, since too many things would be counted as manipulative.)

Also, given that organ sale is less unpleasant and dangerous than many accepted forms of 'risky labour', were we to take this objection seriously, then a wide range of accepted practices should be condemned on similar grounds. What is more, the same line of reasoning might lead us to ban many cases of organ *donation*, for as Harvey points out:

> ... there is financial pressure when the potential [paid] donor is in poverty. And perhaps it may be argued that this alone is sufficient for banning all paid-for donations. But then, in consistency, the same reasoning should be applied to related donors: since some of them are open to heavy psychological and emotional pressure (for example, perhaps by being the submissive and 'guilt'-ridden offspring of an extremely domineering and now ailing parent) ...

If the possibility of (financially) pressuring the organ *seller* is sufficient to warrant a ban on organ sale, then the possibility of (emotionally) pressuring the related organ *donor* must also be sufficient to warrant a ban on organ donation. But since we clearly don't want to ban donation, the possibility of pressuring can't be a sufficient reason to ban sale.

In response to this, it might be argued that financial and emotional pressures are importantly different, in that financial pressure is more erosive of the possibility of genuine consent. This may well be true. The pressure on someone facing starvation (due to poverty) may well be such that an offer to buy her kidney is irresistible. However, a not unreasonable reply is that in those circumstances, *if* the potential seller's plight cannot (or will not) be relieved in any other way, then forbidding her to sell her kidney is more harmful to her than undermining her autonomous consent (by allowing her to sell it). Furthermore, the evil involved here seems to lie not in the sale itself, but in her being allowed to be in such desperate circumstances in the first instance.

Ultimately, our reluctance to treat irreplaceable bodily parts as commodities which may be the subject of buying and selling seems to be grounded both in an intrinsic sense of respect for persons as ends in themselves, and in fears as to the moral climate of any society in which organised trading in organs became the norm. As Bernard Teo writes:

Teo, B, 'Strategies of organ procurement' (1992) 6 Bioethics 113:

... the human body is not like other things. Since human bodiliness is intrinsically tied to human personality and identity, it follows that respect for the human person would also be intrinsically tied to respect for the human body and its parts. In every culture and society, the instinctive revulsion and strong moral aversion toward treating the human body as property and commodity in both religious and secular attitudes is shown by the special respect accorded to the body in elaborate ceremonies and rituals surrounding death and burial. They are signs of respect and reverence for the person who lived. There seems to be that intuitive instinct that the human body has a special moral significance that cannot be equated with other things or commodities. Leon Kass, a physician and philosopher, has warned against trivialising human embodiment. Because human dignity is intrinsically linked to human embodiment, treating the body and its parts as commodities would be to strip the human body of its proper dignity. It would be morally intolerable therefore if human body parts are treated as objects for payment and as commodities of exchange in the market place. Thus it is arguable that placing a monetary value on human body parts would be ethically unacceptable.

Furthermore, in a society where cherished communal values such as altruism and giving are encouraged and cultivated, legalising a commercial market for organs and paying for them would dissolve communal bonds and relationships based on goodwill and altruism. It would transform them into one of contractual buying and selling. Arguably, allowing payment for organs and legalising a market approach would not only dehumanise the transacting parties, but would also undermine the humanitarian character of the transplant undertaking and be an effective dissolvent of community. The wisdom of paying for organs and allowing commercialisation is therefore highly questionable even for the lofty purpose of saving lives.

As the law in the UK stands, of course, commercial dealing in organs (both from live donors and cadavers) is a criminal offence under the Human Organ Transplants Act 1989.

CHAPTER TWELVE

EUTHANASIA

INTRODUCTION

What is euthanasia?

Euthanasia (literally 'an easeful death', from the Greek) describes the practice of bringing about death in a manner that causes the least amount of suffering to the patient. The term is sometimes used narrowly to refer only to the taking of life by positive means, for example, the giving of a lethal injection to a patient whose life is full of unbearable pain. However, in this chapter, we employ it more widely, to encompass, in addition, cases in which a doctor, intending his patient's death, refrains from providing life-prolonging treatment: we thus distinguish between 'active' and 'passive' euthanasia. Though this is ultimately a matter of terminology, the reader should be alert, especially when reading judgments, as to which usage has been adopted in a particular instance. As well as embracing the active/passive distinction, the practice of euthanasia can also assume voluntary and non-voluntary forms depending on whether the patient is competent to request it or not. (Involuntary euthanasia, which consists of imposing/permitting death in a competent patient's best interests, but against his or her own wishes, is not considered here.)

The value of human life

What makes the issue of euthanasia so morally contentious is the enormous value which we place upon human life. In the following extract, Helga Kuhse charts the historical framework in which respect for individual human life attained centrality in Western thought, as well as noting the difficulties encountered by the view in an increasingly secular age:

Kuhse, H, *The Sanctity-of-Life Doctrine in Medicine*, **1987, Oxford: Clarendon Press, pp 16–20:**

Every society known to us subscribes to some principle or principles involving respect for human life. As Georgia Harkness puts it:

> In every society there appears to be an elemental reverence for life which makes the deliberate killing of another person a punishable offence. In all societies there are exceptions ... yet aversion to murder is probably the most universal of all moral attitudes.

But if aversion to murder, or wrongful killing, is universal, there have been great variations between cultural traditions as to what constitutes wrongful killing.

If we turn to the roots of our Western tradition, we find that in Greek and Roman times not all human life was regarded as inviolable and worthy of protection. Slaves and 'barbarians' did not have a full right to life, and human sacrifices and gladiatorial combat were acceptable at different times. Spartan law required that deformed infants be put to death; for Plato, infanticide is one of the regular institutions of the ideal State; Aristotle regards abortion as a desirable option; and the Stoic philosopher Seneca writes unapologetically: 'Unnatural progeny we destroy; we drown even children who at birth are weakly and abnormal.'

Stoic and Epicurean philosophers thought that suicide and euthanasia were acceptable options when life no longer held any value. Once again to quote Seneca:

> I shall not abandon old age, if old age preserves me intact as regards the better part of myself, but if old age begins to shatter my mind, and to pull its various faculties to pieces, if it leaves me, not life, but only the breath of life, I shall rush out of a house that is crumbling and tottering. I shall not avoid illness by seeking death, as long as the illness is curable and does not impede my soul. I shall not lay violent hands upon myself just because I am in pain; for death under such circumstances is defeat. But if I find out that the pain must always be endured, I shall depart, not because of the pain, but because it will be a hindrance to me as regards all my reasons for living.

And whilst there were deviations from these views (one of which is the Hippocratic Oath, briefly to be discussed below), it is probably correct to say that such practices as abortion, infanticide, suicide, and euthanasia were less proscribed in ancient times than they are today. There has been a gradual expansion of the circle protecting human life, outlawing not only the killing of slaves or 'barbarians', gladiatorial combat, and human sacrifice, but also abortion, infanticide, and euthanasia.

Most historians of Western morals agree that the rise of Judaism and even more of Christianity contributed greatly to the general feeling that human life is valuable and worthy of respect.

WEH Lecky gives the now classical account of the sanctity of human life in his *History of European Morals*:

> Considered as immortal beings, destined for the extremes of happiness or of misery, and united to one another by a special community of redemption, the first and most manifest duty of the Christian man was to look upon his fellow men as sacred beings and from this notion grew up the eminently Christian idea of the sanctity of human life ... it was one of the most important services of Christianity that besides quickening greatly our benevolent affections it definitely and dogmatically asserted the sinfulness of all destruction of human life as a matter of amusement, or of simple convenience, and thereby formed a new standard higher than any which then existed in the world ... This minute and scrupulous care for

human life and virtue in the humblest form, in the slave, the gladiator, the savage, or the infant, was indeed wholly foreign to the genius of Paganism. It was produced by the Christian doctrine of the inestimable value of each immortal soul.

Whilst it is true that even before the rise of Christianity some philosophical and religious schools expressed a strong respect for human life, it is generally agreed that such views were only held by a minority. For example, the Hippocratic Oath, which Ludwig Edelstein assigns to the 4th century BC, already strongly disapproves of abortion, euthanasia, and suicide – independently of Judaeo-Christian influence. However, if Edelstein is correct, this oath represented only 'a small segment of Greek opinion' and was not generally accepted until the end of antiquity when Christianity became the dominant religion. Edelstein attributes the oath to the Pythagoreans who strongly condemned suicide on the grounds that 'we are all soldiers of God, placed in an appointed post of duty, which it is a rebellion against our Maker to desert'.

Whatever the importance of the Pythagoreans in the evolution of the idea of the sanctity of human life, it would seem that at least one strand of their view, namely, the belief that we must not take our own life because God has assigned a certain post to us, is continued in the more influential Christian tradition (both Catholic and Protestant), which holds that we are God's property and must not quit our station in life wilfully. Life is, in the Christian tradition, not our own to do with as we like, but is 'entirely an ordination, a loan and a stewardship'. From such presuppositions it follows quite logically that 'only God has the right to take the life of an innocent, and that man ... must wait his appointed time till his charge cometh, till he sinks and is crushed with the weight of his own misery'.

On this view, then, it is not human life as such which is inviolable or has sanctity; it is rather the will of God which has sanctity and must not be violated. As the theologian Karl Barth puts it:

> Life itself does not create this respect. The command of God creates respect for it. It is thus not killing as such which is wrong, but it is wrong to act contrary to the will of God. In other words, killing is not an act wrong either in itself or wrong because of what it does to the victim; rather, killing is wrong simply because it is contrary to the will of God.

... There is no longer a universal acceptance of religion and of the belief that ethics consists in doing what God commands. Conventional attitudes based on these beliefs are, however, still very much with us today. During the long period when Christian beliefs moulded European thought, the sanctity-of-life view became part of an unquestioned moral tradition: it became part of medical ethics and the law. It was, for example, not until 1516 that Sir Thomas More presented the first important defence of mercy killing in the Christian era, and it was not until the 17th and 18th centuries that philosophers began to question the view that ethics requires a religious basis. From such initial philosophical questionings, however, it is a long way to a fundamental change in popular attitudes. Whilst it is today no longer generally believed that life has sanctity in the religious sense, the ethical attitudes to which these religious beliefs gave rise still find expression in the deep-seated belief that human life, irrespective of its quality or kind, is absolutely inviolable and equally valuable; and that we must never take life – either our own or that of anyone else – because life is not ours to do with as we see fit.

But now we must be clear about just what a non-theistic account of the sanctity of human life entails. While it may have made some religious sense to hold that mere bodily life has sanctity because life is a gift from God and has received its value from Him, it makes but poor philosophical sense to say that mere bodily life is intrinsically valuable and absolutely inviolable, for a secular account of the sanctity of human life will be hard put to provide a convincing reason for this view.

'Sanctity of life' and 'vitalism'

Kuhse associates the 'sanctity of life' doctrine, in its strongest form, with the view that human life is of absolute value and should, where possible, be maintained at any cost, including the cost to the individual whose life it is. Thus it is impermissible to shorten (or fail to extend) life, by however small an amount and irrespective of any suffering endured by the person concerned. However, in a recent article, John Keown has denied that the sanctity of life principle, properly understood, commits us to such a conclusion, which he instead ascribes to a separate doctrine, that of 'vitalism':

Keown, J, 'Restoring moral and intellectual shape to the law after *Bland'* (1997) 113 LQR 481:

The principle of the sanctity of life is often advocated but much less often understood. In Western thought, the development of the principle has owed much to the Judaeo-Christian tradition. That tradition's doctrine of the sanctity of life holds that human life is created in the image of God and is, therefore, possessed of an intrinsic dignity which entitles it to protection from unjust attack. With or without that theological underpinning, the doctrine grounds the principle that one ought never intentionally to kill an innocent human being. The 'right to life' is essentially a right not to be intentionally killed.

The dignity of human beings inheres because of the radical capacities, such as for understanding and rational choice, inherent in human nature. Some human beings, such as infants, may not yet possess the ability to exercise these radical capacities. But radical capacities must not be confused with abilities: one may have, for example, the radical capacity but not the ability to speak Swahili. All human beings possess the capacities inherent in their nature even though, because of infancy, disability or senility, they may not yet, not now, or no longer have the ability to exercise them.

As this account of human dignity might suggest, the principle can also be articulated in non-religious terms, in which 'inviolability' might be more apt than 'sanctity'. Indeed, a prohibition on killing is central to the pre-Christian fount of Western medical ethics – the Hippocratic Oath and the modern reaffirmation of that Oath by the (arguably post-Christian) Declaration of Geneva – and many non-believers recognise the right of human beings not to be intentionally killed. Lord Goff of Chieveley noted in *Bland* that the sanctity principle has long been recognised in most, if not all, civilised societies throughout the modem world, as is evidenced by its recognition by international conventions on human rights. Article 2 of the European Convention, for example, provides:

> Everyone's right to life shall be protected by law. No one shall be deprived of his life intentionally save in the execution of a sentence of a court following his conviction of a crime for which this penalty is provided by law.

The right not to be killed is enjoyed regardless of inability or disability. Rejecting any such distinctions as fundamentally arbitrary and inconsistent with a sound concept of justice, the principle (whether in its religious or secular forms) asserts that human life is not only an instrumental good, a necessary precondition of thinking or doing, but a basic good, a fundamental constituent of human flourishing. It is, in other words, not merely good as a means to an end but is, like other integral aspects of a flourishing human life, like friendship and knowledge, something worthwhile in itself. Of course some people, like those who are pictures of health in the prime of life, participate in the good of life and health to a greater extent than others, such as the terminally ill, but even the sick and the dying participate in the good to the extent they are able.

Although life is a basic good it is not an absolute good, a good to which all the other basic goods must be sacrificed in order to ensure its preservation. The sanctity doctrine is not vitalistic. The core of the doctrine is the principle prohibiting intentional killing, not an injunction requiring the preservation of life at all costs. However, although the doctrine denies that human life is an absolute good, the principle that it may never intentionally be taken is an absolute principle, that is, one which has no acceptable exceptions. Although the value of human life is not absolute, the prohibition on taking it is.

Although Keown refers here to the prohibition on 'killing' or 'taking life' as lying at the heart of the sanctity of life principle, it should not be supposed that he wishes to draw any distinction between active and passive euthanasia: in his view (though perhaps this is not the term's standard usage), it is just as possible – and *prima facie* culpable – to 'kill' by an omission as by an act. Rather, the sanctity of life principle acquires flexibility in permitting death in certain circumstances (and is hence saved from unacceptable 'vitalistic' consequences) through a combination of two other sub-principles: these are, respectively, the principle of 'double effect' and the distinction between 'ordinary' and 'extraordinary' treatment. Reliance on these latter principles informs the teachings on euthanasia of the Roman Catholic Church, and has been defended by natural law theorists such as JM Finnis. Nevertheless, both principles have been subjected to powerful criticism. In relation to that of double effect, John Harris has written as follows:

Harris, J, *The Value of Life: An Introduction to Medical Ethics*, 1985, London: Routledge and Kegan Paul, pp 43–45:

... I will take as an authoritative statement of the principle the explanation of it given in a recent Linacre Centre publication:

> ... the term 'double effect' relates to 'side effects' ... The principle of the side effect merely states a possibility: where you may not aim at someone's death, causing it does not necessarily incur guilt – it can be that there are necessities which in the circumstances are great enough or there are legitimate purposes in hand of such a kind to provide a valid excuse for risking or accepting that you cause death. Without such excuse foreseeable killing is either murder or manslaughter.

We should be clear also that you may not aim at someone's death either as an end or a means. There is an immense, and I think insoluble, problem about deciding when a death (or any other consequence) is aimed at as an end or a means and when it is merely a side effect. It all depends on how the action is described, and crucially on how to set limits to the re-description of any action. This can clearly be seen if we examine the Linacre Centre's own example in illustration of the distinction:

> Imagine a potholer stuck with people behind him and water rising to drown them. And suppose two cases: in one he can be blown up; in the other a rock can be moved to open another escape route, but it will crush him to death ...

> There might be people among them who, seeing the consequence, would move the rock, though they would not blow up the man because that would be choosing his death as the means of escape. This is a far from meaningless stance, for they thus show themselves as people who will absolutely reject any policy making the death of innocent people a means or end.

It is difficult to see how anyone could read this and not be impressed by it as an example of the most comprehensive sophistry. If this example has any plausibility, it depends on our accepting that blowing up the potholer can only be described as killing him whereas moving the rock is a complete action description, of which crushing the man is a mere side effect. It is a feature of any action that its description is almost infinitely expandable or contractable. My crooking my finger, is my pulling the trigger, is my shooting at Samson, is my hitting Delilah, is my killing the President, is my orphaning her children, etc, etc. The problem is to set a limit to the legitimacy of characterising the action in one way rather than another. The above description of what went on in the cave could seem plausible only because the whole distinction between direct means and ends on the one hand, and side effects on the other, has already been rigged by a particular choice of action descriptions. This can easily be seen if we change the phraseology slightly:

> Suppose two cases: in one he is crushed leaving room to escape; in the other a hole can be blown in the rock at its weakest point but this will dismember the potholer ...

These descriptions are equally plausible but the impression of which course of action involves direct killing, and which involves death as a side effect of what is done, is different. The crucial point for anyone who wishes to have a realistic appreciation of what is involved in one choice rather than another is surely not: 'which description makes the most undesirable consequence a side effect?' But: 'am I justified in behaving in a way that has these consequences?'

Anyone who thinks that, in the Linacre Centre example, those who choose to save themselves by crushing the potholer rather than by blowing him up are those who 'show themselves as people who will absolutely reject any policy making the death of innocent people a means or end' is simply and comprehensively deceiving himself.

The distinction between effects and side effects, and between effects and double effects, drawn in this way is entirely without moral significance. What matters ... is how our decisions and actions affect the world, not whether that effect is direct or indirect ...

Side effects revisited

I should emphasise that there is a perfectly respectable everyday use of the term 'side effects' and I am not denying that for some purposes it may be useful to distinguish between the direct effects and the side effects of a drug or a course of treatment. But it is important to be clear that this distinction is entirely without moral significance and cannot be used to limit our responsibility for bringing about those side effects.

A usual way of drawing the distinction in medical practice is to characterise the hoped-for result of the treatment as its direct effect, and any unwanted or redundant effects as side effects. So, for example, the degree to which it diminishes pain is the direct effect of an analgesic, and any consequent drowsiness or toxicity a side effect. However, those who administer the analgesic remain responsible for the drowsiness and the toxicity, and will be justified in producing these effects along with the reduction in pain only if, all things considered, the reduction is worth having at the cost of the side effects.

Equally, Jonathan Glover has doubted the analytical and moral propriety of deciding whether to provide life-saving treatment by reference to whether it can be regarded as ordinary or extraordinary:

Glover, J, *Causing Death and Saving Lives*, 1977, Harmondsworth: Penguin, pp 195–97:

The distinction drawn between ordinary and extraordinary means of saving life is not based on the line between what is and is not medically orthodox, but on a cluster of features clearly supposed to be relevant to the question: do the likely results justify the drawbacks of the methods?

In discussions of this distinction, aspects of the means relevant to whether or not they are extraordinary are said to be the degree to which they are expensive, unusual, difficult, painful or dangerous. And the extent to which the outcome is satisfactory is also thought relevant to assessing the 'ordinariness' of the means: it is sometimes suggested that, where the means have many of the drawbacks listed, they are not ordinary if their outcome is to leave the patient severely disabled or a heavy burden on his family.

The trouble with this distinction (whatever its virtues as a rough and ready rule for doctors) is that it tries to do too much at once. The decision about the 'ordinariness' of the means involves assessing how worthwhile the life saved will be, assessing the side effects on the family and the cost in effort and money, and then in the light of all this making an overall assessment of the desirability of the life-saving project. So a stand has to be taken on a number of the largest questions about relative priorities before an answer can be given about ordinariness. It is clear both that there is much room for disagreement about answers here and that to present this cluster of questions as though they were a single one, and almost a technical one concerning 'means' at that, is highly misleading.

The confusion of thought involved in this way of presenting the questions can be seen by looking at those of the factors usually cited that really are to do with the means. We are supposed to assess the extent to which the means are expensive, unusual, difficult, painful or dangerous. The obvious question is what 'unusual' is doing in this list. It seems either redundant or undesirable. For, if the unusual treatment is expensive, difficult, painful or dangerous, we can object to it already on those grounds. But where an effective treatment is cheap, easy, painless and risk-free, only someone whose conventionality verges on dementia will object to it because of its being unusual.

Those who ask whether the outcome will be a high enough chance of a life good enough to justify the pain, or the cost in time, effort or money involved in some life-saving procedure, are asking the unavoidable and central question. What is important is to face this as involving decisions about priorities, and not to slur it over in a way which implies that the answer depends on how often the techniques are used.

Quality of life

Philosophers such as Glover and Harris argue that, in making decisions about ending life, we should be prepared to deploy overt quality of life considerations. Human life is no longer to be regarded as possessing intrinsic value *per se*; rather, what makes life valuable is, crudely, the life-holder's capacity for pleasurable states of consciousness. As Kuhse notes, this value is enhanced where the individual in question is a person with a sense of existing over time and capable of valuing their existence:

Kuhse, H, *The Sanctity-of-Life Doctrine in Medicine,* **1987, Oxford: Clarendon Press, pp 211–14:**

... what is it that gives value to human life, but not – or not to the same degree – to the lives of other living things? Two answers are possible. The first answer is that human life has sanctity simply because it is human life, that is, because it is the life of a member of the species *Homo sapiens*. The second answer is that human life has special value because humans are self-aware, rational, autonomous, purposeful, moral beings, with hopes, ambitions, life purposes, ideals, and so on ... Any of these qualities, or a combination of them, could serve as a basis for a moral distinction between human beings and lettuces or chickens. That such distinguishing qualities are needed is clear: for if the value of life were based on 'mere life', rather than on one or more of the above characteristics, then every life including the earthworm's or the lettuce's would be equally valuable.

It is not difficult to see that the second answer does point to a morally relevant difference between some lives and others. For example, it is quite plausible to hold that the life of a self-aware, rational, purposeful being that sees itself as existing over time is more valuable than the life of an entity or being who lacks these characteristics. But if one takes this approach, then one is not saying that human life has sanctity, but rather that rationality, the capacity to be self-aware, moral or purposeful, and so on, have 'sanctity'. Of course, one may still hold ... that human life has sanctity or special worth, but only in so far as it is a precondition for rationality, purposiveness, or whatever else one takes the valuable characteristic to be. One would not, on this view, be able to argue that the lives of all members of the human species have special value – for example, the lives of the irreversibly comatose, or the lives of severely brain-damaged new-born infants. The second approach, then, does not give us a reason for preserving all human lives, and cannot serve as the basis for the view that all human lives, irrespective of their quality or kind, are equally valuable ...

This conclusion should, in my view ... be applied to decision making in the practice of medicine. What is important is not that a patient is human (and therefore should have her life sustained). Rather, we must ask questions about the quality and kind of the patient's life ...

Quality of life and interests

I start with the assumption that conscious life has value because it enables the existence of pleasurable states of consciousness. Whilst the existence of pleasurable states is not the only value to which human life gives rise, it will be agreed, I think, that it is at least a value that morality ought to take into account. In other words, I am suggesting that life is not an intrinsic good, not a good in itself, but rather a means to something else – for example, pleasurable states of consciousness.

If we were thus to agree that the value of life is not in life *qua* life ('mere life'), but rather has its locus in the value it has for the individual concerned, then it would follow that life is not an unconditional good, but good only in so far as it is of value to its possessor. This means that not all life is equally valuable, as the sanctity-of-life view suggests, nor is it, as I want to suggest, always inviolable. To the extent that we can all envisage situations where we would choose death for ourselves rather than continue living, there will also be situations where any morality based on the Golden Rule or the principle of universalisability would direct that a moral agent take the life of another rather than preserve it ...

As the last sentence of the above passage makes clear, those who take a quality of life approach to euthanasia do not distinguish, other things being equal (ie, leaving aside possible policy reasons of a consequentialist nature, see below, p 649), between active and passive measures designed to terminate life. A positive act of killing, for example, by lethal injection, is regarded as on par with passively allowing death to occur by withholding treatment: in both cases, what is important is the quality of the life in question.

The qualified sanctity of life principle

We now turn to a position which may be regarded as a compromise between the sanctity and quality of life approaches. This 'qualified' sanctity doctrine agrees with the fully fledged sanctity approach that there is something special about human life, such that it is not reducible to the sum of the life-holder's states of consciousness. The respect due to such life is reflected in a (virtual) prohibition on active steps by third parties, including doctors, to terminate it. On the other hand, the doctrine is more relaxed about allowing quality of life considerations to determine when third parties need not act to prolong life.

It is this position which has been adopted by the English courts.

Airedale NHS Trust v Bland [1993] 1 All ER 821

Hoffmann LJ: In my view the choice which the law makes must reassure people that the courts do have full respect for life, but that they do not pursue the principle to the point at which it has become almost empty of any real content and when it involves the sacrifice of other important values such as human dignity and freedom of choice. I think that such reassurance can be provided by a decision, properly explained, to allow Anthony Bland to die ... Is this answer affected by the proposed manner of his death? Some might say that as he is going to die, it does not matter how. Why wait for him to expire for lack of food or be carried off by an untreated infection? Would it not be more humane simply to give him a lethal injection? No one in this case is suggesting that Anthony Bland should be given a lethal injection. But there is concern about ceasing to supply food as against, for example, ceasing to treat an infection with antibiotics. Is there any real distinction? In order to come to terms with our intuitive feelings about whether there is a distinction, I must start by considering why most of us would be appalled if he was given a lethal injection. It is, I think, connected with our view that the sanctity of life entails its inviolability by an outsider. Subject to exceptions like self-defence, human life is inviolate even if the person in question has consented to its violation. That is why although suicide is not a crime, assisting someone to commit suicide is. It follows that, even if we think Anthony Bland would have consented, we would not be entitled to end his life by a lethal injection.

On the other hand, we recognise that, one way or another, life must come to an end. We do not impose on outsiders an unqualified duty to do everything possible to prolong life as long as possible. I think that the principle of inviolability explains why, although we accept that in certain cases it is right to allow a person to die (and the debate so far has been over whether this is such a case) we hold without qualification that no one may introduce an external agency with the intention of causing death.

(For the full facts of this case, and the consideration it received in the House of Lords, see below, p 679.)

The acts/omissions distinction

Whether the law's position is a coherent one turns upon the tenability of the acts/omissions distinction: is there a morally significant distinction between, say, a doctor who gives a lethal injection to a neonate in his care which suffers from severe spina bifida, and a doctor who omits to give such an infant life-saving antibiotics in the face of an infection? This question was the subject of a debate between John Lorber, a Sheffield paediatrician who pioneered a policy of 'selective treatment' for such neonates in the early 1970s, and the philosopher, John Harris:

> **Harris, J, *The Value of Life: An Introduction to Medical Ethics*, 1985, London: Routledge and Kegan Paul, pp 33–39:**
>
> Selective treatment of severely handicapped children is calculated to result in their deaths. I am thinking particularly of the management of children with severe spina bifida. Such a policy has been justified on the hypothesis that it is reasonable to conclude that the child would be better off dead. This paradoxical sounding conclusion means simply that it is judged to be in the child's best interests to die. I am assuming that the children in question are too young, or too severely handicapped, to be themselves consulted. I assume also that this sort of judgment, while difficult to make, is unproblematic in that we can all imagine many cases in which life is so intolerable, so painful, so miserable, so difficult and so utterly without reward, that we would not wish to live such a life and that it is reasonable to suppose that no one would. I assume also that severe spina bifida is such a case.
>
> What is, however, highly problematic is the judgment that it is morally preferable to withhold treatment from such children so that they die slowly, rather than to kill them quickly and painlessly. Since 'selective treatment' in this context usually means not treating and often not feeding either, I will use the term 'selective non-treatment' to refer to this procedure ...
>
> The tragedy is, of course, that these children or their families should suffer unnecessarily for even one month. Lorber sees this and records that 'it is painful to see such infants gradually fading away over a number of weeks or months when everybody hopes for a speedy end'. Lorber's motives are of the highest, he wants to save children and their families as much suffering as in conscience he can, and he has been courageous in pioneering selective non-treatment which is more economical of suffering and of resources than is the active treatment of severe spina bifida. It is therefore particularly poignant that he believes it right to stop short of killing and particularly worthwhile examining his arguments for so doing ...
>
> **The argument from brutalisation**
>
> This argument has two parts which are stated in two sentences, 'active euthanasia may brutalise the person who carries it out ... It would be wrong

for a doctor to order his junior or his nurses to carry out such a task if he cannot bring himself to do it'. To 'brutalise' in this context is, I suppose, to render individuals more insensitive to the pain and suffering of others and more careless of or callous about the value of their lives. Evidence of brutalisation would be very hard to find and Lorber cites none. But what we have to balance here surely is a remote and imponderable danger of sensitive medical staff becoming 'brutalised' to an unknown (but perhaps insignificant) degree, against real and present pain, suffering and distress to the patients, their loving ones, and the medical staff who have to preside over their slow demise. We must also take into account the equally probable brutalising effect of taking responsibility for a slow and distressing rather than a quick and painless end. In the absence of any evidence, it is plausible to suppose that the responsibility of bringing about a slow and distressing death would be more rather than less brutalising than would a quick and merciful killing ...

The argument from lack of consent

'I strongly disagree with active euthanasia,' Lorber states, 'especially for babies and children, who cannot possibly ask for it or give their considered consent'. Consent is worrying, but it is no more worrying for active euthanasia in the cases under consideration, than it is for selective non-treatment. As we have seen, selective non-treatment is intended to result in death and it does, and those who die cannot possibly ask for it or give their considered consent.

The slippery slope argument

> It would be impossible to formulate legislation, however humane are the intentions, that could not be abused by the unscrupulous. There have been plenty of examples in the past, especially in Hitler's Germany. Few just or compassionate persons would wish to give such a dangerous legal power to any individual or group of people.

There are two points that need to be made here. The first is again that Lorber and others already have this power, they decide to act so as to bring about the speedy deaths of their patients and they are very successful. Whatever the dangers of legislation are, it must surely be possible to make them less than those that already exist without specific legislation. The power is awesome but it is already exercised. The second point is about the spectre of Hitler and Nazism. By raising it, Lorber invites us to see the difference between active and passive euthanasia as the difference between humane medical practice in a civilised society and the first step on the road to the holocaust. But the Nazi euthanasia programme was nothing like the possibilities we are considering. Under the Nazis euthanasia was simply one way of exterminating those racially or politically beyond moral consideration. And the Nazis were not short of other ways to achieve the same ends. It is precisely because we care about spina bifida children, precisely because we are in no doubt that they must not suffer, that we are concerned about what it is in their best interests to do. The spectre of Nazism offers no analogy at all and so only fogs the issues.

We must again remind ourselves that doctors already take decisions which result in death with no legal or publicly debated safeguards. If we do not cry 'Nazism' it is simply because we know there is no analogy and we know that all concerned are concerned only about the welfare of their patients. But if we fear even the slimmest chance of abuse, we should take care that all decisions in these areas are taken in the open with the widest possible public debate and scrutiny.

The last door argument

The argument here is that active euthanasia closes the last door on an individual's life whereas 'No treatment with normal nursing care is a safeguard against wrong diagnosis ... If an infant's condition is not as grave as was thought, he will live and he can then be given optimal care ...'. But this is just not true on Lorber's own account of the treatment. If a child selected for non-treatment contracts an infection and dies because it is not given antibiotics or, if it requires resuscitation which is not given and it dies, there will be no opportunity to discover whether the diagnosis was wrong or not. So this 'safeguard' is hit and miss at best. If the child *per* almost *impossible* lives, we may find reason to say the diagnosis was wrong, but if the child dies we cannot say the diagnosis was right unless the non-treatment played no role at all in the death, for otherwise the diagnosis is self-fulfilling. Whether closing a particular door on life chances is closing the last door will be a question of fact in each case. If the child dies of an untreated infection, then the withholding of the antibiotic drugs was in fact the closing of the last door, just as the administering of a lethal injection would be ...

The argument from self-deception

One argument that is sometimes advanced is the suggestion that parents and relatives of severely handicapped children would not accept or consent to anything resembling killing, and so if doctors are to be able to recommend what they see as the most humane course, such a recommendation or, if that is too strong a term, such a possible course of treatment would be useless if it were always rejected by those whose consent is judged necessary. But this, even if true, should not prevent us from seeing clearly what the most humane course of action is and advocating its acceptance. Unless we do so those concerned will continue to deceive themselves as to the reality of what they are doing, or consenting to have done, and will continue to choose a programme which involves weeks and months of avoidable suffering. And we should be clear that it is self-deception unless it can be unequivocally demonstrated that one procedure is of different moral quality to the other. The only palpable differences demonstrated by Lorber are that non-treatment takes longer to bring about death than would active euthanasia and is minimally less certain to result in death. And both these features seem to count against rather than in favour of selective non-treatment, given the reasons which justify its being undertaken at all.

Indeed self-deception is sometimes advanced as itself constituting the moral difference between active and passive euthanasia. The argument here is that it is only because the medical staff and the relatives of the children are able to protect themselves from full awareness of what they are doing that they are able to bring themselves to do what they judge to be morally required by the circumstances. Here the idea that they are only 'letting nature take its course' allows them to distance themselves from the death of the child and fit their part in events more comfortably into their conception of the medical role.

There is a terrible irony here in that the whole practice of medicine might be described as a comprehensive attempt to frustrate the course of nature, of which disease is after all a part, and to prevent 'nature' from killing people in its usual extravagant fashion. There is undoubtedly a widespread, but equally undoubtedly an irrational, respect for what is natural or part of the course of nature. Famines, floods, droughts, storms are all natural and all disastrous. We only, and rightly, want the natural when it's good for us. What is natural is morally inert and progress-dependent. It was only natural for people to die of infected wounds before antibiotics were available and it is only natural for spina bifida children to die if their condition is inoperable, but it is not natural if they are selected for non-treatment, when with full treatment they would live.

It is also perhaps worth emphasising that if we are ever to feel confident that the right thing is for the child to die in these circumstances then we should face the decision under its most stark and 'non-distanced' description. One might say that there is a moral requirement that in matters of such importance where the lives of others are at stake, we should be absolutely sure that we have faced squarely the full import of what we are doing. Whereas if we disguise the facts from ourselves and others by various distancing strategies, we may permanently shield ourselves both from full awareness of what we are about and from the possibility of thinking through all the implications of such consequential decisions.

Equally, James Rachels has produced a pair of well known, and colourful, hypothetical cases to deny the relevance of whether death is caused by action or inaction.

Rachels, J, *The End of Life*, 1986, Oxford: OUP, p 112:

Smith stands to gain a large inheritance if anything should happen to his six year old cousin. One evening while the child is taking his bath, Smith sneaks into the bathroom and drowns the child, and then arranges things so it will look like an accident. No one is the wiser, and Smith gets his inheritance.

Jones also stands to gain if anything should happen to his six year old cousin. Like Smith, Jones sneaks in planning to drown the child in his bath. However, just as he enters the bathroom Jones sees the child slip, hit his head, and fall face down in the water. Jones is delighted; he stands by, ready to push the child's head under if necessary, but it is not necessary. With only a little thrashing about, the child drowns all by himself, 'accidentally', as Jones watches and does nothing. No one is the wiser, and Jones gets his inheritance.

It is certainly true that in many cases the intention of an agent and the consequences of his conduct, in the context of bringing about the death of another individual, will be the same whether active or passive means are adopted. However, as Kuhse notes, a residual difference can be found in the causal relationship between the agent and the death.

Kuhse, H, *The Sanctity-of-Life Doctrine in Medicine*, 1987, Oxford: Clarendon Press, p 79:

... killing and letting die can be distinguished in so far as they involve the agent at different stages of a causal chain – and in the medical setting, generally in different causal chains. The patient's death will either be a consequence of a disease, or a consequence of a lethal agent administered by the doctor.

... [JS] Mill points out that 'many causes may produce death'. And, building on Mill, [John] Mackie draws our attention to the fact that there are many minimally sufficient conditions for a consequence such as death. The act of killing a patient by a lethal injection is an inus condition in one minimally sufficient condition for death, and hence a cause of death; refraining from administering a life-saving course of antibiotics to a patient who is suffering from, say, pneumonia, is an *inus* condition in another minimally sufficient condition for death, and hence another cause. Whilst these two modes of causing death cannot be distinguished in terms of causal efficacy or in terms of causal agency, they can be distinguished in so far as in the first case the physician initiates a course of events that will lead to death, whereas in the second case the doctor refrains from intervening in a course of events not initiated by her that will, coupled with her refraining, also lead to the patient's death.

The approach to causation here, which focuses upon the satisfaction of '*inus* conditions', is effectively the one embodied in the NESS test for causation outlined above, in Chapter 6. In fact, if we recall the latter model, it can be seen that, whereas the agent who *acts* standardly instigates a new causal set sufficient for the death, the agent who *omits* simply allows an existing set to complete itself. (In this regard, it can be argued that Rachels' Smith-and-Jones hypothetical gains its problematic quality from the fact that Jones as well as Smith introduces a new causal set – he is present and ready to pounce – albeit in his case it is pre-empted when he allows a prior set to complete.)

Euthanasia and the State

Leaving aside the difficult question of what moral significance may be derived from these bare causal considerations (Kuhse, herself, denies that there is any), it is apparent that policy arguments also play an important part in the law's adherence to the acts/omissions distinction. Jonathan Glover has commented on this point as follows:

> **Glover, J, *Causing Death and Saving Lives*, 1977, Harmondsworth: Penguin, pp 186–88:**
>
> One [objection to abandoning the distinction] is the suggestion that, if voluntary [active] euthanasia were known to be an option, people might put pressure on their burdensome relations to volunteer. It is hard to evaluate this objection. It seems to me rather implausible, but perhaps I am being too optimistic. In advance of trying a voluntary euthanasia policy, we do not know how people would behave. (Is there any evidence of such pressures in a country where voluntary euthanasia is not illegal?)
>
> A related objection is that, even without pressure being brought by relations, people who felt they were a burden might think that, although they had lives

worth living, they ought to volunteer for euthanasia. This gains some support from the fact that there have been cases of suicide by people whose motive was a reluctance to be a burden on others. Part of the difficulty of evaluating this objection is that it is hard to predict how widespread such feelings would be. Another difficulty is the more fundamental uncertainty about whether it is right in such a case to override the person's autonomy. Where he is wrong in thinking he is a burden, he should not be given euthanasia, but should be persuaded of the truth. (It seems possible that, with so much talk of old people almost as though they were members of another species, many old people who are loved and wanted members of a family do have unnecessary fears that they are a nuisance to the others.) But there are sometimes cases where a person who is old or ill does put a great strain on a family, and where he sees this and would rather die than have the situation continue, it is not obvious that a paternalist refusal to carry out his wishes is justified.

Another possible bad side effect of voluntary euthanasia concerns the treatment of dying patients. Is there a danger that allowing such a policy would hamper the development of the kind of terminal care which would make euthanasia unnecessary? The policy of total rejection of euthanasia may have the advantage of strengthening people's commitment to developing more humane and imaginative forms of terminal care. Certainly some of the most sensitive and impressive work here, such as that of Cicely Saunders and others, has been done in the context of a principled refusal to comply with euthanasia requests. But it is not clear that voluntary euthanasia would seem an alternative rather than a supplement to better terminal care. A hospital with a voluntary euthanasia policy could still have a staff that did all they could to make euthanasia requests unnecessary. The view that voluntary euthanasia would be accepted as an easy alternative to improved care underrates the deep revulsion against killing which most people have, and which often seems especially strong among those in professions like nursing. (Perhaps this is again too optimistic. Is there any clear evidence relevant to this?)

We shall return to such policy concerns later in this chapter when we touch upon the question of law reform in this area.

ACTIVE EUTHANASIA

Background

As we have seen, the law, in holding to its 'qualified sanctity of life' position, draws a fundamental distinction between a positive act which is intended to kill ('active euthanasia') and an omission to act which, equally intentionally, allows the patient's death to occur ('passive euthanasia'). Whereas the former is prohibited in all bar one exceptional case (see below, p 652), the latter is permissible in a somewhat wider set of circumstances. This attitude may be roughly summed up by reference to the Victorian poet AH Clough's sardonic lines: 'thou shalt not kill, but need'st not strive officiously to keep alive'.

A recent example of the law's response to active euthanasia, which also illustrates the point that, generally, the killer's motive in performing the act will be irrelevant, is provided by the case of *R v Cox* (1992).

R v Cox (1992) 12 BMLR 38, Winchester CC (Ogden J)

Dr Cox injected a 70 year old patient, Lillian Boyes, with the lethal poison potassium chloride, after she pleaded with him to put her out of her misery; she was *in extremis*, suffering from the terminal stages of rheumatoid arthritis, and her pain was beyond the control of analgesic drugs. He was charged only with her attempted murder on the basis that, given her condition, Mrs Boyes' death at that time could in fact have been due to her illness (thus pre-empting the operation of the poison):

> **Ogden J** (directing the jury): This is a sad and testing case for all of us involved. The reason is obvious. A distinguished professional man of unblemished reputation and character is now on trial, and the allegation is that he behaved in a way which is a clear repudiation of a doctor's lifelong professional duty, namely to save and not to take life.

> Even the prosecution case acknowledged that he did so only because he was prompted by deep distress at Lillian Boyes' condition; by a belief that she was totally beyond recall and by an intense compassion for her fearful suffering. Nonetheless, members of the jury, if he injected her with potassium chloride for the primary purpose of killing her, of hastening her death, he is guilty of the offence charged, You are therefore tested to the utmost, members of the jury, for you must do your best to put emotion to one side. You must try this case impartially and objectively. You 12 ladies and gentlemen represent the public interest in ensuring that, where it is surely proved, no man of whatever situation or in whatever circumstance can place himself above the law ...

> And so to the charge, ladies and gentlemen. The prosecution allege that Dr Cox attempted to murder Lillian Boyes. They say that be deliberately injected her with potassium chloride in a quantity and in a manner which had no therapeutic purpose and no capacity to afford her any relief from pain and suffering whilst alive. They submit that Dr Cox must have known that, and that, in truth, his conduct in giving that injection was prompted solely, and certainly primarily, by the purpose of bringing her life to an immediate end ...

> If it is proved that Dr Cox injected Lillian Boyes with potassium chloride in circumstances which make you sure that by that act he intended to kill her, then he is guilty of the offence of attempted murder. From the earliest stage it has been admitted that he did indeed inject her intravenously with two ampoules of undiluted potassium chloride, which his note in the medical records clearly indicates ...

> You must understand, members of the jury, that in this highly emotional situation, neither the express wishes of the patient nor of her loving and devoted family can affect the position. Lillian Boyes was fully entitled to decline any further active medical treatment and to specify that thereafter she should only receive painkillers. She did that on 11 August. That was her absolute right and the doctors and nursing staff were obliged to respect her

wishes. A young senior house officer, Dr Byrne, gave evidence before you. He told you that on that day when Lillian Boyes had said 'no more active intervention, please, only painkillers from now on', he had said to her, in effect: 'Thus far and no further. We will stop your positive medical treatment, we will confine ourselves to giving you only analgesics, only painkillers, but we cannot accede to your request that we give you something to kill you.'

Dr Cox was convicted of attempted murder.

That this represents the present state of the law was confirmed, though not without a degree of soul searching, by the House of Lords in *Airedale NHS Trust v Bland*:

> **Lord Goff**: I must however stress, at this point, that the law draws a crucial distinction between cases in which a doctor decides not to provide, or to continue to provide, for his patient treatment or care which could or might prolong his life, and those in which he decides, for example by administering a lethal drug, actively to bring his patient's life to an end ... [T]he former may be lawful, either because the doctor is giving effect to his patient's wishes by withholding the treatment or care, or even in certain circumstances in which ... the patient is incapacitated from stating whether or not he gives his consent. But it is not lawful for a doctor to administer a drug to his patient to bring about his death, even though that course is prompted by a humanitarian desire to end his suffering, however great that suffering may be: see *R v Cox* (unreported), 18 September 1992. So to act is to cross the Rubicon which runs between on the one hand the care of the living patient and on the other hand euthanasia – actively causing his death to avoid or to end his suffering. Euthanasia is not lawful at common law. It is of course well known that there are many responsible members of our society who believe that euthanasia should be made lawful; but that result could, I believe, only be achieved by legislation which expresses the democratic will that so fundamental a change should be made in our law, and can, if enacted, ensure that such legalised killing can only be carried out subject to appropriate supervision and control.
>
> **Lord Browne-Wilkinson**: Finally, the conclusion I have reached will appear to some to be almost irrational. How can it be lawful to allow a patient to die slowly, though painlessly, over a period of weeks from lack of food but unlawful to produce his immediate death by a lethal injection, thereby saving his family from yet another ordeal to add to the tragedy that has already struck them? I find it difficult to find a moral answer to that question. But it is undoubtedly the law and nothing I have said casts doubt on the proposition that the doing of a positive act with the intention of ending life is and remains murder.

Medicines which shorten life

As has been hinted at, there is, however, one exception where a doctor may act in a manner which intentionally shortens his patient's life. This is through the administration of powerful analgesic (pain killing) drugs, such as morphine, which, if ingested in large doses, have the known side effect of accelerating death. The existence of this exception (ie, the fact that a doctor who prescribes such drugs to control pain, though foreseeing his patient's earlier death, will not be guilty of murder) was established in the case of *R v Bodkin Adams*.

R v Bodkin Adams [1957] Crim LR 365 (Devlin J)

Dr Bodkin Adams was charged with murder after increasing the dosage of opiates for an elderly stroke patient, who left him a Rolls-Royce and a chest of silver in her will. Devlin J, commenting upon the doctor's defence that his primary purpose had been to dull the patient's sensation of pain, gave the following direction to the jury.

> **Devlin J**: ... [A] doctor who is aiding the sick and the dying [need not] calculate in minutes, or even in hours, and perhaps not in days or weeks, the effect upon a patient's life of the medicines which he administers or else be in peril of a charge of murder. If the first purpose of medicine, the restoration of health, can no longer be achieved there is still much for a doctor to do, and he is entitled to do all that is proper and necessary to relieve pain and suffering, even if the measures he takes may incidentally shorten life. That is not because there is any special defence for medical men; it is not because doctors are put into any category different from other citizens for this purpose. The law is the same for all, and what I have said to you rests simply upon this: no act is murder which does not cause death. 'Cause' means nothing philosophical or technical or scientific. It means what you 12 men and women sitting as a jury in the jury box would regard in a common sense way as the cause ... If, for example, because a doctor has done something or has omitted to do something death occurs, it can be scientifically proved – if it could – at 11 o'clock instead of 12 o'clock, or even on Monday instead of Tuesday, no people of common sense would say, 'Oh, the doctor caused her death'. They would say the cause of her death was the illness or the injury, or whatever it was, which brought her into hospital, and the proper medical treatment that is administered and that has an incidental effect of determining the exact moment of death, or may have, is not the cause of death in any sensible use of the term. But it remains the fact, and it remains the law, that no doctor, nor any man, no more in the case of the dying man than of the healthy, has the right deliberately to cut the thread of life.

The notion that, in such a case, the doctor may be regarded as not having caused the patient's death is, with respect, difficult to accept (see further on this, in a related context, the passages from the article by David Price extracted below, p 660). More recently, in the *Cox* case, Ogden J preferred to concentrate upon the doctor's intention as providing the key to his possible exculpation.

> **Ogden J**: We all appreciate that some medical treatment, whether of a positive, therapeutic character or solely of an analgesic kind – by which I mean designed solely to alleviate pain and suffering – some treatment carries with it a serious risk to the health or even the life of the patient. Doctors are frequently confronted with, no doubt, distressing dilemmas. They have to

make up their minds as to whether the risk, even to the life of their patient, attendant upon their contemplated form of treatment, is such that the risk is, or is not, medically justified. If a doctor genuinely believes that a certain course is beneficial to his patient, either therapeutically or analgesically, then even though he recognises that that course carries with it a risk to life, he is fully entitled, nonetheless, to pursue it. If in those circumstances the patient dies, nobody could possibly suggest that in that situation the doctor was guilty of murder or attempted murder.

The problem is obviously particularly acute in the case of those who are terminally ill and in considerable pain, if not agony. Such was the case of Lillian Boyes. It was plainly Dr Cox's duty to do all that was medically possible to alleviate her pain and suffering, even if the course adopted carried with it an obvious risk that, as a side effect of that treatment, her death would be rendered likely or even certain.

There can be no doubt that the use of drugs to reduce pain and suffering will often be fully justified notwithstanding that it will, in fact, hasten the moment of death. What can never be lawful is the use of drugs with purpose of hastening the moment of death.

And so, in deciding Dr Cox's intention, the distinction the law requires you to draw is this. Is it proved that in giving that injection, in that form and in those amounts, Dr Cox's primary purpose was to bring the life of Lillian Boyes to an end?

If it was, then he is guilty. If, on the other hand, it was, or may have been, his primary purpose in acting as he did to alleviate her pain and suffering, then he is not guilty. That is so even though he recognised that, in fulfilling that primary purpose, he might or even would hasten the moment of her death ...

Of course, members of the jury, to hasten the death not merely alleviates suffering, it bring it to an end. A dead person suffers no more. But that is not what I mean by alleviation of suffering. Alleviation of suffering means that easing of it for so long as the patient survives; not the easing of it in the throes of, and because of, deliberate purpose killing.

The apparent reliance of this way of regarding the *Bodkin Adams* defence on the principle of double effect (which, as we saw above, has the support of advocates of the full sanctity of life position, but is rejected by most other commentators), has given rise to much debate. It is suggested that the defence is best viewed as a special dispensation to the doctor engaged in the palliative care of a terminally ill patient. Provided he is exercising *bona fide* clinical judgment in easing the dying process, the law will exceptionally limit its focus to the 'narrow intention' of such a doctor, ie, the desire to relieve pain; it is prepared to overlook the fact that, in foreseeing the patient's earlier death, the doctor intends the death in the 'wide' sense sufficient to establish criminal *mens rea* in most other contexts.

In a case brought in August 1997 by a woman, Annie Lindsell, dying from motor neurone disease, Sir Stephen Brown, President of the Family Division of the High Court, confirmed that in his view the same principle will protect doctors who prescribe such analgesics to ease their patients' mental torment (though this was not made the subject of a formal Declaration).

Assisted suicide

In respect of patients who are not already dying, or though dying are not in pain, the doctor is clearly not permitted to do anything that directly shortens life. How far, though, may he furnish the means to allow such patients to kill themselves? It is evident that a doctor who acts thus is not guilty of murder; even one who, say, in the case of a paralysed patient, places a lethal pill in the latter's mouth will (provided the patient knows what is in the pill) at most have assisted in the patient's suicide. The reason is that the latter's voluntary and informed action of swallowing the pill operates as a *novus actus interveniens* which breaks the chain of causation between the doctor's previous act of providing the pill and the patient's death. Instead, the doctor will be guilty of an offence contrary to s 2 of the Suicide Act 1961.

2 **Criminal liability for complicity in another's suicide**

    (1) A person who aids, abets, counsels or procures the suicide of another, or an attempt by another to commit suicide, shall be liable on conviction on indictment to imprisonment for a term not exceeding 14 years.

    (2) If on the trial of an indictment for murder or manslaughter it is proved that the accused aided, abetted, counselled or procured the suicide of the person in question, the jury may find him guilty of that offence.

    ...

    (4) No proceedings shall be instituted for an offence under this section except by or with the consent of the Director of Public Prosecutions.

The ambit of the offence under s 2 of the 1961 Act was tested in the case of *AG v Able* [1984] 1 All ER 277, in which certain members of the Voluntary Euthanasia Society were prosecuted in connection with the distribution of a suicide manual entitled 'A guide to self-deliverance'. Woolf J held that an offence would be committed if, in a particular case, it was known to the defendants that the recipient planned to use the manual to commit suicide (and the latter did so use it).

Given that the main effect of the 1961 Suicide Act was to decriminalise suicide from the point of view of the principal actor, it has often been argued that it is anomalous for assisting the actor to remain an offence. Nevertheless, for the qualified sanctity of life doctrine, it is clear that suicide remains problematic: it is, after all, an act of (self-) killing. That quality of life considerations are here of secondary importance is apparent from the decision of the majority of the Canadian Supreme Court in *Rodriguez v AG of British Columbia*.

Rodriguez v AG of British Columbia **(1993) 82 BCLR (2d) 273**

Sue Rodriguez, aged 42, was suffering from an incurable muscle-wasting disease which was expected to cause complete loss of bodily function within two or three years. Rather than await inevitable death through starvation or suffocation, she applied for a declaration that it would be lawful for her physician to attach her to an intravenous drip containing poison so that, when she felt the time was right, she might activate the drip and die. She claimed to be entitled to such assistance, notwithstanding s 241(b) of the Canadian Criminal Code which prohibited assisted suicide (in similar terms to s 2 of the Suicide Act), on the basis of her right to 'liberty and security of the person' under s 7 of the Canadian Charter of Rights and Freedoms.

> **Sopinka J**: The appellant asserts that it is a principle of fundamental justice that the human dignity and autonomy of individuals be respected, and that to subject her to needless suffering in this manner is to rob her of her dignity ...
>
> Section 241(b) has as its purpose the protection of the vulnerable who might be induced in moments of weakness to commit suicide. This purpose is grounded in the State interest in protecting life and reflects the policy of the state that human life should not be depreciated by allowing life to be taken. This policy finds expression not only in the provisions of our Criminal Code which prohibit murder and other violent acts against others notwithstanding the consent of the victim, but also in the policy against capital punishment and, until its repeal, attempted suicide. This is not only a policy of the State, however, but is part of our fundamental conception of the sanctity of human life. The Law Reform Commission expressed this philosophy appropriately in its Working Paper No 28, *Euthanasia, Aiding Suicide and Cessation of Treatment*, 1982, p 36:
>
>> Preservation of human life is acknowledged to be a fundamental value of our society. Historically, our criminal law has changed very little on this point. Generally speaking, it sanctions the principle of the sanctity of human life. Over the years, however, law has come to temper the apparent absolutism of the principle, to delineate its intrinsic limitations and to define its true dimensions.
>
> As is noted in the above passage, the principle of sanctity of life is no longer seen to require that all human life be preserved at all costs. Rather, it has come to be understood, at least by some, as encompassing quality of life considerations, and to be subject to certain limitations and qualifications reflective of personal autonomy and dignity ...
>
> **Medical care at the end of life**
>
> Canadian courts have recognised a common law right of patients to refuse consent to medical treatment, or to demand that treatment, once commenced, be withdrawn or discontinued ... This right has been specifically recognised to exist even if the withdrawal from or refusal of treatment may result in death (*Nancy B v Hotel-Dieu de Quebec* (1992) 86 DLR (4th) 385, Que SC; *Malette v Shulman* (1990) 72 OR (2d) 417, CA ...

Following Working Paper No 28, the Law Reform Commission recommended in its 1983 Report to the Minister of Justice that the Criminal Code be amended to provide that the homicide provisions not be interpreted as requiring a physician to undertake medical treatment against the wishes of a patient, or to continue medical treatment when such treatment 'has become therapeutically useless', or from requiring a physician to 'cease administering appropriate palliative care intended to eliminate or to relieve the suffering of a person, for the sole reason that such care or measures are likely to shorten the life expectancy of this person' (*Euthanasia: Aiding Suicide and Cessation of Treatment*, Report No 20, 1983, p 35).

The Law Reform Commission had discussed in the Working Paper the possibility of the decriminalisation of assisted suicide in the following terms, pp 53–54:

> First of all, the prohibition in [s 241(b)] is not restricted solely to the case of the terminally ill patient, for whom we can only have sympathy, or solely to his physician or a member of his family who helps him to put an end to his suffering. The section is more general and applies to a variety of situations for which it is much more difficult to feel sympathy. Consider, for example, a recent incident, that of inciting to mass suicide. What of the person who takes advantage of another's depressed state to encourage him to commit suicide, for his own financial benefit? What of the person who, knowing an adolescent's suicidal tendencies, provides him with large enough quantities of drugs to kill him? The accomplice in these cases cannot be considered morally blameless. Nor can one conclude that the criminal law should not punish such conduct. To decriminalise completely the act of aiding, abetting or counselling suicide would therefore not be a valid legislative policy...

> ... It can be seen, therefore, that while the Law Reform Commission of Canada [has] great sympathy for the plight of those who wish to end their lives so as to avoid significant suffering, [it has not been] prepared to recognise that the active assistance of a third party in carrying out this desire should be condoned, even for the terminally ill. The basis for this refusal is twofold it seems – first, the active participation by one individual in the death of another is intrinsically morally and legally wrong, and second, there is no certainty that abuses can be prevented by anything less than a complete prohibition. Creating an exception for the terminally ill might therefore frustrate the purpose of the legislation of protecting the vulnerable because adequate guidelines to control abuse are difficult or impossible to develop.

Recently, in *Washington v Glucksberg* and *Vacco v Quill* 117 S Ct 2258 and 2293 (1997), the US Supreme Court used similar reasoning to justify rulings that State laws prohibiting physician-assisted suicide were not unconstitutional. The question of whether a similar challenge to the provisions of the Suicide Act 1961 would succeed in an English court may soon be significant, given the proposed incorporation into domestic law of the European Convention on Human Rights.

PASSIVE EUTHANASIA

Background

Our concern here is with the more flexible attitude taken by the qualified sanctity of life doctrine in respect of omissions to provide life-sustaining treatment (reflected in the 'need'st not strive officiously' part of AH Clough's couplet).

A preliminary question is what conduct, in the context of providing medical care, will be regarded in law as an *omission* rather than an *act*? For example, a common means of sustaining the life of a critically ill patient in hospital is to place him on a ventilator. If, in a given case, a doctor decides that there is no hope of recovery and switches the machine off, could he not be said to have acted to bring about the patient's death? Lord Goff, however, forcefully rejected this possibility in the *Bland* case:

Lord Goff: Why is it that the doctor who gives his patient a lethal injection which kills him commits an unlawful act and indeed is guilty of murder, whereas a doctor who, by discontinuing life support, allows his patient to die, may not act unlawfully – and will not do so, if he commits no breach of duty to his patient? Professor Glanville Williams has suggested (see his *Textbook of Criminal Law*, 2nd edn, 1983, p 282) that the reason is that what the doctor does when he switches off a life support machine 'is in substance not an act but an omission to struggle', and that 'the omission is not a breach of duty by the doctor, because he is not obliged to continue in a hopeless case'.

I agree that the doctor's conduct in discontinuing life support can properly be categorised as an omission. It is true that it may be difficult to describe what the doctor actually does as an omission, for example where he takes some positive step to bring the life support to an end. But discontinuation of life support is, for present purposes, no different from not initiating life support in the first place. In each case, the doctor is simply allowing his patient to die in the sense that he is desisting from taking a step which might, in certain circumstances, prevent his patient from dying as a result of his pre-existing condition; and as a matter of general principle an omission such as this will not be unlawful unless it constitutes a breach of duty to the patient. I also agree that the doctor's conduct is to be differentiated from that of, for example, an interloper who maliciously switches off a life support machine because, although the interloper may perform exactly the same act as the doctor who discontinues life support, his doing so constitutes interference with the life-prolonging treatment then being administered by the doctor. Accordingly, whereas the doctor, in discontinuing life support, is simply allowing his patient to die of his pre-existing condition, the interloper is actively intervening to stop the doctor from prolonging the patient's life, and such conduct cannot possibly be categorised as an omission.

It is apparent that, for these purposes, the description of a given piece of conduct by the doctor as an *act* turns not upon a narrow criterion of voluntary physical movement, but rather upon whether what he has done amounts to an interference with the natural course of events. Whereas the doctor, in stopping life support, simply brings to a close his own previous and continuing interference in nature, the malicious interloper does interfere, albeit with the 'second' nature (the life-sustaining regime) brought into being by the doctor.

Nevertheless, it would be a grave mistake to conclude that, provided his conduct can be characterised as an omission, the doctor has an automatic free hand in allowing death to occur. The reason why this is not so, and the manner in which the doctor's position differs in this respect from that of the average citizen, is evident from the following passage from Lord Browne-Wilkinson's judgment in *Bland*:

Lord Browne-Wilkinson:

Criminal liability/murder

It is the submission of the Official Solicitor that the withdrawal of artificial feeding would constitute murder. The Official Solicitor has been criticised for using emotive language in this case. In my judgment this criticism is misplaced: much the most difficult question is indeed whether the proposed course of action is, in law, murder notwithstanding the best motives from which everyone concerned is acting.

Murder consists of causing the death of another with intent so to do. What is proposed in the present case is to adopt a course with the intention of bringing about Anthony Bland's death. As to the element of intention or *mens rea*, in my judgment there can be no real doubt that it is present in this case: the whole purpose of stopping artificial feeding is to bring about the death of Anthony Bland.

As to the guilty act, or *actus reus*, the criminal law draws a distinction between the commission of a positive act which causes death and the omission to do an act which would have prevented death. In general an omission to prevent death is not an *actus reus* and cannot give rise to a conviction for murder. But where the accused was under a duty to the deceased to do the act which he omitted to do, such omission can constitute the *actus reus* of homicide, either murder (*R v Gibbins* (1918) 13 Cr App R 134) or manslaughter (*R v Stone* [1977] QB 354) depending upon the *mens rea* of the accused ...

It is apparent, then, that the lawfulness of passive euthanasia revolves around the question: 'When is the doctor released from his normal duty to treat?' In answering this, we shall look at the position of competent and incompetent patients in turn.

Competent patients

Refusals of medical treatment

As we saw above, Chapter 3, it is a cardinal principle of medical law that, in respect of a competent adult patient, treatment may generally not be administered without consent. This is so even in a situation in which, without the treatment, the patient will die. This was made clear, *obiter*, by the Court of Appeal in *Re T (Adult: Refusal of Medical Treatment)* (1992) (in which Lord Donaldson MR gave the leading judgment); and House of Lords *dicta* to the same effect may be found both in *Sidaway v Governors of Royal Bethlem Hospital* [1985] 1 All ER 643 (*per* Lord Templeman, p 666); and in *Airedale NHS Trust v Bland* [1993] 1 All ER 821 (*per* Lord Keith, p 857; Lord Goff, p 866; and Lord Mustill, p 892). Later, the principle formed the *ratio* in the High Court decisions of Thorpe J in *Re C (Adult: Refusal of Treatment)* [1994] 1 All ER 819; and *Secretary of State v Robb* [1995] 2 WLR 722.

On the other hand, as discussed in Chapter 3, it may be that the right to refuse treatment is tempered in certain circumstances by overriding State interests, including the prevention of suicide. In this regard, a natural question to ask is why refusals of life-saving treatment are not construed in general as attempts at suicide which doctors are entitled to thwart? This issue has been analysed by David Price as follows:

Price, DPT, 'Assisted suicide and refusing medical treatment: linguistics, morals and legal contortions' (1996) 4 Med L Rev 370:

A Intention

Does a patient intend to die when he or she refuses further medical treatment definitely resulting in death? The courts typically adopt a narrow construction of intention in this context, equating it with desire, yet seemingly then deny the self-evident truth. In *Bouvia v Superior Court*, for instance, a 28 year old mentally competent quadriplegic woman with cerebral palsy and crippling arthritis, who required others to feed her, refused to allow further food to be administered to her. The trial court said:

> It is fairly clear from the evidence and the court cannot close its eyes to the fact that [petitioner] during her stay in defendant hospital, and for some time prior thereto, had formed an intent to die. She voiced this desire to a member of staff of defendant hospital.

The California Court of Appeal, however, disagreed finding that there was no such intent to die. Similarly, in *McKay v Bergstedt* (1990), involving a 31 year old quadriplegic patient who wished to be disconnected from the life-sustaining respirator. The Nevada Supreme Court found that Kenneth Bergstedt had no intent to take his own life, and thus did not commit suicide, although he realised that death would be the effect of his decision. Yet, he wished to be removed from the respirator because he feared an agonising death and 'despaired over the prospect of life without the attentive care, companionship and love of his devoted father'. It is arguable though that Elizabeth Bouvia did intend to die, even in the sense of wanting to do so – she plainly stated her desire to starve herself to death. Likewise Kenneth Bergstedt, who could not face life without his father. In *Satz v Perlmutter* (1978) the Florida Supreme Court even held that the competent (ventilator-dependent) patient had no intention to die despite having attempted on several occasions to disconnect himself from the respirator, but having been physically prevented from so doing by hospital staff.

1   Intention: desire or more?

In some US cases the courts have rationalised their decision that a request for the removal of life-support equipment does not manifest an intention to die by declaring that the patient really wanted to live. But, even if it is not specious to argue that an individual does not intend to die despite the adoption of a preference for death over life (surely a person may desire, wish or will a result even though it is only the lesser of two evils?), this reasoning relies on the dubious doctrine of double effect. According to the doctrine, all intended, bad ends are morally wrong, and this includes all bad means chosen to achieve ends. Where a consequence is unintended it is perceived as a side effect which, if bad, can be justified according to the totality of the circumstances. The doctrine in this context appeals to the distinction between desiring death for its own sake and intending to avoid continued existence in an unacceptable condition, knowing death is the consequence of the decision. Elizabeth Bouvia wished to avoid continued existence in her quadriplegic and unbearable condition; Kenneth Bergstedt found the thought of life without his father and of experiencing an agonising death unbearable, etc. However, this distinction would lead to treating almost all rational self-killings as non-suicides because it is invariably the case that persons only choose death to avoid some other more undesirable fate, for example, continued existence in unendurable pain or indignity. Indeed, such self-killings are commonly perceived as paradigmatic instances of suicide ...

B   Causation

In *Bouvia* the California Court of Appeal stated that 'her decision to let nature take its course is not equivalent to an election to commit suicide with real parties aiding and abetting therein'. It has been remarked that *Bouvia* establishes that such a refusal does not amount to suicide because the patient does not in law cause his own death. In *Re Conroy*, the New Jersey Supreme Court considered that declining life-sustaining medical treatment is not properly viewed as an attempt to commit suicide and remarked that 'refusing medical intervention merely allows the disease to take its natural course; if death were eventually to occur, it would be the result, primarily, of the underlying disease, and not the result of a self-inflicted injury'. In Canada, in *Nancy B v Hotel-Dieu de Quebec*, the Quebec Superior Court also stated that if the plaintiff's death occurred following the removal of respiratory support, it would result from 'nature taking its course'. This perception is one fostered by many moral philosophers and medical practitioners alike. Nonetheless, despite its pervasiveness, to say the patient is not the cause of his own death is spurious apart from in circumstances where treatment cannot offer a cure or the prolongation of life.

The law distinguishes between *factual* and *legal* causation. A cause will not be a factual cause unless the result would not have occurred but for the defendant's act or omission. There is no doubt though that the patient's refusal of further treatment here is a factual cause of the person's death. In such cases the immediate cause of death is the patient's decision to refuse further life-supporting mechanisms. Death would not have occurred when and as it did without the implementation of the patient's decision. The underlying disease becomes the means of death only. Joseph Fletcher puts it in terms of the natural causes having been 'fatally set in motion' by the patient's decision. Even in cases of terminal illness, medical treatment may still be capable of prolonging life. In fact, in many of the North American cases the patient was not even terminally ill – for instance, in *Bouvia* the patient's life-expectancy was 15–20 years, in *Bergstedt* the patient's condition was non-terminal with artificial support and in *Nancy B* it was stated that with respiratory aid she could live for a 'considerable time'. Whilst from a 'scientific' perspective the underlying illness or condition 'causes' death, the law is not so much concerned with the 'pathological story' as the effects of an individual's behaviour on outcomes. There has never been any need in law for a cause to be a *sufficient* or sole (or even dominant) cause of an outcome. Thus, if any doubt exists with respect to causation, this relates to legal causation only, ie, proximate or imputable cause.

Normally, the role of *legal* causation is to place limits on the on the otherwise endless causes of events and to allocate responsibility for consequences in a fair and even fashion. The inquiry is primarily designed to screen out consequences which are too remote or accidental flowing from the defendant's acts or omissions, assuming that the cause is 'substantial' (ie, significant) – which it clearly would be here. There is rarely, however, any problem stemming from causation where the consequences were intended, which it has been contended above that they are. The individual effectively has sole control over the situation and his or her destiny – it would be surprising if the person did not cause the inevitable results of the decision reached, no matter how understandable or blameless the decision. There is no remoteness or accident implicated in the situations under consideration here. Further, it is an accepted principle of causation that, normally, once a voluntary, informed human act or decision has occurred, there is no need to trace back the causal inquiry beyond it ...

[C]ould it nevertheless be asserted that suicide is incapable of being committed by an omission? It is submitted that, contrary to the views of Glanville Williams, the fact that the patient is (on one view) merely passive and does nothing positive to cause the death is not to the point. One can seemingly commit suicide by falling to act, by deliberately failing to feed oneself for instance. In the Supreme Court of the United States in *Cruzan v Director, Missouri Health Department* (1990), Scalia J stated that:

> ... it would not make much sense to say that one may not kill oneself by walking into the sea, but may sit on the beach until submerged by the incoming tide.

He later added:

> Starving oneself to death is no different from putting a gun to one's temple as far as the common law definition of suicide is concerned; the cause of death in both cases is the suicide's conscious decision to 'put an end to his own existence'.

It is indeed difficult to see what justification could be advanced for a distinction to be drawn between acts and omissions here. The individual is clearly terminating his own life deliberately by either means – it is the ends not the means which are the essence of suicide. Thus, neither lack of intention nor the absence of a causal connection provide a proper basis for the conclusion that the refusal of life-sustaining treatment is not suicide.

Despite the cogency of these arguments, the English courts have made it clear that they will not equate refusals of life-saving medical treatment with suicide (see, in this regard, Lord Goff's speech in *Bland*, p 866 and Thorpe J's judgment in *Secretary of State v Robb*). It is apparent that, in making such judgments, the courts (in accord with their 'qualified sanctity of life' approach) do in fact regard the acts/omissions distinction as crucial: the person who passively declines a life-saving opportunity is distinguished from one who actively engineers his own end. The upshot in the great majority of refusal-of-treatment cases involving competent patients is that, as Lord Goff stated in *Bland*, 'the doctor's duty to act in the best interests of his patient must likewise be qualified'.

Advance directives

A further issue, in relation to refusals of life-saving medical treatment, concerns the time at which they are made. How far will a refusal made by a competent patient at time 1 subsequently bind a doctor who wishes to treat the patient – who in the interim becomes incompetent – at time 2?

Across the Atlantic, the use of 'advance directives' (colloquially termed 'living wills') to refuse treatment has long been commonplace; a good illustration of their operation is provided by the case of *Malette v Shulman*.

Malette v Shulman (1990) 72 OR (2d) 417, Ontario CA

The plaintiff was a Jehovah's Witness who was admitted to hospital unconscious following a road accident. She was found to be carrying a card which (translated from French into English) read as follows:

No blood transfusion!

As one of Jehovah's Witnesses with firm religious convictions, I request that no blood or blood products be administered to me under any circumstances. I fully realise the implications of this position, but I have resolutely decided to obey the Bible command: 'Keep abstaining ... from blood' (Acts 15:28, 29).

However, I have no religious objection to the use of non-blood alternatives, such as Dextran, Haemaccel, PVP, Ringer's Lactate or saline solution.

However, the defendant doctor carried out a life-saving blood transfusion.

Robins JA: On the facts of the present case, Dr Shulman was clearly faced with an emergency. He had an unconscious, critically ill patient on his hands who, in his opinion, needed blood transfusions to save her life or preserve her health. If there were no Jehovah's Witness card he undoubtedly would have been entitled to administer blood transfusions as part of the emergency treatment and could not have been held liable for so doing. In those circumstances he would have had no indication that the transfusions would have been refused had the patient then been able to make her wishes known and, accordingly, no reason to expect that, as a reasonable person, she would not consent to the transfusions.

... Here, the patient, anticipating an emergency in which she might be unable to make decisions about her health care contemporaneous with the emergency, has given explicit instructions that blood transfusions constitute an unacceptable medical intervention and are not to be administered to her. Once the emergency arises, is the doctor nonetheless entitled to administer transfusions on the basis of his honest belief that they are needed to save a patient's life?

The answer, in my opinion, is clearly no. A doctor is not free to disregard a patient's advance instructions any more than he would be free to disregard instructions given at the time of the emergency. The law does not prohibit a patient from withholding consent to emergency medical treatment, nor does the law prohibit a doctor from following his patient's instructions. While the law may disregard the absence of consent in limited emergency circumstances, it otherwise supports the right of competent adults to make decisions concerning their own health care by imposing civil liability on those who perform medical treatment without consent.

The patient's decision to refuse blood ... was made prior to and in anticipation of the emergency. While the doctor would have had the opportunity to dissuade her on the basis of his medical advice, her refusal to accept his advice or her unwillingness to discuss or consider the subject would not relieve him of his obligation to follow her instructions. The principles of self-determination and individual autonomy compel the conclusion that the patient may reject blood transfusions even if harmful consequences may result and even if the decision is generally regarded as foolhardy. Her decision in this instance would be operative after she lapsed into unconsciousness, and the doctor's conduct would be unauthorised. To transfuse a Jehovah's Witness in the face of her explicit instructions to the contrary would, in my opinion, violate her right to control her own body and show disrespect for the religious values by which she has chosen to live her life ...

The plaintiff was awarded $20,000 in damages.

In this country, the concept of advanced directives was supported by the Court of Appeal in *Re T*, where Lord Donaldson MR commented as follows:

Lord Donaldson MR: There seems to be a view in the medical profession that in such emergency circumstances the next of kin should be asked to consent on behalf of the patient and that, if possible, treatment should be postponed until that consent has been obtained. This is a misconception because the next of kin has no legal right either to consent or to refuse consent. This is not to say that it is an undesirable practice if the interests of the patient will not be adversely affected by any consequential delay. I say this because contact with the next of kin may reveal that the patient has made an anticipatory choice which, if clearly established and applicable in the circumstances – two major 'ifs' – would bind the practitioner.

This view was subsequently echoed by the House of Lords in *Bland*. Nevertheless, it is an approach whose justification, at least in the case of a patient who becomes *permanently* incompetent, involves accepting arguments of some philosophical complexity:

Kuczewski, MG, 'Whose will is it, anyway? A discussion of advance directives, personal identity and consensus in medical ethics' (1994) 8 Bioethics 27:

The general problem raised by [John] Robertson and [Rebecca] Dresser can be expressed very simply. They ask, by what warrant/right can we apply the judgments encoded in a living will by a competent person at one time (t1) to the incompetent patient at a later time (t2)? The employment of advance directives has become so common that the question almost seems strange. We are tempted to simply reply, 'by the patient's right of self-determination'. However, to understand the inadequacy of this answer, we need to explore their concept of 'person'.

There are two slightly different versions of the problem put forth by these authors. Robertson's version we shall call the 'weak thesis' because it is the less radical of the two. Robertson's argument rests on the assumption that both the incompetent individual at t2 and the competent person at t1 are the same person but have very different interests. The interests of a person change over the course of her life, sometimes dramatically. Living wills are attempts by the competent person to make treatment decisions for her future based upon her present, rather than future, interests. It may be wrong to base how we treat a patient on interests the person previously possessed rather than her current ones. As Robertson states, 'The values and interests of the competent person no longer are relevant to someone who has lost the rational structure on which those values and interests rested'. Robertson wishes his critique to apply only to situations that involve an incompetent conscious patient. This limitation occurs, presumably, because permanently unconscious patients do not possess significant enough interests to generate a morally weighty conflict with their previous wishes.

Dresser called attention to the fact that one can base an even more radical thesis on the philosophical conception of personal identity advanced by Derek Parfit. Parfit's 'Complex View' stipulates that personal identity is equivalent to psychological continuity. That is, our identity is based on the strength of the connectedness and continuity of our memories, intentions, beliefs, desires, etc.

If the strength of this connectedness falls below a certain minimum threshold, there are philosophical grounds to claim that we are, in fact, dealing with a different person. Thus Dresser employs this background to advance the 'strong or radical thesis' that in applying living wills at t2, we are sometimes applying the directions given by one person to a different person ...

We need to keep in mind that this is not a mere abstract philosophical word game. Rather, it is exactly the warrant of the application of the person's interests at t1 to the person at t2 that is challenged by Dresser and Robertson. It is not empirically obvious why interests in dignity, the financial well being of one's family, bodily integrity, and so on, should be said to survive and be applicable to a person who either no longer exists or cannot cognise and presently appreciate these values. Although present practices regarding the use of living wills may go on despite the failure to justify their employment philosophically, such failure would mean that the consensus was forged on a fictitious account of self-determination. Thus, those who argued in the pre-consensus years for the primacy of the best interest standard as the sole standard of decision making would actually be correct.

It may not be clear which account, that of the consensus or that of the Parfitians, should bear the burden of proof. It is perhaps best to proceed simply on the assumption that we need at least to require each to provide a coherent account in its own terms. Therefore, it is perfectly reasonable to demand from the consensus a way to make sense of the idea of the survival of interests.

In attempting to provide an account of surviving interests, it is easy to agree with the Parfitians that metaphysical vestiges of bygone eras may have infiltrated our thinking. It is only because we still implicitly work with these assumptions that we forget the need to provide a justification for our practices regarding surviving interests. At first, the Parfitian challenge sounds silly to us because we think that it is easy to argue against its momentary sensation-oriented view of the self. Yet, without traditional metaphysics, we do not so easily locate a philosophical foundation for the central concept in our argument. Surviving interests were easily defended on an account of personhood that was tied to eternal entities such as the soul. Since the person, ie, the soul, existed beyond the life of the body, so might their interests ...

The modern counterpart to the Christian soul has been the Cartesian vision of the self as the ultimate foundation of justification and certainty. This notion was brought to moral philosophy in the Kantian understanding of the noumenal self that was posited as the intelligible condition of ethics. However, such a controversial metaphysical basis is clearly unsuitable to serve as the basis of a common sense consensus in this area of clinical practice ... Thus the empirical self must provide the basis of the consensus. It is the elusiveness of this self, as defined empirically, that gives rise to the problem at hand ...

Clearly the surviving interest's origin is in my continuous stream of psychic unity. Where it inheres after this loss of continuity is not made clear. Contractual solutions are not possible because living wills are not contracts.

We have already ruled out theistic conceptions and recourse to a Kantian timeless noumenal self. Therefore, we are going to have to make sense of these surviving interests in terms of some more social (narrative) concept of the self.

We must make clear what it means to say that interests 'survive'. There is an easy suggestion to be made regarding the location of these interests. They survive in the memories, both personal and institutional, of the community. One's interest in his son's education survives because people remember his commitment to it; the arrangements the father made to provide for the education encode these intentions. If all who remember my commitment die and the social arrangements that bear evidence of my intent collapse, my interest cannot be said to 'survive' in any real sense. This is an uncontroversial sense of surviving interest and is operative in last wills and testaments, institutions that are commemoratively named, etc.

Likewise, an individual's interest in dignity, privacy, and bodily integrity is encoded in his living will, in the memory of others, and even in their perceptions of the situation at the time of one's incompetence. I currently remember other people and have an interest in how others remember me in the future. It is this social meaning of interests that best accounts for their survival. It is a narrative sense of interest in that I conceive of myself objectively as part of a larger group that contains a 'part' of me that transcends my individual consciousness and psychological continuity. My story is, to some degree, only complete when told from this vantage point outside of my stream of consciousness. The body that belongs to the incompetent patient at t2 is in some sense 'mine' because other persons will call it by my name and make the story of what happens to it a chapter of the story they tell about 'me'. As such, I attempt to make that chapter embody the values which are presently mine. Through the same type of act of will by which I commit to live today in accordance with dignity, so also, I commit that my final chapter shall embody those values ...

Our intuition to honour living wills is indicative or reflective of the premium our society places on the values of dignity, privacy, and bodily integrity. Thus, we feel the normative force to help individuals bind these values to their narrative identity even after conscious appreciation of them has fled the body ... The answer to the question of the same person is that it is the same person at t1 and t2 mainly because the society recognises and helps constitute this as the case. This recognition has both descriptive and normative components. The normative component is the basis of applying categories such as dignity to the incompetent individual. Society is, in part, the source of individual psychological and narrative continuity and accomplishes this in binding certain features to the individual and fostering their higher commitments. It is this same warrant that is employed in honouring the person's living will.

In its recent report on mental incapacity, the Law Commission has proposed that the legal effect of advance directives be enshrined in legislation. Interestingly, however, it took the view that 'basic care' should be excluded from the ambit of such directives:

Law Commission, *Mental Incapacity*, Report No 231, 1995, London: HMSO:

5.34 In the consultation paper we proposed that an advance directive should never be effective in refusing either pain relief or basic care. On consultation, there was general agreement to the proposition that a patient's right to self-determination could properly be limited by considerations based on public policy. A number of respondents highlighted the effect on staff and other patients if patients were to have power to refuse in advance even the most basic steps to ensure comfort and cleanliness. One respondent argued that since a patient with capacity can refuse all types of treatment the same rule should apply to those making anticipatory refusals, but this minority view did not appeal to us. We were grateful for the assistance of the BMA on the details of the proposed exclusion clause. We accept that patients with capacity regularly refuse certain types or levels of pain relief because they prefer to maintain alertness, and we prefer now to refer only to the alleviation of severe pain. We have also replaced reference to 'spoon feeding' with reference to direct oral feeding, to cater for the administration of nutrition and hydration by syringe or cup. Our proposed definition of 'basic care' reflects a level of care which it would be contrary to public policy to withhold from a patient without capacity.

We recommend that an advance refusal of treatment should not preclude the provision of basic care, namely care to maintain bodily cleanliness and to alleviate severe pain, as well as the provision of direct oral nutrition and hydration.

This approach appears (so far as feeding is concerned) to echo the controversial distinction between ordinary and extraordinary means argued for by holders of the 'full' sanctity of life position. However, as the Commission itself recognises, it is out of kilter with a person's ability under the common law contemporaneously to refuse such feeding: see *Secretary of State v Robb* (1995). At present, the Government is carrying out a process of consultation as to how far these proposals should be implemented (see Green Paper, 'Who decides?', December 1997).

Incompetent patients

General

In addressing the question of when life-saving treatment may be withheld or withdrawn from the incompetent patient, we are within the province of passive *non-voluntary* euthanasia. As already noted, the crucial issue here is the extent of the doctor's duty to employ life-prolonging measures in respect of his patient. It is clear that common sense has never regarded this duty as an absolute one. Moreover, as we have already seen – in the context of John Harris' critique of the policy of 'selective treatment' for infants with spina bifida – such euthanasia has been practised openly at least since the early 1970s. Nevertheless, the first significant English authority in point is a Court of Appeal decision from as recently as 1981.

Re B (A Minor) (Wardship: Medical Treatment) [1981] 1 WLR 1421, CA (Templeman and Dunn LJJ)

B was a baby girl born with Down's syndrome and also suffering from an intestinal blockage. Without an operation to remove the blockage, she would die within a few days. Her parents, however, refused to consent to the treatment and B was made a ward of court. The judge at first instance initially authorised treatment, but revoked his order after speaking to the parents and also hearing that the surgeon appointed to the case was unwilling to operate contrary to their wishes. The health authority appealed.

> **Templeman LJ**: The question which this court has to determine is whether it is in the interests of this child to be allowed to die within the next week or to have the operation, in which case if she lives she will be a mongoloid child, but no one can say to what extent her mental or physical defects will be apparent. No one can say whether she will suffer or whether she will be happy in part. On the one hand the probability is that she will not be a cabbage, as it is called when people's faculties are entirely destroyed. On the other hand it is certain that she will be very severely mentally and physically handicapped.
>
> On behalf of the parents Mr Gray has submitted very movingly, if I may say so, that this is a case where nature has made its own arrangements to terminate a life which would not be fruitful and nature should not be interfered with. He has also submitted that in this kind of decision the views of responsible and caring parents, as these are, should be respected, and that their decision that it is better for the child to be allowed to die should be respected. Fortunately or unfortunately, in this particular case the decision no longer lies with the parents or with the doctors, but lies with the court. It is a decision which of course must be made in the light of the evidence and views expressed by the parents and the doctors, but at the end of the day it devolves on this court in this particular instance to decide whether the life of this child is demonstrably going to be so awful that in effect the child must be condemned to die, or whether the life of this child is still so imponderable that it would be wrong for her to be condemned to die. There may be cases, I know not, of severe proved damage where the future is so certain and where the life of the child is so bound to be full of pain and suffering that the court might be driven to a different conclusion, but in the present case the choice which lies before the court is this: whether to allow an operation to take place which may result in the child living for 20 or 30 years as a mongoloid or whether (and I think this must be brutally the result) to terminate the life of a mongoloid child because she also has an intestinal complaint. Faced with that choice I have no doubt that it is the duty of this court to decide that the child must live. The judge was much affected by the reasons given by the parents and came to the conclusion that their wishes ought to be respected. In my judgment he erred in that the duty of the court is to decide whether it is in the interests of the child that an operation should take place. The evidence in this case only goes to show that if the operation takes place and is successful then the child may live the normal span of a mongoloid child with the handicaps and defects and life of a mongol child, and it is not for this court to say that life of that description ought to be extinguished.

Accordingly the appeal must be allowed and the local authority must be authorised themselves to authorise and direct the operation to be carried out on the little girl.

This decision is an important one, not least because it renders doubtful a well known criminal case of about the same time, *R v Arthur* (1981) 12 BMLR 1, in which a doctor was acquitted of attempting to murder a Down's syndrome baby (whose parents did not wish it to live) after ordering treatment to be withheld: the effect of *Re B* is that, whatever the parents' views, doctors will generally be obliged to treat babies with the standard, albeit serious, handicaps associated with Down's syndrome. However, although Templeman LJ recognised obiter the possibility that, in other cases of more drastic disability, treatment could be withheld, it remained unclear in what circumstances this would be so. Some light was shed on this problem when, subsequently, the Court of Appeal came to deal with a case in which life-prolonging treatment for a baby 'dying' in any event was at issue.

Re C (A Minor) (Wardship: Medical Treatment) [1989] 2 All ER 782, CA (Lord Donaldson MR, Balcombe and Nicholls LJJ)

C was a 16 week old premature baby born with severe hydrocephalus. She suffered from very profound mental and physical handicaps and, despite having a shunt inserted soon after her birth in order to drain fluid from the brain, her prognosis remained extremely poor. At first instance, Ward J declared that it would be lawful for C to be treated in such a way as to 'end her life and die peacefully with the greatest dignity ...'. The case was appealed by the Official Solicitor.

> **Lord Donaldson MR:** In giving the reasons for his decision Ward J said:
>
> > That poor baby has now been nursed and attended by the hospitals with a degree of devotion to duty which deserves the very highest commendation, and I pay tribute to those who have had part in the care of this ward, and I give my thanks to those for so looking after my ward on my behalf. I have had the advantage of a report by an eminent professor of paediatrics, instructed by the Official Solicitor, whom I caused to become involved in this matter to represent the interests of the baby. The professor observes in his report that the outstandingly devoted care she has received could not be replicated in many children's units or in many children's homes, and it is important that that should receive its proper tribute and its proper commendation. Sadly, notwithstanding that devotion this child has not prospered. I have had the benefit of reading the report and hearing the evidence of Dr W, who is the consultant physician at the hospital, a physician of 21 years' experience, and I give him my thanks for the assistance he has given me. He reports to me that this baby has made virtually no progress since her birth.
>
> I omit some other matters and quote again from the judge's judgment, where he said: 'The damage which she has suffered is quite exceptionally severe.' Then he set out the evidence in support of that proposition and continued:

The medical evidence satisfies me that the damage to the cortex of the brain is gross and abnormally severe. The cortex of the brain is that part of the brain which serves the higher functions; those functions of intellect which make human life distinguishable, perhaps, from other forms of life. That damage, moreover, is irreparable, and about that all the medical witnesses are wholly agreed. There is, therefore, no prospect of a happy life for this child, sadly; no prospect whatever. The prognosis, in the conclusion of [the professor], is that it is inconceivable that appreciable skills will ever develop, and that is, of course, confirmed by the total failure of progress in these few short weeks of her life. There is, in the united opinion of the medical experts, no treatment which will alter that prognosis, and the prognosis is therefore one of hopelessness. I am therefore dealing with a child massively handicapped by a mixture of severe or permanent brain lesions, blindness, probable deafness and generalised spastic cerebral palsy of all four limbs.

The judge then referred to the decision of this court in *Re B (A Minor) (Wardship: Medical Treatment)* ... There the facts were very different. The child suffered from Down's syndrome and would be very handicapped mentally and physically. Nevertheless, she could have a life expectancy of 20 to 30 years. She developed an intestinal blockage which would be fatal within a few days unless operated on, but could be cured by operation. There was a difference of medical opinion on whether, in all the circumstances, it was in B's best interests to operate. The parents, who were consulted, thought that it would not. At an earlier stage the judge had taken the view that the operation should be performed but later, when the difference of medical opinion emerged, the judge felt that he should accept the view of the parents. This court disagreed. It held that the judge's duty was to have regard solely to what was in the best interests of the child and that it was not for the court to decide that the child should not have the chance of the normal life span of a mongoloid child with the handicap, defects and life of such a child.

C does not have any such option. She is, as I have already said, dying, and there is no medical or surgical treatment which can alter this fact. The judge continued in his judgment, saying:

But here I am quite satisfied that the damage is severe and irreparable. In so far as I can assess the quality of life, which as a test in itself raises as many questions as it can answer, I adjudge that any quality to life has already been denied to this child because it cannot flow from a brain incapable of even limited intellectual function. Inasmuch as one judges, as I do, intellectual function to be a hallmark of our humanity, her functioning on that level is negligible if it exists at all. Coupled with her total physical handicap, the quality of her life will be demonstrably awful and intolerable ... Asking myself what capacity she has to interact mentally, socially, physically, I answer none. This is her permanent condition.

... All concerned accept that the judge correctly directed himself that the first and paramount consideration was the well being, welfare and interests of C as required by the decision of this court in *Re B (A Minor) (Wardship: Medical*

Treatment) and by the House of Lords in a later and different case with the same name, *Re B (A Minor) (Wardship: Sterilisation)* [1987] 2 All ER 206, p 211 ... *per* Lord Hailsham LC.

Counsel for the local authority nevertheless felt it his duty to direct our attention to a decision of the British Columbia Supreme Court in *Re SD* [1983] 3 WWR 618, while submitting that the facts were very different. In so doing he was fulfilling the fundamental duty of members of the legal profession to assist the courts in the administration of justice, regardless of the views or interests of their client. He was wholly right so to do. In the event, I am fully satisfied that it does nothing to cast doubts on the correctness of his clients', and the judge's, view that the advice of the professor should be accepted. It was another case in which a child suffered from hydrocephalus, but the child concerned was very much older. The child had twice been operated on to implant a shunt and the question was whether he should now undergo a third operation. He was undoubtedly severely handicapped, but not as severely as some in his class at the hospital school. If a third operation were to be performed he would probably continue to live as he had done before and would do so for some years. The parents thought that there should be no operation and that he should be allowed to die at once. The higher court authorised the operation, saying it was too simplistic to say, as did the parents, that the child would be allowed to die in peace. There was a real possibility that, without the operation, the child would endure in a state of progressive disability and pain. That is a wholly different case.

The stress laid by the Master of the Rolls on the fact that C was dying is interesting. As Kennedy and Grubb have pointed out, the medical evidence in the case, though confirming that C's life expectancy was very limited, does not appear to justify such a description of her. However, it seems clear that the court was feeling its way cautiously towards a more open endorsement of passive euthanasia. The decisive step came soon afterwards in the seminal case of *Re J* in 1990.

Re J (A Minor) (Wardship: Medical Treatment) [1990] 3 All ER 930, CA (Lord Donaldson MR, Taylor and Balcombe LJJ)

J was a five month old baby who suffered severe brain damage as a result of his grossly premature birth. He was profoundly handicapped, both mentally and physically, and was unlikely to develop even the most basic functions. He had collapsed on a number of occasions since his birth and the court, pursuant to its wardship jurisdiction, was asked to decide if mechanical ventilation of J should occur in the event of a further collapse.

> **Lord Donaldson MR:** Of the three neonatalogists who have been concerned with [J's] care, the most optimistic is Dr W. His view is that J is likely to develop serious spastic quadriplegia, that is to say, paralysis of both his arms and legs. It is debatable whether he will ever be able to sit up or to hold his head upright. J appears to be blind, although there is a possibility that some degree of sight may return. He is likely to be deaf. He may be able to make sounds which reflect his mood, but he is unlikely ever to be able to speak, even

to the extent of saying Mum or Dad. It is highly unlikely that he will develop even limited intellectual abilities. Most unfortunately of all, there is a likelihood that he will be able to feel pain to the same extent as a normal baby, because pain is a very basic response. It is possible that he may achieve the ability to smile and to cry. Finally, as one might expect, his life expectancy has been considerably reduced, at most into his late teens, but even Dr W would expect him to die long before then ...

The issue here is whether it would be in the best interests of the child to put him on a mechanical ventilator and subject him to all the associated processes of intensive care, if at some future time he could not continue breathing unaided ... The judge has found that the odds are about even whether the need for artificial ventilation, whether mechanical or manual, will ever arise. If it does arise, the very fact that it has arisen will mean that the more optimistic end of the range of prognoses, pessimistic though the whole range is, will have been falsified. On the other hand, the child's state of health might change at any time for the better as well as for the worse, even though there are distinct limits to what could be hoped for, let alone anticipated.

The doctors were unanimous in recommending that there should be no mechanical reventilation in the event of his stopping breathing, subject only to the qualifications injected by Dr W, and accepted by the judge, that in the event of a chest infection, short term manual ventilation would be justified, and that in the event of the child stopping breathing the provisional decision to abstain from mechanical ventilation could and should be revised, if this seemed appropriate to the doctors caring for him in the then prevailing clinical situation.

There can be no criticism of the judge for endorsing this approach on the footing that he was thereby abdicating his responsibility and leaving it to the doctors to decide. He had reviewed and considered the basis of the doctor's views and recommendations in the greatest detail and with the greatest care. Nothing could be more inimical to the interests of the child than the judge should make an order which restricted the doctors' freedom to revise their present view in favour of more active means to preserve the life of the child, if the situation changed and this then seemed to them to be appropriate.

The basis of the doctors' recommendations, approved by the judge, was that mechanical ventilation is itself an invasive procedure which, together with its essential accompaniments, such as the introduction of a nasogastric tube, drips which have to be re-sited and constant blood sampling, would cause the child distress. Furthermore, the procedures involve taking active measures which carry their own hazards, not only to life but in terms of causing even greater brain damage. This had to be balanced against what could possibly be achieved by the adoption of such active treatment. The chances of preserving the child's life might be improved, although even this was not certain, and account had to be taken of the extremely poor quality of life at present enjoyed by the child, the fact that he had already been ventilated for exceptionally long periods, the unfavourable prognosis with or without ventilation and a recognition that if the question of reventilation ever arose, his situation would have deteriorated still further.

Best interests

In the above case, the Court of Appeal invoked the 'best interests' of the infant as the justification for not prolonging his life by further mechanical ventilation. We have previously encountered the 'best interests' test in the context of decisions to provide incompetent patients with treatment of a non-life-saving nature, most notably in sterilisation cases involving mentally disabled women: see above, Chapter 4. In itself the test lacks substance: it is merely a direction that, in reaching the decision whether to treat, the decider should objectively weigh up the factors in favour of treatment against those which militate against it. The factors themselves, and their respective weighting, clearly stand in need of further specification.

An initial question, however, is whether a balancing exercise can be meaningfully performed at all in a context in which one of the options (non-treatment) leads to death. This point was taken by Counsel for the Official Solicitor in *Re J*:

> **Lord Donaldson MR**: [James Munby QC's] first, or absolutist, submission is that a court is never justified in withholding consent to treatment which could enable a child to survive a life-threatening condition, whatever the pain or other side effects inherent in the treatment, and whatever the quality of the life which it would experience thereafter. In making this submission, he distinguishes a case such as that of Baby C ... where the child was dying and no amount of medical skill or care could do more than achieve a brief postponement of the moment of death. He submits, rightly, that in such a case neither the parents nor the court in deciding whether to give or to withhold consent, nor the doctors in deciding what treatment they recommend or would be prepared to administer, are balancing life against death. In such a case, death is inevitable, not in the sense that it is inevitable for all of us, but in the sense that the child is actually dying. What is being balanced is not life against death, but a marginally longer life of pain against a marginally shorter life free from pain and ending in death with dignity ...
>
> In support of this submission, Mr Munby draws attention to the decision of this court in *McKay v Essex HA* [1982] 1 QB 1166. There a child suffered severe and irreversible damage before birth, as a result of her mother contracting rubella (German measles). She sued the health authority claiming damages under two heads. First, she claimed that if her mother had received appropriate treatment her disabilities would have been less. She, therefore, claimed damages based upon the difference between the quality of her life as it was and the quality of life which she would have enjoyed if her mother had received that treatment. That claim was allowed to proceed. However, the child also claimed damages on a different basis. This was founded upon the proposition that her mother should have been advised to seek an abortion and that, if this advice had been given and accepted, she would never have been born at all. The damages claimed under this head were necessarily based upon a comparison between her actual condition and her condition if, as a result of an abortion, she had never been born at all.

This court struck out the second claim as disclosing no cause of action, and it is upon the reasoning which underlay this decision that Mr Munby relies – Stephenson LJ said, p 1180H:

> To impose such a duty towards the child [to give the child's mother an opportunity to terminate the child's life] would, in my opinion, make a further inroad on the sanctity of human life which would be contrary to public policy. It would mean regarding the life of a handicapped child as not only less valuable than the life of a normal child, but so much less valuable that it was not worth preserving.

Later he said, p 1181E:

> But how can a court of law evaluate that second condition [where 'the child's embryonic life has been ended before its life in the world had begun'] and so measure the loss to the child? Even if a court were competent to decide between the conflicting views of theologians and philosophers and to assume an 'after life' or non-existence as the basis for the comparison, how can a judge put a value on the one or the other and compare either alternative with the injured child's life in this world, without the means of knowing what, if anything, it has gained?

... I do not regard this decision as providing us with either guidance or assistance in the context of the present problem. The child was claiming damages, and the decision was that no monetary comparison could be made between the two states. True it is, that it contains an assertion of the importance of the sanctity of human life, but that is not in issue.

Taylor LJ: Despite the court's inability to compare a life afflicted by the most severe disability with death, the unknown, I am of the view that there must be extreme cases in which the court is entitled to say: 'The life which this treatment would prolong would be so cruel as to be intolerable.' If, for example, a child was so damaged as to have negligible use of its faculties and the only way of preserving its life was by the continuous administration of extremely painful treatment such that the child either would be in continuous agony or would have to be so sedated continuously as to have no conscious life at all, I cannot think Mr Munby's absolute test should apply to require the treatment to be given. In those circumstances, without there being any question of deliberately ending the life or shortening it, I consider the court is entitled in the best interests of the child to say that deliberate steps should not be taken artificially to prolong its miserable lifespan.

Assuming that a balancing exercise is possible, it will nevertheless clearly be rather different in form to the comparative assessment of benefits and burdens (the patient's *life with treatment* against her *life without treatment*) familiar from decisions dealing with such matters as sterilisation. In the latter type of case, one can imagine that decisions may sometimes be finely weighted, ultimately turning on apparently marginal differences. By contrast, where without treatment death will occur, the courts will brook no such ambiguity: not only must a life be truly awful for death to seem preferable, but the residual force of the (qualified) sanctity of life principle here asserts itself:

Taylor LJ: Three preliminary principles are not in dispute. First, it is settled law that the court's prime and paramount consideration must be the best interests of the child ...

Secondly, the court's high respect for the sanctity of human life imposes a strong presumption in favour of taking all steps capable of preserving it, save in exceptional circumstances. The problem is to define those circumstances.

Thirdly, and as a corollary to the second principle, it cannot be too strongly emphasised that the court never sanctions steps to terminate life. That would be unlawful. There is no question of approving, even in a case of the most horrendous disability, a course aimed at terminating life or accelerating death. The court is concerned only with the circumstances in which steps should not be taken to prolong life.

What, then, will be the substantive factors relevant to a decision that it is not in a patient's best interests to have their life prolonged? Lord Donaldson MR suggested that 'the critical equation ... cannot be done with mathematical or any precision'. Balcombe LJ also commented as follows:

Balcombe LJ: ... I would deprecate any attempt by this court to lay down such an all-embracing test, since the circumstances of these tragic cases are so infinitely various. I do not know of any demand by the judges who have to deal with these cases at first instance for this court to assist them by laying down any test beyond that which is already the law: that the interests of the ward are the first and paramount consideration ...

On the other hand, Taylor LJ was prepared to be more expansive:

Taylor LJ: At what point in the scale of disability and suffering ought the court to hold that the best interests of the child do not require further endurance to be imposed by positive treatment to prolong its life? Clearly, to justify withholding treatment, the circumstances would have to be extreme. Mr Munby submitted that if the court rejected his absolute test, then at least it would have 'to be certain that the life of the child, were the treatment to be given, would be intolerably awful'.

I consider the correct approach is for the court to judge the quality of life the child would have to endure if given the treatment, and decide whether in all the circumstances such a life would be so afflicted as to be intolerable to that child. I say 'to that child' because the test should not be whether the life would be tolerable to the decider. The test must be whether the child in question, if capable of exercising sound judgment, would consider the life tolerable. This is the approach adopted by McKenzie J in *Re Superintendent of Family and Child Service and Dawson* (1983) 145 DLR (3d) 610 ... It takes account of the strong instinct to preserve one's life even in circumstances which an outsider, not himself at risk of death, might consider unacceptable. The circumstances to be considered would, in appropriate cases, include the degree of existing disability and any additional suffering or aggravation of the disability which the treatment itself would superimpose. In an accident case, as opposed to one involving disablement from birth, the child's pre-accident quality of life and its perception of what has been lost may also be factors relevant to whether the residual life would be intolerable to that child.

Mr Munby argued that, before deciding against treatment, the court would have to be certain that the circumstances of the child's future would comply with the extreme requirements to justify that decision. Certainty as to the future is beyond human judgment. The courts have not, even in the trial of capital offences, required certainty of proof. But, clearly, the court must be satisfied to a high degree of probability.

In the present case, the doctors were unanimous that in his present condition, Baby J should not be put back on to a mechanical ventilator. That condition is very grave indeed. I do not repeat the description of it given by the Master of the Rolls. In reaching his conclusion, the judge no doubt had three factors in mind. First, the severe lack of capacity of the child in all his faculties, which even without any further complication would make his existence barely sentient. Secondly, that, if further mechanical ventilation were to be required, that very fact would involve the risk of a deterioration in J's condition, because of further brain damage flowing from the interruption of breathing. Thirdly, all the doctors drew attention to the invasive nature of mechanical ventilation and the intensive care required to accompany it. They stressed the unpleasant and distressing nature of that treatment. To add such distress and the risk of further deterioration to an already appalling catalogue of disabilities was clearly capable, in my judgment, of producing a quality of life which justified the stance of the doctors and the judge's conclusion.

Recently, Taylor LJ's approach was followed in the High Court in *Re R (Adult: Medical Treatment)*, the first case of this type to involve an adult patient.

Re R (Adult: Medical Treatment) [1996] 2 FLR 99, HC (Sir Stephen Brown P)

R was a 23 year old man who had been born with a serious malformation of the brain and cerebral palsy. He was described as being in a 'low-awareness state' with roughly the perception and cognitive faculties of a new-born infant. During 1995 he was admitted to hospital on no fewer than five occasions and his weight dropped to five stone. The NHS trust responsible for his care sought a declaration that it would be lawful to withhold resuscitation if he collapsed and, subject to the views of his doctors and parents at the relevant time, antibiotics in the face of a life-threatening infection.

> **Sir Stephen Brown P**: All the medical witnesses in this case support the view that CPR would not be appropriate in R's case. Dr S, the responsible consultant, has expressed that view very firmly. Dr Greenwood, a consultant neurologist, has also expressed that view in his report to be found in the documents. Dr John Morgan, a consultant psychiatrist for people with learning disability, in his report says:
>
>> There is a danger that if cardio-pulmonary resuscitation were attempted, he might suffer further brain damage, and his body is relatively fragile and excessive pressure or enthusiasm might lead to damage to his ribs or more serious complications.
>
> Dr Piachaud has also expressed the opinion that CPR would not be appropriate in this patient's case. The Official Solicitor on behalf of the patient R has made a report and counsel on his behalf has made it clear that the

Official Solicitor in the light of his own expert's opinions and all the other evidence before the court supports the view that the procedure of CPR and ventilation would be inappropriate in this patient's case.

So far as the withholding of antibiotics is concerned Dr Andrews stated that this is a matter which can only properly be decided at the time when a potentially life-threatening situation from infection arises. There should not be, as it were, a global 'do not treat' policy. The plaintiff trust has indicated that it is content to accept that position. The decision as to the withholding of the administration of antibiotics in a potentially life-threatening situation is a matter fully within the responsibility of the consultant having the responsibility for treating the patient. It is a matter which should be considered in conjunction with the general practitioner and furthermore in the case of R, with his parents. The Official Solicitor submits that it would be appropriate for the court at this stage to make a declaration that it would be lawful to withhold the administration of antibiotics in the event of the patient developing a potentially life-threatening infection which would otherwise call for the administration of antibiotics, but only if immediately prior to withholding the same:

(a)   the trust is so advised both by the general medical practitioner and by the consultant psychiatrist having the responsibility at the time of the patient's treatment and care; and

(b)   one or other or both of the parents first give their consent thereto.

Such a declaration would recognise the ultimate and effective clinical responsibility of the consultant having responsibility at the time for the patient's treatment and care ...

In this case there is no question of the court being asked to approve a course aimed at terminating life or accelerating death. The court is concerned with circumstances in which steps should not be taken to prolong life. The facts are very different from those in the case of *Airedale NHS Trust v Bland* ... The principle of law to be applied in this case is that of the 'best interests of the patient' as made clear by the Court of Appeal in *Re J (A Minor) (Wardship: Medical Treatment)* ... In the course of his judgment ... Taylor LJ said:

> I consider the correct approach is for the court to judge the quality of life the child would have to endure if given the treatment, and decide whether in all the circumstances such a life would be so afflicted as to be intolerable to that child.

Although this present case concerns a handicapped adult and not a child who is a ward of court the overriding principle in my judgment is the same.

The requirement in the President's order that R's parents agree to any decision to withhold antibiotics is, with respect, not reconcilable with other authorities (for example, *Re T* (1992) and *Re J* itself) which make it clear that ultimately such a decision must be for the doctors (and judges): see further the discussion below, p 686.

Permanently insensate patients

So far our concern has been with patients who have been sensate (ie, capable of experience) but severely impaired. Here it has arguably made sense to conduct a form of comparative exercise in which their quality of life is measured against death (conceived of as permanent unconsciousness). We must now consider a second category of patient for whom no such exercise appears possible, viz, those who, while still alive, become permanently insensate. As Jonathan Glover remarks, citing the German idealist philosopher, Arthur Schopenhauer, in subjective terms such patients are already dead:

> **Glover, J, *Causing Death and Saving Lives*, 1977, Harmondsworth: Penguin, pp 45–46:**
>
> I have no way of refuting someone who holds that being alive, even though unconscious, is intrinsically valuable. But it is a view that will seem unattractive to those of us who, in our own case, see a life of permanent coma as in no way preferable to death. From the subjective point of view, there is nothing to choose between the two. Schopenhauer saw this clearly when he said of the destruction of the body:
>
>> But actually we feel this destruction only in the evils of illness or of old age; on the other hand, for the *subject*, death itself consists merely in the moment when consciousness vanishes, since the activity of the brain ceases. The extension of the stoppage to all the other parts of the organism which follows this is really already an event after death. Therefore, in a subjective respect, death concerns only consciousness.

Legally, of course, such patients are alive: as we saw above, Chapter 11, death is regarded in law as occurring only when the whole of an individual's brainstem has perished. The brainstem is divided into upper and lower parts, the former, together with the cerebral cortex, being necessary for consciousness while the latter controls the body's automatic functions such as breathing, swallowing and other basic reflexes. When the brain is starved of oxygen, the lower brainstem is the last part of it to die, a fact which may give rise to a permanently insensate condition known, medically, as a permanent (formerly 'persistent') vegetative state or 'PVS'.

The issue of whether a patient diagnosed as being in PVS should be subject to a life-sustaining regime of treatment and care fell to be decided by the House of Lords in the most famous passive euthanasia case in English law to date, *Airedale NHS Trust v Bland*.

Airedale NHS Trust v Bland [1993] 1 All ER 821, HL (Keith, Goff, Browne-Wilkinson, Lowry and Mustill LL)

Tony Bland suffered massive and irreversible brain damage in t' Hillsborough football disaster in April 1989. He had lain in a PVS for m than three years and the medical evidence was unanimous that he w never regain any form of awareness. The trust caring for him applied, with his parents' approval, for a declaration that it would be lawful to withhold further life-prolonging treatment and care (artificial nutrition and hydration as well as antibiotics) from him, thus allowing him to die. The order was granted by Sir Stephen Brown P in the High Court and unanimously affirmed by the Court of Appeal (Sir Thomas Bingham MR, Butler-Sloss and Hoffmann LJJ). The Official Solicitor appealed:

> **Lord Keith of Kinkel**: The broad issue raised by the appeal is stated by the parties to be: 'In what circumstances, if ever, can those having a duty to feed an invalid lawfully stop doing so?' The immediate issue, however, is whether in the particular circumstances of Anthony Bland's case those in charge of it would be acting lawfully if they discontinued the particular measures, including feeding by nasogastric tube, which are now being used to maintain Anthony Bland in his existing condition ...
>
> The object of medical treatment and care is to benefit the patient. It may do so by taking steps to prevent the occurrence of illness, or, if an illness does occur, by taking steps towards curing it. Where an illness or the effects of an injury cannot be cured, then efforts are directed towards preventing deterioration or relieving pain and suffering. In Anthony Bland's case the first imperative was to prevent him from dying, as he would certainly have done in the absence of the steps that were taken. If he had died, there can be no doubt that the cause of this would have been the injuries which he had suffered. As it was, the steps taken prevented him from dying, and there was instituted the course of treatment and care which still continues. For a time, no doubt, there was some hope that he might recover sufficiently for him to be able to live a life that had some meaning. Some patients who have suffered damage to the cerebral cortex have, indeed, made a complete recovery. It all depends on the degree of damage. But sound medical opinion takes the view that if a PVS patient shows no signs of recovery after six months, or at most a year, then there is no prospect whatever of any recovery. There are techniques available which make it possible to ascertain the state of the cerebral cortex, and in Anthony Bland's case these indicate that ... it has degenerated into a mass of watery fluid. The fundamental question then comes to be whether continuance of the present regime of treatment and care, more than three years after the injuries that resulted in the PVS, would confer any benefit on Anthony Bland. It is argued for the respondents, supported by the *amicus curiae*, that his best interests favour discontinuance. I feel some doubt about this way of putting the matter. In *Re F (Mental Patient: Sterilisation)* [1990] 2 AC 1 this House held that it would be lawful to sterilise a female mental patient who was incapable of giving consent to the procedure. The ground of the decision was that sterilisation would be in the patient's best interests because her life would be fuller and more agreeable if she were sterilised than if she were not. In *Re J (A Minor) (Wardship: Medical Treatment)* [1991] Fam 33 the Court of Appeal held it to be lawful to withhold life-saving treatment from a very young child in circumstances where the child's life, if saved, would be one irredeemably racked by pain and agony. In both cases it was possible to make a value judgment, as to the consequences to a sensate being, of in the one case

withholding and in the other case administering the treatment in question. In the case of a permanently insensate being, who if continuing to live would never experience the slightest actual discomfort, it is difficult, if not impossible, to make any relevant comparison between continued existence and the absence of it. It is, however, perhaps permissible to say that to an individual with no cognitive capacity whatever, and no prospect of ever recovering any such capacity in this world, it must be a matter of complete indifference whether he lives or dies.

Where one individual has assumed responsibility for the care of another who cannot look after himself or herself, whether as a medical practitioner or otherwise, that responsibility cannot lawfully be shed unless arrangements are made for the responsibility to be taken over by someone else. Thus a person having charge of a baby who fails to feed it, so that it dies, will be guilty at least of manslaughter. The same is true of one having charge of an adult who is frail and cannot look after herself: *R v Stone* [1977] QB 354. It was argued for the guardian *ad litem*, by analogy with that case, that here the doctors in charge of Anthony Bland had a continuing duty to feed him by means of the nasogastric tube and that if they failed to carry out that duty they were guilty of manslaughter, if not murder. This was coupled with the argument that feeding by means of the nasogastric tube was not medical treatment at all, but simply feeding, indistinguishable from feeding by normal means. As regards this latter argument, I am of opinion that regard should be had to the whole regime, including the artificial feeding, which at present keeps Anthony Bland alive. That regime amounts to medical treatment and care, and it is incorrect to direct attention exclusively to the fact that nourishment is being provided. In any event, the administration of nourishment by the means adopted involves the application of a medical technique. But it is, of course, true that in general it would not he lawful for a medical practitioner who assumed responsibility for the care of an unconscious patient simply to give up treatment in circumstances where continuance of it would confer some benefit on the patient. On the other hand a medical practitioner is under no duty to continue to treat such a patient where a large body of informed and responsible medical opinion is to the effect that no benefit at all would be conferred by continuance. Existence in a vegetative state with no prospect of recovery is by that opinion regarded as not being a benefit, and that, if not unarguably correct, at least forms a proper basis for the decision to discontinue treatment and care: *Bolam v Friern Hospital Management Committee* [1957] 1 WLR 582.

Given that existence in the persistent vegetative state is not a benefit to the patient, it remains to consider whether the principle of the sanctity of life, which it is the concern of the State, and the judiciary as one of the arms of the State, to maintain, requires this House to hold that the judgment of the Court of Appeal was incorrect. In my opinion it does not. The principle is not an absolute one. It does not compel a medical practitioner on pain of criminal sanctions to treat a patient, who will die if he does not, contrary to the express wishes of the patient. It does not authorise forcible feeding of prisoners on hunger strike. It does not compel the temporary keeping alive of patients who are terminally ill where to do so would merely prolong their suffering. On the other hand it forbids the taking of active measures to cut short the life of a terminally ill patient. In my judgment it does no violence to the principle to hold that it is lawful to cease to give medical treatment and care to a PVS patient who has been in that state for over three years, considering that to do so involves invasive manipulation of the patient's body to which he has not consented and which confers no benefit upon him ...

My Lords, for these reasons, which are substantially the same as those set out in the speech delivered by my noble and learned friend, Lord Goff of Chieveley, with which I agree, I would dismiss the appeal.

The rest of their Lordships delivered concurring speeches.

The implications of Bland

Best interests in PVS?

As we have seen, there is a philosophical problem in applying the best interests approach to a patient who will never again enjoy any form of experience. For such patients, rather than offering any prospect of release from suffering, death must (as Lord Keith recognised) be a matter of pure indifference. Thus, it might well be argued, it cannot be in their best interests. In the Court of Appeal, Hoffman LJ, drawing on Ronald Dworkin's work, *Life's Dominion*, addressed this difficulty by suggesting that patients in PVS do in fact retain certain interests (*critical* – as opposed to *experiential* – interests, in Dworkinian terms) and that these are served by allowing them to die.

> **Hoffmann LJ**: Counsel for the Official Solicitor argued that however vestigial Anthony Bland's life might be, one could not assume that he would choose to die. Being unconscious, he felt no pain or humiliation and therefore had no interests which suffered from his being kept alive. Anthony Bland was in fact indifferent to whether he lived or died and there was nothing to put in the balance against the intrinsic value of his life.
>
> I think that the fallacy in this argument is that it assumes that we have no interests except in those things of which we have conscious experience. But this does not accord with most people's intuitive feelings about their lives and deaths. At least a part of the reason why we honour the wishes of the dead about the distribution of their property is that we think it would wrong them not to do so, despite the fact that we believe that they will never know that their will has been ignored. Most people would like an honourable and dignified death and we think it wrong to dishonour their deaths, even when they are unconscious that this is happening. We pay respect to their dead bodies and to their memory because we think it an offence against the dead themselves if we do not. Once again I am not concerned to analyse the rationality of these feelings. It is enough that they are deeply rooted in our ways of thinking and that the law cannot possibly ignore them. Thus I think that counsel for the Official Solicitor offers a seriously incomplete picture of Anthony Bland's interests when he confines them to animal feelings of pain or pleasure. It is demeaning to the human spirit to say that, being unconscious, he can have no interest in his personal privacy and dignity, in how he lives or dies ...

This argument has a slightly metaphysical flavour and was not adopted in the House of Lords. Instead, as reflected in Lord Keith's judgment, their Lordships preferred to look at the question from the opposite direction and ask if *treatment* was a benefit to the patient. This approach found its most robust expression in the speech of Lord Mustill.

> **Lord Mustill**: [Anthony Bland] feels no pain and suffers no mental anguish. Stress was laid in argument on the damage to his personal dignity by the continuation of the present medical regime, and on the progressive erosion of the family's happy recollections by month after month of distressing and hopeless care. Considerations of this kind will no doubt carry great weight when parliament comes to consider the whole question in the round. But it seems to me to be stretching the concept of personal rights beyond breaking point to say that Anthony Bland has an interest in ending these sources of others' distress. Unlike the conscious patient he does not know what is happening to his body, and cannot be affronted by it; he does not know of his family's continuing sorrow. By ending his life the doctors will not relieve him of a burden become intolerable, for others carry the burden and he has none. What other considerations could make it better for him to die now rather than later? None that we can measure, for of death we know nothing. The distressing truth which must not be shirked is that the proposed conduct is not in the best interests of Anthony Bland, for he has no best interests of any kind.

> **Best interests: the termination of treatment**

> After much expression of negative opinions I turn to an argument which in my judgment is logically defensible and consistent with the existing law. In essence it turns the previous argument on its head by directing the inquiry to the interests of the patient, not in the termination of life but in the continuation of his treatment. It runs as follows: (i) the cessation of nourishment and hydration is an omission not an act; (ii) accordingly, the cessation will not be a criminal act unless the doctors are under a present duty to continue the regime; (iii) at the time when Anthony Bland came into the care of the doctors, decisions had to be made about his care which he was unable to make for himself. In accordance with *Re F* [1990] 2 AC 1 these decisions were to be made in his best interests. Since the possibility that he might recover still existed his best interests required that he should be supported in the hope that this would happen. These best interests justified the application of the necessary regime without his consent; (iv) all hope of recovery has now been abandoned. Thus, although the termination of his life is not in the best interests of Anthony Bland, his best interests in being kept alive have also disappeared, taking with them the justification for the non-consensual regime and the correlative duty to keep it in being; (v) since there is no longer a duty to provide nourishment and hydration, failure to do so cannot be a criminal offence.

However, though unassailable as a matter of logic, this analysis may be thought to attach too little weight to the general presumption, underpinning the qualified sanctity of life principle, that life should be preserved unless death is unambiguously preferable.

Substituted judgment?

An alternative, and arguably more promising, approach to the dilemma of whether to continue treating those in PVS might be to utilise the doctrine of substituted judgment. As noted in Chapter 4, this test directs attention to the question of whether the patient himself would have wished to receive treatment in such circumstances, and has been used in a number of American cases involving the withdrawal of treatment from permanently insensate patients: see for example, *Re Quinlan* 70 NJ 10 (1976) and *Re Jobes* 529 A 2d 434 (1987). However, in *Bland* Lord Mustill disparaged the test's application in English law.

> **Lord Mustill**: The second method, which is adopted if the evidence is insufficient to justify an inference of what the patient chose in the past so that it can be projected to the present, involves the appointment of a surrogate to make on behalf of the patient the choice which he believes the patient would now make if able to do so. For this purpose the surrogate builds up a picture of the patient's former character, feelings, convictions and so on from which the putative choice is deduced. This process may perhaps have some justification where the patient is sentient but unable to communicate a choice, but it breaks down totally in a case such as the present. To postulate a patient who is in such a condition that he cannot know that there is a choice to be made, or indeed know anything at all, and then ask whether he would have chosen to terminate his life because that condition made it no longer worth living is surely meaningless, as is very clearly shown by the lengths to which the court was driven in *Superintendent of Belchertown State School v Saikewicz* 370 NE 2d 417. The idea is simply a fiction, which I would not be willing to adopt even if there were in the case of Anthony Bland any materials upon which a surrogate could act, which as far as I can see there are not.

(See also the judgment of Lord Goff, pp 871–72, cited in Chapter 4 above.)

Such disapproval is difficult to reconcile with the law's favourable attitude to advance directives, which embody the same underlying rationale of respecting a person's integrity beyond the onset of incompetence – albeit they perform this task with more formality. It may well be that, as Kennedy and Grubb have argued, their Lordships misunderstood the test as applying to those who had never been competent: the reference to the 1977 American case of *Saikewicz* – which concerned the treatment of a sensate 67 year old man who had been incompetent from birth – is revealing. In fact, a close reading of the latter case suggests that the Massachusetts Supreme Court was applying a straightforward best interests test, albeit this made reference to features peculiar to the patient's situation, in particular his inability to comprehend the purpose of (painful) treatment if given: in contrast to the substituted judgment test proper, there is no forensic inquiry into the patient's erstwhile personality here. (The same, incidentally, may be said of the English Court of Appeal's decision in *Re J* (1990) where, despite first appearances – recall Taylor LJ's *dictum* that life, following treatment, should be 'intolerable to that child' – the approach of the court was clearly an objective one.)

Prior to *Bland*, in *Re T*, Lord Donaldson MR appeared more sympathetic to substituted judgment, though he subsumed it within a more general 'best interests' test:

Lord Donaldson MR: Consultation with the next of kin has a further advantage in that it may reveal information as to the personal circumstances of the patient and as to the choice which the patient might have made, if he or she had been in a position to make it. Neither the personal circumstances of the patient nor a speculative answer to the question 'What would the patient have chosen?' can bind the practitioner in his choice of whether or not to treat or how to treat or justify him in acting contrary to a clearly established anticipatory refusal to accept treatment but they are factors to be taken into account by him in forming a clinical judgment as to what is in the best interests of the patient. For example, if he learnt that the patient was a Jehovah's Witness, but had had no evidence of a refusal to accept blood transfusions, he would avoid or postpone any blood transfusion so long as possible.

Subsequently, the Law Commission in its report on mental incapacity has endorsed a similar approach:

Law Commission, *Mental Incapacity*, Report No 231, 1995, London: HMSO, para 328:

We recommend that in deciding what is in a person's best interests regard should be had to:

(1) the ascertainable past and present wishes and feelings of the person concerned, and the factors that person would consider if able to do so;

(2) the need to permit and encourage the person to participate, or to improve his or her ability to participate, as fully as possible in anything done for and any decision affecting him or her;

(3) the views of other people whom it is appropriate and practicable to consult about the person's wishes and feelings and what would be in his or her best interests;

(4) whether the purpose for which any action or decision is required can be as effectively achieved in a manner less restrictive of the person's freedom of action. (Draft Bill, cl 3(2).)

Wishes, feelings and putative factors

3.29 This first element in the checklist establishes the importance of individual views. Realistically, the former views of a person who is without capacity cannot in every case be determinative of the decision which is now to be made. Past wishes and feelings may in any event conflict with feelings the person is still able to express in spite of incapacity. People who cannot make decisions can still experience pleasure and distress. Present wishes and feelings must therefore be taken into account, where necessary balanced with past wishes and feelings. One of the failings of a pure 'substituted judgment' model is the unhelpful idea that a person who cannot make a decision should be treated as if his or her capacity were perfect and unimpaired, and as if present emotions need not also be considered.

The Law Commission's concern here is clearly with patients who, though incompetent, remain sensate. By contrast, there appears to be no reason not to adopt the 'pure' substituted judgment approach in relation to a patient in PVS.

Who decides? – the role of the court

All three of the courts in *Bland* were exercised with the problem of how far a decision by doctors to withdraw treatment from a PVS patient should be subject to judicial sanction. In the House of Lords, Lord Goff commented as follows:

> **Lord Goff**: I turn finally to the extent to which doctors should, as a matter of practice, seek the guidance of the court, by way of an application for declaratory relief, before withholding life-prolonging treatment from a PVS patient. The President considered that the opinion of the court should be sought in all cases similar to the present. In the Court of Appeal, Sir Thomas Bingham MR expressed his agreement with Sir Stephen Brown P in the following words ... pp 815–16:
>
>> This was in my respectful view a wise ruling, directed to the protection of patients, the protection of doctors, the reassurance of patients' families and the reassurance of the public. The practice proposed seems to me desirable. It may very well be that with the passage of time a body of experience and practice will build up which will obviate the need for application in every case, but for the time being I am satisfied that the practice which the President described should be followed.
>
> Before the Appellate Committee, this view was supported both by Mr Munby, for the Official Solicitor, and by Mr Lester, as *amicus curiae*. For the respondents, Mr Francis suggested that an adequate safeguard would be provided if reference to the court was required in certain specific cases, ie, (1) where there was known to be a medical disagreement as to the diagnosis or prognosis, and (2) problems had arisen with the patient's relatives – disagreement by the next of kin with the medical recommendation; actual or apparent conflict of interest between the next of kin and the patient; dispute between members of the patient's family; or absence of any next of kin to give their consent. There is, I consider, much to be said for the view that an application to the court will not be needed in every case, but only in particular circumstances, such as those suggested by Mr Francis. In this connection I was impressed not only by the care being taken by the Medical Ethics Committee to provide guidance to the profession, but also by information given to the Appellate Committee about the substantial number of PVS patients in the country, and the very considerable cost of obtaining guidance from the court in cases such as the present. However, in my opinion this is a matter which would be better kept under review by the President of the Family Division than resolved now by your Lordships' House. I understand that a similar review is being undertaken in cases concerned with the sterilisation of adult women of unsound mind, with a consequent relaxation of the practice relating to applications to the court in such cases. For my part, I would therefore leave the matter as proposed by the Master of the Rolls; but I wish to express the

hope that the President of the Family Division, who will no doubt be kept well informed about developments in this field, will soon feel able to relax the present requirement so as to limit applications for declarations to those cases in which there is a special need for the procedure to be invoked.

However, although good practice, and indeed of comfort to doctors in foreclosing (for all practical purposes) any prospect of criminal liability, it seems that a court declaration is not required as a strict matter of law prior to the discontinuance of life-prolonging measures. The doctor is, at least in the view of a majority of their Lordships, entitled to proceed on such a course in so far as it would be approved by a responsible (Lord Keith suggested it should also be a 'large') body of other doctors, ie, it satisfies the *Bolam* test. The arguably somewhat startling consequences of utilising this test were recognised by Lord Browne-Wilkinson:

> **Lord Browne-Wilkinson:** The answer to the question [whether to withdraw life-sustaining treatment] must of course depend on the circumstances of each case and there will be no single 'right' answer. Different doctors may take different views both on strictly medical issues and the broader ethical issues which the question raises. It follows that the legal question in this case (unlike the question which would arise if there were a *parens patriae* jurisdiction under which the court has to make the decision) is not whether the court thinks it is in the best interests of Anthony Bland to continue to receive intrusive medical care but whether the responsible doctor has reached a reasonable and *bona fide* belief that it is not. The doctor's answer may well be influenced by his own attitude to the sanctity of human life. In cases where there is no strictly medical point in continuing care, if a doctor holds the view that the patient is entitled to stay alive, whatever the quality of such life, he can quite reasonably reach the view that the continuation of intrusive care, being the only way of preserving such life, is in the patient's best interests. But, in the same circumstances another doctor who sees no merit in perpetuating a life of which the patient is unaware can equally reasonably reach the view that the continuation of invasive treatment is not for the patient's benefit. Accordingly, on an application to the court for a declaration that the discontinuance of medical care will be lawful, the court's only concern will be to be satisfied that the doctor's decision to discontinue is in accordance with a respectable body of medical opinion and that it is reasonable.

For his part, however, Lord Mustill was clearly unhappy with the application of the *Bolam* test in such cases:

> **Lord Mustill:** The reasoning which I propose is, I believe, broadly in line with that of your Lordships. But I venture to feel some reservations about the application of the principle of civil liability in negligence laid down in *Bolam v Friern Hospital Management Committee* [1957] 1 WLR 582 to decisions on 'best interests' in a field dominated by the criminal law. I accept without difficulty that this principle applies to the ascertainment of the medical raw material such as diagnosis, prognosis and appraisal of the patient's cognitive functions. Beyond this point, however, it may be said that the decision is ethical, not medical, and that there is no reason in logic why on such a decision the

opinions of doctors should be decisive. If there had been a possibility that this question might make a difference to the outcome of the appeal I would have wished to consider it further, but since it does not I prefer for the moment to express no opinion upon it.

Subsequently, in *Frenchay NHS Trust v S* [1994] 2 All ER 403, a Court of Appeal decision concerning another patient in PVS, Sir Thomas Bingham MR commented as follows:

> **Sir Thomas Bingham MR**: Mr Munby ... submit[s] that the judge erred in attaching too much importance to the judgment of doctors as to what was in the patient's best interests. Mr Munby submits that the House of Lords' decision in *Airedale NHS Trust v Bland* ... left open whether the judgment was finally to be made by the doctors or by the court, his submission being that in the last resort it must be made by the court, albeit with great regard to the opinions of responsible medical men. It is true that the learned judge paid close attention to what members of the House of Lords had said about the subject in the course of their speeches in *Bland's* case and did express the view that the conclusion at which S's consultant had arrived was reasonable and *bona fide*. He regarded the judgments which had been expressed by the doctors in this case as being fully in accord with criteria which their Lordships had laid down. It is, I think, important that there should not be a belief that what the doctor says is the patient's best interest *is* the patient's best interest. For my part I would certainly reserve to the court the ultimate power and duty to review the doctors' decision in the light of all the facts.

A final point of interest is that in *Bland* both Lord Browne-Wilkinson (p 883) and Lord Lowry (p 876) suggested that, if it could clearly be established that life-prolonging treatment were no longer in an incompetent patient's best interests, such treatment would become an unlawful battery. Whatever the strict logic of this proposition, it must be doubtful whether an action against a doctor in such a case would ever be brought, far less succeed: public policy, even in a society in which the qualified nature of the sanctity of life principle is generally accepted, militates against it. (It would be a different matter if the doctor were treating in defiance of a judicial injunction, but in that case the principal issue would be one of contempt of court.)

Resource issues

Our discussion has so far ignored the fact that, in keeping alive patients who enjoy very low (or, in the case of someone in PVS, non-existent) quality of life, there is an 'opportunity cost' in the sense that scarce resources are expended which might otherwise be utilised upon people with a greater capacity to benefit from them. In *Re J (A Minor) (Wardship: Medical Treatment)* [1992] 4 All ER 614 (not to be confused with the case of the same name and similar facts from 1990), the Court of Appeal quashed the trial judge's order that the health authority treat a severely handicapped baby. Balcombe LJ stated:

Balcombe LJ: I would also stress the absolute undesirability of the court making an order which may have the effect of compelling a doctor or health authority to make available scarce resources (both human and material) to a particular child, without knowing whether or not there are other patients to whom those resources might more advantageously be devoted. Lord Donaldson MR has set out in his reasons the condition of J and his very limited future prospects. The effect of the order of Waite J, had it not been immediately stayed by this court, might have been to require the health authority to put J on a ventilator in an intensive care unit, and thereby possibly to deny the benefit of those limited resources to a child who was much more likely than J to benefit from them. At the very least it would in those circumstances have required the health authority to make a further application to the court to vary or discharge the injunction.

In *Bland*, the fact that resource allocation is ultimately an issue that must be faced up to was noted by Lord Mustill:

Lord Mustill:

Best interests of the community

Threaded through the technical arguments addressed to the House were the strands of a much wider position, that it is in the best interests of the community at large that Anthony Bland's life should now end. The doctors have done all they can. Nothing will be gained by going on and much will be lost. The distress of the family will get steadily worse. The strain on the devotion of a medical staff charged with the care of a patient whose condition will never improve, who may live for years and who does not even recognise that he is being cared for, will continue to mount. The large resources of skill, labour and money now being devoted to Anthony Bland might in the opinion of many be more fruitfully employed in improving the condition of other patients, who if treated may have useful, healthy and enjoyable lives for years to come.

This argument was never squarely put, although hinted at from time to time. In social terms it has great force, and it will have to be faced in the end. But this is not a task which the courts can possibly undertake. A social cost-benefit analysis of this kind, which would have to embrace 'mercy killing' to which exactly the same considerations apply, must be for parliament alone, and the outcome of it is at present quite impossible to foresee. Until the nettle is grasped, we must struggle on with the existing law, imperfect as it is.

(See more generally on the resources question the discussion above, Chapter 2.)

Developments since Bland

Following the decision in *Bland*, a number of further applications have been made to the courts for declarations in respect of PVS and other very radically impaired patients, though not the flood predicted by some. The key decisions following *Bland*, and the establishment of further legal safeguards, are described by Mike Hinchcliffe, a Solicitor working in the Official Solicitor's Office:

Hinchcliffe, M, 'Vegetative state patients' (1996) NLJ 1579:

Ten declarations have now been granted. In four other cases, the proceedings were abandoned or the patient died before the hearing. In all the concluded cases, orders were made declaring lawful removing of feeding and hydration. In one case, the patient was ventilator dependent. The parents did not wish for feeding and hydration to be withdrawn and so an order was granted declaring lawful termination of ventilation ... Nine of the concluded cases involved patients in the vegetative state, in part at least, as a result of anoxia (oxygen starvation). All had been unresponsive for at least 12 months, and in one case, an interval as long as seven years had elapsed before the application was made to court. It should be noted that the widely used term 'persistent vegetative state' has now been superseded by 'permanent vegetative state' ...

... Three cases followed [*Bland*] in 1994 – the first [*Frenchay NHS Trust v S* [1994] 2 All ER 403] arose as a matter of great urgency. S, a 24 year old man from the west of England, was said to be in a vegetative state as a result of a drug overdose two and a half years previously. The urgency was due to the fact that his gastrostomy tube became dislodged two days before the hearing and his doctor did not wish to reinstate it. Swinton Thomas J granted a declaration that it would be lawful to refrain from reinstating artificial feeding and hydration. The Official Solicitor unsuccessfully argued in the Court of Appeal for more time to enable him to obtain an independent medical report. The declaration was upheld, the gastrostomy tube was not reinstated and S died a few days later. This is the only case to date where there has not been the opportunity to commission an independent report on behalf of the patient. I think in the light of more recent developments that this would be unlikely to recur, notwithstanding the apparent urgency.

The next case [*Swindon and Marlborough NHS Trust v S* (1994) unreported] also arose as an emergency. In this case, the patient, a woman, had been unresponsive for two and a half years. She went into a coma after neurosurgery to remove a brain tumour. Her husband and children, who had strong religious faith, did not wish for her feeding tube to be unblocked when a problem arose without warning. They felt that it was not right for their loved one to be kept alive in a totally unresponsive state. In this case, although only notified of the emergency late on a Friday afternoon, the Official Solicitor was able to instruct an independent expert in rehabilitation to examine Mrs S and report in time for a hearing which took place before Ward J, as he then was, on the afternoon of Saturday 26 November 1994.

The judge granted the declaration which was sought by the local NHS trust, although Mrs S was cared for by her family at home, the only PVS patient to date who has been in this situation.

Press coverage

In the meantime, [*Re G (Persistent Vegetative State)* [1995] 2 FCR 46,] another case from the South East of England, had been proceeding more slowly. In fact, there had already been a preliminary hearing which established the very important principle that applications for permission to withdraw feeding and hydration from vegetative state patients ought to be heard in open court, to allow public debate about issues of such gravity. [See *Re G (Adult Patient: Publicity)* [1995] 2 FLR 528.] Sir Stephen Brown, the President of the Family Division, went on in his guidelines to declare that the court has power, when sitting in open court, to consider at any stage whether any particular evidence ought to be given in private, and to grant injunctions to protect the anonymity of the patient. It is now clear that such orders can extend to banning the identification of the next of kin and the hospital in which the patient is being cared for, and even the plaintiff NHS trust or health authority, if to identify any of these would risk the identification of the patient.

The case finally came substantively to court before the President in November 1994. G had, at the time of the hearing, been unresponsive for three and a half years following a motorcycle accident in which he sustained severe head injuries. Further brain damage was caused by a cardiac arrest in hospital. G's wife supported the application of the health trust, but his mother opposed it. A professor of neurology instructed by the mother's legal team and a consultant in rehabilitation instructed by the Official Solicitor both confirmed the diagnosis. The President's approach was to say that the mother's views were relevant, but could not prevail. He decided that it was in G's best interests for artificial feeding and hydration to be withdrawn, notwithstanding the strong objections of his mother ...

Future developments

The Official Solicitor's Practice Note [see *Practice Note (Official Solicitor: Vegetative State)* [1996] 2 FLR 375] offers guidance to those contemplating applications to court in vegetative state cases. He has laid particular emphasis on the assessment which must be made before the diagnosis can be confirmed. There is reference to the *Guidelines for Diagnosis and Management of the Permanent Vegetative State*, issued in March 1996 by the Royal College of Physicians, and an acknowledgment of the concerns expressed by Dr Keith Andrews, Medical Director of the Royal Hospital for Neuro-disability, Putney, and others in an article, 'Misdiagnosis of the vegetative state: retrospective study in a rehabilitation unit', published in the British Medical Journal on 6 July 1996. It is noteworthy that emphasis is placed now on the duration of the assessment as well as the experience or training of those carrying it out. Currently there are four more cases being dealt with by the Official Solicitor ...

Subsequently, in *Re D* [1998] 1 FLR 411, Sir Stephen Brown P granted a declaration that it would be lawful not to re-attach the feeding tube of a woman who had been in what was described as 'near PVS' since September 1995. The decision (in March 1997) attracted some concern, not only because Miss D did not satisfy all of the Royal College of Physicians' guidelines for the diagnosis of PVS, but because it coincided with reports in the media of another patient recovering some awareness after ostensibly being in full PVS for nearly eight years. Leaving such diagnostic uncertainties to one side, it may well be thought curious that in this case (as in the *Frenchay* and *Swindon* cases) the application to court was expedited after a problem developed with the patient's feeding tube of its own accord. Such hasty decisions will predictably arouse public concern. Moreover, in legal terms, they are unnecessary: just as it makes no difference whether a doctor removes a patient's feeding tube or fails to reconnect it (both are omissions *per* Lord Goff in *Bland*) equally there is no reason to regard the act of re-attaching the tube as any more of a battery (if that is what it is) than was previously constituted by the regime of artificial feeding.

REFORMING THE LAW

In the wake of the *Bland* case, a Select Committee of the House of Lords was established to look into the current state of English law in relation to euthanasia. Whilst endorsing steps to facilitate the practice of passive euthanasia (though it preferred not to use this term), such as by encouraging the greater use of advance directives, the Committee was of the view that both assisted suicide and active euthanasia should remain offences, the latter continuing to be treated as murder.

> *Report of the Select Committee on Medical Ethics*, **HL Paper No 21, Vol I, 1994, London: HMSO:**
>
> 236   The right to refuse treatment is far removed from the right to request assistance in dying. We spent a long time considering the very strongly held and sincerely expressed views of those witnesses who advocated voluntary euthanasia. Many of us have had the experience of relatives or friends whose dying days were less than peaceful or uplifting, or whose final stages of life were so disfigured that the loved one already seemed lost to us, or who were simply weary of life. Our thinking must inevitably be coloured by such experience. The accounts we received from individual members of the public about such experiences were particularly moving, as were the letters from those who themselves longed for the release of an early death. Our thinking must also be coloured by the wish of every individual for a peaceful and easy death, without prolonged suffering, and by a reluctance to contemplate the possibility of severe dementia or dependence. We gave much thought too to Professor [Ronald] Dworkin's opinion that, for those without religious belief, the individual is best able to decide what manner of death is fitting to the life that has been lived.
>
> 237   Ultimately, however, we do not believe that these arguments are sufficient reason to weaken society's prohibition of intentional killing. That prohibition is the cornerstone of law and social relationships. It protects each of us impartially, embodying the belief that all are equal.

We do not wish that protection to be diminished and we therefore recommend that there be no change in the law to permit euthanasia. We acknowledge that there may be individual cases in which euthanasia may be seen by some to be appropriate. But individual cases cannot reasonably establish the foundation of a policy which would have such serious and widespread repercussions. Moreover dying is not only a personal or individual affair. The death of a person affects the lives of others, often in ways and to an extent that cannot be foreseen. We believe that the issue of euthanasia is one in which the interest of the individual cannot be separated from the interest of society as a whole.

238 One reason for this conclusion is that we do not think it possible to set secure limits on voluntary euthanasia. Some witnesses told us that to legalise voluntary euthanasia was a discrete step which need have no other consequences. But ... issues of life and death do not lend themselves to clear definition, and without that it would not be possible to frame adequate safeguards against non-voluntary euthanasia if voluntary euthanasia were to be legalised. It would be next to impossible to ensure that all acts of euthanasia were truly voluntary, and that any liberalisation of the law was not abused. Moreover to create an exception to the general prohibition of intentional killing would inevitably open the way to its further erosion whether by design, by inadvertence, or by the human tendency to test the limits of any regulation. These dangers are such that we believe that any decriminalisation of voluntary euthanasia would give rise to more, and more grave, problems than those it sought to address. Fear of what some witnesses referred to as a 'slippery slope' could in itself be damaging.

239 We are also concerned that vulnerable people – the elderly, lonely, sick or distressed – would feel pressure, whether real or imagined, to request early death. We accept that, for the most part, requests resulting from such pressure or from remediable depressive illness would be identified as such by doctors and managed appropriately. Nevertheless we believe that the message which society sends to vulnerable and disadvantaged people should not, however obliquely, encourage them to seek death, but should assure them of our care and support in life.

240 Some of those who advocated voluntary euthanasia did so because they feared that lives were being prolonged by aggressive medical treatment beyond the point at which the individual felt that continued life was not a benefit but a burden. But, in the light of the consensus which is steadily emerging over the circumstances in which life-prolonging treatment may be withdrawn or not initiated, we consider that such fears may increasingly be allayed. We welcome moves by the medical professional bodies to ensure more senior oversight of practice in casualty departments, as a step towards discouraging inappropriately aggressive treatment by less experienced practitioners.

241 Furthermore there is good evidence that, through the outstanding achievements of those who work in the field of palliative care, the pain and distress of terminal illness can be adequately relieved in the vast majority of cases. Such care is available not only within hospices: thanks

to the increasing dissemination of best practice by means of home-care teams and training for general practitioners, palliative care is becoming more widely available in the health service, in hospitals and in the community, though much remains to be done. With the necessary political will such care could be made available to all who could benefit from it. We strongly commend the development and growth of palliative care services.

However, the Committee also strongly endorsed the view of a previous Select Committee (*Murder and Life Imprisonment*, Session 1988–89, HL Paper 78, Vol I), that the mandatory life sentence that follows a conviction for murder should be abolished; the discretion over sentencing thereby given to judges would clearly be highly significant in cases where the agent has killed on compassionate grounds ('mercy killing' as it is often termed).

The generally cautious approach in this country, and in particular the strong endorsement of the acts/omissions distinction central to the 'qualified sanctity of life' doctrine, contrasts with that adopted in certain other jurisdictions. Most well known is the policy in Holland of permitting active steps by doctors in some circumstances, which are directly intended to terminate the lives of their patients. The latter development, and the interest it has aroused within our own legal system, has been commented upon extra-judicially by Lord Goff:

Goff, R, 'A matter of life and death' (1995) 3 Med L Rev 1:

The distinction drawn by the House of Lords in the case of Anthony Bland, between on the one hand withholding or withdrawing life sustaining treatment or care and so allowing a patient to die, which may be lawful, and on the other hand actively causing a patient's death, which is not, is one which can readily be understood by lawyers. But it may not be so easily understood by members of the public; and an acute question which has arisen in the aftermath of the cases of Dr Cox and Anthony Bland is whether the distinction is one which is generally acceptable. Taking first the case of Dr Cox, there can be little doubt that, in the last days of her life, if the means had been available to her, Mrs Boyes would have taken her own life; and suicide is, as I have said, now lawful in England. Yet, when she was desperate to take that step because of the terrible nature of her illness, the same illness had the effect that she was unable to obtain the means to do so; furthermore, since in England aiding and abetting another to commit suicide is still a criminal offence, it would have been very difficult for others lawfully to provide her with the necessary assistance ... Then take the case of Anthony Bland. It was there decided that a person in Anthony's condition may lawfully be deprived of life support in the form of artificial feeding, with the inevitable consequence that he will die within a few days; yet, though his doctor has in these circumstances decided that he must inevitably die, the law does not permit him to take the humane step of accelerating that event by giving him a lethal injection. It is for reasons such as these that the two English cases have presented the British public with the question whether the law in its present form is acceptable to them.

To the members of the Voluntary Euthanasia Society, the answer to that question is an emphatic 'No'. The aim of the Society is to make it legal for a competent adult, who is suffering severe distress from an incurable illness, to receive medical help to die at his or her considered and persistent request. In advocating this change in the law, the Society invokes in particular the concept of personal autonomy, which is now reflected in the lawfulness of suicide, and the freedom of choice, inherent in that concept, for an individual to waive the right to his own life ... The Society asks that the law in England should be brought into line with what it believes to be good medical practice, to enable doctors to act in the best interests of their patients without fear of prosecution or the need to dissemble.

The rational force of this argument is very strong. Furthermore, the opinion polls provide at least some evidence of widespread popular support for the Society's proposal ... But certain comments should in any event be made. First, a concordat, such as that adopted in the Netherlands, is difficult to envisage in England; I doubt whether the Director of Public Prosecutions in England would feel free to enter into any such agreement ... The opinion expressed by the House of Lords [in *Bland*] was that only by legislation which expressed the democratic will could so fundamental a change be made in the common law; and attention was drawn to the fact that such legislation, if enacted, could make express provision designed to ensure that any such legalised killing could only be carried out subject to appropriate supervision and control.

Even so, we must be grateful when experiments of this kind are carried out in other jurisdictions, so that we ourselves can learn from them before deciding whether or not to proceed down the same road. I have hitherto regarded the United States as the legal laboratory of the world; but in the case of euthanasia we must all be watching developments in the Netherlands with great interest. However, judging by one account published in a very reputable journal in England ... in 1992, based upon research funded by the British Academy in London [Keown, J, 'The law and practice of euthanasia in the Netherlands' (1992) 108 LQR 51], the established criteria for euthanasia in the Netherlands have proved in practice to be neither so precise nor so strict as originally claimed. The criteria include requirements that the request for euthanasia must come from the patient and must be free and voluntary; that the request must be well considered, durable and persistent; that the patient must be experiencing intolerable (not necessarily physical) suffering; and that the physician must consult with an independent physician colleague who has experience in the field. The first requirement – that the request must be free and voluntary – is, perhaps inevitably, not the subject of further definition, it is not, for example, clear that a request for euthanasia on the ground that the patient is a nuisance to the patient's family is excluded. It is doubtful too whether doctors possess the means, or the expertise, to determine whether the requirement is fulfilled, or indeed the requirement that the request must be well considered, durable and persistent. A survey carried out among general practitioners in the Netherlands in 1990 raised doubts in particular about the efficacy of this latter requirement, revealing that in 22% of cases there had been only one request; in a further 30% of cases, the interval between the first and the last requests as between one hour and one week; and in almost 66% of cases the request was purely oral. The requirement of 'intolerable suffering' has also proved to be imprecise. The survey among general practitioners revealed that, although in 56% of cases the official notification certified intolerable suffering to be the most important reason for euthanasia, only 42% of the patients had mentioned it as a reason, and only 18% as the most important reason. Significantly, 24% of patients gave as their most important reason 'fear/anticipation of mental deterioration', which raises the inevitable but very difficult problem of euthanasia in cases of incipient Alzheimer's disease, a problem not directly addressed in the Dutch criteria. The requirement of consultation also appeared to be of doubtful value in practice, and frequently not complied with ...

In the light of these concerns, together with those identified by the Select Committee in its report, there seems little prospect in the UK that voluntary active euthanasia (let alone the non-voluntary form) will gain legal sanction in the foreseeable future.

INDEX

Index